MAIN COURSES 500

T0159371

MAIN 500
COURSES

Best-ever dishes for family meals, quick suppers, dinner parties and special events, shown in more than 500 tempting photographs

EDITED BY JENNI FLEETWOOD

southwater

This edition is published by Southwater,
an imprint of Anness Publishing Ltd, 108 Great Russell Street,
London WC1B 3NA; info@anness.com

www.southwaterbooks.com; www.annesspublishing.com

If you like the images in this book and would like
to investigate using them for publishing, promotions
or advertising, please visit our website
www.practicalpictures.com for more information.

© Anness Publishing Ltd 2014

A CIP catalogue record for this book is available from
the British Library.

Publisher: Joanna Lorenz
Editor: Joy Wotton
Jacket Design: Nigel Partridge
Copy Editor: Jay Thundercliffe
Production Controller: Steve Lang
Design: SMI

PUBLISHER'S NOTE
Although the advice and information in this book are
believed to be accurate and true at the time of going to press,
neither the authors nor the publisher can accept any legal
responsibility or liability for any errors or omissions that may
have been made nor for any inaccuracies nor for any loss, harm
or injury that comes about from following instructions or
advice in this book.

Notes

Bracketed terms are intended for American readers.

For all recipes, quantities are given in both metric and imperial measures and, where appropriate, in standard cups and spoons.
Follow one set of measures, but not a mixture, because they are not interchangeable.

Standard spoon and cup measures are level. 1 tsp = 5ml, 1 tbsp = 15ml, 1 cup = 250ml/8fl oz. Australian standard tablespoons are
20ml. Australian readers should use 3 tsp in place of 1 tbsp for measuring small quantities.

American pints are 16fl oz/2 cups. American readers should use 20fl oz/2.5 cups in place of 1 pint when measuring liquids.

Electric oven temperatures in this book are for conventional ovens. When using a fan oven, the temperature will probably need to
be reduced by about 10–20°C/20–40°F. Since ovens vary, you should check with your manufacturer's instruction book for guidance.

The nutritional analysis given for each recipe is calculated per portion (i.e. serving or item), unless otherwise stated.
If the recipe gives a range, such as Serves 4–6, then the nutritional analysis will be for the smaller portion size, i.e. 6 servings.
The analysis does not include optional ingredients, such as salt added to taste.
Medium (US large) eggs are used unless otherwise stated.

Main front cover image shows Lamb Shanks in Pearl Barley Broth – for recipe, see page 216.

Contents

Introduction

Main courses were once the most important element of any meal, around which all other courses revolved, but appetizers and desserts began to be seen as more enticing and interesting, and main courses were sadly overlooked. When it comes to planning and preparing a meal, most of us have no difficulty in deciding what to serve for the first or last course – it's what comes between that proves problematic. That's where this book comes in – proving that main courses can be just as exciting and delicious as any other course.

With 500 step-by-step recipes, plus cook's tips and variations, you need never struggle for inspiration again. The difficulty will lie in deciding what to choose from this superb collection, whether it be a colourful salad, a stunning soufflé, a pasta dish or a hearty feast in the form of a meat or chicken roast or a one-pot casserole. Recently, thanks largely to nutritional advice that stresses the importance of a well-balanced diet with small amounts of protein and plenty of vegetables, the main course has returned to its place as the most important part of meal times.

The days of the marathon meal – with an appetizer or soup leading to the fish course, followed by a main dish, a sorbet, dessert, crackers and cheese and, finally, coffee – have largely disappeared thanks to the hectic pace of life. And today it is perfectly acceptable simply to

serve family and dinner guests a satisfying stew with lots of deliciously crusty bread for mopping up the juices, a beautiful baked fish with a pile of buttery new potatoes, or a home-baked pie with a crisp salad. The rule is that there are virtually no rules, so that when you are entertaining at home, you can dispense with soups and appetizers altogether, if you like, or you can simply offer guests canapés with their drinks as they arrive.

Many people don't have the time or inclination to cook more than one course for their main evening meal. The marvellous thing about many main dishes is that they can be prepared in advance and cooked when required. Not only does this keep stress levels low but it also ensures that success levels remain high. Here are literally dozens of slow-cooked dishes, such as roasts, casseroles, stews and curries. They will prove a boon as they need little attention and reward the cook by quietly gaining in flavour as they cook in the oven. In fact many one-pot dishes benefit

from being made a day in advance, giving the delicious flavours time to mingle and combine. Even more convenient for the busy cook is the fact that many of the dishes in this book can be cooked even further ahead and frozen, ready to be defrosted and reheated when needed.

There is no need to follow the classic meat-and-two-veg approach for every main course. People today have a sense of adventure about food, and are happy to explore new ideas and world cuisine. Many have chosen to limit the amount of meat they eat. Today, a main course can be anything you want, and the recipes in this book will give plenty of inspiration in the kitchen. Choose from a meat-free dish, such as Roasted Garlic and Cheese Soufflé or Couscous with Roasted Summer Vegetables, or try a hearty pie such as Steak, Mushroom and Ale Pie, a creamy Pumpkin and Pistachio Risotto, or a substantial soup, such as Chicken Broth with Dumplings.

The international scope of the recipes in this book mean you can delight your diners with main courses taken from some of the best cuisines in the world. Whether you want a fragrant Thai Chicken Curry, the classic Boeuf Bourguignon, or a Mushroom and Pesto Pizza, you are sure to find a delicious main course that reflects the many varied and tasty dishes in this collection with a true global flavour.

You need never feel lost in your search for a new main-course meal again. Here are 500 recipes in one volume, set out in easy-reference sections to help busy cooks find exactly what they want, quickly and easily. From vegetable, meat or fish dishes, hearty soups or substantial salads to meals whose main ingredient is rice, pasta or noodles, you are certain to find the perfect main course.

Roasted Vegetables with Salsa Verde

A simplified salsa verde is perfect with mixed vegetables.

Serves 4
3 courgettes (zucchini),
  sliced lengthways
1 large fennel bulb, cut into wedges
450g/1lb butternut squash, cut
  into 2cm/³⁄₄in chunks
12 shallots
2 red (bell) peppers, seeded and
  cut lengthways into thick slices
4 tomatoes, halved and seeded
45ml/3 tbsp olive oil
2 garlic cloves, crushed
5ml/1 tsp balsamic vinegar
salt and ground black pepper

For the salsa verde
45ml/3 tbsp chopped fresh mint
90ml/6 tbsp chopped fresh flat
  leaf parsley
15ml/1 tbsp Dijon mustard
juice of ¹⁄₂ lemon
30ml/2 tbsp olive oil

For the rice
15ml/1 tbsp vegetable
  or olive oil
75g/3oz/³⁄₄ cup vermicelli,
  broken into short lengths
200g/7oz/1 cup long grain rice
900ml/1¹⁄₂ pints/3³⁄₄ cups
  vegetable stock

1 Preheat the oven to 220°C/425°F/Gas 7. To make the salsa verde, place all the ingredients, except the oil, in a food processor or blender. Blend to a coarse paste, then add the oil, a little at a time, until the mixture forms a smooth purée. Season to taste.

2 To roast the vegetables, toss the courgettes, fennel, squash, shallots, peppers and tomatoes in the oil, garlic and balsamic vinegar. Leave for 10 minutes to allow the flavours to mingle.

3 Place the vegetables, except the squash and tomatoes, on a baking sheet, brush with half the oil mixture and season. Roast for 25 minutes, then turn and brush with more oil mixture. Add the squash and tomatoes and cook for 20–25 minutes.

4 Meanwhile, heat the oil in a heavy pan. Add the vermicelli and fry for 3 minutes. Season to taste. Rinse the rice, then drain and add to the pan. Cook for 1 minute, stirring to coat in oil.

5 Add the stock, then cover the pan and cook for 12 minutes until the water is absorbed. Leave for 10 minutes. Serve the warm rice with the roasted vegetables and salsa verde.

Roasted Courgettes and Peaches

This recipe combines fruit and vegetables to make a colourful medley that is baked rather than deep-fried or grilled. Serve with warm, crusty bread, or as an accompaniment to grilled, broiled or barbecued meats and poultry.

Serves 4
2 courgettes (zucchini)
2 yellow or red (bell) peppers,
  seeded and cut into wedges

120ml/4fl oz/¹⁄₂ cup olive oil
4–6 plum tomatoes
2 firm peaches, peeled, halved
  and stoned (pitted), then cut
  into wedges
30ml/2 tbsp pine nuts
salt and ground black pepper

For the yogurt sauce
500g/1¹⁄₄lb/2¹⁄₄ cups thick and
  creamy natural (plain) yogurt
2–3 garlic cloves, crushed
juice of ¹⁄₂ lemon

1 Preheat the oven to 200°C/400°F/Gas 6. Using a vegetable peeler or a small, sharp knife, peel the courgettes lengthways in stripes like a zebra, then halve and slice them lengthways, or cut into wedges.

2 Place the courgettes and peppers in a baking dish, preferably an earthenware one. Drizzle the oil over them and sprinkle with salt, then bake in the oven for 20 minutes.

3 Take the dish out of the oven and turn the vegetables in the oil, then mix in the tomatoes and peaches. Bake for another 20–25 minutes, until everything is nicely browned.

4 Meanwhile, make the yogurt sauce. In a bowl, beat the yogurt with the garlic and lemon juice. Season with salt and ground black pepper and set aside, or chill in the refrigerator until needed.

5 Dry-roast the pine nuts in a small, heavy pan until they turn golden brown and give off a nutty aroma. Remove from the heat.

6 When the roasted vegetables are ready, remove the dish from the oven and sprinkle the pine nuts over the top. Serve with the yogurt sauce.

Roasted Vegetables Energy 556kcal/2314kJ; Protein 13.3g; Carbohydrate 83.5g, of which sugars 20.5g; Fat 18.9g, of which saturates 2.8g; Cholesterol 0mg; Calcium 173mg; Fibre 9.3g; Sodium 34mg.
Roasted Courgettes Energy 362kcal/1507kJ; Protein 11.7g; Carbohydrate 26.7g, of which sugars 26.3g; Fat 24.1g, of which saturates 3.7g; Cholesterol 2mg; Calcium 284mg; Fibre 4.8g; Sodium 120mg.

Stir-fried Vegetables and Rice

The ginger gives this mixed rice and vegetable dish a wonderful flavour.

Serves 2–4
115g/4oz/generous ½ cup brown basmati rice, rinsed and drained
350ml/12fl oz/1½ cups vegetable stock
2.5cm/1in piece fresh root ginger
1 garlic clove, halved
5cm/2in piece pared lemon rind
115g/4oz/1½ cups shiitake mushrooms
15ml/1 tbsp vegetable oil
175g/6oz baby carrots, trimmed
225g/8oz baby courgettes (zucchini), halved
175–225g/6–8oz/about 1½ cups broccoli, broken into florets
6 spring onions (scallions), diagonally sliced
15ml/1 tbsp light soy sauce
10ml/2 tsp toasted sesame oil

1 Put the rice in a pan and pour in the vegetable stock. Thinly slice the ginger and add it to the pan with the garlic and lemon rind. Slowly bring to the boil, then cover and simmer for 20–25 minutes until the rice is tender. Discard the flavourings and keep the rice hot.

2 Slice the mushrooms, discarding the stems. Heat the oil in a wok and stir-fry the carrots for 4–5 minutes, then add the mushrooms and courgettes and stir-fry for 2–3 minutes. Add the broccoli and spring onions and cook for 3 minutes more, by which time all the vegetables should be tender but should still retain a bit of 'bite'.

3 Add the cooked rice to the vegetables, and toss briefly over the heat to combine the ingredients and heat through. Toss with the soy sauce and sesame oil. Spoon into a bowl and serve immediately.

Cook's Tip
Keep fresh root ginger in the freezer. It can be sliced or grated and thaws very quickly.

Courgette and Jalapeño Chilli Torte

This spicy dish looks rather like a Spanish omelette, which is traditionally served at room temperature. Serve warm or prepare it in advance and leave to cool, but do not refrigerate.

Serves 4–6
500g/1¼lb courgettes (zucchini)
60ml/4 tbsp vegetable oil
1 small onion
3 fresh jalapeño chillies, seeded and cut in strips
3 large eggs
50g/2oz/½ cup self-raising (self-rising) flour
115g/4oz/1 cup grated Monterey Jack or mild Cheddar cheese
2.5ml/½ tsp cayenne pepper
15g/½oz/1 tbsp butter
salt

1 Preheat the oven to 180°C/350°F/Gas 4. Trim the courgettes, then slice them thinly.

2 Heat the oil in a large frying pan. Add the courgettes and cook for a few minutes, turning them over at least once, until they are soft and beginning to brown. Using a slotted spoon, transfer them to a bowl.

3 Slice the onion and add it to the oil remaining in the pan, with most of the jalapeño strips, reserving some for the garnish. Fry until the onions have softened and are golden.

4 Using a slotted spoon, transfer the onions and jalapeños to the bowl with the courgettes.

5 Beat the eggs in a large bowl. Add the self-raising flour, cheese and cayenne. Mix well, then stir in the courgette mixture, with salt to taste.

6 Grease a 23cm/9in round shallow ovenproof dish with the butter. Pour in the courgette mixture and bake in the oven for 30 minutes until it has risen, is firm to the touch and golden brown all over. Allow to cool.

7 Serve the courgette torte in thick wedges, garnished with the remaining jalapeño strips. A fresh tomato salad, sprinkled with chives, makes a colourful accompaniment.

Courgette Torte Energy 421kcal/1747kJ; Protein 18.8g; Carbohydrate 13.2g, of which sugars 3.2g; Fat 32g, of which saturates 12.9g; Cholesterol 216mg; Calcium 356mg; Fibre 1.7g; Sodium 359mg.
Stir-fried Veg Energy 430kcal/1788kJ; Protein 12.5g; Carbohydrate 58.2g, of which sugars 11.2g; Fat 16.2g, of which saturates 2.2g; Cholesterol 0mg; Calcium 127mg; Fibre 6.5g; Sodium 569mg.

Ratatouille

A highly versatile vegetable stew, ratatouille is delicious hot or cold, on its own or with eggs, pasta, fish or meat.

Serves 6

900g/2lb ripe, well-flavoured
  tomatoes
120ml/4fl oz/½ cup olive oil
2 onions, thinly sliced
2 red (bell) peppers, seeded and
  cut into chunks
1 yellow or orange (bell)
  pepper, seeded and cut
  into chunks
1 large aubergine (eggplant),
  cut into chunks
2 courgettes (zucchini), cut into
  thick slices
4 garlic cloves, crushed
2 bay leaves
15ml/1 tbsp chopped young thyme
salt and ground black pepper

1 Plunge the tomatoes into boiling water for 30 seconds, then refresh in cold water. Peel away the skins and chop roughly.

2 Heat a little of the oil in a large, heavy pan and fry the onions for 5 minutes. Add the peppers and fry for a further 2 minutes. Drain. Add the aubergines and more oil and fry gently for 5 minutes. Add the remaining oil and courgettes and fry for 3 minutes. Drain.

3 Add the garlic and tomatoes to the pan with the bay leaves and thyme and a little salt and pepper. Cook gently until the tomatoes have softened and are turning pulpy.

4 Return all the vegetables to the pan and cook gently, stirring frequently, for about 15 minutes, until fairly pulpy but retaining a little texture. Season with more salt and pepper to taste.

> **Cook's Tip**
> There are no specific quantities for the vegetables when making ratatouille so you can, to a large extent, vary the quantities and types of vegetables depending on what you have in the refrigerator. If the tomatoes are a little tasteless, add 30–45ml/2–3 tbsp tomato purée (paste) and a dash of sugar to the mixture along with the tomatoes.

Okra with Tomatoes and Onions

This dish is a popular method of preparing okra. Simple, boiled rice is an ideal accompaniment.

Serves 4–6

90–120ml/6–8 tbsp olive oil
2 onions, thinly sliced
5–8 garlic cloves, roughly chopped
90ml/6 tbsp chopped fresh
  coriander (cilantro) leaves
800g/1¾lb okra
1kg/2¼lb fresh tomatoes, diced
  or 400g/14oz can tomatoes
  plus 30–60ml/2–4 tbsp
  tomato purée (paste)
1.5–2.5ml/¼–½ tsp ground
  cumin
pinch of ground cinnamon
pinch of ground cloves
5ml/1 tsp sugar, or to taste
cayenne pepper
salt and ground black pepper
1 lemon, to serve

1 Heat about half the oil in a heavy pan. Add the onions, garlic and half the coriander and fry for about 10 minutes until the onions are softened and turning brown.

2 Add the okra to the browned onions and stir-fry for about 2–3 minutes.

3 Add the tomatoes, cumin, cinnamon and cloves to the pan, then season to taste with the sugar, cayenne pepper, salt and pepper, and cook until the liquid boils.

4 Reduce the heat to low, then simmer for 20–30 minutes until the okra is tender, stirring occasionally.

5 Taste for spicing and seasoning, and adjust if necessary, then stir in the remaining olive oil and coriander. If serving hot or warm, squeeze in the lemon juice and add to the okra or, if serving cold, cut the lemon into wedges and serve them alongside the okra.

> **Cook's Tips**
> • Trimming the okra and leaving them whole means that they will be succulent and not slimy.
> • Serve with boiled rice or chunks of crusty bread.

Okra with Tomatoes Energy 195kcal/810kJ; Protein 6g; Carbohydrate 14.8g, of which sugars 12.6g; Fat 12.9g, of which saturates 2.1g; Cholesterol 0mg; Calcium 243mg; Fibre 7.9g; Sodium 49mg.
Ratatouille Energy 194kcal/806kJ; Protein 3.9g; Carbohydrate 14.6g, of which sugars 13.1g; Fat 13.7g, of which saturates 2.1g; Cholesterol 0mg; Calcium 49mg; Fibre 4.7g; Sodium 19mg.

Stuffed Vegetables

Colourful peppers and tomatoes make perfect containers for various meat and vegetable stuffings. This rice and herb version uses Mediterranean ingredients.

Serves 4

2 large ripe tomatoes
1 green (bell) pepper
1 yellow or orange (bell) pepper
60ml/4 tbsp olive oil, plus extra
  for sprinkling
2 onions, chopped
2 garlic cloves, crushed
50g/2oz/½ cup blanched
  almonds, chopped
75g/3oz/scant ½ cup long grain
  rice, boiled and drained
15g/½oz mint, roughly chopped
15g/½oz fresh parsley,
  roughly chopped
25g/1oz/2 tbsp sultanas
  (golden raisins)
45ml/3 tbsp ground almonds
salt and ground black pepper
chopped mixed fresh herbs,
  to garnish

1 Preheat the oven to 190°C/375°F/Gas 5. Cut the tomatoes in half and scoop out the pulp and seeds using a teaspoon. Leave the tomatoes to drain on kitchen paper with cut sides down. Roughly chop the tomato pulp and seeds.

2 Halve the peppers, leaving the stalks intact. Scoop out the seeds. Brush the peppers with 15ml/1 tbsp of the oil and bake on a baking tray for 15 minutes.

3 Place the peppers and tomatoes in an ovenproof dish and season with salt and pepper.

4 Fry the onions in the remaining oil for 5 minutes. Add the garlic and chopped almonds and fry for a further minute.

5 Remove the pan from the heat and stir in the rice, chopped tomatoes, mint, parsley and sultanas. Season well and spoon the mixture into the tomatoes and peppers.

6 Pour ⅔ cup boiling water around the tomatoes and peppers and bake, uncovered, for 20 minutes. Scatter with the ground almonds and sprinkle with a little extra olive oil. Return to the oven and bake for 20 minutes more, or until turning golden. Serve garnished with fresh herbs.

Vegetable Stew

This lightly spiced stew is a perfect match for couscous.

Serves 6

45ml/3 tbsp olive oil
250g/9oz shallots
1 large onion, chopped
2 garlic cloves, chopped
5ml/1 tsp cumin seeds
5ml/1 tsp ground coriander seeds
5ml/1 tsp paprika
5cm/2in piece cinnamon stick
2 fresh bay leaves
about 400ml/14fl oz/1⅔ cups
  good vegetable stock
good pinch of saffron strands
450g/1lb carrots, thickly sliced
2 green (bell) peppers, sliced
115g/4oz ready-to-eat dried
  apricots, halved if large
5ml/1 tsp ground toasted
  cumin seeds
450g/1lb squash, cut
  into chunks
pinch of sugar, to taste
salt and ground black pepper
45ml/3 tbsp fresh coriander
  (cilantro) leaves, to garnish

For the tomato sauce

1kg/2¼lb tomatoes, halved
5ml/1 tsp sugar
45ml/3 tbsp olive oil
2 red chillies, seeded and chopped
2–3 garlic cloves, chopped
5ml/1 tsp fresh thyme leaves

1 Preheat the oven to 180°C/350°F/Gas 4. First make the sauce. Place the tomatoes, cut sides up, in a roasting pan. Season well and sprinkle with sugar and oil. Roast for 30 minutes. Mix the chillies, garlic and thyme into the pan and roast for another 30–45 minutes. Cool, then process in a food processor or blender to make a thick sauce. Strain to remove the seeds.

2 Heat 30ml/2 tbsp of the oil in a large pan and cook the shallots gently until browned. Remove and set aside. Cook the onion in the pan and cook for 5–7 minutes, until softened. Stir in the garlic and cumin seeds and cook for 3–4 minutes. Add the ground coriander seeds, paprika, cinnamon stick and bay leaves. Cook for 2 minutes, then mix in the stock, saffron, carrots and peppers. Season, cover and simmer for 10 minutes.

3 Add the apricots and the ground cumin, the shallots and the squash. Stir in the tomato sauce. Cover the pan and cook for 5 minutes. Uncover the pan and continue to cook for 10–15 minutes, until the vegetables are tender. Remove the cinnamon stick and serve sprinkled with the fresh coriander leaves.

Vegetable Stew Energy 166kcal/690kJ; Protein 4.4g; Carbohydrate 18.3g, of which sugars 17.3g; Fat 8.8g, of which saturates 1.4g; Cholesterol 0mg; Calcium 68mg; Fibre 5.5g; Sodium 41mg.
Stuffed Vegetables Energy 234kcal/981kJ; Protein 5.7g; Carbohydrate 32.5g, of which sugars 14.5g; Fat 9.9g, of which saturates 1.2g; Cholesterol 0mg; Calcium 71mg; Fibre 3.6g; Sodium 14mg.

Artichokes with Beans and Almonds

The tender bottoms of globe artichokes are filled with fresh broad beans and flavoured with dill.

Serves 4

175g/6oz/2 cups shelled broad
  (fava) beans
4 large globe artichokes, trimmed
  to their bottoms (see below)

120ml/4fl oz/¹⁄₂ cup olive oil
juice of 1 lemon
10ml/2 tsp sugar
75g/3oz/³⁄₄ cup blanched
  almonds
1 small bunch of fresh dill,
  chopped
2 tomatoes, skinned, seeded
  and diced
salt

1 Put the beans in pan of water and bring to the boil. Lower the heat and simmer for 10–15 minutes or until tender. Drain and refresh under cold running water, then peel off the skins.

2 Place the artichokes in a heavy pan. Mix together the oil, lemon juice and 50ml/2fl oz/¹⁄₄ cup water and pour over the artichokes. Cover and poach gently for about 20 minutes, then add the sugar, beans and almonds. Cover again and continue to poach gently for a further 10 minutes, or until the artichokes are tender. Toss in half the dill, season with salt, and turn off the heat. Leave the artichokes to cool in the pan.

3 Lift the artichokes out of the pan and place them hollow side up in a serving dish. Mix the tomatoes with the beans and almonds, spoon into the middle of the artichokes and around them, and garnish with the remaining dill. Serve the filled artichokes at room temperature.

Cook's Tip

Until ready to use, fresh artichokes should be treated like flowers and put in a jug (pitcher) of water. To prepare them for this dish, cut off the stalks and pull off all the leaves. Dig out the hairy choke from the middle with a spoon, then cut away any hard bits with a small, sharp knife and trim into a neat cup shape. Rub the cups – called bottoms – with a mixture of lemon juice and salt to prevent them from discolouring.

Aromatic Apples with Spicy Pilaff

Vegetables and fruit stuffed with an aromatic pilaff are a great favourite. This recipe is for apples, but you can easily use it to stuff vegetables.

Serves 4

4 cooking apples, or any firm, sour
  apple of your choice
30ml/2 tbsp olive oil
juice of ¹⁄₂ lemon
10ml/2 tsp sugar
salt and ground black pepper

For the filling
30ml/2 tbsp olive oil
a little butter
1 onion, finely chopped

2 garlic cloves
30ml/2 tbsp pine nuts
30ml/2 tbsp currants, soaked in
  warm water for 5–10 minutes
  and drained
5–10ml/1–2 tsp ground cinnamon
5–10ml/1–2 tsp ground allspice
5ml/1 tsp sugar
175g/6oz/scant 1 cup short
  grain rice, thoroughly rinsed
  and drained
1 bunch each of fresh flat leaf
  parsley and dill, finely chopped

To serve
1 tomato
1 lemon
a few fresh mint or basil leaves

1 Make the filling. Heat the oil and butter in a pan, stir in the onion and garlic and cook until softened. Add the pine nuts and currants and cook for 5 minutes. Mix in the spices, sugar and rice. Pour in water to cover the rice – roughly 1–2cm/¹⁄₂–³⁄₄in above the grains – and bring to the boil. Season, then simmer for 10–12 minutes, until almost all the water has been absorbed.

2 Toss in the herbs and turn off the heat. Cover the pan with a dry dish towel and the lid, and leave the rice to steam for 5 minutes. Preheat the oven to 200°C/400°F/ Gas 6.

3 Cut the stalk ends off the apples and keep to use as lids. Core each apple, removing enough flesh to create a cavity. Pack spoonfuls of the rice into the apples. Replace the lids and stand the apples in a small baking dish.

4 Mix together 100ml/3¹⁄₂fl oz/scant ¹⁄₂ cup water with the oil, lemon juice and sugar. Pour over and around the apples, then bake for 30–40 minutes, until the apples are tender. Serve with a tomato and lemon garnish and mint or basil leaves.

Artichokes Energy 351kcal/1455kJ; Protein 8.2g; Carbohydrate 13.4g, of which sugars 8.3g; Fat 29.8g, of which saturates 3.6g; Cholesterol 0mg; Calcium 110mg; Fibre 5.5g; Sodium 29mg.
Aromatic Apples Energy 382kcal/1595kJ; Protein 5g; Carbohydrate 54.1g, of which sugars 18.8g; Fat 16.5g, of which saturates 1.9g; Cholesterol 0mg; Calcium 26mg; Fibre 2.1g; Sodium 4mg.

Imam Bayildi

The aubergines in this Turkish dish are gently poached on top of the stove – when cooked this way they melt in the mouth.

Serves 4

2 large aubergines (eggplants)
sunflower oil, for shallow frying
1 bunch each of fresh flat leaf
   parsley and dill
1 large onion, halved and
   finely sliced
3 tomatoes, skinned and
   finely chopped
2–3 garlic cloves, finely chopped
5ml/1 tsp salt
150ml/¼ pint/⅔ cup olive oil
juice of ½ lemon
15ml/1 tbsp sugar
flat bread and lemon wedges,
   to serve

1 Using a vegetable peeler or a small, sharp knife, peel the aubergines lengthways in stripes like a zebra. Place them in a bowl of salted water for 5 minutes, then drain and pat dry.

2 Heat about 1cm/½in of sunflower oil in a large pan. Fry the aubergines on all sides for a total of 3–5 minutes to soften them. Lift the aubergines out on to a chopping board and slit them open lengthways to create pockets, keeping the bottoms and both ends intact so they look like canoes when stuffed.

3 Reserve a few dill fronds and parsley leaves for the garnish, then chop the rest and mix them in a bowl with the onion, tomatoes and garlic. Add the salt and a little olive oil. Spoon the mixture into the aubergine pockets.

4 Place the aubergines side by side in a deep, heavy pan. Mix the remaining olive oil with 50ml/2fl oz/¼ cup water and the lemon juice. Pour it over the aubergines, and sprinkle with sugar. Cover the pan and place over medium heat to get the oil hot. Lower the heat and cook the aubergines very gently for about 1 hour, basting from time to time. They should be soft and tender, with only a little oil left in the bottom of the pan.

5 Leave the aubergines to cool in the pan, then transfer them to a serving dish and spoon the oil from the bottom of the pan over them. Garnish with the reserved dill and parsley and serve at room temperature, with flat bread and lemon wedges.

Aubergine Tagine

Spiced with coriander, cumin, cinnamon, turmeric and a dash of chilli sauce, this Moroccan-style stew makes a filling supper dish when served with couscous.

Serves 4

1 small aubergine (eggplant),
   cut into 1cm/½in dice
2 courgettes (zucchini),
   thickly sliced
60ml/4 tbsp olive oil
1 large onion, sliced
2 garlic cloves, chopped
150g/5oz/2 cups brown cap
   (cremini) mushrooms, halved
15ml/1 tbsp ground coriander
10ml/2 tsp cumin seeds
15ml/1 tbsp ground cinnamon
10ml/2 tsp ground turmeric
225g/8oz new potatoes,
   quartered
600ml/1 pint/2½ cups passata
   (bottled strained tomatoes)
15ml/1 tbsp tomato purée (paste)
15ml/1 tbsp chilli sauce
75g/3oz/⅓ cup ready-to-eat
   unsulphured dried apricots
400g/14oz/3 cups canned
   chickpeas, drained and rinsed
salt and ground black pepper
15ml/1 tbsp chopped fresh
   coriander (cilantro), to garnish

1 Sprinkle salt over the aubergine and courgettes and leave for 30 minutes. Rinse and pat dry with a dish towel. Heat the grill (broiler) to high. Arrange the courgettes and aubergine on a baking tray and toss in 30ml/2 tbsp of the olive oil. Grill (broil) for 20 minutes, turning occasionally, until tender and golden.

2 Meanwhile, heat the remaining oil in a large heavy pan and cook the onion and garlic for 5 minutes until softened, stirring occasionally. Add the mushrooms and sauté for 3 minutes until tender. Add the spices and cook for 1 minute more, stirring, to allow the flavours to mingle.

3 Add the potatoes and cook for about 3 minutes, stirring. Pour in the passata, tomato purée and 150ml/¼ pint/⅔ cup water. Cover and cook for 10 minutes to thicken the sauce.

4 Add the aubergine, courgettes, chilli sauce, apricots and chickpeas. Season and cook, partially covered, for about 15 minutes until the potatoes are tender. Add a little extra water if the tagine becomes too dry. Sprinkle with chopped fresh coriander to serve.

Imam Bayildi Energy 407kcal/1680kJ; Protein 3g; Carbohydrate 16.7g, of which sugars 14.1g; Fat 37g, of which saturates 5.1g; Cholesterol 0mg; Calcium 67mg; Fibre 4.8g; Sodium 507mg.
Aubergine Tagine Energy 359kcal/1509kJ; Protein 13.9g; Carbohydrate 45g, of which sugars 19.3g; Fat 15g, of which saturates 2.1g; Cholesterol 0mg; Calcium 123mg; Fibre 9.7g; Sodium 597mg.

Chickpea Tagine

The flavour of preserved – or pickled – lemon is wonderful in this dish. Slightly salty, less tart than the fresh fruit, it adds a real zing to the delicate, nutty flavour of the chickpeas.

Serves 4
150g/5oz/³/₄ cup chickpeas, soaked overnight, or 2 x 400g/14oz cans chickpeas, rinsed and drained

30ml/2 tbsp sunflower oil
1 large onion, chopped
1 garlic clove, crushed (optional)
400g/14oz can chopped tomatoes
5ml/1 tsp ground cumin
350ml/12fl oz/1¹/₂ cups vegetable stock
¹/₄ preserved lemon
30ml/2 tbsp chopped fresh coriander (cilantro)

1 If using dried chickpeas, place them in a pan with plenty of water. Boil vigorously for 10–15 minutes, skimming off any scum that rises to the surface. Reduce the heat, then simmer for about 1–1½ hours until tender. Drain well.

2 Place the cooked chickpeas in a bowl of cold water and rub them between your fingers to remove the skins. The skins will float to the surface of the water, making them easy to remove and discard.

3 Heat the oil in a pan or flameproof casserole and fry the onion for 6–8 minutes, until beginning to soften. Add the garlic and cook, stirring frequently, for 4 minutes until the onion has turned golden. Ensure that the garlic does not burn, otherwise it will impart a bitter taste to the dish.

4 Add the cooked or canned chickpeas, tomatoes, cumin and stock to the pan and stir well. Bring the mixture to the boil and simmer, uncovered, for about 30–40 minutes, until the chickpeas are very soft and most of the liquid has evaporated.

5 Rinse the preserved lemon and cut away the flesh and pith. Cut the peel into slivers and stir it into the chickpeas together with the chopped fresh coriander. Serve immediately with warmed flat bread, if you like.

Jamaican Black Bean Pot

Molasses imparts a rich treacly flavour to the spicy sauce, which incorporates a stunning mix of black beans, vibrant red and yellow peppers and orange butternut squash. This dish is delicious served with cornbread or plain rice.

Serves 4
225g/8oz/1¹/₄ cups dried black beans
1 bay leaf
30ml/2 tbsp vegetable oil
1 large onion, chopped
1 garlic clove, chopped

5ml/1 tsp English (hot) mustard powder
15ml/1 tbsp blackstrap molasses
30ml/2 tbsp soft dark brown sugar
5ml/1 tsp dried thyme
2.5ml/¹/₂ tsp dried chilli flakes
5ml/1 tsp vegetable bouillon powder
1 red (bell) pepper, seeded and diced
1 yellow (bell) pepper, seeded and diced
675g/1¹/₂lb/5¹/₄ cups butternut squash or pumpkin, seeded and cut into 1cm/¹/₂in dice
salt and ground black pepper
sprigs of thyme, to garnish

1 Soak the beans overnight in plenty of water, then drain and rinse well. Place in a large pan, cover with fresh water and add the bay leaf. Bring to the boil, then boil rapidly for about 10 minutes. Reduce the heat, cover and simmer for 30 minutes until tender. Drain, reserving the cooking water. Preheat the oven to 180°C/350°F/Gas 4.

2 Heat the oil in the pan and sauté the onion and garlic for about 5 minutes until softened, stirring occasionally. Add the mustard powder, molasses, sugar, thyme and chilli and cook for 1 minute, stirring. Stir in the black beans and spoon the mixture into a flameproof casserole.

3 Add enough water to the reserved cooking liquid to make 400ml/14fl oz/1²/₃ cups, then mix in the bouillon powder and pour into the casserole. Bake in the preheated oven for about 25 minutes.

4 Add the peppers and squash or pumpkin and mix well. Cover, then bake for 45 minutes until the vegetables are tender. Serve garnished with thyme.

Chickpea Tagine Energy 207kcal/871kJ; Protein 9.7g; Carbohydrate 26.4g, of which sugars 7.1g; Fat 7.8g, of which saturates 0.9g; Cholesterol 0mg; Calcium 87mg; Fibre 5.6g; Sodium 56mg.
Jamaican Black Bean Pot Energy 297kcal/1252kJ; Protein 15.1g; Carbohydrate 45.9g, of which sugars 20.3g; Fat 7.1g, of which saturates 1g; Cholesterol 0mg; Calcium 129mg; Fibre 12.6g; Sodium 16mg.

Sweet and Sour Mixed-bean Hotpot

This slow-cooker dish, topped with sliced potatoes, is incredibly easy to prepare, making the most of dried and canned ingredients.

Serves 6

40g/1½oz/3 tbsp butter
4 shallots, peeled and finely
    chopped
40g/1½oz/⅓ cup plain
    (all-purpose) or wholemeal
    (whole-wheat) flour
300ml/½ pint/1¼ cups passata
    (bottled strained tomatoes)
120ml/4fl oz/½ cup unsweetened
    apple juice
60ml/4 tbsp soft light brown sugar

60ml/4 tbsp tomato ketchup
60ml/4 tbsp dry sherry
60ml/4 tbsp cider vinegar
60ml/4 tbsp light soy sauce
400g/14oz can butter (lima) beans
400g/14oz can flageolet (small
    cannellini) beans
400g/14oz can chickpeas
175g/6oz green beans, cut into
    2.5cm/1in lengths
225g/8oz/3 cups mushrooms, sliced
450g/1lb unpeeled potatoes,
    thinly sliced
15ml/1 tbsp olive oil
15ml/1 tbsp chopped fresh thyme
15ml/1 tbsp fresh marjoram
salt and ground black pepper
fresh herbs, to garnish

1 Melt the butter in a pan, add the shallots and fry gently for 5–6 minutes, until soft. Add the flour and cook for 1 minute, stirring, then gradually stir in the passata. Add the apple juice, sugar, ketchup, sherry, vinegar and light soy sauce to the pan and stir in. Bring to the boil, stirring constantly until it thickens.

2 Rinse the beans and chickpeas and drain. Place them in the ceramic cooking pot with the green beans and mushrooms and pour in the sauce. Stir, cover and cook on high for 3 hours.

3 Meanwhile, parboil the potatoes for 4 minutes. Drain well, then toss them in the oil so that they are lightly coated all over.

4 Stir the herbs into the bean mixture and season. Arrange the potato slices on top of the beans, overlapping them slightly so that they completely cover them. Cover the pot and cook for a further 2 hours, or until the potatoes are tender.

5 Place the cooking pot under a medium grill (broiler) and cook for 4–5 minutes to brown. Serve garnished with herbs.

Green Bean Stew

The mild, slightly bitter spiciness of the paprika combines well with the fresh tomatoes and beans in this dish.

Serves 4–6

900g/2lb/6 cups young
    green beans
45ml/3 tbsp olive or
    vegetable oil

3 onions, finely diced
350g/12oz fresh plum tomatoes,
    roughly chopped
5ml/1 tsp paprika
6 garlic cloves, crushed
30ml/2 tbsp chopped fresh flat
    leaf parsley
salt and ground black pepper
a little chopped fresh parsley
    and paprika, to garnish

1 Trim the green beans and cut into 4cm/1½in lengths. Bring a pan of water to the boil.

2 Transfer the green beans into a pan of boiling water. Quickly bring the beans back to the boil, then reduce the heat to a simmer. Cook the beans until just softened, about 5 minutes. Drain well and keep warm.

3 Meanwhile, heat the olive or vegetable oil in a pan and fry the diced onions, stirring frequently, until just starting to turn a pale golden colour.

4 Add the chopped tomatoes and paprika to the cooked onions and mix well.

5 Stir in the green beans and simmer, with the lid on, for about 10–15 minutes.

6 Stir in the garlic and parsley. Season to taste with salt and pepper and serve the beans garnished with a sprinkle of paprika and some parsley.

Cook's Tip
Make sure the beans are stringless or the quality of the dish will be spoiled.

Mixed-bean Hotpot Energy 483kcal/2042kJ; Protein 18.5g; Carbohydrate 73.3g, of which sugars 24.8g; Fat 13.8g, of which saturates 4.5g; Cholesterol 14mg; Calcium 134mg; Fibre 10.9g; Sodium 826mg.
Green Bean Stew Energy 132kcal/545kJ; Protein 2g; Carbohydrate 5.3g, of which sugars 4.4g; Fat 11.6g, of which saturates 1.7g; Cholesterol 0mg; Calcium 34mg; Fibre 2.5g; Sodium 6mg.

Creamy Red Lentil Dhal

This makes a tasty winter supper for vegetarians and meat-eaters alike. The lentils are packed with goodness and are high in fibre and protein. Serve with naan bread, coconut cream and fresh coriander leaves. The coconut cream gives this dish a really rich taste.

Serves 4
15ml/1 tbsp sunflower oil
150g/5oz/²⁄₃ cup red lentils
15ml/1 tbsp hot curry paste
salt and ground black pepper
naan bread, coconut cream and
    fresh coriander (cilantro) leaves,
    to serve

1 Heat the oil in a large pan and add the lentils. Fry for 1–2 minutes, stirring constantly.

2 Stir the curry paste into the lentils for a minute until the aromas are released. Pour in 600ml/1 pint/2½ cups boiling water and stir to combine.

3 Bring the mixture to the boil, then reduce the heat to a gentle simmer. Cover the pan and cook for 15 minutes, stirring occasionally, until the lentils are tender and the mixture has thickened. Add a little more water if necessary.

4 Season the dhal with plenty of salt and ground black pepper to taste, and serve piping hot.

> **Cook's Tip**
> Be sure to carefully pick over the red lentils to remove any small stones or bad lentils. You can do this while running the lentils under cold water in a sieve (strainer).

> **Variation**
> Other lentils or beans can be used in place of the red lentils, if you prefer. Try using green lentils, yellow split peas or mung dhal – all will give different but equally delicious results.

Garlic and Herb Lentils

Dried sage leaves have a really strong herby aroma, and are ideal for this dish, though you could also make it using fresh sage. Serve these lentils with grilled, broiled or barbecued meats, or on their own with a dollop of yogurt seasoned with garlic, salt and pepper.

1 onion, sliced
3–4 plump garlic cloves, roughly
    chopped and bruised
5ml/1 tsp coriander seeds
a handful of dried sage leaves
5–10ml/1–2 tsp sugar
4 carrots, sliced
15–30ml/1–2 tbsp tomato
    purée (paste)
salt and ground black pepper
1 bunch of fresh sage or flat leaf
    parsley, to garnish

Serves 4–6
175g/6oz/¾ cup green lentils
45–60ml/3–4 tbsp fruity olive oil

1 Pick over the lentils, rinse them in cold water and drain. Bring a pan of water to the boil and add the lentils. Lower the heat, partially cover the pan and simmer for 10 minutes.

2 Drain the lentils thoroughly and rinse well under cold running water. Drain again and set aside.

3 Heat the fruity olive oil in a heavy pan, stir in the sliced onion, garlic, coriander seeds, sage and sugar, and cook until the onion begins to soften and colour. Toss in the carrots and cook for 2–3 minutes.

4 Add the drained lentils to the carrots in the pan and pour in 250ml/8fl oz/1 cup water, making sure that the lentils and carrots are covered.

5 Stir in the tomato purée and cover the pan, then cook the lentils and carrots gently for about 20 minutes, until most of the liquid has been absorbed. The lentils and carrots should both be tender but still have some bite.

6 Season the dish with salt and pepper to taste. Transfer to a serving dish and garnish with the fresh sage or flat leaf parsley. Serve hot or at room temperature.

Creamy Red Lentil Dhal Energy 455kcal/1929kJ; Protein 30.1g; Carbohydrate 71.3g, of which sugars 3g; Fat 7.5g, of which saturates 1g; Cholesterol 0mg; Calcium 86mg; Fibre 6.9g; Sodium 61mg.
Garlic Lentils Energy 166kcal/696kJ; Protein 7.6g; Carbohydrate 21.1g, of which sugars 6.7g; Fat 6.2g, of which saturates 0.9g; Cholesterol 0mg; Calcium 38mg; Fibre 4g; Sodium 22mg.

Mushroom and Fennel Hotpot

Hearty and richly flavoured, this tasty slow-cooker stew makes a marvellous vegetarian main dish, but it can also be served as an accompaniment to meat dishes. Dried mushrooms swell up a great deal after soaking, so a little goes a long way in terms of both flavour and quantity.

Serves 4

25g/1oz/¹⁄₂ cup dried shiitake mushrooms
1 small head of fennel
30ml/2 tbsp olive oil
12 shallots, peeled
225g/8oz/3 cups button (white) mushrooms, trimmed and halved
250ml/8fl oz/1 cup dry (hard) cider
25g/1oz/¹⁄₂ cup sun-dried tomatoes
30ml/2 tbsp/¹⁄₂ cup sun-dried tomato purée (paste)
1 bay leaf
salt and ground black pepper
chopped fresh parsley, to garnish

1 Place the dried shiitake mushrooms in a heatproof bowl. Pour over just enough hot water to cover them and set aside to soak for about 15 minutes. Meanwhile, trim and slice the head of fennel.

2 Heat the olive oil in a heavy pan. Add the shallots and fennel, then sauté for about 10 minutes over medium heat, until the vegetables are softened and just beginning to brown. Add the button mushrooms to the pan and cook for a further 2–3 minutes, stirring occasionally.

3 Transfer the vegetable mixture to the ceramic cooking pot. Drain the shiitake mushrooms, adding 30ml/2 tbsp of the soaking liquid to the cooking pot. Chop them and add them to the pot.

4 Pour the cider into the cooking pot and stir in the sun-dried tomatoes and tomato purée. Add the bay leaf. Cover the pot with the lid and cook on high for 3–4 hours, or until the vegetables are tender.

5 Remove the bay leaf and season to taste with salt and black pepper. Serve sprinkled with plenty of chopped parsley.

Aduki Bean Stuffed Mushrooms

Field mushrooms have a rich flavour that goes well with this fragrant stuffing.

Serves 4–6

200g/7oz/1 cup dried or 400g/14oz/2 cups, can aduki beans, drained
45ml/3 tbsp olive oil, plus extra for brushing
1 onion, finely chopped
2 garlic cloves, crushed
30ml/2 tbsp fresh chopped or 5ml/1 tsp dried thyme
8 large field (portobello) mushrooms, stalks finely chopped
50g/2oz/1 cup fresh wholemeal (whole-wheat) breadcrumbs
juice of 1 lemon
185g/6¹⁄₂oz/³⁄₄ cup goat's cheese, crumbled
salt and ground black pepper

For the pine nut tarator
50g/2oz/¹⁄₂ cup pine nuts toasted
50g/2oz/1 cup cubed white bread
2 garlic cloves, chopped
200ml/7fl oz/scant 1 cup semi-skimmed (low-fat) milk
45ml/3 tbsp olive oil
15ml/1 tbsp chopped fresh parsley, to garnish (optional)

1 If using dried beans, soak them overnight, then drain and rinse. Place in a pan, add water to cover and boil for 10 minutes, then reduce the heat, cook for 30 minutes until tender, then drain. If using canned beans, rinse, drain well, then set aside.

2 Preheat the oven to 200°C/400°F/Gas 6. Heat the oil in a frying pan, add the onion and garlic and cook for 5 minutes until softened. Add the thyme and the mushroom stalks and cook for a further 3 minutes, stirring occasionally until tender.

3 Stir in the beans, breadcrumbs and lemon juice, season well, then cook for 2 minutes. Mash two-thirds of the beans with a fork or potato masher, leaving the remaining beans whole.

4 Brush a baking dish and the mushrooms with oil, then top each with bean mixture. Place the mushrooms in the dish, cover with foil and bake for 20 minutes. Top each mushroom with goat's cheese and bake for 15 minutes, or until tender.

5 To make the pine nut tarator, place all the ingredients in a food processor or blender and blend until smooth and creamy. Sprinkle with parsley, if using, and serve with the mushrooms.

Mushroom and Fennel Hotpot Energy 94kcal/394kJ; Protein 2.1g; Carbohydrate 4.2g, of which sugars 4g; Fat 6g, of which saturates 0.9g; Cholesterol 0mg; Calcium 28mg; Fibre 2.4g; Sodium 17mg.
Stuffed Mushrooms Energy 406kcal/1694kJ; Protein 17.5g; Carbohydrate 25.9g, of which sugars 5.9g; Fat 26.6g, of which saturates 8g; Cholesterol 31mg; Calcium 159mg; Fibre 6.1g; Sodium 573mg.

Mixed Vegetables in Coconut Sauce

A vegetable dish is an essential part of an Indian meal, even for a simple occasion, where one or two vegetable dishes may be served with a lentil dhal, a raita, and bread or boiled rice. There are many ways to make a vegetable curry, but this recipe, in which the vegetables are simmered in coconut milk, is typical of South India.

Serves 4

225g/8oz potatoes, cut into 5cm/2in cubes
115g/4oz green beans
150g/5oz carrots, scraped and cut into 5cm/2in cubes
500ml/17fl oz/generous 2 cups hot water
1 small aubergine (eggplant), about 225g/8oz, quartered lengthways
75g/3oz coconut milk powder
5ml/1 tsp salt
30ml/2 tbsp vegetable oil
6–8 fresh or 8–10 curry leaves
1 or 2 dried red chillies, chopped into small pieces
5ml/1 tsp ground cumin
5ml/1 tsp ground coriander
2.5ml/½ tsp ground turmeric
Indian bread, to serve

Bubble and Squeak

Whether you have leftovers, or cook this old-fashioned classic from fresh, be sure to give it a really good 'squeak', or fry, in the pan so it turns a rich honey brown as all the flavours caramelize together. It is known as Colcannon in Ireland, where it is turned in chunks or sections, producing a creamy brown and white cake.

Serves 4

60ml/4 tbsp dripping, bacon fat or vegetable oil
1 onion, finely chopped
450g/1lb floury potatoes, cooked and mashed
225g/8oz cooked cabbage or Brussels sprouts, finely chopped
salt and ground black pepper

1 Heat 30ml/2 tbsp of the dripping, fat or oil in a heavy frying pan. Add the onion and cook, stirring frequently, until softened but not browned.

2 In a large bowl, mix together the potatoes and cooked cabbage or sprouts and season with salt and plenty of pepper to taste. Add the vegetables to the pan with the onions, stir well, then press the vegetable mixture into a large, even cake.

3 Cook over medium heat for about 15 minutes, until the cake is browned underneath.

4 Invert a large plate over the pan, and, holding it tightly against the pan, turn them both over together. Lift off the frying pan, return the pan to the heat and add the remaining dripping, fat or oil. When hot, slide the cake back into the pan, browned side up.

5 Cook over medium heat for 10 minutes, or until the underside is golden brown. Serve hot, in wedges.

1 Put the cubed potatoes, green beans and carrots in a large pan, add 300ml/½ pint/1¼ cups of the hot water and bring to the boil. Reduce the heat a little, cover the pan and continue to cook for 5 minutes.

2 Cut the aubergine quarters into 5cm/2in pieces. Rinse well and add to the pan.

3 Blend the coconut milk powder with the remaining hot water and add to the vegetables, with the salt. Bring to a slow simmer, cover and cook for 6–7 minutes.

4 In a small pan, heat the oil over medium heat and add the curry leaves and the dried red chillies. Immediately follow with the ground cumin, coriander and turmeric.

5 Stir-fry the spices together for 15–20 seconds and pour the entire contents of the pan over the vegetables. Stir to distribute the spices evenly and remove the pan from the heat. Serve the mixed vegetables with rice, dhal or any Indian bread.

> **Cook's Tip**
> If you don't have leftover cooked cabbage or Brussels sprouts, shred raw cabbage and cook both in boiling salted water until tender. Drain, then chop.

Bubble and Squeak Energy 205kcal/857kJ; Protein 3.5g; Carbohydrate 23.3g, of which sugars 4.2g; Fat 11.5g, of which saturates 1.2g; Cholesterol 0mg; Calcium 34mg; Fibre 3g; Sodium 15mg.
Mixed Vegetables Energy 92kcal/384kJ; Protein 2.9g; Carbohydrate 5.8g, of which sugars 5.3g; Fat 6.6g, of which saturates 0.9g; Cholesterol 6mg; Calcium 30mg; Fibre 2.3g; Sodium 77mg.

Tofu and Pepper Kebabs

A simple coating of ground, dry-roasted peanuts provides plenty of flavour.

Serves 4
250g/9oz firm tofu, cubed

50g/2oz/½ cup dry-roasted peanuts, ground
2 red and 2 green (bell) peppers, seeded and cut into large chunks
60ml/4 tbsp sweet chilli dipping sauce

1 Preheat the grill (broiler) to medium. Turn the tofu cubes in the ground nuts to coat thoroughly on all sides.

2 Thread the pepper and tofu on to skewers and place on a grill (broiler) rack. Grill (broil) for 10–12 minutes. Serve with the sauce.

Potato Rösti and Tofu

Although this dish features various components, it is not difficult to make.

Serves 4
425g/15oz/3¾ cups tofu, cubed
4 large potatoes, peeled, parboiled and grated
sunflower oil, for frying
salt and ground black pepper
30ml/2 tbsp sesame seeds, toasted

For the marinade
30ml/2 tbsp dark soy sauce
15ml/1 tbsp clear honey
2 garlic cloves, crushed
4cm/1½in piece fresh root ginger, grated
5ml/1 tsp toasted sesame oil

For the sauce
15ml/1 tbsp olive oil
8 tomatoes, seeded and chopped

1 Mix the marinade ingredients in a bowl and add the tofu. Chill for 1 hour. Preheat the oven to 200°C/400°F/Gas 6. Drain the tofu and spread on a baking tray. Bake for 20 minutes until crisp.

2 For the sauce, simmer the oil, marinade and tomatoes in a pan for 10 minutes. Pass through a sieve (strainer) and keep warm.

3 For the rösti, season the potatoes and form four cakes. Heat a little oil in a frying pan. Cook the cakes until golden on both sides. Sprinkle with seeds and serve with the tofu and sauce.

Green Beans with Tofu and Chilli

Another name for snake beans is yardlong beans. This is something of an exaggeration but they do grow to 35cm/14in and more. Look for them in Asian stores and markets, but if you have trouble finding them, substitute other green beans, such as French beans, in their place.

Serves 4
500g/1¼lb snake beans (yardlong beans), thinly sliced

200g/7oz silken tofu, cut into cubes
2 shallots, thinly sliced
200ml/7fl oz/scant 1 cup coconut milk
115g/4oz/1 cup roasted peanuts, chopped
juice of 1 lime
10ml/2 tsp palm sugar (jaggery) or light muscovado (brown) sugar
60ml/4 tbsp soy sauce
5ml/1 tsp dried chilli flakes

1 Bring a pan of lightly salted water to the boil. Add the beans and blanch them for 30 seconds.

2 Drain the beans immediately, then refresh under cold running water and drain again, shaking them well to remove as much water as possible. Place in a serving bowl and set aside until needed.

3 Put the tofu and shallots in a heavy pan, then add the coconut milk. Heat gently, stirring constantly, until the tofu begins to crumble.

4 Add the roasted peanuts, lime juice, sugar, soy sauce and chilli flakes to the pan. Heat, stirring frequently, until the sugar has dissolved. Pour the sauce over the prepared beans, toss to combine and serve immediately.

Variation
The sauce also works very well with mangetouts (snow peas) and sugarsnap peas. Alternatively, stir in sliced yellow or red (bell) pepper for a brightly coloured dish.

Tofu Kebabs Energy 175kcal/730kJ; Protein 10g; Carbohydrate 12.9g, of which sugars 11.4g; Fat 9.6g, of which saturates 1.6g; Cholesterol 0mg; Calcium 339mg; Fibre 3.6g; Sodium 108mg.
Potato Rösti Energy 433kcal/1811kJ; Protein 15g; Carbohydrate 42.3g, of which sugars 8.6g; Fat 23.7g, of which saturates 3.3g; Cholesterol 0mg; Calcium 618mg; Fibre 4.6g; Sodium 46mg.
Green Beans Energy 263kcal/1091kJ; Protein 14.5g; Carbohydrate 13.3g, of which sugars 10g; Fat 17.2g, of which saturates 3g; Cholesterol 0mg; Calcium 335mg; Fibre 4.7g; Sodium 1353mg.

Baked Potatoes and Three Fillings

Potatoes baked in their skins make an excellent and nourishing meal on their own. For an even better treat, add one of these three delicious and easy toppings to your potato.

Serves 4
4 medium baking potatoes
olive oil
sea salt
filling of your choice (see below)

Stir-fry vegetables
45ml/3 tbsp groundnut (peanut) or sunflower oil
2 leeks, thinly sliced
2 carrots, cut into sticks
1 courgette (zucchini), thinly sliced
115g/4oz baby corn, halved

115g/4oz/1½ cup button (white) mushrooms, sliced
45ml/3 tbsp soy sauce
30ml/2 tbsp dry sherry or vermouth
15ml/1 tbsp sesame oil
sesame seeds, to garnish

Red bean chillies
425g/15oz can red kidney beans, drained
200g/7oz/scant 1 cup low-fat cottage or cream cheese
30ml/2 tbsp mild chilli sauce
5ml/1 tsp ground cumin

Cheese and creamy corn
425g/15oz can creamed corn
115g/4oz/1 cup hard cheese, freshly grated
5ml/1 tsp mixed dried herbs
fresh parsley sprigs, to garnish

1 Preheat the oven to 200°C/400°F/Gas 6. Score the potatoes with a cross and rub all over with the oil. Bake for 45 minutes to 1 hour until tender. Cut the potatoes open along the score lines and push up the flesh. Season and top with a filling.

2 For the vegetables, heat the groundnut or sunflower oil in a wok or frying pan until hot. Add the leeks, carrots, courgette and baby corn and stir-fry for about 2 minutes, then add the mushrooms and stir-fry for 1 minute. Add the soy sauce, sherry or vermouth and sesame oil. Heat through until bubbling and sprinkle with sesame seeds.

3 For the red beans, heat the beans in a pan and stir in the cottage or cream cheese, chilli sauce and cumin.

4 For the creamy corn, heat the corn gently in a pan with the cheese and herbs. Garnish with the parsley sprigs.

Wild Mushroom Gratin with Beaufort Cheese, New Potatoes and Walnuts

This is one of the simplest and most delicious ways of cooking mushrooms. Serve this dish as the Swiss do, with new potatoes and gherkins.

Serves 4
900g/2lb small new or salad potatoes
50g/2oz/4 tbsp unsalted (sweet) butter or 60ml/4 tbsp olive oil

350g/12oz/5 cups assorted wild and cultivated mushrooms, thinly sliced
175g/6oz Beaufort or Fontina cheese, thinly sliced
50g/2oz/½ cup broken walnuts, toasted
salt and ground black pepper
12 gherkins and mixed green salad leaves, to serve

1 Put the potatoes in a large pan. Add water to cover and bring to the boil. Add a little salt, then simmer for about 15 minutes, or until the potatoes are tender, but do not let them get too soft.

2 Drain the potatoes thoroughly and return them to the pan. Add a knob (pat) of butter or a splash of olive oil and cover the pan to keep the potatoes warm.

3 Heat the remaining butter or the olive oil in a large frying pan over medium-high heat. Add the mushrooms and fry until their juices appear.

4 Increase the heat under the pan and cook the mushrooms briskly until most of their juices have cooked away. Season with salt and black pepper.

5 Meanwhile, preheat the grill (broiler). Arrange the cheese on top of the mushroom slices, place the pan under the grill and cook until bubbly and golden brown.

6 Sprinkle the mushroom gratin with the broken walnuts and serve immediately with the buttered potatoes and sliced gherkins. Serve a side dish of mixed green salad, if you like, to complete this meal.

Baked Potatoes Energy 304kcal/1290kJ; Protein 10.6g; Carbohydrate 60.5g, of which sugars 12.8g; Fat 3.9g, of which saturates 1.7g; Cholesterol 5mg; Calcium 121mg; Fibre 3.5g; Sodium 393mg.
Mushroom Gratin Energy 529kcal/2207kJ; Protein 18.4g; Carbohydrate 37g, of which sugars 3.5g; Fat 34.2g, of which saturates 17.3g; Cholesterol 71mg; Calcium 356mg; Fibre 3.7g; Sodium 440mg.

Potatoes Baked with Tomatoes

This simple, hearty dish from the south of Italy is best when tomatoes are in season and bursting with lots of flavour, but it can also be made with canned plum tomatoes.

Serves 6

2 large red or yellow onions, thinly sliced

1kg/2¼lb baking potatoes, thinly sliced

450g/1lb tomatoes, fresh or canned, sliced, with their juice

90ml/6 tbsp olive oil

115g/4oz/1 cup Parmesan or Cheddar cheese, freshly grated

a few fresh basil leaves

50ml/2fl oz/¼ cup water

salt and ground black pepper

1 Preheat the oven to 180°C/350°F/Gas 4. Brush a large baking dish generously with oil.

2 Arrange a layer of some onions in the base of the dish, followed by some layers of potatoes and tomatoes, alternating them to make the dish look colourful.

3 Pour a little of the olive oil over the surface, and sprinkle with some of the grated cheese. Season with salt and ground black pepper.

4 Continue to layer the vegetables in the dish until they are all used up. You should end with an overlapping layer of potatoes and tomatoes.

5 Tear the basil leaves into small pieces, and add them here and there among the vegetables, saving a few for garnish. Sprinkle the top with the remaining grated cheese and oil.

6 Pour the water over the dish. Bake in the oven for 1 hour until the vegetables are tender.

7 Check the potato dish towards the end of cooking and if the top begins to brown too much, place a sheet of foil or baking parchment, or a flat baking tray on top of the dish. Garnish the dish with the remaining fresh basil leaves, once it is cooked, and serve immediately.

Baked Scalloped Potatoes with Feta Cheese and Olives

Thinly sliced potatoes are cooked with Greek feta cheese and black and green olives in olive oil. This dish is a good one to serve with toasted pitta bread.

Serves 4

900g/2lb main crop potatoes

150ml/¼ pint/⅔ cup olive oil

1 sprig rosemary

275g/10oz/2½ cups feta cheese, crumbled

115g/4oz/1 cup pitted black and green olives

300ml/½ pint/1¼ cups hot vegetable stock

salt and ground black pepper

1 Preheat the oven to 200°C/400°F/Gas 6. Cook the potatoes in plenty of boiling water for 15 minutes. Drain and cool slightly.

2 When the potatoes are cool enough to handle, peel them and cut into thin slices.

3 Lightly grease the base and sides of a 1.5-litre/2½-pint/6¼-cup rectangular ovenproof dish with a little of the olive oil.

4 Layer the potatoes in the base of the dish. Break up the rosemary sprig and sprinkle over the potatoes along with the feta cheese and olives.

5 Drizzle with the remaining olive oil and pour over the stock. Season with salt and plenty of ground black pepper.

6 Bake in the oven for about 35 minutes, covering with foil to prevent the potatoes from getting too brown. Serve hot, straight from the dish.

> **Cook's Tip**
> Make sure you choose good-quality Greek feta cheese, which has a different texture to the feta cheese that is produced in other countries.

Potatoes Baked Energy 309kcal/1290kJ; Protein 9.8g; Carbohydrate 31.7g, of which sugars 8g; Fat 16.7g, of which saturates 4.9g; Cholesterol 15mg; Calcium 211mg; Fibre 3.2g; Sodium 189mg.
Scalloped Potatoes Energy 584kcal/2429kJ; Protein 14.8g; Carbohydrate 37.3g, of which sugars 4g; Fat 42.7g, of which saturates 13.7g; Cholesterol 48mg; Calcium 279mg; Fibre 3.1g; Sodium 1662mg.

Spicy Potato Strudel

Wrap up a tasty mixture of vegetables in a spicy, creamy sauce with crisp filo pastry. Serve with a good selection of chutneys or a spicy yogurt sauce.

Serves 4

1 onion, chopped
2 carrots, coarsely grated
1 courgette (zucchini), chopped
350g/12oz firm potatoes, finely chopped
65g/2½ oz/5 tbsp butter
10ml/2 tsp mild curry paste
2.5ml/½ tsp dried thyme
150ml/¼ pint/⅔ cup water
1 egg, beaten
30ml/2 tbsp single (light) cream
50g/2oz/¼ cup Cheddar cheese, grated
8 sheets filo pastry, thawed if frozen
sesame seeds, for sprinkling
salt and ground black pepper

1 In a large frying pan, cook the onion, carrots, courgette and potatoes in 25g/1oz/2 tbsp of the butter for 5 minutes, tossing frequently so they cook evenly. Add the curry paste and stir in. Continue to cook the vegetables for a further minute or so.

2 Add the thyme, water and seasoning. Bring to the boil, then reduce the heat and simmer for about 10 minutes until tender, stirring occasionally.

3 Remove from the heat and leave to cool. Transfer the mixture into a large bowl and then mix in the egg, cream and cheese. Chill until ready to fill the filo pastry.

4 Preheat the oven to 190°C/375°F/Gas 5. Melt the remaining butter and lay out four sheets of filo pastry, slightly overlapping them to form a fairly large rectangle. Brush with some melted butter and fit the other sheets on top. Brush again.

5 Spoon the filling along one long side, then roll up the pastry. Form it into a circle and set on a baking sheet. Brush again with the last of the butter and sprinkle over the sesame seeds.

6 Bake the strudel in the oven for about 25 minutes until golden and crisp. Leave to stand for 5 minutes before cutting.

Vegetable Casserole with Dumplings

Light courgette dumplings spiced with caraway complete this hearty slow-cooker dish.

Serves 3

300ml/½ pint/1¼ cups dry (hard) cider
175ml/6fl oz/¾ cup boiling vegetable stock
2 leeks, cut into 2cm/¾in slices
2 carrots, cut into chunks
2 parsnips, cut into chunks
225g/8oz potatoes, cut into chunks
1 sweet potato, cut into chunks

1 bay leaf
7.5ml/1½ tsp cornflour (cornstarch)
115g/4oz full-fat soft cheese with garlic and herbs
salt and ground black pepper

For the dumplings

115g/4oz/1 cup self-raising (self-rising) flour
5ml/1 tsp caraway seeds
50g/2oz/½ cup shredded vegetable suet (chilled, grated shortening)
1 courgette (zucchini), grated
about 75ml/5 tbsp cold water

1 Reserve 15ml/1 tbsp of the cider and pour the rest into the ceramic cooking pot with the stock. Cover and switch to high.

2 Add the vegetables to the ceramic cooking pot with the bay leaf. Cover with the lid and cook for 3 hours.

3 In a small bowl, blend the cornflour with the reserved cider. Add the cheese and mix together until combined, then gradually blend in a few spoonfuls of the cooking liquid. Pour over the vegetables and stir until thoroughly mixed. Season with salt and black pepper. Cover and cook for a further 1–2 hours, or until the vegetables are almost tender.

4 Towards the end of the cooking time, make the dumplings. Sift the flour into a large mixing bowl and stir in the caraway seeds, suet, courgette, salt and black pepper. Stir in the water, adding a little more if necessary, to make a soft dough. With floured hands, shape the mixture into 12 dumplings, about the size of walnuts.

5 Carefully place the dumplings on top of the casserole, cover and cook for a further hour, or until the vegetables and dumplings are cooked. Serve in warmed deep soup plates.

Cheesy Leek and Couscous Cake

The tang of sharp Cheddar cheese goes perfectly with the sweet taste of leeks. The cheese melts into the couscous and helps it stick together, making a firm cake that is easy to cut into wedges. Serve with a crisp green salad.

Serves 4

300g/11oz/1¾ cups couscous
45ml/3 tbsp olive oil
2 leeks, sliced
200g/7oz mature (sharp)
 Cheddar or Monterey
 Jack, grated
salt and ground black pepper

1 Put the couscous in a large heatproof bowl and pour over 450ml/¾ pint/scant 2 cups boiling water. Cover and set aside for about 15 minutes, or until all the water has been absorbed.

2 Heat 15ml/1 tbsp of the oil in a 23cm/9in non-stick frying pan. Add the leeks and cook over medium heat for about 4–5 minutes, stirring occasionally, until tender and golden.

3 Remove the leeks with a slotted spoon and stir them into the couscous. Add the grated cheese and some salt and pepper and stir through.

4 Heat the remaining oil in the pan and add the couscous and leek mixture. Pat down firmly to form a cake and cook over a fairly gentle heat for 15 minutes, or until the underside is crisp and golden.

5 Slide the couscous cake on to a plate, then invert it back into the pan to cook the other side. Cook for a further 5–8 minutes, or until golden, then remove from the heat. Slide on to a board and serve cut into wedges.

Variation
There are endless variations on this tangy, tasty cake but choose a cheese that melts well because it will help the cake to stick together. Try using caramelized onions and blue cheese in place of the leeks and Cheddar.

Cauliflower Cheese

The use of flour to thicken sauces began in France in the 17th century – hence the name 'roux' for the mixture of flour and fat that forms the basis of a white sauce – but cheese sauce made in this way has become a staple of English cuisine.

Serves 4

1 medium cauliflower
25g/1oz/2 tbsp butter
25g/1oz/4 tbsp plain
 (all-purpose) flour
300ml/½ pint/1¼ cups milk
115g/4oz/1 cup mature (sharp)
 Cheddar cheese, grated
salt and ground black pepper

1 Trim the cauliflower and cut it into florets. Bring a pan of lightly salted water to the boil, drop in the cauliflower and cook for 5–8 minutes, or until just tender. Drain and transfer the florets into an ovenproof dish.

2 To make the sauce, melt the butter in a pan, stir in the flour and cook gently, stirring constantly, for about 1 minute (do not allow it to brown). Remove from the heat and gradually stir in the milk.

3 Return the pan containing the sauce to the heat and cook, stirring constantly, until the mixture thickens and comes to the boil. Simmer for 1–2 minutes.

4 Stir three-quarters of the cheese into the sauce and season to taste with salt and pepper. Spoon the sauce over the cauliflower florets and sprinkle the remaining cheese on top. Put under a hot grill (broiler) until the cheese topping bubbles and turns golden brown.

Variations
• *Boost the cheese flavour by adding a little English (hot) mustard to the cheese sauce.*
• *As an alternative to Cheddar cheese, use a blue cheese such as Stilton. You will not need as much.*
• *Cauliflower cheese is delicious with strips of crisp fried bacon, either served on the side or crumbled into the sauce.*

Cheesy Leek Cake Energy 475kcal/1973kJ; Protein 18.6g; Carbohydrate 41.4g, of which sugars 2.3g; Fat 25.9g, of which saturates 12.1g; Cholesterol 49mg; Calcium 408mg; Fibre 2.2g; Sodium 361mg.
Cauliflower Energy 318kcal/1318kJ; Protein 17.4g; Carbohydrate 4.4g, of which sugars 3.9g; Fat 25.8g, of which saturates 16.3g; Cholesterol 71mg; Calcium 371mg; Fibre 1.8g; Sodium 453mg.

Grilled Polenta with Onions, Radicchio and Taleggio Cheese

Slices of grilled polenta are tasty topped with slowly caramelized onions and bubbling Taleggio cheese.

Serves 4
900ml/1½ pints/3¾ cups water
5ml/1 tsp salt
150g/5oz/generous 1 cup polenta
50g/2oz/⅓ cup freshly grated
  Parmesan cheese
5ml/1 tsp chopped fresh thyme
90ml/6 tbsp olive oil

675g/1½lb onions, halved
  and sliced
2 garlic cloves, chopped
a few fresh thyme sprigs
5ml/1 tsp brown sugar
15–30ml/1–2 tbsp balsamic
  vinegar
2 heads radicchio, cut into thick
  slices or wedges
225g/8oz Taleggio cheese,
  sliced
salt and ground black pepper

1 In a large pan, bring the water to the boil and add the salt. Stirring all the time, add the polenta in a steady stream, then bring to the boil. Cook over low heat, stirring frequently, for 30–40 minutes, until thick and smooth. Beat in the Parmesan and thyme, then turn on to a board. Spread evenly, then cool.

2 Heat 30ml/2 tbsp of the oil in a frying pan over medium heat. Add the onions and stir to coat in the oil, then cover and cook over a very low heat for 15 minutes, stirring occasionally.

3 Add the garlic and most of the thyme sprigs and cook for 10 minutes. Add the sugar, 15ml/1 tbsp of the vinegar and season. Cook for another 5–10 minutes, until soft and browned.

4 Preheat the grill (broiler). Cut the polenta into thick slices and brush with a little oil, then grill (broil) until crusty and golden. Turn the polenta and add the radicchio to the grill rack. Brush the radicchio with oil. Grill for 5 minutes, until the polenta and radicchio are browned. Drizzle a little vinegar over.

5 Heap the onions on to the polenta. Sprinkle the cheese and a few sprigs of thyme over both polenta and radicchio. Grill until the cheese is bubbling. Season and serve immediately.

Mushroom Stroganoff

This creamy mushroom dish is ideal for a dinner party.

Serves 8
25g/1oz/2 tbsp butter
900g/2lb mixed mushrooms, cut
  into bitesize pieces

350ml/12fl oz/1½ cups white
  wine sauce
250ml/8fl oz/1 cup sour cream
chopped chives, to garnish
boiled white rice, to serve

1 Melt the butter in a large pan and cook the mushrooms for 8–10 minutes until they are tender and brown.

2 Add the wine sauce to the cooked mushrooms in the pan and bring to the boil, stirring. Stir in the sour cream and season to taste. Serve with the boiled rice, garnished with the chives.

Mushroom Polenta

Polenta is delicious topped with cheesy mushrooms.

Serves 4
250g/9oz/2¼ cups
  quick-cook polenta

50g/2oz/¼ cup butter
400g/14oz/5½ cups brown cap
  (cremini) mushrooms, sliced
175g/6oz/1½ cups grated
  Gruyère cheese
salt and ground black pepper

1 Line a 28 × 18cm/11 × 7in baking tin (pan) with baking parchment. Bring 1 litre/1¾ pints/4 cups water with 5ml/1 tsp salt to the boil in a large pan. Add the polenta and cook for 5 minutes until smooth. Place in the tin and leave to cool.

2 Preheat the oven to 200°C/400°F/Gas 6. Melt the butter in a pan and cook the mushrooms for 5 minutes until golden.

3 Place the polenta on a chopping board and remove the parchment. Cut into large squares and place in an ovenproof dish. Sprinkle with half the cheese, season, then pour the mushrooms and juices over the top. Sprinkle with the remaining cheese and bake for 20 minutes until the cheese is melted.

Grilled Polenta Energy 617kcal/2563kJ; Protein 26.5g; Carbohydrate 43.9g, of which sugars 12.6g; Fat 36.6g, of which saturates 13.9g; Cholesterol 52mg; Calcium 676mg; Fibre 4.3g; Sodium 705mg.
Stroganoff Energy 556kcal/2316kJ; Protein 13.3g; Carbohydrate 80.4g, of which sugars 7.2g; Fat 21.7g, of which saturates 11.4g; Cholesterol 51mg; Calcium 96mg; Fibre 2.5g; Sodium 897mg.
Mushroom Energy 518kcal/2155kJ; Protein 18.9g; Carbohydrate 46.2g, of which sugars 0.3g; Fat 27.2g, of which saturates 16.1g; Cholesterol 69mg; Calcium 334mg; Fibre 2.5g; Sodium 397mg.

Baked Cheese Polenta with Tomato Sauce

Polenta, or cornmeal, is a staple food in Italy. It is cooked like a sort of porridge, and eaten soft, or set, cut into shapes then baked or grilled.

Serves 4
5ml/1 tsp salt
250g/9oz/2¼ cups quick-cook polenta
5ml/1 tsp paprika
2.5ml/½ tsp ground nutmeg
30ml/2 tbsp olive oil
1 large onion, finely chopped
2 garlic cloves, crushed
2 x 400g/14oz cans chopped tomatoes
15ml/1 tbsp tomato purée (paste)
5ml/1 tsp sugar
75g/3oz Gruyère cheese, grated
oil or melted butter, for greasing
salt and ground black pepper

1 Preheat the oven to 200°C/400°F/Gas 6. Line a 28 x 18cm/11 x 7in baking tin (pan) with clear film (plastic wrap). Bring 1 litre/1¾ pints/4 cups water to the boil with the salt.

2 Pour in the polenta in a steady stream and cook, stirring constantly, for 5 minutes. Beat in the paprika and nutmeg, then pour into the prepared tin and smooth the surface. Set aside to cool.

3 Heat the oil in a pan and cook the onion and garlic, stirring frequently, over medium heat for about 6–8 minutes until soft.

4 Add the chopped tomatoes, tomato purée and sugar. Season with salt and pepper. Simmer for 20 minutes.

5 Turn out the polenta on to a chopping board and cut into 5cm/2in squares. Lightly brush an ovenproof dish with a little oil or melted butter.

6 Place half the polenta squares into the greased ovenproof dish. Spoon over half the tomato sauce, and sprinkle with half the Gruyère cheese. Repeat the layers until all the ingredients are used up. Bake in the oven for about 25 minutes, until golden. Serve immediately.

Baked Sweet Potatoes with Leeks

This dish tastes wonderful and looks stunning if you buy orange-fleshed sweet potatoes. They score low on the glycaemic index and promote a healthy, steady rise in blood sugar.

Serves 4
4 large sweet potatoes, scrubbed
30ml/2 tbsp olive oil
2 large leeks, washed and sliced
115g/4oz Gorgonzola cheese, thinly sliced
salt and ground black pepper

1 Preheat the oven to 190°C/375°F/Gas 5. Dry the sweet potatoes with kitchen paper and rub them all over with about 15ml/1 tbsp of the oil.

2 Place the sweet potatoes on a baking tray and sprinkle with salt. Bake in the preheated oven for about 45 minutes to 1 hour, or until tender.

3 Meanwhile, heat the remaining oil in a frying pan and add the sliced leeks. Cook for 3–4 minutes, or until softened and just beginning to turn golden.

4 Cut the potatoes in half lengthways and place them cut side up on the baking tray. Top with the cooked leeks and season.

5 Lay the cheese slices on top and grill (broil) under a hot grill (broiler) for 2–3 minutes, until the cheese is melted and bubbling. Serve immediately.

Cook's Tip
Ensure that the potatoes are completely cooked by inserting a sharp knife or a metal skewer into the centre of the potato.

Variation
Use other cheeses if you like. Mature (sharp) Cheddar would work well, or go for another blue cheese such as Stilton or Dolcelatte, if you prefer.

Sweet Potatoes Energy 338kcal/1425kJ; Protein 9.5g; Carbohydrate 44.8g, of which sugars 13.1g; Fat 14.8g, of which saturates 6.6g; Cholesterol 22mg; Calcium 206mg; Fibre 6.5g; Sodium 432mg.
Cheese Polenta Energy 415kcal/1734kJ; Protein 13.4g; Carbohydrate 57.5g, of which sugars 10g; Fat 14g, of which saturates 4.9g; Cholesterol 18mg; Calcium 180mg; Fibre 3.6g; Sodium 707mg.

Spiced Couscous with Halloumi and Courgette Ribbons

Couscous forms the foundation of this dish and is topped with griddled sliced courgettes and halloumi.

Serves 4

275g/10oz/1²/3 cups couscous
1 bay leaf
1 cinnamon stick
30ml/2 tbsp olive oil, plus extra
  for brushing
1 large red onion, chopped
2 garlic cloves, chopped
5ml/1 tsp mild chilli powder
5ml/1 tsp ground cumin
5ml/1 tsp ground coriander
5 cardamom pods, bruised
50g/2oz/¼ cup whole
  almonds, toasted
1 peach, stoned (pitted)
  and diced
25g/1oz/2 tbsp butter
3 courgettes (zucchini), sliced
  lengthways into ribbons
225g/8oz halloumi cheese, sliced
salt and ground black pepper
chopped fresh flat leaf parsley,
  to garnish

1 Place the couscous in a bowl and pour over 500ml/17fl oz/ generous 2 cups boiling water. Add the bay leaf and cinnamon stick and season with salt. Leave the couscous for 10 minutes until the water is absorbed, then fluff up the grains with a fork.

2 Meanwhile, heat the oil in a large heavy pan, add the onion and garlic and cook, stirring, for about 7 minutes until soft.

3 Stir in the chilli powder, cumin, coriander and cardamom pods, and cook for 3 minutes. Add the couscous, almonds, diced peach and butter, and heat through for 2 minutes.

4 Brush a grill (broiling) pan with oil and heat until very hot. Turn down the heat to medium, then place the courgettes on the grill and cook for 5 minutes until tender and slightly charred. Turn the courgettes over, add the halloumi and continue cooking for 5 minutes, turning the halloumi halfway through.

5 Remove the cinnamon stick, bay leaf and cardamom pods from the couscous, then arrange it on a plate and season well. Top with the halloumi and courgettes. Sprinkle the parsley over the top and serve.

Roast Mediterranean Vegetables with Pecorino Cheese

Aubergines, courgettes, peppers and tomatoes make a marvellous medley when roasted and served drizzled with fragrant olive oil. Shavings of sheep's milk Pecorino add the perfect finishing touch.

Serves 4–6

1 aubergine (eggplant), sliced
2 courgettes (zucchini), sliced
2 red or yellow (bell) peppers,
  seeded and quartered
1 large onion, thickly sliced
2 large carrots, cut into sticks
4 firm plum tomatoes, halved
extra virgin olive oil, for brushing
  and sprinkling
45ml/3 tbsp chopped fresh parsley
45ml/3 tbsp pine nuts,
  lightly toasted
125g/4oz piece of Pecorino cheese
salt and ground black pepper

1 Layer the aubergine slices in a colander, sprinkling each layer with a little salt. Leave the aubergine to drain over a sink or plate for about 20 minutes.

2 Preheat the oven to 220°C/425°F/Gas 7. Rinse the aubergine slices thoroughly under cold running water, drain well and pat dry with kitchen paper.

3 Spread out the aubergine slices, courgettes, peppers, onion, carrots and tomatoes in one or two large roasting pans. Brush the vegetables lightly with olive oil and roast them in the oven for about 20 minutes or until they are lightly browned and the skins on the peppers have begun to blister.

4 Transfer the vegetables to a large serving platter. If you like, peel the peppers. Trickle over any vegetable juices from the pan and season to taste with salt and pepper.

5 As the roasted vegetables cool, sprinkle them with a little more oil. When the vegetables reach room temperature, mix in the parsley and pine nuts.

6 Using a vegetable peeler, shave the Pecorino and sprinkle the shavings over the vegetables. Serve immediately.

Roast Vegetables Energy 202kcal/839kJ; Protein 12g; Carbohydrate 10g, of which sugars 9.3g; Fat 12.9g, of which saturates 4.8g; Cholesterol 21mg; Calcium 300mg; Fibre 4g; Sodium 244mg.
Spiced Couscous Energy 515kcal/2138kJ; Protein 19.9g; Carbohydrate 42.7g, of which sugars 6.1g; Fat 30.3g, of which saturates 12.5g; Cholesterol 46mg; Calcium 290mg; Fibre 2.9g; Sodium 264mg.

Couscous with Roasted Summer Vegetables

To add a flicker of fire to this dish, serve it with a spoonful of harissa. To cool the palate, offer a bowl of thick yogurt.

Serves 6

3 red onions, peeled and quartered
2–3 courgettes (zucchini), halved lengthways and cut across into 2–3 pieces
2–3 red, green or yellow (bell) peppers, seeded and quartered
2 aubergines (eggplants), cut into 6–8 long segments
2–3 leeks, cut into long strips
2–3 sweet potatoes, halved lengthways and cut into long strips
4–6 tomatoes, quartered
6 garlic cloves, crushed
25g/1oz fresh root ginger, sliced
a few large fresh rosemary sprigs
150ml/¼ pint/⅔ cup olive oil
10ml/2 tsp clear honey
salt and ground black pepper
natural (plain) yogurt or harissa and bread, to serve

For the couscous

500g/1¼lb/3 cups couscous
5ml/1 tsp salt
600ml/1 pint/2½ cups warm water
45ml/3 tbsp sunflower oil
25g/1oz/2 tbsp butter, diced

1 Preheat the oven to 200°C/400°F/Gas 6. Arrange all the vegetables in a roasting pan. Add the garlic, ginger and rosemary.

2 Drizzle the vegetables with the oil and honey, season and then roast for about 1½ hours until they are tender and slightly caramelized. Turn them in the oil occasionally.

3 When the vegetables are nearly ready, put the couscous in a bowl. Stir the salt into the water, then stir it into the couscous. Leave to stand for 10 minutes to plump up then, using your fingers, rub the sunflower oil into the grains. Transfer the couscous into an ovenproof dish, arrange the butter over the top, cover with foil and heat in the oven for about 20 minutes.

4 To serve, pile the couscous on a large dish and shape into a mound with a little pit at the top. Spoon vegetables into the pit and around the dish. Pour the oil from the pan over the couscous. Serve with yogurt or harissa and bread.

Summer Vegetable Kebabs with Harissa and Yogurt Dip

This simple and tasty vegetarian dish is delicious served with couscous and a fresh, crispy green salad. It also makes an excellent side dish to accompany meat-based main courses. Vegetable and fish kebabs are becoming increasingly popular in Morocco.

Serves 4

2 aubergines (eggplants), part-peeled and cut into chunks
2 courgettes (zucchini), cut into chunks
2–3 red or green (bell) peppers, cut into chunks
12–16 cherry tomatoes
4 small red onions, quartered
60ml/4 tbsp olive oil
juice of ½ lemon
1 garlic clove, crushed
5ml/1 tsp ground coriander
5ml/1 tsp ground cinnamon
10ml/2 tsp clear honey
5ml/1 tsp salt

For the harissa and yogurt dip

450g/1lb/2 cups natural (plain) yogurt
30–60ml/2–4 tbsp harissa
small bunch of fresh coriander (cilantro), finely chopped
small bunch of mint, finely chopped
salt and ground black pepper

1 Preheat the grill (broiler) on the hottest setting. Put all the vegetables in a bowl.

2 Mix the olive oil, lemon juice, garlic, ground coriander, cinnamon, honey and salt, and pour the mixture over the vegetables. Turn the vegetables gently in the marinade, then thread them on to metal skewers. Cook the kebabs under the grill, turning them occasionally until the vegetables are nicely browned all over.

3 To make the dip, put the yogurt in a bowl and beat in the harissa, making it as fiery as you like by adding more harissa.

4 Add most of the coriander and mint, reserving a little to garnish, and season well with salt and pepper. Serve the vegetables on the skewers while they are still hot. Garnish with the reserved herbs and serve with the yogurt dip.

Couscous Energy 561kcal/2340kJ; Protein 10.4g; Carbohydrate 78.8g, of which sugars 18.7g; Fat 24.6g, of which saturates 3.5g; Cholesterol 0mg; Calcium 101mg; Fibre 7.3g; Sodium 51mg
Summer Kebabs Energy 274kcal/1144kJ; Protein 11.1g; Carbohydrate 28.8g, of which sugars 26.2g; Fat 13.7g, of which saturates 2.5g; Cholesterol 1mg; Calcium 303mg; Fibre 5.9g; Sodium 111mg.

Roasted Aubergines with Feta and Coriander

This is a perfect dish for a summer lunch or picnic that will appeal to everyone. Aubergines take on a lovely smoky flavour when grilled on a barbecue. Choose a good quality Greek feta cheese for the best flavour.

Serves 6
3 medium aubergines (eggplants)
400g/14oz feta cheese
a small bunch of coriander
 (cilantro), roughly chopped,
 plus extra sprigs to garnish
60ml/4 tbsp extra virgin olive oil
salt and ground black pepper

1 Prepare a barbecue. When the flames have died down and the coals are grey, cook the aubergines for 20 minutes, turning occasionally, until charred and soft. Remove from the barbecue and cut in half lengthways.

2 Carefully scoop out the aubergine flesh and place it into a bowl, reserving the skins. Mash the flesh roughly with a fork.

3 Crumble the feta cheese, then stir it into the mashed aubergine with the chopped coriander and olive oil. Season with salt and ground black pepper to taste.

4 Spoon the aubergine and feta mixture back into the skins and return to the barbecue for 5 minutes to warm through. Serve immediately, garnished with a few coriander sprigs.

Variations
• If you prefer, or if the weather outside is not suited to a barbecue, this dish can be made using a grill (broiler).
• Use fresh parsley in place of the fresh coriander (cilantro), if you prefer.

Cook's Tip
Most modern varieties of aubergine (eggplant) do not need salting before cooking as they are not as bitter as they once were.

Smoked Aubergines in Cheese Sauce

This dish features aubergines baked in the oven with a cheese sauce and topped with Parmesan. It is a warming and nourishing dish that is popular with children. Serve it as a main dish for lunch or supper with chunks of fresh, crusty bread and a juicy, fresh green salad.

Serves 4
2 large aubergines (eggplants)
50g/2oz/1/4 cup butter
30ml/2 tbsp plain
 (all-purpose) flour
600ml/1 pint/2 1/2 cups milk
 (you may need a little more)
115g/4oz Cheddar cheese, grated
salt and ground black pepper
finely grated Parmesan cheese,
 for the topping

1 Preheat the oven to 200°C/400°F/Gas 6. Put the whole aubergines directly on the gas flame on top of the stove, or under a conventional grill (broiler), and turn them until the skin is charred on all sides and the flesh feels soft. Place in a plastic bag and leave for a few minutes.

2 When the aubergines are cool enough to handle, hold each one by the stalk under cold running water and gently peel off the charred skin.

3 Squeeze the flesh with your fingers to get rid of any excess water and place on a chopping board. Remove the stalks and chop the flesh to a pulp.

4 Make the sauce. Melt the butter in a heavy pan, remove from the heat and stir in the flour. Slowly beat in the milk, then return the pan to medium heat and cook, stirring constantly, until the sauce is smooth and thick.

5 Beat in the grated Cheddar cheese a little at a time, then beat in the aubergine pulp and season with salt and pepper.

6 Transfer the mixture into a deep baking dish and sprinkle a generous layer of Parmesan over the top.

7 Bake in the oven for about 25 minutes, until the top is nicely crisped and browned. Serve immediately.

Roasted Aubergines Energy 257kcal/1066kJ; Protein 12g; Carbohydrate 4.2g, of which sugars 3.9g; Fat 21.5g, of which saturates 10.3g; Cholesterol 47mg; Calcium 286mg; Fibre 3.3g; Sodium 968mg.
Smoked Aubergines Energy 322kcal/1344kJ; Protein 14.1g; Carbohydrate 15.2g, of which sugars 9.3g; Fat 22.7g, of which saturates 14.5g; Cholesterol 63mg; Calcium 415mg; Fibre 2.2g; Sodium 350mg.

Roasted Squash with Sun-dried Tomatoes and Goat's Cheese

Gem squash has a sweet, subtle flavour that contrasts well with olives and sun-dried tomatoes in this recipe. The rice adds substance without changing any of the flavours.

Serves 2

4 whole gem squashes
225g/8oz/2 cups cooked white
    long grain rice
75g/3oz/1½ cups sun-dried
    tomatoes, chopped
50g/2oz/½ cup pitted black
    olives, chopped
60ml/4 tbsp soft goat's cheese
15ml/1 tbsp chopped fresh
    basil leaves, plus basil sprigs,
    to serve
30ml/2 tbsp olive oil
natural (plain) yogurt and mint
    dressing or green salad, to
    serve (optional)

1 Preheat the oven to 180°C/350°F/Gas 4. Trim away the base of each squash to create a flat surface so they will stand up. Slice off the top and, using a spoon, scoop out and discard the seeds, creating a cavity for the filling.

2 Place the rice, tomatoes, olives, cheese, the basil and half the olive oil in a large mixing bowl. Stir until all the ingredients are thoroughly combined.

3 Brush a shallow baking dish with the remaining oil. The dish should be just large enough to hold the squash side by side. Divide the rice mixture among the squash and pack it down into the cavity. Place them in the dish.

4 Cover with foil and bake in the oven for 45–50 minutes until the squash is tender when pierced with a skewer. Garnish with basil sprigs and serve with a yogurt and mint dressing or a salad.

Variation
This filling can be used to stuff other vegetables such as marrow (large zucchini), aubergines (eggplants), or (bell) peppers. Adjust the baking time in the oven depending on the vegetable used.

Barley Risotto with Squash and Leeks

This is more like a pilaff, made with slightly chewy, nutty-flavoured pearl barley, than a classic risotto. Sweet leeks and roasted squash are superb with this earthy grain.

Serves 4–5

200g/7oz/1 cup pearl barley
1 butternut squash, peeled,
    seeded and cut into chunks
10ml/2 tsp chopped fresh thyme
60ml/4 tbsp olive oil
25g/1oz/2 tbsp butter
4 leeks, cut into fairly thick
    diagonal slices
2 garlic cloves, finely chopped
175g/6oz/2½ cups brown cap
    (cremini) mushrooms, sliced
2 carrots, coarsely grated
about 120ml/4fl oz/½ cup
    vegetable stock
30ml/2 tbsp chopped fresh flat
    leaf parsley
50g/2oz Pecorino cheese, grated
    or shaved
45ml/3 tbsp pumpkin seeds,
    toasted, or chopped walnuts
salt and ground black pepper

1 Rinse the barley, then cook it in simmering water, keeping the pan part-covered, for 35–45 minutes, or until tender. Drain. Preheat the oven to 200°C/400°F/Gas 6.

2 Place the squash in a roasting pan with half the thyme. Season with ground black pepper and toss with half the oil. Roast, stirring once, for 30–35 minutes, until tender and beginning to brown.

3 Heat half the butter with the remaining oil in a large frying pan. Cook the leeks and garlic gently for 5 minutes, stirring frequently. Add the mushrooms and remaining thyme, then cook until the liquid from the mushrooms evaporates and they begin to fry.

4 Stir in the carrots and cook for 2 minutes, then add the barley and most of the stock. Season well and part-cover the pan. Cook for a further 5 minutes. Pour in the remaining stock if the mixture seems dry.

5 Stir in the parsley, the remaining butter and half the Pecorino. Then stir in the squash. Season and serve sprinkled with the toasted pumpkin seeds or walnuts and the remaining Pecorino.

Roasted Squash Energy 337kcal/1416kJ; Protein 11.5g; Carbohydrate 43.5g, of which sugars 7.1g; Fat 14.2g, of which saturates 5.9g; Cholesterol 23mg; Calcium 206mg; Fibre 5.3g; Sodium 613mg.
Barley Risotto Energy 263kcal/1110kJ; Protein 8.1g; Carbohydrate 38.6g, of which sugars 6.1g; Fat 9.5g, of which saturates 3.3g; Cholesterol 11mg; Calcium 134mg; Fibre 4.5g; Sodium 77mg.

Cheese and Leek Rissoles with Tomato, Garlic and Chilli Sauce

These rissoles are based on the Welsh speciality, Glamorgan sausages. They are usually made with breadcrumbs alone, but mashed potato lightens the mix. Here they are served with a lively tomato sauce.

Serves 4
25g/1oz/2 tbsp butter
175g/6oz leeks, finely chopped
90ml/6 tbsp cold mashed potato
115g/4oz/2 cups fresh white or
  wholemeal (whole-wheat)
  breadcrumbs
150g/5oz/1¼ cups grated
  Caerphilly or Lancashire cheese
30ml/2 tbsp chopped fresh parsley
5ml/1 tsp chopped fresh sage
2 large eggs, beaten

cayenne pepper
65g/2½oz/1 cup dry white
  breadcrumbs
oil for shallow frying

For the sauce
30ml/2 tbsp olive oil
2 garlic cloves, thinly sliced
1 fresh red chilli, seeded and
  finely chopped, or a good pinch
  of dried red chilli flakes
1 small onion, finely chopped
500g/1¼lb tomatoes, peeled,
  seeded and chopped
few fresh thyme sprigs
10ml/2 tsp balsamic vinegar
  or red wine vinegar
pinch of light brown sugar
15–30ml/1–2 tbsp chopped
  fresh oregano
salt and ground black pepper

1 Melt the butter and fry the leeks for 4–5 minutes, until softened. Mix with the mashed potato, fresh breadcrumbs, cheese, parsley and sage. Add sufficient beaten egg (about two-thirds) to bind. Season well and add a good pinch of cayenne. Shape the mixture into 12 rissoles. Dip in the remaining egg, then coat with the dry breadcrumbs. Chill the coated rissoles.

2 To make the sauce, heat the oil over low heat in a pan, add the garlic, chilli and onion and cook for 3–4 minutes. Add the tomatoes, thyme and vinegar. Add salt, pepper and sugar. Cook for 40–50 minutes, until reduced. Remove the thyme and purée in a blender. Reheat with the oregano, and adjust the seasoning.

3 Fry the rissoles in shallow oil until golden brown on all sides. Drain on kitchen paper and serve with the sauce.

Provençal Rice

One of the glorious things about food from the south of France is its colour, and this dish is no exception.

Serves 4
2 onions
90ml/6 tbsp olive oil
175g/6oz/scant 1 cup brown long
  grain rice
10ml/2 tsp mustard seeds
475ml/16fl oz/2 cups
  vegetable stock
1 large or 2 small red (bell) peppers,
  seeded and cut into chunks
1 small aubergine (eggplant), cut
  into cubes

2–3 courgettes (zucchini), sliced
12 cherry tomatoes
5–6 fresh basil leaves, torn
  into pieces
2 garlic cloves, finely chopped
60ml/4 tbsp white wine
60ml/4 tbsp passata (bottled
  strained tomatoes) or
  tomato juice
2 hard-boiled eggs, cut
  into wedges
8 stuffed green olives, sliced
15ml/1 tbsp capers
3 drained sun-dried tomatoes in
  oil, sliced (optional)
butter
sea salt and ground black pepper

1 Preheat the oven to 200°C/400°F/Gas 6. Finely chop one onion. Heat 30ml/2 tbsp of the oil in a pan and fry the chopped onion over medium heat for 5–6 minutes until softened.

2 Add the rice and mustard seeds. Cook, stirring, for 2 minutes. Add the stock and a little salt. Bring to the boil, then lower the heat, cover and simmer for 35 minutes until the rice is tender.

3 Meanwhile, cut the remaining onion into wedges. Place in a roasting pan with the peppers, aubergine, courgettes and cherry tomatoes. Sprinkle over the basil and garlic. Pour over the remaining oil and season. Roast for 15–20 minutes, stirring once. Reduce the oven temperature to 180°C/350°F/Gas 4.

4 Spoon the rice into an earthenware casserole. Put the roasted vegetables on top, together with any juices from the pan, then pour over the wine and passata or tomato juice.

5 Arrange the egg wedges on top, with the olives, capers and sun-dried tomatoes, if using. Dot with butter, cover and cook for 15–20 minutes until heated through. Serve immediately.

Cheese Rissoles Energy 580kcal/2416kJ; Protein 19.2g; Carbohydrate 35.5g, of which sugars 6.9g; Fat 40.3g, of which saturates 15.2g; Cholesterol 164mg; Calcium 361mg; Fibre 3.6g; Sodium 604mg.
Provençal Rice Energy 359kcal/1511kJ; Protein 9.5g; Carbohydrate 59.2g, of which sugars 12.1g; Fat 10g, of which saturates 1.8g; Cholesterol 48mg; Calcium 74mg; Fibre 5.7g; Sodium 114mg.

Green Beans with Eggs

This is an unusual way of cooking green beans, but tastes delicious. Try this dish for a light supper or as an accompaniment to a simple roast. Served solo, it is a good source of protein and would make a quick, easy and attractive-looking vegetarian meal.

Serves 6
300g/11oz string beans, topped, tailed and halved
30ml/2 tbsp vegetable oil
1 onion, halved and thinly sliced
3 eggs
50g/2oz/¹/₂ cup grated Monterey Jack or mild Cheddar cheese
salt and ground black pepper
strips of lemon rind, to garnish

1 Bring a pan of water to the boil, add the beans and cook for 5–6 minutes or until tender. Drain in a colander, rinse under cold water to preserve the bright colour, then drain the beans once more, shaking the colander several times.

2 Heat the oil in a frying pan and fry the onion slices for 3–4 minutes until soft and translucent.

3 Break the eggs into a mixing bowl and beat them with salt and ground black pepper.

4 Add the egg mixture to the cooked onion. Cook slowly over medium heat, stirring constantly so that the egg becomes lightly scrambled. The egg should be moist throughout. Do not overcook; the consistency must be creamy.

5 Add the beans to the pan and cook for a few minutes until warmed through. Transfer the mixture into a heated serving dish, top with the grated cheese and garnish with lemon rind.

> **Variations**
> • *Freshly grated Parmesan can be used instead of the Monterey Jack or Cheddar cheese for a sharper flavour.*
> • *Garnish with strips of red (bell) pepper instead of lemon rind for a more colourful finish, or use a mixture of peppers.*
> • *For a more substantial dish, add cooked spaghetti.*

Onions Stuffed with Goat's Cheese and Sun-dried Tomatoes

Roasted onions and goat's cheese are a winning combination. These stuffed onions make an excellent main course when served with a rice or cracked wheat pilaff.

Serves 4
4 large onions
150g/5oz goat's cheese, crumbled or cubed
50g/2oz fresh breadcrumbs
8 sun-dried tomatoes in olive oil, drained and chopped
1–2 garlic cloves, finely chopped
2.5ml/¹/₂ tsp chopped fresh thyme
30ml/2 tbsp chopped fresh parsley
1 small egg, beaten
45ml/3 tbsp pine nuts, toasted
30ml/2 tbsp olive oil (use oil from the tomatoes)
salt and ground black pepper

1 Bring a large pan of lightly salted water to the boil. Add the whole onions in their skins and boil for 10 minutes. Drain and cool, then cut each onion in half horizontally and peel.

2 Using a teaspoon, remove the centre of each onion, leaving a thick shell. Reserve the flesh and place the shells in an oiled baking dish. Preheat the oven to 190°C/375°F/Gas 5.

3 Chop the scooped-out onion flesh and place in a bowl. Add the goat's cheese, breadcrumbs, sun-dried tomatoes, garlic, thyme, parsley and egg. Mix well, then season with salt and pepper and add the toasted pine nuts.

4 Divide the stuffing among the onions and cover with foil. Bake for about 25 minutes. Uncover, drizzle with the oil and cook for another 30–40 minutes, until bubbling and well cooked. Baste occasionally during cooking.

> **Variation**
> *Use feta cheese in place of the goat's cheese and substitute chopped mint, currants and pitted black olives for the other flavourings, if you like.*

Green Beans Energy 126kcal/519kJ; Protein 6.7g; Carbohydrate 2.7g, of which sugars 1.9g; Fat 9.0g, of which saturates 3.3g; Cholesterol 104mg; Calcium 106mg; Fibre 1.4g; Sodium 102mg.
Stuffed Onions Energy 400kcal/1659kJ; Protein 14g; Carbohydrate 19g, of which sugars 7.3g; Fat 30.4g, of which saturates 9.2g; Cholesterol 82mg; Calcium 115mg; Fibre 2.4g; Sodium 345mg.

Baked Herb Crêpes

Add fresh herbs, such as parsley or basil, to make crêpes something special, then fill them with spinach, pine nuts and ricotta cheese and serve with a garlicky tomato sauce.

Serves 4
25g/1oz/½ cup chopped
    fresh herbs
15ml/1 tbsp sunflower oil, plus
    extra for frying and greasing
120ml/4fl oz/½ cup milk
3 eggs
25g/1oz/¼ cup plain
    (all-purpose) flour
pinch of salt

For the sauce
30ml/2 tbsp olive oil
1 small onion, chopped
2 garlic cloves, crushed
400g/14oz can
    chopped tomatoes
pinch of soft light brown sugar

For the filling
450g/1lb fresh spinach, cooked
175g/6oz/¾ cup ricotta cheese
25g/1oz/¼ cup pine nuts, toasted
5 sun-dried tomatoes in olive oil,
    drained and chopped
30ml/2 tbsp chopped fresh basil
salt, nutmeg and ground
    black pepper
4 egg whites

1 To make the crêpes, place the herbs and oil in a food processor and blend until smooth. Add the milk, eggs, flour and salt and process again. Leave to rest for 30 minutes. Heat a small frying pan and add a little oil. Add a ladleful of batter. Swirl around to cover the base. Cook for 2 minutes, turn and cook for 2 minutes. Make seven more crêpes.

2 To make the sauce, heat the oil in a pan, add the onion and garlic and cook gently for 5 minutes. Add the tomatoes and sugar and cook for about 10 minutes, or until thickened. Purée in a blender, then strain and set aside.

3 Preheat the oven to 190°C/375°F/Gas 5. To make the filling, mix the spinach with the ricotta, pine nuts, tomatoes and basil. Season with salt, nutmeg and pepper. Whisk the egg whites until stiff. Fold one-third into the mixture, then gently fold in the rest.

4 Place one crêpe at a time on a lightly oiled baking sheet, add a spoonful of filling and fold into quarters. Bake for 12 minutes until set. Reheat the sauce and serve with the crêpes.

Courgette, Feta and Chilli Fritters

Ideal for lunch, supper, a savoury snack or appetizer, these tasty patties are incredibly versatile. You can even make miniature versions and serve them as tasty finger food with drinks at a party. If you like a little more fire on your tongue, you can add extra fresh red chillies.

Serves 4–6
3 firm courgettes (zucchini)
30–45ml/2–3 tbsp olive oil
1 large onion, halved lengthways,
    halved again crossways, and
    sliced along the grain
4 garlic cloves, chopped
45ml/3 tbsp plain (all-purpose) flour
3 eggs, beaten
225g/8oz feta cheese, crumbled
1 bunch each of fresh flat leaf
    parsley, mint and dill, chopped
1 fresh red chilli, seeded
    and chopped
sunflower oil, for shallow frying
salt and ground black pepper
mint leaves, to garnish

1 Wash the courgettes and trim off the ends. Hold them at an angle and grate them, then put them in a colander or sieve (strainer) and sprinkle with a little salt. Leave them to weep for about 5 minutes.

2 Squeeze the grated courgettes in your hand to extract the juices. Heat the olive oil in a heavy frying pan, stir in the courgettes, onion and garlic and fry until they begin to take on colour. Remove from the heat and leave to cool.

3 Place the flour into a large bowl and gradually beat in the eggs to form a smooth batter. Beat in the cooled courgette mixture. Add the feta cheese, herbs and chilli, and season with a little pepper. Add salt if you like, but usually the feta is quite salty. Mix well.

4 Heat enough sunflower oil for shallow frying in a heavy, non-stick pan. Drop four spoonfuls of the mixture into the hot oil, leaving space between each one, then fry over medium heat for 6–8 minutes, or until firm to the touch and golden brown on both sides. Remove from the pan with a slotted spoon and drain on kitchen paper while you fry the remainder. Serve while still warm, garnished with mint leaves.

Baked Herb Crêpes Energy 434kcal/1800kJ; Protein 14.9g; Carbohydrate 15.1g, of which sugars 9.8g; Fat 35.4g, of which saturates 8.3g; Cholesterol 161mg; Calcium 251mg; Fibre 5g; Sodium 229mg.
Fritters Energy 327kcal/1354kJ; Protein 12.3g; Carbohydrate 12.4g, of which sugars 5.4g; Fat 25.7g, of which saturates 7.9g; Cholesterol 121mg; Calcium 214mg; Fibre 2.3g; Sodium 581mg.

Soufflé Omelette with Mushrooms

This soufflé omelette makes an ideal meal for one, especially with this delicious filling, but be warned – when others smell it cooking they are likely to demand their share. Thankfully it is easy to increase the quantities to feed more people.

Serves 1
2 eggs, separated
15g/¹⁄₂oz/1 tbsp butter
flat leaf parsley or coriander
(cilantro) leaves, to garnish

For the mushroom sauce
15g/¹⁄₂oz/1 tbsp butter
75g/3oz/generous 1 cup
button (white) mushrooms,
thinly sliced
15ml/1 tbsp plain
(all-purpose) flour
85–120ml/3–4fl oz/¹⁄₃–¹⁄₂ cup
semi-skimmed (low-fat) milk
5ml/1 tsp chopped fresh parsley
salt and ground black pepper

1 To make the mushroom sauce, melt the butter in a pan or frying pan and add the sliced mushrooms. Fry gently for 4–5 minutes, stirring occasionally. The mushrooms will exude quite a lot of liquid, but this will rapidly be reabsorbed.

2 Stir in the flour, then gradually add the milk, stirring all the time. Cook until the sauce boils and thickens. Add the parsley, if using, and season with salt and pepper. Keep warm.

3 Make the omelette. Beat the egg yolks with 15ml/1 tbsp water and season with a little salt and pepper. Whisk the egg whites until stiff, then fold into the egg yolks. Preheat the grill (broiler) for at least 3 minutes.

4 Meanwhile, melt the butter in a large frying pan. Pour in the egg mixture. Cook over a gentle heat for 2–4 minutes.

5 Place the frying pan under the grill and cook for a further 3–4 minutes until the top of the omelette has puffed up and has turned a golden brown colour.

6 Slide the omelette on to a warmed serving plate, pour the mushroom sauce over the top and fold the omelette in half. Serve, garnished with parsley.

Spanish Omelette

The traditional Spanish omelette consists simply of potatoes, onions and eggs. This one has other vegetables and white beans and makes a substantial vegetarian meal.

Serves 6
30ml/2 tbsp olive oil, plus extra
for drizzling
1 Spanish (Bermuda)
onion, chopped
1 small red (bell) pepper, seeded
and diced
2 celery sticks, chopped
225g/8oz potatoes, peeled, diced
and cooked
400g/14oz can cannellini
beans, drained
8 eggs
salt and ground black pepper
sprigs of oregano, to garnish
green salad and olives, to serve

1 Heat the olive oil in a 30cm/12in frying pan or paella pan. Add the onion, red pepper and celery, and cook for 3–5 minutes until the vegetables are soft but not coloured.

2 Add the potatoes and beans, and cook for several minutes to heat through.

3 In a small bowl, beat the eggs with a fork, then season well and pour over the ingredients in the pan.

4 Stir the egg mixture with a wooden spatula until it begins to thicken, then allow it to cook over low heat for about 8 minutes. The omelette should be firm, but still moist in the middle. Cool slightly, then invert on to a serving plate.

5 Cut the omelette into thick wedges. Serve warm or cool with a green salad and olives and a little olive oil. Garnish with sprigs of oregano.

Cook's Tip
In Spain, this omelette is often served as a tapas dish or appetizer. It is delicious served cold, cut into bitesize pieces and accompanied with a chilli sauce or mayonnaise for dipping.

Omelette Energy 838kcal/3514kJ; Protein 45.5g; Carbohydrate 53.7g, of which sugars 42.1g; Fat 51.4g, of which saturates 28.3g; Cholesterol 497mg; Calcium 1150mg; Fibre 1.3g; Sodium 707mg.
Spanish Omelette Energy 223kcal/937kJ; Protein 15.2g; Carbohydrate 25.1g, of which sugars 5.4g; Fat 7.7g, of which saturates 1.9g; Cholesterol 190mg; Calcium 82mg; Fibre 6.8g; Sodium 86mg.

34

VEGETABLE DISHES

Soft Tacos with Spiced Omelette

Served hot, warm or cold,
these tacos make easy food
on the move for younger
members of the family, when
they need something
nourishing to take on a
picnic, hike or cycle ride.

Serves 4
30ml/2 tbsp sunflower oil
50g/2oz/¼ cup beansprouts
50g/2oz carrots, cut into thin sticks

25g/1oz Chinese leaves (Chinese
  cabbage), chopped
15ml/1 tbsp light soy sauce
4 eggs
1 small spring onion (scallion),
  finely sliced
5ml/1 tsp Cajun seasoning
25g/1oz/2 tbsp butter
4 soft flour tortillas, warmed in
  the oven or microwave
salt and ground black pepper

1 Heat the oil in a small frying pan and stir-fry the beansprouts,
carrot sticks and chopped cabbage until they begin to soften.
Add the soy sauce, stir to combine and set aside.

2 Place the eggs, sliced spring onion, Cajun seasoning, salt
and ground black pepper in a bowl, and beat together.
Melt the butter in a small pan until it sizzles. Add the beaten
eggs and cook over a gentle heat, stirring constantly,
until almost firm.

3 Divide the vegetables and scrambled egg among
the tortillas, fold up into cones or parcels and serve.
For travelling, the tacos can be wrapped in foil.

Variation
*Fill warm pitta breads with this spicy omelette mixture. Mini
pitta breads are perfect for younger children who may find the
folded tacos difficult to handle.*

Cook's Tip
*You can buy fresh soft tortillas in large supermarkets. They
freeze well, so keep a packet or two in the freezer.*

Frittata with Sun-dried Tomatoes

Like a Spanish omelette,
a frittata is cooked until
firm enough to be cut into
wedges. Italian in origin,
it is served hot or cold.

Serves 3–4
6 sun-dried tomatoes
60ml/4 tbsp olive oil

1 small onion, finely chopped
pinch of fresh thyme leaves
6 eggs
50g/2oz/⅔ cup freshly grated
  Parmesan cheese
salt and ground black pepper
sprigs of thyme, to garnish
shavings of Parmesan,
  to serve

1 Place the tomatoes in a small bowl and pour over enough
hot water to just cover them. Leave to soak for about
15 minutes.

2 Lift the tomatoes out of the water and pat dry using kitchen
paper. Reserve the soaking water. Cut each tomato into
thin strips.

3 Heat the oil in a large frying pan. Stir in the chopped onion
and cook for 5–6 minutes or until softened and golden.

4 Stir the sun-dried tomatoes and thyme into the onions, and
cook over medium heat for a further 2–3 minutes, stirring from
time to time. Season with salt and ground black pepper.

5 Break the eggs into a bowl and beat lightly. Stir in 45ml/3 tbsp
of the tomato-soaking water and the Parmesan. Raise the heat
under the frying pan. When the oil is sizzling, add the eggs.
Mix quickly into the other ingredients, then stop stirring.
Lower the heat to medium and cook for 4–5 minutes, or until
the base is golden and the top puffed.

6 Take a large plate, place it upside down over the pan and,
holding it firmly with oven gloves, turn the pan and the frittata
over on to it. Slide the frittata back into the pan, and continue
cooking for 3–4 minutes until golden brown on the second side.

7 Remove the pan from the heat. Cut the frittata into wedges,
garnish with sprigs of thyme and serve immediately.

Soft Tacos Energy 280kcal/1168kJ; Protein 9.5g; Carbohydrate 24.2g, of which sugars 2g; Fat 16.7g, of which saturates 5.5g; Cholesterol 204mg; Calcium 80mg; Fibre 1.5g; Sodium 217mg.
Frittata Energy 170kcal/705kJ; Protein 5.7g; Carbohydrate 3g, of which sugars 2.6g; Fat 15.2g, of which saturates 4.1g; Cholesterol 13mg; Calcium 158mg; Fibre 0.6g; Sodium 167mg.

Potato, Onion and Feta Frittata

This Italian omelette is cooked with vegetables, including red onion and new potatoes, and feta cheese. The finished dish is served flat, like a Spanish tortilla. Cut it into wedges and serve it with crusty bread and a tomato salad.

Serves 2–4
25ml/1½ tbsp olive oil
1 red onion, sliced
350g/12oz cooked new potatoes, halved or quartered, if large
6 eggs, lightly beaten
115g/4oz/1 cup feta cheese, diced
salt and ground black pepper

1 Heat the oil in a large heavy, flameproof frying pan. Add the sliced onion and cook for about 5 minutes until softened, stirring occasionally.

2 Add the potatoes and cook for a further 5 minutes until golden, stirring to prevent them sticking. Spread the mixture evenly over the base of the pan.

3 Preheat the grill (broiler) to high. Season the beaten eggs, then pour them over the onion and potatoes. Sprinkle the cheese on top and cook over a moderate heat for 5–6 minutes until the eggs are set and the base of the frittata is lightly golden.

4 Place the pan under the preheated grill (protect the pan handle with a double layer of foil if it is not flameproof) and cook the top of the omelette for about 3 minutes until it is set and lightly golden. Serve the frittata warm or cold, cut into big wedges.

Cook's Tip
Eggs are an important source of vitamin B12, which is vital for the nervous system and the development of red blood cells. They also supply other B vitamins, zinc and selenium and a useful amount of iron. It is beneficial to eat a food rich in vitamin C at the same time in order to help the absorption of iron. Do not eat too many eggs, though – no more than a maximum of three per week.

Roasted Garlic and Cheese Soufflé

The mellow flavour of roasted garlic pervades this simple soufflé.

Serves 4
2 large heads of garlic
3 fresh thyme sprigs
15ml/1 tbsp olive oil
250ml/8fl oz/1 cup milk
1 fresh bay leaf
2 x 1cm/½in thick onion slices
2 cloves
50g/2oz/¼ cup butter
40g/1½oz/⅓ cup plain (all-purpose) flour, sifted
cayenne pepper
3 eggs, separated, plus 1 egg white
150g/5oz goat's cheese, crumbled
50g/2oz/⅔ cup freshly grated Parmesan cheese
2.5–5ml/½–1 tsp chopped fresh thyme
2.5ml/½ tsp cream of tartar
salt and ground black pepper

1 Preheat the oven to 180°C/350°F/Gas 4. Place the garlic and thyme sprigs on a piece of foil. Sprinkle with oil and close the foil, then bake for 1 hour, until the garlic is soft. Leave to cool.

2 Squeeze the garlic out of its skin. Discard the thyme and garlic skins, then purée the garlic flesh with the oil. Place the milk, bay leaf, onion slices and cloves in a pan. Bring to the boil, then remove from the heat. Leave for 30 minutes.

3 Melt 40g/1½oz/3 tbsp of the butter in a pan. Stir in the flour and cook for 2 minutes, stirring. Reheat and strain the milk, then gradually stir it into the flour and butter. Simmer for 10 minutes, stirring frequently. Season with salt, pepper and a pinch of cayenne. Cool slightly. Preheat the oven to 200°C/400°F/Gas 6.

4 Beat in the egg yolks one at a time. Then beat in the goat's cheese, all but 15ml/1 tbsp of the Parmesan and the chopped thyme. Grease four large ramekins (about 250ml/8fl oz/1 cup).

5 Whisk the egg whites and cream of tartar in a clean bowl until firm. Stir 45ml/3 tbsp of the whites into the sauce, then fold in the remainder. Pour the mixture into the ramekins. Run a knife around the edges. Sprinkle with the reserved Parmesan.

6 Place on a baking sheet and bake for 20 minutes. They should be risen and firm to a light touch. Serve immediately.

Potato Frittata Energy 289kcal/1207kJ; Protein 15.5g; Carbohydrate 15.7g, of which sugars 2.4g; Fat 18.9g, of which saturates 7g; Cholesterol 306mg; Calcium 155mg; Fibre 1.1g; Sodium 529mg.
Soufflé Energy 563kcal/2338kJ; Protein 28.8g; Carbohydrate 16.5g, of which sugars 5.8g; Fat 42.9g, of which saturates 24.1g; Cholesterol 294mg; Calcium 422mg; Fibre 0.7g; Sodium 710mg.

Leek, Cheese and Walnut Roulade

This roulade is surprisingly easy to prepare and it makes a good main course.

Serves 4–6
butter or oil, for greasing
30ml/2 tbsp fine breadcrumbs
75g/3oz/1 cup finely grated
  Parmesan cheese
50g/2oz/¼ cup butter
2 leeks, thinly sliced
40g/1½oz/⅓ cup plain
  (all-purpose) flour
250ml/8fl oz/1 cup milk

5ml/1 tsp Dijon mustard
1.5ml/¼ tsp freshly grated nutmeg
2 large eggs, plus 1 egg white
2.5ml/½ tsp cream of tartar
salt and ground black pepper
rocket (arugula) and balsamic
  dressing, to serve

For the filling
2 large red (bell) peppers
350g/12oz/1½ cups curd cheese
90g/3½oz chopped walnuts
4 spring onions (scallions), chopped
15g/½oz fresh basil leaves

1 Grease and line a 30 x 23cm/12 x 9in Swiss roll tin (jelly roll pan), then sprinkle with the breadcrumbs and 30ml/2 tbsp of the grated Parmesan. Preheat the oven to 190°C/375°F/Gas 5.

2 Melt the butter in a pan and fry the leeks for 5 minutes. Stir in the flour and cook for 2 minutes, then add the milk. Cook for 4 minutes, stirring constantly. Add the mustard and nutmeg and season. Reserve 30–45ml/2–3 tbsp Parmesan, then stir the rest into the sauce. Cool slightly, then beat in the egg yolks.

3 In a scrupulously clean bowl, whisk the egg whites and cream of tartar until stiff. Stir 2–3 spoonfuls of the egg white into the leek mixture, then fold in the remaining egg white. Pour into the tin. Bake for 15–18 minutes, until risen and just firm.

4 Heat the grill (broiler). Halve and seed the peppers. Cook, skin side up, until black. Peel off the skin and cut into strips. Beat the cheese with the walnuts and spring onions. Chop half the basil and beat it into the mixture. Season to taste.

5 Sprinkle a sheet of baking parchment with the remaining Parmesan. Turn out the roulade and strip off the paper. Spread the filling over it and top with the pepper strips. Tear the basil over the top. Roll up the roulade. Serve with rocket and dressing.

Spinach and Goat's Cheese Roulade

This twice-baked roulade is really a Swiss roll soufflé.

Serves 4
300ml/½ pint/1¼ cups milk
50g/2oz/½ cup plain
  (all-purpose) flour
150g/5oz/⅔ cup butter
100g/3¾oz chèvre (goat's
  cheese), chopped

40g/1½oz/½ cup freshly grated
  Parmesan cheese, plus extra
  for dusting
4 eggs, separated
250g/9oz/2¼ cups fresh shiitake
  mushrooms, sliced
275g/10oz baby spinach
  leaves, washed
45ml/3 tbsp crème fraîche
salt and ground black pepper

1 Preheat the oven to 190°C/375°F/Gas 5. Line a 30 x 20cm/12 x 8in Swiss roll tin (jelly roll pan) with baking parchment so that the edges rise above the sides of the tin. Grease lightly.

2 Mix the milk, flour and 50g/2oz/¼ cup of the butter in a large pan. Bring to the boil over low heat, whisking until thick. Simmer for 2 minutes, then mix in the chèvre and half the Parmesan. Cool for 5 minutes, then beat in the egg yolks, and season.

3 Whisk the egg whites in a grease-free bowl until soft peaks form. Gently fold the whites into the chèvre mixture, using a large metal spoon. Spoon into the prepared tin, spread gently to level, then bake for 15 minutes until the top feels just firm.

4 Let the roulade cool for a short time. Meanwhile, dust a sheet of baking parchment with a little Parmesan cheese and carefully invert the roulade on to the paper. Tear the lining paper away from the base of the roulade, in strips. Roll up in the baking parchment and set aside to cool completely.

5 Make the filling. Melt the remaining butter in a pan, reserving 30ml/2 tbsp. Add the mushrooms and stir-fry for 3 minutes. In a separate pan, cook the spinach until it wilts. Drain, add to the mushrooms and stir in the crème fraîche. Season, then cool.

6 Unroll the roulade and spread over the filling. Roll up again and place on a baking sheet. Brush with the reserved butter and sprinkle with the Parmesan. Bake for 15 minutes until risen.

Spinach Roulade Energy 625kcal/2589kJ; Protein 22.7g; Carbohydrate 15.3g, of which sugars 5.6g; Fat 52.9g, of which saturates 31.7g; Cholesterol 321mg; Calcium 423mg; Fibre 2.5g; Sodium 691mg.
Leek Roulade Energy 401kcal/1667kJ; Protein 21.9g; Carbohydrate 14.9g, of which sugars 9.2g; Fat 29.4g, of which saturates 12g; Cholesterol 123mg; Calcium 324mg; Fibre 2.9g; Sodium 493mg.

Leek, Spinach and Courgette Kugel

Fresh dill, spring onions and garlic give their flavours to the fresh greens of leeks, spinach and courgette in this crisp kugel.

Serves 6–8

90ml/6 tbsp olive oil
2 large leeks, thinly sliced
500g/1¼lb spinach, washed
1 courgette (zucchini),
  coarsely grated
1 baking potato
3 garlic cloves, chopped
3 spring onions (scallions),
  chopped or thinly sliced
1–2 pinches of ground turmeric
about 45ml/3 tbsp medium
  matzo meal
15–30ml/1–2 tbsp chopped fresh
  dill, plus extra to garnish
3 eggs, lightly beaten
salt and ground black pepper
lemons wedges, to serve

1 Preheat the oven to 200°C/400°F/Gas 6. Heat half the oil in a pan, add the leeks and fry until tender. Remove from the heat.

2 Cook the spinach in the water that clings to it after washing until just tender. Drain and, when cool enough to handle, roughly chop. Add the spinach and courgette to the leeks, and stir to combine.

3 Peel and coarsely grate the potato, then squeeze in your hands to remove excess starch and liquid. Add to the leeks with the garlic, spring onions, turmeric and plenty of salt and pepper.

4 Add enough matzo meal to the vegetable mixture to form a thick dough consistency. Stir the dill into the eggs, then add to the vegetable mixture.

5 Pour the remaining oil into a baking tin (pan) and heat in the oven for about 5 minutes. When the oil is hot, spoon the vegetable mixture evenly into the tin, letting the hot oil bubble up around the sides and on to the top.

6 Bake the kugel for about 15 minutes, then reduce the oven temperature to 180°C/350°F/Gas 4 and bake for a further 15–20 minutes, until the kugel is firm to the touch and the top is golden brown. Sprinkle with chopped dill to garnish and serve hot or warm with the lemon wedges for squeezing over.

Couscous with Eggs and Tomato

This tasty vegetarian dish is quick to make with the easy-to-use couscous available today.

Serves 4

675g/1½lb plum tomatoes,
  roughly chopped
4 garlic cloves, chopped
75ml/5 tbsp olive oil
½ fresh red chilli, seeded
  and chopped
10ml/2 tsp soft light brown sugar
4 eggs
1 large onion, chopped
2 celery sticks, finely sliced
50g/2oz/⅓ cup sultanas
  (golden raisins)
200g/7oz/generous 1 cup
  ready-to-use couscous
350ml/12fl oz/1½ cups hot
  vegetable stock
salt and ground black pepper

1 Preheat the oven to 200°C/400°F/Gas 6. Spread out the tomatoes and garlic in a roasting pan, drizzle with 30ml/2 tbsp of the oil, sprinkle with the chopped chilli and sugar, salt and pepper, and roast for 20 minutes.

2 Meanwhile, cook the eggs in boiling water for 4 minutes, then plunge them straight into cold water and leave until cold. Carefully peel off the shells.

3 Heat 15–30ml/1–2 tbsp of the remaining olive oil in a large pan and fry the onion and celery until softened. Add the sultanas, couscous and hot stock, and set aside until all the liquid has been absorbed. Stir gently, adding extra hot stock if necessary, and season to taste. Turn the mixture into a large heated serving dish, bury the eggs in the couscous and cover with foil. Keep warm in the oven.

4 Remove the tomato mixture from the oven and press it through a sieve (strainer) placed over a bowl. Add 15ml/1 tbsp boiling water and the rest of the olive oil and stir to make a smooth, rich sauce.

5 Remove the couscous mixture from the oven and locate the eggs. Spoon the couscous on to four serving plates, top each with an egg and a little tomato sauce. Serve immediately, with the rest of the sauce offered to diners separately.

Leek Kugel Energy 172kcal/714kJ; Protein 6.4g; Carbohydrate 11.2g, of which sugars 2.9g; Fat 11.5g, of which saturates 1.9g; Cholesterol 71mg; Calcium 138mg; Fibre 3.1g; Sodium 118mg.
Couscous Energy 418kcal/1744kJ; Protein 12.1g; Carbohydrate 49.3g, of which sugars 21g; Fat 20.6g, of which saturates 3.7g; Cholesterol 190mg; Calcium 85mg; Fibre 3.4g; Sodium 99mg.

Savoury Nut Loaf

Ideal as an alternative to the traditional meat roast, this slow-cooker dish is perfect for special occasions.

Serves 4

30ml/2 tbsp olive oil, plus extra
  for greasing
1 onion, finely chopped
1 leek, finely chopped
2 celery sticks, finely chopped
225g/8oz/3 cups mushrooms,
  chopped
2 garlic cloves, crushed

425g/15oz can lentils, drained
115g/4oz/1 cup mixed nuts, such
  as hazelnuts, cashew nuts and
  almonds, finely chopped
50g/2oz/¹⁄₂ cup plain
  (all-purpose) flour
50g/2oz/¹⁄₂ cup grated mature
  (sharp) Cheddar cheese
1 egg, beaten
45–60ml/3–4 tbsp chopped fresh
  mixed herbs
salt and ground black pepper
chives and sprigs of fresh flat leaf
  parsley, to garnish

1 Place an upturned saucer or metal pastry ring in the base of the ceramic cooking pot. Pour in about 2.5cm/1in hot water and switch the slow cooker to high.

2 Grease the base and sides of a 900g/2lb loaf tin (pan) or terrine – first making sure it will fit in the slow cooker – and line the base and sides of the tin with baking parchment.

3 Heat the oil in a large pan, add the onion, leek, celery, mushrooms and garlic, then cook for 10 minutes, until the vegetables have softened. Do not let them brown.

4 Remove the pan from the heat, then stir in the lentils, mixed nuts and flour, grated cheese, beaten egg and herbs. Season well with salt and black pepper and mix thoroughly.

5 Spoon the mixture into the tin or terrine. Level the surface with a fork, then cover with a piece of foil. Place the tin in the ceramic cooking pot and pour in enough near-boiling water to come just over halfway up the side of the dish. Cover with the lid and cook for 3–4 hours, or until the loaf is firm to the touch.

6 Leave to cool in the tin for 15 minutes. Serve the loaf hot or cold, cut into slices and garnished with chives and parsley.

Kidney Bean and Gari Loaf

Kidney beans and peppers are used to make this tasty, nutritious loaf.

Serves 4–6

225g/8oz/1¹⁄₄ cups dried red
  kidney beans, soaked overnight
15g/¹⁄₂oz/1 tbsp butter
1 onion, finely chopped
2 garlic cloves, crushed

¹⁄₂ red and ¹⁄₂ green (bell)
  pepper, seeded and chopped
1 fresh green chilli, seeded and
  finely chopped
5ml/1 tsp chopped fresh
  mixed herbs
2 eggs, beaten
15ml/1 tbsp lemon juice
75ml/5 tbsp gari (see Cook's Tip)
salt and ground black pepper

1 Drain the kidney beans, then place them in a pan, cover with water and boil rapidly for 15 minutes. Reduce the heat and continue boiling for about 1 hour, until the beans are tender. Drain, reserving the cooking liquid. Preheat the oven to 190°C/375°F/Gas 5 and grease a 900g/2lb loaf tin (pan).

2 Melt the butter in a large frying pan and fry the onion, garlic and peppers for 5 minutes. Add the chilli, mixed herbs and a little salt and pepper and stir to mix.

3 Place the beans in a large bowl, blender or food processor and mash or process to a pulp. Add the onion and pepper mix and stir well. Cool slightly, then stir in the eggs and lemon juice.

4 Place the gari in a separate bowl and sprinkle generously with warm water. The gari should become soft and fluffy after about 5 minutes. Stir the gari into the bean mixture. Spoon the mixture evenly into the prepared loaf tin and bake in the oven for 35–45 minutes, until firm to the touch.

5 Cool the loaf in the tin, and then turn it out on to a plate. Cut into thick slices and serve.

> **Cook's Tip**
> Gari is a coarse-grained flour, made from a starchy root vegetable, cassava, which is first dried, then ground.

Nut Loaf Energy 484Kcal/2019kJ; Protein 23.7g; Carbohydrate 34.1g, of which sugars 5.1g; Fat 29g, of which saturates 5.4g; Cholesterol 69mg; Calcium 238mg; Fibre 8.7g; Sodium 128mg.
Bean and Gari Loaf Energy 303Kcal/1275kJ; Protein 18g; Carbohydrate 42.5g, of which sugars 5g; Fat 7.5g, of which saturates 2.9g; Cholesterol 103mg; Calcium 79mg; Fibre 10.2g; Sodium 70mg.

Bean Chilli with Cornbread Topping

The delicious cornbread topping to this slow-cooker dish makes this a really great one-pot meal.

Serves 4
115g/4oz/generous ½ cup dried red kidney beans, soaked overnight
115g/4oz/generous ½ cup dried black-eyed beans (peas), soaked overnight
1 bay leaf
15ml/1 tbsp vegetable oil
1 large onion, finely chopped
1 garlic clove, crushed
5ml/1 tsp ground cumin
5ml/1 tsp chilli powder
5ml/1 tsp mild paprika
2.5ml/½ tsp dried marjoram
450g/1lb mixed vegetables such as potatoes, carrots, aubergines (eggplants), parsnips and celery, cut into 2cm/¾in chunks
1 vegetable stock (bouillon) cube
400g/14oz can chopped tomatoes
15ml/1 tbsp tomato purée (paste)
salt and ground black pepper

For the cornbread topping
250g/9oz/2¼ cups fine cornmeal
30ml/2 tbsp wholemeal (whole-wheat) flour
7.5ml/1½ tsp baking powder
1 egg, plus 1 egg yolk lightly beaten
300ml/½ pint/1¼ cups milk

1 Drain the beans and rinse, then place in a pan with 600ml/1 pint/2½ cups of cold water and the bay leaf. Bring to the boil and boil rapidly for 10 minutes. Leave to cool slightly, then place into the ceramic cooking pot and switch the slow cooker to high.

2 Heat the oil in a pan, add the onion and cook for 7–8 minutes. Add the garlic, cumin, chilli powder, paprika and marjoram and cook for 1 minute. Transfer into the ceramic cooking pot and stir. Add the vegetables to the mixture. Cover with the lid and cook for 3 hours, or until the beans are tender.

3 Add the stock cube and chopped tomatoes to the cooking pot, then stir in the tomato purée and season with salt and ground black pepper. Replace the lid and cook for a further 30 minutes until the mixture is at boiling point.

4 To make the topping, mix the cornmeal, flour, baking powder and a pinch of salt in a bowl. Make a well in the centre and add the egg, egg yolk and milk. Mix, then spoon over the chilli. Cover and cook for 1 hour until the topping is firm and cooked.

Baked Peppers with Egg and Lentils

These oven-baked eggs with a difference make a tasty vegetarian meal packed with protein and fibre.

Serves 4
75g/3oz/½ cup Puy lentils
2.5ml/½ tsp ground turmeric
2.5ml/½ tsp ground coriander
2.5ml/½ tsp paprika
450ml/¾ pint/1¾ cups vegetable stock
2 large (bell) peppers, halved lengthways and seeded
a little oil
15ml/1 tbsp chopped fresh mint
4 eggs
salt and ground black pepper
sprigs of coriander (cilantro), to garnish

1 Put the lentils in a pan with the spices and stock. Bring to the boil, stirring occasionally, and simmer for 30–40 minutes. If necessary, add more water during cooking.

2 Preheat the oven to 190°C/375°F/Gas 5. Brush the peppers lightly with oil and place them close together on a baking tray. Stir the chopped mint into the lentils, then fill the peppers with the mixture.

3 Crack the eggs, one at a time, into a small jug (pitcher) and carefully pour into the middle of a pepper. Stir into the lentils and sprinkle with seasoning. Bake for 10 minutes until the egg white is just set. Garnish with coriander and serve.

Cook's Tip
Puy lentils have a blue-green speckled colour. They are more expensive than normal lentils but have a superior taste.

Variations
• Use beef tomatoes instead of (bell) peppers. Cut a lid off the tomatoes and scoop out their middles using a spoon. Fill with lentils and eggs and bake as before.
• Add a little extra flavour to the lentil mixture by adding chopped onion and tomatoes sautéed in olive oil.

Bean Chilli Energy 613kcal/2595kJ; Protein 29.6g; Carbohydrate 97.4g, of which sugars 15.8g; Fat 14.5g, of which saturates 3.4g; Cholesterol 112mg; Calcium 257mg; Fibre 13.4g; Sodium 413mg.
Baked Peppers Energy 188kcal/788kJ; Protein 11.8g; Carbohydrate 16.3g, of which sugars 5.9g; Fat 9g, of which saturates 2.1g; Cholesterol 190mg; Calcium 58mg; Fibre 2.6g; Sodium 82mg.

Broccoli and Cheese Mina

A mina is a type of pie, prepared from layered matzos and a savoury sauce, and topped with beaten egg, which holds it all together.

Serves 4

1 large broccoli head
pinch of salt
pinch of sugar
8 matzo squares
50g/2oz/¹/₂ cup butter, plus extra
   for greasing

1 onion, chopped
250g/9oz/2¹/₄ cups grated
   Cheddar cheese
250g/9oz/generous 1 cup
   cottage cheese
65g/2¹/₂oz/³/₄ cup freshly grated
   Parmesan cheese
2 spring onions (scallions), chopped
30–45ml/2–3 tbsp chopped
   fresh dill
4 eggs
30ml/2 tbsp water
8 garlic cloves, chopped

1 Preheat the oven to 190°C/375°F/Gas 5. Remove the tough part of the stem from the broccoli, then cut the broccoli head into even-size florets. Cook the broccoli by either steaming above or boiling in water to which you have added a pinch of salt and sugar. Cook until bright green, then remove from the pan with a slotted spoon.

2 Wet four matzos and leave to soak for 2–3 minutes. Butter a baking sheet that is large enough to hold four matzo pieces in a single layer. If necessary, use two baking sheets.

3 Place the dampened matzos on the baking sheet, then top evenly with the broccoli, onion, Cheddar cheese, cottage cheese, Parmesan cheese, spring onions and dill.

4 In a bowl, lightly beat together the eggs and water, then pour about half the egg over the cheese and broccoli mixture. Wet the remaining matzos and place on top of the broccoli. Pour the remaining egg over the top, dot with half the butter and sprinkle half the chopped garlic over the top.

5 Bake the mina for 20 minutes. Dot the remaining butter on top and sprinkle over the remaining chopped garlic. Return to the oven and bake for about 10 minutes more, or until the mina is golden brown and crisp on top. Serve hot or warm.

Carrot and Parsnip Gratin

This gratin is deliciously sweet-tasting and succulent. It is perfect for serving with meats such as pork and turkey, or on its own with a salad or crusty bread.

Serves 4

25g/1oz/2 tbsp butter, plus extra
   for greasing
1 large onion, halved and sliced

1 garlic clove, crushed
350g/12oz carrots, grated
350g/12oz parsnips, grated
2 eggs, beaten
150ml/¹/₄ pint/²/₃ cup single
   (light) cream
freshly grated nutmeg
25g/1oz/¹/₂ cup soft white
   breadcrumbs
salt and ground black pepper

1 Preheat the oven to 180°C/350°F/Gas 4. Heat the butter in a large frying pan or pan until it melts. Add the sliced onion and crushed garlic and cook gently until tender and transparent. Mix in the grated carrots and parsnips, cook for a few minutes, then season with plenty of salt and ground black pepper.

2 Butter a shallow, ovenproof dish and spoon the vegetable mixture into it, smoothing down the top with the spoon.

3 In a large jug (pitcher), beat the eggs with the cream, nutmeg and seasoning. Pour the egg mixture over the cooked grated vegetables and sprinkle with the breadcrumbs. Place the dish in the oven and bake for about 30 minutes until the gratin is firm to the touch and turning golden brown.

Variation
Try cooking other mixtures of root vegetables in this way, such as carrot and swede (rutabaga) or celeriac and parsnip.

Cook's Tip
If you can, use organic vegetables for this recipe. As well as being healthier, organic vegetables can save you time as they do not need to be peeled and can simply be scrubbed and grated.

Broccoli Mina Energy 687kcal/2852kJ; Protein 42.4g; Carbohydrate 23g, of which sugars 4.2g; Fat 45.6g, of which saturates 26.6g; Cholesterol 304mg; Calcium 816mg; Fibre 2.8g; Sodium 969mg.
Carrot Gratin Energy 414kcal/1734kJ; Protein 6.2g; Carbohydrate 52.8g, of which sugars 38.9g; Fat 21.3g, of which saturates 12.4g; Cholesterol 124mg; Calcium 47mg; Fibre 2.3g; Sodium 175mg.

Roasted Ratatouille Moussaka

A classic vegetable dish that tastes of the Mediterranean.

Serves 4–6
2 red (bell) peppers, seeded and cut into large chunks
2 yellow (bell) peppers, seeded and cut into large chunks
2 aubergines (eggplants), cut into large chunks
3 courgettes (zucchini), thickly sliced
45ml/3 tbsp olive oil
3 garlic cloves, crushed
400g/14oz can chopped tomatoes
30ml/2 tbsp sun-dried tomato purée (paste)
45ml/3 tbsp chopped fresh basil
15ml/1 tbsp balsamic vinegar
1.5ml/¼ tsp soft light brown sugar
salt and ground black pepper
basil leaves, to garnish

For the topping
25g/1oz/2 tbsp butter
25g/1oz/¼ cup plain (all-purpose) flour
300ml/½ pint/1¼ cups milk
1.5ml/¼ tsp freshly grated nutmeg
250g/9oz ricotta cheese
3 eggs, beaten
25g/1oz/⅓ cup freshly grated Parmesan cheese

1 Preheat the oven to 230°C/450°F/Gas 8. Arrange the peppers, aubergines and courgettes in a large roasting pan. Season well. Mix together the oil and garlic and pour over the vegetables.

2 Roast in the oven for 15–20 minutes until slightly charred, lightly tossing the vegetables once. Remove from the oven and set aside. Reduce the oven temperature to 200°C/400°F/Gas 6.

3 Put the tomatoes, tomato purée, basil, vinegar and sugar in a pan and heat to boiling point. Simmer, uncovered for 10–15 minutes. Season to taste. Transfer the roasted vegetables to the pan of tomato sauce. Mix well and spoon into an ovenproof dish.

4 To make the topping, melt the butter in a large pan over a gentle heat. Stir in the flour and cook for 1 minute. Pour in the milk, stirring constantly. Add the nutmeg and whisk over a gentle heat until thickened. Cook for a further 2 minutes, then set aside.

5 Mix the ricotta cheese and beaten eggs. Season to taste. Spoon over the vegetables and sprinkle with the Parmesan. Bake for 30–35 minutes until the topping is golden brown. Serve immediately, garnished with basil leaves.

Tomato Bread and Butter Pudding

This is a great family dish and is ideal when you don't have time to cook on the day because the pudding can be prepared in advance. It makes a wonderful warming supper for a winter meal.

Serves 4
50g/2oz/4 tbsp butter, softened
15ml/1 tbsp red pesto sauce
1 garlic and herb foccacia
150g/5oz mozzarella cheese, thinly sliced
2 large ripe tomatoes, sliced
300ml/½ pint/1¼ cups milk
3 large eggs
5ml/1 tsp fresh chopped oregano, plus extra to garnish
50g/2oz Pecorino Romano or Fontina cheese, grated
salt and ground black pepper

1 Preheat the oven to 180°C/350°F/Gas 4. Blend together the butter and pesto sauce in a small bowl.

2 Slice the garlic and herb bread and spread one side of each slice with the pesto mixture.

3 In an oval ovenproof dish, layer the bread slices with the mozzarella and tomatoes, overlapping each new layer of ingredients with the next.

4 Beat together the milk, eggs and oregano in a large bowl. Season well with salt and ground black pepper and pour over the bread. Leave to stand for 5 minutes.

5 Sprinkle over the grated cheese and bake the pudding in the preheated oven for about 40–45 minutes, or until golden brown and just set.

6 When the pudding is ready, serve it immediately, straight from the dish, sprinkled liberally with more coarsely chopped fresh oregano.

> **Cook's Tip**
> If you like, you can use other cheeses, such as Beaufort, Bel Paese or Taleggio, in this pudding.

Bread Pudding Energy 642kcal/2693kJ; Protein 32.1g; Carbohydrate 57.3g, of which sugars 8.4g; Fat 33.5g, of which saturates 18g; Cholesterol 242mg; Calcium 573mg; Fibre 2.8g; Sodium 1066mg.
Moussaka Energy 570kcal/2367kJ; Protein 22.1g; Carbohydrate 27.5g, of which sugars 21.7g; Fat 42.1g, of which saturates 20.3g; Cholesterol 223mg; Calcium 339mg; Fibre 7.1g; Sodium 447mg.

Stir-fried Prawns with Rice Noodles

One of the most appealing aspects of Asian food is its appearance. Ingredients are carefully chosen so that each dish, even a simple stir-fry such as this one, is balanced in terms of colour, texture and flavour.

Serves 4
130g/4½oz rice noodles
30ml/2 tbsp groundnut
  (peanut) oil
1 large garlic clove, crushed
150g/5oz large prawns (shrimp),
  peeled and deveined
15g/½oz dried shrimp
1 piece mooli (daikon), about
  75g/3oz, grated
15ml/1 tbsp fish sauce
30ml/2 tbsp soy sauce
30ml/2 tbsp light muscovado
  (brown) sugar
30ml/2 tbsp lime juice
90g/3½oz/⅓ cup beansprouts
40g/1½oz/⅓ cup peanuts,
  chopped
15ml/1 tbsp sesame oil
chopped coriander (cilantro),
  5ml/1 tsp dried chilli flakes
  and 2 shallots, finely chopped,
  to garnish

1 Soak the noodles in a bowl of boiling water for 5 minutes, or according to the packet instructions. Heat the oil in a wok or large frying pan. Add the garlic, and stir-fry over medium heat for 2–3 minutes, until golden brown.

2 Add the prawns, dried shrimp and grated mooli and stir-fry for a further 2 minutes. Stir in the fish sauce, soy sauce, sugar and lime juice.

3 Drain the noodles thoroughly, then snip them into smaller lengths with scissors. Add to the wok or pan with the beansprouts, peanuts and sesame oil. Toss to mix, then stir-fry for 2 minutes. Serve immediately, garnished with the coriander, chilli flakes and shallots.

Cook's Tip
Some cooks salt the mooli and leave it to drain, then rinse and dry before use.

Prawn and Potato Omelette

More like a Spanish tortilla than a French omelette, this dish makes a delicious lunch when served with a fresh leafy green salad. The sweet prawns are cooked gently inside the omelette, staying tender and succulent.

Serves 6
200g/7oz potatoes, peeled
  and diced
30ml/2 tbsp olive oil
1 onion, finely sliced
2.5ml/½ tsp paprika
2 large tomatoes, peeled,
  seeded and chopped
200g/7oz peeled raw
  prawns (shrimp)
6 eggs
2.5ml/½ tsp baking powder
salt

1 Cook the potatoes in a pan of salted boiling water for about 10 minutes or until tender.

2 Meanwhile, pour the oil into a 23cm/9in frying pan that can safely be used under the grill (broiler). Place the pan over medium heat.

3 Add the onion slices and stir well to coat evenly in the oil. Cook for 5 minutes until the onions begin to soften but not turn brown. Sprinkle over the paprika and cook for a further 1 minute, stirring constantly.

4 Stir in the tomatoes. Drain the cooked potatoes thoroughly and add them to the pan. Stir gently to mix. Increase the heat and cook for 10 minutes, or until the mixture has thickened and the potatoes have absorbed the flavour of the tomatoes.

5 Remove the pan from the heat. Add the prawns and stir gently to combine with the other ingredients.

6 Preheat the grill. Beat the eggs in a separate bowl, stir in the baking powder and salt. Pour the egg mixture into the pan and mix thoroughly.

7 Cover the pan and cook for 8–10 minutes until the omelette has almost set, then finish under the grill. Serve hot in wedges.

Stir-fried Prawns Energy 397kcal/1675kJ; Protein 21.3g; Carbohydrate 56.5g, of which sugars 3.2g; Fat 11.1g, of which saturates 2.4g; Cholesterol 89mg; Calcium 72mg; Fibre 3.3g; Sodium 567mg.
Prawn Omelette Energy 247kcal/1031kJ; Protein 19.6g; Carbohydrate 10.8g, of which sugars 3g; Fat 14.5g, of which saturates 3.3g; Cholesterol 383mg; Calcium 93mg; Fibre 1.2g; Sodium 211mg.

Grilled Langoustines with Herbs

This simple cooking method enhances both the delicate colour and flavour of the langoustines. Choose the largest you can find (or afford) for this dish, and allow five or six per serving.

Serves 4–6
60ml/4 tbsp extra virgin olive oil
60ml/4 tbsp hazelnut oil
15ml/1 tbsp each finely chopped fresh basil, chives, chervil, parsley and tarragon
pinch of ground ginger
20–24 large langoustines, preferably live
lemon wedges and rocket (arugula) leaves, to garnish
salt and ground black pepper

1 Preheat the grill (broiler) to very hot. Mix together the olive and hazelnut oils in a small bowl. Add the herbs, a pinch of ground ginger and salt and pepper to taste. Whisk thoroughly until slightly thickened and emulsified.

2 If you are using live langoustines, immerse them in a large pan of boiling water for 1–2 minutes, then drain and leave them to cool.

3 Split the langoustines lengthways using a large sharp knife and arrange them on a foil-lined grill (broiling) pan. Spoon over the herb-flavoured oil.

4 Grill (broil) for 8–10 minutes, basting the langoustines two or three times until they are cooked and lightly browned.

5 Arrange the langoustines on a warmed serving dish, pour the juices from the grill pan over and serve immediately garnished with lemon wedges and rocket leaves.

Cook's Tips
• Don't forget to provide your guests with fingerbowls of warm water and plenty of paper napkins.
• If you use cooked langoustines, then grill (broil) them for just 2–3 minutes to warm them through.

Sweet Potato, Pumpkin and Prawn Cakes

This unusual Asian combination makes a delicious dish that needs only a fish sauce or soy sauce to dip into as an accompaniment. Serve with noodles or fried rice for a more substantial meal.

Serves 4
200g/7oz/1¾ cups strong white bread flour
2.5ml/½ tsp salt
2.5ml/½ tsp dried yeast
175ml/6fl oz/¾ cup warm water
1 egg, beaten
200g/7oz raw prawns (shrimp)
225g/8oz pumpkin, peeled, seeded and grated
150g/5oz sweet potato, grated
2 spring onions (scallions), chopped
50g/2oz water chestnuts, chopped
2.5ml/½ tsp chilli sauce
1 garlic clove, crushed
juice of ½ lime
vegetable oil, for deep-frying
lime wedges, to serve

1 Sift together the flour and salt into a large mixing bowl and make a well in the centre. In a separate container, dissolve the yeast in the water until creamy, then pour into the centre of the flour and salt mixture. Pour in the egg and set aside for a few minutes until bubbles start to appear. Mix the ingredients to form a smooth batter.

2 Peel the prawns, if necessary, then place in a pan with just enough boiling water to cover. Simmer for about 2 minutes or until the prawns have turned pink. Drain, rinse in cold water and drain again well. Coarsely chop the prawns, then place in a bowl with the pumpkin and sweet potato.

3 Add the spring onions, water chestnuts, chilli sauce, garlic and lime juice and mix well. Fold into the batter mixture carefully until evenly mixed.

4 Heat a 1cm/½in layer of oil in a large frying pan until really hot. Spoon in the batter in heaps, leaving space between each one, and cook until golden brown on both sides. Drain well on kitchen paper and keep warm as you cook the rest. Serve hot with the lime wedges.

Sweet Potato Energy 317kcal/1346kJ; Protein 18.2g; Carbohydrate 57.6g, of which sugars 9.1g; Fat 3.2g, of which saturates 0.9g; Cholesterol 145mg; Calcium 216mg; Fibre 6g; Sodium 383mg.
Langoustines Energy 128kcal/536kJ; Protein 14.3g; Carbohydrate 0g, of which sugars 0g; Fat 7.8g, of which saturates 1.2g; Cholesterol 175mg; Calcium 72mg; Fibre 0g; Sodium 1000mg.

Mussels with Fennel, Herbs and Cream

This recipe is quite similar to moules marinière but has the additional flavouring of fennel and mild curry. Traditionally the mussels are shelled and piled into scallop shells, but nothing beats a bowlful of steaming hot, garlicky mussels, served in their own shells.

Serves 6
1.8kg/4lb fresh mussels
250ml/8fl oz/1 cup dry
 white wine
good pinch of grated nutmeg
3 thyme sprigs
2 bay leaves
1 small onion, finely chopped
50g/2oz/¼ cup butter
1 fennel bulb, thinly sliced
4 garlic cloves, crushed
2.5ml/½ tsp curry paste
 or powder
30ml/2 tbsp plain
 (all-purpose) flour
150ml/¼ pint/⅔ cup double
 (heavy) cream
ground black pepper
chopped fresh dill, to garnish

1 Scrub the mussels, discarding any that are damaged or open ones that do not close when tapped with a knife.

2 Put the wine, nutmeg, thyme, bay leaves and onion in a large pan and bring just to the boil. Add the mussels and cover with a lid. Cook for 4–5 minutes until the mussels have opened.

3 Drain the mussels, reserving all the juices. Discard any mussels that remain closed.

4 Melt the butter in a large clean pan and gently fry the fennel slices and garlic for about 5 minutes until softened.

5 Stir in the curry paste or powder and flour and cook for 1 minute. Remove from the heat and gradually blend in the cooking juices from the mussels. Return to the heat and cook, stirring, for 2 minutes.

6 Stir in the cream and a little pepper. Add the mussels to the pan and heat through for 2 minutes. Serve hot, garnished with chopped fresh dill.

Clam Stovies

This is a delicious clam version of the classic Scottish potato dish. Limpets or cockles can also be used in place of the clams if you can buy them very fresh or collect them yourself along the seashore.

Serves 4
2.5 litres/4 pints/10 cups clams
potatoes (see step 3)
oil, for greasing
chopped fresh flat leaf parsley,
 to garnish
50g/2oz/¼ cup butter
salt and ground black pepper

1 Wash the clams and soak them overnight in fresh cold water. This will clean them out and get rid of any grains of sand and other detritus.

2 Preheat the oven to 190°C/375°F/Gas 5. Put the clams into a large pan, cover with water and bring to the boil. Add a little salt, then simmer until the shells open. Reserve the cooking liquor. Shell the clams, reserving a few whole.

3 Weigh the shelled clams. You will need approximately three times the weight of the clams in unpeeled potatoes.

4 Peel and slice the potatoes thinly. Lightly oil the base and sides of a flameproof, ovenproof dish.

5 Arrange a layer of potatoes in the base of the dish, then add a layer of the clams and season with a little salt and ground black pepper. Repeat the layering process until the ingredients are all used, finishing with a layer of potatoes on top. Finally, season lightly with more salt and black pepper.

6 Pour in some of the reserved cooking liquor to come about halfway up the dish. Dot the top with the butter, then cover the dish tightly with foil. Bring to the boil on top of the stove over medium-high heat, then transfer to the preheated oven and bake for about 2 hours until the potatoes are tender and the top is golden brown.

7 Serve the bake immediately, garnished with chopped fresh flat leaf parsley.

Mussels Energy 314kcal/1308kJ; Protein 16.6g; Carbohydrate 6g, of which sugars 1.9g; Fat 22.2g, of which saturates 13g; Cholesterol 87mg; Calcium 207mg; Fibre 1.1g; Sodium 246mg.
Clam Stovies Energy 320kcal/1348kJ; Protein 17.3g; Carbohydrate 36.7g, of which sugars 3.3g; Fat 12.6g, of which saturates 7g; Cholesterol 57mg; Calcium 188mg; Fibre 2.9g; Sodium 262mg.

Clams and Mussels with Lemon Grass and Coconut Cream

Lemon grass has an incomparable aromatic flavour and is widely used with all kinds of seafood in Thailand as the flavours marry so perfectly.

Serves 6

1.8kg/4lb fresh mussels
450g/1lb baby clams
120ml/4fl oz/½ cup dry
   white wine
1 bunch spring onions
   (scallions), chopped
2 lemon grass stalks, chopped
6 kaffir lime leaves, chopped
10ml/2 tsp Thai green
   curry paste
200ml/7fl oz/scant 1 cup
   coconut cream
30ml/2 tbsp chopped fresh
   coriander (cilantro)
salt and ground black pepper
garlic chives, to garnish

1 Scrub the mussel shells with a stiff brush and rinse under cold running water. Scrape off any barnacles and remove the 'beards' with a small knife. Rinse well. Scrub the clams. Discard any mussels or clams that are damaged or broken or which do not close immediately when tapped sharply.

2 Put the wine in a large pan with the spring onions, lemon grass and lime leaves. Stir in the curry paste. Simmer until the wine has almost evaporated.

3 Add the mussels and clams to the pan and increase the heat to high. Cover tightly and steam the shellfish for 5–6 minutes, until they open.

4 Using a slotted spoon, transfer the mussels and clams to a heated serving bowl, cover and keep hot. Discard any shellfish that remain closed. Strain the cooking liquid into a clean pan through a sieve (strainer) lined with muslin (cheesecloth) and simmer briefly to reduce the liquid to about 250ml/8fl oz/1 cup.

5 Stir the coconut cream and chopped coriander into the sauce and season to taste with salt and pepper. Heat through. Pour the sauce over the shellfish, garnish with the garlic chives and serve immediately.

Oysters with a Herb Crust

When buying oysters that are already shucked (opened and lifted out from the shells), try and retain their juices so you can spoon some back into the shells for the cooking process. It is also nice to put a teaspoonful of laverbread in with each oyster before adding the breadcrumb and cheese topping.

Serves 2

6–8 oysters
½ lemon
sweet chilli sauce (optional)
50g/2oz/1 cup fresh breadcrumbs
50g/2oz/½ cup grated
   hard cheese
15ml/1 tbsp finely chopped chives
15ml/1 tbsp finely
   chopped parsley
50g/2oz/¼ cup butter
salt and ground black pepper

1 Scrub and open the oysters. Lay them, in the deep shells, in a grill (broiler) pan and squeeze a little lemon juice on to each one. Add a tiny drop of chilli sauce to each shell, if using.

2 Preheat the grill (broiler). Mix the breadcrumbs with the cheese, herbs, and a little seasoning. Spoon the mixture on top of the oysters and dot with tiny pieces of butter.

3 Cook under the grill (not too close) for about 5 minutes, or until the topping is crisp golden brown and bubbling around the edges. Serve immediately.

> **Variation**
> *Laverbread is a traditional Welsh delicacy made from the edible seaweed laver. To make laverbread, the seaweed is boiled for several hours, then minced (ground) or puréed. A spoonful of this paste can be added to the oysters before the topping.*

> **Cook's Tip**
> *To open a live oyster, hold it in a clean cloth firmly with one hand and, with a special pointed knife, prise (pry) open at the hinge of the shell.*

Clams and Mussels Energy 177Kcal/745kJ; Protein 21.8g; Carbohydrate 1.9g, of which sugars 1.2g; Fat 7.8g, of which saturates 5.3g; Cholesterol 58mg; Calcium 212mg; Fibre 0.3g; Sodium 594mg.
Oysters Energy 433kcal/1804kJ; Protein 18.3g; Carbohydrate 21.9g, of which sugars 1g; Fat 30.4g, of which saturates 18.6g; Cholesterol 123mg; Calcium 349mg; Fibre 1g; Sodium 933mg.

Seared Scallops with Chive Sauce

Scallops are partnered with a chive sauce and a pilaff of wild and white rice with leeks and carrots.

Serves 4
12–16 shelled scallops
45ml/3 tbsp olive oil
50g/2oz/⅓ cup wild rice
65g/2½oz/5 tbsp butter
4 carrots, cut into long thin strips
2 leeks, cut into diagonal slices
1 small onion, finely chopped
115g/4oz/⅔ cup long grain rice
1 fresh bay leaf
200ml/7fl oz/scant 1 cup white wine
450ml/¾ pint/scant 2 cups fish stock
60ml/4 tbsp double (heavy) cream
a little lemon juice
25ml/5 tsp chopped fresh chives
30ml/2 tbsp chervil sprigs
salt and ground black pepper

1 Lightly season the scallops, brush with 15ml/1 tbsp of the olive oil and set aside. Cook the wild rice in plenty of boiling water for about 30 minutes, until tender, then drain.

2 Melt half the butter in a frying pan and cook the carrots for 5 minutes. Add the leeks and fry for 2 minutes. Season and add 30–45ml/2–3 tbsp water, then cover and cook for a few minutes more. Uncover and cook until the liquid has reduced.

3 Melt half the rest of the butter with 15ml/1 tbsp of the remaining oil in a pan. Fry the onion for 3–4 minutes. Add the long grain rice and bay leaf and stir-fry for 3–4 minutes.

4 Pour in half the wine and half the stock. Season with salt and bring to the boil. Stir, then cover and simmer for 15 minutes, or until the liquid is absorbed and the rice is cooked and tender. Stir the carrots, leeks and wild rice into the long grain rice. Boil the remaining wine and stock in a pan until reduced by half.

5 Heat a frying pan over high heat. Add the remaining butter and oil. Sear the scallops for 1–2 minutes each side, then set aside. Pour the reduced stock and cream into the pan and boil until thick. Season and stir in the lemon juice, chives and scallops.

6 Stir the chervil into the rice and pile it on to plates. Arrange the scallops on top and spoon the sauce over the rice.

Cockle Cakes

One of the simplest ways to serve cockles is to toss them in fine oatmeal and briefly fry them. Here, they are made into small cakes, nicest when cooked in bacon fat, though you could, of course, simply fry them in oil or butter. They are particularly good topped with scrambled, poached or fried egg, or as part of a full breakfast.

Serves 4–8
125g/4¼oz/generous 1 cup plain (all-purpose) flour
1 egg
150ml/¼ pint/⅔ cup milk
ground black pepper
100g/3½oz shelled cooked cockles (small clams)
15–30ml/1–2 tbsp chopped fresh chives (optional)
6 bacon rashers (slices)
oil for cooking

1 Sift the flour into a large mixing bowl, make a well in the centre and break the egg into it.

2 Mix the egg into the flour, and gradually stir in the milk to make a smooth batter.

3 Season the batter with ground black pepper and stir in the cockles and chopped fresh chives (if using).

4 Heat a little oil in a pan, add the bacon and fry quickly. Lift out and keep warm.

5 Add tablespoonfuls of batter to the hot bacon fat, leaving them space to spread. Cook until crisp and golden, turning over once. Drain and serve with the bacon.

> **Cook's Tip**
> Cockles, which have always been more popular in Europe than the United States, can be eaten raw or cooked, as with clams or oysters. They have a tendency to be quite gritty and must be washed thoroughly to remove any grains of sand before cooking. They should be cooked in a pan of boiling water for about 5–6 minutes. Ensure that they are not overcooked, otherwise they will become tough.

Cockle Cakes Energy 137kcal/572kJ; Protein 7g; Carbohydrate 13.1g, of which sugars 1.2g; Fat 6.6g, of which saturates 1.7g; Cholesterol 40mg; Calcium 63mg; Fibre 0.5g; Sodium 322mg.
Seared Scallops Energy 598kcal/2489kJ; Protein 30.8g; Carbohydrate 38.9g, of which sugars 6.3g; Fat 32g, of which saturates 15.3g; Cholesterol 108mg; Calcium 88mg; Fibre 3.1g; Sodium 321mg.

Scallops with Bacon

In the 19th century, scallops were dredged in large numbers along England's Sussex coast. Today, they are fished off the Isle of Man. Like oysters, scallops are often believed to be an aphrodisiac. They are best when cooked quickly and briefly, and go very well with crisp, salty bacon.

Serves 4
15ml/1 tbsp olive oil
4 streaky (fatty) bacon rashers (strips), cut into 2.5cm/1in pieces
2–3 fresh sage leaves, chopped
small piece of butter
8 large or 16 small scallops
15ml/1 tbsp fresh lemon juice
100ml/3½fl oz/scant ½ cup dry (hard) cider or dry white wine

1 Heat the oil in a frying pan. Add the bacon and sage and cook, stirring occasionally, until the bacon is golden brown. Lift out and keep warm.

2 Add the butter to the pan and when hot add the scallops. Cook quickly for about 1 minute on each side until browned. Lift out and keep warm.

3 Add the lemon juice and cider or white wine to the pan and, scraping up any sediment remaining in the pan, bring just to the boil.

4 Continue to gently simmer the mixture until it has reduced to just a few tablespoons of syrupy sauce.

5 Serve the scallops and bacon on heated individual plates with the cider or wine sauce drizzled over.

Cook's Tip
In summer, some fishmongers sell marsh samphire (glasswort), which grows around the coast of England and makes a good accompaniment to this dish. To prepare samphire, wash it well and pick off the soft fleshy branches, discarding the thicker woody stalks. Drop it into boiling water for just 1 minute before draining and serving.

Chilli Crab Cakes

Crab meat makes wonderful fish cakes, as shown by these gutsy morsels. Served with a rich tomato dip, they make great party food.

Makes about 15
225g/8oz white crab meat (fresh, frozen or canned)
115g/4oz cooked floury potatoes, mashed
30ml/2 tbsp fresh herb seasoning
2.5ml/½ tsp mild mustard
2.5ml/½ tsp ground black pepper
½ fresh hot chilli, finely chopped
5ml/1 tsp fresh oregano
1 egg, beaten
plain (all-purpose) flour, for dredging

vegetable oil, for frying
lime wedges and coriander (cilantro) sprigs, to garnish
fresh whole chilli peppers, to garnish

For the tomato dip
15g/½oz/1 tbsp butter or margarine
½ onion, finely chopped
2 canned plum tomatoes, chopped
1 garlic clove, crushed
150ml/¼ pint/⅔ cup water
5–10ml/1–2 tsp malt vinegar
15ml/1 tbsp chopped fresh coriander (cilantro)
½ hot fresh chilli, chopped

1 Mix together the crab meat, potatoes, herb seasoning, mustard, pepper and chilli, oregano and egg in a large bowl. Chill the mixture for at least 30 minutes.

2 Meanwhile, make the tomato dip. Melt the butter or margarine in a small pan over medium heat. Add the onion, tomatoes and garlic and cook for about 5 minutes until the onion is tender. Add the water, vinegar, coriander and fresh chilli.

3 Bring to the boil, reduce the heat and simmer for about 10 minutes. Transfer the mixture to a food processor or blender and blend to a smooth purée.

4 Shape the chilled crab mixture into rounds and dredge with flour, shaking off the excess. Heat a little oil in a frying pan and fry, a few cakes at a time, for 2–3 minutes on each side. Drain on kitchen paper and keep warm in a low oven while cooking the remainder. Garnish with lime wedges, coriander sprigs and whole chillies and serve with the tomato dip.

Scallops Energy 208kcal/867kJ; Protein 15.6g; Carbohydrate 2.4g, of which sugars 0.7g; Fat 14.5g, of which saturates 5.9g; Cholesterol 53mg; Calcium 19mg; Fibre 0g; Sodium 445mg.
Chilli Crab Cakes Energy 70kcal/290kJ; Protein 3.5g; Carbohydrate 2.9g, of which sugars 0.7g; Fat 5g, of which saturates 1.1g; Cholesterol 26mg; Calcium 24mg; Fibre 0.3g; Sodium 95mg.

Chilli Crab and Tofu Stir-fry

For a light healthy meal, this speedy stir-fry is the ideal choice. The silken tofu has a fairly bland taste on its own but is excellent for absorbing all the delicious flavours of this dish – the crab meat, garlic, chillies, spring onions and soy sauce.

Serves 2

250g/9oz silken tofu
60ml/4 tbsp vegetable oil
2 garlic cloves, finely chopped

115g/4oz white crab meat
130g/4¹⁄₂oz/generous 1 cup baby corn, halved lengthways
2 spring onions (scallions), chopped
1 fresh red chilli, seeded and finely chopped
30ml/2 tbsp soy sauce
15ml/1 tbsp Thai fish sauce
5ml/1 tsp palm sugar (jaggery) or light muscovado (brown) sugar
juice of 1 lime
small bunch fresh coriander (cilantro), chopped, to garnish

1 Using a sharp knife, cut the silken tofu into 1cm/½in cubes.

2 Heat the oil in a wok or large, heavy frying pan. Add the tofu cubes and stir-fry until they are golden all over, taking care not to break them up while cooking. Remove from the pan with a slotted spoon and set aside.

3 Add the garlic to the wok or pan and stir-fry until just golden. Ensure that it does not burn, otherwise it will have a slightly bitter taste.

4 Add the crab meat, tofu, corn, spring onions, chilli, soy sauce, fish sauce and sugar to the pan. Cook, stirring constantly, until the vegetables are just tender.

5 Stir in the lime juice, transfer to warmed bowls, sprinkle with the coriander and serve immediately.

> **Cook's Tip**
> This is a very economical dish to prepare as you need only a small amount of crab meat. The canned variety can also be used in this recipe, which will make it even cheaper.

Lobster Thermidor

One of the classic French dishes, Lobster Thermidor makes a little lobster go a long way. It is best to use one big rather than two small lobsters, as a larger lobster will contain a higher proportion of flesh and the meat will be sweeter.

Serves 2

1 large lobster, about 800g–1kg/1¾–2¹⁄₄lb, boiled
45ml/3 tbsp brandy
25g/1oz/2 tbsp butter

2 shallots, finely chopped
115g/4oz/1¹⁄₂ cups button (white) mushrooms, thinly sliced
15ml/1 tbsp plain (all-purpose) flour
105ml/7 tbsp fish or shellfish stock
120ml/4fl oz/¹⁄₂ cup double (heavy) cream
5ml/1 tsp Dijon mustard
2 egg yolks, beaten
45ml/3 tbsp dry white wine
45ml/3 tbsp grated Parmesan
salt, ground black pepper and cayenne pepper
steamed rice and salad, to serve

1 Split the lobster in half lengthways; crack the claws. Discard the stomach sac; keep the coral for another dish. Keeping each half-shell intact, extract the meat from the tail and claws, then cut into large dice. Place in a shallow dish; sprinkle over the brandy. Cover and set aside. Wipe and dry the half-shells and set them aside.

2 Melt the butter in a pan and cook the shallots over low heat until soft. Add the mushrooms and cook, stirring, until tender. Stir in the flour and a pinch of cayenne. Cook for 2 minutes. Add the stock, stirring until the sauce boils and thickens.

3 Stir in the cream and mustard and continue to cook until the sauce is smooth and thick. Season to taste with salt, black pepper and cayenne. Pour half the sauce on to the egg yolks, stir well and return the mixture to the pan. Stir in the wine; adjust the seasoning, being generous with the cayenne.

4 Preheat the grill (broiler) to medium-high. Stir the diced lobster and the brandy into the sauce. Arrange the lobster half-shells in a grill (broiling) pan and divide the mixture among them. Sprinkle with Parmesan and place under the grill until browned. Serve with steamed rice and mixed salad leaves.

Chilli Crab Stir-fry Energy 370kcal/1532kj; Protein 23.3g; Carbohydrate 6.2g, of which sugars 5.1g; Fat 28.1g, of which saturates 1g; Cholesterol 210mg; Calcium 185mg; Fibre 1.2g; Sodium 2487mg.
Lobster Thermidor Energy 859kcal/3573kj; Protein 56g; Carbohydrate 9.8g, of which sugars 2g; Fat 59.6g, of which saturates 33.8g; Cholesterol 536mg; Calcium 488mg; Fibre 1.2g; Sodium 976mg.

Grilled Lobster with Tarragon Cream

Lobsters are at their best prepared simply to make the most of their firm sweet meat. Fresh herbs, cream and butter are among the best accompaniments.

Serves 4
2 live lobsters, about
   675–800g/1½–1¾lb

grated rind of 1 orange
75g/3oz/6 tbsp unsalted
   (sweet) butter
pinch of cayenne pepper
50ml/2fl oz/¼ cup whipping
   cream
2 sprigs of fresh tarragon
salt and ground black pepper

1 Dispatch or freeze the lobsters before cooking, if you like, then bring a large pan of water to the boil. Add the grated orange rind and plunge the whole lobsters into the pan. Bring the water back to a rolling boil, then boil for about 5 minutes.

2 Drain the lobsters and, when cool, split them down the middle with a knife. Remove the stomach sac from the head and the intestine tract from down the tail. Remove and crack open the claws. Remove the meat and place it in the head.

3 Melt the butter and brush it liberally over the four half lobsters. Season lightly with salt and a little cayenne pepper.

4 Preheat the grill (broiler) to high. Pour the cream into a pan over low heat and add the sprigs of tarragon, stirring it in gently. Bring the cream to just below boiling point, turn the heat right down, and then leave the cream for 10 minutes.

5 Put the lobsters under the preheated grill for about 7 minutes, and then pour off the juices into the cream and stir gently.

6 Add the buttery lobster juices from the grill (broiling) pan and turn the heat up a fraction. Bring the cream mixture to the boil, whisking to combine the ingredients. Strain the sauce.

7 Place half a lobster on each warmed serving plate, and gently spoon over the cream sauce, letting it spill over on to the plate. Serve immediately.

Lobster with Mustard and Cream

Tender, sweet lobster meat is transformed by the addition of whisky, cream and mustard.

Serves 2
1 lobster, about 500g/1¼lb
10ml/2 tsp butter
splash of whisky (grain not malt)
1 shallot or ½ onion, chopped

50g/2oz button (white) mushrooms
splash of white wine
175ml/6fl oz/¾ cup double
   (heavy) cream
5ml/1 tsp wholegrain mustard
10ml/2 tsp chopped fresh chervil
   and a little tarragon
60ml/4 tbsp butter, melted
salt and ground black pepper
breadcrumbs to garnish

1 Cook the lobster in boiling salted water for about 7 minutes, then set aside to cool. Once cool, cut the lobster down the middle, top to bottom, and remove the intestines down the back. Remove the meat from the tail, taking care not to let it break into pieces.

2 Cut the tail meat into diagonal slices. Remove the meat from the claws, keeping it as whole as possible. Wash the two half-shells out and set aside.

3 Heat a frying pan over low heat and add the butter. Gently add the lobster meat and colour lightly. Pour in the whisky. If you have a gas stove, allow the flames to get inside the pan to briefly flame the pieces and burn off the alcohol. Remove the lobster meat.

4 Add the chopped shallot or onion and the mushrooms, and cook gently over a medium-low heat for a few minutes until soft and the onion or shallot is transparent. Add a little white wine, then the cream, and allow to simmer to reduce to a light coating texture. Then add the mustard and the chopped herbs and mix well. Season to taste. Meanwhile, preheat the grill (broiler) to high.

5 Place the two lobster half-shells on the grill (broiling) pan. Distribute the lobster meat evenly throughout the two half-shells and spoon the sauce over. Sprinkle with breadcrumbs, drizzle with melted butter and brown under the grill. Serve immediately.

Grilled Lobster Energy 284kcal/1180kJ; Protein 20.8g; Carbohydrate 0.8g, of which sugars 0.8g; Fat 22.1g, of which saturates 13.2g; Cholesterol 153mg; Calcium 91mg; Fibre 0.6g; Sodium 421mg.
Lobster with Mustard Energy 812kcal/3357kJ; Protein 23.6g; Carbohydrate 12g, of which sugars 3.7g; Fat 74.9g, of which saturates 46g; Cholesterol 287mg; Calcium 127mg; Fibre 0.9g; Sodium 580mg.

Steamed Lettuce-wrapped Sole

If you can afford it, use Dover sole fillets for this recipe; if not, lemon sole, trout, plaice, flounder and brill are all excellent cooked this way.

Serves 4

2 large sole fillets, skinned
15ml/1 tbsp sesame seeds
15ml/1 tbsp sunflower or groundnut (peanut) oil
10ml/2 tsp sesame oil
2.5cm/1in piece fresh root ginger, peeled and grated
3 garlic cloves, finely chopped
15ml/1 tbsp soy sauce or Thai fish sauce
juice of 1 lemon
2 spring onions (scallions), thinly sliced
8 large soft lettuce leaves
12 large fresh mussels, scrubbed and bearded

1 Cut the sole fillets in half lengthways. Season; set aside. Prepare a steamer.

2 Heat a heavy frying pan until hot. Toast the sesame seeds lightly but do not allow them to burn. Set aside in a bowl until required.

3 Heat the oils in the frying pan over medium heat. Add the ginger and garlic and cook until lightly coloured; stir in the soy sauce or fish sauce, lemon juice and spring onions. Remove from the heat; stir in the toasted sesame seeds.

4 Lay the pieces of fish on baking parchment, skinned side up. Spread each piece evenly with the ginger mixture. Roll up each piece, starting at the tail end. Place on a baking sheet.

5 Plunge the lettuce leaves into the boiling water you have prepared for the steamer and immediately lift them out with tongs or a slotted spoon. Lay them out flat on kitchen paper and gently pat them dry. Wrap each sole parcel in two lettuce leaves, making sure that the filling is well covered to keep it in place.

6 Arrange the fish parcels in a steamer basket, cover and steam over simmering water for 8 minutes. Add the mussels and steam for 2–4 minutes, until opened. Discard any that remain closed. Put the parcels on individual warmed plates, halve and garnish with mussels. Serve immediately.

Seafood and Spring Onion Skewers

Serve these tasty skewers with the tartare sauce dip.

Serves 4

675g/1½lb monkfish tail, filleted, skinned and membrane removed
1 bunch thick spring onions (scallions)
75ml/5 tbsp olive oil
1 garlic clove, finely chopped
15ml/1 tbsp lemon juice
5ml/1 tsp dried oregano
30ml/2 tbsp chopped fresh flat leaf parsley
12–18 small scallops or large raw prawns (shrimp)
75g/3oz/1½ cups fine fresh breadcrumbs
salt and ground black pepper

For the tartare sauce
2 egg yolks
300ml/½ pint/1¼ cups olive oil, or vegetable and olive oil mixed
15–30ml/1–2 tbsp lemon juice
5ml/1 tsp French mustard
15ml/1 tbsp chopped gherkin
15ml/1 tbsp chopped capers
30ml/2 tbsp chopped fresh flat leaf parsley
30ml/2 tbsp chopped fresh chives
5ml/1 tsp chopped fresh tarragon

1 Soak nine bamboo skewers in cold water for 30 minutes. Make the tartare sauce. Whisk the egg yolks and a pinch of salt. Whisk in the oil, a drop at a time at first. When about half the oil is incorporated, add it in a thin stream, whisking all the time. Stop when the mayonnaise is very thick.

2 Whisk in 15ml/1 tbsp lemon juice, then a little more oil. Stir in all the mustard, gherkin, capers, parsley, chives and tarragon. Add lemon juice and seasoning to taste.

3 Cut the monkfish into 18 pieces and cut the spring onions into 18 pieces about 5–6cm/2–2½in long. Mix the oil, garlic, lemon juice, oregano and half the parsley with seasoning. Add the seafood and spring onions, then marinate for 15 minutes.

4 Mix the breadcrumbs and remaining parsley together. Toss the seafood and spring onions in the mixture to coat.

5 Preheat the grill (broiler). Thread the seafood and spring onions on to the skewers. Drizzle with marinade, then cook for 5–6 minutes in total, turning once and drizzling with more marinade. Serve immediately with the tartare sauce.

Steamed Sole Energy 118kcal/492kJ; Protein 15.3g; Carbohydrate 0.9g, of which sugars 0.9g; Fat 5.9g, of which saturates 0.7g; Cholesterol 41mg; Calcium 46mg; Fibre 0.3g; Sodium 359mg.
Seafood Skewers Energy 385kcal/1598kJ; Protein 20.3g; Carbohydrate 7.8g, of which sugars 0.7g; Fat 30.5g, of which saturates 4g; Cholesterol 67mg; Calcium 43mg; Fibre 0.6g; Sodium 139mg.

Fillets of Turbot with Oysters

This luxurious dish is ideal for special occasions. Keep the head, bones and trimmings for stock. Sole, brill and halibut can all be substituted for the turbot.

Serves 4
12 Pacific oysters
115g/4oz/1/2 cup butter
2 carrots, cut into julienne strips
200g/7oz celeriac, cut into julienne strips
the white parts of 2 leeks, cut into julienne strips
375ml/13fl oz/generous 1 1/2 cups champagne or dry white sparkling wine (about 1/2 bottle)
105ml/7 tbsp whipping cream
1 turbot, about 1.75kg/4–4 1/2 lb, filleted and skinned
salt and ground white pepper

1 Using an oyster knife, open the oysters over a bowl to catch the juices, then carefully remove them from their shells, and place them in a separate bowl. Set aside until required.

2 Melt 25g/1oz/2 tbsp of the butter in a shallow pan, add the vegetable julienne and cook over low heat until tender. Pour in half the champagne or sparkling wine and cook very gently until all the liquid has evaporated.

3 Strain the oyster juices into a pan and add the cream and the remaining champagne or sparkling wine. Place over medium heat until the mixture has reduced to the consistency of thin cream. Dice half the remaining butter and whisk it into the sauce, one piece at a time, until smooth. Season to taste, then pour the sauce into a blender and process until velvety smooth.

4 Return the sauce to the pan, bring it to just below boiling point, then drop in the oysters. Poach for 1 minute to warm but barely cook. Keep warm, but do not let the sauce boil.

5 Season the turbot fillets. Heat the remaining butter in a large frying pan until foaming, then cook the fillets over medium heat for 2–3 minutes on each side until cooked through and golden.

6 Cut each fillet into three and arrange on individual warmed plates. Pile the vegetables on top, place three oysters around the turbot fillets on each plate and pour the sauce over.

Fisherman's Casserole

This delicious seafood casserole combines fish fillets with shellfish and new potatoes in a creamy sauce.

Serves 4
500g/1 1/4lb mixed fish fillets, such as haddock, bass, red mullet, salmon
500g/1 1/4lb mixed shellfish, such as squid strips, mussels, cockles (small clams) and prawns (shrimp)
15ml/1 tbsp oil
25g/1oz/2 tbsp butter
1 medium onion, finely chopped
1 carrot, finely chopped
3 celery sticks, finely chopped
30ml/2 tbsp plain (all-purpose) flour
600ml/1 pint/2 1/2 cups fish stock
300ml/1/2 pint/1 1/4 cups dry (hard) cider
350g/12oz new potatoes, halved
150ml/1/4 pint/2/3 cup double (heavy) cream
small handful of chopped mixed herbs, such as parsley, chives and dill
salt and ground black pepper

1 Wash the fish fillets and dry on kitchen paper. Remove the skin and any bones. Cut the fish into large, even chunks.

2 Shell the prawns if necessary. Scrub the mussels and cockles, discarding any with broken shells or that do not close when given a sharp tap. Pull off the black beards on the mussels.

3 Heat the oil and butter in a large pan, add the onion, carrot and celery and cook over medium heat, stirring occasionally, until beginning to soften. Add the flour, and cook for 1 minute.

4 Remove the pan from the heat and gradually stir in the fish stock and cider. Return the pan to the heat and cook, stirring constantly, until the mixture comes to the boil and thickens.

5 Add the potatoes. Bring the sauce back to the boil, then cover and simmer gently for 10–15 minutes until the potatoes are nearly tender. Add all the fish and shellfish and stir in gently.

6 Stir in the cream. Bring back to a gentle simmer, then cover and cook gently for 5–10 minutes or until the fish is cooked through, then discard any unopened shells. Adjust the seasoning to taste and gently stir in the herbs. Serve immediately.

Fillets of Turbot Energy 752kcal/3125kJ; Protein 66.7g; Carbohydrate 9.2g, of which sugars 8g; Fat 44.1g, of which saturates 23.9g; Cholesterol 106mg; Calcium 252mg; Fibre 1.4g; Sodium 370mg.
Casserole Energy 583kcal/2439kJ; Protein 49.3g; Carbohydrate 25.3g, of which sugars 6.1g; Fat 30.2g, of which saturates 16.5g; Cholesterol 354mg; Calcium 199mg; Fibre 2.5g; Sodium 404mg.

Stir-fried Squid with Ginger

There is an ancient belief that a well-loved wok holds the memory of all the dishes that have ever been cooked in it. Give yours something to think about by introducing it to this classic combination of baby squid in soy sauce, ginger and lemon juice. Spring onions add a crunchy texture that is very welcome.

Serves 2

4 ready-prepared baby squid, total
    weight about 250g/9oz
15ml/1 tbsp vegetable oil
2 garlic cloves, finely chopped
30ml/2 tbsp soy sauce
2.5cm/1in piece fresh root ginger,
    peeled and finely chopped
juice of ½ lemon
5ml/1 tsp sugar
2 spring onions (scallions),
    chopped

1 Rinse the squid well and pat dry with kitchen paper. Place on a board and use a sharp knife to cut the bodies into rings. Halve the tentacles, if necessary.

2 Heat the oil in a wok or large frying pan and cook the garlic, stirring constantly, until it turns golden brown, but do not let it burn. Add the squid pieces to the pan and stir-fry for a further 30 seconds over high heat.

3 Add the soy sauce, ginger, lemon juice, sugar and spring onions. Stir-fry for a further 30 seconds, then spoon into individual heated bowls and serve.

Cook's Tip
Squid has an undeserved reputation for having an unpleasant rubbery texture. This is always a result of overcooking it, so ensure that you watch the timings carefully.

Variation
This dish is often prepared with fresh galangal rather than ginger and works well with most kinds of seafood, including prawns (shrimp) and scallops.

Grilled Squid with Chorizo Sausage and Tomatoes

The best way to cook this dish is on a griddle or in a ridged griddle pan. If you can only find medium-size squid, allow two per serving and halve them lengthways.

Serves 6
24 small squid, cleaned
150ml/¼ pint/⅔ cup extra
    virgin olive oil

300g/11oz cooking chorizo,
    cut into 12 slices
3 tomatoes, halved and seasoned
    with salt and pepper
24 cooked new potatoes,
    halved
fresh rocket (arugula) leaves
juice of 1 lemon
salt and ground black
    pepper
lemon slices, to garnish

1 Separate the body and tentacles of the squid and cut the bodies in half lengthways if they are large.

2 Pour half the oil into a bowl, season with salt and pepper, then toss all the squid in the oil. Heat a ridged griddle (grill) pan or grill (broiler) to very hot.

3 Cook the prepared squid bodies for about 45 seconds on each side until the flesh is opaque and tender. Then transfer to a plate and keep hot. Grill the tentacles for about 1 minute on each side, then place them on the plate.

4 Grill the chorizo slices for about 30 seconds on each side, until golden brown, then set them aside with the squid. Grill the tomato halves for 1–2 minutes on each side, until they are softened and browned. Place the potatoes and a handful of rocket in a large bowl.

5 Pour the lemon juice into a bowl and whisk in the remaining oil. Season. Reserve 30ml/2 tbsp of this dressing. Pour the dressing over the potatoes and rocket, toss lightly and divide among six serving plates. Pile a portion of the squid, tomatoes and chorizo on each salad, and drizzle over the reserved dressing. Garnish each plate with lemon slices and serve immediately.

Stir-fried Squid Energy 165kcal/694kJ; Protein 19.7g; Carbohydrate 4.8g, of which sugars 3.2g; Fat 7.6g, of which saturates 1.2g; Cholesterol 281mg; Calcium 20mg; Fibre 0g; Sodium 1206mg.
Grilled Squid Energy 629kcal/2630kJ; Protein 39.3g; Carbohydrate 30.6g, of which sugars 4g; Fat 39.7g, of which saturates 10.6g; Cholesterol 417mg; Calcium 41mg; Fibre 2.2g; Sodium 1106mg.

Grilled Spicy Fish Brochettes

Serve these delicious skewers with seasonal new potatoes and marinated aubergine slices. Accompany them with a spicy chilli and tomato sauce and a stack of warm, soft pitta breads or flour tortillas.

Serves 4–6
5 garlic cloves, chopped
2.5ml/½ tsp paprika
2.5ml/½ tsp ground cumin
2.5–5ml/½–1 tsp salt
2–3 pinches of cayenne pepper
60ml/4 tbsp olive oil
30ml/2 tbsp lemon juice
30ml/2 tbsp chopped fresh
coriander (cilantro) or parsley
675g/1½lb firm-fleshed white
fish, such as haddock, halibut,
sea bass, snapper or turbot, cut
into 2.5–5cm/1–2in cubes
3–4 green (bell) peppers, cut into
2.5–5cm/1–2in pieces
2 lemon wedges, to serve

1 Put the chopped garlic, paprika, cumin, salt, cayenne pepper, oil, lemon juice and coriander or parsley in a large bowl and mix together.

2 Add the fish and toss to coat. Marinate the fish for 30 minutes to 2 hours, at room temperature, or chill overnight in a refrigerator.

3 About 40 minutes before you are going to cook the brochettes, light the barbecue. The barbecue is ready when the coals have turned white and grey.

4 Meanwhile, thread the fish cubes and pepper pieces alternately on to wooden or metal skewers.

5 Grill the brochettes on the barbecue for 2–3 minutes on each side, or until the fish is tender and lightly browned. Serve with lemon wedges.

> **Cook's Tip**
> If you are threading the fish on to bamboo or wooden skewers, soak the skewers in cold water for 30 minutes before use to stop them burning.

Poached Fish in Spicy Tomato Sauce

A selection of white fish fillets are used in this deliciously spicy dish – cod, haddock, hake or halibut are all good to use. Serve the fish with flat breads, such as pitta, and a spicy tomato relish. It is also good served with couscous or plain boiled rice and a green salad with a refreshing lemon juice dressing.

Serves 8
600ml/1 pint/2½ cups fresh
tomato sauce
2.5–5ml/½–1 tsp harissa
60ml/4 tbsp chopped fresh
coriander (cilantro) leaves
1.5kg/3¼lb mixed white fish
fillets, cut into chunks
salt and ground black pepper
2 fresh red chillies (optional),
finely sliced, to garnish
pitta bread, to serve

1 Heat the tomato sauce with the harissa and coriander in a large pan. Add salt and pepper to taste and bring to the boil.

2 Remove the pan from the heat and add the fish fillets to the hot tomato sauce. Return to the heat and bring the sauce to the boil again.

3 Reduce the heat and simmer the fish very gently for about 5 minutes, or until the pieces are tender. (Test with a fork: if the flesh flakes easily, then it is cooked.)

4 Taste the sauce and adjust the seasoning, adding more harissa if necessary.

5 Warm the pitta bread under the grill (broiler) and serve with the fish, garnished with the chilli slices, if using.

> **Cook's Tip**
> Harissa is a chilli paste spiced with cumin, garlic and coriander. It is fiery and should be used with care until you are familiar with the flavour. Start by adding a small amount, and then add more after tasting the sauce.

Fish Brochettes Energy 276kcal/1157kJ; Protein 33.3g; Carbohydrate 8g, of which sugars 7.6g; Fat 12.5g, of which saturates 1.9g; Cholesterol 61mg; Calcium 34mg; Fibre 2g; Sodium 118mg.
Poached Fish Energy 219kcal/923kJ; Protein 36.2g; Carbohydrate 6.7g, of which sugars 3.2g; Fat 5.5g, of which saturates 1.5g; Cholesterol 94mg; Calcium 46mg; Fibre 1.4g; Sodium 370mg.

Deep-fried Marinated Small Fish

This delicious selection of crispy fried fish has a Japanese-inspired marinade that is spiced with chillies to give a tongue-tingling effect.

Serves 4

450g/1lb sprats (US small whitebait or smelts)
plain (all-purpose) flour, for dusting
1 small carrot
1/3 cucumber
2 spring onions (scallions)
4cm/1 1/2in piece fresh root ginger, peeled
1 dried red chilli
75ml/5 tbsp rice vinegar
60ml/4 tbsp shoyu
15ml/1 tbsp mirin
30ml/2 tbsp sake
vegetable oil, for deep-frying

1 Wipe the fish dry with paper, then put them in a plastic bag with a handful of flour. Seal and shake to coat.

2 Cut the carrot and cucumber into thin strips. Cut the spring onions into three, then slice into thin, lengthways strips. Slice the ginger into thin, lengthways strips and rinse in cold water. Drain. Seed and chop the chilli into thin rings.

3 In a mixing bowl, mix the rice vinegar, shoyu, mirin and sake together to make a marinade. Add the chilli and all the sliced vegetables. Stir well.

4 Pour plenty of vegetable oil into a deep pan and heat to 180°C/350°F. Deep-fry the fish, five or six at a time, until golden brown. Drain on layered kitchen paper, then plunge the hot fish into the marinade. Leave the fish to marinate for at least an hour. Serve the fish cold in a shallow bowl topped with the marinated vegetables.

Variation
You can prepare small sardines in this way, too. They have tougher bones and need to be deep-fried twice. Heat the oil and deep-fry until the outside of the fish is just crisp but still pale. Drain and wait for 5 minutes, then put them back into the hot oil again and cook until golden brown.

Fish Tagine

Serve this aromatic dish with couscous flavoured with fresh mint.

Serves 8

1.3kg/3lb firm fish fillets, skinned and cut into 5cm/2in chunks
30ml/2 tbsp olive oil
4 onions, chopped
1 large aubergine (eggplant), cut into 1cm/1/2in cubes
2 courgettes (zucchini), cut into 1cm/1/2in cubes
400g/14oz can chopped tomatoes
400ml/14fl oz/1 2/3 cups passata (bottled strained tomatoes)
200ml/7fl oz/scant 1 cup fish stock
1 preserved lemon, chopped
90g/3 1/2oz/scant 1 cup pitted olives
60ml/4 tbsp chopped fresh coriander (cilantro)
salt and ground black pepper
fresh coriander sprigs, to garnish

For the harissa

3 large fresh red chillies, seeded and chopped
3 garlic cloves, peeled
15ml/1 tbsp ground coriander
30ml/2 tbsp ground cumin
5ml/1 tsp ground cinnamon
grated rind of 1 lemon
30ml/2 tbsp sunflower oil

1 To make the harissa, process everything together in a blender or food processor to form a smooth paste. Set aside.

2 Put the chunks of fish in a wide bowl and add 30ml/2 tbsp of the harissa. Toss to coat, then cover and chill for at least 1 hour.

3 Heat 15ml/1 tbsp oil in a shallow pan. Cook the onions gently for 10 minutes. Stir in the remaining harissa, and cook for 5 minutes.

4 Heat the remaining oil in a separate shallow pan. Add the aubergine cubes and cook for 10 minutes, or until they are golden brown. Add the courgettes and cook for a further 2 minutes.

5 Add the aubergines and courgettes to the onions, then stir in the chopped tomatoes, passata and fish stock. Bring to the boil, then reduce the heat and simmer for about 20 minutes.

6 Add the fish, lemon and olives to the pan. Cover and simmer gently for 15–20 minutes until cooked through. Stir in the chopped coriander. Season to taste and garnish with coriander.

Deep-fried Fish Energy 307kcal/1273kJ; Protein 17.4g; Carbohydrate 4.2g, of which sugars 4g; Fat 23.7g, of which saturates 3.6g; Cholesterol 83mg; Calcium 91mg; Fibre 0.2g; Sodium 961mg.
Fish Tagine Energy 174kcal/735kJ; Protein 33.7g; Carbohydrate 6.1g, of which sugars 5.9g; Fat 1.8g, of which saturates 0.4g; Cholesterol 81mg; Calcium 32mg; Fibre 2.5g; Sodium 134mg.

Classic Fish Pie

Originally a fish pie was based on the 'catch of the day'. Now we can choose either the fish we like best, or the variety that offers best value for money.

Serves 4

450g/1lb mixed fish, such as
  cod or salmon fillets and
  peeled prawns (shrimp)
finely grated rind of 1 lemon
450g/1lb floury potatoes
25g/1oz/2 tbsp butter, plus extra
  for greasing
salt and ground black pepper
1 egg, beaten

For the sauce
15g/½oz/1 tbsp butter
15ml/1 tbsp plain
  (all-purpose) flour
150ml/¼ pint/⅔ cup milk
45ml/3 tbsp chopped fresh parsley

1 Preheat the oven to 220°C/425°F/Gas 7. Grease an ovenproof dish and set aside. Cut the fish into bitesize pieces. Season the fish, sprinkle over the lemon rind and place in the base of the dish. Set aside while you make the topping.

2 Cook the potatoes in a pan of boiling salted water for about 10–15 minutes until tender.

3 Meanwhile, make the sauce. Melt the butter in a pan, add the flour and cook, stirring, for a few minutes. Remove from the heat and gradually whisk in the milk. Return to the heat and bring to the boil, then reduce the heat and simmer, whisking all the time, until the sauce has thickened and achieved a smooth consistency. Add the parsley and season to taste. Pour over the fish mixture.

4 Drain the potatoes well, and then mash with the butter. Pipe or spoon the potatoes on top of the fish mixture. Brush the beaten egg over the potatoes. Bake for 45 minutes until the top is golden brown. Serve hot.

> **Cook's Tip**
> If using frozen fish, defrost it thoroughly first, as lots of water from the fish will ruin your pie.

Hoki Stir-fry

Any firm white fish, such as monkfish, hake or cod, can be used for this attractive stir-fry. You can vary the vegetables according to what is available, but try to include at least three different colours.

Serves 4–6

675g/1½lb hoki fillet, skinned
pinch of five-spice powder
2 carrots
115g/4oz/1 cup small
  mangetouts (snow peas)
115g/4oz asparagus spears
4 spring onions (scallions)
45ml/3 tbsp groundnut (peanut) oil
2.5cm/1in piece fresh root ginger,
  peeled and cut into thin slivers
2 garlic cloves, finely chopped
300g/11oz/scant 1½ cups
  beansprouts
8–12 small baby corn cobs
15–30ml/1–2 tbsp light soy sauce
salt and ground black pepper

1 Cut the hoki into finger-size strips and season with salt, pepper and five-spice powder. Cut the carrots diagonally into slices as thin as the mangetouts.

2 Trim the mangetouts. Trim the asparagus spears and cut in half crossways. Trim the spring onions and cut them diagonally into 2cm/¾in pieces, keeping the white and green parts separate. Set aside.

3 Heat a wok or large frying pan, then pour in the oil. As soon as the oil is hot, add the ginger and garlic. Stir-fry for 1 minute, then add the white parts of the spring onions and cook for a further 1 minute.

4 Add the hoki strips to the pan and stir-fry for 2–3 minutes, until all the pieces of fish are opaque.

5 Add the beansprouts to the pan and toss them around to coat them in the oil, then put in the carrots, mangetouts, asparagus and corn. Continue to stir-fry for 3–4 minutes, by which time the fish should be cooked through, but all the vegetables are still crunchy.

6 Add soy sauce to taste, toss everything quickly together, then stir in the green parts of the spring onions. Serve immediately.

Fish Pie Energy 573kcal/2401kJ; Protein 36.8g; Carbohydrate 41g, of which sugars 7.3g; Fat 31.2g, of which saturates 4.7g; Cholesterol 92mg; Calcium 270mg; Fibre 1.2g; Sodium 1084mg.
Hoki Stir-fry Energy 183kcal/764kJ; Protein 22.4g; Carbohydrate 5g, of which sugars 3.8g; Fat 8.2g, of which saturates 1.1g; Cholesterol 0mg; Calcium 49mg; Fibre 2.3g; Sodium 295mg.

Chilli-spiced Fried Plaice

In this beautiful Japanese dish the flesh of the fish and also the skeleton is deep-fried to such crispness that you can eat it all.

Serves 4
4 small plaice or flounder, about
    500–675g/1¼–1½lb total
    weight, gutted
60ml/4 tbsp cornflour
    (cornstarch)
vegetable oil, for deep-frying
salt

For the condiment
130g/4½oz mooli (daikon), peeled
4 dried chillies, seeded
1 bunch of chives, finely chopped,
    plus whole chives to garnish

For the sauce
20ml/4 tsp rice vinegar
20ml/4 tsp shoyu

1 Use a very sharp knife to make deep cuts around the gills and across the tail of the fish. Cut through the skin from the head down to the tail along the centre. Slide the tip of the knife under the flesh near the head and gently cut the fillet from the bone. Fold the fillet with your hand as you cut, as if peeling it from the bone. Keep the knife horizontal.

2 Repeat for the other half, then turn the fish over and do the same to get four fillets from each fish. Place in a dish and sprinkle with a little salt on both sides. Keep the bony skeletons.

3 For the condiment, pierce the mooli with a skewer in four places to make holes, then insert the chillies. Leave for 15 minutes, then grate finely. Squeeze out the moisture with your hand. Press a quarter of the grated mooli and chilli into an egg cup, then turn out on to a plate. Make three more mounds.

4 Cut the fish fillets into four slices crossways and coat in cornflour. Heat the oil in a wok or pan to 175°C/345°F. Deep-fry the fillets, two to three at a time, until light golden brown. Raise the temperature to 180°C/350°F. Dust the skeletons with cornflour and cook until crisp. Drain and sprinkle with salt.

5 For the sauce, mix the rice vinegar and shoyu in a bowl. Arrange the fish on the plates with the mooli moulds and chives. To eat, mix the condiment and fish with the sauce.

Fried Flat Fish with Lemon and Capers

Several species of flat fish are caught in the Mediterranean and they are most commonly simply fried and served with lemon wedges to squeeze over the top. Intensely flavoured capers make a pleasant tangy addition to the very simple and quickly made sauce in this recipe. For a special occasion, try to find whole flat fish, small enough to serve one per diner.

Serves 2
30–45ml/2–3 tbsp plain
    (all-purpose) flour
4 sole, plaice or flounder fillets,
    or 2 whole small flat fish
45ml/3 tbsp olive oil
25g/1oz/2 tbsp butter
60ml/4 tbsp lemon juice
30ml/2 tbsp pickled
    capers, drained
salt and ground black pepper
fresh flat leaf parsley, to garnish
lemon wedges, to serve

1 Sift the flour on to a plate and season well with salt and ground black pepper. Dip the fish fillets into the flour to coat them evenly on both sides.

2 Heat the oil and butter in a large shallow pan until foaming. Add the fish fillets and fry over medium heat for 2–3 minutes on each side.

3 Lift out the fillets carefully with a metal spatula and place them on a warmed serving platter. Season with salt and ground black pepper.

4 Add the lemon juice and capers to the pan, heat through and pour over the fish. Garnish with parsley and serve immediately with lemon wedges.

> **Cook's Tip**
> This is a tasty and very quick way to prepare any small flat fish, or fillets of any white fish. The delicate flavour is enhanced by the lemon juice and capers without being overwhelmed.

Chilli-spiced Plaice Energy 219kcal/911kJ; Protein 13.8g; Carbohydrate 13.3g, of which sugars 1.7g; Fat 12.6g, of which saturates 1.6g; Cholesterol 34mg; Calcium 60mg; Fibre 1g; Sodium 808mg.
Fried Flat Fish Energy 425kcal/1773kJ; Protein 34.2g; Carbohydrate 5.9g, of which sugars 0.2g; Fat 29.7g, of which saturates 9.3g; Cholesterol 111mg; Calcium 103mg; Fibre 0.3g; Sodium 316mg.

Pan-fried Skate Wings with Black Butter

Skate can be quite inexpensive and this classic dish is perfect for a family supper. The sweet flesh is easily removed from the unthreatening soft bones, and it is a good choice for children as well as senior members of the family. Serve it with steamed leeks and plain boiled potatoes.

Serves 4
4 skate wings, about
  225g/8oz each
60ml/4 tbsp red wine vinegar
  or malt vinegar
30ml/2 tbsp drained capers in
  vinegar, chopped if large
30ml/2 tbsp chopped
  fresh parsley
150g/5oz/²⁄₃ cup butter
salt and ground black pepper

I Put the skate wings in a large, shallow pan, cover with cold water and add a pinch of salt and 15ml/1 tbsp of the red wine or malt vinegar.

2 Bring to the boil, skim the surface, then lower the heat and simmer gently for about 10–12 minutes, until the skate flesh comes away from the bone easily. Carefully drain the skate and peel off the skin.

3 Transfer the skate to a warmed serving dish, season with salt and ground black pepper and sprinkle over the capers and parsley. Keep hot.

4 In a small pan, heat the butter until it foams and turns a rich nutty brown. Pour it over the skate.

5 Pour the remaining vinegar into the pan and boil until reduced by about two-thirds. Drizzle over the skate and serve.

> **Cook's Tip**
> *Despite the title of the recipe, the butter should be a rich golden brown. It should never be allowed to blacken, or it will taste unpleasantly bitter.*

Skate Wings with Capers

This sophisticated way of serving skate wings is perfect for a dinner party. Serve them with a light, green salad.

Serves 6
50g/2oz/¹⁄₄ cup butter
6 small skate wings

grated rind and juice of
  2 limes
30ml/2 tbsp salted capers,
  rinsed and drained
salt and ground black pepper
handful of rocket (arugula),
  to garnish

I Heat the butter in a large frying pan and add one of the skate wings. Fry for 4–5 minutes on each side, until golden and cooked through.

2 Using a metal spatula, carefully transfer the cooked skate wing to a warmed serving plate and keep warm while you cook each of the remaining skate wings in the same way.

3 Return the pan to the heat and add the lime rind and juice, and capers. Season with salt and ground black pepper to taste and allow to bubble for 1–2 minutes.

4 Place the skate wings on warmed serving plates. Spoon a little of the juices and the capers over each skate wing, garnish with rocket and serve immediately.

> **Variation**
> *If fresh limes are not available, then fresh lemons can be used instead in their place.*

> **Cook's Tip**
> • *Do not be put off by the faint ammonia smell of skate. It vanishes when the fish is cooked.*
> • *Skate wings can vary greatly in size. If all you can find is large wings, then simply serve half a wing per diner.*

Pan-fried Skate Energy 411kcal/1709kJ; Protein 30.8g; Carbohydrate 0.6g, of which sugars 0.5g; Fat 31.8g, of which saturates 19.5g; Cholesterol 80mg; Calcium 112mg; Fibre 0.6g; Sodium 472mg.
Skate Wings Energy 300kcal/1256kJ; Protein 26.4g; Carbohydrate 7g, of which sugars 6.7g; Fat 14.3g, of which saturates 8.8g; Cholesterol 36mg; Calcium 114mg; Fibre 1.2g; Sodium 272mg.

Grilled Sole with Chive Butter

The very best way of transforming simple grilled fish into a luxury dish is by topping it with a flavoured butter, as in this recipe.

Serves 4
115g/4oz/½ cup unsalted
  (sweet) butter, softened, plus
  extra, melted
5ml/1 tsp diced lemon grass
pinch of finely grated lime rind
1 kaffir lime leaf, very finely
  shredded (optional)
45ml/3 tbsp chopped chives or
  chopped chive flowers, plus
  extra chives or chive flowers
  to garnish
2.5–5ml/½–1 tsp Thai fish sauce
4 sole, skinned
salt and ground black pepper
lemon or lime wedges, to serve

1 Put the butter in a bowl and cream it with a wooden spoon. Add the lemon grass, lime rind, lime leaf, if using, and chives or chive flowers. Mix well, making sure all the ingredients are thoroughly combined, then season to taste with Thai fish sauce, salt and pepper.

2 Chill the butter mixture to firm it a little, then form it into a roll and wrap in foil or clear film (plastic wrap). Chill until firm. Preheat the grill (broiler).

3 Brush the fish with melted butter. Place it on the grill (broiling) rack and season. Grill (broil) for about 5 minutes on one side.

4 Carefully turn the pieces of fish over and grill the other side for 4–5 minutes, until the fish is firm and just cooked. Test the flesh with a fork, it should flake easily.

5 Meanwhile, cut the chilled butter into thin slices. Put the fish on individual plates and top with the butter. Garnish with chives and serve with lemon or lime wedges.

> **Cook's Tips**
> • Finer white fish fillets, such as plaice, can be cooked in this way, but reduce the cooking time slightly.
> • The flavoured butter can be made ahead and frozen.

Grilled Hake with Lemon and Chilli

Nothing could be simpler than perfectly grilled fish with a dusting of chilli and lemon rind. This is an ideal meal for those occasions when something light is called for and you want to prepare a quick fast meal.

Serves 4
4 hake fillets, about 150g/5oz each
30ml/2 tbsp olive oil
finely grated rind and juice
  of 1 lemon
15ml/1 tbsp crushed
  chilli flakes
salt and ground black pepper

1 Preheat the grill (broiler) to high. Lightly brush the hake fillets with the olive oil and place them all, skin side up, on a large baking tray.

2 Grill (broil) the fish for 4–5 minutes, until the skin is crispy, then carefully turn the fillets over in the pan, using a metal spatula or two spoons.

3 Sprinkle the fillets with the lemon rind and chilli flakes and season with salt and ground black pepper.

4 Grill the fillets for a further 2–3 minutes, or until the hake is cooked through. (Test using the point of a sharp knife; the flesh should flake.) Transfer the fillets of hake to individual plates and squeeze over the lemon juice just before serving.

> **Cook's Tip**
> A pastry brush is the ideal implement for coating fish with oil, but keep one specifically for the purpose, unless you want your apple pie to taste slightly fishy. Draw a fish on the handle with a marker pen to distinguish it from your pastry brush.

> **Variation**
> Any firm white fish can be cooked in this simple, low-fat way. Try cod, halibut or hoki. If you do not have any chilli flakes, brush the fish with chilli oil instead of olive oil.

Grilled Sole Energy 349kcal/1447kJ; Protein 27.4g; Carbohydrate 0.5g, of which sugars 0.5g; Fat 26.3g, of which saturates 15g; Cholesterol 136mg; Calcium 49mg; Fibre 0g; Sodium 591mg.
Grilled Hake Energy 188kcal/786kJ; Protein 27g; Carbohydrate 0.1g, of which sugars 0.1g; Fat 8.8g, of which saturates 1.2g; Cholesterol 35mg; Calcium 22mg; Fibre 0g; Sodium 150mg.

John Dory with Light Curry Sauce

The curry taste of this dish should be very subtle, so use a mild curry powder. Serve the fish with pilau rice and mango chutney.

Serves 4

4 John Dory fillets, about
    175g/6oz each, skinned
15ml/1 tbsp sunflower oil
25g/1oz/2 tbsp butter
salt and ground black pepper
15ml/1 tbsp fresh coriander
    (cilantro) leaves and 1 small
    mango, diced, to garnish
pilau rice and mango chutney,
    to serve

For the curry sauce
30ml/2 tbsp sunflower oil
1 carrot, chopped
1 onion, chopped
1 celery stick, chopped
white of 1 leek, chopped
2 garlic cloves, crushed
50g/2oz creamed coconut
    (coconut cream), crumbled
2 tomatoes, peeled, seeded
    and diced
2.5cm/1in piece fresh root
    ginger, grated
15ml/1 tbsp tomato purée (paste)
5–10ml/1–2 tsp mild curry powder
500ml/17fl oz/generous 2 cups
    chicken or fish stock

1 Make the sauce. Heat the oil in a pan; add the vegetables and garlic. Cook gently until soft but not brown.

2 Add the coconut, tomatoes and ginger. Cook for 1–2 minutes, then stir in the tomato purée and curry powder to taste. Add the stock, stir and season.

3 Bring to the boil, then lower the heat, cover the pan and cook over the lowest heat for about 50 minutes. Stir once or twice to prevent burning. Leave to cool, then pour into a food processor or blender and process until smooth. Return to a clean pan and reheat gently, adding a little water if too thick.

4 Season the fish fillets with salt and pepper. Heat the oil in a large frying pan, add the butter and heat until sizzling. Put in the fish and cook for about 2–3 minutes on each side, until pale golden and cooked through. Drain on kitchen paper.

5 Serve on a bed of rice. Arrange the fillets on individual warmed plates and pour the sauce around. Garnish with finely diced mango and coriander leaves, and serve with chutney.

Hake au Poivre with Pepper Relish

This version of the classic steak au poivre can be made with monkfish or cod.

Serves 4

30–45ml/2–3 tbsp mixed
    peppercorns (black, white, pink
    and green)
4 hake steaks, 175g/6oz each
30ml/2 tbsp olive oil

For the (bell) pepper relish
2 red (bell) peppers, halved, cored
    and seeded

15ml/1 tbsp olive oil
2 garlic cloves, chopped
4 ripe tomatoes, peeled, seeded
    and quartered
4 drained canned anchovy
    fillets, chopped
5ml/1 tsp capers
15ml/1 tbsp balsamic vinegar,
    plus extra for drizzling
12 fresh basil leaves, shredded,
    plus a few extra to garnish
salt and ground black pepper

1 Put the peppercorns in a mortar and crush them coarsely with a pestle. Season the hake fillets lightly with salt, then coat them on both sides with the crushed peppercorns. Set aside.

2 Make the relish. Cut the peppers into 1cm/½in strips. Heat the oil in a frying pan that has a lid. Add the peppers and stir them for about 5 minutes, until they are slightly softened. Stir in the chopped garlic, tomatoes and anchovies, then cover the pan and simmer the mixture very gently for about 20 minutes, until the peppers are very soft.

3 Transfer the contents of the pan into a food processor and process to a coarse purée. Transfer to a bowl and season to taste with salt and pepper. Stir in the capers, balsamic vinegar and basil. Keep the relish hot.

4 Heat the olive oil in a shallow pan, add the hake steaks and cook them, in batches if necessary, for 5 minutes on each side, turning them once or twice, until they are just cooked through.

5 Place the fish steaks on individual plates and spoon a little red pepper relish on to the side of each plate. Garnish with basil leaves and drizzle with a little extra balsamic vinegar. Serve the rest of the relish separately.

Hake au Poivre Energy 283kcal/1186kJ; Protein 33.7g; Carbohydrate 8.2g, of which sugars 8g; Fat 13g, of which saturates 1.9g; Cholesterol 42mg; Calcium 47mg; Fibre 2.3g; Sodium 304mg.
John Dory Energy 333kcal/1391kJ; Protein 34.9g; Carbohydrate 12.5g, of which sugars 11.5g; Fat 16.3g, of which saturates 4.9g; Cholesterol 13mg; Calcium 102mg; Fibre 2.6g; Sodium 291mg.

Halibut with Leek and Ginger

Generally, fish needs to be absolutely fresh, but halibut needs to mature for a day or two to bring out the flavour. Serve with a tasty leek and ginger mixure and mashed potatoes to mop up all the juices.

Serves 4

2 leeks
50g/2oz piece fresh root ginger
4 halibut steaks, about 175g/6oz
each (see Cook's Tip)
15ml/1 tbsp olive oil
75g/3oz/6 tbsp butter
salt and ground black pepper

1 Trim the leeks, discarding the coarse outer leaves, the very dark green tops and the root end. Cut them into 5cm/2in lengths, then slice into thin matchsticks. Wash thoroughly.

2 Peel the fresh ginger as best you can, then slice it very thinly and cut the slices into thin sticks.

3 Dry the halibut on kitchen paper. Heat a large pan with the oil and add 50g/2oz/¼ cup of the butter. As it begins to bubble, place the steaks carefully in the pan, skin side down. Allow the halibut to colour – about 3–4 minutes. Then turn the steaks over, reduce the heat and cook for about a further 10 minutes.

4 Remove the fish from the pan, set aside and keep warm. Add the leeks and ginger to the pan, stir to mix, then allow the leeks to soften (they may colour slightly but this is fine). Once softened, season with a little salt and ground black pepper. Cut the remaining butter into small pieces then, off the heat, gradually stir into the pan.

5 To serve, place the halibut steaks on individual warmed plates and strew the leek and ginger mixture over the fish. Accompany with mashed potato, if you like.

> **Cook's Tip**
> Ask your fishmonger for flattish halibut steaks and not too thick as you want to cook them in a pan on the stove and not in the oven. Also ask him or her to skin them for you.

Grilled Halibut with Sauce Vierge

Any thick white fish fillets can be cooked in this dish; turbot, brill and John Dory are especially delicious, but the flavoursome sauce also gives humbler fish such as haddock or hake a real lift.

Serves 4

105ml/7 tbsp olive oil
2.5ml/½ tsp fennel seeds
2.5ml/½ tsp celery seeds
5ml/1 tsp mixed peppercorns
675–800g/1½–1¾lb middle cut
of halibut, about 3cm/1¼in
thick, cut into 4 pieces
coarse sea salt
5ml/1 tsp fresh thyme
leaves, chopped
5ml/1 tsp fresh rosemary
leaves, chopped
5ml/1 tsp fresh oregano or
marjoram leaves, chopped
cooked green cabbage, to serve

For the sauce
105ml/7 tbsp extra virgin olive oil
juice of 1 lemon
1 garlic clove, finely chopped
2 tomatoes, peeled, seeded
and diced
5ml/1 tsp small capers
2 drained canned anchovy
fillets, chopped
5ml/1 tsp chopped fresh chives
15ml/1 tbsp shredded fresh
basil leaves
15ml/1 tbsp chopped fresh chervil

1 Heat a ridged griddle (grill) pan or preheat the grill (broiler) to high. Brush the griddle pan or grill pan with a little of the olive oil. Mix the fennel and celery seeds with the peppercorns in a mortar. Crush with a pestle, and then stir in the coarse sea salt to taste. Spoon the mixture into a shallow dish and stir in the herbs and the remaining olive oil.

2 Add the halibut pieces to the olive oil mixture, turning them to coat them thoroughly, then arrange them with the dark skin uppermost in the oiled griddle pan or grill pan. Cook or grill (broil) for about 6–8 minutes, until the fish is cooked all the way through and the skin has browned.

3 Combine all the sauce ingredients except the herbs in a pan and heat gently until warm but not hot. Stir in the chives, basil and chervil.

4 Place the halibut on four warmed plates. Spoon the sauce around and over the fish and serve with green cabbage.

Halibut with Leek Energy 364kcal/1520kJ; Protein 39.1g; Carbohydrate 2.7g, of which sugars 2.1g; Fat 21.9g, of which saturates 10.8g; Cholesterol 101mg; Calcium 75mg; Fibre 1.9g; Sodium 221mg.
Grilled Halibut Energy 410kcal/1709kJ; Protein 37.3g; Carbohydrate 1.8g, of which sugars 1.4g; Fat 28.3g, of which saturates 4.1g; Cholesterol 60mg; Calcium 72mg; Fibre 0.5g; Sodium 165mg.

Halibut with Coconut Milk

This aromatic dish, known locally as moqueca, comes from the state of Bahia, on the east coast of Brazil. Cooked and served in an earthenware dish, it is usually accompanied by white rice and flavoured cassava flour to soak up the delicious sauce.

Serves 6

6 halibut, cod, haddock or
   monkfish fillets, about
   115g/4oz each
juice of 2 limes
8 fresh coriander (cilantro) sprigs
2 red chillies, seeded and chopped
3 tomatoes, sliced into thin rounds
1 red (bell) pepper, seeded and
   sliced into thin rounds
1 green (bell) pepper, seeded and
   sliced into thin rounds
1 small onion, sliced into
   thin rounds
200ml/7fl oz/scant 1 cup
   coconut milk
60ml/4 tbsp palm oil
salt
cooked white rice, to serve

**For the flavoured
cassava flour**
30ml/2 tbsp palm oil
1 medium onion, thinly sliced
250g/9oz/2¼ cups cassava flour

1 Place the fish in a large, shallow dish and pour over water to cover. Pour in the lime juice and set aside for 30 minutes. Drain the fish and pat dry with kitchen paper. Arrange the fish in a single layer in a heavy pan that has a tight-fitting lid.

2 Sprinkle the coriander and chillies over the fish, then top with a layer each of tomatoes, peppers and onion. Pour the coconut milk over, cover and leave to stand for 15 minutes.

3 Season with salt, then place the pan over high heat and cook until the coconut milk comes to the boil. Lower the heat and simmer for 5 minutes. Remove the lid, pour in the palm oil, cover again and simmer for 10 minutes.

4 Meanwhile, make the flavoured cassava flour. Heat the oil in a large frying pan. Add the onion and cook for 8–10 minutes until soft. Stir in the cassava flour and cook, stirring, for 1–2 minutes until toasted and evenly coloured by the oil. Season with salt.

5 Serve the fish with the rice and flavoured cassava flour.

Jamaican Fish Curry

Although the rice is simply boiled, it is an integral part of this dish and is a good example of how plain rice takes on the flavour of the sauce with which it is served.

Serves 4

2 halibut steaks, total weight
   about 500–675g/1¼–1½lb
30ml/2 tbsp groundnut (peanut) oil
2 cardamom pods
1 cinnamon stick
6 allspice berries
4 cloves
1 large onion, chopped
3 garlic cloves, crushed
10–15ml/2–3 tsp grated fresh
   root ginger
10ml/2 tsp ground cumin
5ml/1 tsp ground coriander
2.5ml/½ tsp cayenne pepper
   or to taste
4 tomatoes, peeled, seeded
   and chopped
1 sweet potato, about 225g/8oz,
   cut into 2cm/¾in cubes
475ml/16fl oz/2 cups fish stock
   or water
115g/4oz piece of creamed
   coconut or 120ml/4 fl oz/
   ½ cup coconut cream
1 bay leaf
225g/8oz/generous 1 cup white
   long grain rice
salt

1 Rub the halibut steaks well with salt and set aside. Heat the oil in a flameproof casserole and stir-fry the cardamom pods, cinnamon stick, allspice berries and cloves for 3 minutes.

2 Add the onion, garlic and ginger. Cook for 4–5 minutes over a gentle heat, until the onion is fairly soft, stirring frequently. Add the cumin, coriander and cayenne pepper and cook briefly.

3 Stir in the tomatoes, sweet potato, stock or water, coconut and bay leaf. Season with salt. Bring to the boil, then cover and simmer for 15–18 minutes, until the sweet potato is tender.

4 Cook the rice according to your preferred method. Meanwhile, add the fish steaks to the pan of curry sauce and spoon the sauce over them. Put a lid on the pan and simmer for about 10 minutes, until the fish is just tender and flakes easily.

5 Spoon the rice into a warmed serving dish, spoon over the sauce and arrange the steaks on top. Serve immediately.

Halibut with Coconut Energy 336kcal/1410kJ; Protein 41.9g; Carbohydrate 8.4g, of which sugars 8.1g; Fat 15.2g, of which saturates 2.1g; Cholesterol 66mg; Calcium 73mg; Fibre 2.2g; Sodium 622mg.
Fish Curry Energy 639kcal/2669kJ; Protein 34.1g; Carbohydrate 62g, of which sugars 8.3g; Fat 28.4g, of which saturates 18.7g; Cholesterol 44mg; Calcium 74mg; Fibre 2.4g; Sodium 115mg.

Pan-fried Sea Bream with Lime and Tomato Salsa

The most popular way of cooking a fresh piece of fish is to pan-fry it or grill it. In this recipe a simple salsa is flashed in the pan at the end of cooking, to make a light sauce for the fish.

Serves 4

4 sea bream fillets
juice of 2 limes
30ml/2 tbsp chopped
   coriander (cilantro)
1 fresh red chilli, seeded and
   finely chopped
2 spring onions (scallions),
   sliced
45ml/3 tbsp olive oil, plus extra
   to serve
2 large tomatoes, diced
salt
cooked white rice, to serve

1 Place the fish fillets in a shallow china or glass dish large enough to hold them all in a single layer.

2 Mix the lime juice, coriander, chilli and spring onions in a jug (pitcher). Stir in half the oil, then pour this marinade over the fish. Cover and marinate for around 15–20 minutes. Do not be tempted to marinate the fish for longer than this or the acid in the marinade will start to 'cook' it.

3 Heat the remaining oil in a large heavy frying pan over high heat. Lift each piece of fish from the marinade and pat dry with kitchen paper.

4 Season the fish with salt and place in the hot pan, skin side down. Cook for 2 minutes, then turn with a metal spatula and cook for a further 2 minutes, until the flesh is opaque all the way through.

5 Add the marinade and the chopped tomatoes to the pan. Bring the sauce gently to the boil and cook, stirring constantly, for about 1 minute, until the tomatoes are lightly cooked but still retain their shape.

6 Drizzle a little olive oil over the fish and serve on individual warm plates, with white rice and the tomato salsa.

Roast Monkfish with Garlic

Monkfish tied up and cooked in this way is known in French as a 'gigot', because it resembles a leg of lamb. The combination of monkfish and garlic is superb. For a contrast in colour, serve it with vibrant green beans.

Serves 4–6

1kg/2¼lb monkfish tail,
   skinned
14 fat garlic cloves
5ml/1 tsp fresh thyme leaves
30ml/2 tbsp olive oil
juice of 1 lemon
2 bay leaves
salt and ground black pepper

1 Preheat the oven to 220°C/425°F/Gas 7. Remove any membrane from the monkfish tail and cut out the central bone. Peel two garlic cloves and cut them into thin slivers. Sprinkle a quarter of these and half the thyme leaves over the cut side of the fish, then close it up and use kitchen string to tie it into a neat shape. Pat dry with kitchen paper.

2 Make incisions on either side of the fish and push in the remaining garlic slivers. Heat half the olive oil in a frying pan that can safely be used in the oven. When the oil is hot, put in the monkfish and brown it all over for about 5 minutes, until evenly coloured. Season with salt and pepper, sprinkle with lemon juice and sprinkle over the remaining thyme.

3 Tuck the bay leaves under the monkfish, arrange the remaining (unpeeled) garlic cloves around it and drizzle the remaining oil over the fish and the garlic. Transfer the pan to the oven for 20–25 minutes, until the fish is cooked through.

4 Place on a warmed serving dish with the garlic and some green beans. To serve, remove the string and cut the monkfish into 2cm/¾in thick slices.

Cook's Tips
• The garlic heads can be used whole.
• When serving the monkfish, invite each guest to pop out the soft garlic pulp with a fork and spread it over the monkfish.

Roast Monkfish Energy 259kcal/1091kJ; Protein 45.7g; Carbohydrate 4.1g, of which sugars 0.4g; Fat 6.7g, of which saturates 1.1g; Cholesterol 40mg; Calcium 27mg; Fibre 1g; Sodium 51mg.
Pan-fried Sea Bream Energy 166kcal/698kJ; Protein 27.3g; Carbohydrate 2g, of which sugars 2g; Fat 5.5g, of which saturates 0.2g; Cholesterol 57mg; Calcium 84mg; Fibre 1g; Sodium 173mg.

Sea Bass with Parsley and Lime Butter

The delicate but firm, sweet flesh of sea bass goes beautifully with citrus flavours. Serve with roast fennel and sautéed diced potatoes or, for a summer lunch, with new potatoes and salad.

Serves 6
50g/2oz/¼ cup butter
6 sea bass fillets, about
  150g/5oz each
grated rind and juice of
  1 large lime
30ml/2 tbsp chopped fresh parsley
salt and ground black pepper

1 Heat the butter in a large frying pan and add three of the sea bass fillets, skin side down. Cook for 3–4 minutes, or until the skin has turned crisp and golden. Turn the fish over and cook for a further 2–3 minutes, or until cooked through. If the flesh flakes easily when tested with a knife, it is cooked.

2 Carefully remove the fillets from the pan with a metal spatula. Place each on a serving plate and keep them warm. Cook the remaining fish in the same way and transfer to serving plates.

3 Add the lime rind and juice to the pan with the chopped parsley, and season with salt and black pepper. Allow to bubble for 1–2 minutes, then pour a little over each fish portion and serve immediately.

Variation
Instead of serving this with sautéed diced potatoes, offer fat home-made oven chips (French fries) with fresh herbs and a little lime to echo the flavouring used in the butter for the fish. Slice 4 large waxy potatoes thickly and spread them in a single layer in a roasting pan. Sprinkle with 30ml/2 tbsp chopped fresh herbs and the finely grated rind of 1 lime. Drizzle with 30ml/2 tbsp olive oil and dot with the same quantity of butter. Cover with foil and bake at 200°C/400°F/Gas 6 for 1–1¼ hours, removing the foil after 30 minutes and stirring the chips at least twice.

Cod Plaki

Greece has so much coastline, it is no wonder that fish is popular all over the country. Generally, it is treated very simply, but this recipe is a little more involved, baking the fish with onions and tomatoes. Other firm, white fish steaks can be used in place of the cod, if you prefer, such as haddock or hake.

Serves 6
300ml/½ pint/1¼ cups olive oil
2 onions, thinly sliced
3 large well-flavoured tomatoes,
  roughly chopped
3 garlic cloves, thinly sliced
5ml/1 tsp sugar
5ml/1 tsp chopped fresh dill
5ml/1 tsp chopped fresh mint
5ml/1 tsp chopped fresh
  celery leaves
15ml/1 tbsp chopped
  fresh parsley
6 cod steaks
juice of 1 lemon
salt and ground black pepper
extra dill, mint or parsley,
  to garnish

1 Heat the olive oil in a large frying pan or flameproof dish. Add the sliced onions and cook, stirring occasionally, for about 6–8 minutes until pale golden and soft.

2 Add the chopped tomatoes, sliced garlic, sugar, dill, mint, celery leaves and parsley to the pan. Pour in about 300ml/ ½ pint/1¼ cups water. Bring the mixture gently to the boil.

3 Season with salt and ground black pepper. Reduce the heat and simmer, uncovered, for 25 minutes, until the liquid has reduced by one-third.

4 Add the fish steaks to the pan, ensuring they are evenly distributed and submerged in the sauce. Cook gently for about 10–12 minutes, until the fish is just cooked through.

5 Remove the pan from the heat and stir in the lemon juice. Cover the pan and set aside to stand for about 20 minutes before serving.

6 Arrange the cod in a dish and spoon the sauce over. Garnish with herbs and serve warm or cold.

Sea Bass Energy 213kcal/890kJ; Protein 29g; Carbohydrate 0g, of which sugars 0g; Fat 11g, of which saturates 5g; Cholesterol 138mg; Calcium 199mg; Fibre 0.1g; Sodium 200mg.
Cod Plaki Energy 492kcal/2041kJ; Protein 37.7g; Carbohydrate 6.7g, of which sugars 5.6g; Fat 35g, of which saturates 5g; Cholesterol 92mg; Calcium 36mg; Fibre 1.4g; Sodium 128mg.

Salt Cod with Chilli and Olives

This tasty, spicy dish is enjoyed on Christmas Eve throughout Mexico.

Serves 6

450g/1lb dried salt cod
105ml/7 tbsp extra virgin olive oil
1 onion, halved and thinly sliced
4 garlic cloves, crushed
2 x 400g/14oz cans chopped
   tomatoes in tomato juice
75g/3oz/3/4 cup slivered almonds
75g/3oz/1/2 cup pickled jalapeño
   chilli slices
115g/4oz/1 cup green olives
   stuffed with pimiento
small bunch of fresh parsley,
   finely chopped
salt and ground black pepper
fresh flat leaf parsley,
   to garnish
crusty bread, to serve

1 Put the cod in a large bowl and pour over enough cold water to cover. Soak for 24 hours, changing the water at least five times during this period. Drain the cod and remove the skin using a large sharp knife. Shred the flesh finely using two forks, and put it into a bowl. Set it aside.

2 Heat half the oil in a large frying pan. Add the onion and fry until softened and translucent. Remove the onion and oil from the pan and set aside. In the same pan, add the remaining oil. When hot, add the crushed garlic and fry gently for 2 minutes.

3 Add the tomatoes and their juice to the pan with the garlic. Cook over a medium-high heat for about 20 minutes, stirring occasionally, until the mixture has reduced and thickened.

4 Meanwhile, spread out the slivered almonds in a single layer in a large heavy frying pan. Toast them over medium heat for a few minutes, shaking the pan lightly throughout the process so that they turn golden brown all over. Do not let them burn.

5 Add the jalapeño chilli slices and stuffed olives to the toasted almonds. Mix in the fish and cook for 20 minutes more, stirring occasionally, until the mixture is almost dry.

6 Season to taste, add the parsley and cook for a further 2–3 minutes. Garnish with parsley leaves and serve in heated bowls, with crusty bread.

Classic Fish and Chips

Quintessentially English, this is fish and chips as it should be, with tender flakes of fish in a crisp batter, and home-made chips.

Serves 4

450g/1lb potatoes
groundnut (peanut) oil, for
   deep-frying
4 x 175g/6oz cod fillets, skinned
lemon wedges, to serve

For the batter
75g/3oz/2/3 cup plain
   (all-purpose) flour
1 egg yolk
10ml/2 tsp oil
175ml/6fl oz/3/4 cup water
salt

1 To make the chips, cut the potatoes into slices about 5mm/1/4in thick. Then cut the slices into 5mm/1/4in fingers or chips. Rinse the slices thoroughly, drain well, and then dry in a clean dish towel.

2 Heat the oil in a deep fat fryer to 180°C/350°F. Add the chips in the basket to the fryer and cook for 3 minutes. Lift out and shake off excess fat.

3 To make the batter, sift the flour into a bowl. Add a pinch of salt. Make a well in the middle of the flour and add the egg yolk, oil and a little of the water. Mix the yolk with the liquid, then add the remaining water and incorporate the surrounding flour to make a smooth batter. Cover and set aside.

4 Reheat the oil in the fryer and cook the chips again for about 5 minutes, until they are golden and crisp. Drain on kitchen paper and season with salt. Keep hot in a low oven.

5 Dip the pieces of fish fillet into the batter and turn them to make sure they are evenly coated. Allow any excess batter to drip off before carefully lowering the fish into the hot oil.

6 Cook the fish for 5 minutes, turning once, if necessary, so that the batter browns evenly all over. The batter should be crisp and golden. Remove with a slotted spoon and drain well on kitchen paper. Serve the hot fish immediately, with lemon wedges and the chips.

Salt Cod Energy 229kcal/954kJ; Protein 29.6g; Carbohydrate 2.2g, of which sugars 1.5g; Fat 11.3g, of which saturates 1.3g; Cholesterol 69mg; Calcium 40mg; Fibre 0.9g; Sodium 92mg.
Fish and Chips Energy 645kcal/2700kJ; Protein 32.6g; Carbohydrate 54.3g, of which sugars 0.7g; Fat 34.5g, of which saturates 4.2g; Cholesterol 0mg; Calcium 130mg; Fibre 3.4g; Sodium 294mg.

Roast Cod Wrapped in Prosciutto

Wrapping chunky fillets of cod in wafer-thin slices of prosciutto keeps the fish succulent and moist, at the same time adding flavour and visual impact. Serve with baby new potatoes and a herb salad for a stylish supper or lunch dish.

Serves 4
2 thick skinless cod fillets, about
375g/13oz each
75ml/5 tbsp extra virgin olive oil
75g/3oz prosciutto,
thinly sliced
400g/14oz tomatoes,
on the vine
salt and ground black pepper

1 Preheat the oven to 220°C/425°F/Gas 7. Pat the fish dry on kitchen paper and remove any stray bones. Season lightly on both sides with salt and pepper.

2 Place one fillet in an ovenproof dish and drizzle 15ml/1 tbsp of the oil over it. Cover with the second fillet, laying the thick end on top of the thin end of the lower fillet.

3 Lay the ham over the fish, overlapping the slices to cover the fish in an even layer. Tuck the ends of the ham under the fish and tie it in place at intervals with fine string.

4 Using kitchen scissors, snip the tomato vines into four portions and add to the dish. Drizzle the tomatoes and ham with the remaining oil and season lightly.

5 Roast for 35 minutes, until the tomatoes are tender and the fish is cooked through. Test the fish by piercing one end of the parcel with the tip of a sharp knife to check that it flakes easily.

6 Slice the fish and transfer the portions to warmed plates, adding the tomatoes. Spoon over the cooking juices from the dish and serve immediately.

> **Variation**
> *You can use Serrano ham, or other air-dried ham, in place of the prosciutto, if you prefer.*

Fish Pie with Sweet Potato Topping

This dish is full of tasty flavours – the slightly spicy sweet potato complements the mild-flavoured fish.

Serves 4
175g/6oz/scant 1 cup basmati
rice, soaked and drained
450ml/³⁄₄ pint/scant 2 cups
well-flavoured stock
175g/6oz/1¹⁄₂ cups podded
broad (fava) beans
675g/1¹⁄₂lb haddock or cod
fillets, skinned
450ml/³⁄₄ pint/scant 2 cups milk
15g/¹⁄₂oz/1 tbsp butter

For the sauce
25g/1oz/2 tbsp butter
30–45ml/2–3 tbsp plain
(all-purpose) flour
15ml/1 tbsp chopped
fresh parsley
salt and ground black pepper

For the topping
450g/1lb sweet potatoes, peeled
and cut in large chunks
450g/1lb floury white potatoes,
peeled and cut in large chunks
milk and butter, for mashing
10ml/2 tsp freshly chopped parsley
5ml/1 tsp freshly chopped dill

1 Preheat the oven to 190°C/375°F/Gas 5. Put the rice in a pan with the stock. Bring to the boil, then cover and simmer for 10 minutes until tender. Cook the beans in lightly salted water until tender, then drain. When cool, remove their skins.

2 For the topping, cook the sweet and white potatoes separately in boiling salted water until tender. Drain, then mash with milk and butter and spoon into separate bowls. Beat the parsley and dill into the sweet potatoes.

3 Place the fish in a pan and pour in milk to cover. Dot with 15g/¹⁄₂oz/1 tbsp of the butter and season. Simmer for 5 minutes until tender. Remove from the pan. Make up the cooking liquid to 450ml/³⁄₄ pint/scant 2 cups with the remaining milk.

4 Make a white sauce. Melt the butter in a pan, stir in the flour and cook for 1 minute. Gradually add the milk mixture, stirring, until a white sauce forms. Stir in the parsley, taste and season.

5 Spread the rice on the bottom of a gratin dish. Add the beans and fish and pour over the sauce. Top with the mashed potatoes and bake for 15 minutes until browned.

Roast Cod Energy 281kcal/1172kJ; Protein 32.8g; Carbohydrate 3.1g, of which sugars 3.1g; Fat 15.3g, of which saturates 2.3g; Cholesterol 81mg; Calcium 23mg; Fibre 1g; Sodium 116mg.
Fish Pie Energy 604kcal/2545kJ; Protein 41.6g; Carbohydrate 88g, of which sugars 8.6g; Fat 10.7g, of which saturates 5.7g; Cholesterol 99mg; Calcium 94mg; Fibre 6.9g; Sodium 223mg.

Trout with Tamarind and Chilli Sauce

Sometimes trout can taste rather bland, but this spicy sauce really gives it a zing. If you like your food very spicy, add an extra chilli.

Serves 4

4 trout, cleaned
6 spring onions (scallions), sliced
60ml/4 tbsp soy sauce
15ml/1 tbsp vegetable oil
30ml/2 tbsp chopped fresh
   coriander (cilantro) and strips
   of fresh red chilli, to garnish

For the sauce
50g/2oz tamarind pulp
105ml/7 tbsp boiling water
2 shallots, coarsely chopped
1 fresh red chilli, seeded
   and chopped
1cm/½in piece fresh root ginger,
   peeled and chopped
5ml/1 tsp soft light brown sugar
45ml/3 tbsp Thai fish sauce

1 Slash the trout diagonally four or five times on each side. Place them in a shallow dish that is large enough to hold them all in a single layer.

2 Fill the cavity of each trout with spring onions and douse each fish with soy sauce. Carefully turn the fish over to coat both sides with the sauce. Sprinkle any remaining spring onions over the top.

3 To make the sauce, put the tamarind pulp in a small bowl and pour over the boiling water. Mash well with a fork until softened and combined.

4 Transfer the tamarind mixture to a food processor or blender, and add the shallots, fresh chilli, ginger, sugar and fish sauce. Process to a coarse pulp. Scrape into a bowl.

5 Heat the oil in a large frying pan or wok and cook the trout, one at a time if necessary, for about 5 minutes on each side, until the skin is crisp and browned and the flesh cooked.

6 Transfer the trout to warmed serving plates and spoon over some of the sauce. Sprinkle with the coriander and chilli and serve with the remaining sauce.

Pan-fried Citrus Trout with Basil

The clean taste of oranges and lemons and the aromatic scent of basil combine beautifully in this recipe to create a light and tangy sauce for trout fillets.

Serves 4

4 trout fillets, about 200g/7oz
   each

2 lemons
3 oranges
105ml/7 tbsp olive oil
45ml/3 tbsp plain
   (all-purpose) flour
25g/1oz/2 tbsp butter
5ml/1 tsp soft light brown sugar
15g/½ oz/½ cup fresh
   basil leaves
salt and ground black pepper

1 Arrange the trout fillets in a single layer in the base of a non-metallic shallow dish.

2 Grate the rind from one lemon and two of the oranges, then squeeze these fruits and pour the combined juices into a jug (pitcher). Slice the remaining fruits and set aside to use as a garnish.

3 Add 75ml/5 tbsp of the oil to the citrus juices. Beat with a fork and pour over the fish. Cover and leave to marinate in the refrigerator for at least 2 hours.

4 Preheat the oven to 150°C/300°F/Gas 2. Using a metal spatula, carefully remove the trout from the marinade. Season the fish and coat each in flour.

5 Heat the remaining oil in a frying pan and add the trout. Fry for 2–3 minutes on each side until cooked, then transfer to a plate and keep hot in the oven.

6 Add the butter and the marinade to the pan and heat gently, stirring until the butter has melted. Season with salt and pepper, then stir in the sugar. Continue cooking gently for 4–5 minutes until the sauce has thickened slightly.

7 Finely shred half the basil leaves and add them to the pan. Pour the sauce over the fish and garnish with the remaining basil and the orange and lemon slices.

Pan-fried Trout Energy 266kcal/1119kJ; Protein 40.5g; Carbohydrate 7.9g, of which sugars 7.7g; Fat 8.3g, of which saturates 0.2g; Cholesterol 0mg; Calcium 140mg; Fibre 1.7g; Sodium 177mg.
Trout with Tamarind Energy 82kcal/346kJ; Protein 12g; Carbohydrate 2g, of which sugars 1.6g; Fat 3g, of which saturates 0.6g; Cholesterol 48mg; Calcium 24mg; Fibre 0.3g; Sodium 245mg.

Trout a la Navarra

This trout dish is named after the Spanish region of Navarre and features tender fish wrapped in slices of dry-cured ham.

Serves 4

4 brown or rainbow trout, about
    250g/9oz each, cleaned
50g/2oz/¼ cup melted butter,
    plus extra for greasing
16 thin slices Serrano ham, about
    200g/7oz
salt and ground black pepper
buttered potatoes, to
    serve (optional)

1 Extend the belly cavity of each trout, cutting up one side of the backbone. Slip a knife behind the rib bones to loosen them (sometimes just flexing the fish will make the bones pop up). Chop these off from both sides with scissors, and season the fish well inside.

2 Preheat the grill (broiler) to high, with a shelf in the top position. Line a baking tray with kitchen foil and grease it with a little butter.

3 Working with the fish on the foil, fold a piece of ham into each belly. Use smaller or broken bits of ham for this, and reserve the eight best slices.

4 Brush each trout with a little butter, seasoning the outside lightly with salt and ground black pepper. Wrap two slices of ham around each one, crossways, tucking the ends into the belly of the fish.

5 Grill (broil) the trout for about 4 minutes, then carefully turn them over with a metal spatula, rolling them across on the belly, so the ham wrapping does not come loose, and grill for a further 4 minutes until cooked through – the flesh will flake easily when tested with the tip of a knife.

6 Serve the trout very hot, with any spare butter spooned over the top and around the sides. Diners should open the trout on their plates, and eat them from the inside, pushing the flesh off the skin.

Cheese-topped Trout

Succulent strips of filleted trout are topped with a mixture of Parmesan, pine nuts, herbs and breadcrumbs before being drizzled with lemon butter and grilled.

Serves 4

50g/2oz/1 cup fresh white
    breadcrumbs
50g/2oz Parmesan cheese, grated
25g/1oz/⅓ cup pine nuts,
    chopped
15ml/1 tbsp chopped fresh parsley
15ml/1 tbsp chopped fresh
    coriander (cilantro)
30ml/2 tbsp olive oil
4 thick trout fillets, about
    225g/8oz each
40g/1½oz/3 tbsp butter
juice of 1 lemon
salt and ground black pepper
lemon slices, to garnish
steamed baby asparagus and
    carrots, to serve

1 In a mixing bowl, combine the breadcrumbs, Parmesan cheese, pine nuts, parsley and coriander. Add the oil.

2 Cut each trout fillet into two strips. Firmly press the breadcrumb mixture on to the top of each strip of trout.

3 Preheat the grill (broiler) to high. Grease the grill (broiling) pan with 15g/½oz of the butter. Melt the remaining butter in a small pan and stir in the lemon juice.

4 Place the breadcrumb-topped fillets on the greased grill pan and pour the lemon butter over.

5 Grill (broil) the trout for 10 minutes or until the fillets are just cooked. Place two trout strips on each plate, garnish with lemon slices and serve with steamed asparagus and carrots.

Variations
• If you don't have any fresh coriander (cilantro), increase the amount of fresh parsley.
• Dried peaches or apricots could be chopped finely and added to the stuffing, with perhaps a little finely grated lemon rind to enhance the fruity flavour.

Cheese-topped Trout Energy 524kcal/2185kJ; Protein 51.3g; Carbohydrate 10.3g, of which sugars 0.9g; Fat 31.1g, of which saturates 8.9g; Cholesterol 34mg; Calcium 214mg; Fibre 1g; Sodium 422mg.
Trout a la Navarra Energy 369kcal/1546kJ; Protein 48g; Carbohydrate 0.6g, of which sugars 0.6g; Fat 19.4g, of which saturates 8.8g; Cholesterol 216mg; Calcium 66mg; Fibre 0g; Sodium 821mg.

Salmon Parcels with Lemon and Herb Butter

A delicious fish with a delicate flavour, salmon needs to be served simply. Here, fresh dill and lemon are combined to make a slightly piquant butter.

Serves 4
50g/2oz/¼ cup butter, softened, plus extra for greasing
finely grated rind of
  1 lemon
15ml/1 tbsp lemon juice
15ml/1 tbsp chopped
  fresh dill
4 salmon steaks
2 lemon slices, halved
4 sprigs of fresh dill
salt and ground
  black pepper

1 Place the softened butter, lemon rind, lemon juice and chopped fresh dill in a small bowl and mix together with a fork until thoroughly blended. Season to taste with salt and ground black pepper.

2 Spoon the butter on to a piece of baking parchment and roll up, smoothing with your hands into a sausage shape. Twist the ends tightly, wrap in clear film (plastic wrap) and put in the freezer for 20 minutes, until firm.

3 Meanwhile, preheat the oven to 190°C/375°F/Gas 5. Cut out four even squares of foil to encase the salmon steaks and grease each one with butter. Place a salmon steak into the centre of each.

4 Remove the herb butter from the freezer and slice into eight equal rounds. Place two rounds of butter on top of each salmon steak with a halved lemon slice in the centre and a sprig of dill on top. Lift up the edges of the foil and crinkle them together until well sealed. Place the foil parcels on a large baking tray.

5 Bake the salmon parcels in the preheated oven for about 20 minutes. Place the unopened parcels on warmed plates. Open the parcels and slide the contents on to the plates with the juices, or let diners do it themselves.

Teriyaki Salmon Fillets with Ginger Strips

Bottles of teriyaki sauce – a lovely rich Japanese glaze – are available in most large supermarkets and Asian stores. Serve the salmon with sticky rice or soba noodles for a healthy, light meal.

Serves 4
4 salmon fillets, 150g/5oz each
75ml/5 tbsp teriyaki marinade
150ml/¼ pint/⅔ cup
  sunflower oil
5cm/2in piece of fresh root
  ginger, peeled and cut
  into matchsticks

1 Put the salmon in a shallow, non-metallic dish and pour over the teriyaki marinade. Cover with clear film (plastic wrap) and chill for 2 hours.

2 Meanwhile, heat the sunflower oil in a small pan and add the ginger. Fry for 1–2 minutes, stirring constantly, until golden brown and crisp. Remove with a slotted spoon and drain on kitchen paper. Set aside until ready to serve the salmon.

3 Heat a griddle (grill) pan until smoking hot. Remove the salmon from the marinade and add, skin side down, to the pan. Cook for 2–3 minutes, then turn over and cook for a further 1–2 minutes, or until cooked through.

4 Remove from the pan and divide among four serving plates. Top the salmon fillets with the crispy fried ginger.

5 Pour the marinade into the pan and cook for 1–2 minutes. Pour over the salmon and serve immediately.

Cook's Tip
In Japanese cuisine, teriyaki sauce is traditionally made by mixing and heating soy sauce, sake or mirin, and a sweetener such as sugar or honey. The sauce is reduced, then used to marinate meat which is then grilled (broiled). Sometimes ginger or garlic is added to the sauce.

Salmon with Butter Energy 409kcal/1700kJ; Protein 35.6g; Carbohydrate 0.2g, of which sugars 0.2g; Fat 29.6g, of which saturates 9.8g; Cholesterol 114mg; Calcium 47mg; Fibre 0.2g; Sodium 156mg.
Teriyaki Salmon Energy 239kcal/995kJ; Protein 24.8g; Carbohydrate 2.1g, of which sugars 1.7g; Fat 13.3g, of which saturates 2.3g; Cholesterol 58mg; Calcium 93mg; Fibre 0.3g; Sodium 323mg.

Hot Smoked Salmon with Spicy Fruit Salsa

This is a fantastic way of smoking salmon on a barbecue in no time at all. The spicy fruit salsa makes a mildly spicy companion.

Serves 6

6 salmon fillets, about 175g/6oz each, with skin
15ml/1 tbsp sunflower oil
salt and ground black pepper
2 handfuls hickory wood chips, soaked in cold water for as much time as you have available, preferably 30 minutes

For the fruit salsa

1 ripe mango, diced
4 drained canned pineapple slices, diced
1 small red onion, finely chopped
1 fresh long mild red chilli, seeded and finely chopped
15ml/1 tbsp good-quality sweet chilli sauce
grated rind and juice of 1 lime
leaves from 1 small lemon basil plant or 45ml/3 tbsp fresh coriander (cilantro) leaves, shredded or chopped

1 First, make the salsa by putting the mango and diced pineapple in a bowl. Add the chopped onion and seeded and chopped chilli, and stir to mix. Add the chilli sauce, lime rind and juice, and the herb leaves. Stir to mix well. Cover tightly with clear film (plastic wrap) and leave in a cool place until needed.

2 Rinse the salmon fillets and pat dry, then brush each with a little oil. Place the fillets skin side down on a lightly oiled grill (broiler) rack over medium-hot coals. Cover the barbecue with a lid or a tent made of heavy-duty foil and cook the fish for 3–5 minutes.

3 Drain the hickory chips into a colander and sprinkle about a third of them as evenly as possible over the coals. Carefully drop them through the slats in the grill racks, taking care not to sprinkle the ash as you do so.

4 Replace the barbecue cover and continue cooking for a further 8 minutes, adding a small handful of hickory chips twice more during this time. Serve the salmon hot or cold, with the mango and pineapple salsa.

Roasted Salmon with Honey and Mustard

The clear, unpolluted Norwegian fjords produce salmon of the highest quality. Norwegian salmon has an international reputation and is exported all over the world. Chefs everywhere like to experiment with new ways of presenting this delicious, highly prized fish.

Serves 4

30ml/2 tbsp olive oil
15ml/1 tbsp honey
30ml/2 tbsp wholegrain French mustard
grated rind ½ lemon
4 salmon fillets, about 150g/5oz each
salt and ground black pepper

1 To make the marinade, put the olive oil, honey, wholegrain mustard and lemon rind in a small bowl and mix together until well combined. Season the marinade with salt and ground black pepper to taste.

2 Put the salmon fillets in a shallow ovenproof dish or on a baking sheet lined with a sheet of baking parchment. Spread the marinade over each fillet, rubbing it in with your fingers. Leave to marinate for 30 minutes.

3 Preheat the oven to 200°C/400°F/Gas 6. Roast the fish in the oven for 10–12 minutes, until the flesh flakes easily. Serve hot.

> **Variation**
> This dish also tastes great using trout fillets in place of the salmon, which come from the same family of fish as salmon. Rainbow trout is best but brown trout can also be used.

> **Cook's Tip**
> Choose the best salmon you can find to really elevate this dish. Look for wild salmon rather than the farmed variety.

Hot Salmon Energy 364kcal/1519kJ; Protein 35.9g; Carbohydrate 7.8g, of which sugars 7.4g; Fat 21.2g, of which saturates 3.6g; Cholesterol 88mg; Calcium 58mg; Fibre 1.3g; Sodium 82mg.
Roasted Salmon Energy 296kcal/1231kJ; Protein 25.9g; Carbohydrate 3.2g, of which sugars 3.2g; Fat 20g, of which saturates 3.2g; Cholesterol 63mg; Calcium 36mg; Fibre 0.4g; Sodium 178mg.

Salmon with Tequila Cream Sauce

Use tequila that is lightly aged for this sauce. It has a smooth flavour, which goes well with the cream.

Serves 4
3 fresh jalapeño chillies
45ml/3 tbsp olive oil
1 small onion, finely chopped
150ml/¼ pint/⅔ cup fish stock
grated rind and juice of 1 lime
120ml/4fl oz/½ cup single (light) cream
30ml/2 tbsp reposada tequila
1 firm avocado
4 salmon fillets
salt and ground white pepper
strips of green (bell) pepper and fresh flat leaf parsley, to garnish

1 Roast the chillies in a frying pan until the skins blister, being careful not to let the flesh burn. Put them in a strong plastic bag and tie the top to keep the steam in. Set aside for 20 minutes.

2 Heat 15ml/1 tbsp of the oil in a pan. Add the onion and fry for 3–4 minutes, then add the stock, lime rind and juice. Cook for 10 minutes, until the stock reduces. Remove the chillies from the bag, peel off the skins, slit and scrape out the seeds.

3 Stir the cream into the onion and stock mixture. Slice the chilli flesh into strips and add to the pan. Cook over a gentle heat, stirring constantly, for 2–3 minutes. Season to taste with salt and white pepper.

4 Stir the tequila into the onion and chilli mixture. Leave the pan over a very low heat. Peel the avocado, remove the stone (pit) and slice the flesh. Brush the salmon fillets on one side with a little of the remaining oil.

5 Heat a frying pan or ridged grill (griddle) pan until very hot and add the salmon, oiled side down. Cook for 2–3 minutes, until the underside is golden, then brush the top with oil, turn each fillet over and cook the other side until the fish is cooked and flakes easily when tested with the tip of a sharp knife.

6 Serve on a pool of sauce, with the avocado slices. Garnish with strips of green pepper and a sprinkling of fresh parsley. This is good served with fried potatoes.

Baked Salmon with Watercress Sauce

Baking the whole salmon in foil produces a flesh rather like that of a poached fish but with the ease of baking.

Serves 6–8
2–3kg/4½–6¾lb salmon, cleaned with head and tail left on
3–5 spring onions (scallions), thinly sliced
1 lemon, thinly sliced
1 cucumber, thinly sliced
fresh dill sprigs, to garnish
lemon wedges, to serve

For the watercress sauce
3 garlic cloves, chopped
200g/7oz watercress leaves, finely chopped
40g/1½oz fresh tarragon, finely chopped
300g/11oz/1⅓ cups mayonnaise
15–30ml/1–2 tbsp freshly squeezed lemon juice
200g/7oz/scant 1 cup unsalted (sweet) butter, melted
salt and ground black pepper

1 Preheat the oven to 180°C/350°F/Gas 4. Rinse the salmon and lay it on a large piece of foil. Stuff the fish with the sliced spring onions and layer the lemon slices inside and around the fish, then sprinkle with plenty of salt and ground black pepper. Loosely fold the foil around the fish and fold the edges over to seal. Bake for about 1 hour.

2 Remove the fish from the oven. Leave to stand, wrapped in the foil, for 15 minutes, then unwrap and leave to cool. When cool, lift it on to a large plate, still covered with lemon slices. Wrap in clear film (plastic wrap) and chill for several hours.

3 Before serving, discard the lemon slices around the fish. Using a blunt knife to lift up the edge of the skin, carefully peel the skin away from the flesh, avoiding tearing the flesh, and pull out any fins at the same time. Arrange the cucumber in overlapping rows along the length of the fish to resemble large fish scales.

4 To make the sauce, put the garlic, watercress, tarragon, mayonnaise and lemon juice in a food processor or blender or a bowl, and process or mix to combine. Add the butter, a little at a time, processing or stirring, until the sauce is thick and smooth. Cover and chill before serving. Serve the fish, garnished with dill, with the sauce and lemon wedges.

Salmon Tequila Energy 2895kcal/12052kJ; Protein 304.5g; Carbohydrate 2.3g, of which sugars 1.6g; Fat 183.1g, of which saturates 33.7g; Cholesterol 764mg; Calcium 345mg; Fibre 1.1g; Sodium 685mg.
Baked Salmon Energy 783kcal/3242kJ; Protein 38.7g; Carbohydrate 1g, of which sugars 0.9g; Fat 69.3g, of which saturates 21.3g; Cholesterol 173mg; Calcium 102mg; Fibre 0.5g; Sodium 418mg.

Salmon with Hollandaise Sauce

A whole poached fish makes an elegant party dish and served cold it is perfect for a summer buffet.

Serves 8–10

300ml/½ pint/1¼ cups dry (hard) cider or white wine
1 large carrot, roughly chopped
2 medium onions, roughly chopped
2 celery sticks, roughly chopped
2 bay leaves
a few black peppercorns
sprig of parsley
sprig of thyme
2–2.5kg/4½–5½lb whole salmon, gutted, washed and dried

For the hollandaise sauce

175g/6oz/¾ cup unsalted butter
5ml/1 tsp sugar
3 egg yolks
10ml/2 tsp cider vinegar or white wine vinegar
10ml/2 tsp lemon juice
salt and ground white pepper

1 Put all the ingredients except the salmon into a large pan and add 1 litre/1¾ pints/4 cups water. Bring to the boil and simmer gently for 30–40 minutes. Strain and leave to cool.

2 About 30 minutes before serving, pour the cooled stock into a fish kettle. Lay the salmon on the rack and lower it into the liquid. Heat until the stock almost comes to the boil, cover and simmer very gently for 20–25 minutes until the fish is just cooked through – test the thickest part with a knife.

3 Meanwhile, to make the hollandaise sauce, heat the butter with the sugar until the butter has melted and the mixture is hot but not sizzling.

4 Put the egg yolks, vinegar, lemon juice and seasonings into a processor or blender and blend on high speed for about 15 seconds, or until the mixture is creamy.

5 Keep the processor or blender on high speed and add the hot butter mixture in a slow stream until the sauce is thick, smooth and creamy.

6 Lift the salmon out of its cooking liquid. Remove the skin carefully, and lift the salmon on to a warmed serving plate. Garnish with watercress and serve with the warm hollandaise.

Grilled Butterflied Salmon

Ask your fishmonger to bone the salmon for butterflying. If you order the fish in advance, and give the supplier plenty of time, most will be happy to oblige.

Serves 6–8

25ml/1½ tbsp dried juniper berries
10ml/2 tsp dried green peppercorns
5ml/1 tsp caster (superfine) sugar
45ml/3 tbsp vegetable oil, plus extra for greasing
30ml/2 tbsp lemon juice
2.25kg/5lb salmon, scaled, cleaned and boned for butterflying
salt
lemon wedges and fresh parsley sprigs, to garnish

1 Coarsely grind the juniper berries and peppercorns in a spice mill or in a mortar with a pestle. Put the ground spices in a small bowl and stir in the caster sugar, vegetable oil, lemon juice and salt to taste.

2 Open the salmon like a book, skin side down. Spread the juniper mixture evenly over the flesh. Fold the salmon closed again and place it on a large plate. Cover and marinate in the refrigerator for at least 1 hour.

3 Preheat the grill (broiler). Open up the salmon again and place it, skin side down, on a large oiled baking sheet. Spoon any juniper mixture left on the plate over the fish.

4 Grill (broil) the salmon, keeping it about 10cm/4in from the heat, for 8–10 minutes or until the salmon is cooked and the flesh is opaque. Serve immediately, garnished with the lemon wedges and parsley.

> **Cook's Tip**
> It is worth keeping a jar of juniper berries in the spice rack, not merely so you can try this recipe, but also for using with game, or to give chicken or rabbit a gamy flavour. Juniper berries are also delicious with red cabbage.

Salmon Energy 450kcal/1868kJ; Protein 34.6g; Carbohydrate 0.5g, of which sugars 0.5g; Fat 34.4g, of which saturates 12.8g; Cholesterol 182mg; Calcium 44mg; Fibre 0g; Sodium 183mg.
Grilled Salmon Energy 532kcal/2220kJ; Protein 55.7g; Carbohydrate 0g, of which sugars 0g; Fat 34.2g, of which saturates 6.3g; Cholesterol 138mg; Calcium 59mg; Fibre 0g; Sodium 124mg.

Barbecued Red Mullet with Chilli

Red mullet are simple to cook on a barbecue, with bay leaves for flavour and a dribble of tangy dressing instead of a marinade. Serve the fish with a green salad dressed with parsley and lemon juice.

Serves 4

4 red mullet or snapper, about
   225–275g/8–10oz each,
   cleaned and descaled if cooking
   under a grill (broiler)

olive oil, for brushing
fresh herb sprigs, such as fennel,
   dill, parsley, or thyme
2–3 dozen fresh or dried
   bay leaves

For the dressing
90ml/6 tbsp olive oil
6 garlic cloves, finely
   chopped
½ dried chilli, seeded
   and chopped
juice of ½ lemon
15ml/1 tbsp parsley

1 Prepare the barbecue or preheat the grill (broiler) with the shelf 15cm/6in from the heat source.

2 Brush each fish with oil and stuff the cavities with the herb sprigs. Brush the grill pan with oil and lay bay leaves across the cooking rack. Place the fish on top and cook for 15–20 minutes until cooked through, turning once.

3 To make the dressing, heat the olive oil in a small pan and fry the chopped garlic with the dried chilli. Add the lemon juice and strain the dressing to remove the garlic and chilli. Add the chopped parsley and stir to combine. Serve the fish on warmed plates, drizzled with the dressing.

Cook's Tips
• Nicknamed the woodcock of the sea, red mullet are one of the fish that are classically cooked uncleaned to give them extra flavour. In this recipe, however, the fish are cleaned and herbs are used to add extra flavour.
• If you are cooking the fish on a barbecue, light the barbecue well in advance. Before cooking, the charcoal or wood should be grey, with no flames.

Marinated Red Mullet

Snapper, sea bream or tilapia are all good alternatives to mullet in this recipe.

Serves 6

7.5ml/1½ tsp mild Spanish
   paprika, preferably Spanish
   smoked pimentón
45ml/3 tbsp plain
   (all-purpose) flour
120ml/4fl oz/½ cup
   olive oil
6 red mullet or snapper,
   weighing about 300g/11oz
   each, filleted

2 aubergines (eggplants), sliced or
   cut into long wedges
2 red or yellow (bell) peppers,
   seeded and thickly sliced
1 large red onion, thinly sliced
2 garlic cloves, sliced
15ml/1 tbsp sherry vinegar
juice of 1 lemon
brown sugar, to taste
15ml/1 tbsp chopped
   fresh oregano
18–24 black olives
45ml/3 tbsp chopped fresh
   flat leaf parsley
salt and ground black pepper

1 Mix 5ml/1 tsp of the paprika with the flour and season well with salt and pepper.

2 Heat half the oil in a large frying pan. Dip the fish into the flour, turning to coat both sides, and fry for 4–5 minutes, until browned on each side. Place the fish in a glass or china dish suitable for marinating it.

3 Add 30ml/2 tbsp of the remaining oil to the pan and fry the aubergines until softened and browned. Drain on kitchen paper and add to the fish.

4 Add another 30ml/2 tbsp oil to the pan and cook the peppers and onion gently for 6–8 minutes, until softened. Add the garlic and remaining paprika, then cook for 2 minutes. Stir in the vinegar and lemon juice with 30ml/2 tbsp water and heat until simmering. Season to taste with a pinch of sugar.

5 Stir in the oregano and olives, then spoon over the fish. Set aside to cool, then cover and chill for several hours or overnight.

6 About 30 minutes before serving, bring the fish and vegetables to room temperature. Stir in the parsley and serve.

Red Mullet Energy 290kcal/1207kJ; Protein 22.7g; Carbohydrate 2.2g, of which sugars 0.3g; Fat 21.3g, of which saturates 2.4g; Cholesterol 0mg; Calcium 91mg; Fibre 0.7g; Sodium 114mg.
Marinated Mullet Energy 335kcal/1406kJ; Protein 31.9g; Carbohydrate 18.4g, of which sugars 11.5g; Fat 15.5g, of which saturates 1.4g; Cholesterol 0mg; Calcium 166mg; Fibre 4.6g; Sodium 347mg.

Haddock in Cheese Sauce

A relative of cod, haddock is a popular white fish, though unfortunately supplies in some regions of the world have declined considerably in recent years. Other white fish can be used instead in this flavourful dish – try hake, coley or whiting.

Serves 4
1kg/2¼lb haddock fillets
300ml/½ pint/1¼ cups milk
1 small onion, thinly sliced
2 bay leaves
a few black peppercorns

For the sauce
25g/1oz/2 tbsp butter
25g/1oz/2 tbsp flour
5ml/1 tsp English (hot) mustard
115g/4oz mature (sharp) hard cheese such as Cheddar, grated
salt and ground black pepper

1 Put the fish in a pan large enough to hold it in a single layer. Add the milk, onion, bay leaves and peppercorns and heat slowly until small bubbles are rising to the surface.

2 Cover and simmer very gently for 5–8 minutes, until the fish is just cooked. Lift out with a slotted spoon, straining and reserving the cooking liquid. Flake the fish, removing any bones and skin.

3 To make the sauce, melt the butter in a pan, stir in the flour and cook gently, stirring all the time, for about 1 minute (do not allow it to brown). Remove from the heat and gradually stir in the strained milk. Return the pan to the heat and cook, stirring, until the mixture thickens and comes to the boil. Stir in the mustard and three-quarters of the cheese and season to taste.

4 Gently stir the fish into the sauce and spoon the mixture into individual flameproof dishes. Sprinkle the remaining cheese over the top. Put under a hot grill (broiler) until bubbling and golden. Serve with crusty bread.

> **Cook's Tip**
> The fish can be left whole if you prefer. Simply spoon the sauce over them before grilling (broiling).

Haddock with Mustard Cabbage

This simple dish takes less than twenty minutes to make and is quite delicious. Ensure that you buy smoked haddock that is undyed, not the bright yellow variety. Serve it with new potatoes.

Serves 4
1 Savoy or pointu cabbage
675g/1½lb undyed smoked haddock fillet
300ml/½ pint/1¼ cups milk
½ onion, sliced into rings
2 bay leaves
½ lemon, sliced
4 white peppercorns
4 ripe tomatoes
50g/2oz/¼ cup butter
30ml/2 tbsp wholegrain mustard
juice of 1 lemon
salt and ground black pepper
30ml/2 tbsp chopped fresh parsley, to garnish

1 Cut the cabbage in half, remove the central core and thick ribs, then shred the cabbage. Cook in a pan of lightly salted, boiling water, or steam over boiling water for about 10 minutes, until just tender. Leave in the pan or steamer until required.

2 Meanwhile, put the haddock fillet in a large shallow pan with the milk, onion rings and bay leaves. Add the lemon slices and peppercorns to the pan. Bring to simmering point, cover and poach until the fish flakes easily when tested with the tip of a sharp knife. Depending on the thickness of the fish, this will be about 8–10 minutes. Remove the pan from the heat. Preheat the grill (broiler).

3 Cut the tomatoes in half horizontally, season them with salt and pepper and grill (broil) until lightly browned. Drain the cabbage, refresh under cold water and drain again.

4 Melt the butter in a shallow pan or wok, add the cabbage and toss over the heat for 2 minutes. Mix in the mustard and season to taste, then transfer the cabbage into a warmed serving dish.

5 Drain the haddock. Skin and cut the fish into four pieces. Place on top of the cabbage with some onion rings and grilled tomato halves. Pour on the lemon juice, then sprinkle with chopped parsley and serve.

Haddock with Cabbage Energy 319kcal/1340kJ; Protein 36.1g; Carbohydrate 14.2g, of which sugars 13.7g; Fat 13.1g, of which saturates 7.3g; Cholesterol 90mg; Calcium 146mg; Fibre 4.2g; Sodium 1512mg.
Haddock in Cheese Sauce Energy 430kcal/1809kJ; Protein 58.2g; Carbohydrate 9.6g, of which sugars 4.5g; Fat 17.4g, of which saturates 10.6g; Cholesterol 136mg; Calcium 351mg; Fibre 0.4g; Sodium 446mg

Grilled Swordfish Steaks

Crisp grilled asparagus with a shoyu and sake coating is an excellent accompaniment for the marinated swordfish steaks in this dish.

Serves 4
4 swordfish steaks, about
   175g/6oz each
2.5ml/½ tsp salt
300g/11oz shiro miso

45ml/3 tbsp sake
oil, for brushing

For the asparagus
25ml/1½ tbsp shoyu
25ml/1½ tbsp sake
8 asparagus spears, the hard
   ends discarded, each spear
   cut into three

1 Place the swordfish in a shallow container. Sprinkle with the salt on both sides and leave for 2 hours. Drain and wipe the fish with kitchen paper.

2 Mix the miso and sake, then spread half across the bottom of the cleaned container. Cover with a sheet of muslin (cheesecloth) the size of a dish towel, folded in half, then open the fold.

3 Place the swordfish, side by side, on top, and cover with the muslin. Spread the rest of the miso mixture on the muslin. Make sure the muslin is touching the fish. Marinate for 2 days in the coolest part of the refrigerator.

4 Remove the fish from the refrigerator and allow to come to room temperature. Preheat the grill (broiler) to medium. Oil the wire rack and grill (broil) the fish gently for about 8 minutes on each side, turning every 2 minutes. If the steaks are thin, check every time you turn the fish to see if they are ready.

5 For the asparagus. mix the shoyu and sake in a small bowl. Grill the asparagus for 2 minutes on each side, then dip into the bowl. Return to the grill for 2 minutes more on each side. Dip into the sauce again and set aside.

6 Serve the steak hot on four individual serving plates, accompanied by the drained, grilled asparagus.

Shark Steaks in Spicy Marinade

A meaty, firm-fleshed fish, shark is widely available, either fresh or frozen. It needs careful watching during cooking, as overcooking will make it dry and tough, but the flavour is excellent. The Mexican-style marinade in this recipe uses achiote seed, a vivid red spice also known as annatto.

Serves 4
grated rind and juice of 1 orange
juice of 1 small lime

45ml/3 tbsp white wine
30ml/2 tbsp olive oil
2 garlic cloves, crushed
10ml/2 tsp ground achiote seed
   (annatto powder)
2.5ml/½ tsp cayenne pepper
2.5ml/½ tsp dried marjoram
5ml/1 tsp salt
4 shark steaks
fresh oregano leaves, to garnish
4 wheat flour tortillas and any
   suitable salsa, to serve

1 Put the orange rind and juice in a shallow non-metallic dish that is large enough to hold all the shark steaks in a single layer. Add the lime juice, white wine, olive oil, garlic, ground achiote, cayenne, marjoram and salt. Mix well.

2 Add the shark steaks to the dish and spoon the marinade evenly over the top. Cover with clear film (plastic wrap) and set aside for 1 hour, turning once.

3 Heat a griddle (grill) pan until very hot and cook the shark steaks for 2–3 minutes on each side. Alternatively, they are very good cooked on the barbecue, so long as they are cooked after the coals have lost their fierce initial heat.

4 Garnish the shark steaks with oregano and serve with the tortillas and salsa. A green vegetable would also go well.

Cook's Tip
Shark flesh freezes successfully, with little or no loss of flavour on thawing, making it ideal to use frozen steaks in this dish if you cannot buy the fresh fish.

Swordfish Energy 240kcal/1009kJ; Protein 37g; Carbohydrate 2.8g, of which sugars 2.5g; Fat 8.2g, of which saturates 1.8g; Cholesterol 81mg; Calcium 18mg; Fibre 0.3g; Sodium 2269mg.
Shark Steaks Energy 222kcal/931kJ; Protein 35g; Carbohydrate 1.4g, of which sugars 0.1g; Fat 7.7g, of which saturates 1g; Cholesterol 66mg; Calcium 60mg; Fibre 1.2g; Sodium 233mg.

Tuna and Mascarpone Bake

A one-dish meal ideal for informal entertaining that marries the smoky flavour of seared tuna with a sweet and herby Italian sauce. The dish has a grated potato base as well as a topping made of diced potato chunks.

Serves 4
4 tuna steaks, about 175g/6oz each

400g/14oz can chopped
 tomatoes, drained
2 garlic cloves, crushed
30ml/2 tbsp chopped
 fresh basil
250g/9oz/generous 1 cup
 mascarpone cheese
3 large potatoes
25g/1oz/2 tbsp
 butter, diced
salt and ground black pepper

1 Preheat the oven to 200°C/400°F/Gas 6. Heat a griddle (grill) pan on the stove and sear the fish steaks for 2 minutes on each side, seasoning with a little black pepper. Set aside while you prepare the sauce.

2 Mix the chopped tomatoes, garlic, basil and cheese together in a bowl and season to taste with salt and plenty of ground black pepper.

3 Peel the potatoes, then grate half of them and dice the other half. Blanch them in separate pans of lightly salted water for about 3 minutes. Drain thoroughly and set aside to cool slightly. When the grated potato is cool enough to handle, squeeze out any excess moisture.

4 Lightly grease a 1.75 litre/3 pint/7½ cup ovenproof dish. Spoon a little sauce and some grated potato into it. Lay the tuna over the grated potato with more sauce and the remaining grated potato. Sprinkle the diced butter and the diced potatoes over the top. Bake for 30 minutes until cooked through and brown on top. Serve immediately.

Variation
This dish can easily be made into a side dish, simply leave out the tuna and prepare the other ingredients as before.

Tuna Steaks with Red Onion Salsa

Red onions are ideal for this salsa, not only for their mild and sweet flavour, but also because they look so appetizing. Salad, rice or bread and a bowl of thick yogurt flavoured with chopped fresh herbs are good accompaniments.

Serves 4
4 tuna loin steaks, about
 175–200g/6–7oz each
5ml/1 tsp cumin seeds, toasted
 and crushed
pinch of dried red chilli flakes
grated rind and juice of 1 lime
30–60ml/2–4 tbsp extra virgin
 olive oil
salt and ground black pepper

lime wedges and fresh coriander
 (cilantro) sprigs, to garnish

For the salsa
1 small red onion, finely chopped
200g/7oz red or yellow cherry
 tomatoes, roughly chopped
1 avocado, peeled, stoned (pitted)
 and chopped
2 kiwi fruit, peeled and chopped
1 fresh red chilli, seeded and
 finely chopped
15g/½oz fresh coriander,
 chopped
6 fresh mint sprigs, leaves
 only, chopped
5–10ml/1–2 tsp Thai fish sauce
about 5ml/1 tsp muscovado
 (molasses) sugar

1 Wash the tuna steaks and pat dry. Sprinkle with half the cumin, the dried chilli, salt, pepper and half the lime rind. Rub in 30ml/2 tbsp of the oil and set aside in a glass or china dish for about 30 minutes.

2 Meanwhile, make the salsa. Mix the onion, tomatoes, avocado, kiwi fruit, chilli, coriander and mint. Add the remaining cumin, the rest of the lime rind and half the lime juice. Add the fish sauce and sugar to taste. Leave for 15–20 minutes, then add more Thai fish sauce, lime juice and olive oil if required.

3 Heat a ridged, cast iron grill (griddle) pan. Cook the tuna, allowing about 2 minutes on each side for rare tuna or a little longer for a medium result.

4 Serve the tuna steaks garnished with lime wedges and coriander sprigs. Serve the salsa separately or spoon on to the plates with the tuna.

Tuna Steaks Energy 389kcal/1628kJ; Protein 43.2g; Carbohydrate 7.9g, of which sugars 6.8g; Fat 20.7g, of which saturates 4.4g; Cholesterol 49mg; Calcium 55mg; Fibre 2.5g; Sodium 180mg.
Tuna Bake Energy 520kcal/2185kJ; Protein 51g; Carbohydrate 29.3g, of which sugars 6.9g; Fat 22.9g, of which saturates 11.2g; Cholesterol 89mg; Calcium 65mg; Fibre 2.6g; Sodium 178mg.

Barbecued Sardines with Orange and Parsley

Sardines are ideal for the barbecue – the meaty flesh holds together well, the skin crisps up nicely and there are no lingering cooking smells in the house. Look for whole sardines with a firm flesh and bright eyes for freshness. Serve them with a selection of salads and crusty bread.

Serves 6

6 whole sardines, gutted
1 orange, sliced
a small bunch of fresh flat leaf
 parsley, chopped
60ml/4 tbsp extra virgin
 olive oil
salt and ground black pepper

1 Arrange the sardines and orange slices in a single layer in a shallow, non-metallic dish. Sprinkle over the chopped parsley and season with salt and pepper.

2 Drizzle the olive oil over the sardines and orange slices and gently stir to coat well. Cover the dish with clear film (plastic wrap) and chill for 2 hours.

3 Meanwhile, prepare the barbecue. Remove the sardines and orange slices from the marinade and cook the fish over the barbecue for 7–8 minutes on each side, until cooked through. Serve immediately.

Variation
If you do not have any fresh parsley, then other fresh herbs can be substituted. Try using the same quantity of dill, coriander (cilantro) or tarragon.

Cook's Tip
If no barbecue is available, or the weather is bad, cook these sardines under a medium grill (broiler) indoors.

Sardine Frittata with Parsley and Chives

It may seem odd to cook sardines in an omelette, but they are surprisingly delicious this way. Frozen sardines are fine for this dish. Serve the frittata with crisp sautéed potatoes and thinly sliced cucumber crescents.

Serves 4

4 fat sardines, cleaned, filleted
 and with heads removed,
 thawed if frozen

juice of 1 lemon
45ml/3 tbsp olive oil
6 large (US extra large) eggs
30ml/2 tbsp chopped
 fresh parsley
30ml/2 tbsp chopped
 fresh chives
1 garlic clove, chopped
salt, ground black pepper
 and paprika

1 Open out the sardines and sprinkle the fish with lemon juice, a little salt and paprika. Heat 15ml/1 tbsp olive oil in a frying pan and fry the sardines for about 1–2 minutes on each side to seal them. Drain on kitchen paper, trim off the tails and set aside until required.

2 Separate the eggs. In a bowl, whisk the yolks lightly with the parsley, chives and a little salt and pepper. Beat the whites in a separate bowl with a pinch of salt until fairly stiff. Preheat the grill (broiler) to medium-high.

3 Heat the remaining olive oil in a large frying pan, add the garlic and cook over low heat until just golden. Gently mix together the egg yolks and whites and ladle half the mixture into the pan. Cook gently until just beginning to set on the base, then lay the sardines on the frittata and sprinkle lightly with paprika.

4 Pour over the remaining egg mixture and cook until the frittata has browned underneath and is beginning to set on top.

5 Put the pan under the grill and cook until the top of the frittata is golden. Cut into wedges and serve immediately.

Barbecued Sardines Energy 156kcal/649kJ; Protein 13.1g; Carbohydrate 1.7g, of which sugars 1.7g; Fat 10.8g, of which saturates 2.3g; Cholesterol 0mg; Calcium 73mg; Fibre 0.3g; Sodium 72mg.
Sardine Frittata Energy 342kcal/1422kJ; Protein 28.9g; Carbohydrate 0.2g, of which sugars 0.2g; Fat 25.3g, of which saturates 6g; Cholesterol 285mg; Calcium 137mg; Fibre 0.4g; Sodium 220mg.

Grilled Mackerel with Gooseberry Relish

With a variety of health benefits, mackerel is a nutritious fish, and the tart gooseberries give you a serving of fruit, too.

Serves 4
4 whole mackerel

60ml/4 tbsp olive oil

For the sauce
250g/9oz gooseberries
*25g/1oz/2 tbsp soft light
   brown sugar*
5ml/1 tsp wholegrain mustard
salt and ground black pepper

1 For the sauce, wash and trim the gooseberries, and then chop them roughly, so that some pieces that are larger than others.

2 Cook the gooseberries in a little water with the sugar in a small pan. A thick and chunky purée will form. Add the mustard and season to taste with salt and ground black pepper.

3 Preheat the grill (broiler) to high and line the grill (broiling) pan with foil. Using a sharp knife, slash the fish two or three times down each side, then season and brush with the olive oil.

4 Place the fish in the grill pan and cook for about 4 minutes on each side until cooked. You may need to cook them for a few minutes longer if they are particularly large. The slashes will open up to speed cooking and the skin should be lightly browned. To check that they are cooked properly, use a small sharp knife to pierce the skin and check for uncooked flesh.

5 Place the mackerel on warmed plates and spread generous dollops of the gooseberry relish over them. Pass the remaining sauce around at the table.

> **Cook's Tip**
> *Turn the grill (broiler) on well in advance as the fish need a fierce heat to cook quickly. If you like the fish but hate the smell, try barbecuing outside.*

Roast Mackerel with Spicy Chermoula Paste

Chermoula is a marinade used in African cooking. There are many variations on the flavourings used, but it is usually based on a blend of coriander, lemon and garlic, and often includes saffron and paprika. It is popular with fish, but can be used with poultry and meat.

Serves 4
*4 whole mackerel, cleaned
   and gutted*
*30–45ml/2–3 tbsp chermoula
   paste*
75ml/5 tbsp olive oil
2 red onions, sliced
salt and ground black pepper

1 Preheat the oven to 190°C/375°F/Gas 5. Place each fish on a large sheet of baking parchment. Using a sharp knife, slash into the flesh of each fish several times.

2 In a small bowl, mix the chermoula with the olive oil, and spread the paste over the skin of the mackerel, rubbing the mixture into the cuts.

3 Sprinkle the red onions over the mackerel, and season with salt and pepper. Scrunch the ends of the baking parchment together to seal. Place the four parcels on a baking tray.

4 Bake for 20 minutes, until the mackerel is cooked through. Serve the fish on warmed plates, still in their paper parcels, to be unwrapped at the table.

> **Cook's Tips**
> • *Buy only very fresh mackerel: they should be firm with a bright eye and smell of the sea.*
> • *Chermoula paste is now readily available in most large supermarkets. It can be mixed with oil and other ingredients and used as a marinade, or simply brushed on to fish and meat before cooking.*

Mackerel Energy 576kcal/2390kJ; Protein 38.1g; Carbohydrate 8.4g, of which sugars 8.4g; Fat 43.5g, of which saturates 8.2g; Cholesterol 108mg; Calcium 43mg; Fibre 1.5g; Sodium 128mg.
Roast Mackerel Energy 422kcal/1753kJ; Protein 31.8g; Carbohydrate 1.9g, of which sugars 0.1g; Fat 31.9g, of which saturates 6g; Cholesterol 86mg; Calcium 51mg; Fibre 1.3g; Sodium 117mg.

Poussins with Courgette and Apricot

These poussins are stuffed with courgettes and apricots.

Serves 4
4 small poussins
about 40g/1½oz/3 tbsp butter, at room temperature
5–10ml/1–2 tsp ground coriander
1 red (bell) pepper, cut into strips
1 fresh red chilli, thinly sliced
15–30ml/1–2 tbsp olive oil
120ml/4fl oz/½ cup chicken stock
30ml/2 tbsp cornflour (cornstarch)
salt and ground black pepper
fresh flat leaf parsley, to garnish

For the stuffing
525ml/17fl oz/2¼ cups chicken or vegetable stock
275g/10oz/generous 1½ cups couscous
2 small courgettes (zucchini), coarsely grated
8 ready-to-eat dried apricots, roughly chopped
15ml/1 tbsp chopped fresh flat leaf parsley
15ml/1 tbsp chopped fresh coriander (cilantro)
juice of ½ lemon

1 First make the stuffing. Bring the stock to the boil and pour it over the couscous in a large bowl. Stir once, and then set aside for 10 minutes. Preheat the oven to 200°C/400°F/Gas 6.

2 Fluff up the couscous with a fork and spoon 90ml/6 tbsp into a large bowl. Add the courgettes, apricots, chopped herbs, lemon juice and seasoning and stir. Spoon the stuffing loosely into the body cavities of the poussins and secure with string. Place the birds in a roasting pan, rub the butter into the skins and sprinkle with ground coriander and a little salt and pepper.

3 Place the red pepper and chilli in the roasting pan around the poussins, and then spoon over the olive oil. Roast for 20 minutes, then reduce the oven to 180°C/350°F/Gas 4. Pour the stock around the poussins and baste each one with the stock. Return the pan to the oven and roast for 30–35 minutes, until the poussins are cooked through and the meat juices run clear.

4 Transfer the poussins to a serving plate. Blend the cornflour with 45ml/3 tbsp cold water, stir into the stock and peppers in the roasting pan and heat gently, stirring, until the sauce is thickened. Season to taste, and then pour over the poussins. Garnish with parsley and serve with the remaining couscous.

Glazed Poussins

Golden poussins make an impressive main course. Serve with a simple mushroom risotto and side salad.

Serves 4
50g/2oz/¼ cup butter
10ml/2 tsp mixed spice (pumpkin pie spice)
grated rind and juice of 2 clementines
30ml/2 tbsp clear honey
4 poussins, each weighing about 450g/1lb
1 onion, finely chopped
1 garlic clove, chopped
15ml/1 tbsp plain (all-purpose) flour
50ml/2fl oz/¼ cup Marsala
300ml/½ pint/1¼ cups chicken stock
small bunch of fresh coriander (cilantro), to garnish

1 Preheat the oven to 220°C/425°F/Gas 7. Heat the butter, mixed spice, clementine rind and juice and honey until the butter has melted, stirring to mix well. Remove from the heat.

2 Place the poussins in a roasting pan, brush them with the glaze, then roast for 40 minutes. Brush with any remaining glaze and baste occasionally with the pan juices during cooking. Transfer the poussins to a serving platter, cover with foil and stand for 10 minutes.

3 Skim off all but 15ml/1 tbsp of the fat from the roasting pan. Add the onion and garlic to the juices in the pan and cook on the stove until beginning to brown. Stir in the flour, then gradually pour in the Marsala, followed by the stock, whisking all the time. Bring to the boil and simmer for 3 minutes to make a smooth, rich gravy.

4 Transfer the poussins to warm plates or a platter and garnish with coriander. Offer the gravy separately.

> **Variation**
> To give the poussins extra flavour, stuff each poussin before roasting with a quartered clementine and one or two garlic cloves, then skewer the legs with sprigs of fresh rosemary.

Glazed Poussins Energy 544kcal/2264kJ; Protein 36.2g; Carbohydrate 5.8g, of which sugars 5.8g; Fat 42.1g, of which saturates 14.5g; Cholesterol 215mg; Calcium 16mg; Fibre 0g; Sodium 207mg.
Poussins Energy 593kcal/2477kJ; Protein 28.1g; Carbohydrate 59.4g, of which sugars 10.2g; Fat 28.5g, of which saturates 10.1g; Cholesterol 137mg; Calcium 64mg; Fibre 2.5g; Sodium 156mg.

Grilled Chicken Balls on Skewers

These little morsels make a great low-fat snack or finger food at a drinks party.

Serves 4
300g/11oz skinless chicken, minced (ground)
2 eggs
2.5ml/ ½ tsp salt
10ml/2 tsp plain (all-purpose) flour
10ml/2 tsp cornflour (cornstarch)

90ml/6 tbsp dried breadcrumbs
2.5cm/1in piece fresh root ginger, grated

For the yakitori sauce
60ml/4 tbsp sake
75ml/5 tbsp shoyu
15ml/1 tbsp mirin
15ml/1 tbsp sugar
2.5ml/ ½ tsp cornflour (cornstarch) blended with 5ml/1 tsp water

1 Soak eight bamboo skewers for about 30 minutes in water. Put all the ingredients for the chicken balls, except the ginger, in a food processor and process to blend well.

2 Shape some of the mixture into a small ball about half the size of a golf ball using your hands. Make a further 30–32 balls in the same way.

3 Using your hands, squeeze out the juice from the grated ginger into a small mixing bowl. Discard the remaining pulp. Preheat the grill (broiler).

4 Add the ginger juice to a small pan of boiling water. Add the chicken balls, and boil for about 7 minutes, or until the colour of the meat changes and the balls float to the surface of the water. Scoop the balls out using a slotted spoon and drain on kitchen paper.

5 In a small pan, mix all the ingredients for the yakitori sauce, except the cornflour liquid. Bring to the boil, then simmer until the sauce has reduced slightly. Add the cornflour liquid and stir until thickened. Transfer to a small bowl.

6 Drain the skewers and thread 3–4 balls on each. Grill (broil) for a few minutes, turning frequently, until they brown. Brush with sauce and return to the heat. Repeat twice, then serve.

Chilli-spiced Poussin

When you are short of time these spicy poussins make a quick alternative to a traditional roast. Ask your butcher to prepare the birds for spatchcocking by removing the backbone.

Serves 4
2 poussins, 675g/1½lb each, ready for spatchcocking
15ml/1 tbsp chilli powder
15ml/1 tbsp ground cumin
45ml/3 tbsp olive oil
salt and ground black pepper

1 Lay out one of the poussins. Push a metal skewer through the wings and breast, then push a second skewer through the thighs and breast. Prepare the other poussin in the same way.

2 Preheat the grill (broiler). Combine the chilli, cumin, oil and seasoning. Brush over the poussins. Lay the birds, skin side down, on a grill (broiling) rack and cook for 15 minutes. Turn over and grill (broil) for 15 minutes until cooked. Remove the skewers and halve each bird along the breastbone. Serve drizzled with the pan juices.

Chicken Fillets with Serrano Ham

Serve these fillets with new potatoes and broccoli.

Serves 4
4 skinless chicken breast fillets
4 slices Serrano ham
75g/3oz/6 tbsp butter

30ml/2 tbsp chopped capers
30ml/2 tbsp fresh thyme leaves
1 large lemon, cut lengthways into 8 slices
a few small fresh thyme sprigs
salt and ground black pepper

1 Preheat the oven to 200°C/400°F/Gas 6. Place each fillet in a plastic bag and flatten slightly with a rolling pin. Arrange the fillets in an ovenproof dish and top with a slice of Serrano ham.

2 Mix the butter with the capers, thyme and seasoning. Divide into quarters, then place on each ham-topped fillet. Arrange two lemon slices on the butter and sprinkle with thyme. Bake for 25 minutes, or until the chicken is cooked through. Serve immediately with the buttery juices spooned over the top.

Chilli-spiced Poussin Energy 465kcal/1936kJ; Protein 36.6g; Carbohydrate 1.3g, of which sugars 0g; Fat 35.1g, of which saturates 8.4g; Cholesterol 189mg; Calcium 20mg; Fibre 0g; Sodium 131mg.
Chicken Fillets Energy 343kcal/1432kJ; Protein 37.8g; Carbohydrate 0.6g, of which sugars 0.5g; Fat 21.1g, of which saturates 11.9g; Cholesterol 122mg; Calcium 45mg; Fibre 0.6g; Sodium 553mg.
Chicken Balls Energy 332kcal/1398kJ; Protein 30.4g; Carbohydrate 29g, of which sugars 7.4g; Fat 9.7g, of which saturates 2.6g; Cholesterol 339mg; Calcium 84mg; Fibre 0.6g; Sodium 325mg.

Chicken Satay

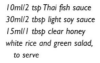

These miniature kebabs are popular all over South-east Asia, and they are delicious when cooked on a barbecue. The peanut dipping sauce is a perfect partner for the marinated chicken.

Serves 4

4 skinless, boneless chicken
  breast portions

For the marinade
2 garlic cloves, crushed
2.5cm/1in piece fresh root ginger,
  finely grated

10ml/2 tsp Thai fish sauce
30ml/2 tbsp light soy sauce
15ml/1 tbsp clear honey
white rice and green salad,
  to serve

For the satay sauce
90ml/6 tbsp crunchy
  peanut butter
1 fresh red chilli, seeded and
  finely chopped
juice of 1 lime
60ml/4 tbsp coconut milk
salt

1 First, make the satay sauce. Put all the ingredients in a food processor or blender. Process until smooth, then check the seasoning and add more salt or lime juice if necessary. Spoon the sauce into a bowl, cover with clear film (plastic wrap) and set aside.

2 Using a sharp knife, slice each chicken breast portion into four long strips. Put all the marinade ingredients in a large bowl and mix well, then add the chicken strips and toss together until thoroughly coated. Cover and leave for at least 30 minutes in the refrigerator to marinate.

3 Meanwhile, soak 16 wooden satay sticks or kebab skewers in water for 30 minutes, to prevent them from burning during cooking. Preheat the grill (broiler) to high or prepare the barbecue. Drain the satay sticks or skewers. Drain the chicken strips. Thread one strip on to each satay stick or skewer. Grill (broil) for 3 minutes on each side, or until the chicken is golden brown and cooked through.

4 Serve immediately with the satay sauce, white rice and a fresh green salad.

Stuffed Chicken Rolls

In this unusual dish, tender, delicate chicken is perfect with the more robust flavours of Parma ham and wild mushrooms.

Serves 4
25g/1oz/2 tbsp butter
1 garlic clove, chopped
150g/5oz/1¼ cups cooked white
  long grain rice
45ml/3 tbsp ricotta cheese
10ml/2 tsp chopped fresh flat
  leaf parsley

5ml/1 tsp chopped fresh tarragon
4 skinless chicken breast fillets
3–4 slices Parma ham
15ml/1 tbsp olive oil
120ml/4fl oz/½ cup
  white wine
salt and ground black pepper
fresh flat leaf parsley sprigs,
  to garnish
cooked tagliatelle and sautéed
  blewit or other wild
  mushrooms, to serve

1 Preheat the oven to 180°C/350°F/Gas 4. Melt 10g/¼oz/2 tsp of the butter in a pan and fry the garlic for a few seconds. Spoon into a bowl, add the rice, ricotta, parsley and tarragon and season with salt and pepper. Stir to mix.

2 Place each chicken breast in turn between two sheets of clear film (plastic wrap) and flatten by beating lightly, but firmly, with a rolling pin or steak mallet. Divide the slices of Parma ham between the chicken fillets, trimming them to fit.

3 Place a spoonful of the rice stuffing at the wider end of each ham-topped breast. Roll up carefully and tie in place with string or secure with a cocktail stick (toothpick).

4 Heat the oil and the remaining butter in a frying pan and lightly fry the chicken rolls until browned on all sides. Place side by side in a shallow baking dish and pour over the white wine.

5 Cover the dish with baking parchment and cook in the oven for 30–35 minutes until the chicken is tender.

6 Cut the rolls into slices and serve on a bed of tagliatelle with sautéed wild mushrooms and a generous grinding of black pepper. Garnish with sprigs of flat leaf parsley.

Chicken Satay Energy 48kcal/200kJ; Protein 4.8g; Carbohydrate 2.2g, of which sugars 2.1g; Fat 2.2g, of which saturates 0.4g; Cholesterol 13mg; Calcium 3mg; Fibre 0.1g; Sodium 105mg.
Chicken Rolls Energy 329kcal/1375kJ; Protein 30g; Carbohydrate 21.3g, of which sugars 1.3g; Fat 11.5g, of which saturates 5.1g; Cholesterol 95mg; Calcium 65mg; Fibre 1.3g; Sodium 257mg.

Soy Sauce and Star Anise Chicken

Although the chicken cooks quickly, it does benefit from being marinated first. This only takes a moment and ensures that there is no last-minute work to do when guests arrive.

Serves 4
4 skinless chicken breast fillets
2 whole star anise
45ml/3 tbsp olive oil
30ml/2 tbsp soy sauce
ground black pepper

1 Put the chicken breast fillets in a shallow, non-metallic dish and add the star anise.

2 In a small bowl, whisk together the olive oil and soy sauce and season with ground black pepper to make a marinade. Extra salt will not be necessary as the soy sauce is salty.

3 Pour the marinade over the chicken and stir to coat each breast fillet all over. Cover the dish with clear film (plastic wrap) and set aside for as much time as you have. If you are able to make it ahead, leave the chicken in the marinade for around 6–8 hours as the flavour will constantly improve. Place the covered dish in the refrigerator. When ready to cook, preheat the grill (broiler), while the fillets come to room temperature.

4 Cook the chicken under the grill, turning occasionally. It will need about 7–10 minutes on each side depending on the thickness. Place each piece of chicken on a warmed plate and serve immediately.

Variation
If you prefer, cook on a barbecue. When the coals are dusted with ash, spread them out evenly. Remove the chicken breasts from the marinade and cook for 8 minutes on each side, spooning over the marinade from time to time, until the chicken is cooked through. The chicken can also be cooked on the top of the stove on a ridged griddle (grill) pan. Get the pan very hot first, add the chicken and turn the pieces after a few minutes so that they are branded in a criss-cross fashion.

Chicken Stuffed with Cheese

This is one of those dishes that makes you feel good about cooking for friends. It does not require any effort but looks and tastes as if you have gone to huge amounts of trouble. Serve grilled Mediterranean vegetables, or use simply dressed salad leaves with the chicken.

Serves 4–6
4–6 skinless chicken breast fillets, preferably from a corn-fed bird
115g/4oz firm goat's cheese
60ml/4 tbsp chopped fresh oregano
20ml/4 tsp maple syrup
juice of 1 lemon
oil for brushing
salt and ground black pepper

1 Slash a pocket horizontally in each chicken fillet. Mix the goat's cheese, chopped oregano and 10ml/2 tsp of the maple syrup in a small bowl. Stuff the pockets in the chicken with the mixture. Do not overfill the pockets.

2 Put the remaining maple syrup into a shallow dish large enough to hold the stuffed chicken fillets in a single layer. Stir in the lemon juice and add the chicken pieces. Rub them all over with the mixture, then cover and leave in a cool place for 20 minutes, turning them occasionally. Season with salt and pepper and marinate for 10 minutes more.

3 Prepare the barbecue. Once the flames have died down, rake the hot coals to one side and insert a drip tray flat beside them. Position a lightly oiled grill (broiler) rack over the coals to heat. When the coals are ready they will have a light coating of ash over them. Lay the chicken breast fillets skin side up, on the grill rack over the drip tray. Cover the chicken with a lid or tented heavy-duty foil.

4 Grill (broil) the chicken for about 15 minutes in total, turning and moving the pieces around the grill rack so that they cook evenly without getting too charred. Baste with any remaining marinade 5 minutes before the end of cooking.

5 Transfer the chicken to a dish to rest and keep warm for about 5 minutes before serving.

Chicken with Cheese Energy 234kcal/980kJ; Protein 33.1g; Carbohydrate 2.8g, of which sugars 2.8g; Fat 10.1g, of which saturates 4.9g; Cholesterol 75mg; Calcium 40mg; Fibre 0g; Sodium 220mg.
Star Anise Chicken Energy 237kcal/992kJ; Protein 36.2g; Carbohydrate 0.6g, of which sugars 0.6g; Fat 9.9g, of which saturates 1.6g; Cholesterol 105mg; Calcium 9mg; Fibre 0g; Sodium 624mg.

Chicken Strips with Lemon and Garlic

These chicken strips make an unusual first course for four, and only need to be cooked at the last moment. Serve them as a main course for two with fried or baked potatoes.

Serves 2–4
2 skinless chicken breast fillets
30ml/2 tbsp olive oil

1 shallot, finely chopped
4 garlic cloves, finely chopped
5ml/1 tsp paprika
juice of 1 lemon
30ml/2 tbsp chopped
  fresh parsley
salt and ground black pepper
fresh flat leaf parsley,
  to garnish
lemon wedges and fried potatoes
  (optional), to serve

1 Remove the little fillet from the back of each breast portion. If the large fillet still looks fatter than a finger, bat it with a rolling pin to make it thinner. Slice all the chicken meat into strips.

2 Heat the oil in a large frying pan. Stir-fry the chicken with the shallot, garlic and paprika over high heat for 3 minutes until cooked through.

3 Add the lemon juice and parsley and season to taste. Serve immediately, with lemon wedges and fried potatoes, if using. Garnish with flat leaf parsley.

Variation
You can use strips of turkey breast fillet or pork fillet (tenderloin), if you prefer. They will need slightly longer cooking than the chicken.

Cook's Tip
Chicken breast fillets have a little fillet strip that easily becomes detached. Collect these in a bag or container in the freezer. You will not miss them and will soon have sufficient for this dish.

Mustard Baked Chicken

In this recipe, a mild, aromatic wholegrain mustard makes a tasty way of cooking chicken. Speciality mustards, such as the whiskey variety used here, are widely available from supermarkets and food stores. Serve the chicken with new potatoes and peas or sugarsnap peas.

Serves 4–6
8–12 chicken joints, or
  1 medium chicken, about
  1kg/2¼lb, jointed
juice of ½ lemon
15–30ml/2–3 tbsp
  whiskey mustard
10ml/2 tsp chopped
  fresh tarragon
sea salt and ground
  black pepper

1 Preheat the oven to 190°C/375°F/Gas 5. Place the chicken joints into a large shallow baking dish in a single layer. There should be a slight space between each joint.

2 Sprinkle the lemon juice over the chicken to flavour the skin. Season well with sea salt and black pepper.

3 Spread the mustard evenly over the joints and sprinkle with the chopped tarragon.

4 Bake in the preheated oven for 20–30 minutes or until thoroughly cooked, depending on the size of the chicken pieces. Serve immediately.

Variation
A whole chicken can also be baked this way. Allow 1½ hours in an oven preheated to 180°C/350°F/Gas 4. When cooked, the juices will run clear without any trace of blood.

Cook's Tip
If you can't find whiskey mustard, you can easily make up a home-made version by mixing 5ml/1 tsp of whiskey into every 15ml/1 tbsp of normal wholegrain mustard.

Chicken Strips Energy 139kcal/580kJ; Protein 18.6g; Carbohydrate 1.5g, of which sugars 1.1g; Fat 6.5g, of which saturates 1g; Cholesterol 53mg; Calcium 33mg; Fibre 0.8g; Sodium 50mg.
Mustard Baked Chicken Energy 426kcal/1768kJ; Protein 40.3g; Carbohydrate 0g, of which sugars 0g; Fat 29.3g, of which saturates 8.1g; Cholesterol 215mg; Calcium 13mg; Fibre 0g; Sodium 146mg.

Spiced Barbecued Chicken

In this recipe, the marinade is strongly scented with cumin and cinnamon, with a large amount of lemon juice to balance the sweetness of the spices. Slash the skin of the chicken to allow the flavours to penetrate.

Serves 4
5 garlic cloves, chopped
30ml/2 tbsp ground cumin
7.5ml/1½ tsp ground cinnamon
5ml/1 tsp paprika
juice of 1 lemon
30ml/2 tbsp olive oil
1.3kg/3lb chicken, cut into
    8 portions
salt and ground black pepper
fresh coriander (cilantro) leaves,
    to garnish
warmed pitta bread, salad and
    lemon wedges, to serve

1 In a bowl, combine the garlic, cumin, cinnamon, paprika, lemon juice, oil, salt and pepper.

2 Add the chicken and turn to coat thoroughly. Leave to marinate for at least 1 hour, or cover and place in the refrigerator overnight.

3 Light the barbecue and leave for about 40 minutes. It will be ready for cooking when the flames have died away and the coals have a covering of ash.

4 Arrange the pieces of dark meat on the grill (broiler) and cook for 10 minutes, turning once and basting from time to time with the marinade.

5 Place the remaining chicken pieces on the grill and cook for about 7–10 minutes, turning occasionally, until golden brown and the juices run clear when pricked with a skewer. Serve the chicken immediately, with pitta breads, lemon wedges and a fresh mixed salad.

> **Variation**
> For a different flavour, use 7.5ml/1½ tsp turmeric and a pinch of ground cardamom in place of the cinnamon.

Crumbed Chicken with Caper and Herb Mayonnaise

The contrast between crisp crumb and tender chicken is what makes this dish so successful. Caper mayonnaise is traditional but mayo flavoured with wasabi would be good too.

Serves 4
4 chicken breast fillets,
    about 200g/7oz each
juice of 1 lemon
5ml/1 tsp paprika
plain (all-purpose) flour, for dusting
1–2 eggs
dried breadcrumbs, for coating
about 60ml/4 tbsp olive oil
salt and ground black pepper
lemon wedges (optional),
    to serve

For the mayonnaise
120ml/4fl oz/½ cup mayonnaise
30ml/2 tbsp pickled capers,
    drained and chopped
30ml/2 tbsp chopped fresh parsley

1 Remove the skin from the chicken breast fillets. Lay them outside down and, with a sharp knife, cut horizontally, almost through, from the rounded side. Open each fillet up like a book. Press gently with your hand to make a roundish shape the size of a side plate. Sprinkle the surface of the chicken with lemon juice and paprika.

2 Set out three shallow bowls. Sprinkle flour over one, seasoning it well. Beat the egg with a little salt and pour into the second. Sprinkle the third with dried breadcrumbs.

3 Dip the chicken fillets first into the flour on both sides, then into the egg, then into the breadcrumbs, turning to coat them evenly in the ingredients.

4 Put the mayonnaise ingredients in a large bowl and mix well until thoroughly combined.

5 Heat the oil in a heavy frying pan over high heat. Fry the breast fillets two at a time, turning after 4 minutes, until golden on both sides and cooked through. Add more oil for the second batch if needed. Serve immediately, on individual plates, with the mayonnaise and lemon wedges, if using.

Crumbed Chicken Energy 582kcal/2428kJ; Protein 51.5g; Carbohydrate 10.3g, of which sugars 0.8g; Fat 37.6g, of which saturates 6g; Cholesterol 210mg; Calcium 43mg; Fibre 0.5g; Sodium 369mg.
Barbecued Chicken Energy 481kcal/1997kJ; Protein 40.8g; Carbohydrate 1g, of which sugars 0.1g; Fat 34.8g, of which saturates 8.9g; Cholesterol 215mg; Calcium 14mg; Fibre 0.3g; Sodium 147mg.

Barbecue Chicken with Lemon Grass

When cooked on a barbecue, this is the perfect dish for a summer party, but you can also cook this tasty chicken in the oven if the weather proves disappointing.

Serves 4–6
1.6kg/3–3½lb chicken, cut into 8–10 pieces
lime wedges and fresh red chillies, to garnish

For the marinade
2 lemon grass stalks, roots trimmed
2.5cm/1in piece fresh root ginger, peeled and thinly sliced
6 garlic cloves, coarsely chopped
4 shallots, coarsely chopped
½ bunch coriander (cilantro) roots, chopped
15ml/1 tbsp palm sugar (jaggery) or light muscovado (brown) sugar
120ml/4fl oz/½ cup coconut milk
30ml/2 tbsp Thai fish sauce
30ml/2 tbsp light soy sauce

1 To make the marinade, cut off the lower 5cm/2in of the lemon grass stalks and chop them coarsely. Put into a food processor with the ginger, garlic, shallots, coriander, sugar, coconut milk and sauces and process until smooth.

2 Place the chicken pieces in a dish, pour over the marinade and stir to mix well. Cover the dish and leave in a cool place to marinate for at least 4 hours, or preferably leave it in the refrigerator overnight.

3 Prepare the barbecue or preheat the oven to 200°C/400°F/Gas 6. Drain the chicken, reserving the marinade. If you are cooking in the oven, arrange the chicken pieces in a single layer on a rack set over a roasting pan.

4 Cook the chicken on the barbecue over moderately hot coals or bake in the oven for 20–30 minutes. Turn the pieces and brush with the marinade once or twice during cooking.

5 As soon as the chicken pieces are golden brown and cooked through, transfer them to a serving platter, garnish with the lime wedges and red chillies and serve immediately.

Chicken with Fennel and Peas

This Italian dish strongly reflects the traditions of Mediterranean cuisine.

Serves 4
4 skinless chicken breast fillets
plain (all-purpose) flour, for dusting
30–45ml/2–3 tbsp olive oil
1–2 onions, chopped
¼ fennel bulb, chopped (optional)
15ml/1 tbsp chopped fresh parsley, plus extra to garnish
7.5ml/1½ tsp fennel seeds
75ml/5 tbsp dry Marsala
120ml/4fl oz/½ cup chicken stock
300g/11oz/2¼ cups petits pois (baby peas)
juice of 1½ lemons
2 egg yolks
salt and ground black pepper

1 Season the chicken with salt and pepper, then dust generously with flour. Shake off the excess flour; set aside.

2 Heat 15ml/1 tbsp oil in a pan, add the onions, fennel, if using, parsley and fennel seeds. Cook for 5 minutes.

3 Add the remaining oil and the chicken to the pan and cook for about 2–3 minutes on each side, until lightly browned. Remove the chicken and onion mixture from the pan and set aside.

4 Deglaze the pan by pouring in the Marsala and cooking over high heat until reduced to about 30ml/2 tbsp, then pour in the chicken stock. Add the peas and return the chicken and onion mixture to the pan. Cook over very low heat while you prepare the egg mixture.

5 In a bowl, beat the lemon juice and egg yolks together, then slowly add about 120ml/4fl oz/½ cup of the hot liquid from the chicken and peas, stirring well to combine.

6 Return the mixture to the pan and cook over low heat, stirring, until the mixture thickens slightly. (Do not allow the mixture to boil or the eggs will curdle and spoil the sauce.) Serve the chicken immediately, sprinkled with a little extra chopped fresh parsley.

Barbecue Chicken Energy 229Kcal/959kJ; Protein 31.3g; Carbohydrate 4.3g, of which sugars 3.4g; Fat 9.7g, of which saturates 1.4g; Cholesterol 94mg; Calcium 32mg; Fibre 0.5g; Sodium 397mg.
Chicken with Fennel Energy 375kcal/1567kJ; Protein 43.4g; Carbohydrate 14.9g, of which sugars 7g; Fat 13.9g, of which saturates 2.6g; Cholesterol 206mg; Calcium 51mg; Fibre 4.5g; Sodium 99mg.

Chicken with Summer Vegetables

This is an all-in-the-pot dish, with the chicken cooking liquid providing the stock for the rest of the cooking and the sauce.

Serves 4
1.8kg/4lb boiling fowl
  (stewing chicken)
I onion, peeled, studded
  with 6 cloves
I bay leaf
a sprig each of thyme and parsley

10 black peppercorns
12 small potatoes, washed
8 small shallots, peeled
vegetables of your choice, such as
  carrots, courgettes (zucchini),
  broad (fava) beans, peas,
  mangetouts (snow peas)
25g/1oz/2 tbsp butter
30ml/2 tbsp plain
  (all-purpose) flour
60ml/4 tbsp chopped
  fresh tarragon

1 Wash the chicken and dry with kitchen paper. Place in a large pan with the onion, bay leaf, thyme, parsley and peppercorns, with water to cover. Bring to the boil, then reduce the heat and simmer gently for 1½ hours.

2 Remove the chicken from the pan and keep warm. Remove all the seasonings, either with a slotted spoon or by straining the mixture, then bring the cooking liquid back to the boil. Use a spoon to skim off any fat that may have appeared on the top of the stock.

3 Cook the vegetables in the liquid, putting the potatoes in first for a few minutes, then adding the shallots and carrots, if using, and finally any green vegetables that take no time at all. When the vegetables are cooked, place the chicken on a serving dish and surround with all the vegetables.

4 In a small pan, melt the butter, add the flour and stir to create a roux. Slowly add some liquor from the large pan until a sauce is created – about 600ml/1 pint/2½ cups – and allow to simmer for a few minutes to reduce down and strengthen the flavour.

5 Stir the chopped fresh tarragon into the sauce, then ladle over the chicken and vegetables. Serve immediately.

Bacon, Chicken and Leek Pudding

Old-fashioned suet puddings are still a favourite, and this one is bursting with flavour.

Serves 4
200g/7oz unsmoked lean, rindless
  bacon, preferably in one piece
400g/14oz skinless boneless
  chicken, preferably thigh meat
2 medium leeks, finely chopped

30ml/2 tbsp finely chopped
  fresh parsley
175g/6oz/1¼ cups self-raising
  (self-rising) flour
75g/3oz/½ cup shredded suet
  (US chilled, grated shortening)
120ml/4fl oz chicken or
  vegetable stock, or water
ground black pepper
butter for greasing

1 Cut the bacon and chicken into bitesize pieces. Mix them in a bowl with the leeks and half the parsley. Season with pepper.

2 Sift the flour into another large bowl and stir in the suet and the remaining parsley. Stir in sufficient cold water to make a soft dough. On a lightly floured surface, roll out the dough to a circle measuring about 33cm/13in across. Cut out one quarter of the circle, like a wedge, roll up and reserve.

3 Lightly butter a 1.2 litre/2 pint/5 cup heatproof bowl. Use the rolled out dough to line the buttered bowl, pressing the cut edges together to seal them and allowing the pastry to overlap the top of the bowl slightly.

4 Carefully spoon the bacon and chicken mixture into the bowl, packing it neatly. Pour the chicken or vegetable stock over the bacon mixture, making sure it does not overfill the bowl.

5 Roll out the reserved pastry into a circle to form a lid and lay it over the filling, pinching the edges together to seal them well. Cover with baking parchment (pleated in the centre to allow the pudding to rise), and then a large sheet of foil (again pleated at the centre). Tuck the edges under and press them tightly to the sides of the bowl until well sealed.

6 Steam the pudding over boiling water for about 3½ hours. Check the water level occasionally. Uncover the pudding, slide a knife around the sides and turn out on to a serving plate.

Chicken with Vegetables Energy 713kcal/2973kJ; Protein 51.2g; Carbohydrate 39.3g, of which sugars 13g; Fat 40g, of which saturates 12.9g; Cholesterol 261mg; Calcium 103mg; Fibre 5.4g; Sodium 251mg.
Chicken Pudding Energy 535kcal/2236kJ; Protein 28.2g; Carbohydrate 39.4g, of which sugars 2.9g; Fat 31.3g, of which saturates 14.8g; Cholesterol 86mg; Calcium 111mg; Fibre 4g; Sodium 999mg.

Coq au Vin

This rustic, one-pot casserole contains chunky pieces of chicken, slowly simmered in a rich red wine sauce until tender.

Serves 6

45ml/3 tbsp light olive oil
12 shallots
225g/8oz rindless streaky (fatty) bacon rashers (strips), chopped
3 garlic cloves, finely chopped
225g/8oz small mushrooms, halved
6 boneless chicken thighs
3 chicken breast fillets, halved

1 bottle red wine
salt and ground black pepper
45ml/3 tbsp chopped fresh parsley, to garnish
boiled potatoes, to serve

For the bouquet garni
3 sprigs each parsley, thyme and sage
1 bay leaf
4 peppercorns

For the beurre manié
25g/1oz/2 tbsp butter, softened
25g/1oz/¼ cup plain (all-purpose) flour

1 Heat the oil in a flameproof casserole and cook the shallots for 5 minutes until golden. Increase the heat, then add the bacon, garlic and mushrooms and cook, stirring, for 10 minutes.

2 Transfer the cooked ingredients to a plate, then brown the chicken pieces in the oil remaining in the pan, turning them until golden brown all over. Return the shallots, garlic, mushrooms and bacon to the casserole and pour in the red wine.

3 Tie the ingredients for the bouquet garni in a bundle in a piece of muslin (cheesecloth) and add to the casserole. Bring to the boil. Reduce the heat, cover and simmer for 30–40 minutes.

4 To make the beurre manié, cream the butter and flour together in a bowl using your fingers to make a smooth paste. Add small lumps of the paste to the casserole, stirring well until each piece has melted. When all the paste has been added, bring the casserole back to the boil and simmer for 5 minutes.

5 Season the casserole to taste with salt and pepper. Serve immediately, garnished with chopped fresh parsley and accompanied by boiled potatoes.

Stoved Chicken

The word 'stoved' is derived from the French étuver – to cook in a covered pot – and originates from the time of the Franco/Scottish Alliance in the 17th century. Instead of buying chicken joints, you can also choose either thighs or drumsticks.

Serves 4
900g/2lb potatoes, cut into 5mm/¼ in slices

2 large onions, thinly sliced
15ml/1 tbsp chopped fresh thyme
25g/1oz/¼ stick butter
15ml/1 tbsp oil
2 large bacon rashers (strips), chopped
4 large chicken joints, halved
1 bay leaf
600ml/1 pint/2½ cups chicken stock
salt and ground black pepper

1 Preheat the oven to 150°C/300°F/Gas 2. Make a layer of half the potato slices in the base of a large casserole, then cover with half the onion. Sprinkle with half the thyme and season.

2 Heat the butter and oil in a large frying pan, then brown the bacon and chicken. Using a slotted spoon, transfer the chicken and bacon to the casserole. Reserve the fat in the pan.

3 Tuck the bay leaf in between the chicken. Sprinkle the remaining thyme over, then cover with the remaining onion, followed by a neat layer of overlapping potato slices. Season.

4 Pour the stock into the casserole. Brush the top layer of potatoes with the reserved fat, then cover and cook in the oven for 2 hours, or until the chicken is cooked and tender.

5 Preheat the grill (broiler) to high. Uncover the casserole, place it under the grill and cook until the slices of potato are beginning to brown and crisp. Serve hot.

Variation
You can use tarragon instead of the thyme: French tarragon has a superior flavour to the Russian variety.

Coq au Vin Energy 630kcal/2618kJ; Protein 42.8g; Carbohydrate 19.3g, of which sugars 7.4g; Fat 41g, of which saturates 17.3g; Cholesterol 209mg; Calcium 67mg; Fibre 2.6g; Sodium 480mg.
Stoved Chicken Energy 630kcal/2653kJ; Protein 69.2g; Carbohydrate 48.2g, of which sugars 8.9g; Fat 19.2g, of which saturates 7.2g; Cholesterol 195mg; Calcium 57mg; Fibre 3.9g; Sodium 574mg.

Chicken Casserole with Spiced Figs

This is a delicious dish that is perfect for an informal gathering or as a tasty alternative to the usual roast chicken on a Sunday. Joints of chicken are cooked with bacon in a beautifully spiced sauce, which goes perfectly with a glass or two of red wine.

Serves 4
50g/2oz bacon lardons or pancetta, diced
15ml/1 tbsp olive oil
1.3–1.6kg/3–3½lb free-range or corn-fed chicken, jointed into eight pieces

120ml/4fl oz/½ cup white wine
finely pared rind of ½ lemon
50ml/2fl oz/¼ cup chicken stock
salt and ground black pepper
green salad, to serve

For the figs
150g/5oz/¾ cup sugar
120ml/4fl oz/½ cup white wine vinegar
1 lemon slice
1 cinnamon stick
120ml/4fl oz/½ cup water
450g/1lb fresh figs

1 Prepare the figs. In a heavy pan, simmer the sugar, vinegar, lemon and cinnamon with the water for about 5 minutes. Add the figs and cook for a further 10 minutes. Remove the pan from the heat and leave to stand for 3 hours.

2 Heat a large frying pan without any oil. Fry the bacon or pancetta, stirring frequently, for 6–8 minutes until golden. Transfer to an ovenproof dish.

3 Add the olive oil to the pan. Season the chicken, then add to the pan and quickly brown on both sides. Transfer the joints to the ovenproof dish.

4 Preheat the oven to 180°C/350°F/Gas 4. Drain the figs. Add the wine and lemon rind to the pan and boil until the wine has reduced and is syrupy. Pour over the chicken.

5 Cook the chicken in the oven, uncovered, for 20 minutes, then add the figs and chicken stock. Cover and return to the oven for a further 10 minutes. Serve with a green salad.

Colombian Chicken Hotpot

Traditionally, three native varieties of potatoes are used in this traditional dish.

Serves 8
1.6kg/3½lb chicken
3 spring onions (scallions)
2 bay leaves
6 fresh coriander (cilantro) sprigs
6 whole black peppercorns
675g/1½lb floury potatoes, peeled and cut into 1cm/½in chunks
675g/1½lb waxy potatoes, peeled and cut into 1cm/½in chunks

675g/1½lb baby new potatoes
2 corn cobs, each cut into 4 pieces
salt
capers and sour cream, to serve

For the avocado salsa
1 hard-boiled egg
1 large ripe avocado
1 spring onion (scallion), chopped
15ml/1 tbsp chopped fresh coriander (cilantro)
1 fresh green chilli, seeded and finely chopped
salt

1 Put the chicken in a large pan and cover with water. Add the onions, bay, coriander and peppercorns. Season, bring to the boil and skim the surface. Reduce to a gentle simmer, cover and cook for 1 hour or until the chicken is fully cooked and tender. Remove from the heat and allow to cool. Drain the chicken, reserving the liquid, and cut into eight pieces, discarding the carcass.

2 Skim the fat from the liquid, then strain it into a clean pan. Bring to the boil. Add the floury and waxy potatoes and simmer for 15 minutes. Stir in the baby new potatoes and corn and simmer for a further 20 minutes.

3 The waxy potatoes should be soft and partly broken. The new or salad potatoes should be tender but still whole. Return the chicken pieces to the pan and reheat gently but thoroughly.

4 Make the fresh avocado salsa. Peel and chop the hard-boiled egg. Using a fork, mash it in a small bowl. Just before serving, cut the avocado in half and scoop the flesh into a bowl. Mash well with a fork, then stir in the egg. Add the spring onion, fresh coriander and chilli, mix well, then season to taste with salt.

5 Serve the chicken mixture with the avocado salsa, capers and sour cream on the side, if you like.

Chicken Casserole Energy 811kcal/3396kJ; Protein 44g; Carbohydrate 69.8g, of which sugars 69.8g; Fat 39.2g, of which saturates 10.9g; Cholesterol 215g; Calcium 183mg; Fibre 4.3g; Sodium 394mg.
Chicken Hotpot Energy 505kcal/2113kJ; Protein 31g; Carbohydrate 42g, of which sugars 4.1g; Fat 24.7g, of which saturates 7g; Cholesterol 152mg; Calcium 37mg; Fibre 3.7g; Sodium 566mg.

Seville Chicken

Oranges and almonds are a favourite ingredient in southern Spain, especially around Seville, where the orange and almond trees are a familiar and wonderful sight.

Serves 4

1 orange
8 chicken thighs
plain (all-purpose) flour, seasoned
    with salt and pepper
45ml/3 tbsp olive oil
1 large Spanish (Bermuda) onion,
    roughly chopped
2 garlic cloves, crushed
1 red (bell) pepper, seeded
    and sliced
1 yellow (bell) pepper, seeded
    and sliced
115g/4oz chorizo sausage, sliced
50g/2oz/½ cup flaked
    (sliced) almonds
225g/8oz/generous 1 cup brown
    basmati rice
about 600ml/1 pint/2½ cups
    chicken stock
400g/14oz can chopped
    tomatoes
175ml/6fl oz/¾ cup white wine
generous pinch of dried thyme
salt and ground black pepper
fresh thyme sprigs, to garnish

1 Pare a thin strip of peel from the orange and set it aside. Peel the orange, then cut it into segments, working over a bowl to catch the juice. Dust the chicken thighs with seasoned flour.

2 Heat the oil in a large frying pan and fry the chicken pieces on both sides until nicely brown. Transfer to a plate. Add the onion and garlic to the pan and fry for 4–5 minutes until the onion begins to brown. Add the red and yellow peppers and fry, stirring occasionally, until slightly softened.

3 Add the chorizo, stir-fry for a few minutes, then sprinkle over the almonds and rice. Cook, stirring, for 1–2 minutes.

4 Pour in the chicken stock, tomatoes and wine and add the orange strip and thyme. Season well. Bring to simmering point, stirring, then return the chicken pieces to the pan.

5 Cover tightly and cook over very low heat for 1–1¼ hours until the rice and chicken are tender. Just before serving, add the orange segments and allow to cook briefly to heat through. Garnish with fresh thyme and serve.

Spicy Spanish Chicken

This chicken dish has a spicy red pepper sauce. In the past, the dried choricero pepper – the one that gives chorizos their colour and spice – was used alone, but nowadays the dish is often made with fresh red peppers, spiced with chilli.

Serves 4

675g/1½lb red (bell) peppers
10ml/2 tsp paprika
4 free-range chicken portions
30ml/2 tbsp olive oil
1 large onion, chopped
2 garlic cloves, finely chopped
200g/7oz Serrano or other ham, in
    one piece, or a gammon chop
200g/7oz can chopped tomatoes
1 dried guindilla or other hot
    dried chilli, chopped, or 2.5ml/
    ½ tsp chilli powder, to taste
salt and ground black pepper
chopped fresh parsley, to garnish
small new potatoes, to serve

1 Preheat the grill (broiler) to high. Put the peppers on a baking sheet and grill (broil) for 10 minutes, turning occasionally, until the skins have blistered and blackened. Place the peppers in a bowl, cover with clear film (plastic wrap) and leave to cool.

2 Rub salt and paprika into the chicken portions. Heat the oil in a large frying pan and add the chicken portions, skin side down. Fry over medium-low heat, turning until golden on all sides.

3 Meanwhile, select a casserole into which the chicken will fit comfortably. Spoon in 45ml/3 tbsp fat from the other pan. Fry the onion and garlic until soft. Dice the ham or gammon and add, stirring occasionally, for a few minutes.

4 Add the chopped tomatoes to the casserole, with the chopped dried chilli or chilli powder. Cook for 4–5 minutes.

5 Peel the skins off the peppers and discard. Put the peppers into a blender and strain in the juices, discarding the seeds. Process, then add the paste to the casserole. Heat through.

6 Add the chicken pieces to the casserole, bedding them down in the sauce. Cook, covered, for 15 minutes and check the seasonings, adding more if necessary. Garnish with a little parsley and serve with small new potatoes.

Seville Chicken Energy 861kcal/3598kJ; Protein 65.3g; Carbohydrate 67.1g, of which sugars 17.1g; Fat 34g, of which saturates 5.6g; Cholesterol 155g; Calcium 172mg; Fibre 6.3g; Sodium 453mg.
Spicy Chicken Energy 332kcal/1396kJ; Protein 47.6g; Carbohydrate 13.8g; of which sugars 12.4g; Fat 10g, of which saturates 2.1g; Cholesterol 134mg; Calcium 33mg; Fibre 3.2g; Sodium 702mg.

Chicken Pie with Olives and Raisins

This is a great family meal, which is perfect for a Sunday lunch.

Serves 6

1.6kg/3½lb 1 chicken
6 peppercorns
1 bay leaf
3 fresh parsley sprigs
30ml/2 tbsp olive oil
1 large onion, finely chopped
2 hard-boiled eggs, chopped
2 tomatoes, roughly chopped

50g/2oz/½ cup pitted green
  olives, roughly chopped
15ml/1 tbsp drained bottled capers
65g/2½oz/scant ½ cup raisins
salt and ground black pepper

For the topping
500g/1¼lb/3⅓ cups drained
  canned corn kernels
90g/3½oz butter
10ml/2 tsp caster (superfine) sugar
3 eggs, lightly beaten
salt

1 Put the chicken in a large, heavy pan and add water to cover. Add the peppercorns, bay leaf and parsley and bring to the boil. Lower the heat, cover and simmer gently for 1 hour.

2 Allow the chicken to cool in the cooking liquid. When cold enough to handle, lift the chicken out of the pan and, using two forks, shred the flesh roughly. Discard the skin and bones.

3 Make the topping. Transfer the corn kernels into a blender or food processor and purée until smooth. Melt the butter in a pan over low heat. Stir in the corn and sugar. Season with salt and cook, stirring, for 10 minutes, until the mixture thickens. Remove from the heat and leave to cool for 10 minutes, then gradually stir in the beaten eggs. Set the topping mixture aside.

4 Preheat the oven to 180°C/350°F/Gas 4. Heat the oil in a frying pan and stir in the onion. Cook gently for 5 minutes, until soft, and season with salt and pepper to taste.

5 Stir in the hard-boiled eggs, tomatoes, olives, capers and raisins. Fold in the shredded chicken. Spoon the pie filling into a 25 x 20cm/10 x 8in baking dish. Using a spoon, spread the corn topping evenly over the top of the chicken filling and bake for 45 minutes, until golden brown. Leave to stand for 10 minutes before serving on warmed plates.

Paprika Chicken with Rice

This Spanish rice dish with chicken is a casserole, intended to be more liquid than a paella. You can vary the recipe by adding seasonal vegetables, and peas and corn can also be included if you wish. The paprika and the slices of chorizo give the rice a warm spicy flavour.

Serves 4

60ml/4 tbsp olive oil
6 chicken thighs, halved along
  the bone
5ml/1 tsp paprika
1 large Spanish (Bermuda) onion,
  roughly chopped
2 garlic cloves, finely chopped
1 chorizo sausage, sliced

115g/4oz Serrano or cooked
  ham, diced
1 red (bell) pepper,
  roughly chopped
1 yellow (bell) pepper,
  roughly chopped
225g/8oz/1 generous cup paella
  rice, washed and drained
2 large tomatoes, chopped
  or 200g/7oz can
  chopped tomatoes
120ml/4fl oz/½ cup
  amontillado sherry
750ml/1¼ pints/3 cups
  chicken stock
5ml/1 tsp dried oregano or thyme
1 bay leaf
salt and ground black pepper
15 green olives and chopped
  fresh flat leaf parsley,
  to garnish

1 Heat the oil in a wide flameproof casserole. Season the chicken pieces with salt and paprika. Fry until nicely brown all over, then reserve on a plate.

2 Add the onion and garlic to the pan and fry gently until beginning to soften. Add the sliced chorizo and ham or gammon and stir-fry. Add the chopped peppers and cook until they begin to soften.

3 Sprinkle in the rice and cook, stirring, for 1–2 minutes. Add the tomatoes, sherry, chicken stock and dried herbs and season well. Arrange the chicken pieces deep in the mixture, and tuck in the bay leaf.

4 Cover and cook over very low heat for 30–40 minutes, until the chicken and rice are done. Stir, then garnish with olives and chopped parsley and serve.

Paprika Chicken Energy 194kcal/813kJ; Protein 26g; Carbohydrate 2.1g, of which sugars 1.6g; Fat 9.1g, of which saturates 1.4g; Cholesterol 74mg; Calcium 42mg; Fibre 1.1g; Sodium 69mg.
Chicken Pie Energy 516kcal/2162kJ; Protein 36g; Carbohydrate 32.5g, of which sugars 18.3g; Fat 28g, of which saturates 12g; Cholesterol 265mg; Calcium 57mg; Fibre 2g; Sodium 698mg.

Chicken Chilli Parcels

These fried burritos are a common sight on street stalls and in cafés along the Mexican border with Texas, but are not so well known farther south.

Serves 4

2 skinless chicken breast fillets
1 chipotle chilli, seeded
15ml/1 tbsp vegetable oil
2 onions, finely chopped
4 garlic cloves, crushed
2.5ml/½ tsp ground cumin
2.5ml/½ tsp ground coriander
2.5ml/½ tsp ground cinnamon
2.5ml/½ tsp ground cloves
300g/11oz/scant 2 cups drained canned tomatillos
400g/14oz/2¾ cups cooked pinto beans
8 x 20–25cm/8–10in fresh wheat flour tortillas
salt and ground black pepper

1 Put the chicken in a large pan, pour over water to cover and add the chilli. Bring to the boil, and then simmer for 10 minutes or until the chicken is cooked and the chilli has softened. Remove the chilli and chop finely. Transfer the chicken on to a plate. Leave to cool slightly, then shred with two forks.

2 Heat half the oil in a frying pan. Fry the onions until translucent, then add the garlic and ground spices and cook for 3 minutes. Add the tomatillos and pinto beans. Cook over medium heat for 5 minutes, stirring to break up the tomatillos and some of the beans. Simmer for 5 minutes. Add the chicken and season.

3 Wrap the tortillas in foil and place them on a plate. Stand the plate over boiling water for about 5 minutes until the tortillas are pliable. Alternatively, wrap them in microwave-safe clear film (plastic wrap) and heat in a microwave on full power for 1 minute.

4 Spoon one-eighth of the bean filling into the centre of a tortilla, fold in both sides, then fold the bottom of the tortilla up and the top down to form a neat parcel. Secure with a cocktail stick (toothpick).

5 Heat the remaining oil in a large frying pan and fry the tortilla parcels in batches until crisp, turning once. Remove them from the oil with a slotted spoon and drain on kitchen paper. Serve hot.

Chicken Fajitas

The perfect dish for casual entertaining, fajitas are a self-assembly dish: warm flour tortillas are brought to the table and everyone adds their own fillings.

Serves 6

3 skinless, chicken breast fillets
finely grated rind and juice
of 2 limes
30ml/2 tbsp caster
(superfine) sugar
10ml/2 tsp dried oregano
2.5ml/½ tsp cayenne pepper
5ml/1 tsp ground cinnamon
2 onions
3 (bell) peppers (1 red, 1 yellow
or orange and 1 green)
12 ready-made soft tortillas
45ml/3 tbsp vegetable oil
guacamole, salsa and sour cream,
to serve

1 Slice the chicken into 2cm/¾in wide strips and place them in a large bowl. Add the lime rind and juice, caster sugar, oregano, cayenne and cinnamon. Mix thoroughly. Set aside to marinate for at least 30 minutes.

2 Cut the onions in half and slice them thinly. Cut the peppers in half, remove the cores and seeds, then slice the flesh into 1cm/½in wide strips.

3 Heat a large frying pan or griddle (grill) pan and warm each tortilla in turn for about 30 seconds on each side, or until the surface colours and begins to blister. Keep the tortillas warm and pliable by wrapping them in a clean, dry dish towel.

4 Heat the oil in a large frying pan. Stir-fry the marinated chicken for 5–6 minutes, then add the peppers and onions and cook for 3–4 minutes more, until the chicken is cooked through and the vegetables are tender, but still juicy. Spoon the chicken mixture into a serving bowl and take it to the table with the warm tortillas and bowls of guacamole, salsa and sour cream.

5 To eat, take a tortilla, spread it with a little salsa, add a spoonful of guacamole and pile some of the chicken mixture in the centre. The final touch is to add a small dollop of sour cream. The tortilla is then folded and ready to eat.

Chicken Fajitas Energy 485kcal/2044kJ; Protein 26g; Carbohydrate 67.4g, of which sugars 15.3g; Fat 14.2g, of which saturates 3.8g; Cholesterol 60mg; Calcium 118mg; Fibre 4g; Sodium 53mg.
Chicken Chilli Parcels Energy 468kcal/1968kJ; Protein 27.5g; Carbohydrate 51.1g; of which sugars 6g; Fat 18.5g; of which saturates 2.3g; Cholesterol 61mg; Calcium 105mg; Fibre 3.3g; Sodium 271mg.

Chicken and Prawn Jambalaya

The mixture of chicken, seafood and rice makes a quick and easy feast for the whole family. Jambalayas are a colourful mixture of highly flavoured ingredients, and are always popular.

Serves 10

2 chickens, each about
   1.5kg/3–3½lb
450g/1lb piece raw gammon
   (smoked or cured ham)
50g/2oz/4 tbsp lard or bacon fat
50g/2oz/½ cup plain
   (all-purpose) flour
3 medium onions, finely sliced
2 green (bell) peppers, seeded
   and sliced
675g/1½lb tomatoes, peeled
   and chopped
2–3 garlic cloves, crushed
10ml/2 tsp chopped fresh thyme
   or 5ml/1 tsp dried thyme
24 raw prawns (shrimp), peeled
   and deveined
500g/1¼lb/3 cups white long
   grain rice
1.2 litres/2 pints/5 cups water
2–3 dashes Tabasco sauce
45ml/3 tbsp chopped fresh flat
   leaf parsley, plus tiny fresh
   parsley sprigs, to garnish
salt and ground black pepper

1 Cut each chicken into 10 pieces and season with salt and pepper. Dice the gammon, discarding the rind and fat.

2 Melt the lard or bacon fat in a heavy frying pan. Add the chicken pieces in batches, brown them all over, then lift them out with a slotted spoon and set them aside.

3 Reduce the heat. Sprinkle the flour into the fat in the pan and stir until the roux turns golden brown. Return the chicken pieces to the pan. Add the gammon, onions, peppers, tomatoes, garlic and thyme. Cook, stirring regularly, for 10 minutes, then add the prawns and mix lightly.

4 Stir the rice into the pan and pour in the water. Season with salt, pepper and Tabasco sauce. Bring to the boil, then cook gently until the rice is tender and all the liquid has been absorbed. Add a little extra boiling water if the rice looks like drying out before it is cooked.

5 Mix the parsley into the finished dish, garnish with tiny sprigs of flat leaf parsley and serve immediately.

Drunken Chicken

This dish has a delicious sweet-and-sour flavour. Serve with rice and tortillas to mop up the sauce.

Serves 4

150g/5oz/scant 1 cup raisins
120ml/4fl oz/½ cup sherry
115g/4oz/1 cup plain
   (all-purpose) flour
2.5ml/½ tsp salt
2.5ml/½ tsp ground black pepper
45ml/3 tbsp vegetable oil
8 skinless chicken thighs, bone-in
1 onion, halved and thinly sliced
3 garlic cloves, crushed
2 tart eating apples, such as
   Granny Smith
115g/4oz/1 cup slivered almonds
1 ripe plantain, peeled and sliced
350ml/12fl oz/1½ cups
   well-flavoured chicken stock
250ml/8fl oz/1 cup tequila
fresh herbs, chopped, to garnish

1 Put the raisins in a bowl and pour the sherry over. Set aside to plump up. Season the flour and spread it out on a large, flat dish or soup plate. Heat 30ml/2 tbsp of the oil in a large frying pan. Dip each chicken thigh in turn in the seasoned flour, then fry in the hot oil until browned, turning occasionally. Drain on kitchen paper.

2 Heat the remaining vegetable oil in a large, deep frying pan. Add the onion slices and crushed garlic and cook for 2–3 minutes. Meanwhile, peel, core and dice the apples.

3 Add the diced apple to the onion mixture with the almonds and plantain slices. Cook, stirring occasionally, for 3–4 minutes, then add the soaked raisins, with any free sherry. Add the chicken pieces to the pan.

4 Pour the chicken stock and tequila over the chicken mixture. Cover the pan with a lid and cook for 15 minutes, then take off the lid and cook for 10 minutes more or until the sauce has reduced by about half.

5 Check that the chicken thighs are cooked by lifting one out of the pan and piercing it in the thickest part with a sharp knife or skewer. Any juices that come out should be clear. If necessary, cook the chicken for a little longer before serving, sprinkled with chopped fresh herbs.

Drunken Chicken Energy 608kcal/2552kJ; Protein 35.4g; Carbohydrate 52.7g, of which sugars 29g; Fat 17.6g, of which saturates 1.9g; Cholesterol 82mg; Calcium 107mg; Fibre 3.7g; Sodium 97mg.
Chicken Jambalaya Energy 748kcal/3117kJ; Protein 54.9g; Carbohydrate 50.3g, of which sugars 5.5g; Fat 36.2g, of which saturates 10.8g; Cholesterol 262mg; Calcium 70mg; Fibre 2g; Sodium 588mg.

Yogurt Chicken and Rice Cake

This unusual dish is packed with Middle Eastern flavours.

Serves 6

40g/1½oz/3 tbsp butter
1 chicken, about 1.5kg/3–3½lb
1 large onion, chopped
250ml/8fl oz/1 cup chicken stock
2 eggs, beaten
475ml/16fl oz/2 cups natural
  (plain) yogurt
2–3 saffron strands, dissolved in
  15ml/1 tbsp warm water
5ml/1 tsp ground cinnamon
450g/1lb/2⅓ cups basmati rice
1.2 litres/2 pints/5 cups
  hot water
75g/3oz/¾ cup cranberries
50g/2oz/½ cup flaked
  (sliced) almonds
salt and ground black pepper
herb and radicchio salad, to serve

1 Melt two-thirds of the butter in a flameproof casserole. Joint the chicken and fry with the onion for 4–5 minutes. Add the stock and season. Bring to the boil, then simmer for 45 minutes until the chicken is cooked and the stock has reduced by half.

2 Drain the chicken, reserving the stock. Cut the flesh into large pieces and place in a bowl. In another bowl, mix the eggs with the yogurt. Add the saffron water and cinnamon. Season lightly. Stir into the chicken, cover and leave for up to 2 hours.

3 Preheat the oven to 160°C/325°F/Gas 3. Grease a large baking dish. Place the rice in a pan, add the hot water and a little salt. Bring back to the boil, and then simmer gently for 10 minutes. Drain, rinse thoroughly in warm water and drain once more.

4 Lift the chicken from the marinade and mix half the rice into the marinade. Spread the mixture on the bottom of the dish. Place the chicken on top, then cover with half the plain rice. Add the cranberries, then cover with the remaining rice. Pour over the reserved stock, sprinkle with almonds and the remaining butter. Cover with foil and bake for 35–45 minutes.

5 Leave the dish to cool for a few minutes, then place it on a cold, damp dish towel (to help lift the rice from the bottom of the dish). Run a knife around the inside rim, invert a large, flat plate over the dish and turn out the rice 'cake'. Cut into six wedges and serve hot, with a herb and radicchio salad.

West African Chicken and Rice

This West African dish is usually made in large quantities, using jointed whole chickens. This version is somewhat more sophisticated, but still has the traditional flavour.

Serves 4

2 garlic cloves, crushed
5ml/1 tsp dried thyme
4 skinless chicken breast fillets
30ml/2 tbsp palm or vegetable oil
400g/14oz can chopped tomatoes
15ml/1 tbsp tomato purée (paste)
1 onion, chopped
450ml/¾ pint/scant 2 cups
  chicken stock
30ml/2 tbsp dried shrimps or
  crayfish, ground
1 fresh green chilli, seeded and
  finely chopped
350g/12oz/1¾ cups white long
  grain rice
750ml/18fl oz/2½ cups water
chopped fresh thyme, to garnish

1 Mix the garlic and thyme in a bowl. Rub the mixture into the chicken breast fillets. Heat the oil in a frying pan and add the chicken fillets to the pan to brown in the oil, then remove to a plate. Add the chopped tomatoes, tomato purée and onion to the pan. Cook over medium heat, stirring occasionally, for 15 minutes until the tomatoes are well reduced.

2 Lower the heat a little, return the chicken pieces to the pan and stir well to coat with the sauce. Cook for 10 minutes, stirring, then add the stock, the shrimps or crayfish and the chilli. Bring to the boil, then simmer for 5 minutes, or until the chicken is cooked, stirring occasionally.

3 Meanwhile, put the rice in a separate pan. Pour in 750ml/ 18 fl oz/2½ cups of water, and top up with the sauce from the chicken. Bring to the boil, then lower the heat and cover the pan. Cook over low heat for 12–15 minutes until the liquid has been absorbed and the rice is tender.

4 Pack the rice in four individual moulds and set aside. Lift out the chicken fillets from the sauce and put them on a board. If the sauce is runny, cook it over high heat to reduce it a little. Unmould a rice timbale on each of four serving plates. Spoon the sauce around, then quickly slice the chicken fillets and fan them on the sauce. Garnish with thyme sprigs and serve.

Yogurt Chicken Energy 682kcal/2843kJ; Protein 43.4g; Carbohydrate 69g, of which sugars 8.2g; Fat 25.7g, of which saturates 10.2g; Cholesterol 220mg; Calcium 198mg; Fibre 0.6g; Sodium 250mg.
West African Chicken Energy 719kcal/2998kJ; Protein 44.1g; Carbohydrate 76.3g, of which sugars 5.4g; Fat 25.9g, of which saturates 7.4g; Cholesterol 163mg; Calcium 54mg; Fibre 1.3g; Sodium 187mg.

Chicken Korma with Saffron Rice

Mild and fragrant, this dish is an old favourite.

Serves 4
75g/3oz/¾ cup flaked (sliced) almonds
15ml/1 tbsp butter
about 15ml/1 tbsp sunflower oil
675g/1½lb skinless chicken breast fillets, cut into bitesize pieces
1 onion, chopped
4 green cardamom pods
2 garlic cloves, crushed
10ml/2 tsp ground cumin
5ml/1 tsp ground coriander
1 cinnamon stick
good pinch of chilli powder
175ml/6fl oz/¾ cup chicken stock
300ml/½ pint/1¼ cups coconut milk
5ml/1 tsp tomato purée (paste)
75ml/5 tbsp single (light) cream
15–30ml/1–2 tbsp fresh lime juice
10ml/2 tsp grated lime rind
5ml/1 tsp garam masala
salt and ground black pepper
fresh coriander (cilantro) sprigs, to garnish
poppadums, to serve (optional)

For the saffron rice
275g/10oz/1½ cups basmati rice
750ml/1¼ pints/3 cups chicken stock
generous pinch of saffron strands, soaked in hot water

1 Dry-fry the almonds in a pan until pale golden. Transfer two-thirds to a plate and dry-fry the remainder until they are slightly deeper in colour. Set aside the darker almonds for the garnish. Grind the paler almonds in a spice grinder or coffee mill.

2 Heat the butter and oil in a frying pan. Fry the chicken for 5 minutes, then set aside. Fry the onion for 2 minutes, then add the cardamom and garlic and fry for 3–4 minutes. Stir in the ground almonds, cumin, coriander, cinnamon and chilli powder and fry for 1 minute. Stir in the stock, coconut milk and tomato purée. Add the chicken and season. Cover and simmer for 10 minutes until the chicken is tender. Set aside.

3 Place the rice in a pan. Add the stock and the saffron. Bring to the boil over medium heat, then cover and cook over low heat for 10 minutes. Just before the rice is ready, reheat the korma and stir in the cream, the lime juice and rind and the garam masala. Pile the rice into a serving dish and spoon the korma into another dish. Garnish with the reserved almonds and coriander sprigs, and serve with poppadums, if you like.

Tandoori Chicken

The word tandoori refers to a method of cooking in a charcoal-fired clay oven called a tandoor. Warm naan bread and mango chutney may be offered with the chicken and rice.

Serves 4
30ml/2 tbsp vegetable oil
2 small onions, cut into wedges
2 garlic cloves, sliced
4 skinless chicken breast fillets, cut into cubes
100ml/3½fl oz/⅓ cup water
300g/11oz jar tandoori sauce
salt and ground black pepper
fresh coriander (cilantro) sprigs, to garnish

To serve
5ml/1 tsp ground turmeric
350g/12oz/1⅔ cups basmati rice

1 Heat the oil in a flameproof casserole. Add the onions and garlic, and cook for about 3 minutes, or until the onion is beginning to soften, stirring frequently.

2 Add the cubes of chicken fillet to the casserole and cook for about 6 minutes. Stir the water into the tandoori sauce and pour it over the chicken. Bring to the boil, then reduce the heat and simmer for 10 minutes, or until the chicken pieces are cooked through and tender and the tandoori sauce is slightly reduced and thickened.

3 Meanwhile, bring a large pan of lightly salted water to the boil, add the turmeric and rice and bring back to the boil. Stir once, reduce the heat to prevent the water from boiling over, and simmer the rice for 12 minutes, or according to the time suggested on the packet, until tender.

4 Drain the rice well and serve with the tandoori chicken on warmed individual serving plates, garnished with the sprigs of fresh coriander.

Cook's Tip
You will find jars of ready-made tandoori sauce in many large supermarkets and Asian stores.

Chicken Korma Energy 671kcal/2805kJ; Protein 52.2g; Carbohydrate 62.2g, of which sugars 2.1g; Fat 23.7g, of which saturates 6.1g; Cholesterol 136mg; Calcium 110mg; Fibre 1.6g; Sodium 137mg.
Tandoori Chicken Energy 592kcal/2479kJ; Protein 44g; Carbohydrate 77.5g, of which sugars 4.5g; Fat 11.4, of which saturates 1.1g; Cholesterol 105mg; Calcium 54mg; Fibre 0.4g; Sodium 826mg.

Thai Fried Chicken Rice

This substantial dish is based on Thai fragrant rice, which is sometimes known as jasmine rice. Chicken, red pepper and corn add colour and extra flavour.

Serves 4
475ml/16fl oz/2 cups water
50g/2oz/½ cup coconut
 milk powder
350g/12oz/1¾ cups Thai
 fragrant rice, rinsed
30ml/2 tbsp groundnut (peanut) oil
2 garlic cloves, chopped
1 small onion, finely chopped
2.5cm/1in piece of fresh root
 ginger, grated
225g/8oz skinless chicken breast
 fillets, cut into 1cm/½in dice
1 red (bell) pepper, seeded
 and sliced
115g/4oz/1 cup drained canned
 corn kernels
5ml/1 tsp chilli oil
5ml/1 tsp hot curry powder
2 eggs, beaten
salt
spring onion (scallion) shreds,
 to garnish

1 Pour the water into a pan and whisk in the coconut milk powder. Add the rice and bring to the boil. Lower the heat, cover and cook for 12 minutes or until the rice is tender and the liquid has been absorbed. Spread the rice on a baking sheet and leave until cold.

2 Heat the oil in a wok, add the garlic, onion and ginger and stir-fry over medium heat for 2 minutes.

3 Push the vegetables to the sides of the wok, add the chicken to the centre and stir-fry for 2 minutes. Add the rice and stir-fry over high heat for about 3 minutes more.

4 Stir in the sliced red pepper, corn, chilli oil and curry powder, with salt to taste. Toss over the heat for 1 minute. Stir in the beaten eggs and cook for 1 minute more. Garnish with spring onion shreds and serve immediately.

> **Cook's Tip**
> It is important that the rice is completely cold before being fried and the oil is very hot, or the rice will absorb too much oil.

Special Chicken Chow Mein with Chinese Sausage and Chilli

Lap cheong is a spicy Chinese sausage.

Serves 4–6
450g/1lb egg noodles
45ml/3 tbsp vegetable oil
2 garlic cloves, sliced
5ml/1 tsp chopped fresh root ginger
2 fresh red chillies, seeded
 and chopped
2 lap cheong or spicy sausage,
 about 75g/3oz in total, rinsed
 and sliced
1 skinless chicken breast fillet,
 thinly sliced
16 uncooked tiger prawns (jumbo
 shrimp), peeled, tails left intact,
 and deveined
115g/4oz/2 cups green beans
225g/8oz/1 cup beansprouts
small bunch garlic chives,
 about 50g/2oz
30ml/2 tbsp soy sauce
15ml/1 tbsp oyster sauce
15ml/1 tbsp sesame oil
salt and ground black pepper
2 shredded spring onions
 (scallions) and fresh coriander
 (cilantro) leaves, to garnish

1 Cook the noodles in a large pan of boiling water, according to the instructions on the packet. Drain well.

2 Heat 15ml/1 tbsp of the oil in a wok or large frying pan. Add the garlic, ginger and chillies and stir-fry for about 2 minutes. Add the lap cheong or spicy sausage, chicken, prawns and beans. Stir-fry over high heat for a further 2 minutes, or until the chicken and prawns are cooked through. Transfer the mixture to a bowl, then set aside.

3 Heat the rest of the oil in the wok. Toss in the beansprouts and garlic chives and stir-fry for 1–2 minutes. Add the drained noodles and toss over the heat to mix. Season with the soy sauce, oyster sauce and salt and pepper to taste.

4 Return the prawn mixture to the wok. Mix well with the noodles and toss until heated through.

5 Stir the sesame oil into the noodles. Spoon into a warmed bowl and serve immediately, garnished with the spring onions and coriander leaves.

Chow Mein Energy 624kcal/2631kj; Protein 29.3g; Carbohydrate 84.5g; of which sugars 4.6g; Fat 21.2g; of which saturates 4.2g; Cholesterol 107mg; Calcium 76mg; Fibre 4.8g; Sodium 808mg.
Thai Fried Rice Energy 508kcal/2127kj; Protein 24.7g; Carbohydrate 83.9g, of which sugars 8.7g; Fat 8g, of which saturates 1.6g; Cholesterol 135mg; Calcium 57mg; Fibre 1.3g; Sodium 204mg.

Thai Chicken Curry

This flavourful and fragrant, creamy curry is quite easy to make.

Serves 6

400ml/14oz can unsweetened
   coconut milk
6 skinless chicken breast fillets,
   finely sliced
225g/8oz can bamboo shoots,
   drained and sliced
30ml/2 tbsp fish sauce
15ml/1 tbsp soft light brown sugar
cooked jasmine rice, to serve

For the green curry paste
4 fresh green chillies, seeded

1 lemon grass stalk, sliced
1 small onion, sliced
3 garlic cloves
1cm/½in piece galangal or
   fresh root ginger, peeled
grated rind of ½ lime
5ml/1 tsp coriander seeds
5ml/1 tsp cumin seeds
2.5ml/½tsp fish sauce

To garnish
1 fresh red chilli, seeded and cut
   into fine strips
finely pared rind of ½ lime,
   finely shredded
fresh Thai purple basil or
   coriander (cilantro), chopped

1 First make the green curry paste: place all the paste ingredients in a food processor or blender and process to a thick paste. Set aside.

2 Bring half the coconut milk to the boil in a large frying pan, then reduce the heat and simmer for about 5 minutes, or until reduced by half. Stir in the green curry paste and simmer for a further 5 minutes.

3 Add the finely sliced chicken breast fillets to the pan with the remaining coconut milk, bamboo shoots, fish sauce and sugar. Stir well to combine all the ingredients.

4 Bring the curry back to simmering point, then simmer gently for about 10 minutes, or until the chicken slices are cooked through. The mixture will look grainy or curdled during cooking; this is quite normal.

5 Spoon the curry and rice into warmed serving bowls, garnish with the chilli strips, shredded lime rind, and basil or coriander, and serve immediately.

Stir-fried Chicken with Pepper and Cashews

Although it is not native to South-east Asia, the cashew tree is highly prized in Thailand and the classic partnership of these slightly sweet nuts with chicken is immensely popular both in Thailand and abroad.

Serves 4–6
450g/1lb chicken breast fillets
1 red (bell) pepper

2 garlic cloves
4 dried red chillies
30ml/2 tbsp vegetable oil
30ml/2 tbsp oyster sauce
15ml/1 tbsp soy sauce
pinch of sugar
1 bunch spring onions (scallions),
   cut into 5cm/2in lengths
175g/6oz/1½ cups cashew
   nuts, roasted
coriander (cilantro) leaves,
   to garnish

1 Remove and discard the skin from the chicken breasts and trim off any excess fat. With a sharp knife, cut the chicken into bitesize pieces and set aside.

2 Halve the red pepper, scrape out the seeds and membranes and discard, then cut the flesh into 2cm/¾in dice. Peel and thinly slice the garlic and chop the dried red chillies.

3 Preheat a wok, and then heat the oil. The best way to do this is to drizzle the oil around the inner rim, so that it runs down and coats the entire wok.

4 Add the garlic and dried chillies to the wok and stir-fry over medium heat until golden. Do not let the garlic burn, otherwise it will taste bitter.

5 Add the chicken to the wok and stir-fry until it is cooked through, then add the red pepper. If the mixture is very dry, add a little water.

6 Stir in the oyster sauce, soy sauce and sugar. Add the spring onions and cashew nuts. Stir-fry for 1–2 minutes more, until heated through. Spoon into a warm dish and serve immediately, garnished with the coriander leaves.

Thai Chicken Curry Energy 236kcal/991kJ; Protein 33.8g; Carbohydrate 7.2g, of which sugars 5.9g; Fat 8.3g, of which saturates 1.6g; Cholesterol 165mg; Calcium 149mg; Fibre 3.1g; Sodium 253mg.
Stir-fried Chicken Energy 458kcal/1909kJ; Protein 37.1g; Carbohydrate 17.7g, of which sugars 17.6g; Fat 7.1g; of which saturates 1.2g; Cholesterol 79mg; Calcium 26mg; Fibre 0g; Sodium 447mg.

Chicken Strips with Walnut and Bread Sauce

This chicken and walnut dish is popular in Turkey. It is ideal for lunch or supper, or would be lovely as part of a buffet spread.

Serves 6
1 chicken, trimmed of excess fat
3 slices of day-old white bread, crusts removed
150ml/¼ pint/⅔ cup milk
175g/6oz/1½ cup shelled walnuts
4–6 garlic cloves
salt and ground black pepper

For the stock
1 onion, quartered
1 carrot, chopped
2 celery sticks, chopped
4–6 cloves
4–6 allspice berries
4–6 black peppercorns
2 bay leaves
5ml/1 tsp coriander seeds
1 small bunch of fresh flat leaf parsley, stalks bruised and tied together

For the garnish
30ml/2 tbsp butter
5ml/1 tsp Turkish red pepper or paprika
a few fresh coriander (cilantro) leaves

1 Put the chicken into a deep pan with all the ingredients for the stock. Add water to just cover the chicken and bring to the boil. Lower the heat, cover and simmer for about 1 hour.

2 Remove the chicken from the pan and boil the stock with the lid off for about 15 minutes until reduced, then strain and season. When the chicken has cooled a little, discard the skin and tear the flesh into thin strips. Put them into a large bowl.

3 In a shallow dish, soak the bread in the milk for a few minutes until the milk is absorbed. Using a mortar and pestle, pound the walnuts and the garlic to a paste. Beat in the bread, then add to the chicken mixture. Beat in spoonfuls of the warm stock to bind the mixture until it is light and creamy.

4 Spoon the mixture into a mound in a serving dish. Melt the butter and stir in the red pepper or paprika, then pour it in a cross shape over the mound. Garnish with coriander leaves.

Pot-roasted Chicken with Preserved Lemons

Roasting chicken and potatoes in this way gives an interesting variety of textures. The chicken and potatoes on the top crisp up, while underneath they stay soft and juicy. Serve with steamed carrots or curly kale.

Serves 4–6
30ml/2 tbsp olive oil
675g/1½lb potatoes, unpeeled and cut into chunks
6–8 pieces of preserved lemon
corn-fed chicken, about 1.3kg/3lb, jointed
salt and ground black pepper

1 Preheat the oven to 190°C/375°F/Gas 5. Drizzle the olive oil into the bottom of a roasting pan that is large enough to hold all the ingredients.

2 Spread the chunks of potato in a single layer in the pan and tuck in the pieces of preserved lemon.

3 Pour about 1cm/½in of cold water into the roasting pan. Arrange the chicken pieces on top and season with plenty of salt and ground black pepper.

4 Place the pan in the preheated oven and roast for about 45 minutes to 1 hour, or until the chicken is cooked through. The cooking time will depend on the size of the chicken pieces.

5 Leave the chicken to rest for 5 minutes before serving with the potatoes accompanied by carrots and curly kale, if you like.

Cook's Tip
It is important to ensure that the chicken is thoroughly cooked through. To check, insert a skewer or knife into the thickest part of the chicken joints – usually the thigh pieces. The juices that emerge should run clear with no hint of pink. If the juices have a pinkish tinge, then return the chicken to the oven and cook for a further 5 minutes before checking again.

Chicken Strips Energy 222kcal/937kJ; Protein 34.1g; Carbohydrate 7.6g, of which sugars 1.6g; Fat 6.4g, of which saturates 3.3g; Cholesterol 105mg; Calcium 53mg; Fibre 0.2g; Sodium 324mg.
Pot-roasted Chicken Energy 536kcal/2233kJ; Protein 28.3g; Carbohydrate 26.8g, of which sugars 2.2g; Fat 35.7g, of which saturates 8.4g; Cholesterol 133mg; Calcium 21mg; Fibre 1.7g; Sodium 123mg.

Roast Chicken with Ginger, Garlic and Cinnamon

This dish, with its blend of spices and sweet fruit, is inspired by Moroccan flavours. Serve with couscous, mixed with a handful of cooked chickpeas.

Serves 4
1–1.6kg/2¼–3½lb chicken
115–130g/4–4½oz fresh root ginger, grated
6–8 garlic cloves, roughly chopped
juice of 1 lemon
about 30ml/2 tbsp olive oil
2–3 large pinches of ground cinnamon
500g/1¼lb seedless red and green grapes
5–7 shallots, chopped
about 250ml/8fl oz/1 cup chicken stock
salt and ground black pepper

1 Rub the chicken with half of the ginger, the garlic, half the lemon juice, the olive oil, cinnamon, salt and plenty of pepper. Leave to marinate. Cut half the grapes in half.

2 Preheat the oven to 180°C/350°F/Gas 4. Heat a heavy frying pan or flameproof casserole until hot. Remove the chicken from the marinade, add to the pan and cook until browned on all sides. Add a little extra oil if necessary.

3 Put some of the shallots into the chicken cavity with the garlic and ginger from the marinade and as many of the whole grapes as will fit inside. Roast in the oven for 40–60 minutes, or until the chicken is tender.

4 Remove the chicken from the pan and cover. Pour off any oil from the pan, reserving the juices in the pan. Add the remaining shallots to the pan and cook for about 5 minutes until softened.

5 Add half of the halved grapes, the remaining ginger, the stock and any juices from the roast chicken and cook over medium-high heat until the grapes have cooked down to a thick sauce. Season with salt, ground black pepper and the remaining lemon juice to taste. Strain the sauce if you prefer to remove the grape skins. Carve the chicken and serve on a warmed serving dish, surrounded by the sauce and the reserved grapes.

Roast Chicken with Leek, Laver and Lemon Stuffing

Leek, lemon and laver (a type of seaweed) complement each other beautifully to make a light stuffing that goes perfectly with chicken.

Serves 4–6
1.3–1.8kg/3–4lb oven-ready chicken
1 small onion, quartered
½ lemon, roughly chopped
2 garlic cloves, halved
olive oil or melted butter

For the stuffing
30ml/2 tbsp olive oil
2 rindless bacon rashers (slices), finely chopped
1 small leek, thinly sliced
1 garlic clove, crushed or finely chopped
30ml/2 tbsp laverbread
150g/5½oz/1¼ cups fresh breadcrumbs
finely grated rind and juice of ½ lemon
salt and ground black pepper

1 To make the stuffing, put the oil and bacon into a pan and cook over medium heat, stirring occasionally, for 3 minutes. Add the leek and garlic and cook for 3–5 minutes until soft. Remove from the heat and stir in the laverbread, breadcrumbs, lemon rind and juice, and seasoning. Leave to cool.

2 Preheat the oven to 200°C/400°F/Gas 6. Rinse the chicken inside and out, and then pat dry with kitchen paper. Spoon the stuffing into the neck cavity of the chicken and fold the skin over and under. Any excess stuffing can be put under the breast skin – loosen it carefully by sliding your fingers underneath.

3 Put the onion, lemon and garlic into the main cavity of the chicken. Sit the bird in a roasting pan and brush it all over with olive oil or melted butter. Cover the breasts with a piece of foil.

4 Roast for about 1½ hours, or until the chicken is cooked through (insert a sharp knife in the thick part of the thigh, the juices should run clear, not pink). Remove the foil for the final 30 minutes of cooking to allow the skin to brown and crisp.

5 Leave to rest for 15–20 minutes before carving. Reheat the pan juices and serve them spooned over the chicken.

Chicken with Leek Energy 486kcal/2027kJ; Protein 33.4g; Carbohydrate 22.3g, of which sugars 1.2g; Fat 29.7g, of which saturates 8.1g; Cholesterol 154mg; Calcium 54mg; Fibre 1g; Sodium 461mg.
Chicken with Ginger Energy 595kcal/2489kJ; Protein 32.4g; Carbohydrate 48g, of which sugars 46.8g; Fat 31.7g, of which saturates 8.3g; Cholesterol 160mg; Calcium 64mg; Fibre 2.5g; Sodium 138mg.

Chicken with Herb Stuffing

Nothing beats a traditional roast chicken dinner.

Serves 6

1.8kg/4lb large chicken, with
  giblets and neck if possible
1 small onion, sliced
1 small carrot, sliced
small bunch of parsley and thyme
15g/½oz/1 tbsp butter
30ml/2 tbsp oil
6 rashers (strips) bacon
15ml/1 tbsp plain (all-purpose) flour
salt and ground black pepper

For the stuffing

1 onion, finely chopped
50g/2oz/¼ cup butter
150g/5oz/2½ cups fresh
  white breadcrumbs
15ml/1 tbsp fresh chopped parsley
15ml/1 tbsp fresh chopped mixed
  herbs, such as thyme, marjoram
  and chives
grated rind and juice of ½ lemon
1 small (US medium) egg,
  lightly beaten

1 Remove the giblets from the chicken and set the liver aside to use in the gravy. Put the giblets and neck into a pan with the onion, carrot, parsley, thyme and season. Add cold water to cover, bring to the boil and simmer for 1 hour. Strain the stock and discard the giblets. Preheat the oven to 200°C/400°F/Gas 6.

2 For the stuffing, cook the onion in butter in a pan over low heat until soft. Remove from the heat and add the breadcrumbs, herbs and lemon rind. Mix in the lemon juice and egg and season.

3 Loosely pack the stuffing into the neck cavity and secure. Spread the breast with butter, pour the oil into a roasting pan and lay in the bird. Place the bacon over the top of the bird.

4 Weigh the stuffed chicken and allow 20 minutes per 450g/1lb and 20 minutes over. After 20 minutes in the oven, reduce to 180°C/350°F/Gas 4. Place on a serving dish and rest for 10 minutes.

5 For the gravy, pour off the excess fat from the pan, chop and add the liver and cook for 1 minute. Sprinkle in enough flour to absorb the fat and add a little giblet stock. Bring to the boil, adding more stock until the consistency is right. Season to taste.

6 Carve the chicken and serve with the herb stuffing and gravy.

Roast Chicken with Sweet Potatoes

This chicken is delicately flavoured with lime, garlic, turmeric and coriander.

Serves 4

4 garlic cloves, 2 finely chopped
  and 2 bruised but left whole
small bunch coriander (cilantro),
  with roots, coarsely chopped
10ml/2 tsp salt
5ml/1 tsp ground turmeric

5cm/2in piece fresh turmeric
1.5kg/3¼lb roasting chicken
1 lime, cut in half
4 medium/large sweet potatoes,
  peeled and cut into wedges
300ml/½ pint/1¼ cups chicken
  or vegetable stock
30ml/2 tbsp soy sauce
salt and ground black pepper

1 Preheat the oven to 190°C/375°F/Gas 5. Calculate the cooking time for the chicken: allow 20 minutes per 500g/1¼lb, plus 20 minutes. Using a mortar and pestle or food processor, grind the chopped garlic, coriander, salt and turmeric to a paste.

2 Place the chicken in a roasting pan and smear it with the herb paste. Squeeze the lime juice over and place the lime halves and garlic cloves in the cavity. Cover with foil and place in the oven.

3 Meanwhile, bring a pan of water to the boil and par-boil the sweet potatoes for 10–15 minutes, until just tender. Drain well and place them around the chicken in the pan. Baste with the cooking juices and season. Replace the foil and return to the oven. About 20 minutes before the end of cooking, remove the foil and baste the chicken. Turn the sweet potatoes over.

4 When the chicken is cooked, lift it out of the pan and drain out the juices collected inside the bird into the pan. Place on a chopping board, cover with foil and leave to rest before carving. Transfer the sweet potatoes to a serving dish and keep them hot in the oven while you make the gravy.

5 Pour away the oil from the roasting pan but keep the juices. Place on the stove and heat until bubbling. Pour in the stock and bring to the boil, stirring constantly. Stir in the soy sauce and check the seasoning before straining the gravy into a sauceboat. Serve with the carved meat and the sweet potatoes.

Chicken Energy 562kcal/2342kJ; Protein 40.9g; Carbohydrate 23.2g, of which sugars 2.7g; Fat 34.5g, of which saturates 11.9g; Cholesterol 216mg; Calcium 72mg; Fibre 1.5g; Sodium 381mg.
Roast Chicken Energy 529kcal/2201kJ; Protein 47.3g; Carbohydrate 8.7g, of which sugars 2.7g; Fat 34g, of which saturates 9.4g; Cholesterol 248mg; Calcium 26mg; Fibre 0.9g; Sodium 840mg.

Chicken with Gravy and Bread Sauce

This is a traditional dish which tastes wonderful and makes a perfect family meal.

Serves 4

50g/2oz/¼ cup butter
I onion, chopped
75g/3oz/1½ cups fresh
  white breadcrumbs
grated rind of I lemon
30ml/2 tbsp chopped fresh parsley
30ml/2 tbsp chopped
  fresh tarragon
I egg yolk
1.5kg/3¼lb oven-ready chicken
175g/6oz rindless streaky (fatty)
  bacon rashers (strips)
salt and ground black pepper

For the bread sauce
I onion, studded with 6 cloves
I bay leaf
300ml/½ pint/1¼ cups milk
150ml/¼ pint/⅔ cup single
  (light) cream
115g/4oz/2 cups fresh
  white breadcrumbs
knob of butter

For the gravy
10ml/2 tsp plain (all-purpose)
  flour
300ml/½ pint/1¼ cups
  well-flavoured chicken stock
dash of Madeira or sherry

1 Preheat the oven to 200°C/400°F/Gas 6. First make the stuffing. Melt half the butter in a pan and fry the onion for about 5 minutes, or until softened but not coloured.

2 Remove the pan from the heat and add the breadcrumbs, lemon rind, parsley and half the chopped tarragon. Season, then mix in the egg yolk to bind the ingredients into a moist stuffing.

3 Fill the neck end of the chicken with stuffing, then truss the chicken neatly and weigh it. To calculate the cooking time, allow 20 minutes per 450g/1lb, plus 20 minutes. Put the chicken in a roasting pan and season well. Beat together the remaining butter and tarragon, then smear this over the bird.

4 Lay the bacon rashers over the top of the chicken (this helps stop the light breast meat from drying out) and roast for the calculated time. Baste the bird every 30 minutes during cooking and cover with buttered foil if the bacon begins to overbrown.

5 Meanwhile, make the bread sauce. Put the clove-studded onion, bay leaf and milk in a small, heavy pan and bring slowly to the boil. Remove from the heat and leave the milk to stand for 30 minutes so the flavours mingle.

6 Strain the milk into a clean pan (discard the other ingredients) and add the cream and breadcrumbs. Bring to the boil, stirring constantly, then simmer for 5 minutes. Keep warm while you make the gravy and carve the chicken, then stir in the butter and seasoning just before serving. Transfer the cooked chicken to a serving dish, cover with foil and leave for 10 minutes.

7 To make the gravy, pour off all but 15ml/1 tbsp fat from the roasting pan. Place the pan on the stove and stir in the flour. Cook for 1 minute, then gradually add the stock and Madeira or sherry. Bring to the boil, stirring, then simmer for 3 minutes until thickened. Add seasoning and strain into a warm sauceboat.

8 Carve the chicken and serve immediately with the stuffing, gravy and hot bread sauce.

Chicken Livers in Sherry

This is a very popular, traditional Spanish dish. It makes a delicious little tapas and is particularly good eaten with bread or on toast. For a more elegant presentation, serve piled on top of little rice tortitas.

Serves 4

225g/8oz chicken livers, thawed
  if frozen, trimmed
15ml/1 tbsp olive oil
I small onion, finely chopped
2 small garlic cloves,
  finely chopped
5ml/1 tsp fresh thyme leaves
30ml/2 tbsp sweet oloroso sherry
30ml/2 tbsp crème fraîche or
  double (heavy) cream
2.5ml/½ tsp paprika
salt and ground black pepper
fresh thyme, to garnish

1 Carefully trim the chicken livers, removing and discarding any green spots and sinews. Set aside the livers until you are ready to cook them.

2 Heat the olive oil in a large, heavy frying pan and fry the onion and garlic, stirring constantly, for about 4–6 minutes until the onions begin to soften and turn translucent. Ensure that the garlic does not burn otherwise it will impart a bitter flavour to the dish.

3 Add the chicken livers to the pan along with the thyme and cook, stirring occasionally, for a further 3 minutes.

4 Stir the sherry into the livers, add the crème fraîche and cook briefly until the mixture starts to bubble. Season with salt, ground black pepper and paprika, garnish with fresh thyme and serve immediately.

> **Cook's Tip**
> If you can't find any fresh chicken livers, then look for frozen ones in the supermarket, but ensure they are fully defrosted before using.

Chicken Energy 673kcal/2814kJ; Protein 41.8g; Carbohydrate 46.3g, of which sugars 7.9g; Fat 35.4g, of which saturates 13.3g; Cholesterol 246mg; Calcium 215mg; Fibre 1.7g; Sodium 537mg.
Chicken Livers Energy 131kcal/545kJ; Protein 10.4g; Carbohydrate 2.1g, of which sugars 1.5g; Fat 8.2g, of which saturates 3.3g; Cholesterol 224mg; Calcium 14mg; Fibre 0.2g; Sodium 46mg.

Quail Hotpot with Merlot and Winter Vegetables

Sweet, slightly tangy grapes are a classic ingredient for accompanying quail, and here they bring a fresh, fruity flavour to the rich red wine sauce. Creamy mashed potatoes are an excellent accompaniment for this dish.

Serves 4

4 quails
150g/5oz seedless red grapes
50g/2oz/¼ cup butter
4 shallots, halved
175g/6oz baby carrots, scrubbed
175g/6oz baby turnips
450ml/¾ pint/scant 2 cups
   Merlot or other red wine
salt and ground black pepper
fresh flat leaf parsley, to garnish

For the croûtes

4 slices white bread,
   crusts removed
60ml/4 tbsp olive oil

1 Preheat the oven to 220°C/425°F/Gas 7. Season the birds and stuff with grapes. Melt the butter in a flameproof casserole and brown the birds. Lift out and set aside.

2 Add the shallots, carrots and turnips to the fat remaining in the casserole and cook until they are just beginning to colour. Replace the quails, breast side down, and pour in the Merlot or other red wine. Cover the casserole and transfer it to the oven. Cook for about 30 minutes, or until the quails are tender.

3 Meanwhile, make the croûtes. Use a 10cm/4in plain cutter to stamp out rounds from the bread. Heat the oil in a frying pan and cook the bread until golden on both sides. Drain on kitchen paper and keep warm.

4 Place the croûtes on plates. Use a draining spoon to set a quail on each croûte. Arrange the vegetables around the quails, cover and keep hot.

5 Boil the cooking juices hard until reduced to syrupy consistency. Skim off as much butter as possible, then season the sauce to taste. Drizzle the sauce over the quails and garnish with parsley, then serve immediately.

Hen in a Pot with Parsley Sauce

Although hard to find nowadays, a boiling fowl is ideal in this recipe. A large chicken could replace the boiling fowl. Serve with potatoes and cabbage.

Serves 6

1.6–1.8kg/3½–4lb boiling fowl
   (stewing chicken)
½ lemon, sliced
small bunch of parsley and thyme
675g/1½lb carrots, cut into chunks
12 shallots, left whole
salt and ground pepper
fresh parsley sprigs, to garnish

For the sauce

50g/2oz/¼ cup butter
50g/2oz/½ cup plain
   (all-purpose) flour
15ml/1 tbsp lemon juice
60ml/4 tbsp finely chopped
   fresh parsley
150ml/¼ pint/⅔ cup milk

1 Put the boiling fowl into a large pan with enough water to cover. Add the lemon, parsley and thyme, and season well. Cover the fowl and bring to the boil, then reduce the heat and simmer over a gentle heat for 2½ hours, turning several times during cooking.

2 Add the carrots and whole onions to the pot and cook for 30–40 minutes, or until the fowl and the vegetables are tender.

3 Using a slotted spoon, lift the fowl on to a warmed serving dish, arrange the vegetables around it and keep warm. Remove the herbs and lemon slices from the cooking liquid and discard.

4 Bring the liquid back to the boil and boil it, uncovered, to reduce the liquid by about a third. Strain and leave to settle for 1–2 minutes, then skim the fat off the surface.

5 Melt the butter in a pan, add the flour and cook, stirring, for 1 minute. Gradually stir in the stock and bring to the boil. Add the lemon juice, parsley and milk. Adjust the seasoning and simmer the sauce for another 1–2 minutes.

6 To serve, pour a little of the sauce over the fowl and the vegetables, then garnish with sprigs of fresh parsley and take to the table for carving. Pour the remaining sauce into a sauceboat.

Quail Hotpot Energy 506kcal/2118kJ; Protein 44.6g; Carbohydrate 19.7g, of which sugars 6.8g; Fat 19.9g, of which saturates 3.7g; Cholesterol 0mg; Calcium 127mg; Fibre 2.8g; Sodium 280mg.
Hen in a Pot Energy 509kcal/2114kJ; Protein 36.2g; Carbohydrate 20.1g, of which sugars 12.2g; Fat 31.9g, of which saturates 11.4g; Cholesterol 195mg; Calcium 109mg; Fibre 4g; Sodium 214mg.

Chargrilled Quails in a Chilli and Pomegranate Marinade

This is a simple and tasty way of serving small birds, such as quails, poussins or grouse. The sharp marinade tenderizes the meat, as well as enhancing its flavour. Served straight off the charcoal grill with warm flat bread and a crunchy salad, they are delicious for lunch or supper, or you may like to include them in a barbecue spread.

Serves 4

4 quails, cleaned and boned
juice of 4 pomegranates
juice of 1 lemon
30ml/2 tbsp olive oil
5–10ml/1–2 tsp Turkish red pepper,
   or 5ml/1 tsp chilli powder
30–45ml/2–3 tbsp thick and
   creamy natural (plain) yogurt
salt
1 bunch of fresh flat leaf parsley
seeds of $^1/_2$ pomegranate,
   to garnish

1 Soak eight wooden skewers in hot water for about 30 minutes, then drain. Thread one skewer through the wings of each bird and a second skewer through the legs to keep them together.

2 Place the skewered birds in a wide, shallow dish. Beat the pomegranate and lemon juice with the oil and red pepper or chilli powder, pour over the quails and rub it into the skin. Cover with foil and leave to marinate in the refrigerator for 2–3 hours, turning the birds over from time to time.

3 Get the barbecue ready for cooking. Lift the birds out of the marinade and pour what is left of it into a bowl. Beat the yogurt into the leftover marinade and add a little salt.

4 Brush some of the yogurt mixture over the birds and place them on the prepared barbecue.

5 Cook for 4–5 minutes on each side, brushing with the yogurt as they cook to form a crust.

6 Chop some of the parsley and lay the rest on a serving dish. Place the cooked quails on the parsley and garnish with the pomegranate seeds and the chopped parsley. Serve hot.

Guinea Fowl with Cream Sauce

Served with creamy sweet potato mash and whole baby leeks, guinea fowl is superb with a rich, creamy whisky sauce.

Serves 4

2 guinea fowl, each weighing
   about 1kg/2$^1/_4$lb

90ml/6 tbsp whisky
150ml/$^1/_4$ pint/$^2/_3$ cup well-
   flavoured chicken stock
150ml/$^1/_4$ pint/$^2/_3$ cup double
   (heavy) cream
20 baby leeks
salt and ground black pepper
fresh thyme sprigs, to garnish
mashed sweet potatoes, to serve

1 Preheat the oven to 200°C/400°F/Gas 6. Brown the guinea fowl on all sides in a roasting pan on the stove, then turn it breast uppermost and transfer the pan to the oven. Roast for about 1 hour, until the guinea fowl are golden and cooked through. Transfer the guinea fowl to a warmed serving dish, cover with foil and keep warm.

2 Pour off the excess fat from the pan, then heat the juices on the stove and stir in the whisky. Bring to the boil and cook until reduced. Add the stock and cream and simmer again until reduced slightly. Strain and season to taste.

3 Meanwhile, trim the leeks so that they are roughly the same length as the guinea fowl breasts, then cook them whole in boiling salted water for about 3 minutes, or until tender but not too soft. Drain the leeks in a colander.

4 Carve the guinea fowl. To serve, arrange portions of mashed sweet potato on warmed serving plates, then add the carved guinea fowl and the leeks. Garnish with sprigs of fresh thyme, and season with plenty of ground black pepper. Spoon a little of the sauce over each portion and serve the rest separately.

> **Variation**
> If you dislike the flavour of whisky, then substitute brandy, Madeira or Marsala. Or, to make a non-alcoholic version, use freshly squeezed orange juice instead.

Chargrilled Quails Energy 288kcal/1207kJ; Protein 37.4g; Carbohydrate 5.8g, of which sugars 5.8g; Fat 13g, of which saturates 2.7g; Cholesterol 0mg; Calcium 84mg; Fibre 0.5g; Sodium 111mg.
Guinea Fowl Energy 854kcal/3568kJ; Protein 110.6g; Carbohydrate 0.6g, of which sugars 0.6g; Fat 41.7g, of which saturates 18g; Cholesterol 51mg; Calcium 159mg; Fibre 0g; Sodium 308mg.

Pheasant Cooked in Port with Mushrooms

This warming dish is delicious served with mashed root vegetables and shredded cabbage or leeks. Marinating the pheasant in port helps to moisten and tenderize the meat. If you prefer, marinate the bird in a full-bodied red wine and use button mushrooms.

Serves 4
2 pheasants, cut into portions
300ml/¹/₂ pint/1¹/₄ cups port
50g/2oz/¹/₄ cup butter
300g/11oz brown cap (cremini) mushrooms, halved if large
salt and ground black pepper

1 Place the pheasant in a bowl and pour over the port. Cover and marinate for 3–4 hours or overnight, turning occasionally.

2 Drain the meat thoroughly, reserving the marinade. Pat the portions dry on kitchen paper and season lightly with salt and pepper. Melt three-quarters of the butter in a frying pan and cook the pheasant portions on all sides for about 5 minutes, until deep golden. Drain well, transfer to a plate, then cook the mushrooms in the fat remaining in the pan for 3 minutes.

3 Return the pheasant to the pan and pour in the reserved marinade with 200ml/7fl oz/scant 1 cup water. Bring to the boil, reduce the heat and cover, then simmer gently for about 45 minutes, until the pheasant is tender.

4 Using a slotted spoon, carefully remove the pheasant portions and mushrooms from the frying pan and keep warm. Bring the cooking juices to the boil and boil vigorously for about 5 minutes, until they are reduced and slightly thickened.

5 Strain the juices through a fine sieve (strainer) and return them to the pan. Whisk in the remaining butter over gentle heat until it has melted. Season to taste with salt and ground black pepper, then pour the juices over the pheasant and mushrooms and serve immediately.

Jungle Curry of Guinea Fowl

This is a traditional curry from the northern region of Thailand. Ready-made curry paste is an excellent way to reduce the preparation time of this dish, and many versions are very good.

Serves 4
1 guinea fowl or similar game bird
15ml/1 tbsp vegetable oil
10ml/2 tsp green curry paste
15ml/1 tbsp Thai fish sauce
2.5cm/1in piece fresh galangal, peeled and finely chopped
15ml/1 tbsp fresh green peppercorns
3 kaffir lime leaves, torn
15ml/1 tbsp whisky
300ml/¹/₂ pint/1¹/₄ cups chicken stock
50g/2oz snake beans or yard-long beans, cut into 2.5cm/1in lengths (about ¹/₂ cup)
225g/8oz/3¹/₄ cups chestnut mushrooms, sliced
1 piece drained canned bamboo shoot, about 50g/2oz, shredded
5ml/1 tsp dried chilli flakes, to garnish (optional)

1 Cut up the guinea fowl, remove and discard the skin, then take all the meat off the bones. Chop the meat into bitesize pieces and set aside.

2 Heat the oil in a wok or frying pan and add the curry paste. Stir-fry over medium heat for 30 seconds, until the paste gives off its aroma.

3 Add the fish sauce and the guinea fowl meat and stir-fry until the meat is browned all over. Add the galangal, peppercorns, lime leaves and whisky, then pour in the stock.

4 Bring the mixture to the boil. Add the vegetables to the pan, return to a simmer and cook gently for 2–3 minutes, until they are just cooked. Spoon into a dish, sprinkle with chilli flakes, if you like, and serve immediately.

> **Cook's Tip**
> Fresh green peppercorns are simply unripe berries. They are sold on the stem and look rather like miniature Brussels sprout stalks. Look for them at Thai supermarkets.

Jungle Curry Energy 321kcal/1345kJ; Protein 42.2g; Carbohydrate 1.1g, of which sugars 0.7g; Fat 50.4g, of which saturates 12.8g; Cholesterol 240mg; Calcium 91mg; Fibre 1.5g; Sodium 305mg.
Pheasant in Port Energy 457kcal/1910kJ; Protein 46.2g; Carbohydrate 6.4g, of which sugars 4.5g; Fat 23.1g, of which saturates 6.1g; Cholesterol 9mg; Calcium 102mg; Fibre 2g; Sodium 483mg.

Pheasant and Wild Mushroom Ragoût

Pheasants make especially good eating when combined with smoky, aromatic wild mushrooms and a glass of rich port.

Serves 4

4 pheasant breast fillets, skinned
12 shallots, halved
2 garlic cloves, crushed
75g/3oz wild mushrooms, sliced
75ml/2½fl oz/⅓ cup port
150ml/¼ pint/⅔ cup
    chicken stock
sprigs of fresh parsley
    and thyme
1 bay leaf
grated rind of 1 lemon
200ml/7fl oz/scant 1 cup
    double (heavy) cream
oil, for frying
salt and ground black pepper

1 Dice and season the pheasant breast fillets. Heat a little oil in a heavy frying pan and cook the pheasant meat for 5–6 minutes, stirring frequently until evenly browned. Remove from the pan and set aside.

2 Add the shallots to the pan, fry quickly to colour them a little, then add the garlic and sliced mushrooms. Reduce the heat and cook gently for 5 minutes.

3 Pour the port and stock into the pan and add the herbs and lemon rind. Bring to the boil, then simmer, uncovered, until the sauce has reduced and thickened a little. When the shallots are nearly cooked add the cream, reduce to thicken, then return the meat to the pan. Allow to cook for a few minutes before serving.

> **Cook's Tip**
> Serve with pilaff rice: fry a chopped onion, stir in 2.5cm/1in cinnamon stick, 2.5ml/½ tsp crushed cumin seeds, 2 crushed cardamom pods, a bay leaf and 5ml/1 tsp turmeric. Add 225g/8oz/generous 1 cup long grain rice. Stir until well coated. Pour in 600ml/1 pint/2½ cups boiling water, cover, then simmer gently for 15 minutes. Transfer to a serving dish, cover with a dish towel and leave for 5 minutes.

Pigeons Cooked in Spiced Vinegar

This is a Spanish recipe using pigeon marinated in spiced vinegar and red wine. It works well with chicken thighs. Cabbage is a familiar partner to pigeon, but puréed celeriac also goes very well.

Serves 4

4 pigeons (US squabs), about
    225g/8oz each, cleaned
30ml/2 tbsp olive oil
1 onion, roughly chopped
225g/8oz/3 cups brown cap
    (cremini) mushrooms, sliced
plain (all-purpose) flour, for dusting
300ml/½ pint/1¼ cups beef or
    game stock
30ml/2 tbsp chopped fresh
    parsley
salt and ground black pepper
fresh flat leaf parsley, to garnish

For the marinade
15ml/1 tbsp olive oil
1 onion, chopped
1 carrot, chopped
1 celery stick, chopped
3 garlic cloves, sliced
6 allspice berries, bruised
2 bay leaves
8 black peppercorns, bruised
120ml/4fl oz/½ cup red
    wine vinegar
150ml/¼ pint/⅔ cup
    red wine

1 Starting a day before you want to eat the dish, combine all the ingredients for the marinade in a large dish. Add the pigeons and turn them in the marinade, then cover and chill for 12 hours, turning occasionally.

2 Preheat the oven to 150°C/300°F/Gas 2. Heat the oil in a large, flameproof casserole and cook the onion and mushrooms for about 5 minutes, until the onion has softened.

3 Meanwhile, remove the pigeons to a plate using a slotted spoon and strain the marinade into a bowl, then set both aside separately.

4 Sprinkle the flour on the pigeons and add them to the casserole, breast side down. Pour in the marinade and stock, and add the parsley and seasoning. Cover and cook for about 1½ hours or until tender.

5 Check the seasoning, then serve the pigeons on warmed plates with the sauce, garnished with fresh parsley.

Pheasant Energy 530kcal/2200kJ; Protein 34.1g; Carbohydrate 7.4g, of which sugars 5.9g; Fat 33g, of which saturates 20.2g; Cholesterol 69mg; Calcium 91mg; Fibre 1.1g; Sodium 114mg.
Pigeons Energy 361kcal/1502kJ; Protein 34.2g; Carbohydrate 4.2g, of which sugars 3.3g; Fat 20.3g, of which saturates 1.7g; Cholesterol 0mg; Calcium 57mg; Fibre 1.6g; Sodium 119mg.

Pan-fried Pheasant with Oatmeal and Cream Sauce

Rolled oats are often used for coating fish before pan-frying, but this treatment is equally good with tender poultry. Sweet, slightly tangy redcurrant jelly is used to bind the oatmeal to the tender pheasant breast fillets.

Serves 4

115g/4oz/generous 1 cup
  medium rolled oats
4 skinless pheasant breast fillets
45ml/3 tbsp redcurrant
  jelly, melted
50g/2oz/¼ cup butter
15ml/1 tbsp olive oil
45ml/3 tbsp wholegrain
  mustard
300ml/½ pint/1¼ cups double
  (heavy) cream
salt and ground black pepper

1 Place the medium rolled oats on a shallow plate and season with salt and ground black pepper.

2 Brush the skinned pheasant breast fillets with the melted redcurrant jelly, then turn them in the oats to coat evenly. Shake off any excess oats and set aside.

3 Heat the butter and oil in a frying pan until foaming. Add the pheasant breast fillets and cook over high heat, turning frequently, until they are golden brown on all sides.

4 Reduce the heat under the pan to medium and cook the pheasant fillets for a further 8–10 minutes, turning once or twice, until the meat is thoroughly cooked. Remove from the pan and keep warm while you make the sauce.

5 Add the mustard and cream to the frying pan, stirring to combine with the cooking juices from the pheasant fillets. Bring slowly to the boil, then simmer for 6–8 minutes over low heat, or until the sauce has thickened to a good consistency.

6 To serve, spoon the sauce on to four warmed serving plates. Slice each pheasant breast fillet into three, place on the sauce and serve, accompanied by seasonal greens, if you like.

Roast Pheasant

Pheasant contains very little fat, so it is must stay moist during cooking. A layer of bacon helps the meat to stay succulent.

Serves 2

1 hen pheasant
25g/1oz/2 tbsp butter
115g/4oz rindless streaky (fatty)
  bacon rashers (strips)
salt and ground black pepper
thinly cut chips (French fries),
  to serve
For the stuffing
25g/1oz/2 tbsp butter
1 leek, chopped
115g/4oz peeled, cooked
  chestnuts, coarsely chopped
30ml/2 tbsp chopped fresh flat
  leaf parsley

For the gravy
15ml/1 tbsp cornflour
  (cornstarch)
300ml/½ pint/1¼ cups well-
  flavoured chicken stock
50ml/2fl oz/¼ cup port

1 Preheat the oven to 190°C/375°F/Gas 5. Season the pheasant inside and out. Loosen and lift the skin covering the breast and rub the butter between the skin and flesh.

2 To make the stuffing, melt the butter in a pan and, when foaming, add the leek. Cook for 5 minutes, or until softened but not coloured. Remove the pan from the heat, and mix in the cooked, chopped chestnuts, parsley and seasoning to taste.

3 Spoon the stuffing into the body cavity of the pheasant and secure the opening with skewers. Arrange the bacon rashers in a lattice pattern over the breast. Place in a roasting pan. Roast the pheasant for 1–1½ hours, or until the juices run clear when the bird is pierced with a skewer in the thickest part of the leg.

4 Remove the pheasant from the oven. Cover with foil and leave to stand for 15 minutes. Meanwhile, heat the juices in the roasting pan on the stove and stir in the cornflour. Gradually pour in the stock and port, stirring constantly. Bring to the boil, then reduce the heat and simmer for 5 minutes until the gravy thickens. Strain into a sauceboat and keep warm.

5 Carve the pheasant, then serve the meat with the stuffing and gravy, accompanied by the chips.

Pan-fried Pheasant Energy 847kcal/3520kJ; Protein 37.1g; Carbohydrate 30.1g, of which sugars 9.1g; Fat 59g, of which saturates 35.1g; Cholesterol 129mg; Calcium 105mg; Fibre 2g; Sodium 205mg.
Roast Pheasant Energy 560kcal/2328kJ; Protein 45.2g; Carbohydrate 3.2g, of which sugars 1.7g; Fat 39.3g, of which saturates 20.1g; Cholesterol 75mg; Calcium 107mg; Fibre 0.1g; Sodium 501mg.

Roast Young Grouse

Rowan jelly goes very well with this meat. Young grouse can be identified by their pliable breastbone, legs and feet, and their claws will be sharp. The birds have very little fat so bacon is used here to protect the breasts during the initial roasting.

Serves 2
2 young grouse
6 rashers (strips) bacon

2 sprigs of rowanberries or
  ½ lemon, quartered, plus
  30ml/2 tbsp extra
  rowanberries (optional)
50g/2oz/¼ cup butter
150ml/¼ pint/⅔ cup
  red wine
150ml/¼ pint/⅔
  cup water
5ml/1 tsp rowan jelly
salt and ground black pepper

1 Preheat the oven to 200°C/400°F/Gas 6. Wipe the grouse with kitchen paper and place in a roasting pan. Lay the bacon over the breasts.

2 If you have rowanberries, place one sprig in the cavity of each grouse as well as half the butter. Otherwise put a lemon quarter and half the butter in each cavity.

3 Roast the grouse in the preheated oven for 10 minutes, then remove the bacon and pour in the wine. Return to the oven for 10 minutes.

4 Baste the birds with the juices and cook for a further 5 minutes. Remove the birds from the pan and keep warm.

5 Add the water and rowan jelly to the pan and simmer until the jelly melts. Strain into another pan, add the rowanberries, if using, and simmer until the sauce just begins to thicken. Season with salt and pepper, then serve alongside the grouse.

Cook's Tip
Serve grouse with the traditional accompaniments of bread sauce and thinly cut chips, if you like.

Grouse with Marsala and Orchard Fruit Stuffing

Tart apples, plums and pears combined with shallots and spice make a fabulous orchard fruit stuffing that perfectly complements the rich gamy flavour of grouse.

Serves 2
juice of ½ lemon
2 young grouse
50g/2oz/¼ cup butter
4 Swiss chard leaves

50ml/2fl oz/¼ cup Marsala
salt and ground black pepper

For the stuffing
2 shallots, finely chopped
1 cooking apple, peeled, cored
  and chopped
1 pear, peeled, cored and chopped
2 plums, halved, stoned (pitted)
  and chopped
large pinch of mixed spice (apple
  pie spice)

1 Sprinkle the lemon juice over the grouse and season well. Melt half the butter in a large flameproof casserole, add the grouse and cook for 10 minutes, turning occasionally. Use tongs to remove the grouse from the casserole and set aside.

2 For the stuffing, add the shallots to the fat in the casserole and cook until softened. Add the apple, pear, plums and spice, and cook for 5 minutes. Remove the casserole from the heat and spoon the hot fruit mixture into the body cavities of the birds.

3 Truss the birds neatly with string. Smear the remaining butter over the birds and wrap them in the chard leaves, then replace them in the casserole.

4 Pour in the Marsala and heat until simmering. Cover tightly and simmer for 20 minutes, or until the birds are tender. Leave to rest in a warm place for about 10 minutes before serving.

Cook's Tip
There isn't a lot of liquid in the casserole for cooking the birds – they are steamed rather than boiled, so it is very important that the casserole is heavy with a tight lid.

Roast Young Grouse Energy 423kcal/1763kJ; Protein 43.8g; Carbohydrate 1.5g, of which sugars 1.5g; Fat 24g, of which saturates 10.8g; Cholesterol 51mg; Calcium 43mg; Fibre 0g; Sodium 902mg.
Grouse Energy 521kcal/2191kJ; Protein 76.5g; Carbohydrate 17.5g, of which sugars 17.3g; Fat 13.5g, of which saturates 3g; Cholesterol 0mg; Calcium 302mg; Fibre 5.8g; Sodium 404mg.

Turkey Patties

Minced turkey makes deliciously light patties, which are ideal for summer meals. The recipe is a flavourful variation on a classic burger and they can also be made using minced lamb, pork or beef.

Serves 6
675g/1½lb minced (ground) turkey
1 small red onion, finely chopped
grated rind and juice of 1 lime
small handful of fresh thyme leaves
flour, for dusting
15–30ml/1–2 tbsp olive oil
salt and ground black pepper

1 Mix together the turkey, onion, lime rind and juice, thyme and seasoning. Cover and chill for up to 4 hours to allow the flavours to mingle.

2 Divide the turkey mixture into six equal portions. Shape into round patties with lightly floured hands.

3 Preheat a griddle (grill) pan. Brush the patties with oil, then place them on the pan and cook on one side for 10–12 minutes. Turn the patties over with a metal spatula, brush with more oil and cook for a further 10–12 minutes on the second side, or until cooked through. Serve immediately.

> **Cook's Tip**
> Serve the patties in split and toasted buns or pieces of crusty bread, with chutney, salad leaves and chunky fries.

> **Variations**
> • Minced (ground) chicken or minced pork can be used instead of turkey in these burgers.
> • You can also try chopped oregano, parsley or basil in place of the thyme, and lemon rind instead of lime.

Turkey Croquettes

Enjoy these crisp patties of smoked turkey mixed with potato and spring onions and rolled in breadcrumbs.

115g/4oz/2 cups fresh white breadcrumbs
vegetable oil, for deep frying
salt and ground black pepper

Serves 4
450g/1lb potatoes, diced
3 eggs
30ml/2 tbsp milk
175g/6oz smoked turkey rashers (strips), finely chopped
2 spring onions (scallions), finely sliced

For the sauce
15ml/1 tbsp olive oil
1 onion, finely chopped
400g/14oz can tomatoes, drained
30ml/2 tbsp tomato purée (paste)
15ml/1 tbsp chopped fresh parsley

1 Boil the potatoes for 20 minutes or until tender. Drain and return the pan to low heat to evaporate the excess water.

2 Mash the potatoes with two eggs and the milk. Season well with salt and black pepper. Stir in the turkey and spring onions. Chill for 1 hour.

3 Meanwhile, to make the sauce, heat the oil in a frying pan and fry the onion for 5 minutes until soft. Add the tomatoes and purée, stir and simmer for 10 minutes. Stir in the parsley, season with salt and pepper and keep warm until needed.

4 Remove the potato mixture from the refrigerator and divide into eight pieces. Shape each piece into a sausage shape, and dip in the remaining beaten egg, and then the breadcrumbs.

5 Heat the oil in a pan or deep-fat fryer to 175°C/330°F and deep-fry the croquettes for 5 minutes, or until golden and crisp. Serve with the sauce.

> **Cook's Tip**
> Test the oil temperature by dropping a cube of bread into it. If it sinks, rises and sizzles in 10 seconds, the oil is ready to use.

Turkey Croquettes Energy 404kcal/1698kJ; Protein 19.4g; Carbohydrate 47g, of which sugars 7.7g; Fat 16.7g, of which saturates 2.4g; Cholesterol 73mg; Calcium 93mg; Fibre 3.3g; Sodium 315mg.
Turkey Patties Energy 141kcal/596kJ; Protein 24.8g; Carbohydrate 0.8g, of which sugars 0.60g; Fat 4.4g, of which saturates 1.1g; Cholesterol 69mg; Calcium 15mg; Fibre 0.2g; Sodium 62mg.

Roast Turkey with Fruit Stuffing

The sausagemeat inside this bird is black morcilla, and prunes and raisins make it even more sweet and fruity. The sauce is flavoured with sweet grape juice and an intriguing splash of anis.

Serves 8
3kg/6½lb bronze or black turkey, weighed without the giblets
60ml/4 tbsp oil
200g/7oz rashers (strips) streaky (fatty) bacon

For the stuffing
45ml/3 tbsp olive oil
1 onion, chopped
2 garlic cloves, finely chopped
115g/4oz fatty bacon lardons
150g/5oz morcilla or black pudding (blood sausage), diced
1 turkey liver, diced
50g/2oz½ cup Muscatel raisins, soaked in 45ml/3 tbsp anis spirit, such as Ricard, and chopped

115g/4oz ready-to-eat pitted prunes, chopped
50g/2oz½ cup almonds, chopped
1.5ml/¼ tsp dried thyme
finely grated rind of 1 lemon
freshly grated nutmeg
60ml/4 tbsp chopped fresh parsley
1 large (US extra large) egg, beaten
60ml/4 tbsp cooked rice or stale breadcrumbs
salt and ground black pepper

For the sauce
45ml/3 tbsp plain (all-purpose) flour
350ml/12fl oz/1½ cups turkey giblet stock, warmed
350ml/12fl oz/1½ cups red grape juice
30ml/2 tbsp anis spirit, such as Ricard
salt and ground black pepper

1 First make the stuffing. Heat 30ml/2 tbsp olive oil in a pan and fry the onion, garlic and baconfor 3–4 minutes. Transfer to a large bowl. Add the remaining oil to the pan and fry the morcilla or black pudding for 3–4 minutes and the liver for 2–3 minutes.

2 Add the raisins, prunes, almonds, thyme, lemon rind, nutmeg, seasoning and parsley to the pan. Stir in the egg and rice or breadcrumbs.

3 About 3 hours before serving, preheat the oven, with a low shelf, to 200°C/400°F/Gas 6. Remove the turkey's wishbone, running fingernails up the two sides of the neck to find it. Just nick it out. Season the turkey inside with salt and black pepper, stuff and retruss it. Season outside. Keep at room temperature.

4 Heat a roasting pan in the oven with 60ml/4 tbsp oil. Put in the turkey and baste the outside. Lay the bacon over the breast and legs. Reduce the oven temperature to 180°C/350°F/Gas 4 and roast for 2¼–2½ hours, basting once. To test, insert a skewer into the thickest part of the inside leg. The juices should run clear. Remove the trussing thread and transfer the turkey to a heated serving plate. Keep warm.

5 Make the sauce. Skim as much fat as possible from the juices in the roasting pan. Sprinkle in the flour and cook gently for a few minutes, stirring constantly. Stir in the warm turkey stock and bring to simmering point. Add the grape juice and anis, and bring back to simmering point. Taste for seasoning and pour into a warmed jug (pitcher) or sauceboat. Carve the turkey and serve with the sauce.

Roast Turkey

This classic dish will star at any celebration.

Serves 8
4.5kg/10lb oven-ready turkey, with giblets
1 large onion, peeled and studded with 6 whole cloves
50g/2oz/4 tbsp butter, softened
10 chipolata sausages
salt and ground black pepper

For the stuffing
225g/8oz rindless, streaky (fatty) bacon, chopped

1 large onion, finely chopped
450g/1lb pork sausagemeat (bulk sausage)
25g/1oz/⅓ cup rolled oats
30 ml/2 tbsp chopped fresh parsley
10ml/2 tsp dried mixed herbs
1 large (US extra large) egg, beaten
115g/4oz ready-to-eat dried apricots, finely chopped

For the gravy
25g/1oz/2 tbsp plain (all-purpose) flour
450ml/¾ pint/scant 2 cups giblet stock

1 Preheat the oven to 200°C/400°F/Gas 6. For the stuffing, cook the bacon and onion in a frying pan until done. Mix with the other ingredients and season well.

2 Stuff the neck-end of the turkey and secure with a small skewer. Shape the remaining stuffing into balls. Put the clove-studded onion in the body cavity. Weigh the stuffed bird and calculate the cooking time; allow 15 minutes per 450g/1lb plus 15 minutes.

3 Place the bird in a large roasting pan. Spread the turkey with butter and season well. Cover loosely with foil and cook for 30 minutes. Lower the oven to 180°C/350°F/Gas 4. Baste every 30 minutes. Remove the foil for the last hour.

4 Place the stuffing balls and sausages into ovenproof dishes. Put in the oven 20 minutes before the end of cooking time.

5 Transfer the turkey to a serving plate, cover with foil and leave to stand for 15 minutes. To make the gravy, spoon off the fat from the roasting pan, leaving the meat juices. Blend in the flour and cook for 2 minutes. Stir in the stock, bring to the boil and transfer to a gravy jug (pitcher). To serve, carve the turkey and surround with sausages and stuffing balls.

Roast Turkey Energy 828kcal/3452kJ; Protein 73.1g; Carbohydrate 19.4g, of which sugars 7g; Fat 51.3g, of which saturates 18.1g; Cholesterol 292mg; Calcium 77mg; Fibre 1.8g; Sodium 1267mg.
Turkey with Stuffing Energy 662kcal/2772kJ; Protein 66.3g; Carbohydrate 27.9g, of which sugars 15.5g; Fat 31.5g, of which saturates 8.1g; Cholesterol 274mg; Calcium 104mg; Fibre 2.2g; Sodium 658mg.

Roasted Duckling on a Bed of Honeyed Potatoes

The rich flavour of duck combined with these sweetened potatoes glazed with honey makes a great treat for a special occasion.

Serves 4

1 duckling, giblets removed
60ml/4 tbsp light soy sauce
150ml/¼ pint/⅔ cup fresh
   orange juice
3 large floury potatoes, cut
   into chunks
30ml/2 tbsp clear honey
15ml/1 tbsp sesame seeds
salt and ground black pepper

1 Preheat the oven to 200°C/400°F/Gas 6. Place the duckling in a roasting pan. Prick the skin well all over with a fork.

2 Mix the soy sauce and orange juice together and pour over the duck. Cook in the oven for 20 minutes.

3 Place the potato chunks in a bowl, stir in the honey and toss to mix well. Remove the duckling from the oven and spoon the potatoes all around and under the duckling.

4 Roast for a further 35 minutes and remove from the oven. Toss the potatoes in the juices so the underside will be cooked and turn the duck over. Place back in the oven and cook for a further 30 minutes.

5 Remove the duckling from the oven and carefully scoop off the excess fat, leaving the juices behind.

6 Sprinkle the sesame seeds over the potatoes, season with salt and pepper and turn the duckling back over, breast side up, and cook for a further 10 minutes. Remove the duckling and potatoes from the oven and keep warm, allowing the duck to stand for a few minutes.

7 Pour off the excess fat and simmer the juices on the stove for a few minutes. Serve the juices with the carved duckling and the potatoes.

Chinese Duck Curry

The duck in this dish is best marinated for as long as possible, such as overnight, although it tastes good even if you only have time to marinate it briefly.

Serves 4

4 duck breast portions, skin
   and bones removed
30ml/2 tbsp five-spice powder
30ml/2 tbsp sesame oil
grated rind and juice of 1 orange
1 medium butternut squash,
   peeled and cubed
10ml/2 tsp Thai red curry paste
30ml/2 tbsp Thai fish sauce
15ml/1 tbsp palm sugar
   (jaggery) or light muscovado
   (brown) sugar
300ml/½ pint/1¼ cups
   coconut milk
2 fresh red chillies, seeded
4 kaffir lime leaves, torn
small bunch coriander (cilantro),
   chopped, to garnish

1 Cut the duck meat into bitesize pieces and place in a bowl with the five-spice powder, sesame oil and orange rind and juice. Stir well to mix all the ingredients and coat the duck in the marinade. Cover and marinate for at least 10 minutes.

2 Meanwhile, cook the squash in boiling water for 10 minutes, until just tender. Drain and set aside.

3 Pour the marinade from the duck into a wok and heat until boiling. Stir in the curry paste and cook for 1 minute, until well blended and fragrant. Add the duck and cook for 3 minutes, stirring constantly, until browned on all sides.

4 Add the fish sauce and palm sugar and cook for 1 minute more. Stir in the coconut milk until the mixture is smooth, then add the cooked squash with the chillies and lime leaves. Simmer gently, stirring frequently, for 2 minutes, then spoon into a dish, sprinkle with the coriander and serve.

Cook's Tip
You can save a little time and effort by buying prepared butternut in bags from the supermarket. Small cubes are best, since they will cook more quickly.

Roasted Duckling Energy 806kcal/3341kJ; Protein 20.8g; Carbohydrate 32.3g, of which sugars 6.4g; Fat 66.8g, of which saturates 17.9g; Cholesterol 0mg; Calcium 53mg; Fibre 2.1g; Sodium 403mg.
Duck Curry Energy 295kcal/1241kJ; Protein 31.4g; Carbohydrate 13.3g, of which sugars 10g; Fat 10.5g, of which saturates 2.3g; Cholesterol 165mg; Calcium 65mg; Fibre 1.8g; Sodium 546mg.

Roast Duck with Marmalade and Soy Sauce

Sweet-and-sour flavours, such as marmalade and soy sauce, complement the rich, fatty taste of duck beautifully. Serve these robustly flavoured duck breast fillets with simple accompaniments, such as steamed sticky rice and pak choi.

Serves 6
6 duck breast fillets
45ml/3 tbsp fine-cut marmalade
45ml/3 tbsp light soy sauce
salt and ground black pepper

1 Preheat the oven to 190°C/375°F/Gas 5. Place the duck breast fillets skin side up on a grill (broiling) rack and place in the sink. Pour boiling water all over the duck. This shrinks the skin and helps it crisp during cooking. Pat the duck dry with kitchen paper and transfer to a roasting pan.

2 Whisk together the marmalade and soy sauce in a bowl, and brush the mixture over the duck. Season with a little salt and some black pepper and roast in the preheated oven for about 20–25 minutes, basting occasionally with the marmalade mixture in the pan.

3 Remove the duck breast fillets from the oven and leave to rest for 5 minutes. Slice the duck breast fillets and serve drizzled with any juices left in the pan.

Variations
• Marmalade gives the duck a lovely citrus flavour, but this recipe also works well if you substitute black cherry jam. Use a little plum sauce instead of the light soy sauce, if you like, but not too much as the flavour of the cherries will be swamped.
• If the occasion calls for a little ceremony, roast a whole duck. You will need to prick the skin of the bird all over before roasting, so that the fat, which is trapped in a layer beneath the skin, will be released during cooking. This excess oily matter can then be drained off during cooking.

Duck and Sesame Stir-fry

For a special family meal that is a guaranteed success, this is ideal. It tastes fantastic and cooks fast.

Serves 4
250g/9oz boneless
    duck meat
15ml/1 tbsp sesame oil
15ml/1 tbsp vegetable oil

4 garlic cloves, finely sliced
2.5ml/½ tsp dried chilli flakes
15ml/1 tbsp Thai fish sauce
15ml/1 tbsp light soy sauce
120ml/4fl oz/½ cup water
1 head broccoli, cut into
    small florets
coriander (cilantro) and 15ml/
    1 tbsp toasted sesame seeds,
    to garnish

1 Cut all the duck meat into bitesize pieces. Heat the oils in a wok or large, heavy frying pan and stir-fry the garlic over medium heat until it is golden brown – do not let it burn otherwise it will give the food a bitter taste.

2 Add the duck to the pan and stir-fry for a further 2 minutes, until the meat begins to brown.

3 Stir in the chilli flakes, fish sauce, soy sauce and water. Add the broccoli and continue to stir-fry for about 2 minutes, until the duck is just cooked through.

4 Serve on warmed plates, garnished with coriander and the toasted sesame seeds.

Cook's Tip
Broccoli has excited interest recently since it is claimed that eating this dark green vegetable regularly can help to reduce the risk of some cancers. Broccoli is a source of protein, calcium, iron and magnesium, as well as vitamins A and C.

Variation
Pak choi (bok choy) or Chinese flowering cabbage can be used instead of broccoli.

Roast Duck Energy 160kcal/672kJ; Protein 19.9g; Carbohydrate 5.8g, of which sugars 5.8g; Fat 6.5g, of which saturates 2g; Cholesterol 110mg; Calcium 16mg; Fibre 0.1g; Sodium 645mg.
Duck and Sesame Stir-fry Energy 165kcal/686kJ; Protein 17.4g; Carbohydrate 2.3g, of which sugars 2g; Fat 10.6g, of which saturates 1.8g; Cholesterol 69mg; Calcium 72mg; Fibre 2.9g; Sodium 345mg.

Duck with Damson and Ginger Sauce

This is a variation of classic Llanover salt duck, a recipe collected by Lady Llanover, a 19th-century patron of the Welsh culture and language. Simple pan-fried duck breast fillets go well with a fruit sauce too, as in this recipe.

Serves 4

250g/9oz fresh damsons
5ml/1 tsp ground ginger
45ml/3 tbsp sugar
10ml/2 tsp wine vinegar or
 sherry vinegar
4 duck breast fillets
15ml/1 tbsp oil
salt and ground black pepper

1 Put the damsons in a pan with the ginger and 45ml/3 tbsp water. Bring to the boil, cover and simmer gently for 5 minutes, or until the fruit is soft. Stir frequently and add a little extra water if the fruit looks as if it is drying out or sticking to the bottom of the pan.

2 Stir in the sugar and vinegar. Press the mixture through a sieve (strainer) to remove stones (pits) and skin. Taste the sauce and add more sugar, if necessary, and seasoning to taste.

3 Meanwhile, with a sharp knife, score the fat on the duck breast fillets in several places without cutting into the meat. Brush the oil over both sides of the duck. Sprinkle a little salt and pepper on the fat side only.

4 Preheat a griddle (grill) pan or heavy frying pan. When hot, add the duck breast fillets, skin side down, and cook over medium heat for about 5 minutes or until the fat is evenly browned and crisp. Turn over and cook the meat side for 4–5 minutes. Lift out and leave to rest for 5–10 minutes.

5 Slice the duck on the diagonal and serve immediately, accompanied by the sauce.

> **Cook's Tip**
> Both the duck and the sauce are good served cold too. Serve with simple steamed vegetables or crisp salads.

Duck with Plum Sauce

This is an updated version of an old English dish that was traditionally served in the late summer and early autumn, when Victoria plums are ripe and abundant. The sharp, fruity flavour of the plums balances the richness of the duck.

Serves 4

4 duck quarters
1 large red onion, finely chopped
500g/1¼lb ripe plums, quartered
 and stoned (pitted)
30ml/2 tbsp redcurrant jelly
salt and ground black pepper

1 Prick the duck skin all over with a fork to release the fat during cooking and help give a crisp result, then place the portions in a heavy frying pan, skin side down.

2 Cook the duck pieces for about 8–10 minutes on each side, or until they are golden brown and cooked right through. Remove the duck from the frying pan, using tongs or a draining spoon, and keep warm.

3 Pour away all but 30ml/2 tbsp of the duck fat, then stir-fry the onion for 5 minutes, or until golden. Add the plums and cook for a further 5 minutes, stirring. Add the redcurrant jelly.

4 Return the duck portions to the pan and cook for a further 5 minutes or until thoroughly reheated. Season with salt and pepper to taste before serving.

> **Cook's Tip**
> Make sure the plums are very ripe, otherwise the mixture may be too dry and the sauce extremely tart.

> **Variations**
> • The red onion can be replaced with a white or a brown one.
> • Fine-cut orange marmalade makes a tangy alternative to the redcurrant jelly.

Duck with Plum Energy 608kcal/2515kJ; Protein 15.1g; Carbohydrate 17.4g, of which sugars 17g; Fat 53.5g, of which saturates 14.5g; Cholesterol 0mg; Calcium 35mg; Fibre 2.2g; Sodium 102mg.
Duck with Damson Energy 275kcal/1157kJ; Protein 29.9g; Carbohydrate 17.5g, of which sugars 17.5g; Fat 12.5g, of which saturates 2.4g; Cholesterol 165mg; Calcium 39mg; Fibre 1.1g; Sodium 167mg.

Roast Mallard

The roast mallard is especially tasty served on a potato cake bed. Traditional accompaniments include thinly cut chips and apple sauce or rowan jelly; puréed Jerusalem artichokes are also an unusual and excellent accompaniment for game birds.

Serves 2–3
1 oven-ready mallard
1 small onion studded
    with cloves
a few apple slices
25g/1oz/2 tbsp butter,
    softened
5 streaky (fatty) bacon
    rashers (strips)
salt and ground black pepper

1 Thoroughly wash the bird inside and out under cold running water and wipe dry on kitchen paper.

2 Weigh the mallard and calculate the cooking time at 15 minutes per 450g/1lb for rare meat, 20 minutes per 450g/1lb if you prefer the meat well done. Preheat the oven to 200°C/400°F/Gas 6.

3 Put the clove-studded onion and a few apple slices inside the bird. Spread the butter all over the skin, and season.

4 Cover with the bacon and place the bird in a roasting pan with 30ml/2 tbsp water and roast for the time estimated. Remove the rashers for the last 10 minutes to allow the skin to brown.

5 To serve, carve the meat and arrange on heated plates, leaving the legs whole.

Cook's Tips
• *Wild fowl from coastal areas can have a fishy flavour. To offset this, put the oven-ready bird into a pan of cold, salted water and bring to the boil; leave to simmer for 15–20 minutes, then remove the bird and wash and dry both inside and out before proceeding.*
• *Wildfowl are often served rare; the meat is lean and will be dry unless slowly cooked to retain moisture.*

Roast Goose with Apples

Goose is popular at Christmas, but it should be enjoyed at any time of year.

Serves 8
1 oven-ready goose weighing
    about 5.5kg/12lb, with giblets
1 small onion, sliced
2 small carrots, sliced
2 celery sticks, sliced
small bunch of parsley and thyme

450/1lb black pudding (blood
    sausage), crumbled or chopped
1 large garlic clove, crushed
2 large cooking apples, peeled,
    cored and finely chopped
250ml/8fl oz/1 cup dry (hard) cider
about 15ml/1 tbsp flour
salt and ground black pepper
roast potatoes and freshly cooked
    seasonal vegetables, to serve

1 Remove the goose liver from the giblets and put the rest of the giblets into a pan with the onion, carrots, celery and herbs. Cover with water, season and simmer for 30–45 minutes. Chop the liver finely and mix it with the black pudding, garlic and apples. Season, then sprinkle in 75ml/2½fl oz/⅓ cup cider.

2 Preheat the oven to 200°C/400°F/Gas 6. Wipe out the goose and pack with the stuffing. Season and prick the skin all over. Weigh the stuffed goose and calculate the cooking time at 15 minutes per 450g/1lb and 15 minutes over. Put the goose on a rack in a roasting pan, cover with foil and roast for 1 hour.

3 Remove the goose from the oven and pour off the hot fat. Pour the remaining cider over the goose, replace the foil, and return to the oven. Half an hour before the end of the cooking time, remove the foil and baste with the juices. Return to the oven, uncovered, and allow the skin to brown and crisp. Transfer to a serving plate, and rest for 20 minutes before carving.

4 Meanwhile, make the gravy. Pour off any excess fat from the roasting pan, leaving 30ml/2 tbsp, then sprinkle in enough flour to absorb it. Stir for 1 minute, then strain in enough giblet stock to make a gravy. Bring to the boil and simmer for 4 minutes, stirring. Season to taste and pour the gravy into a sauceboat.

5 Carve the goose into slices at the table and serve with the gravy, roast potatoes and some seasonal vegetables.

Roast Mallard Energy 486kcal/2028kJ; Protein 49.6g; Carbohydrate 0.1g, of which sugars 0.1g; Fat 32g, of which saturates 14.1g; Cholesterol 278mg; Calcium 28mg; Fibre 0g; Sodium 1.08g.
Roast Goose Energy 822kcal/3437kJ; Protein 54.8g; Carbohydrate 44.1g, of which sugars 21.8g; Fat 48.7g, of which saturates 0.9g; Cholesterol 0mg; Calcium 87mg; Fibre 3.1g; Sodium 486mg.

Pork Patties with Lemon Grass

Lemon grass lends a citrus flavour to pork, enhanced by the fresh zing of ginger. Serve these patties in burger buns with slices of tomato, crisp lettuce and a splash of chilli sauce.

Serves 4
450g/1lb/2 cups minced (ground) pork
15ml/1 tbsp fresh root ginger, grated
1 lemon grass stalk
salt and ground black pepper

1 Mix the pork with the ginger and season. Remove the tough outer layers from the lemon grass stalk and discard. Chop the centre part as finely as possible and mix into the pork. Shape into four patties and chill for about 20 minutes.

2 Heat the oil in a large, non-stick frying pan and add the patties. Fry for 3–4 minutes on each side over a gentle heat, until cooked through. Remove from the pan with a metal spatula and drain on kitchen paper, then serve.

Sticky Glazed Pork Ribs

These ribs have a great sweet-and-sour flavour and are popular with children and adults alike. Serve with fresh bread to mop up all the juices.

Serves 4
900g/2lb pork spare ribs
75ml/5 tbsp clear honey
75ml/5 tbsp light soy sauce
salt and ground black pepper

1 Preheat the oven to 190°C/375°F/Gas 5. Put the spare ribs in a roasting pan and season well with salt and pepper.

2 In a small bowl, mix together the honey and soy sauce and pour over the ribs. Turn the ribs several times, spooning over the mixture until thoroughly coated.

3 Bake the spare ribs for 30 minutes, then increase the oven temperature to 220°C/425°F/Gas 7 and cook for a further 10 minutes, or until the marinade turns into a thick, sticky glaze.

Pan-fried Pork with Thyme and Garlic Risotto

Lean pork chump chops are delicious served with smooth, creamy, but robust, risotto in this quick and contemporary meal.

Serves 4
4 large pork chump or loin chops, each weighing about 175g/6oz, rind removed
1 garlic clove, finely chopped
juice of ½ lemon
5ml/1 tsp soft light brown sugar

25g/1oz/2 tbsp butter
fresh thyme sprigs, to garnish

For the risotto
25g/1oz/2 tbsp butter
15ml/1 tbsp olive oil
2 shallots, chopped
2 garlic cloves, finely chopped
250g/9oz/1½ cups risotto rice
15ml/1 tbsp fresh thyme leaves
900ml/1½ pints/3¾ cups boiling pork or chicken stock
salt and ground black pepper

1 Put the chops in a shallow dish, sprinkle the garlic over. To make the marinade, mix the lemon juice and soft light brown sugar together, and drizzle this over the chops. Turn the chops to coat both sides with the lemon mixture, then cover the dish and leave the chops to marinate in the refrigerator while making the risotto.

2 To make the risotto, heat the butter with the oil in a large, heavy pan until foaming. Cook the shallots and garlic gently until the shallots are softened, but not coloured. Add the rice and thyme and stir until the grains are coated with butter and oil.

3 Add a ladleful of hot stock and cook gently, stirring occasionally. When the stock is absorbed, add another ladleful. Continue in this way until all the stock is absorbed. The whole process should take 25–30 minutes. Season to taste.

4 Cook the chops when the risotto is half cooked. Melt the butter in a heavy frying pan. Remove the chops from the marinade and fry them for 3–4 minutes on each side.

5 Divide the risotto among four plates and arrange the chops on top. Serve immediately, garnished with fresh thyme.

Pork Patties Energy 234kcal/974kJ; Protein 21.6g; Carbohydrate 0g, of which sugars 0g; Fat 16.4g, of which saturates 4.7g; Cholesterol 74mg; Calcium 8mg; Fibre 0g; Sodium 74mg.
Pork Ribs Energy 358kcal/1509kJ; Protein 48.5g; Carbohydrate 21.8g, of which sugars 16.4g; Fat 9.1g, of which saturates 3.2g; Cholesterol 142mg; Calcium 25mg; Fibre 0.2g; Sodium 436mg.
Pan-fried Pork Energy 747kcal/3116kJ; Protein 61.4g; Carbohydrate 52.2g, of which sugars 2g; Fat 32.1g, of which saturates 13.6g; Cholesterol 219mg; Calcium 34mg; Fibre 0.2g; Sodium 223mg.

Pork Kebabs with Barbecue Sauce

Pork fillet is the best cut for these kebabs because it is lean and tender and will cook quickly.

Serves 4

500g/1¼lb lean pork
  fillet (tenderloin)
8 large, thick spring
  onions (scallions)
120ml/4fl oz/½ cup
  barbecue sauce
1 lemon, cut into wedges,
  to garnish

1 Cut the pork into 2.5cm/1in cubes. Cut the spring onions into 2.5cm/1in-long sticks.

2 Preheat the grill (broiler) to high. Oil the wire rack and spread out the pork cubes on it. Grill (broil) the pork until the juices drip, then dip the pieces in the barbecue sauce and put back on the grill. Grill until cooked through, repeating the dipping process twice more. Set aside and keep warm.

3 Trim the spring onions and place them on the grill rack. Gently grill them until soft and slightly brown on the outside. Do not dip them into the barbecue sauce. Thread about four pieces of cooked pork and three spring onion pieces on to each of the eight bamboo skewers.

4 Arrange the skewers on a platter. Squeeze a little lemon juice over each skewer. Serve immediately, offering the remaining lemon wedges separately, so that guests can squeeze the juice over their meat.

> **Variation**
> *This is an unusual kebab recipe, in that the cubes of pork are threaded on to the skewers only after cooking. This is because the meat is regularly dipped in glaze, and it is easier to get an all-round coating if the cubes of pork are free. If you prefer to assemble the skewers first and cook them on the barbecue, do so. Use metal skewers, which will not char, and baste frequently with the sauce.*

Noisettes of Pork with Creamy Calvados and Apple Sauce

This dish gives the impression of being far more difficult to prepare than it really is, so it is ideal as part of a formal menu to impress guests. Buttered gnocchi or griddled polenta and red cabbage are suitable accompaniments.

Serves 4

30ml/2 tbsp plain
  (all-purpose) flour
4 noisettes of pork, about
  175g/6oz each, firmly tied
25g/1oz/2 tbsp butter
4 baby leeks, finely sliced
5ml/1 tsp mustard seeds,
  coarsely crushed
30ml/2 tbsp Calvados
150ml/¼ pint/⅔ cup dry
  white wine
2 Golden Delicious apples, peeled,
  cored and sliced
150ml/¼ pint/⅔ cup double
  (heavy) cream
30ml/2 tbsp chopped
  fresh parsley
salt and ground black pepper

1 Place the flour in a bowl or on a plate and add plenty of salt and black pepper. Turn the noisettes of pork in the flour mixture to coat them lightly.

2 Melt the butter in a heavy frying pan and cook the noisettes until golden on both sides. Lift the noisettes out of the pan and set aside somewhere warm.

3 Add the sliced leeks to the fat remaining in the pan and cook for 5 minutes, stirring frequently.

4 Stir the mustard seeds into the frying pan. Pour in the Calvados, then carefully ignite it to burn off the alcohol. When the flames have died down, pour in the dry white wine and return the pork noisettes to the pan. Cook gently for about 10 minutes, turning the pork frequently.

5 Add the sliced apples and double cream and simmer for 5 minutes, or until the apples are tender and the sauce is thick, rich and creamy. Taste for seasoning, then stir in the chopped parsley and serve immediately.

Stir-fried Pork with Mushrooms

Pork fillet, also called tenderloin, is the perfect cut for stir-frying – it is lean and cooks in minutes when cut into fine strips.

Serves 4
30ml/2 tbsp sesame oil
450g/1lb lean pork fillet
  (tenderloin), cut into
  fine strips
1 onion, halved and sliced
1 green chilli, seeded and chopped
2 garlic cloves, sliced
150g/5oz oyster mushrooms,
  sliced
200g/7oz runner beans or green
  beans, sliced
2 oranges, peeled and cut
  into segments
15ml/1 tbsp clear honey
30ml/2 tbsp sherry

To serve
350g/12oz egg noodles, cooked
30ml/2 tbsp sesame oil

1 Heat the oil in a wok or large frying pan until very hot. Stir-fry the pork in three batches for 2 minutes each, or until crisp. Remove each batch in turn.

2 Add the onion, chilli, garlic, mushrooms and runner beans or green beans. Stir-fry the vegetables for 3–5 minutes.

3 Return the pork to the wok or pan. Add the orange segments, honey and sherry, and cook for a further 2 minutes, stirring frequently.

4 Prepare the egg noodles in a separate pan or wok. Heat the oil and stir-fry the cooked noodles for 2–3 minutes, or until hot, then divide them among individual warm serving bowls and spoon the pork stir-fry on top. Serve immediately.

Cook's Tips
• When stir-frying, cut the ingredients into similar size strips so that they cook evenly and quickly, and prepare all the ingredients before you begin cooking.
• The wok or frying pan for stir-frying has to be very hot to cook the food correctly. The oil should be on the verge of starting to smoke before you add the first ingredients.

Paprika Pork

This chunky, goulash-style pork dish is rich with mixed peppers and paprika. Grilling the peppers before adding them to the meat really brings out their sweet, vibrant flavour. Rice or buttered boiled potatoes go particularly well with the rich pork.

Serves 4
2 red, 1 yellow and 1 green
  (bell) peppers
500g/1¼lb lean pork
  fillet (tenderloin)
45ml/3 tbsp paprika
300g/11oz jar or tub of tomato
  sauce with herbs or garlic
boiled plain rice, to serve
salt and ground black pepper

1 Preheat the grill (broiler). Cut the peppers in half, remove the seeds and discard, then chop the halves into thick strips and sprinkle in a single layer on a foil-lined grill (broiling) rack.

2 Cook the peppers under the preheated grill for about 20–25 minutes, turning frequently until the edges of the strips are lightly charred.

3 Meanwhile, cut the pork into chunks. Season with salt and ground black pepper. Heat a heavy, non-stick frying pan without any oil. When hot, add the pork to the pan and cook for about 5 minutes, turning occasionally, until beginning to brown.

4 Transfer the meat to a heavy pan and add the paprika, tomato sauce, 300ml/½ pint/1¼ cups water and a little seasoning. Bring to the boil, reduce the heat, cover the pan and simmer gently for 30 minutes.

5 Add the grilled (broiled) peppers to the pan and cook for a further 10–15 minutes, stirring occasionally, until the meat is tender. Taste for seasoning and serve immediately with boiled plain rice.

Cook's Tip
Fresh, ready-made tomato sauce is widely available in the chiller section of supermarkets and food stores.

Paprika Pork Energy 533kcal/2248kJ; Protein 50.1g; Carbohydrate 60.2g, of which sugars 17.8g; Fat 11.9, of which saturates 3.3g; Cholesterol 110mg; Calcium 127mg; Fibre 10.7g; Sodium 659mg.
Stir-fried Pork Energy 243kcal/1016kJ; Protein 26.6g; Carbohydrate 10g, of which sugars 9.1g; Fat 10.5g, of which saturates 2.3g; Cholesterol 71mg; Calcium 61mg; Fibre 2.8g; Sodium 85mg.

Curried Pork with Pickled Garlic

This very rich curry is best accompanied by lots of plain rice and perhaps a light vegetable dish. It can serve four with a vegetable curry on the side, and perhaps some freshly steamed greens, such as pak choi or curly kale.

Serves 2

130g/4¹/₂oz lean pork steaks
30ml/2 tbsp vegetable oil
1 garlic clove, crushed
15ml/1 tbsp red curry paste

130ml/4¹/₂fl oz/generous ¹/₂ cup coconut cream
2.5cm/1in piece fresh root ginger, finely chopped
30ml/2 tbsp vegetable or chicken stock
30ml/2 tbsp fish sauce
5ml/1 tsp sugar
2.5ml/¹/₂ tsp ground turmeric
10ml/2 tsp lemon juice
4 pickled garlic cloves, finely chopped
strips of lemon and lime rind, to garnish

1 Place the pork steaks in the freezer for 30–40 minutes, until firm, then, using a sharp knife, cut the meat into fine slivers, trimming off any excess fat.

2 Heat the oil in a wok or large, heavy frying pan and cook the garlic over low to medium heat until golden brown. Do not let it burn. Add the curry paste and stir it in well.

3 Add the coconut cream and stir until the liquid begins to reduce and thicken. Stir in the pork. Cook for 2 minutes more, until the pork is cooked through.

4 Add the ginger, stock, fish sauce, sugar and turmeric to the wok or pan, stirring constantly, then add the lemon juice and pickled garlic and heat through. Serve in warmed bowls, garnished with strips of rind.

Cook's Tip
Asian stores sell pickled garlic. It is well worth seeking out and investing in, as the taste is sweet and delicious. It will also keep for a long time in your kitchen.

Spanish Pork and Sausage Casserole

This delicious pork dish from the Catalan region of Spain uses the spicy butifarra sausage. You can find these sausages in some Spanish delicatessens, or you can substitute some sweet Italian sausages.

Serves 4

30ml/2 tbsp olive oil
4 boneless pork chops, about 175g/6oz

4 butifarra or sweet Italian sausages
1 onion, chopped
2 garlic cloves, chopped
120ml/4fl oz/¹/₂ cup dry white wine
4 plum tomatoes, chopped
1 bay leaf
30ml/2 tbsp chopped fresh parsley
salt and ground black pepper
green salad and baked potatoes, to serve

1 Heat the oil in a large deep frying pan. Cook the pork chops over high heat until browned on both sides, then transfer to a plate and set aside.

2 Add the sausages, onion and garlic to the pan and cook over medium heat for about 6–8 minutes, turning the sausages two or three times during cooking. When the sausages are evenly browned and the onion has softened, return the browned chops to the pan.

3 Stir the wine, tomatoes and bay leaf into the pan, and season with salt and pepper. Add the parsley. Cover the pan and cook for 30 minutes.

4 Remove the sausages from the pan and cut into thick slices. Return them to the pan and heat through for a minute or two. Serve immediately, accompanied by a fresh green salad and baked potatoes.

Cook's Tip
Vine tomatoes, which are making a welcome appearance in our supermarkets, can be used instead of the plum tomatoes in this recipe, if you prefer.

Curried Pork Energy 227kcal/947kJ; Protein 16.3g; Carbohydrate 9.8g, of which sugars 6.1g; Fat 14g, of which saturates 2.4g; Cholesterol 41mg; Calcium 30mg; Fibre 1g; Sodium 474mg.
Spanish Pork Energy 431kcal/1803kJ; Protein 44.3g; Carbohydrate 12.5g, of which sugars 7g; Fat 20.8g, of which saturates 6.5g; Cholesterol 127mg; Calcium 78mg; Fibre 2.4g; Sodium 618mg.

Porchetta

This is a simplified version of a traditional Italian festive dish. Make sure the piece of belly pork has a good amount of crackling – because this is the best part, which guests will just love. Serve with plenty of creamy mashed potatoes and a seasonal green vegetable.

Serves 8
2kg/4½lb boned belly pork
45ml/3 tbsp fresh rosemary
   leaves, roughly chopped
50g/2oz/⅔ cup freshly grated
   Parmesan cheese
15ml/1 tbsp olive oil
salt and ground black pepper

1 Preheat the oven to 180°C/350°F/Gas 4. Lay the belly pork skin side down on a chopping board.

2 Spread the chopped rosemary leaves over the meat, pushing it in a little with your hand, and sprinkle with the grated Parmesan cheese. Season with salt and plenty of ground black pepper and drizzle over the olive oil.

3 Starting from one end, roll the pork up firmly and tie string around it at 2.5cm/1in intervals to secure. Transfer the rolled pork to a roasting pan and cook for about 3 hours, or until cooked through.

4 Transfer the pork to a chopping board and leave it to rest for about 10 minutes. This will improve the texture and flavour of the meat after the heating process. Carve the pork into slices and serve immediately.

> **Cook's Tip**
> To help ensure that you have crisp crackling on the pork you should dry and score the skin. Pat the outside of the pork with kitchen paper or a clean dish towel to dry it. The skin will already have a few cuts in it but it does not hurt to add a few more. Use a very sharp paring knife or use a craft knife with a sharp, clean blade and score the skin in a few places, ensuring that you have cut just through to the fat beneath the skin.

Roast Pork with Sage Stuffing

Sage and onion make a classic stuffing for roast pork.

Serves 6–8
1.6kg/3½lb boneless loin of pork
60ml/4 tbsp fine, dry breadcrumbs
10ml/2 tsp chopped fresh sage
25ml/1½ tbsp plain
   (all-purpose) flour
300ml/½ pint/1¼ cups cider
150ml/¼ pint/⅔ cup water
5–10ml/1–2 tsp crab apple or
   redcurrant jelly

salt and ground black pepper
sprigs of thyme, to garnish

For the stuffing
25g/1oz/2 tbsp butter
50g/2oz bacon, finely chopped
2 large onions, finely chopped
75g/3oz/1½ cups fresh
   white breadcrumbs
30ml/2 tbsp chopped fresh sage
5ml/1 tsp chopped fresh thyme
10ml/2 tsp grated lemon rind
1 small egg, beaten

1 Preheat the oven to 220°C/425°F/Gas 7. For the stuffing, melt the butter in a frying pan. Cook the bacon until it browns, then add the onions and cook until they soften. Mix with the breadcrumbs, sage, thyme, lemon rind, egg and salt and pepper.

2 Cut the rind off the joint of pork in one piece and score it well. Place the pork fat side down and season. Add a layer of stuffing, then roll up and tie. Lay the rind over the pork and rub in 5ml/1 tsp salt. Roast for 2–2½ hours, basting once or twice. Reduce the oven to 190°C/375°F/Gas 5 after 20 minutes.

3 Shape the remaining stuffing into balls and add to the pan for the last 30 minutes. When the pork is done, remove the rind, increase the oven to 220°C/425°F/Gas 7 and roast the rind for 20–25 minutes, until crisp.

4 Mix the dry breadcrumbs and sage and press them into the fat on the pork. Cook the pork for 10 minutes, then cover and set aside in a warm place for 15–20 minutes.

5 For the gravy, remove all but 30–45ml/2–3 tbsp of the fat from the roasting pan and place it on the stove. Stir in the flour, followed by the cider and water. Simmer for 10 minutes. Strain into a pan and add the jelly. Season and cook for 5 minutes. Serve with slices of pork and crackling, garnished with thyme.

Porchetta Energy 773kcal/3216kJ; Protein 65.2g; Carbohydrate 0g, of which sugars 0g; Fat 56.9g, of which saturates 20g; Cholesterol 219mg; Calcium 98mg; Fibre 0g; Sodium 293mg.
Roast Pork Energy 390kcal/1637kJ; Protein 47.9g; Carbohydrate 21.6g, of which sugars 4.8g; Fat 12.9g, of which saturates 5.2g; Cholesterol 164mg; Calcium 62mg; Fibre 1.3g; Sodium 434mg.

Chorizo and Spring Onion Hash

This is a great dish to use up any leftover boiled potatoes, if you have them. The potatoes will absorb some of the delicious spicy flavours of the chorizo.

450g/1lb cooked potatoes, cut into small chunks
1 bunch of spring onions (scallions), sliced
salt and ground black pepper

Serves 4
450g/1lb fresh chorizo sausages
15ml/1 tbsp olive oil

1 Heat a large frying pan over medium heat and add the sausages. Cook for 8–10 minutes, turning occasionally, until cooked through. Remove from the pan and set aside.

2 Add the olive oil to the fat released by the chorizo slices in the frying pan. Add the small cubes of potatoes and cook them over low heat for about 5–8 minutes, turning the chunks occasionally until golden.

3 Meanwhile, cut the chorizo sausages into bitesize chunks and add to the pan with the potatoes.

4 Add the spring onions to the frying pan and cook, stirring frequently, for a couple more minutes, until they are piping hot. Season with salt and plenty of ground black pepper, and serve immediately.

> **Cook's Tip**
> • Fresh chorizo sausages are available from good butchers or from Spanish delicatessens and larger supermarkets. They often come in different varieties, with some being hotter and spicier than others – choose those that match your taste.
> • If you do not have any leftover cooked potatoes, then simply boil some from scratch in plenty of salted water until tender. Leave them to cool completely before cutting into small chunks and adding to the frying pan, as specified above.

Potato and Pepperoni Tortilla

Cooked potatoes are delicious with spicy pepperoni in this thick Spanish-style omelette. Salad and crusty bread are excellent accompaniments.

75g/3oz pepperoni, sliced
3 spring onions (scallions), sliced
115g/4oz Fontina cheese, cut into cubes
115g/4oz/1 cup frozen peas, thawed
6 eggs
30ml/2 tbsp chopped fresh parsley
salt and ground black pepper

Serves 4
30ml/2 tbsp olive oil
225g/8oz potatoes, cooked and cut into cubes

1 Heat the oil in a non-stick frying pan and add the potatoes, pepperoni and spring onions. Cook over high heat for about 5 minutes, stirring occasionally, until the pepperoni releases some of its fat and the onions have softened. Add the cheese and peas, and stir to combine.

2 In a medium bowl, beat the eggs with the parsley and seasoning, then pour the mixture over the ingredients in the frying pan. Stir well to distribute the egg mixture around the ingredients. Cook gently, without stirring, for about 10 minutes, or until the egg mixture is golden underneath.

3 When the mixture has almost set, cover the pan with a large plate and carefully invert the pan and its cover to turn out the tortilla. Slide the tortilla back into the pan and continue cooking for a further 10 minutes, or until browned underneath.

4 Carefully turn out the tortilla on to a large, flat serving platter and serve hot or warm, cut into slices. Alternatively, leave until cold.

> **Cook's Tip**
> If you do not have the confidence to invert the tortilla and replace it in the pan, simply finish cooking it under a preheated grill (broiler) for 5–8 minutes, or until just set.

Spicy Chorizo Hash Energy 522kcal/2172kJ; Protein 14.4g; Carbohydrate 29.6g, of which sugars 3.7g; Fat 39.3g, of which saturates 14.3g; Cholesterol 53mg; Calcium 63mg; Fibre 2.1g; Sodium 869mg.
Potato Tortilla Energy 321kcal/1333kJ; Protein 13.1g; Carbohydrate 19.6g, of which sugars 10.2g; Fat 21.1g, of which saturates 8.3g; Cholesterol 123mg; Calcium 256mg; Fibre 3g; Sodium 254mg.

Sausages with Mash and Gravy

Tangy mustard mash and onion gravy are the perfect accompaniments to sausages.

Serves 4
12 pork and leek sausages
salt and ground black pepper

For the onion gravy
30ml/2 tbsp olive oil
25g/1oz/2 tbsp butter
8 onions, sliced

5ml/1 tsp caster (superfine) sugar
15ml/1 tbsp plain
   (all-purpose) flour
300ml/½ pint/1¼ cups
   beef stock

For the mash
1.5kg/3¼lb potatoes
50g/2oz/¼ cup butter
150ml/¼ pint/⅔ cup double
   (heavy) cream
15ml/1 tbsp wholegrain mustard

1 For the gravy, heat the oil and butter in a large pan. Add the onions and mix well to coat them in the fat. Cover and cook gently for about 30 minutes, stirring frequently. Add the sugar and cook for 5 minutes, or until the onions are softened.

2 Stir the flour into the pan, then gradually stir in the stock. Bring to the boil, stirring, then simmer for 3 minutes, or until thickened. Season with salt and pepper.

3 Meanwhile, cook the potatoes in a pan of boiling salted water for 20 minutes, or until tender.

4 Drain the potatoes well and mash them with the butter, double cream and wholegrain mustard. Season to taste.

5 While the potatoes are cooking, preheat the grill (broiler) to medium. Arrange the pork and leek sausages in the grill (broiling) pan and cook for 15–20 minutes, or until cooked and evenly brown. Serve the sausages with the mustard mash and plenty of onion gravy.

> **Variation**
> Instead of the mustard, add 15ml/1 tbsp pesto, 2 crushed garlic cloves and a little olive oil.

Toad-in-the-Hole

This is one of those dishes that is classic comfort food – remembered as a childhood favourite and perfect for lifting the spirits on cold days. Use only the best sausages for this grown-up version, which has chives added to the batter.

30ml/2 tbsp chopped fresh
   chives (optional)
2 eggs
300ml/½ pint/1¼ cups milk
50g/2oz/⅓ cup white vegetable
   fat or lard
450g/1lb Cumberland sausages
   or good-quality pork sausages
salt and ground black pepper

Serves 4–6
175g/6oz/1½ cups plain
   (all-purpose) flour

1 Preheat the oven to 220°C/425°F/Gas 7. Sift the flour into a large bowl with a pinch of salt and pepper. Make a well in the centre of the flour.

2 Whisk the chives, if using, with the eggs and milk, then pour this into the well in the flour. Gradually whisk the flour into the liquid to make a smooth batter. Cover and leave to stand for at least 30 minutes.

3 Put the vegetable fat or lard into a small roasting pan and place in the oven for 3–5 minutes until very hot.

4 Add the sausages to the pan and cook in the oven for about 15 minutes. Turn the sausages twice during cooking.

5 Pour the batter over the sausages, ensuring it is spread out evenly, and cook for about 20 minutes, or until the batter is risen and turned golden. Serve immediately.

> **Variation**
> For a young children's supper, omit the chives from the batter and cook cocktail sausages in muffin pans until golden. Add the batter and cook for 10–15 minutes, or until puffed and golden.

Sausages Energy 939kcal/3913kJ; Protein 19.9g; Carbohydrate 85g, of which sugars 16.7g; Fat 60g, of which saturates 28.6g; Cholesterol 133mg; Calcium 179mg; Fibre 6.6g; Sodium 942mg.
Toad-in-the-Hole Energy 497kcal/2070kJ; Protein 14.5g; Carbohydrate 32.1g, of which sugars 3.8g; Fat 35.4g, of which saturates 13.6g; Cholesterol 109mg; Calcium 141mg; Fibre 1.3g; Sodium 616mg.

Bacon with Parsley Sauce

Boiled bacon makes a very easy and delicious supper dish. Serve with small new potatoes, sautéed with leeks for a splendid meal.

Serves 6–8
1.35kg/3lb piece of bacon, such
 as corner or collar
1 large onion, thickly sliced
1 large carrot, thickly sliced
2 celery sticks, roughly chopped

6 black peppercorns
4 whole cloves
2 bay leaves

For the parsley sauce
600ml/1 pint/2½ cups milk
25g/1oz/2 tbsp butter
25g/1oz/¼ cup plain
 (all-purpose) flour
handful of fresh parsley,
 finely chopped
salt and ground black pepper

1 Put the bacon in a large pan and cover it with cold water. Bring the water slowly to the boil, then drain off and discard it. If necessary, rinse the pan and replace the bacon.

2 Add the onion, carrot, celery, peppercorns, cloves and bay leaves to the pan. Pour in enough cold water to cover the bacon by about 2.5cm/1in or slightly more.

3 Bring slowly to the boil and, if necessary, skim any scum off the surface. Cover and simmer very gently for 1½ hours.

4 To make the parsley sauce, put the milk, butter and flour into a pan. Stirring continually with a whisk, cook over medium heat until the sauce thickens and comes to the boil. Stir in the parsley and let the sauce bubble gently for 1–2 minutes before seasoning to taste with salt and pepper.

5 Lift the bacon on to a warmed serving plate, cover with foil and leave to rest for 15 minutes before slicing and serving with the parsley sauce.

> **Cook's Tip**
> Use the stock from the bacon to make the Welsh dish cawl, a soup–stew with vegetables and dried lentils, peas or beans.

Ham and Vegetables with Eggs

This delicious dish is incredibly simple to make and is hearty enough to serve as a meal in itself. The eggs are not beaten, but are broken into the vegetable mixture and cooked whole.

Serves 4
30ml/2 tbsp olive oil
1 onion, roughly chopped
2 garlic cloves, finely chopped
175g/6oz cooked ham
225g/8oz courgettes (zucchini)

1 red (bell) pepper, seeded and
 thinly sliced
1 yellow (bell) pepper, seeded
 and thinly sliced
10ml/2 tsp paprika
400g/14oz can chopped
 tomatoes
15ml/1 tbsp sun-dried tomato
 purée (paste)
4 large (US extra large) eggs
115g/4oz/1 cup coarsely grated
 Cheddar cheese
salt and ground black pepper
crusty bread, to serve

1 Heat the olive oil in a deep frying pan. Add the onion and garlic and cook for 4 minutes, stirring frequently, until the onions have softened but not browned.

2 Meanwhile, cut the piece of cooked ham and the courgettes into 5cm/2in batons.

3 Add the slices of courgette and pepper to the pan and cook over medium heat, stirring frequently, for about 3–4 minutes until beginning to soften.

4 Stir the paprika, tomatoes, tomato purée and ham into the pan. Season with plenty of salt and ground black pepper. Bring the mixture to a simmer and cook gently for 15 minutes.

5 Reduce the heat to low. Make four wells in the tomato mixture and carefully break an egg into each well. Season with salt and pepper and cook over low heat until the white of the eggs begins to set. Preheat the grill (broiler).

6 Sprinkle the cheese over the mixture in the pan and cook under the hot grill for about 5 minutes until the eggs are set. Serve immediately.

Bacon Energy 467kcal/1937kJ; Protein 32.7g; Carbohydrate 5.7g, of which sugars 3.7g; Fat 34.8g, of which saturates 14.4g; Cholesterol 87mg; Calcium 118mg; Fibre 0.4g; Sodium 2045mg.
Ham Energy 357kcal/1487kJ; Protein 24.8g; Carbohydrate 12.2g, of which sugars 10.7g; Fat 23.1g, of which saturates 9.4g; Cholesterol 244mg; Calcium 280mg; Fibre 3.1g; Sodium 817mg.

Leeks Baked with Ham, Cream and Mint

Choose leeks that are not too thick for this very easy but delicious supper dish. Serve good bread to mop up the sauce and a green salad to refresh the palate.

Serves 4

8–12 slender leeks
8–12 large, medium-thick slices
  Parma or Serrano ham

15g/½oz/1 tbsp butter
75g/3oz/1 cup freshly grated
  Parmesan cheese
250ml/8fl oz/1 cup double
  (heavy) cream
15ml/1 tbsp chopped fresh mint
pinch of cayenne pepper
45ml/3 tbsp fine white
  breadcrumbs
salt and ground black pepper

1 Trim the leeks so that they are all the same size. Bring a large pan of lightly salted water to the boil, add the leeks and cook for 5–8 minutes. Test the leeks with the tip of a sharp knife to check if they are cooked. Drain, reserving 60ml/4 tbsp of the cooking water. Squeeze the excess water out of the leeks. Preheat the oven to 190°C/375°F/Gas 5.

2 Wrap each leek in a slice of ham. Butter an ovenproof gratin dish just large enough to take the leeks in one layer and arrange the leeks in it. Season to taste with salt and pepper and scatter half the grated Parmesan cheese over the leeks.

3 Mix the cream, cooking water and mint. Season with salt, pepper and cayenne and pour over the leeks. Scatter the breadcrumbs and the remaining Parmesan on top. Bake for 30–35 minutes, until bubbling and browned. Serve immediately.

> **Variation**
> Wrap the cooked leeks in fried, but not crisp, bacon. Then pour over a cheese sauce made with equal quantities of the reserved cooking water and milk. Season to taste with Dijon mustard, grated Cheddar cheese and a little nutmeg. Sprinkle with Parmesan and white breadcrumbs and bake as above.

Pan-fried Gammon with Cider

Gammon and cider are a delicious combination, since the sweet, tangy flavour of cider complements the gammon perfectly. Serve with mustard mashed potatoes and a dark green vegetable, such as steamed Savoy cabbage, green beans or lightly cooked Brussels sprouts.

Serves 4

30ml/2 tbsp sunflower oil
4 gammon (smoked or cured
  ham) steaks, 225g/8oz each
150ml/¼ pint/⅔ cup dry
  (hard) cider
45ml/3 tbsp double (heavy) cream
salt and ground black pepper
flat leaf parsley, to garnish
mustard mashed potatoes,
  to serve

1 Heat the oil in a large frying pan until hot. Neatly snip the rind on the gammon steaks to stop them curling up and add them to the pan.

2 Cook the steaks for 3–4 minutes on each side, then pour in the cider. Allow to boil for a couple of minutes,

3 Stir the cream into the pan and simmer for 1–2 minutes, or until the sauce has thickened slightly. Season with salt and pepper, and serve with mashed potato. Garnish with parsley.

> **Variation**
> The Irish dish champ makes a great alternative to mustard mashed potatoes: Cook 900g/2lb peeled potatoes in boiling salted water until tender. Meanwhile, heat 120ml/4fl oz/½ cup creamy milk with 6 finely chopped spring onions (scallions). Mash the potatoes with the milk and onions and 50g/2oz/ ¼ cup butter. Pile the champ in a dish, make a well in the centre, and place another 50g/2oz/¼ cup butter in the well.

> **Cook's Tip**
> Cooking gammon (smoked or cured ham) in a liquid is a good way of ensuring it stays moist and soft-textured.

Leeks Energy 386kcal/1603kJ; Protein 18.1g; Carbohydrate 13.4g, of which sugars 4.2g; Fat 31.4g, of which saturates 17.7g; Cholesterol 98mg; Calcium 289mg; Fibre 2.7g; Sodium 784mg.
Pan-fried Gammon Energy 429kcal/1784kJ; Protein 39.6g; Carbohydrate 1.2g, of which sugars 1.2g; Fat 28.4g, of which saturates 10.1g; Cholesterol 67mg; Calcium 24mg; Fibre 0g; Sodium 1985mg.

Cider-glazed Ham

This wonderful ham glazed with cider is traditionally served with cranberry sauce and is ideal for Christmas.

Serves 8–10

2kg/4½lb middle gammon (smoked or cured ham) joint
1 large or 2 small onions
about 30 whole cloves
3 bay leaves
10 black peppercorns
1.3 litres/2¼ pints/5⅔ cups medium-dry cider
45ml/3 tbsp soft light brown sugar
flat leaf parsley, to garnish

For the cranberry sauce
350g/12oz/3 cups cranberries
175g/6oz/¾ cup soft light brown sugar
grated rind and juice of 2 clementines
30ml/2 tbsp port

1 Weigh the ham and calculate the cooking time at 20 minutes per 450g/1lb, then place it in a large casserole or pan. Stud the onion or onions with 5–10 of the cloves and add to the casserole or pan with the bay leaves and peppercorns.

2 Add 1.2 litres/2 pints/5 cups of the cider and enough water just to cover the ham. Heat until simmering, and then skim off the scum that rises to the surface. Start timing the cooking from the moment the stock simmers. Cover with a lid or foil and simmer gently for the calculated time. Towards the end of the cooking time, preheat the oven to 220°C/425°F/Gas 7.

3 Heat the sugar and remaining cider in a pan until the sugar has dissolved. Simmer for 5 minutes to make a dark, sticky glaze. Leave to cool for 5 minutes.

4 Lift the ham out of the casserole or pan. Carefully and evenly, cut the rind off, then score the fat into a neat diamond pattern. Place the ham in a roasting pan or ovenproof dish. Press a clove into the centre of each diamond, then carefully spoon over the glaze. Bake for 20–25 minutes, or until the fat is brown, glistening and crisp.

5 Simmer all the cranberry sauce ingredients in a heavy pan for 15–20 minutes, stirring frequently. Transfer to a sauceboat. Serve the ham hot or cold, garnished with parsley and with the sauce.

Ham with Mustard Sauce and Crispy Cabbage

This is an updated version of the traditional boiled bacon and cabbage, in which the meat – either gammon or any cut of boiling bacon – is cooked in milk. This helps to counteract the saltiness and imparts a delicious flavour.

Serves 4–6

1.3kg/3lb piece of gammon (smoked or cured ham) or boiling bacon
30ml/2 tbsp oil
2 large onions, sliced
1 bay leaf
750ml/1¼ pints/3 cups milk, plus extra if necessary
15ml/1 tbsp cornflour (cornstarch), dissolved in 15ml/1 tbsp milk
45ml/3 tbsp wholegrain mustard
15–30ml/2–3 tbsp single (light) cream (optional)
1 head of cabbage, such as Savoy, trimmed, ribs removed and leaves finely sliced
ground black pepper

1 Soak the bacon joint in cold water overnight. To cook, heat 15ml/1 tbsp oil in a large pan, add the onions and cook gently for a few minutes.

2 Place the joint on the bed of onions. Add the bay leaf and milk, and season with pepper. Bring to the boil, cover with a tight-fitting lid and cook over a gentle heat for about 1½ hours. When the meat is cooked, the skin will peel off easily.

3 Remove the meat from the pan and keep warm. Strain the cooking liquid. Reserve 300ml/½ pint/1¼ cups for the sauce and put the remainder aside for soup. Add the cornflour mixture to the reserved liquid and bring up to the boil, stirring constantly. As it begins to thicken, stir in the wholegrain mustard and cream, if using.

4 Rinse the cabbage in cold running water and drain well. Heat the remaining oil in a wok or large frying pan and stir-fry the cabbage for 2–3 minutes until cooked but still crunchy. Slice the ham and serve on warmed serving plates with the mustard sauce and crisply cooked cabbage.

Cider-glazed Ham Energy 368kcal/1541kJ; Protein 39.6g; Carbohydrate 15.2g, of which sugars 15.2g; Fat 16.9g, of which saturates 5.6g; Cholesterol 52mg; Calcium 25mg; Fibre 0.6g; Sodium 1982mg.
Ham with Mustard Sauce Energy 541Kcal/2253kJ; Protein 58.4g; Carbohydrate 7.4g, of which sugars 5g; Fat 30.8g, of which saturates 9.4g; Cholesterol 77mg; Calcium 76mg; Fibre 2.1g; Sodium 2.87g.

Marinated Lamb with Oregano and Basil

Yogurt Shish Kebabs

This is the ultimate kebab –
chargrilled meat on bread
with yogurt and tomatoes.

Serves 4

12 plum tomatoes
30ml/2 tbsp butter
4 pitta, cut into bitesize chunks
5ml/1 tsp ground sumac
5ml/1 tsp dried oregano
225g/8oz/1 cup thick and creamy
    natural (plain) yogurt
salt and ground black pepper
1 bunch fresh flat leaf parsley,
    chopped, to garnish

For the sauce
30ml/2 tbsp olive oil
15ml/1 tbsp butter

1 onion, finely chopped
2 garlic cloves, finely chopped
1 fresh green chilli, seeded and
    finely chopped
5–10ml/1–2 tsp sugar
400g/14oz can chopped tomatoes

For the kebabs
500g/1¼lb/2¼ cups lean
    minced (ground) lamb
2 onions, finely chopped
1 fresh green chilli, seeded and
    finely chopped
4 garlic cloves, crushed
5ml/1 tsp paprika
5ml/1 tsp ground sumac
1 bunch fresh flat leaf parsley,
    finely chopped

1 Make the kebabs. Put the lamb in a bowl with the other ingredients and mix to combine. Cover and chill for 15 minutes.

2 Make the sauce. Heat the oil and butter in a heavy pan, stir in the onion, garlic and chilli and cook for 5 minutes. Add the sugar and tomatoes and cook for 30 minutes until quite thick. Season to taste, remove from the heat and keep warm.

3 Prepare the barbecue and shape the kebabs. Cook the kebabs on the barbecue for 6–8 minutes, turning once. Thread the tomatoes on to four skewers and cook until charred.

4 Melt the butter in a pan and fry the bread until golden. Sprinkle with some sumac and oregano, then spread out on a serving dish. Spoon a little sauce and half the yogurt on top.

5 Cut the meat into bitesize pieces and place on the pitta with the tomatoes. Season with salt, sumac and oregano, garnish with the parsley and top with yogurt and the remaining sauce.

Lamb leg steaks are chunky
with a sweet flavour and go
well with fresh oregano
and basil in this deliciously
simple meal. However, you
can also use finely chopped
rosemary or thyme. Serve
the lamb with couscous
or boiled rice.

Serves 4
4 large or 8 small lamb leg steaks
60ml/4 tbsp garlic-infused
    olive oil
1 small bunch of fresh oregano,
    roughly chopped
1 small bunch of fresh
    basil, torn
salt and ground black pepper

1 Place all the lamb steaks in a shallow, non-metallic dish. In a small bowl, mix 45ml/3 tbsp of the oil with the fresh oregano, basil and some salt and black pepper, reserving some of the herbs for the garnish.

2 Pour the herb oil over the lamb steaks and turn to coat them thoroughly in the marinade. Cover and chill in the refrigerator for up to 8 hours.

3 Heat the remaining olive oil in a large frying pan. Remove the lamb steaks from the marinade and cook over medium heat for about 5–6 minutes on each side, until browned on the outside but still slightly pink in the centre.

4 Add the marinade to the frying pan and cook for a further 1–2 minutes until warmed through and beginning to bubble. Divide the steaks between warmed serving plates, pour over a little sauce and garnish with the reserved herbs.

> ### Cook's Tip
> You can make your own garlic-infused oil if you prefer. You will need a whole garlic bulb and a bottle of olive oil, about 500ml/17fl oz/generous 2 cups. Simply peel all the cloves from a garlic bulb and place in the bottle of oil. Leave for a week or two before using.

Marinated Lamb Energy 466kcal/1938kJ; Protein 40g; Carbohydrate 0.7g, of which sugars 0.6g; Fat 33.7g, of which saturates 12g; Cholesterol 152mg; Calcium 66mg; Fibre 1.3g; Sodium 180mg.
Kebabs Energy 642kcal/2688kJ; Protein 35.2g; Carbohydrate 52.8g, of which sugars 24.1g; Fat 33.9g, of which saturates 15.1g; Cholesterol 121mg; Calcium 253mg; Fibre 6.3g; Sodium 456mg.

Harissa-spiced Koftas

Serve these spicy koftas
in pitta breads with sliced
tomatoes, cucumber and
mint leaves, with a drizzle
of natural (plain) yogurt.
Harissa is a fiery-hot sauce,
originally from Tunisia,
usually made from chillies,
garlic, cumin, coriander,
caraway and olive oil.

Serves 4
*450g/1lb/2 cups minced
  (ground) lamb
1 small onion, finely
  chopped
10ml/2 tsp harissa paste
salt and ground black pepper*

1 Place eight wooden skewers in a bowl of cold water and
leave to soak for at least 30 minutes.

2 Put the lamb in a large bowl and add the chopped onion
and harissa. Mix well to combine, and season with plenty of salt
and ground black pepper.

3 Using wet hands, divide the mixture into eight equal pieces
and press on to the skewers in a long sausage shape to make
the lamb koftas.

4 Prepare a barbecue. Cook the skewered koftas over the hot
coals for about 10 minutes, turning occasionally, until cooked
through. Serve immediately.

> **Variation**
> *These koftas can be made with other minced (ground) meat
> such as beef or pork, if you prefer.*

> **Cook's Tip**
> *If you use wooden or bamboo skewers, then soaking them in
> water for 30 minutes is necessary to stop the skewers from
> burning during the cooking process. You can avoid this by
> investing in a set of metal skewers.*

Lamb Chops with a Mint Jelly Crust

Mint and lamb are classic
partners, and the fresh
white breadcrumbs used
here add extra texture. They
will make an unusual and
tasty alternative to a
traditional Sunday dinner.

Serves 4
*8 lamb chops, about
  115g/4oz each
50g/2oz/1 cup fresh white
  breadcrumbs
30ml/2 tbsp mint jelly
salt and ground black pepper*

1 Preheat the oven to 190°C/375°F/Gas 5. Place the lamb
chops on a baking sheet and season with plenty of salt and
ground black pepper, pressing the seasoning into the chops a
little with your hands.

2 Put the fresh white breadcrumbs and mint jelly in a small
bowl and mix together to combine. Season with a little salt and
black pepper.

3 Carefully spoon the breadcrumb mixture on top of the
chops, pressing down firmly with the back of a spoon to make
sure they stick to the chops.

4 Bake the lamb chops in the preheated oven for about
20–30 minutes, or until they are just cooked through. They
should be slightly pink in the middle. Serve immediately.

> **Variation**
> *This dish will work with other cuts of lamb, such as leg or
> shoulder steaks. Avoid any cut that is too fatty, such as breast
> steaks, or too lean, such as the fillets from the neck.*

> **Cook's Tip**
> *Serve the chops with sweet potatoes baked in their skins and
> some steamed green vegetables.*

Harissa-spiced Koftas Energy 233kcal/972kJ; Protein 22.1g; Carbohydrate 2.1g, of which sugars 0.9g; Fat 15.3g, of which saturates 7g; Cholesterol 87mg; Calcium 28mg; Fibre 0.2g; Sodium 79mg.
Lamb Chops Energy 551kcal/2309kJ; Protein 64.1g; Carbohydrate 11.3g, of which sugars 2g; Fat 27.9g, of which saturates 13.3g; Cholesterol 248mg; Calcium 46mg; Fibre 0.3g; Sodium 316mg.

Sumac-spiced Burgers with Relish

A sharp-sweet red onion relish works well with burgers based on Middle-Eastern style lamb. Serve with pitta bread and tabbouleh or a green salad.

Serves 4
25g/1oz/3 tbsp bulgur wheat
500g/1¼lb lean minced
  (ground) lamb
1 small red onion, finely chopped
2 garlic cloves, finely chopped
1 green chilli, seeded and
  finely chopped
5ml/1 tsp ground cumin seeds
2.5ml/½ tsp ground sumac
15g/½oz chopped fresh parsley
30ml/2 tbsp chopped fresh mint

olive oil, for frying
salt and ground black pepper

For the relish
2 red (bell) peppers, halved
2 red onions, cut into 5mm/¼in
  thick slices
75–90ml/5–6 tbsp virgin olive oil
350g/12oz cherry tomatoes,
  chopped
½–1 fresh red or green chilli,
  seeded and finely chopped
30ml/2 tbsp chopped mint
30ml/2 tbsp chopped parsley
15ml/1 tbsp chopped oregano
2.5–5ml/½–1 tsp each ground
  toasted cumin and sumac
juice of ½ lemon
caster (superfine) sugar, to taste

1 Pour 150ml/¼ pint/⅔ cup hot water over the bulgur wheat and leave to stand for 15 minutes, then drain.

2 Place the bulgur in a bowl and add the minced lamb, onion, garlic, chilli, cumin, sumac, parsley and mint. Mix together thoroughly, then season with 5ml/1 tsp salt and plenty of black pepper. Form the mixture into eight burgers and set aside while you make the relish.

3 Grill (broil) the peppers, until the skin chars and blisters. Peel off the skin, dice and place in a bowl. Brush the onions with oil and grill until browned. Chop. Add the onions, tomatoes, chilli, mint, parsley, oregano and 2.5ml/½ tsp each of the cumin and sumac to the peppers. Stir in 60ml/4 tbsp oil and 15ml/1 tbsp of the lemon juice and salt, pepper and sugar to taste. Set aside.

4 Heat a frying pan over high heat and grease with olive oil. Cook the burgers for about 5–6 minutes on each side. Serve immediately with the relish.

Barbecued Lamb with Red Pepper Salsa

Vibrant red pepper salsa brings out the best in succulent lamb steaks to make a dish that looks as good as it tastes. Serve with a selection of salads and crusty bread.

Serves 6
6 lamb steaks
about 15g/1½oz/½ cup fresh
  rosemary sprigs
2 garlic cloves, sliced

60ml/4 tbsp olive oil
30ml/2 tbsp maple syrup
salt and ground black pepper
fresh flat leaf parsley, to garnish
green salad, to serve

For the salsa
200g/7oz red (bell) peppers,
  roasted, peeled, seeded
  and chopped
1 garlic clove, crushed
15ml/1 tbsp chopped chives
30ml/2 tbsp extra virgin olive oil

1 Place the lamb steaks in a shallow dish that will hold them all in one layer. Season with salt and pepper. Pull the leaves off the rosemary and sprinkle them over the meat.

2 Add the slices of garlic, then drizzle the olive oil and maple syrup over the top. Cover and chill until ready to cook. If you have time, the lamb steaks can be left to marinate in the refrigerator for 12 hours or up to 24 hours.

3 Prepare a barbecue or preheat the grill (broiler). Make sure that the steaks are liberally coated with the marinating ingredients, then cook them over the hot coals on the barbecue or under the grill for about 2–5 minutes on each side. The cooking time will depend on the heat of the barbecue coals and the thickness of the steaks as well as the result required – rare, medium or well cooked.

4 While the lamb steaks are cooking, mix together all the ingredients for the salsa in a large bowl. Serve the salsa spooned on to the serving plates with the meat or in a small serving dish on the side. Garnish the lamb with sprigs of flat leaf parsley and pass around a cool, crisp salad – iceberg lettuce would be ideal.

Burgers Energy 537kcal/2228kJ; Protein 27.2g; Carbohydrate 19g, of which sugars 13.4g; Fat 39.6g, of which saturates 11.1g; Cholesterol 96mg; Calcium 83mg; Fibre 4.2g; Sodium 105mg.
Barbecued Lamb Energy 390kcal/1627kJ; Protein 44.1g; Carbohydrate 2.1g, of which sugars 2g; Fat 22.8g, of which saturates 6.8g; Cholesterol 158mg; Calcium 33mg; Fibre 0.5g; Sodium 106mg.

Lamb Steaks with Redcurrant Glaze

Good and meaty, but thin enough to cook quickly, lamb leg steaks are a good choice for the cook short on time. The redcurrant and rosemary glaze looks gorgeous, especially with a fresh redcurrant garnish.

Serves 4
4 large fresh rosemary sprigs
4 lamb leg steaks
75ml/5 tbsp redcurrant jelly
30ml/2 tbsp raspberry or
*   red wine vinegar*
salt and ground black pepper
peas and new potatoes, to serve

1 Reserve the tips of the rosemary sprigs and finely chop the remaining leaves. Rub the chopped rosemary, salt and ground black pepper all over the lamb steaks. Cover and set aside to let the flavours mingle.

2 Preheat the grill (broiler). Heat the redcurrant jelly gently in a small pan with 30ml/2 tbsp water and a little seasoning. Stir in the raspberry or red wine vinegar.

3 Place the lamb steaks on a foil-lined grill (broiling) rack and brush with a little of the redcurrant glaze. Cook under the grill (broiler) for about 5 minutes on each side, until deep golden, brushing frequently with more redcurrant glaze.

4 Transfer the lamb to warmed serving plates. Pour any juices from the foil into the remaining glaze and heat through gently.

5 Pour the glaze over the lamb and serve immediately with peas and new potatoes garnished with rosemary sprigs.

Cook's Tip
This is a good recipe for the barbecue. Wait until the fierce heat has subsided and the coals are dusted with white ash, then place the rosemary-rubbed steaks directly on the grill (broiling) rack. Brush frequently with the glaze as they cook. If you grow your own rosemary, try sprinkling some over the coals. As the oil in the herb warms, the scent of rosemary will perfume the air and stimulate the appetite.

Barnsley Lamb Chops with Mustard Sauce

Named after the UK town of Barnsley, these double-sized lamb chops are cut from the saddle – the two loins with the backbone intact between them. If you can't get any, then double up on normal loin chops or ask your butcher to cut extra thick chops. The tangy mustard sauce is a favourite with lamb.

Serves 4
15ml/1 tbsp tender
*   rosemary leaves*
60ml/4 tbsp olive oil
4 Barnsley chops or 8 lamb
*   loin chops*
100ml/3½fl oz/scant ½ cup
*   lamb or beef stock*
30ml/2 tbsp wholegrain mustard
5ml/1 tsp Worcestershire sauce
salt and ground black pepper

1 Chop the rosemary very finely and mix with the oil. Rub the mixture over the chops and leave to stand, covered, for 30 minutes, or longer if refrigerated. Season lightly with salt and ground black pepper.

2 Heat a large frying pan, add the chops, in batches, and cook over medium heat for 5–8 minutes on each side until cooked through and tender. Lift the chops out of the pan, and set aside to keep warm.

3 Pour the stock into the hot pan, scraping up any sediment, and add the mustard. Heat until the mixture comes to the boil, then bubble gently until the sauce is reduced by about a third.

4 Stir the Worcestershire sauce into the sauce and adjust the seasoning to taste. Serve the chops with the mustard sauce spooned over.

Variation
For a richer variation of this dish, make a mustard cream sauce, by stirring in 150ml/¼ pint/⅔ cup sour cream at the end of step 3 and bubble gently for 2–3 minutes.

Lamb Steaks Energy 362kcal/1518kJ; Protein 34.4g; Carbohydrate 13g, of which sugars 13g; Fat 19.6g, of which saturates 9.1g; Cholesterol 133mg; Calcium 16mg; Fibre 00g; Sodium 156mg.
Lamb Chops Energy 582kcal/2401kJ; Protein 18.8g; Carbohydrate 0.9g, of which sugars 0.8g; Fat 55.9g, of which saturates 23.6g; Cholesterol 96mg; Calcium 17mg; Fibre 00g; Sodium 313mg.

Roast Leg of Lamb

Roast lamb is a year-round family favourite.

Serves 6
1.5kg/3¼lb leg of lamb
4 garlic cloves, sliced
2 fresh rosemary sprigs
30ml/2 tbsp light olive oil
300ml/½ pint/1¼ cups red wine
5ml/1 tsp honey
45ml/3 tbsp redcurrant jelly
salt and ground black pepper

For the roast potatoes
45ml/3 tbsp white vegetable fat
    or lard
1.3kg/3lb potatoes, cut into chunks

For the mint sauce
about 15g/½oz fresh mint
10ml/2 tsp caster (superfine) sugar
15ml/1 tbsp boiling water
30ml/2 tbsp white wine vinegar

1 Preheat the oven to 220°C/425°F/Gas 7. Make small slits into the lamb and press a slice of garlic and a few rosemary leaves into each slit. Place the joint in a roasting pan and season well. Drizzle the oil over the lamb and roast for about 1 hour.

2 Meanwhile, mix the wine, honey and redcurrant jelly in a pan and heat until the jelly melts. Bring to the boil, then reduce the heat and simmer until reduced by half. Spoon this glaze over the lamb and return it to the oven for 30–45 minutes.

3 To make the potatoes, put the fat in a roasting pan on the shelf above the meat. Boil the potatoes for 5–10 minutes, then drain them and fluff up the surface of each with a fork. Add them to the pan and baste well. Roast them for 40–50 minutes.

4 Meanwhile, make the mint sauce. Place the mint on a chopping board and sprinkle the sugar over the top. Chop the mint finely, then transfer the mint and sugar to a bowl.

5 Add the boiling water and stir until the sugar has dissolved. Add 15ml/1 tbsp vinegar and taste the sauce before adding the remaining vinegar. Leave to stand until you are ready to serve.

6 Cover the lamb with foil and set it aside in a warm place to rest for 10–15 minutes before carving. Serve with the crisp roast potatoes, mint sauce and seasonal vegetables.

Lamb Casserole with Garlic and Broad Beans

This recipe has a Spanish influence and makes a substantial meal, served with potatoes. It's based on stewing lamb with a large amount of garlic and sherry – the addition of broad beans gives colour.

Serves 6
45ml/3 tbsp olive oil
1.5kg/3–3½lb fillet lamb, cut into
    5cm/2in cubes
1 large onion, chopped
6 large garlic cloves, unpeeled
1 bay leaf
5ml/1 tsp paprika
120ml/4fl oz/½ cup dry sherry
115g/4oz shelled fresh or frozen
    broad (fava) beans
30ml/2 tbsp chopped
    fresh parsley
salt and ground black pepper
mashed or boiled potatoes,
    to serve (optional)

1 Heat 30ml/2 tbsp of the oil in a large flameproof casserole. Add half the lamb cubes to the pan and cook for 45 minutes until evenly browned on all sides. Transfer to a plate and set aside. Brown the rest of the meat in the same way and remove from the casserole.

2 Heat the remaining oil in the pan, add the onion and cook for about 5 minutes until softened and just beginning to turn brown. Return the browned lamb cubes to the casserole and stir in with the onion.

3 Add the garlic cloves, bay leaf, paprika and sherry to the casserole. Season with salt and ground black pepper. Bring the mixture to the boil, then reduce the heat. Cover the pan with a tight-fitting lid and simmer very gently for 1½–2 hours, until the meat is tender.

4 About 10 minutes before the end of the cooking time, stir in the broad beans. Re-cover the pan and place back in the oven until the meat and beans are tender.

5 Stir in the chopped parsley just before serving. Accompany the casserole with mashed or boiled potatoes, if you like.

Roast Leg of Lamb Energy 518kcal/2177kJ; Protein 61.3g; Carbohydrate 18.1g, of which sugars 1.5g; Fat 22.8g, of which saturates 8.2g; Cholesterol 200mg; Calcium 21mg; Fibre 1.1g; Sodium 138mg.
Lamb Casserole Energy 541kcal/2258kJ; Protein 50.8g; Carbohydrate 3.5g, of which sugars 1.2g; Fat 33.7g, of which saturates 13.8g; Cholesterol 190mg; Calcium 45mg; Fibre 1.6g; Sodium 221mg.

Herb-crusted Rack of Lamb

This roast is quick and easy to prepare, yet impressive when served: the perfect choice when entertaining. Boiled or steamed new potatoes and lightly cooked broccoli or sugar snap peas are suitable accompaniments for the lamb. Serve with a light red wine.

Serves 4
2 x 6-bone racks of lamb, chined
50g/2oz/1 cup fresh white
  breadcrumbs
2 large garlic cloves, crushed
90ml/6 tbsp chopped mixed fresh
  herbs, such as rosemary, thyme,
  flat leaf parsley and marjoram,
  plus extra sprigs to garnish
50g/2oz/¼ cup butter, melted
salt and ground black pepper

For the puy lentils
1 red onion, chopped
30ml/2 tbsp olive oil
400g/14oz can Puy or green
  lentils, rinsed and drained
400g/14oz can chopped
  tomatoes
30ml/2 tbsp chopped
  fresh parsley

1 Preheat the oven to 220°C/425°F/Gas 7. Trim any excess fat from the racks of lamb, and season well all over with salt and ground black pepper.

2 Mix together the breadcrumbs, garlic, herbs and butter in a bowl, and press on to the fat sides of the lamb. Place the racks in a roasting pan and roast for 25 minutes. When cooked, cover with foil and leave to stand for 5 minutes before carving.

3 Meanwhile, cook the onion in the olive oil until softened. Add the lentils and tomatoes and cook for 5 minutes, or until the lentils are piping hot. Stir in the parsley and season to taste.

4 Cut each rack of lamb in half and serve with the lentils and new potatoes. Garnish with herb sprigs.

> **Cook's Tip**
> Puy lentils, also called French green lentils, are a dark, speckled blue-green colour. They are more expensive than the more common green lentil but have a superior taste and texture.

Lamb, New Potato and Red Chilli Curry

This dish makes the most of an economical cut of meat by cooking it slowly until the meat is falling from the bone. Chillies and coconut cream give it lots of flavour.

Serves 4
25g/1oz/2 tbsp butter
4 garlic cloves, crushed
2 onions, sliced into rings
2.5ml/½ tsp each ground cumin,
  ground coriander, turmeric and
  cayenne pepper
2–3 red chillies, seeded and
  finely chopped
300ml/½ pint/1¼ cups hot
  chicken stock
200ml/7fl oz/scant 1 cup
  coconut cream
4 lamb shanks, all excess
  fat removed
450g/1lb new potatoes, halved
6 ripe tomatoes, quartered
salt and ground black pepper
coriander (cilantro) leaves,
  to garnish
spicy rice, to serve

1 Preheat the oven to 160°C/325°F/Gas 3. Melt the butter in a large flameproof casserole, add the garlic and onions and cook over low heat for 15 minutes, until golden. Stir in the spices and chillies, then cook for a further 2 minutes.

2 Add the hot stock and coconut cream. Place the lamb shanks in the liquid and cover the casserole with foil. Cook in the oven for 2 hours, turning the shanks twice, first after about an hour or so and again about half an hour later.

3 Par-boil the potatoes for 10 minutes, drain and add to the casserole with the tomatoes, then cook uncovered in the oven for a further 35 minutes. Season to taste with salt and pepper, garnish with coriander leaves and serve with the spicy rice.

> **Cook's Tip**
> Make this dish a day in advance if possible. Cool and chill overnight, then skim off the excess fat that has risen to the surface. Reheat the curry thoroughly before you serve it.

Rack of Lamb Energy 639kcal/2673kJ; Protein 51.5g; Carbohydrate 28.2g, of which sugars 1.9g; Fat 36.4g, of which saturates 16.7g; Cholesterol 171mg; Calcium 89mg; Fibre 4.9g; Sodium 294mg.
Lamb Curry Energy 364kcal/1528kJ; Protein 23.5g; Carbohydrate 30.5g, of which sugars 12.1g; Fat 17.4g, of which saturates 8.8g; Cholesterol 89mg; Calcium 58mg; Fibre 3.5g; Sodium 205mg.

Dhansak

Serve this tasty curry with basmati rice and Indian bread.

Serves 4–6
90ml/6 tbsp vegetable oil
5 fresh green chillies, chopped
2.5cm/1in piece fresh root ginger, grated
3 garlic cloves, crushed, plus 1 garlic clove, sliced
2 bay leaves
5cm/2in piece cinnamon stick
900g/2lb lean lamb, cubed
600ml/1 pint/2½ cups water
175g/6oz/¾ cup red whole lentils, washed and drained
50g/2oz/¼ cup each chana dhal, husked moong dhal and red lentils, washed and drained
2 potatoes, chopped
1 aubergine (eggplant), chopped
4 onions, finely sliced, deep-fried and drained
50g/2oz fresh spinach, trimmed, washed and chopped
25g/1oz fenugreek leaves, fresh or dried
115g/4oz carrots or pumpkin
115g/4oz fresh coriander (cilantro), chopped
50g/2oz fresh mint, chopped, or 15ml/1 tbsp mint sauce
30ml/2 tbsp dhansak masala
30ml/2 tbsp sambhar masala
10ml/2 tsp soft light brown sugar
60ml/4 tbsp tamarind juice
salt

1 Heat 45ml/3 tbsp of the oil in a large pan. Fry the chillies, ginger, crushed garlic, bay leaves and cinnamon for 2 minutes. Add the lamb pieces and the water. Bring to the boil, then simmer, covered, until the lamb is half cooked.

2 Strain the stock into another pan. Add the lentils and cook for 25–30 minutes. Add the potatoes and aubergine. Reserve a little of the fried onions and stir the remainder into the pan with the spinach, fenugreek and carrot or pumpkin. Cook until the vegetables are tender, then coarsely mash with a spoon.

3 Heat 15ml/1 tbsp of oil in a large frying pan. Reserve a few coriander and mint leaves and fry the remaining leaves with the dhansak and sambhar masala, salt and sugar. Add the lamb pieces and fry gently for 5 minutes. Stir into the lentils and vegetables with the tamarind juice. Cover and simmer for 10–15 minutes.

4 Fry the sliced garlic in oil until golden, then garnish the dhansak with the garlic, onion, and reserved coriander and mint leaves.

Moussaka

This Greek dish with layered lamb, potatoes and aubergines is topped with a rich, cheesy sauce to make a substantial meal.

Serves 6
30ml/2 tbsp olive oil
30ml/2 tbsp chopped fresh oregano
1 large onion, finely chopped
675g/1½lb lean minced (ground) lamb
1 large aubergine (eggplant), sliced
2 x 400g/14oz cans chopped tomatoes
45ml/3 tbsp tomato purée (paste)
1 lamb stock (bouillon) cube, crumbled
2 floury main crop potatoes, halved
115g/4oz/1 cup Cheddar cheese, grated
150ml/¼ pint/⅔ cup single (light) cream
salt and ground black pepper
fresh bread, to serve

1 Preheat the oven to 180°C/350°F/Gas 4. Heat the olive oil in a large deep-sided frying pan. Fry the oregano and onions over low heat, stirring frequently, for about 5 minutes or until the onions have softened.

2 Stir in the lamb and cook for 10 minutes until browned. Meanwhile, grill (broil) the aubergine slices for 5 minutes until browned, turning once.

3 Stir the tomatoes and purée into the meat mixture, and crumble the stock cube over it, stir well, season with salt and pepper and simmer uncovered for a further 15 minutes.

4 Meanwhile, cook the potatoes in lightly salted boiling water for 5–10 minutes until just tender. Drain, and when cool enough to handle, cut into thin slices.

5 Layer the aubergines, lamb and potatoes in a 1.75 litre/3 pint/7½ cup oval ovenproof dish, finishing with a layer of potatoes.

6 Mix the cheese and cream together in a bowl and pour over the top of the other ingredients in the dish. Cook for around 45–50 minutes until the moussaka is bubbling and golden on the top. Serve straight from the dish, while hot, with plenty of fresh, crusty bread.

Dhansak Energy 627kcal/2626kJ; Protein 43.6g; Carbohydrate 48.6g, of which sugars 12g; Fat 30.3g, of which saturates 9.4g; Cholesterol 114mg; Calcium 141mg; Fibre 6.5g; Sodium 177mg.
Moussaka Energy 588Kcal/2444kJ; Protein 37.9g; Carbohydrate 14.8g, of which sugars 3.7g; Fat 40.9g, of which saturates 18.2g; Cholesterol 206mg; Calcium 379mg; Fibre 2.4g; Sodium 506mg.

Haggis with Clapshot Cake

This is a traditional haggis recipe served with turnip and potato clapshot – a variation on the usual dish of 'haggis with neeps and tatties', or boiled turnips and potatoes.

Serves 4
1 large haggis, approximately 800g/1¾lb
450g/1lb peeled turnip or swede (rutabaga)
225g/8oz peeled potatoes
120ml/4fl oz/½ cup milk
1 garlic clove, crushed with 5ml/1 tsp salt
175ml/6fl oz/¾ cup double (heavy) cream
freshly grated nutmeg
ground black pepper
butter, for greasing

1 Preheat the oven to 180°C/350°F/Gas 4. Wrap the haggis in foil, covering it completely and folding over the edges of the foil. Place the haggis in a roasting pan with 2.5cm/1in water. Heat through in the preheated oven for 30–40 minutes.

2 Slice the turnip or swede and potatoes quite finely. A mandolin or food processor is quite handy for this as both vegetables tend to be difficult to cut finely with a knife.

3 Put the sliced vegetables in a large pan and add the milk and garlic. Stir gently over low heat until the potatoes begin to break down and the liquid thickens slightly.

4 Add the cream and nutmeg and some pepper into the mixture. Stir gently but thoroughly. Slowly bring to the boil, reduce the heat and simmer gently for a few minutes.

5 Butter a deep round 18cm/7in dish or a small roasting pan. Transfer the mixture to the dish or pan. It should not come up too high as it will rise slightly and bubble. Bake in the oven for about 1 hour, or until the top is golden brown.

6 Remove the foil from the haggis, place on a warmed serving dish and bring out to the table for your guests to witness the cutting. Use a sharp knife to cut through the skin, then spoon out the haggis on to warmed plates. Serve the clapshot cake in slices with the haggis, spooning any juices over.

Lancashire Hotpot

This famous hotpot was traditionally cooked in a farmhouse oven, in time for supper at the end of the day. The ingredients would have been layered straight into the pot, but here the meat is first browned to add colour and extra flavour to the dish.

Serves 4
15–30ml/1–2 tbsp oil
8–12 lean best end of neck (cross rib) lamb chops
about 175g/6oz lamb's kidneys, skin and core removed and cut into pieces
2 medium onions, thinly sliced
few sprigs of fresh thyme or rosemary
900g/2lb potatoes, thinly sliced
600ml/1 pint/2½ cups lamb or vegetable stock
25g/1oz/2 tbsp butter, in small pieces
salt and ground black pepper

1 Preheat the oven to 180°C/350°F/Gas 4. Heat the oil in a large frying pan and brown the lamb chops quickly on all sides. Remove the meat from the pan and set aside.

2 Add the pieces of kidney to the hot pan and brown lightly over high heat. Lift out.

3 In a casserole, layer the chops and kidneys with the onions, herbs and potatoes, seasoning each layer.

4 Finish off with a layer of potatoes. Pour over the stock, sprinkle with herbs and dot the top with butter. Cover, put into the preheated oven and cook for 2 hours.

5 Remove the lid, increase the oven to 220°C/425°F/Gas 7 and cook, uncovered, for a further 30 minutes until the potatoes on top are crisp. Serve immediately.

> **Variation**
> Add sliced carrots or mushrooms to the layers. Replace 150ml/ ¼ pint/⅔ cup of stock with dry (hard) cider or dry white wine.

Hotpot Energy 810kcal/3400kJ; Protein 76.7g; Carbohydrate 43.7g, of which sugars 9.3g; Fat 37.8g, of which saturates 13.2g; Cholesterol 363mg; Calcium 140mg; Fibre 6.2g; Sodium 285mg.
Haggis Energy 918kcal/3819kJ; Protein 24.9g; Carbohydrate 55.3g, of which sugars 8.5g; Fat 67.9g, of which saturates 30.2g; Cholesterol 244mg; Calcium 180mg; Fibre 3.1g; Sodium 1586mg.

Veal in a Wheat Beer Sauce

The bitterness of the beer in this stew is matched by the sweet onions and carrots.

Serves 4

900g/2lb boned shoulder or leg of
   veal, cut into 5cm/2in cubes
45ml/3 tbsp plain (all-purpose)
   flour, seasoned
65g/2¹/₂oz/5 tbsp butter
3 shallots, finely chopped
I celery stick
fresh parsley sprig
2 fresh bay leaves
5ml/I tsp caster (superfine) sugar,
   plus a good pinch
250ml/8fl oz/I cup wheat beer
475ml/16fl oz/2 cups veal stock
20–25 large silverskin onions or
   small pickling (pearl) onions
450g/1lb carrots, thickly sliced
2 large egg yolks
105ml/7 tbsp double (heavy) cream
a little lemon juice (optional)
30ml/2 tbsp chopped fresh parsley
salt and ground black pepper

I Dust the veal with the flour. Heat 25g/1oz/2 tbsp of the butter in a frying pan, add the veal and quickly cook until just golden. Remove the veal and set aside. Add 15g/½oz/1 tbsp butter to the pan and gently cook the shallots for 5–6 minutes.

2 Replace the veal. Tie the celery, parsley and 1 bay leaf, then add to the pan with a pinch of sugar. Pour in the beer and bubble briefly, then pour in the stock. Season, then cover and simmer for 40–50 minutes, or until the veal is cooked.

3 Meanwhile, melt the remaining butter in another frying pan. Cook the onions until golden all over. Remove from the pan and set aside. Add the carrots, 5ml/1 tsp sugar, a pinch of salt, the bay leaf and enough water to cover. Bring to the boil and cook for 10–12 minutes. Add the onions and continue to cook until the onions and carrots are tender and slightly caramelized.

4 Transfer the veal to a bowl and discard the celery and herb bundle. Mix the egg yolks and cream in another bowl, then add a ladleful of carrot liquid. Return this mixture to the pan and cook over very low heat, stirring, until the sauce has thickened.

5 Add the veal to the sauce, add the onions and carrots and reheat until warmed through. Season to taste, adding lemon juice, if necessary, then serve, sprinkled with the parsley.

Osso Bucco with Risotto Milanese

Osso bucco, literally meaning 'bone with a hole', is an Italian stew of veal, onions and leeks in wine.

Serves 4

50g/2oz/1/4 cup butter
15ml/1 tbsp olive oil
I large onion, chopped
I leek, finely chopped
45ml/3 tbsp plain
   (all-purpose) flour
4 large portions of veal shin,
   hind cut
600ml/1 pint/2¹/₂ cups dry
   white wine
salt and ground black pepper

For the risotto
25g/1oz/2 tbsp butter
I onion, finely chopped
350g/12oz/1²/₃ cups risotto rice
I litre/1³/₄ pints/4 cups boiling
   chicken stock
2.5ml/½ tsp saffron strands
60ml/4 tbsp white wine
50g/2oz/²/₃ cup Parmesan
   cheese, coarsely grated

For the gremolata
grated rind of I lemon
30ml/2 tbsp chopped
   fresh parsley
I garlic clove, finely chopped

I Heat the butter and oil in a frying pan. Add the onion and leek, and cook for 5 minutes without browning. Season the flour and dust the veal, then cook over high heat until browned.

2 Gradually stir in the wine and heat until simmering. Cover the pan and simmer for 1½ hours, stirring occasionally, until the meat is very tender. Use a draining spoon to transfer the veal to a warmed dish, then boil the sauce until reduced a little.

3 Make the risotto about 30 minutes before the stew is ready. Melt the butter in a large pan and cook the onion until softened. Stir in the rice to coat all the grains in butter. Add a ladleful of stock and mix well. Add the stock a ladleful at a time, as it is absorbed by the rice.

4 Pound the saffron strands in a mortar, then stir in the wine. Pour into the risotto and cook for a final 5 minutes. Remove the pan from the heat and stir in the Parmesan.

5 Make the gremolata by mixing the lemon rind, parsley and garlic. Serve the risotto and veal, sprinkled with the gremolata.

Veal Energy 672kcal/2801kJ; Protein 53.4g; Carbohydrate 32.4g, of which sugars 17.4g; Fat 36.2g, of which saturates 19.5g; Cholesterol 358mg; Calcium 147mg; Fibre 5.4g; Sodium 389mg.
Osso Bucco Energy 901kcal/3764kJ; Protein 49.1g; Carbohydrate 92g, of which sugars 8g; Fat 25.9g, of which saturates 13.7g; Cholesterol 130mg; Calcium 248mg; Fibre 2.9g; Sodium 349mg.

Chunky Burgers with Spicy Relish

Burgers are easy to make and these taste terrific – far better than any ready-made ones you can buy. Use lean minced beef so that the burgers are not fatty.

Serves 4
450g/1lb lean minced
(ground) beef
1 shallot, chopped
30ml/2 tbsp chopped fresh flat
leaf parsley
30ml/2 tbsp tomato ketchup
salt and ground black pepper

For the spicy relish
15ml/1 tbsp olive oil
1 shallot, chopped
1 garlic clove, crushed
1 small fresh green chilli, seeded
and finely chopped
400g/14oz can ratatouille

To serve
4 burger buns
1 Little Gem (Bibb) lettuce heart,
separated into leaves

1 Mix the lean minced beef, chopped shallot, chopped fresh flat leaf parsley, ketchup and seasoning in a mixing bowl until thoroughly combined.

2 Divide the mixture into quarters and shape into four chunky burgers, pressing them firmly between the palms of your hands. Place the burgers on a plate and set aside until ready to cook.

3 To make the spicy relish, heat the olive oil in a frying pan and cook the shallot, garlic and chilli for a few minutes, stirring frequently, until softened. Stir in the ratatouille and simmer for about 5 minutes.

4 Meanwhile, preheat the grill (broiler), a griddle (grill) pan or frying pan. Grill (broil) or fry the burgers for about 5 minutes on each side, or until cooked through.

5 Split the burger buns and toast them, if you like. Arrange a few lettuce leaves on the bun bases, then top with the burgers and add a little of the warm spicy relish. Add the bun tops and serve immediately, offering the remaining relish and any extra lettuce leaves separately. Serve with chunky chips (French fries) or baked potatoes.

Sliced Seared Beef

These Japanese beef rolls make an excellent light lunch or supper treat.

Serves 4
generous pinch of salt
500g/1¼lb chunk of beef thigh
(a long, thin chunk looks better
than a thick, round chunk)
10ml/2 tsp vegetable oil

For the marinade
175ml/6fl oz/¼ cup rice vinegar
70ml/4½ tbsp sake
150ml/¼ pint/⅔ cup shoyu
15ml/1 tbsp sugar
1 garlic clove, thinly sliced
1 small onion, thinly sliced
sansho

For the garnish
about 15cm/6in Japanese or
ordinary salad cucumber, cut
into matchsticks
6 shiso leaves and shiso flowers,
cut into thin strips
½ lemon, thinly sliced
1 garlic clove, grated (optional)

1 Mix the marinade ingredients in a small pan and warm through until the sugar has dissolved. Set aside to cool. Rub the salt into the meat. Leave for 3 minutes, then rub the oil in.

2 Fill a bowl with cold water. Put a mesh grill tray over the heat on the stove, or heat a griddle (grill) pan. Sear the beef, turning frequently until about 5mm/¼in is cooked. Dip into the water briefly, pat dry, and then submerge in the marinade for 1 day.

3 Remove the meat and strain the marinade, reserving the liquid and the marinated onions and garlic. Cut the beef into 5mm/¼in slices.

4 Heap the cucumber sticks on a large serving plate and put the marinated onion and garlic on top. Arrange the beef slices alongside or on the bed of cucumber and other vegetables.

5 Fluff the shiso strips and put on top of the beef. Decorate with shiso flowers, if using. Lightly sprinkle with the lemon rings, and serve with the reserved marinade in individual bowls.

6 To eat, take a few beef slices on to individual plates. Roll a slice with your choice of garnish, then dip it into the marinade. Add a little grated garlic, if using.

Sliced Seared Beef Energy 258kcal/1079kJ; Protein 28.7g; Carbohydrate 9.8g, of which sugars 9.8g; Fat 11.7g, of which saturates 4.8g; Cholesterol 73mg; Calcium 20mg; Fibre 0.3g; Sodium 82mg.
Chunky Burgers Energy 484kcal/2021kJ; Protein 27.9g; Carbohydrate 30.2g, of which sugars 7.7g; Fat 28.8g, of which saturates 9.3g; Cholesterol 68mg; Calcium 120mg; Fibre 2.2g; Sodium 473mg.

Spicy Corned Beef and Egg Hash

This is real nursery, or comfort, food at its best. Whether you remember Gran's version, or prefer this American-style hash, it turns corned beef into a supper fit for any guest.

Serves 4

30ml/2 tbsp vegetable oil
25g/1oz/2 tbsp butter
1 onion, finely chopped
1 green (bell) pepper, diced
2 large firm boiled potatoes,
   cut into small chunks
350g/12oz can corned beef, cut
   into small cubes
1.5ml/¼ tsp grated nutmeg
1.5ml/¼ tsp paprika
4 eggs
salt and ground black pepper
deep-fried parsley, to garnish
sweet chilli sauce or tomato
   sauce, to serve

1 Heat the oil and butter together in a large frying pan. Add the onion and fry for 5–6 minutes until softened.

2 In a bowl, mix together the green pepper, potatoes, corned beef, nutmeg and paprika and season well with salt and black pepper. Add to the pan and toss gently to distribute the cooked onion. Press down lightly and fry without stirring on medium heat for about 3–4 minutes until a golden brown crust has formed on the underside.

3 Stir the mixture through to distribute the brown crust, then repeat the frying and breaking up process twice more, until the mixture is well browned.

4 Make four wells in the hash and carefully crack an egg into each. Cover and cook gently for about 4–5 minutes until the egg whites are set.

5 Sprinkle with deep-fried parsley and cut into quarters. Serve hot with sweet chilli sauce or tomato sauce.

Cook's Tip
Chill the can of corned beef for about half an hour before use – it will be easier to cut it into cubes.

Pan-fried Steak with Warm Tomato Salsa

A tangy salsa of tomatoes, spring onions and balsamic vinegar makes a colourful topping for chunky, pan-fried steaks cooked just the way you like them.

Serves 2

2 steaks, about 2cm/¾in thick
4 large plum tomatoes
2 spring onions (scallions)
30ml/2 tbsp balsamic vinegar
salt and ground black pepper

1 Trim any excess fat from the steaks, then season on both sides with salt and pepper. Heat a non-stick frying pan and cook the steaks for about 3 minutes on each side for medium rare. Cook for a little longer if you like your steak well cooked.

2 Meanwhile, put the tomatoes in a heatproof bowl, cover with boiling water and leave for 1–2 minutes.

3 When the tomato skins start to split, drain and peel them, then halve the tomatoes and scoop out the seeds. Dice the tomato flesh.

4 When the steaks are cooked to your taste, remove from the pan with a fish slice or metal spatula, to drain off any excess oil, and transfer them to plates. Keep the steaks warm on a very low oven temperature while you prepare the salsa.

5 Thinly slice the spring onions and add them to the cooking juices in the frying pan with the diced tomato, balsamic vinegar, 30ml/2 tbsp water and a little seasoning. Stir briefly until warm, scraping up any meat residue. Spoon the salsa over the steaks, dividing it equally between them, and serve.

Cook's Tip
Choose rump (round), sirloin or fillet steak (beef tenderloin). If you prefer to grill (broil) the steak, the timing will be the same as the recipe, though you must take into account the thickness of the meat.

Hash Energy 1683kcal/7030kJ; Protein 123.4g; Carbohydrate 67.9g, of which sugars 21.6g; Fat 104.6g, of which saturates 42.2g; Cholesterol 1108mg; Calcium 260mg; Fibre 6.6g; Sodium 3483mg.
Pan-fried Steak Energy 207kcal/872kJ; Protein 33.9g; Carbohydrate 3.4g, of which sugars 3.4g; Fat 6.5g, of which saturates 2.7g; Cholesterol 89mg; Calcium 17mg; Fibre 1.2g; Sodium 100mg.

The Gaucho Barbecue

There is no better way of enjoying the prestigious Pampas beef than with a traditional barbecue. The meat is cooked simply, with no need for rubs or marinades, then enjoyed with a delicious selection of salads and salsas.

Serves 6
50g/2oz/¼ cup coarse sea salt
200ml/7fl oz/ scant 1 cup
   warm water
6 pork sausages
1kg/2¼lb beef short ribs
1kg/2¼lb rump (round) steak, in
   one piece
salads, salsas and breads, to serve

1 Dissolve the sea salt in the warm water in a bowl. Leave to cool. Meanwhile, prepare the barbecue. If you are using a charcoal grill, light the coals about 40 minutes before you want to start cooking. Wait until the coals are no longer red but are covered in white ash. Occasionally add coals to the barbecue to maintain this temperature.

2 Start by cooking the sausages, which should take about 15–20 minutes depending on the size. Once cooked on all sides, slice the sausages thickly and arrange on a plate. Let guests help themselves while you cook the remaining meats.

3 The short ribs should be placed bony side down on the grill. Cook for 15 minutes, turn, brush the cooked side of each rib with brine and grill for a further 25–30 minutes. Slice and transfer to a plate for guests to help themselves.

4 Place the whole rump steak on the grill and cook for 5 minutes, then turn over and baste the browned side with brine. Continue turning and basting in this way for 20–25 minutes in total, until the meat is cooked to your liking. Allow the meat to rest for 5 minutes, then slice thinly and serve with plenty of salad, salsa and bread.

Cook's Tip
Regularly basting the meat with brine, which is salted water, helps to keep it moist and succulent.

Collops of Fillet Steak with Shallots

Caramelized shallots are delicious. The time needed for cooking the steaks will depend upon how thick they are. Rare meat will feel soft to the touch; medium will have some resistance; well done will feel firm.

Serves 4
4 fillet steaks (beef tenderloins)
15ml/1 tbsp olive oil
50g/2oz/¼ cup butter
20 shallots, peeled
5ml/1 tsp caster (superfine) sugar
150ml/¼ pint/⅔ cup beef stock
salt and ground black pepper

1 Take the steaks out of the refrigerator well before you need them and dry with kitchen paper. Heat the oil and butter in a large frying pan then cook the steaks allowing 3–4 minutes for rare, 4–5 minutes for medium or 5–6 minutes for well-done meat.

2 Once cooked remove the steaks from the pan and keep warm. Put the shallots in the pan and brown lightly in the meat juices.

3 Add the sugar to the shallots, and then stir in the stock. Reduce the heat to low and allow the liquid to evaporate, shaking the pan from time to time to stop the shallots from sticking.

4 The shallots will end up slightly soft, browned and caramelized with a shiny glaze. Season to taste with salt and ground black pepper.

5 Serve the steaks on warmed plates and spoon over the caramelized shallots and juices from the pan.

Cook's Tip
Serve with sautéed potatoes. Cook unpeeled baby potatoes in boiling salted water for about 20 minutes until just tender. Drain, cool, then remove the skins. Slice thickly. Heat a mixture of olive oil and butter in a frying pan and cook the potato slices until browned and crisp. Drain on kitchen paper and serve.

Gaucho Barbecue Energy 785kcal/3283kJ; Protein 97.5g; Carbohydrate 4.8g, of which sugars 0.7g; Fat 41.9g, of which saturates 17.4g; Cholesterol 257mg; Calcium 42mg; Fibre 0.3g; Sodium 575mg.
Collops of Fillet Steak Energy 424kcal/1767kJ; Protein 43.2g; Carbohydrate 6.1g, of which sugars 4.6g; Fat 25.4g, of which saturates 12.5g; Cholesterol 149mg; Calcium 27mg; Fibre 0.9g; Sodium 166mg.

Fillet Steak with Pickled Walnuts

This is a traditional way of cooking beef, which makes it go a little further with the use of the onions. Fillet mignons are the small pieces from the end of the fillet.

Serves 4
15ml/1 tbsp vegetable oil
75g/3oz/6 tbsp butter
8 slices of beef fillet (fillet mignon)
4 onions, sliced
15ml/1 tbsp pickled walnuts
salt and ground black pepper

1 Heat the oil and half the butter in a frying pan and cook the steaks until almost done – about 3–4 minutes on each side depending on thickness and preference (see Cook's Tip). Keep them warm and set aside.

2 Once you have taken your steaks out of the pan, melt the remaining butter, then add the sliced onions. Increase the heat and stir to brown and soften the onions, scraping the base of the pan.

3 Add the pickled walnuts and juice and cook for a few minutes. Season to taste with salt and ground black pepper. Serve the beef on warmed plates and spoon the onions and juices over.

Variation
If you prefer, use mushroom sauce instead of pickled walnuts. and serve with button (white) mushrooms fried in butter.

Cook's Tip
Be sure to cook the steaks how you and your guests like them. For many people the sight of bloody juices coming from their steak is a bit off-putting. For rare steaks, cook as in step 1 and perhaps for a minute or two longer. For medium rare, cook for an additional 2–3 minutes or 4–5 minutes for well done – although exact cooking times will depend on the thickness of the steaks and the heat of your pan. To be on the extra safe side, you may have to cut into your steak to check.

Steak Béarnaise

Béarnaise sauce is a classic accompaniment for griddled, grilled or pan-fried steak. Tarragon complements the steak. Roasted vegetables make a good accompaniment.

Serves 4
4 sirloin steaks, about 225g/8oz each, trimmed
salt and ground black pepper

For the Béarnaise sauce
90ml/6 tbsp white wine vinegar
12 black peppercorns
2 bay leaves
2 shallots, finely chopped
4 fresh tarragon sprigs
4 egg yolks
225g/8oz/1 cup unsalted (sweet) butter, diced
30ml/2 tbsp chopped tarragon
ground white pepper

1 For the sauce, put the vinegar, peppercorns, bay leaves, shallots and tarragon sprigs in a small pan and simmer until reduced to 30ml/2 tbsp. Strain the vinegar. Beat the egg yolks with salt and white pepper in a heatproof bowl. Stand the bowl over a pan of simmering water, then beat in the vinegar.

2 Gradually beat in the butter, one piece at a time, allowing each addition to melt before adding the next. Do not allow the water to heat beyond a gentle simmer or the sauce will overheat and curdle. Beat the chopped fresh tarragon into the sauce and remove the pan from the heat. The sauce should be smooth, thick and glossy.

3 Cover the surface of the sauce with clear film (plastic wrap) or dampened baking parchment to prevent a skin forming, and leave over the pan of hot water, still off the heat, to keep warm while you cook the steak.

4 Season the steaks with salt and plenty of ground black pepper. Cook the steaks for 2–4 minutes on each side. The cooking time depends on the thickness of the steaks and the extent to which you want to cook them. As a guide, 2–4 minutes will give a medium-rare result.

5 Serve the steaks on warmed plates. Peel the clear film or dampened baking parchment off the sauce and stir it lightly, then spoon it over the steaks.

Fillet Steak Energy 490kcal/2036kJ; Protein 43.4g; Carbohydrate 6.1g, of which sugars 4.3g; Fat 32.6g, of which saturates 17g; Cholesterol 167mg; Calcium 31mg; Fibre 1.1g; Sodium 219mg.
Steak Béarnaise Energy 796kcal/3297kJ; Protein 51.1g; Carbohydrate 0.5g, of which sugars 0.4g; Fat 65.5g, of which saturates 37.2g; Cholesterol 459mg; Calcium 50mg; Fibre 0.2g; Sodium 450mg.

Boeuf Bourguignon

The is a classic French dish of beef cooked in Burgundy style, with red wine, pieces of bacon, shallots and mushrooms. It is baked in a low oven for hours until the meat is deliciously tender and succulent.

Serves 6

175g/6oz rindless streaky
  (fatty) bacon rashers
  (strips), chopped
900g/2lb lean braising steak,
  such as top rump
  (round) steak

30ml/2 tbsp plain
  (all-purpose) flour
45ml/3 tbsp sunflower oil
25g/1oz/2 tbsp butter
12 shallots
2 garlic cloves, crushed
175g/6oz/2¹⁄₃ cups mushrooms,
  sliced
450ml/³⁄₄ pint/scant 2 cups
  robust red wine
150ml/¹⁄₄ pint/²⁄₃ cup beef stock
  or consommé
1 bay leaf
2 sprigs each of fresh thyme,
  parsley and marjoram
salt and ground black pepper

1 Preheat the oven to 160°C/325°F/Gas 3. Heat a large flameproof casserole, then add the chopped bacon and cook, stirring occasionally, until the pieces are crisp and golden brown.

2 Meanwhile, cut the beef into 2.5cm/1in cubes. Season the flour and use to coat the meat. Use a slotted spoon to remove the bacon from the casserole and set aside. Add the oil, and then fry the beef in batches until light browned all over. Set aside with the bacon.

3 Add the butter to the fat remaining in the casserole. Cook the shallots and garlic until they are just beginning to colour, then add the mushrooms and cook for a further 5 minutes.

4 Return the bacon and beef to the casserole, and stir in the red wine and the beef stock or consommé. Tie the herbs together to create a bouquet garni and add to the casserole.

5 Cover with a tight fitting lid and cook in the oven for about 1½–2 hours, or until the meat is tender, stirring once or twice during the cooking time. Season to taste and serve with creamy mashed root vegetables, such as celeriac and potatoes.

Fillet of Beef Stroganoff

Legend has it that this famous Russian recipe was devised to use beef that was frozen by the Siberian climate. The only way it could be cooked was in very thin strips. The strips of lean beef were served in a sour cream sauce flavoured with brandy.

Serves 8

1.2kg/2½lb fillet of beef
30ml/2 tbsp plain
  (all-purpose) flour

large pinch each of cayenne
  pepper and paprika
75ml/5 tbsp sunflower oil
1 large onion, chopped
3 garlic cloves, finely chopped
450g/1lb/6½ cups brown cap
  (cremini) mushrooms, sliced
75ml/5 tbsp brandy
300ml/½ pint/1¼ cups beef
  stock or consommé
300ml/½ pint/1¼ cups
  sour cream
45ml/3 tbsp chopped fresh flat
  leaf parsley
salt and ground black pepper

1 Thinly slice the fillet of beef across the grain, then cut it into fine strips. Season the flour with the cayenne pepper and paprika.

2 Heat half the oil in a large frying pan, add the onion and garlic, and cook gently, stirring occasionally, for 6–8 minutes until the onion has softened.

3 Add the mushrooms and stir-fry over high heat. Transfer the vegetables and their juices to a dish and set aside.

4 Wipe the pan, then add and heat the remaining oil. Coat a batch of meat with flour, then stir-fry over high heat until browned. Remove from the pan, then coat and stir-fry another batch. When the last batch of steak is cooked, replace all the meat and vegetables. Add the brandy and simmer until it has almost evaporated.

5 Stir in the stock or consommé and seasoning and cook for 10–15 minutes, stirring frequently, or until the meat is tender and the sauce is thick and glossy. Add the sour cream and sprinkle with chopped parsley. Serve immediately with rice and a simple salad.

Boeuf Bourguignon Energy 749kcal/3117kJ; Protein 63.3g; Carbohydrate 15.2g, of which sugars 8.8g; Fat 40.3g, of which saturates 14g; Cholesterol 167mg; Calcium 69mg; Fibre 2.8g; Sodium 868mg.
Beef Stroganoff Energy 399kcal/1659kJ; Protein 34.6g; Carbohydrate 6.5g, of which sugars 3g; Fat 23.9g, of which saturates 9.8g; Cholesterol 114mg; Calcium 56mg; Fibre 1.1g; Sodium 85mg.

Stir-fried Beef in Oyster Sauce

Mouthwatering tender rump steak is cooked here in a delicious combination with shiitake, oyster and straw mushrooms flavoured with garlic, ginger and chilli.

Serves 4–6

450g/1lb rump (round) steak
30ml/2 tbsp soy sauce
15ml/1 tbsp cornflour
   (cornstarch)
45ml/3 tbsp vegetable oil
15ml/1 tbsp chopped garlic
15ml/1 tbsp chopped fresh
   root ginger
225g/8oz/3¼ cups mixed
   mushrooms, such as shiitake,
   oyster and straw
30ml/2 tbsp oyster sauce
5ml/1 tsp sugar
4 spring onions (scallions), cut into
   short lengths
ground black pepper
2 fresh red chillies, seeded and
   cut into strips, to garnish

1 Place the steak in the freezer for about 30–40 minutes, until firm since this will help when slicing it. Using a sharp knife, slice it on the diagonal into thin strips.

2 Mix together the soy sauce and cornflour in a large bowl. Add the steak, turning to coat well, cover with clear film (plastic wrap) and leave to marinate at room temperature for 1–2 hours.

3 Heat half the oil in a wok or large, heavy frying pan. Add the garlic and ginger and cook for 1–2 minutes, until fragrant. Drain the steak, add it to the wok or pan and stir well to separate the strips. Cook, stirring frequently, for a further 1–2 minutes, until the steak is browned all over and tender. Remove from the wok or pan and set aside.

4 Heat the remaining oil in the wok or pan. Add the mushrooms and stir-fry over medium heat until golden brown.

5 Return the steak to the wok and mix it with the mushrooms. Spoon in the oyster sauce and sugar, mix well, then add ground black pepper to taste. Toss over the heat until all the ingredients are thoroughly combined. Stir in the spring onions. Transfer the mixture on to a serving platter, garnish with the strips of red chilli and serve.

Stir-fried Beef and Mushrooms

The combination of garlic and black beans is a classic Cantonese seasoning for beef. Serve boiled rice as an accompaniment.

Serves 4

30ml/2 tbsp soy sauce
30ml/2 tbsp Chinese rice wine or
   dry sherry
10ml/2 tsp cornflour (cornstarch)
10ml/2 tsp sesame oil
450g/1lb fillet or rump (round)
   steak, trimmed of fat
12 dried shiitake mushrooms
25ml/1½ tbsp salted black beans
5ml/1 tsp sugar
120ml/4fl oz/½ cup groundnut
   (peanut) oil
4 garlic cloves, thinly sliced
2.5cm/1in piece fresh root ginger,
   cut into fine strips
200g/7oz open cap
   mushrooms, sliced
1 bunch spring onions (scallions),
   sliced diagonally
1 fresh red chilli, seeded and
   finely sliced
salt and ground black pepper

1 In a bowl, mix half the soy sauce, half the rice wine or sherry, half the cornflour and all the sesame oil with 15ml/1 tbsp cold water and season. Very thinly slice the beef and stir into the cornflour mixture. Set aside for 30 minutes.

2 Pour boiling water over the dried mushrooms and soak for 25 minutes. Drain, reserving 45ml/3 tbsp of the soaking water. Remove and discard the hard stalks and cut the caps in half. Mash the black beans and sugar in a bowl. Mix the remaining cornflour, soy sauce and wine or sherry in another bowl.

3 Heat the groundnut oil in a wok until very hot. Stir-fry the beef for 30–45 seconds, until just brown. Transfer to a plate. Pour off some oil to leave about 45ml/3 tbsp in the wok. Stir-fry the garlic and ginger for 1 minute, then add the shiitake and fresh mushrooms for 2 minutes. Set aside a handful of the green spring onion tops, then add the rest to the wok. Stir, add the mashed black beans and stir-fry for another 1–2 minutes.

4 Stir the beef back into the wok, then add the reserved shiitake water. Stir the cornflour mixture into the wok and simmer until the sauce thickens. Sprinkle the chilli and reserved spring onions over the beef and serve immediately.

Beef in Oyster Sauce Energy 160Kcal/670kJ; Protein 17.6g; Carbohydrate 2.9g, of which sugars 2.7g; Fat 8.8g, of which saturates 2g; Cholesterol 44mg; Calcium 10mg; Fibre 0.6g; Sodium 485mg.
Beef and Mushrooms Energy 208kcal/873kJ; Protein 25.9g; Carbohydrate 4.7g, of which sugars 1.5g; Fat 8.8g, of which saturates 3.5g; Cholesterol 69mg; Calcium 20mg; Fibre 1.1g; Sodium 590mg.

Garlic and Chilli Marinated Beef

Fruity and smoky chillies combine well with garlic in this marinade for steak. Cornmeal makes a crisp coating for the onion rings.

Serves 4

20g/³⁄₄oz mild dried red chillies (such as mulato or pasilla), stalks and seeds removed
2 garlic cloves, plain or smoked, finely chopped
5ml/1 tsp ground toasted cumin seeds
5ml/1 tsp dried oregano
60ml/4 tbsp olive oil
4 x 175–225g/6–8oz beef steaks
salt and ground black pepper

For the onion rings
2 onions, sliced into rings
250ml/8fl oz/1 cup milk
75g/3oz/³⁄₄ cup coarse cornmeal
2.5ml/¹⁄₂ tsp dried red chilli flakes
5ml/1 tsp ground toasted cumin seeds
5ml/1 tsp dried oregano
vegetable oil, for deep-frying

1 Dry-fry the chillies in a frying pan for 2–4 minutes, until they give off their aroma. Transfer to a bowl, cover with warm water and leave for 20–30 minutes. Drain and reserve the water.

2 Process the chillies with the garlic, cumin, oregano and oil in a food processor. Add a little soaking water, if needed. Season with pepper. Wash and dry the steaks, rub the chilli paste all over them and leave to marinate for up to 12 hours.

3 For the onion rings, soak the onion slices in the milk for 30 minutes. Mix the cornmeal, chilli, cumin and oregano and season with salt and pepper. Heat the oil for deep-frying to 160–180°C/325–350°F, or until a cube of day-old bread turns brown in about a minute.

4 Drain the onion rings and coat each one in the cornmeal mixture. Fry for 2–4 minutes, until browned and crisp. Do not overcrowd the pan, but cook in batches. Lift the onion rings out of the pan with a slotted spoon and drain on kitchen paper.

5 Heat a barbecue or cast-iron griddle (grill) pan. Season the steaks with salt and grill (broil) for 4 minutes on each side for a medium result; reduce or increase this time according to how rare or well done you like steak. Serve with the onion rings.

Beef Enchiladas with Chilli Sauce

Enchiladas are usually made with corn tortillas, although in parts of northern Mexico flour tortillas may be used. The chilli sauce gives this dish a satisfying kick.

Serves 3–4

500g/1¹⁄₄lb rump (round) steak, cut into 5cm/2in cubes
2 ancho chillies, seeded
2 pasilla chillies, seeded
2 garlic cloves, crushed
10ml/2 tsp dried oregano
2.5ml/¹⁄₂ tsp ground cumin
30ml/2 tbsp vegetable oil
7 fresh corn tortillas
sliced onion and flat leaf parsley, to garnish
mango and chilli salsa, to serve

1 Put the steak in a deep frying pan and cover with water. Bring to the boil, then lower the heat and simmer for about 1–1¹⁄₂ hours, or until very tender.

2 Meanwhile, put the dried chillies in a small bowl and just cover with hot water. Leave to soak for 30 minutes, then transfer the chillies to a blender and blend, gradually adding some of the soaking water to make a smooth paste.

3 Drain the steak and leave to cool, reserving 250ml/8fl oz/1 cup of the cooking liquid. Meanwhile, fry the garlic, oregano and cumin in the oil for 2 minutes.

4 Stir in the chilli paste and the reserved cooking liquid from the beef. Tear one of the tortillas into small pieces and add it to the mixture. Bring to the boil, then lower the heat. Simmer for 10 minutes, stirring occasionally, until the sauce has thickened.

5 Shred the steak, using two forks, and stir the meat into the sauce. Heat through for a few minutes. Meanwhile, wrap the tortillas in kitchen foil and steam them on a plate over boiling water until pliable.

6 Spoon some of the meat mixture on to each tortilla and roll it up to make an enchilada. Keep the enchiladas in a warmed dish until you have rolled them all. Garnish with shreds of onion and fresh flat leaf parsley, and then serve immediately with mango and chilli salsa.

Marinated Beef Energy 428kcal/1787kj; Protein 44.2g; Carbohydrate 17.4g, of which sugars 3g; Fat 20g, of which saturates 5.4g; Cholesterol 91mg; Calcium 51mg; Fibre 0.8g; Sodium 136mg.
Beef Enchiladas Energy 503kcal/2121kj; Protein 43g; Carbohydrate 51.9g, of which sugars 2.9g; Fat 15.1g, of which saturates 3.7g; Cholesterol 98mg; Calcium 101mg; Fibre 2.5g; Sodium 335mg.

Taquitos with Beef

In this Mexican dish, home-made corn tortillas are moulded around a tasty filling of tender steak in a spicy, flavoursome sauce.

Serves 12
500g/1½lb rump (round) steak, diced into 1cm/½in pieces
2 garlic cloves, peeled
750ml/1¼ pints/3 cups beef stock
150g/5oz/1 cup masa harina
pinch of salt
120ml/4fl oz/½ cup warm water
7.5ml/1½ tsp dried oregano
2.5ml/½ tsp ground cumin
30ml/2 tbsp tomato purée (paste)
2.5ml/½ tsp caster (superfine) sugar
salt and ground black pepper
shredded lettuce and onion relish, to serve

1 Put the beef and whole garlic cloves in a large pan and cover with the beef stock. Bring to the boil, lower the heat and simmer for 10–15 minutes, until the meat is tender. Using a slotted spoon, transfer the meat to a clean pan and set it aside. Reserve the stock.

2 Mix the masa harina and salt in a bowl. Add the warm water, a little at a time, to make a dough that can be worked into a ball. Knead on a floured surface for 3–4 minutes until smooth, then wrap in clear film (plastic wrap) and leave for 1 hour.

3 Divide the dough into 12 small balls. Line the tortilla press with plastic (this can be cut from a new plastic sandwich bag). Put a ball on the press and bring the top down to flatten it into a 5–6cm/2–2½in round. Repeat with the remaining dough balls.

4 Heat a griddle (grill) or frying pan until hot. Cook each tortilla for 15–20 seconds on each side, and then for a further 15 seconds on the first side. Keep warm by folding inside a dish towel.

5 Add the oregano, cumin, tomato purée and caster sugar to the pan containing the beef, with a couple of tablespoons of the reserved beef stock. Cook gently for a few minutes to combine the flavour. To assemble, place a little of the lettuce on a warm tortilla, top with a little filling, shredded lettuce and onion relish, and fold in half. Serve immediately.

Spicy Meatballs with Tomato Sauce

Wherever you go in Latin America, you will find a different interpretation of this hearty family dish. Spanish in origin, the meatballs are often made with pork or veal, or a mixture of meats, and are known as albondigas.

Serves 4
500g/1¼lb minced (ground) beef
3 garlic cloves, crushed
1 small onion, finely chopped
50g/2oz/1 cup fresh breadcrumbs
2.5ml/½ tsp ground cumin
1 egg, beaten
50g/2oz/½ cup plain (all-purpose) flour
60ml/4 tbsp olive oil
salt
cooked white rice, to serve

For the sauce
30ml/2 tbsp olive oil
1 small onion, thinly sliced
2 red (bell) peppers, seeded and diced
2 fresh red chillies, seeded and chopped
2 garlic cloves, crushed
165g/5½ oz/⅔ cup canned chopped tomatoes
400ml/14fl oz/1⅔ cups light beef stock
ground black pepper

1 Place all the meatball ingredients, except the flour and oil, in a large bowl. Using your hands, mix until thoroughly combined. Season with salt and shape the mixture into even balls. Wet your hands to prevent the mixture from sticking. Dust the balls lightly with flour.

2 Heat the oil in a large frying pan and cook the meatballs, in batches, for 6–8 minutes or until golden. When all the meatballs have been browned, wipe the pan clean with kitchen paper.

3 For the sauce, pour the olive oil into the pan and cook the onion and peppers over low heat for 10 minutes, until soft. Add the chillies and garlic, and cook for a further 2 minutes. Pour in the tomatoes and stock, and bring to the boil. Lower the heat, cover the pan and simmer for 15 minutes. Season to taste.

4 Add the meatballs to the pan and spoon the sauce over them. Bring back to the boil, then cover and simmer for 10 minutes. Serve with rice.

Taquitos with Beef Energy 291kcal/1222kJ; Protein 31.5g; Carbohydrate 26.5g, of which sugars 1.8g; Fat 6.3g, of which saturates 2.1g; Cholesterol 74mg; Calcium 10mg; Fibre 1.1g; Sodium 97mg.
Spicy Meatballs Energy 335kcal/1394kJ; Protein 17.8g; Carbohydrate 11.9g, of which sugars 6.8g; Fat 24.6g, of which saturates 7.7g; Cholesterol 58mg; Calcium 45mg; Fibre 1.9g; Sodium 522mg.

Baked Potatoes with Chilli

Classic chilli beef tops crisp, floury-centred baked potatoes. Easy to prepare and great for a simple yet substantial family supper.

Serves 4

2 large baking potatoes
15ml/1 tbsp vegetable oil, plus more for brushing
1 garlic clove, crushed
1 small onion, chopped
1/2 red (bell) pepper, chopped
225g/8oz lean minced (ground) beef
1/2 small fresh red chilli, seeded and chopped
5ml/1 tsp ground cumin
pinch of cayenne pepper
200g/7oz can chopped tomatoes
30ml/2 tbsp tomato purée (paste)
2.5ml/1/2 tsp fresh oregano
2.5ml/1/2 tsp fresh marjoram
200g/7oz can red kidney beans, drained
15ml/1 tbsp chopped fresh coriander (cilantro)
salt and ground black pepper
chopped fresh marjoram, to garnish
lettuce leaves, to serve
60ml/4 tbsp sour cream, to serve

1 Preheat the oven to 220°C/425°F/Gas 7. Brush or rub the potatoes with a little of the oil, and then pierce them with skewers. Place the potatoes on the top shelf of the oven and bake them for 30 minutes before beginning to cook the chilli.

2 Heat the oil in a large heavy pan and add the garlic, onion and pepper. Fry gently for 4–5 minutes until softened.

3 Add the beef and fry until browned, then stir in the chilli, cumin, cayenne pepper, tomatoes, tomato purée, 60ml/4 tbsp water and the herbs. Bring to a boil, then reduce the heat, cover and simmer for about 25 minutes, stirring occasionally.

4 Stir in the kidney beans and cook, uncovered, for 5 minutes. Remove from the heat and stir in the chopped coriander. Season well and set aside.

5 Cut the baked potatoes in half and place them in serving bowls. Top with the chilli mixture and a dollop of sour cream. Garnish with chopped fresh marjoram and serve hot, accompanied by a few lettuce leaves.

Chilli con Carne

This famous Tex-Mex stew has become an international favourite. Serve with rice or baked potatoes to complete this hearty meal.

Serves 8

1.2kg/2 1/2lb lean braising steak
30ml/2 tbsp sunflower oil
1 large onion, chopped
2 garlic cloves, finely chopped
15ml/1 tbsp plain (all-purpose) flour
300ml/1/2 pint/1 1/4 cups red wine
300ml/1/2 pint/1 1/4 cups beef stock
30ml/2 tbsp tomato purée (paste)
fresh coriander (cilantro) leaves, to garnish
salt and ground black pepper

For the beans

30ml/2 tbsp olive oil
1 onion, chopped
1 red chilli, seeded and chopped
2 x 400g/14oz cans red kidney beans, drained and rinsed
400g/14oz can chopped tomatoes

For the topping

6 tomatoes, peeled and chopped
1 fresh green chilli, seeded and chopped
30ml/2 tbsp chopped fresh chives
30ml/2 tbsp chopped fresh coriander (cilantro)
150ml/1/4 pint/2/3 cup sour cream

1 Cut the meat into cubes. Heat the oil in a large, flameproof casserole. Add the onion and garlic, and cook until softened. Season the flour, place on a plate, then toss the meat in it.

2 Remove the onion from the pan, then add a batch of beef and cook over high heat until evenly browned. Remove from the pan and set aside, then brown another batch.

3 Return all the meat with the onion to the pan. Stir in the wine, stock and tomato purée. Bring to the boil, reduce the heat and simmer for 45 minutes, or until the beef is tender.

4 Meanwhile, for the beans, heat the oil in a frying pan and cook the onion and chilli until softened. Add the beans and tomatoes and simmer for 20–25 minutes, or until thickened.

5 Mix the tomatoes, chilli, chives and coriander for the topping. Ladle the meat on to plates. Add a layer of beans and tomato topping. Finish with sour cream and garnish with the coriander.

Chilli con Carne Energy 289kcal/1216kJ; Protein 27.3g; Carbohydrate 24.7g, of which sugars 7.9g; Fat 9.7g, of which saturates 2.8g; Cholesterol 45mg; Calcium 61mg; Fibre 7.8g; Sodium 65mg.
Baked Potatoes Energy 327kcal/1369kJ; Protein 17.7g; Carbohydrate 30.6g, of which sugars 8.2g; Fat 15.7g, of which saturates 6.4g; Cholesterol 43mg; Calcium 71mg; Fibre 5.2g; Sodium 277mg.

Spicy Mexican Pie

Spiced beef is mixed with
rice and layered between
tortillas, with a salsa sauce.

Serves 4
1 onion, chopped
2 garlic cloves, crushed
1 fresh red chilli, seeded and sliced
350g/12oz rump (round) steak,
    cut into small cubes
15ml/1 tbsp oil
225g/8oz/2 cups cooked rice
beef stock, to moisten
3 large wheat tortillas

For the salsa picante
2 x 400g/14oz cans
    chopped tomatoes

2 garlic cloves, halved
1 onion, quartered
1–2 fresh red chillies, seeded and
    roughly chopped
5ml/1 tsp ground cumin
2.5–5ml/¹/₂–1 tsp cayenne pepper
5ml/1 tsp fresh oregano or
    2.5ml/¹/₂ tsp dried oregano
tomato juice or water, if required

For the cheese sauce
50g/2oz/4 tbsp butter
50g/2oz/¹/₂ cup plain
    (all-purpose) flour
600ml/1 pint/2¹/₂ cups milk
115g/4oz/1 cup grated
    Cheddar cheese
salt and ground black pepper

1 Preheat the oven to 180°C/350°F/Gas 4. Make the salsa
picante. Place the tomatoes, garlic, onion and chillies in a blender
or food processor and process until smooth. Pour into a small pan,
add the spices and oregano and season with salt. Bring to the boil,
stirring occasionally. Boil for 1–2 minutes, then cover and simmer
for 15 minutes. Add a little tomato juice or water if necessary.

2 For the cheese sauce, melt the butter and stir in the flour.
Cook for 1 minute. Add the milk and cook until it thickens. Stir
in all but 30ml/2 tbsp of the cheese and season. Set aside.

3 Mix the onion, garlic and chilli in a bowl. Add the beef and
mix well. Heat the oil in a frying pan and stir-fry the mixture for
10 minutes. Stir in the rice and beef stock. Season to taste.
Pour a quarter of the cheese sauce into an ovenproof dish.
Add a tortilla. Spread over half the salsa, then half the meat.

4 Repeat these layers, then add half the remaining sauce and
the last tortilla. Pour over the last of the sauce and sprinkle the
reserved cheese on top. Bake for 15–20 minutes until golden.

Cannelloni Stuffed with Meat

This is a rich and substantial
dish, which takes quite a
long time to prepare. Serve
it for a party – it can be
made a day ahead up to the
baking stage.

Serves 6
15ml/1 tbsp olive oil
1 small onion, finely chopped
450g/1lb minced (ground) beef
1 garlic clove, finely chopped
5ml/1 tsp dried mixed herbs
120ml/4fl oz/¹/₂ cup beef stock
1 egg
75g/3oz cooked ham or
    mortadella sausage, chopped
45ml/3 tbsp fine fresh white
    breadcrumbs
150g/5oz/1²/₃ cups freshly grated
    Parmesan cheese

18 quick-cook cannelloni tubes
salt and ground black pepper

For the tomato sauce
30ml/2 tbsp olive oil
1 small onion, finely chopped
¹/₂ carrot, finely chopped
1 celery stick, finely chopped
1 garlic clove, crushed
400g/14oz can chopped Italian
    plum tomatoes
a few sprigs of fresh basil
2.5ml/¹/₂ tsp dried oregano

For the white sauce
50g/2oz/¹/₄ cup butter
50g/2oz/¹/₂ cup plain
    (all-purpose) flour
900ml/1¹/₂ pints/3³/₄ cups milk
nutmeg

1 Heat the olive oil in a frying pan and cook the onion over
low heat, stirring occasionally, for about 5 minutes until softened.
Add the beef and garlic and cook gently for 10 minutes. Add
the herbs, and season to taste, then moisten with half the stock.
Cover the pan and simmer for 25 minutes, stirring from time to
time and adding more stock as the mixture reduces. Spoon into
a bowl and leave to cool.

2 For the tomato sauce, heat the olive oil in a medium pan,
add the vegetables and garlic and cook over medium heat,
stirring frequently, for 10 minutes. Add the canned tomatoes.
Fill the empty can with water, pour it into the pan, then stir in the
basil, with salt and pepper to taste. Bring to the boil, lower the heat,
cover and simmer for 25–30 minutes, stirring occasionally. Purée
the tomato sauce in a blender or food processor.

3 Add the egg, ham or mortadella, the breadcrumbs and
90ml/6 tbsp of the grated Parmesan to the meat and stir well
to mix. Taste for seasoning.

4 Spread a little tomato sauce over the bottom of a baking
dish. Fill the cannelloni tubes with the meat mixture and place
them in a single layer in the dish on top of the tomato sauce.
Pour the remaining tomato sauce over the top.

5 Preheat the oven to 190°C/375°F/Gas 5. Make the white
sauce. Melt the butter in a pan, add the flour and cook, stirring,
for 1–2 minutes. Add the milk a little at a time, whisking after
each addition. Bring to the boil and cook, stirring, until the sauce
is smooth and thick. Grate in nutmeg to taste and season with a
little salt and pepper. Whisk well, then remove from the heat.

6 Pour the white sauce over the cannelloni, then sprinkle with
the remaining Parmesan. Bake for 40–45 minutes or until the
cannelloni tubes feel tender when pierced with a skewer.
Leave the cannelloni for 10 minutes before serving.

Spicy Pie Energy 595kcal/2516kJ; Protein 30.3g; Carbohydrate 91.2g; of which sugars 11.3g; Fat 14.7g; of which saturates 4.7g; Cholesterol 53mg; Calcium 153mg; Fibre 4.0g; Sodium 379mg.
Cannelloni Energy 455kcal/1905kJ; Protein 25.5g; Carbohydrate 41.7g; of which sugars 6.4g; Fat 21.8g; of which saturates 7.8g; Cholesterol 76mg; Calcium 203mg; Fibre 1.6g; Sodium 571mg.

Lasagne from Bologna

This is the classic Italian lasagne al forno, based on a traditional rich, meaty sauce. It makes a fine supper and is equally good the next day.

Serves 6
12 quick-cook dried lasagne sheets
50g/2oz/²/₃ cup freshly grated
   Parmesan cheese

For the white sauce
50g/2oz/¹/₄ cup butter
50g/2oz/¹/₂ cup plain
   (all-purpose) flour
900ml/1¹/₂ pints/3³/₄ cups hot milk
salt and ground black pepper

For the Bolognese sauce
45ml/3 tbsp olive oil
1 onion, finely chopped
1 small carrot, finely chopped
1 celery stick, finely chopped
2 garlic cloves, finely chopped
400g/14oz minced (ground) beef
120ml/4fl oz/¹/₂ cup red wine
200ml/7fl oz/scant 1 cup passata
   (bottled strained tomatoes)
15ml/1 tbsp tomato purée (paste)
5ml/1 tsp dried oregano
15ml/1 tbsp chopped fresh flat
   leaf parsley
about 350ml/12fl oz/1¹/₂ cups
   beef stock
salt and ground black pepper

1 Preheat the oven to 190°C/375°F/Gas 5.

2 Make the white sauce. Melt the butter in a medium pan, add the flour and cook, stirring, for 1–2 minutes. Whisk in the milk a little at a time. Bring to the boil and cook, stirring, until the sauce is smooth and thick. Season to taste and remove from the heat.

3 Make the Bolognese sauce. Heat the oil in a large pan, add the vegetables and cook over a low heat for 5–7 minutes. Stir in the beef and cook for 5 minutes. Add the wine, passata, tomato purée, herbs and 60ml/4tbsp stock. Bring to the boil and cook gently for 30 minutes, adding more stock as necessary. Season to taste.

4 Spread a third of the Bolognese sauce over the bottom of a baking dish. Cover with a quarter of the white sauce, followed by four lasagne sheets. Repeat the layers twice more, then cover the top layer of lasagne with the remaining white sauce and sprinkle the Parmesan evenly over the top.

5 Bake for 40–45 minutes or until the pasta feels tender when pierced with a skewer. Stand for 10 minutes before serving.

Pot-roasted Brisket

This big, pot-roasted beef dish includes a heavy, sausage-shaped dumpling, which is added to the pot and cooked with the meat.

Serves 6–8
5 onions, sliced
3 bay leaves
1–1.6kg/2¹/₄–3¹/₂lb beef brisket
1 garlic head, broken into cloves
4 carrots, thickly sliced
5–10ml/1–2 tsp paprika
500ml/17fl oz/generous 2 cups
   beef stock
3–4 potatoes, quartered
salt and ground black pepper

For the dumpling
about 90cm/36in sausage casing
250g/9oz/2¹/₄ cups plain
   (all-purpose) flour
75g/3oz/¹/₂ cup semolina
   or couscous
10–15ml/2–3 tsp paprika
1 carrot, grated and 2 carrots,
   diced (optional)
250ml/8fl oz/1 cup rendered
   chicken fat
30ml/2 tbsp crisp, fried onions
¹/₂ onion, grated and 3 onions,
   thinly sliced
3 garlic cloves, chopped

1 Preheat the oven to 180°C/350°F/Gas 4. Put a third of the onions and a bay leaf in an ovenproof dish, then top with the beef. Sprinkle over the garlic, carrots and the remaining bay leaves. Add salt, pepper and paprika, then top with the remaining onions. Pour in stock to fill the dish to about 5–7.5cm/2–3in from the rim and cover with foil. Cook in the oven for 2 hours.

2 Meanwhile, make the dumpling. In a bowl, combine all the ingredients, season and stuff the mixture into the casing, leaving space for it to expand. Tie into sausage-shaped lengths.

3 When the meat has cooked for about 2 hours, add the dumpling and potatoes to the pan, re-cover and cook for a further 1 hour, or until the meat and potatoes are tender.

4 Remove the foil from the dish and increase the oven temperature to 190–200°C/375–400°F/Gas 5–6. Move the onions away from the top of the meat to the side of the dish and return to the oven for a further 30 minutes, or until the meat, onions and potatoes are beginning to brown and become crisp. Serve hot or cold.

Lasagne Energy 472kcal/1994kJ; Protein 20.5g; Carbohydrate 66g, of which sugars 10.4g; Fat 16g, of which saturates 8.8g; Cholesterol 43mg; Calcium 316mg; Fibre 2g; Sodium 296mg.
Pot-roasted Brisket Energy 586kcal/2453kJ; Protein 33.2g; Carbohydrate 55.5g, of which sugars 9.6g; Fat 27.3g, of which saturates 10.8g; Cholesterol 85mg; Calcium 93mg; Fibre 3.8g; Sodium 93mg.

Stuffed Butterfly of Beef with Cheese and Chilli Sauce

This recipe had its origins in northern Mexico or in New Mexico, which is beef country. It is a good way to cook steaks, either under the grill or on the barbecue.

Serves 4

4 fresh serrano chillies
4 fillet steaks (beef tenderloins),
   at least 2.5cm/1 in thick
115g/4oz/½ cup full-fat (whole)
   soft cheese
30ml/2 tbsp tequila
30ml/2 tbsp oil
1 onion, chopped
2 garlic cloves, sliced
5ml/1 tsp dried oregano
2.5ml/½ tsp salt
2.5ml/½ tsp ground black pepper
175g/6oz/1½ cups grated
   medium Cheddar cheese

1 Dry roast the chillies in a griddle (grill) pan over medium heat, turning them frequently until the skins are blistered but not burnt. Place in a plastic bag and tie the top to keep the steam in. Set aside for 20 minutes. Cut each steak almost in half across its width, so that it can be opened out, butterfly-fashion.

2 Remove the chillies from the bag, slit them and scrape out the seeds with a sharp knife. Cut the flesh into long narrow strips, then cut each strip into several shorter strips.

3 Put the soft cheese in a small heavy pan and stir over low heat until it has melted. Add the chilli strips and the tequila and stir to make a smooth sauce. Keep warm over a very low heat.

4 Heat the oil in a frying pan and gently fry the onion, garlic and oregano for 5 minutes, stirring frequently until the onion has browned. Season with the salt and pepper. Remove the pan from the heat and stir in the grated cheese so that it melts into the onion. Preheat the grill (broiler) to its highest setting.

5 Spoon a quarter of the cheese and onion filling on to one side of each steak and close the other side over it. Place the steaks in a grill (broiling) pan and cook for 3–5 minutes on each side, depending on how you like your steak. Serve on warmed plates with fried potatoes and the cheese sauce poured over.

Steak and Kidney Pudding

This dish, a 19th-century invention, has become one of England's most famous and popular dishes.

Serves 6

500g/1¼lb lean stewing steak,
   cut into cubes
225g/8oz beef kidney or lamb's
   kidneys, skin and core removed
   and cut into small cubes
1 medium onion, finely chopped
30ml/2 tbsp chopped fresh herbs,
   such as parsley and thyme
30ml/2 tbsp plain
   (all-purpose) flour
275g/10oz/2½ cups self-raising
   (self-rising) flour
150g/5oz/1 cup shredded suet
   (US chilled, grated shortening)
finely grated rind of 1 small lemon
butter, for greasing
120ml/4fl oz/½ cup beef stock
salt and ground black pepper

1 Put the steak into a large bowl and mix in the kidneys, onion and herbs. Mix in the plain flour and seasoning.

2 To make the pastry, sift the self-raising flour into a large bowl. Stir in the suet and lemon rind. Add sufficient cold water to bind the ingredients and gather into a soft dough. Knead on a lightly floured surface, and then roll out to make a circle about 35cm/14in across. Cut out one-quarter, roll up and set aside.

3 Lightly butter a 1.75 litre/3 pint/7½ cup heatproof bowl. Line with the rolled out dough, pressing the cut edges together and allowing the pastry to overlap the top of the bowl slightly. Carefully spoon the steak mixture into the bowl.

4 Pour stock over the steak mixture to reach no more than three-quarters of the way up the filling. Roll out the reserved pastry into a circle to form a lid and lay it over the filling, pinching the edges together to seal them well.

5 Cover with baking parchment, pleated in the centre to allow the pudding to rise, and then with a large sheet of pleated foil. Tuck the edges under and press tightly to the sides of the bowl until securely sealed. Steam for about 5 hours.

6 Remove the foil and paper, slide a knife around the sides of the pudding and turn out on to a warmed serving plate.

Steak Pudding Energy 436kcal/1835kJ; Protein 31.1g; Carbohydrate 49.5g, of which sugars 4.8g; Fat 13.9g, of which saturates 3.6g; Cholesterol 166mg; Calcium 201mg; Fibre 1.9g; Sodium 380mg.
Butterfly of Beef Energy 640kcal/2659kJ; Protein 56.1g; Carbohydrate 1.3g, of which sugars 1g; Fat 44.8g, of which saturates 23.5g; Cholesterol 201mg; Calcium 329mg; Fibre 0.2g; Sodium 508mg.

Cottage Pie

This classic British pie is so good that it is difficult to know when second or third helpings are enough. Serve with a selection of fresh vegetables.

Serves 4

30ml/2 tbsp olive oil
1 onion, finely chopped
1 carrot, finely chopped
115g/4oz mushrooms, chopped
500g/1¼lb lean chuck steak, minced (ground)
300ml/½ pint/1¼ cups brown veal stock or water
15ml/1 tbsp plain (all-purpose) flour
bay leaf
15ml/3 tsp Worcestershire sauce
15ml/1 tbsp tomato purée (paste)
675g/1½lb potatoes, boiled
25g/1oz/2 tbsp butter
45ml/3 tbsp hot milk
15ml/1 tbsp chopped fresh tarragon
salt and ground black pepper

1 Heat the olive oil in a large pan, add the onion, carrot and mushrooms and cook, stirring occasionally, until browned. Stir the minced beef into the pan and cook, stirring to break up the lumps, until lightly browned.

2 Blend a few spoonfuls of the stock or water with the flour, then stir this mixture into the pan. Stir in the remaining stock or water and bring to a simmer, stirring.

3 Add the bay leaf, Worcestershire sauce and tomato purée to the pan. Stir well, then cover the pan with a lid and simmer very gently for about 1 hour, stirring occasionally. Uncover the pan towards the end of cooking to allow any excess water to evaporate, if necessary.

4 Preheat the oven to 190°C/375°F/Gas 5. Gently heat the potatoes for a couple of minutes, then mash with the butter, milk and seasoning.

5 Add the tarragon and seasoning to the mince, then pour into a pie dish. Cover the mince with an even layer of potato and mark the top with the prongs of a fork. Bake in the preheated oven for about 25 minutes, until golden brown. Serve with a selection of seasonal vegetables, if you like.

Roast Beef with Peppercorns and Juniper Berries

This joint looks spectacular, and served with roast potatoes and seasonal vegetables, it makes a perfect celebration meal.

Serves 8–10

45ml/3 tbsp mixed peppercorns
15ml/1 tbsp juniper berries
2.75kg/6lb rolled rib of beef
30ml/2 tbsp Dijon mustard
15ml/1 tbsp olive oil
20 shallots
5 garlic cloves, peeled
60ml/4 tbsp light olive oil
15ml/1 tbsp caster (superfine) sugar
flat leaf parsley, to garnish

For the gravy
150ml/¼ pint/⅔ cup red wine
600ml/1 pint/2½ cups beef stock
salt and ground black pepper

1 Preheat the oven to 230°C/450°F/Gas 8. Coarsely crush the peppercorns and juniper berries. Sprinkle half the spices over the meat, then transfer to a roasting pan and roast for 30 minutes.

2 Reduce the oven temperature to 180°C/350°F/Gas 4. Mix the mustard and oil into the remaining crushed spices and spread the resulting paste over the meat. Roast the meat for a further 1¼ hours for rare, 1 hour 50 minutes for medium-rare or 2 hours 25 minutes for well done. Baste frequently.

3 An hour before the beef is due to be ready, mix the shallots and garlic cloves with the light olive oil and spoon into the roasting pan around the beef. After 30 minutes, sprinkle the caster sugar over the shallots and garlic. Stir the shallots and garlic two or three times during cooking.

4 Transfer the meat to a large serving platter, cover tightly with foil and set aside to rest in a warm place for 20–30 minutes.

5 To make the gravy, simmer the wine and stock in a pan for about 5 minutes to intensify the flavour. Skim the fat from the roasting pan, then pour in the wine mixture, scraping up all the residue from the bottom. Simmer until the gravy is reduced and thickened slightly. Season to taste. Carve the beef and serve with the shallots and gravy, garnished with the parsley.

Cottage Pie Energy 426kcal/1788kJ; Protein 33.9g; Carbohydrate 39.2g, of which sugars 6.3g; Fat 15.9g, of which saturates 5.9g; Cholesterol 0mg; Calcium 66mg; Fibre 3.7g; Sodium 240mg.
Roast Beef Energy 561kcal/2338kJ; Protein 62.9g; Carbohydrate 4.8g, of which sugars 3.8g; Fat 31.2g, of which saturates 11.2g; Cholesterol 160mg; Calcium 26mg; Fibre 0.6g; Sodium 178mg.

Braised Rabbit with Paprika

This is an updated version of a classic Spanish rabbit stew. Its Spanish name, salmorejo, refers to the traditional ingredients – pounded garlic, bread and vinegar; the wine is a modern addition.

Serves 4
675g/1½lb rabbit, jointed
300ml/½ pint/1¼ cups dry
  white wine
15ml/1 tbsp sherry vinegar
several oregano sprigs
2 bay leaves
30ml/2 tbsp plain
  (all-purpose) flour
90ml/6 tbsp olive oil
175g/6oz baby (pearl) onions,
  peeled and left whole
4 garlic cloves, sliced
150ml/¼ pint/⅔ cup
  chicken stock
1 dried chilli, seeded and
  finely chopped
10ml/2 tsp paprika
salt and ground black pepper

1 Put the rabbit in a bowl. Add the wine, vinegar, oregano and bay leaves and toss together. Marinate for several hours or overnight in the refrigerator. Drain the rabbit, reserving the marinade, and pat the pieces dry with kitchen paper. Season the flour and use to dust the marinated rabbit.

2 Heat the oil in a large, wide flameproof casserole or frying pan. Fry the rabbit pieces until golden on all sides, then remove them and set aside. Fry the onions until they are beginning to colour, then reserve on a separate plate.

3 Add the garlic to the pan and fry, then add the strained marinade, with the chicken stock, chilli and paprika. Return the rabbit to the pan with the onions. Bring to a simmer, then cover and simmer gently for about 45 minutes until the rabbit is tender. Check the seasoning, adding more vinegar and paprika if necessary, and serve.

Cook's Tip
If you prefer, rather than cooking on the stove, transfer the stew to an ovenproof dish and bake in the oven at 180°C/350°F/ Gas 4 for about 50 minutes.

Hare with Beetroot and Crowdie

Crowdie is a cream cheese made on every homestead up to the middle of the last century. For a less rich dish, you can use plain yogurt in place of the crowdie.

Serves 4
2 saddles of hare
10ml/2 tsp olive oil
350g/12oz cooked beetroot (beet)
30ml/2 tbsp chopped shallot
30ml/2 tbsp white wine vinegar
50g/2oz/¼ cup crowdie
5ml/1 tsp English (hot) mustard
salt and ground black pepper

For the marinade
600ml/1 pint/2½ cups red wine
1 carrot, finely diced
1 onion, finely diced
generous pinch of mixed herbs
pinch of salt
8 peppercorns
8 juniper berries
2 cloves

1 Using a flexible knife, remove the membrane covering the saddles. Mix all the ingredients for the marinade together and coat the saddles, then leave for one day, turning occasionally.

2 Preheat the oven to 240°C/475°F/Gas 9. Dry the saddles with kitchen paper. Strain the marinade and set aside.

3 Heat the olive oil in a large ovenproof pan. Brown the saddles all over, then cook in the preheated oven for 10–15 minutes. They should still be pink. Leave in a warm place to rest.

4 Remove most of the fat from the pan. Add the beetroot and cook for 1–2 minutes, then add the shallot and cook for about 2 minutes to soften.

5 Add the vinegar and 30ml/2 tbsp of the marinade and stir in thoroughly. Reduce the liquid until a coating texture is nearly achieved. Reduce the heat to low and add the crowdie. Whisk it in until completely melted, then add the mustard and season to taste. Set aside and keep warm.

6 To serve, remove the fillets from the top and bottom of the saddles and slice lengthways. Place on four warmed plates and arrange the beetroot mixture on top. Reheat the sauce, without boiling, and hand around separately.

Braised Rabbit Energy 311kcal/1294kJ; Protein 23.2g; Carbohydrate 9.5g, of which sugars 2.6g; Fat 20.4g, of which saturates 4.1g; Cholesterol 83mg; Calcium 65mg; Fibre 0.9g; Sodium 52mg.
Hare Energy 352kcal/1471kJ; Protein 41g; Carbohydrate 9.6g, of which sugars 8.7g; Fat 13.1g, of which saturates 6.5g; Cholesterol 136mg; Calcium 84mg; Fibre 1.9g; Sodium 255mg.

Home-made Venison Sausages

Venison sausages have an excellent flavour, a much lower fat content than most sausages, and they are easy to make if you forget about sausage skins and just shape the mixture.

Makes 1.4kg/3lb
900g/2lb finely minced
   (ground) venison
450g/1lb finely minced
   (ground) belly of pork
15ml/1 tbsp salt

10ml/2 tsp ground black pepper
1 garlic clove, crushed
5ml/1 tsp dried thyme
1 egg, beaten
plain (all-purpose) flour,
   for dusting
oil, for frying

To serve
fried onions
grilled (broiled) tomatoes
grilled (broiled) field (portobello)
   mushrooms
fresh basil, to garnish

1 Combine all the sausage ingredients, except the flour and oil, in a bowl.

2 Take a small piece of the mixture and fry it in a little oil in a heavy frying pan, then taste to check the seasoning for the batch. Adjust if necessary.

3 Pinch off small balls of the mixture and form into chipolata-size sausages, using floured hands.

4 Heat the oil in a large, heavy frying pan and shallow-fry the sausages for 10 minutes or until they are golden brown and cooked right through.

5 Fry some onion rings alongside the sausages. At the same time, grill (broil) mushrooms and halved tomatoes to serve on the side. Garnish with shredded basil.

> **Cook's Tip**
> If you find yourself with more sausages than you need for one meal, freeze the surplus in a container for no more than a month. Be sure to thaw the sausages before cooking.

Roast Loin of Boar with Prunes

Once hunted, farmed 'wild' boar is becoming a popular alternative to pork as it has a tastier, more gamy flavour. Suggested accompaniments include mashed potato with black pudding and cooked cabbage with some apple sauce.

Serves 4–6
8 pitted prunes
1 glass poitín or Irish whiskey
675g/1½lb boned loin of
   boar, any excess fat removed
salt and coarsely ground
   black pepper

1 Soak the prunes overnight in enough poitín or whiskey to cover. Use a skewer to make a circular incision along the loin of boar and stuff with the prunes.

2 Place a large square of foil on a flat surface. Place a large square of clear film (plastic wrap) on top of the foil. Place the loin on one end of the clear film and roll up tightly. Refrigerate for 2 hours.

3 Preheat the oven to 200°C/400°F/Gas 6. Remove the foil and clear film and cut the loin into steaks. Heat a heavy pan and sear the meat on both sides until brown. Season with salt and coarsely ground black pepper.

4 Transfer the meat to a roasting pan and cook in the oven for 7–10 minutes. Leave the boar to rest for 5–10 minutes before serving on heated plates.

> **Cook's Tips**
> • To prepare the mash add 225g/8oz cooked black pudding (blood sausage) to 1kg/2¼lb cooked mash potatoes. Mash with cream and butter. Stir in 15ml/1 tbsp mustard and season.
> • Poitín, or Poteen, is an Irish distilled spirit, traditionally made from malted barley grain or potatoes. It is one of the strongest alcoholic drinks available (90–95% ABV), hence the reason why it was illegal for centuries in Ireland. It may be hard to get hold of, but can be replaced with Irish whiskey instead.

Roast Boar Energy 290kcal/1214kJ; Protein 36.6g; Carbohydrate 6.8g, of which sugars 6.8g; Fat 6.8g, of which saturates 2.4g; Cholesterol 106mg; Calcium 19mg; Fibre 1.2g; Sodium 120mg.
Venison Sausages Energy 1747kcal/7356kJ; Protein 302.4g; Carbohydrate 0g, of which sugars 0g; Fat 65.3g, of which saturates 17.6g; Cholesterol 924mg; Calcium 105mg; Fibre 0g; Sodium 880mg.

Venison Medallions with Dumplings

Venison is lean and full-flavoured. This recipe makes a spectacular dinner party dish – it gives the appearance of being difficult to make but is actually very easy.

Serves 4
600ml/1 pint/2½ cups
   venison stock
120ml/4fl oz/½ cup port
15ml/1 tbsp sunflower oil
4 x 175g/6oz medallions
   of venison

chopped parsley, to garnish
steamed baby vegetables, such as
   carrots, courgettes (zucchini)
   and turnips, cooked, to serve

For the dumplings
75g/3oz/⅔ cup self-raising
   (self-rising) flour
40g/1½oz beef suet (US chilled,
   grated shortening)
15ml/1 tbsp chopped fresh
   mixed herbs
5ml/1 tsp creamed horseradish
45–60ml/3–4 tbsp water

1 First make the dumplings: mix the flour, suet and herbs and make a well in the middle. Add the horseradish and water, then mix to make a soft but not sticky dough. Shape the dough into walnut-size balls and chill in the refrigerator for up to 1 hour.

2 Place the venison stock in a large pan. Bring to the boil and simmer vigorously until the stock has reduced by half.

3 Add the port to the stock and continue boiling the mixture until reduced again by half, then pour the reduced stock into a large frying pan.

4 Heat the stock until it is simmering and add the dumplings. Poach them gently for 5–10 minutes, or until risen and cooked through. Use a draining spoon to remove the dumplings from the pan.

5 Smear the sunflower oil over a non-stick griddle (grill) pan, and heat until very hot. Add the venison medallions and cook for 2–3 minutes on each side.

6 Place the venison medallions on warm serving plates and pour the sauce over. Serve with the dumplings and the vegetables, garnished with parsley.

Venison Casserole

Low in fat but high in flavour, venison is an excellent choice for healthy, yet rich, casseroles that make warming winter suppers. Cranberries and orange bring a festive fruitiness to this recipe, and the addition of allspice gives the sauce a complex, spicy depth of flavour. It is delicious served with small baked potatoes and steamed green vegetables.

Serves 4
30ml/2 tbsp olive oil
1 onion, chopped
2 celery sticks, sliced
10ml/2 tsp ground allspice
15ml/1 tbsp plain
   (all-purpose) flour
675g/1½lb stewing
   venison, cubed
225g/8oz cranberries
grated rind and juice of 1 orange
900ml/1½ pints/3¾ cups beef
   or venison stock
salt and ground black pepper

1 Heat the olive oil in a flameproof casserole. Add the onion and celery and cook for 5 minutes until softened.

2 Meanwhile, mix the ground allspice with the flour and either spread the mixture out on a large plate or place in a large plastic bag. Toss the venison in the flour mixture a few pieces at a time (to prevent them from becoming soggy) until all the meat is lightly coated.

3 When the onion and celery are softened, remove from the casserole using a slotted spoon and set aside. Add the venison pieces to the casserole in batches and cook until browned and sealed on all sides.

4 Add the cranberries and orange rind and juice to the casserole. Pour in the beef or venison stock and stir well.

5 Return the vegetables and all the venison to the casserole and heat until simmering, then cover tightly and reduce the heat. Simmer, stirring occasionally, for 45 minutes, or until the meat is tender.

6 Season the venison casserole to taste with salt and pepper before serving.

Venison Medallions Energy 393kcal/1651kJ; Protein 29.1g; Carbohydrate 33.4g, of which sugars 6.4g; Fat 16.3g, of which saturates 7.5g; Cholesterol 67mg; Calcium 136mg; Fibre 2.3g; Sodium 189mg.
Venison Casserole Energy 242kcal/1025kJ; Protein 38.3g; Carbohydrate 10.4g, of which sugars 7.2g; Fat 6.6g, of which saturates 1.8g; Cholesterol 84mg; Calcium 27mg; Fibre 1.4g; Sodium 105mg.

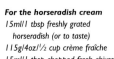

Buffalo Steaks with Horseradish Cream

The flavour of buffalo is very like that of beef so, not surprisingly, it goes very well with horseradish cream – one of the classic accompaniments for beef.

15ml/1 tbsp sunflower oil
salt and ground black pepper
a few whole chives, to garnish
mixed salad leaves, to serve

For the horseradish cream
15ml/1 tbsp freshly grated
horseradish (or to taste)
115g/4oz/¹/₂ cup crème fraîche
15ml/1 tbsp chopped fresh chives

Serves 4
4 buffalo steaks, about
150g/5oz each
25g/1oz/2 tbsp butter

1 Season the buffalo steaks on both sides with salt and plenty of ground black pepper.

2 Heat the butter and oil in a frying pan until sizzling. Add the steaks and cook for 3–4 minutes on each side, turning once.

3 Meanwhile, make the horseradish cream. Mix the horseradish, crème fraîche and chopped chives in a small bowl.

4 Serve the steaks with a dollop of horseradish cream, garnish with chives and serve with a mixed leaf salad.

Venison Pie

This is a variation on cottage or shepherd's pie and the result, using rich venison, is particularly tasty. Serve with lightly steamed green vegetables, such as kale or cabbage.

Serves 6
30ml/2 tbsp olive oil
2 leeks, washed, chopped
1kg/2¹/₄lb minced (ground) venison

30ml/2 tbsp chopped fresh parsley
300ml/¹/₂ pint/1¹/₄ cups game
consommé
salt and ground black pepper

For the topping
1.4kg/3¹/₄lb mixed root
vegetables, such as sweet
potatoes, parsnips and swede
(rutabaga), coarsely chopped
15ml/1 tbsp horseradish sauce
25g/1oz/2 tbsp butter

1 Heat the oil in a pan over medium heat. Add the leeks and cook for 8 minutes until softened and beginning to brown.

2 Add the minced venison to the pan and cook over medium heat, stirring frequently, for about 10 minutes or until the venison is thoroughly browned all over.

3 Add the chopped fresh parsley and stir it in thoroughly, then add the consommé and season with salt and ground black pepper. Stir well. Bring the mixture to the boil, then reduce the heat to low, cover and simmer gently for 20 minutes, stirring occasionally.

4 Meanwhile, preheat the oven to 200°C/400°F/Gas 6 and prepare the pie topping. Cook the chopped root vegetables in boiling salted water to cover for 15–20 minutes.

5 Drain the vegetables and put them in a bowl. Mash them together with the horseradish sauce, butter and black pepper.

6 Spoon the venison mixture into a large ovenproof dish and cover the top evenly with the mashed vegetables. It is often easier to spoon it over in small quantities rather than pouring it on, and then smooth it out.

7 Bake in the oven for 20 minutes, or until piping hot and beginning to brown. Serve with steamed green vegetables.

> **Cook's Tips**
> • Surprisingly tender and with a taste similar to lean beef, buffalo meat has no pronounced gamy flavour. It is growing in popularity and can be found on restaurant menus and is available from large supermarkets and speciality meat markets.
> • The cuts of meat from a buffalo are similar to those from beef and can be substituted for beef in most recipes. Buffalo is high in iron and lower in fat and cholesterol than most cuts of beef and chicken as well as some fish.
> • Fresh horseradish is available in many supermarkets. The roots should be firm with no sign of blemishes or withering. The root should be refrigerated, wrapped in a plastic bag, and peeled before using.

Venison Pie Energy 307kcal/1291kJ; Protein 39.8g; Carbohydrate 13.2g, of which sugars 12.5g; Fat 12g, of which saturates 4.1g; Cholesterol 93mg; Calcium 154mg; Fibre 5.8g; Sodium 176mg.
Buffalo Steaks Energy 331kcal/1378kJ; Protein 32.7g; Carbohydrate 5.8g, of which sugars 4.9g; Fat 19.7g, of which saturates 8.3g; Cholesterol 110mg; Calcium 21mg; Fibre 0.8g; Sodium 409mg.

Classic Quick-cook Margherita Pizza with Mozzarella

Bought pizza base mixes are a great kitchen stand-by. A margherita pizza makes a lovely simple supper, but of course you can add any extra toppings you like. Prosciutto and rocket make a great addition – just add them to the pizza after it is cooked.

Serves 2

half a 300g/11oz packet pizza
   base mix
15ml/1 tbsp herb-infused olive oil
45ml/3 tbsp ready-made tomato
   and basil sauce
150g/5oz mozzarella, sliced
salt and ground black pepper
basil leaves, to garnish

1 Make the pizza base according to the instructions on the packet. Preheat the oven to 220°C/425°F/Gas 7.

2 Brush the pizza base with a little of the herb-infused olive oil. Spread the tomato and basil sauce evenly over the base, using the back of a spoon, not quite to the edges.

3 Arrange the slices of mozzarella evenly on top of the pizza. Place on a baking sheet and bake in the preheated oven for about 20–25 minutes, or until the pizza dough is golden and the cheese is melted and bubbling.

4 Drizzle the remaining oil on top of the pizza, season to taste with salt and black pepper and serve immediately, garnished with fresh basil leaves.

> **Cook's Tip**
> You can make your own herb-infused oil, if you prefer. You will need a whole bunch of fresh herbs such as rosemary, thyme, basil, coriander (cilantro) or parsley and a bottle of olive oil, about 500ml/17fl oz/generous 2 cups. Simply bruise all the fresh herbs with a rolling pin to release their aromas and stuff them into the bottle of oil. Leave the oil for a week or two before using.

Polenta Pan-pizza with Red Onions

This yeast-free pizza is cooked in a frying pan rather than the oven.

Serves 2
30ml/2 tbsp olive oil
1 large red onion, sliced
3 garlic cloves, crushed
115g/4oz/1½ cups brown cap
   (cremini) mushrooms, sliced
5ml/1 tsp dried oregano
115g/4oz mozzarella cheese
15ml/1 tbsp pine nuts (optional)

For the pizza base
50g/2oz/½ cup unbleached plain
   (all-purpose) flour, sifted
2.5ml/½ tsp salt
115g/4oz/1 cup fine polenta
5ml/1 tsp baking powder
1 egg, beaten
150ml/¼ pint/⅔ cup milk
25g/1oz/⅓ cup freshly grated
   Parmesan cheese
2.5ml/½ tsp dried chilli flakes
15ml/1 tbsp olive oil

1 To make the topping, heat half the oil in a frying pan. Cook the onion for 10 minutes until tender. Remove the onion from the pan and set aside. Add the remaining oil to the pan. Fry the garlic for 1 minute, then add the sliced mushrooms and oregano and cook for 5 minutes more until the mushrooms are tender.

2 To make the pizza base, mix together the flour, salt, polenta and baking powder in a bowl. Make a well in the centre and add the egg. Gradually add the milk, and mix well to make into a thick, smooth batter. Stir in the Parmesan and chilli flakes.

3 Heat the olive oil in a 25cm/10in heavy flameproof frying pan until hot. Spread in the batter and cook over medium heat for about 3 minutes or until the base is set.

4 Remove from the heat and run a knife around the edge of the pizza base. Place a plate over the pan and flip over. Slide the base back into the pan on its uncooked side and cook for 2 minutes until golden.

5 Preheat the grill (broiler) to high. Spoon the onions over the base, then top with the mushroom mixture. Crumble the mozzarella cheese on top, then grill (broil) until the cheese has melted. Sprinkle over the pine nuts, if using, and grill until golden. Serve in wedges.

Margherita Pizza Energy 420kcal/1761kJ; Protein 7.6g; Carbohydrate 49.8g, of which sugars 7.8g; Fat 22.6g, of which saturates 2.2g; Cholesterol 2mg; Calcium 133mg; Fibre 3.4g; Sodium 130mg.
Pan-pizza Energy 782kcal/3262kJ; Protein 31.9g; Carbohydrate 77.1g, of which sugars 12.4g; Fat 39.1g, of which saturates 14.5g; Cholesterol 145mg; Calcium 540mg; Fibre 4.8g; Sodium 439mg.

Potato, Smoked Mozzarella and Garlic Pizza

New potatoes, smoked mozzarella and garlic make this pizza unique.

Serves 2–3

350g/12oz small new or
    salad potatoes
45ml/3 tbsp olive oil
2 garlic cloves, crushed
1 pizza base, about 25–30cm/
    10–12in diameter

1 red onion, thinly sliced
150g/5oz/1¼ cups smoked
    mozzarella cheese, grated
10ml/2 tsp chopped fresh
    rosemary or sage
salt and ground black pepper
30ml/2 tbsp freshly grated
    Parmesan cheese, to garnish

1 Preheat the oven to 220°C/425°F/Gas 7. Put the potatoes in a large pan. Add water to cover and bring to the boil. Add salt, then simmer for about 5 minutes, or until the potatoes are just becoming tender. Drain thoroughly and leave to cool.

2 When the potatoes are cool enough to handle, peel and slice them thinly.

3 Heat 30ml/2 tbsp of the oil in a frying pan. Add the sliced potatoes and garlic and fry for 5–8 minutes, turning frequently until tender.

4 Brush the pizza base with the remaining oil. Sprinkle the onion over, then arrange the potatoes on top.

5 Sprinkle over the mozzarella and rosemary or sage and plenty of black pepper. Bake for 15–20 minutes until golden. Remove from the oven, sprinkle with Parmesan and more ground black pepper.

Variation
For non-vegetarians, you can add sliced smoked pork sausage or pastrami to the pizza to make it even more substantial.

Mushroom and Pesto Pizza

Home-made Italian-style pizzas are a little time-consuming to make but the results are worth the effort.

Serves 4

For the pizza base
350g/12oz/3 cups strong plain
    (all-purpose) flour
1.5ml/¼ tsp salt
15g/½oz easy-blend (rapid-rise)
    dried yeast
15ml/1 tbsp olive oil

For the topping
50g/2oz dried porcini mushrooms
25g/1oz/¾ cup fresh basil
25g/1oz/⅓ cup pine nuts
40g/1½oz Parmesan cheese,
    thinly sliced
105ml/7 tbsp olive oil
2 onions, thinly sliced
225g/8oz brown cap (cremini)
    mushrooms, sliced
salt and ground black pepper

1 To make the pizza base, put the flour in a bowl with the salt, dried yeast and olive oil. Add 250ml/8fl oz/1 cup hand-hot water and mix to a dough using a round-bladed knife.

2 Turn on to a work surface and knead for 5 minutes until smooth. Place in a clean bowl, cover with clear film (plastic wrap) and leave in a warm place until doubled in bulk.

3 Meanwhile, make the topping. Soak the dried mushrooms in hot water for 20 minutes. Place the basil, pine nuts, Parmesan and 75ml/5 tbsp of the olive oil in a blender or food processor and process to make a smooth pesto paste. Set the pesto aside.

4 Fry the onions in the remaining olive oil for 3–4 minutes until just browning. Fry the brown cap mushrooms for 2 minutes. Stir in the drained porcini mushrooms and season lightly.

5 Preheat the oven to 220°C/425°F/Gas 7. Lightly grease a large baking sheet. Turn the pizza dough on to a floured surface and roll out to a 30cm/12in round. Place on the baking sheet.

6 Spread the pesto mixture to within 1cm/½in of the edges of the pizza base. Spread the mushroom mixture on top. Bake the pizza in the oven for 35–40 minutes until risen and golden. Serve in wedges with a crisp green salad, if you like.

Potato Pizza Energy 413kcal/1727kJ; Protein 14.1g; Carbohydrate 39.5g, of which sugars 3.7g; Fat 23.1g, of which saturates 8.5g; Cholesterol 29mg; Calcium 222mg; Fibre 2.1g; Sodium 302mg
Mushroom Pizza Energy 631kcal/2642kJ; Protein 15.6g; Carbohydrate 76.6g, of which sugars 7.4g; Fat 31.3g, of which saturates 5.7g; Cholesterol 10mg; Calcium 285mg; Fibre 5.3g; Sodium 120mg

Fiorentina Pizza

An egg adds the finishing touch to this classic Italian spinach pizza; try not to overcook it though, as it is best when the yolk is still slightly soft in the middle.

Serves 2–3
45ml/3 tbsp olive oil
1 small red onion, thinly sliced
175g/6oz fresh spinach,
 stalks removed
1 pizza base, about
 25–30cm/10–12in in diameter
1 small jar pizza sauce
freshly grated nutmeg
150g/5oz mozzarella cheese
1 egg
25g/1oz/¼ cup Gruyère
 cheese, grated

1 Heat 15ml/1 tbsp of the oil and fry the onion until soft. Add the spinach and fry until wilted. Drain any excess liquid.

2 Preheat the oven to 220°C/425°F/Gas 7. Brush the pizza base with half the remaining olive oil.

3 Spread the pizza sauce evenly over the base, using the back of a spoon, then top with the spinach mixture. Sprinkle a little freshly grated nutmeg over the surface of the spinach.

4 Thinly slice the mozzarella and arrange the slices evenly over the spinach topping. Drizzle the remaining oil over the pizza. Bake in the preheated oven for 10 minutes, then remove from the oven.

5 Make a small well in the centre of the pizza topping and carefully break the egg into the hole.

6 Sprinkle over the grated Gruyère cheese and return the pizza to the oven for a further 5–10 minutes until crisp and golden. Serve immediately, in wedges.

> **Variation**
> A calzone is like a pizza but is folded in half to conceal the filling. Add the egg with the rest of the pizza topping, fold over the dough, seal the edges and bake for 20 minutes.

Pissaladière

This famous onion and anchovy dish is most delicious eaten lukewarm rather than piping hot. Serve with a salad and fresh bread.

Serves 6
250g/9oz/2¼ cups strong plain
 (all-purpose) white flour, plus
 extra for dusting
50g/2oz/⅓ cup fine polenta
 or semolina
5ml/1 tsp salt
175ml/6fl oz/¾ cup
 lukewarm water
5ml/1 tsp active dried yeast

5ml/1 tsp sugar
30ml/2 tbsp extra virgin olive oil

For the topping
60–75ml/4–5 tbsp extra virgin
 olive oil
6 large sweet Spanish (Bermuda)
 onions, thinly sliced
2 large garlic cloves, thinly sliced
5ml/1 tsp chopped fresh thyme,
 plus several sprigs
1 fresh rosemary sprig
1–2 x 50g/2oz cans anchovies in
 olive oil, drained
50–75g/2–3oz small black olives
salt and ground black pepper

1 Mix the flour, polenta or semolina and salt in a large bowl. Pour half the water into a bowl. Add the yeast and sugar, then leave in a warm place for 10 minutes, until frothy. Pour into the flour mixture with the remaining water and the olive oil.

2 Mix all the ingredients together to form a dough, then turn out and knead until smooth and elastic. Return the dough to the clean, floured bowl and place it in a plastic bag. Set aside at room temperature until doubled in size.

3 Meanwhile, prepare the topping. Heat 45ml/3 tbsp of the olive oil in a large pan and stir in the onions. Cover and cook over very low heat for 20–30 minutes. Add the garlic, chopped thyme and rosemary and a little salt. Cook for 15–25 minutes. Remove and discard the rosemary. Set the onions aside to cool.

4 Preheat the oven to 220°C/425°F/Gas 7. Roll out the dough and place on a baking sheet. Spread the onions over the dough. Cut the anchovies in half lengthways and arrange in a lattice pattern over the onions. Sprinkle the olives and thyme sprigs over and drizzle with the remaining olive oil. Bake for about 20–25 minutes. Season with pepper and serve warm in slices.

Fiorentina Pizza Energy 503kcal/2100kJ; Protein 20.8g; Carbohydrate 40.3g, of which sugars 5.9g; Fat 29.7g, of which saturates 10.9g; Cholesterol 101mg; Calcium 417mg; Fibre 2.8g; Sodium 668mg.
Pissaladière Energy 436kcal/1815kJ; Protein 5.9g; Carbohydrate 37.4g, of which sugars 5.8g; Fat 31.1g, of which saturates 1.5g; Cholesterol 0mg; Calcium 77mg; Fibre 1.5g; Sodium 542mg.

Hot Pepperoni Pizza

There is nothing better than a home-baked pizza, especially when the topping includes pepperoni and red chillies.

Serves 4

225g/8oz/2 cups strong white bread flour
10ml/2 tsp easy-blend (rapid-rise) dried yeast
5ml/1 tsp sugar
5ml/½ tsp salt
15ml/1 tbsp olive oil, plus extra for greasing
175ml/6fl oz/¾ cup mixed hand-hot milk and water

For the topping
400g/14oz can chopped tomatoes, well drained
2 garlic cloves, crushed
1 tsp dried oregano, plus extra to garnish
225g/8oz mozzarella cheese, coarsely grated
2 dried red chillies, crumbled
225g/8oz pepperoni, sliced
30ml/2 tbsp drained capers

1 Sift the flour into a bowl. Stir in the yeast, sugar and salt. Make a well in the centre. Stir the olive oil into the milk and water, then stir the mixture into the flour. Mix to a soft dough.

2 Knead the dough on a lightly floured surface for 5-10 minutes until it is smooth and elastic. Return it to the clean, lightly oiled, bowl and cover with clear film (plastic wrap). Leave in a warm place until the dough has doubled in size.

3 Preheat the oven to 220°C/425°F/Gas 7. Turn the dough out on to a lightly floured surface and knead for 1 minute. Divide it in half and roll each piece out to a 25cm/10in circle. Place on oiled baking sheets.

4 To make the topping, mix the tomatoes, garlic and oregano in a bowl. Spread half the mixture over each base. Set half the mozzarella aside. Divide the rest between the pizzas. Bake for 7–10 minutes until the dough rim on each pizza is pale golden.

5 Sprinkle the crumbled chillies over the pizzas, then arrange the pepperoni slices and capers on top. Sprinkle with the remaining mozzarella, then return the pizzas to the oven and bake for 7–10 minutes more. Sprinkle over the oregano and serve immediately.

Bresaola and Rocket Pizza

Although the Armenians initiated the idea of topping flattened dough with savoury ingredients before baking it, it was the Italians – the Neapolitans in particular – who developed the pizza in the 1830s.

Serves 4

150g/5oz packet pizza base mix
120ml/4fl oz/½ cup lukewarm water
225g/8oz/3¼ cups mixed wild mushrooms
25g/1oz/2 tbsp butter
2 garlic cloves, coarsely chopped
60ml/4 tbsp pesto
8 slices bresaola
4 tomatoes, sliced
75g/3oz/⅓ cup full-fat (whole) cream cheese
25g/1oz rocket (arugula)

1 Preheat the oven to 200°C/400°F/Gas 6. Place the packet of pizza base mix into a large mixing bowl and pour in enough of the water to mix to a soft, not sticky, dough.

2 Turn out the dough on to a lightly floured surface and knead for about 5 minutes, or until smooth and elastic. Divide the dough into two equal pieces, knead lightly to form two balls, then pat out the balls of dough into flat rounds.

3 Roll out each piece of dough on a lightly floured surface to a 23cm/9in round and transfer to baking sheets.

4 Slice the wild mushrooms. Melt the butter in a frying pan and cook the garlic for 2 minutes. Add the mushrooms and cook over a high heat for about 5 minutes, or until the mushrooms have softened but are not overcooked.

5 Spread pesto on the pizza bases to within 2cm/¾in of the edge of each one. Arrange the bresaola and tomato slices around the rims of the pizzas, then spoon the cooked mushrooms into the middle.

6 Dot the cream cheese on top of the pizzas and bake for 15–18 minutes, or until the bases are crisp. Top each pizza with a handful of rocket leaves just before serving. Serve immediately.

Pepperoni Pizza Energy 631kcal/2640kJ; Protein 28.8g; Carbohydrate 47.6g, of which sugars 4.7g; Fat 37.6g, of which saturates 16.8g; Cholesterol 80mg; Calcium 318mg; Fibre 2.7g; Sodium 1499mg.
Bresaola Pizza Energy 448kcal/1873kJ; Protein 16.6g; Carbohydrate 34.7g, of which sugars 6g; Fat 28g, of which saturates 12.8g; Cholesterol 56mg; Calcium 179mg; Fibre 3.5g; Sodium 213mg.

Puff Pastry Tarts with Tomato and Tapenade

These easy-to-make individual tarts are delicious and look and taste fantastic, despite the fact that they demand very little time or effort. The mascarpone cheese topping melts as it cooks to make a smooth, creamy sauce.

Serves 4
oil, for greasing
500g/1¼lb puff pastry, thawed
*   if frozen*
60ml/4 tbsp olive tapenade
500g/1¼lb cherry tomatoes
90g/3½oz/scant ½ cup
*   mascarpone cheese*
salt and ground black pepper

1 Preheat the oven to 220°C/425°F/Gas 7. Lightly grease a large baking sheet and sprinkle it with water. Roll out the pastry on a lightly floured surface. Cut out four 16cm/6½in rounds, using a bowl or small plate as a guide, and transfer to the baking sheet.

2 Using the tip of a sharp knife, mark a shallow cut 1cm/½in in from the edge of each pastry round to form a rim.

3 Reserve half the tapenade and spread the rest over the pastry rounds, keeping the paste inside the marked rim. Cut half the tomatoes in half. Pile all the tomatoes, whole and halved, on the pastry, again keeping them inside the rim. Season lightly.

4 Bake for 20 minutes, until the pastry is well risen and golden. Dot with the remaining tapenade. Spoon a little mascarpone on the centre of the tomatoes and season with black pepper. Bake for a further 10 minutes, until the mascarpone has melted to make a sauce. Serve the tarts warm.

Variations
• *Cherry tomatoes have a delicious sweet flavour with a low acidity, but plum tomatoes or vine-ripened tomatoes are also suitable for these tarts and will give delicious results.*
• *Red pesto can be used instead of the tapenade if you prefer a subtler flavour.*

Leek and Goat's Cheese Tart

This delicious and tangy tart is best served hot. If your cheese is particularly strong, use the smaller quantity listed in the ingredients.

Serves 6
85g/3oz/¾ cup hazelnuts, skinned
175g/6oz/1½ cups plain
*   (all-purpose) flour*

115g/4oz/½ cup butter, chilled
*   and cut into small cubes*
15ml/1 tbsp olive oil
350g/12oz leeks, thinly sliced
5 eggs, lightly beaten
425ml/¾ pint single (light) cream
2.5ml/½ tbsp wholegrain mustard
175–225g/6–8oz/1½–2 cups
*   hard goat's cheese, grated*
salt and ground black pepper

1 Toast the hazelnuts in a dry frying pan until golden. Leave to cool, roughly chop half and finely chop the rest.

2 Sift the flour and seasoning into a large bowl and stir in the finely chopped nuts. Add the butter. Using your fingertips, rub the butter into the flour until it resembles fine breadcrumbs. Sprinkle over about 45ml/3 tbsp cold water, mix until the crumbs stick together and then gather the mixture into a ball.

3 Roll out the pastry and line a 25cm/10in flan tin (pan). Chill for 10–25 minutes to rest (or leave it there until required). Put a baking sheet in the oven and preheat to 200°C/400°F/Gas 6.

4 Put the oil and leeks into a pan and cook until soft, stirring occasionally. Meanwhile, prick the base of the pastry case (pie shell) and line with baking parchment and dried beans. Put on to the hot baking sheet and cook for 10 minutes. Remove the paper and beans and brush the pastry with beaten egg. Return to the oven for 3–4 minutes.

5 Meanwhile, mix together the remaining eggs with the cream, mustard, half the cheese and a little seasoning. Stir the mixture into the leeks and pour into the hot pastry case. Sprinkle the rest of the cheese on top and sprinkle the remaining (roughly chopped) hazelnuts over the top or around the edges.

6 Put into the hot oven and cook for about 30 minutes until set and golden. Serve hot or at room temperature.

Puff Pastry Tarts Energy 543kcal/2269kJ; Protein 10.2g; Carbohydrate 50.8g, of which sugars 6.2g; Fat 35.9g, of which saturates 2.4g; Cholesterol 9mg; Calcium 91mg; Fibre 1.7g; Sodium 736mg.
Leek Tart Energy 683kcal/2835kJ; Protein 20.7g; Carbohydrate 26.9g, of which sugars 4g; Fat 55g, of which saturates 27.3g; Cholesterol 267mg; Calcium 381mg; Fibre 3.1g; Sodium 409mg.

Leek and Roquefort Tart with Walnut Pastry

Mild leeks go exceptionally well with the salty flavour of the Roquefort cheese. Serve with a green salad of rocket, mizuna or watercress.

Serves 4–6

25g/1oz/2 tbsp butter
450g/1lb leeks, sliced
175g/6oz Roquefort cheese, sliced
2 large eggs
250ml/8fl oz/1 cup double
  (heavy) cream
10ml/2 tsp chopped fresh tarragon
salt and ground black pepper

For the pastry
175g/6oz/1½ cups plain
  (all-purpose) flour
5ml/1 tsp soft dark brown sugar
50g/2oz/¼ cup butter
75g/3oz walnuts, ground
15ml/1 tbsp lemon juice
30ml/2 tbsp iced water

1 First make the pastry. Sift the flour and 2.5ml/½ tsp salt into a bowl. Add some black pepper and the sugar. Rub in the butter until the mixture looks like breadcrumbs, then stir in the walnuts. Bind with the lemon juice and iced water. Gather into a ball, wrap in clear film (plastic wrap)and chill for 30 minutes.

2 Preheat the oven to 190°C/375°F/Gas 5. Roll out the pastry and use to line a 21–23cm/8½–9in loose-based flan tin (pan). Protect the sides of the pastry with foil, prick the base with a fork and bake for 15 minutes. Remove the foil and bake for a further 5–10 minutes, until just firm to the touch. Reduce the oven temperature to 180°C/350°F/Gas 4.

3 Meanwhile, make the filling. Melt the butter in a pan, add the leeks, cover and cook for 10 minutes. Season and cook for a further 10 minutes. Leave to cool a little, then spoon into the pastry and arrange the Roquefort on top. Beat the eggs with the cream and season with pepper. Beat in the tarragon and carefully pour the mixture into the tart.

4 Bake the tart in the oven for 30–40 minutes, until the filling has risen and browned and become firm to a gentle touch. Allow to cool for 10 minutes before serving.

Caramelized Onion Tart

Served warm with a mixed leaf salad, this classic tart makes a perfect light lunch.

Serves 6

15ml/1 tbsp unsalted (sweet)
  butter, plus extra for greasing
15ml/1 tbsp olive oil
500g/1¼lb onions, sliced
large pinch of ground nutmeg
5ml/1 tsp soft dark brown sugar
2 eggs
150ml/¼ pint/⅔ cup single
  (light) cream
50g/2oz/½ cup Gruyère
  cheese, grated
salt and ground black pepper

For the pastry
75g/3oz/⅔ cup unbleached plain
  (all-purpose) flour
75g/3oz/⅔ cup wholemeal
  (whole-wheat) flour
75g/3oz/6 tbsp unsalted
  (sweet) butter
1 egg yolk

1 To make the pastry, rub together the plain and wholemeal flours and butter until the mixture resembles fine breadcrumbs. Mix in the egg yolk and enough cold water to form a dough.

2 Turn out the dough on to a lightly floured work surface and form into a smooth ball, then cover and chill for 30 minutes.

3 Meanwhile, make the filling. Heat the butter and oil in a frying pan. Cook the onions over low heat for 30 minutes until very soft, stirring often. Add the nutmeg, sugar and seasoning. Cook for 5 minutes until the onions are caramelized. Set aside.

4 Preheat the oven to 220°C/425°F/Gas 7. Lightly grease a loose-based 35 × 12cm/14 × 4½in fluted baking tin (pan). Roll out the pastry and use to line the prepared tin. Trim the top, then chill for 20 minutes.

5 Prick the pastry base with a fork, then line with baking parchment and baking beans and bake blind for 10 minutes. Remove the paper and the beans, then spoon in the onions.

6 Beat the eggs with the cream, then add the cheese and season to taste. Pour the mixture over the onions and bake for 30 minutes until set and golden.

Leek Tart Energy 683kcal/2835kJ; Protein 20.7g; Carbohydrate 26.9g, of which sugars 4g; Fat 55g, of which saturates 27.3g; Cholesterol 267mg; Calcium 381mg; Fibre 3.1g; Sodium 409mg.
Onion Tart Energy 905kcal/3748kJ; Protein 15g; Carbohydrate 36.7g, of which sugars 3g; Fat 78.2g, of which saturates 47.1g; Cholesterol 384mg; Calcium 272mg; Fibre 1.6g; Sodium 383mg.

Wild Mushroom and Fontina Tart

This tart makes a tasty vegetarian main course, when served with a green salad and fresh crusty bread. Consider using any types of wild mushrooms you like – chanterelles, morels, horns of plenty and ceps all have wonderful flavours from earthy to very delicate.

Serves 6
225g/8oz ready-made shortcrust pastry, thawed if frozen
50g/2oz/¼ cup butter
350g/12oz/5 cups mixed wild mushrooms, sliced if large
150g/5oz fontina cheese, sliced
salt and ground black pepper

1 Preheat the oven to 190°C/375°F/Gas 5. Roll out the pastry on a lightly floured surface.

2 Use the rolled dough to a line a 23cm/9in loose-bottomed flan tin (pan). Chill the pastry for 30 minutes, then line the pastry case (pie shell) with baking parchment, add a layer of baking beans and bake in the oven for 15 minutes. Remove the beans and parchment, and bake for a further 5 minutes, until light golden brown on the edges. Set aside.

3 Heat the butter in a large frying pan until foaming. Add the mushrooms and season with salt and ground black pepper. Cook over medium heat for 4–5 minutes, moving the mushrooms about and turning them occasionally with a wooden spoon, until golden.

4 Arrange the mushrooms in the cooked pastry case with the fontina. Return the tart to the oven for 10 minutes, or until the cheese is golden and bubbling. Serve hot.

> **Cook's Tip**
> *Picking your own wild mushrooms is a rewarding experience. If you are in any doubt as to the variety, then you should not eat them as there are many poisonous mushrooms out there. While picking, you should carry the mushrooms in a basket so they will release their spores back on to the ground.*

Red Onion Tart

Cornmeal gives the pastry a crumbly texture to contrast with the juiciness of the onions. A tomato and basil salad is good with the tart.

Serves 5–6
60ml/4 tbsp olive oil
1kg/2¼lb red onions, thinly sliced
2–3 garlic cloves, thinly sliced
5ml/1 tsp chopped fresh thyme, plus a few whole sprigs
5ml/1 tsp soft dark brown sugar
10ml/2 tsp sherry vinegar
225g/8oz fontina cheese, thinly sliced
salt and ground black pepper

For the pastry
115g/4oz/1 cup plain (all-purpose) flour
75g/3oz/¾ cup fine cornmeal
5ml/1 tsp soft dark brown sugar
5ml/1 tsp chopped fresh thyme
90g/3½oz/7 tbsp butter
1 egg yolk
30–45ml/2–3 tbsp iced water

1 To make the pastry, sift the plain flour and cornmeal into a bowl with 5ml/1 tsp salt. Add black pepper and stir in the sugar and thyme. Rub in the butter until it looks like breadcrumbs. Beat the egg yolk with 30ml/2 tbsp tbsp iced water and use to bind the pastry, adding another 15ml/1 tbsp iced water, if necessary. Gather the dough into a ball with your fingertips, wrap in clear film (plastic wrap) and chill it for 30–40 minutes.

2 Heat 45ml/3 tbsp of the oil in a frying pan. Gently cook the onions, covered, for 20–30 minutes, stirring occasionally. Add the garlic and chopped thyme, then cook, stirring occasionally, for another 10 minutes. Add the sugar and sherry vinegar. Cook, uncovered, for 5–6 minutes, until the onions start to caramelize slightly. Season with salt and pepper. Cool.

3 Preheat the oven to 190°C/375°F/Gas 5. Roll out the pastry and use to line a 25cm/10in loose-based metal flan tin (pan). Prick the pastry all over with a fork and support the sides with foil. Bake for 12–15 minutes, until lightly coloured.

4 Remove the foil and spread the onions evenly over the base. Add the fontina and thyme sprigs. Drizzle over the remaining oil, then bake for 15–20 minutes, until the filling is hot and the cheese is bubbling. Garnish with thyme and serve immediately.

Red Onion Tart Energy 494kcal/2051kJ; Protein 13.2g; Carbohydrate 38.9g, of which sugars 11.3g; Fat 31.7g, of which saturates 16g; Cholesterol 100mg; Calcium 172mg; Fibre 3.2g; Sodium 307mg.
Mushroom Tart Energy 409kcal/1701kJ; Protein 10.2g; Carbohydrate 21.9g, of which sugars 2.3g; Fat 31g, of which saturates 13.4g; Cholesterol 143mg; Calcium 121mg; Fibre 2.3g; Sodium 199mg.

Summer Herb Ricotta Flan

Simple to make and infused with fresh aromatic herbs, this delicate flan makes a delightful lunch dish.

Serves 4
olive oil, for greasing and glazing
800g/1¾lb/3½ cups
  ricotta cheese
75g/3oz/1 cup finely grated
  Parmesan cheese
3 eggs, separated
60ml/4 tbsp torn fresh
  basil leaves
60ml/4 tbsp chopped fresh chives
45ml/3 tbsp fresh oregano leaves
2.5ml/½ tsp salt
2.5ml/½ tsp paprika
ground black pepper
fresh herb leaves, to garnish

For the tapenade
400g/14oz/3½ cups pitted black
  olives, rinsed and halved,
  reserving a few whole to
  garnish (optional)
5 garlic cloves, crushed
75ml/5 tbsp/⅓ cup olive oil

1 Preheat the oven to 180°C/350°F/Gas 4 and lightly grease a 23cm/9in springform cake tin (pan) with oil.

2 Mix together the ricotta, Parmesan and egg yolks in a food processor or blender. Add the herbs and seasoning, and blend until smooth and creamy.

3 Whisk the egg whites in a large bowl until they form soft peaks. Gently fold the egg whites into the ricotta mixture, taking care not to knock out too much air. Spoon the ricotta mixture into the tin and smooth the top.

4 Bake in the preheated oven for 1 hour 20 minutes or until the flan is risen and the top golden.

5 Remove the tin from the oven and brush the top of the flan lightly with olive oil, then sprinkle with paprika. Leave the flan to cool before removing from the tin.

6 Make the tapenade. Place the olives and garlic in a food processor or blender and process until finely chopped. Gradually add the olive oil and blend to a coarse paste, then transfer to a serving bowl. Garnish the flan with fresh herb leaves and serve with the tapenade.

Cheese and Asparagus Flan

The distinctive taste of fresh asparagus comes through in this tasty flan.

Serves 5–6
300g/11oz small asparagus
  spears weighed after trimming,
  cooked until tender
75g/3oz mature (sharp) Cheddar
  cheese, grated
3 spring onions (scallions), sliced
2 eggs
300ml/½ pint/1¼ cups double
  (heavy) cream
freshly grated nutmeg
salt and ground black pepper

For the pastry
175g/6oz/1½ cups plain (all-
  purpose) flour
pinch of salt
40g/1½oz/3 tbsp lard or white
  cooking fat, diced
40g/1½oz/3 tbsp butter, diced

1 To make the pastry, sift the flour and salt into a bowl and rub in the lard or fat and butter until the mixture resembles fine breadcrumbs. Stir in about 45ml/3 tbsp cold water and gather together into a ball. Wrap the pastry and chill for 30 minutes.

2 Put a flat baking sheet in the oven and preheat to 200°C/400°F/Gas 6. Roll out the pastry on a lightly floured work surface and use it to line a 20cm/8in flan tin (pan). Line the pastry case (pie shell) with baking parchment and add a layer of baking beans. Bake on the sheet for 10–15 minutes.

3 Remove the beans and parchment, and bake for a further 5 minutes, until light golden brown on the edges. Remove the flan and reduce the temperature to 180°C/350°F/Gas 4.

4 Cut the cooked asparagus spears into 2.5cm/1in lengths, leaving the tips whole. Sprinkle half the cheese in the base of the pastry case and add the asparagus and the spring onions.

5 Beat the eggs with the cream and season with salt, black pepper and nutmeg. Pour over the asparagus and top with the remaining cheese.

6 Return the flan to the hot baking sheet in the oven and cook for about 30 minutes or until just set. Leave the flan to settle for 5 minutes before cutting and serving.

Cheese Flan Energy 547kcal/2266kJ; Protein 10.4g; Carbohydrate 24.7g, of which sugars 2.4g; Fat 45.6g, of which saturates 26.2g; Cholesterol 165mg; Calcium 184mg; Fibre 1.8g; Sodium 167mg.
Ricotta Flan Energy 730kcal/3021kJ; Protein 32.7g; Carbohydrate 8.6g, of which sugars 6.7g; Fat 63g, of which saturates 26.7g; Cholesterol 245mg; Calcium 335mg; Fibre 4g; Sodium 2512mg.

Tuna and Egg Galette

This flaky pastry tart combines soft-centred eggs and a slightly piquant fish filling. It makes a wonderful dish for a summer supper.

Serves 4

2 sheets of ready-rolled puff pastry
flour, for rolling
beaten egg, to glaze
60ml/4 tbsp olive oil

175g/6oz tuna steak
2 onions, sliced
1 red (bell) pepper, chopped
2 garlic cloves, crushed
45ml/3 tbsp capers, drained
5ml/1 tsp grated lemon rind
30ml/2 tbsp lemon juice
5 eggs
salt and ground black pepper
30ml/2 tbsp chopped flat leaf
    parsley, to garnish

1 Preheat the oven to 190°C/375°F/Gas 5. Lay one sheet of puff pastry on a lightly floured baking tray and cut it to a 28 x 18cm/11 x 7in rectangle. Brush the whole sheet with beaten egg.

2 Cut the second sheet of pastry to the same size. Cut out a rectangle from the centre and discard, leaving a 2.5cm/1in border. Carefully lift the border on to the first sheet. Brush the border with beaten egg and prick the base. Bake the pastry case (pie shell) for about 15 minutes until golden and well risen.

3 Heat 30ml/2 tbsp of the oil in a frying pan and fry the tuna steak for 2–3 minutes on each side until golden but still pale pink in the middle. Transfer the steak to a plate and flake into small pieces.

4 Add the remaining oil to the pan and fry the onions, red pepper and garlic for about 6–8 minutes until softened, stirring occasionally. Remove the pan from the heat and stir in the flaked tuna, capers and lemon rind and juice. Season well with salt and black pepper.

5 Spoon the filling into the pastry case and level the surface with the back of a spoon. Break the eggs into the filling and return the galette to the oven for about 10 minutes, or until the eggs have just cooked through. Garnish with chopped parsley and serve immediately.

Smoked Salmon Quiche

The ingredients in this light quiche perfectly complement the melt-in-the-mouth pastry made with potatoes.

Serves 6
For the pastry
115g/4oz floury maincrop
    potatoes, diced
225g/8oz/2 cups plain
    (all-purpose) flour, sifted
115g/4oz/½ cup butter, diced
½ egg, beaten
10ml/2 tsp chilled water

salad leaves and chopped fresh
    dill, to serve

For the filling
275g/10oz smoked salmon
6 eggs, beaten
150ml/¼ pint/⅔ cup full-cream
    (whole) milk
300ml/½ pint/1¼ cups double
    (heavy) cream
30–45ml/2–3 tbsp chopped
    fresh dill
30ml/2 tbsp capers, chopped
salt and ground black pepper

1 Boil the potatoes in a pan of salted water for 15 minutes or until tender. Drain well and return to the pan. Mash the potatoes until smooth and set aside to cool completely.

2 Place the flour in a bowl and rub in the butter to form fine crumbs. Beat in the potatoes and egg. Bring the mixture together, adding chilled water if needed.

3 Roll the pastry out on a floured surface and use to line a deep 23cm/9in round, loose-based, fluted flan tin (pan). Chill in the refrigerator for 1 hour.

4 Preheat the oven to 200°C/400°F/Gas 6. Place a baking sheet in the oven to preheat it. Chop the salmon into bite-size pieces and set aside.

5 For the filling, beat the eggs, milk and cream together. Then stir in the dill and capers and season with pepper. Add in the salmon and stir to combine.

6 Prick the base of the pastry case (pie shell) with a fork and pour the mixture into it. Bake on a baking sheet for about 35–45 minutes until cooked through. Serve warm with salad leaves and some dill.

Tuna and Egg Galette Energy 544kcal/2263kJ; Protein 21.7g; Carbohydrate 27.7g, of which sugars 4.6g; Fat 39.5g, of which saturates 10.1g; Cholesterol 260mg; Calcium 102mg; Fibre 1.9g; Sodium 320mg.
Salmon Quiche Energy 338kcal/1413kJ; Protein 24.3g; Carbohydrate 17.9g, of which sugars 10.2g; Fat 19.4g, of which saturates 7g; Cholesterol 199mg; Calcium 167mg; Fibre 0.7g; Sodium 665mg.

Onion and Sausage Tarte Tatin

Toulouse sausages have a garlicky flavour that is delicious with fried onions.

Serves 4
45ml/3 tbsp sunflower oil
450g/1lb Toulouse sausages
2 large onions, sliced
250g/9oz ready-made puff pastry, thawed if frozen
salt and ground black pepper

1 Heat the oil in a 23cm/9in non-stick frying pan with an ovenproof handle, and add the sausages. Cook over a gentle heat, turning occasionally, for 7–10 minutes, or until golden and cooked through. Remove from the pan and set aside.

2 Preheat the oven to 190°C/375°F/Gas 5. Heat the remaining oil in the frying pan. Gently cook the onions for 10 minutes, stirring occasionally, until caramelized. Season well.

3 Slice each sausage into four or five chunks and stir into the onions. Remove from the heat and set aside.

4 Roll out the puff pastry and cut out a circle slightly larger than the frying pan. Lay the pastry over the sausages and onions, tucking the edges in all the way around. Bake for 20 minutes, or until the pastry is risen and golden. Turn out on to a board, pastry side down, cut into wedges and serve.

Haggis, Potato and Apple Tart

Apple combines well with haggis as its tart and sweet taste cuts through the richness of the meat.

Serves 4
450g/1lb peeled potatoes, sliced
1 garlic clove
5ml/1 tsp salt
freshly grated nutmeg
400g/14oz ready-made puff pastry
300g/11oz haggis
2 cooking apples, cored
1 egg, beaten
salt and ground black pepper

1 Preheat the oven to 220°C/425°F/Gas 7. Mix the potatoes with the garlic crushed with 5ml/1 tsp salt. Season with nutmeg, salt and pepper to taste.

2 Roll out the puff pastry into two discs, one about 25cm/10in in diameter and the other a little larger. Place the smaller pastry disc on a baking tray and spread half the potatoes over it, leaving a rim of about 2cm/¾in all the way round.

3 Cut the haggis open and crumble the meat on top. Slice the apple into circles and spread over the haggis. Top with the rest of the potatoes. Brush the egg all around the exposed pastry rim then place the other pastry circle on top, pushing down to seal. Use a fork to tidy up the edges and then press down around the edge again to create a firm seal. Leave to rest for 10 minutes.

4 Brush over with more egg and bake for 10 minutes to set the pastry. Then reduce the oven to 200°C/400°F/Gas 6 and bake for 40 minutes until evenly browned and cooked. Serve in slices.

Quiche Lorraine

This classic quiche from eastern France has some traditional characteristics that are often forgotten in modern recipes, namely very thin pastry, a really creamy and light, egg-rich filling,

Serves 4–6
175g/6oz/1½ cups plain (all-purpose) flour, sifted, plus extra for dusting
pinch of salt
115g/4oz/½ cup unsalted (sweet) butter, at room temperature, diced
3 eggs, plus 3 yolks
6 smoked streaky (fatty) bacon rashers (strips), rinds removed
300ml/½ pint/1¼ cups double (heavy) cream
25g/1oz/2 tbsp unsalted (sweet) butter
salt and ground black pepper

1 Place the flour, salt, butter and 1 egg yolk in a food processor and process until blended. Place on to a lightly floured surface and form into a ball. Leave to rest for 20 minutes.

2 Lightly flour a deep 20cm/8in round flan tin (pan), and place it on a baking tray. Roll out the pastry and use to line the tin, trimming off any overhang. Press the pastry into the corners of the tin. If the pastry breaks up, gently push it into shape. Chill for 20 minutes. Preheat the oven to 200°C/400°F/Gas 6.

3 Cut the bacon into strips and grill (broil). Arrange the bacon in the pastry case (pie shell). Mix the cream, remaining eggs and yolks and seasoning, and pour into the pastry case.

4 Bake in the oven for 15 minutes, then reduce the heat to 180°C/350°F/Gas 4 and bake for a further 15–20 minutes. When the filling is puffed up and golden brown and the pastry edges are crisp, remove from the oven and top with knobs of butter. Stand for 5 minutes before serving.

> **Cook's Tip**
> To prepare the quiche in advance, bake for 5–10 minutes less than recommended, until the filling is just set. Reheat later at 190°C/375°F/Gas 5 for about 10 minutes.

Tarte Tatin Energy 765kcal/3176kJ; Protein 17g; Carbohydrate 43.7g, of which sugars 9.4g; Fat 59.9g, of which saturates 14.7g; Cholesterol 53mg; Calcium 114mg; Fibre 2.3g; Sodium 1053mg.
Haggis Tart Energy 698kcal/2919kJ; Protein 15.8g; Carbohydrate 72.9g, of which sugars 6.1g; Fat 41.2g, of which saturates 5.8g; Cholesterol 68mg; Calcium 88mg; Fibre 1.9g; Sodium 901mg.
Quiche Lorraine Energy 670kcal/2775kJ; Protein 13g; Carbohydrate 23.7g, of which sugars 1.4g; Fat 58.9g, of which saturates 32.9g; Cholesterol 302mg; Calcium 94mg; Fibre 0.9g; Sodium 611mg.

Heart of Palm Pie

The delicate creamy filling in this pie contrasts beautifully with the crumbly pastry.

Serves 8
500g/1¼lb/5 cups plain
  (all-purpose) flour, plus extra
  for dusting
5ml/1 tsp salt
175g/6oz/¾ cup butter
75g/3oz/6 tbsp lard or white
  cooking fat
1 egg yolk
45ml/3 tbsp cold water

For the filling
25g/1oz/2 tbsp butter
1 large onion, finely chopped
4 garlic cloves, crushed

15ml/1 tbsp plain
  (all-purpose) flour
200ml/7fl oz/scant 1 cup full-fat
  (whole) milk
2 hard-boiled eggs, chopped
1 large tomato, peeled, seeded
  and cubed
1 fresh red chilli, seeded and
  finely chopped
2 x 400g/14oz cans heart of
  palm, drained and cut into
  2cm/¾in slices
15ml/1 tbsp chopped fresh flat
  leaf parsley
salt and ground black pepper

For the glaze
1 egg yolk
15ml/1 tbsp water

1 Place the flour, salt, butter and lard or fat in a food processor and process until the mixture resembles fine breadcrumbs. With the motor still running, add the egg yolk and the cold water. As soon as the mixture comes together, transfer to a floured surface. Knead the pastry lightly until smooth. Divide the pastry into two rounds, one slightly larger than the other, wrap both in cling film (plastic wrap) and place in the refrigerator.

2 Melt the butter in a frying pan over low heat. Stir in the onion and cook for 5 minutes until soft. Add the garlic and cook for a further 2 minutes. Stir in the flour and cook, stirring, for 1 minute. Remove from the heat and slowly pour in the milk, a little at a time, stirring to break up any lumps.

3 Return to the heat and cook, stirring, for 2 minutes to make a thin white sauce. Remove from the heat and stir in the chopped eggs, tomato, chilli, palm hearts and parsley. Season with salt and pepper. Preheat the oven to 190°C/375°F/Gas 5. Place a large baking sheet in the oven so that it heats up.

4 On a floured surface, roll out the larger piece of pastry and line the base and sides of a 23cm/9in round loose-based quiche pan. The pastry will be very crumbly, so it may tear in a few places. Should this happen, use your fingers to push the pastry together again. There should be no gaps.

5 Add the filling, then roll out the remaining pastry and use to top the pie. Do not worry about any small gaps in the pastry, as they add to the rustic character of the dish.

6 Make the glaze by mixing the egg yolk with the water. Using a pastry brush, glaze the pastry, then place the pan on the baking sheet and bake for 45 minutes, until the pastry is golden.

7 Leave the pie to cool for 5 minutes on a wire rack before removing it from the pan and putting it on to a large plate. Serve warm or at room temperature.

Mediterranean One-crust Pie

This free-form pie encases a rich tomato and bean filling.

Serves 4
1 red (bell) pepper
30ml/2 tbsp olive oil, plus extra
  for greasing
1 large onion, finely chopped
500g/1¼lb aubergine
  (eggplant), cubed
1 courgette (zucchini), sliced
2 garlic cloves, crushed
15ml/1 tbsp fresh oregano or
  5ml/1 tsp dried, plus extra
  fresh oregano to garnish
200g/7oz/1½ cups canned red
  kidney beans, drained and rinsed

115g/4oz/1 cup pitted black
  olives, rinsed
375g/13oz/1⅔ cup passata
  (bottled strained tomatoes)
1 egg, beaten, or a little milk
30ml/2 tbsp semolina
salt and ground black pepper

For the pastry
75g/3oz/⅔ cup unbleached plain
  (all-purpose) flour
75g/3oz/⅔ cup wholemeal
  (whole-wheat) flour
75g/3oz/6 tbsp vegetable
  margarine
50g/2oz/⅔ cup freshly grated
  Parmesan cheese

1 Preheat the oven to 220°C/425°F/Gas 7. To make the pastry, sift the the flours into a large bowl. Rub in the margarine until the mixture resembles breadcrumbs, then stir in the grated Parmesan. Mix in enough cold water to form a firm dough. Turn out the dough on to a lightly floured surface and form into a smooth ball. Wrap the dough and chill for 30 minutes.

2 Place the pepper on a baking tray and roast in the oven for 20 minutes. Put the pepper in a plastic bag and leave until cool enough to handle. Peel and seed, then dice the flesh. Set aside. Heat the oil in a frying pan. Fry the onion for 5 minutes until soft. Add the aubergine for 5 minutes until tender. Add the courgettes, garlic and oregano, and cook for 5 minutes. Then add the beans, olives, passata and pepper. Simmer until hot, then set aside.

3 Roll out the pastry on a floured surface to form a 30cm/12in round. Place on an oiled baking sheet. Brush with beaten egg or milk, sprinkle over the semolina, leaving a 4cm/1½in border, then spoon over the filling. Gather up the edges of the pastry a little. Brush with more egg or milk and bake for 30–35 minutes until golden. Garnish with oregano and serve.

Heart of Palm Pie Energy 710kcal/2955kJ; Protein 9.9g; Carbohydrate 54.8g, of which sugars 6g; Fat 51.7g, of which saturates 30.5g; Cholesterol 193mg; Calcium 178mg; Fibre 3.6g; Sodium 434mg.
Mediterranean Pie Energy 554kcal/2318kJ; Protein 17.7g; Carbohydrate 56.6g, of which sugars 15.7g; Fat 30.2g, of which saturates 4.2g; Cholesterol 13mg; Calcium 295mg; Fibre 11.6g; Sodium 1353mg.

Egg and Spinach Pie

This pie makes an excellent picnic dish as it can be made in advance and travels well.

Serves 10–12

oil, for greasing
115g/4oz/½ cup butter, melted
1 bunch spring onions (scallions), finely chopped
675g/1½lb fresh or frozen spinach, cooked and chopped
30ml/2 tbsp fresh marjoram or oregano, chopped or 10ml/2 tsp dried
350g/12oz ricotta cheese
45ml/3 tbsp freshly grated Parmesan cheese
60ml/4 tbsp double (heavy) cream, whipped
5ml/1 tsp grated fresh nutmeg
450g/1lb filo pastry
2 egg whites, stiffly whisked
8 eggs, hard-boiled and peeled
salt and ground black pepper

1 Lightly grease a deep 20 x 25cm/8 x 10in roasting pan. Preheat the oven to 190°C/375°F/Gas 5.

2 Heat 30ml/2 tbsp butter in a large pan and fry the onions until softened. Stir in the spinach and herb, and season with salt and pepper to taste. Mix until well blended and the spinach is quite soft and smooth. In a bowl, beat the ricotta cheese with the Parmesan, cream, nutmeg and seasoning until really smooth.

3 Use just over half the sheets of filo pastry for the base: brush each sheet with melted butter, and layer neatly in the pan, allowing any excess pastry to hang over the edges. Keep the rest of the pastry covered with a damp cloth.

4 Whisk the egg whites, then fold into the cheese. Fold in the spinach until evenly mixed. Spoon half the mixture into the pan and arrange the eggs on top. Cover with the rest of the filling and fold over any excess pastry edges.

5 Brush the remaining sheets of pastry with butter and place over the top. Brush with more butter, then bake for 1 hour until the pastry is golden and the pie feels quite firm. Allow the pie to cool slightly, then carefully invert it on to a clean surface, and serve warm or leave to cool completely and serve cold.

Chestnut, Stilton and Ale Pie

This hearty dish has a rich gravy and a herb pastry top.

Serves 4

30ml/2 tbsp sunflower oil
2 large onions, chopped
500g/1¼lb/8 cups button (white) mushrooms, halved
3 carrots, sliced
1 parsnip, cut into thick slices
15ml/1 tbsp fresh thyme or 5ml/1 tsp dried
2 bay leaves
250ml/8fl oz/1 cup Guinness
120ml/4fl oz/½ cup vegetable stock
5ml/1 tsp Worcestershire sauce
5ml/1 tsp soft dark brown sugar
350g/12oz/3 cups canned chestnuts, halved
30ml/2 tbsp unbleached plain (all-purpose) flour
150g/5oz/1½ cups Stilton, cubed
1 egg, beaten, or milk, to glaze
salt and ground black pepper

For the pastry

115g/4oz/1 cup wholemeal (whole-wheat) flour
a pinch of salt
50g/2oz/4 tbsp unsalted (sweet) butter or vegetable margarine
15ml/1 tbsp fresh thyme or 5ml/1 tsp dried

1 To make the pastry, rub the flour, salt and butter or margarine until it resembles fine breadcrumbs. Add the thyme and enough water to form a soft dough. Turn out on to a floured surface and knead to a smooth dough. Wrap and chill for 30 minutes.

2 Make the filling. Heat the oil in a heavy pan and fry the onions for 5 minutes until softened. Add the mushrooms and cook for 3 minutes, then add the carrots, parsnip and herbs. Cover and cook for 3 minutes, then pour in the Guinness, stock and Worcestershire sauce. Add the sugar and seasoning. Simmer, covered, for 5 minutes, then add the chestnuts.

3 Mix the flour to a paste with 30ml/2 tbsp water. Add to the pan and cook, uncovered, for 5 minutes until the sauce thickens. Stir in the cheese and heat until melted, stirring constantly.

4 Preheat the oven to 220°C/425°F/Gas 7. Roll out the pastry to fit the top of a 1.5 litre/2½ pint/6¼ cup pie dish. Spoon in the filling, dampen the edges of the dish and cover with the pastry. Seal, trim and crimp the edges. Cut a slit in the top, brush with egg or milk and bake for 30 minutes until golden.

Egg and Spinach Pie Energy 378kcal/1580kJ; Protein 16.1g; Carbohydrate 25.4g, of which sugars 1.2g; Fat 24.5g, of which saturates 13.6g; Cholesterol 204mg; Calcium 265mg; Fibre 2.5g; Sodium 322mg.
Chestnut Pie Energy 666kcal/2782kJ; Protein 18.9g; Carbohydrate 70.3g, of which sugars 22.6g; Fat 32.7g, of which saturates 16.6g; Cholesterol 62mg; Calcium 238mg; Fibre 11g; Sodium 415mg.

Filo Fish Pies

These light filo-wrapped fish pies can be made with any firm white fish fillets, such as orange roughy, cod, halibut or hoki. Serve with salad leaves and mayonnaise.

Serves 6

400g/14oz spinach, trimmed
1 egg, lightly beaten
2 garlic cloves, crushed
450g/1lb orange roughy or other white fish fillet
juice of 1 lemon
50g/2oz/¼ cup butter, melted
8–12 filo pastry sheets, thawed if frozen, quartered
15ml/1 tbsp finely chopped chives
200ml/7fl oz/scant 1 cup half-fat crème fraîche
15ml/1 tbsp chopped fresh dill
salt and ground black pepper

1 Preheat the oven to 190°C/375°F/Gas 5. Wash the spinach, then cook it in a lidded heavy pan with just the water that clings to the leaves. As soon as the leaves are tender, drain, squeeze as dry as possible and chop. Put the spinach in a bowl, add the egg and garlic, season with salt and pepper and set aside. Dice the fish and place it in a bowl. Stir in the lemon juice. Season with salt and pepper and toss lightly.

2 Brush the inside of six 13cm/5in tartlet tins (muffin pans) with a little of the melted butter. Fit a piece of filo pastry into the tins, draping it so that it hangs over the sides. Brush with butter, then add another sheet at right-angles to the first. Brush with butter. Continue to line the tins in this way.

3 Spread the spinach evenly over the pastry. Add the diced fish and season well. Stir the chives into the crème fraîche and spread the mixture over the top of the fish. Sprinkle with dill.

4 Draw the overhanging pieces of pastry together and scrunch lightly to make a lid. Brush with butter. Bake for about 15–20 minutes, until golden brown. Serve immediately.

Variation
To make one large pie, use a 20cm/8in tin (pan) and bake in the oven for 45 minutes.

Trout with Pastry and Almond Crust

Beautiful presentation is a real plus when it comes to serving fish, and this trout is as pretty as a picture with its filo wrapping dusted with almonds. Almonds are used in the delicious stuffing, too, making this a tasty and filling main course.

Serves 4

4 whole trout, about 175g/6oz each, cleaned
40g/1½oz/3 tbsp butter
1 small onion, finely chopped
115g/4oz/1 cup ground almonds
30ml/2 tbsp chopped fresh parsley
finely grated rind of 1 lemon
12 sheets filo pastry
salt and ground black pepper
lemon slices and parsley sprigs, to garnish

1 Preheat the oven to 200°C/400°F/Gas 6. Season the trout generously with salt and black pepper.

2 Melt 25g/1oz/2 tbsp of the butter in a large pan and cook the onion for 1–2 minutes until soft and translucent. Do not allow the onion to brown.

3 Stir 75g/3oz/¾ cup of the ground almonds into the onions in the pan, then add the chopped parsley and the lemon rind. Stir well to combine.

4 Gently stuff the cavity of each trout with one-quarter of the mixture. Press the mixture down firmly to mould it to the shape of the cavity.

5 Melt the remaining butter. Cut three sheets of filo pastry into long strips and brush with the melted butter. Wrap the strips around one fish, with the buttered side inside. Leave the head and the tail free. Place on a baking sheet. Wrap the other trout.

6 Brush the top of the pastry casing with melted butter and sprinkle the remaining ground almonds over the fish. Bake for 20–25 minutes until the pastry is golden brown. Place on warmed individual serving dishes, garnish with the lemon slices and parsley sprigs and serve.

Filo Fish Pies Energy 233kcal/972kJ; Protein 18.4g; Carbohydrate 9.1g, of which sugars 2.2g; Fat 14g, of which saturates 8.2g; Cholesterol 84mg; Calcium 170mg; Fibre 1.7g; Sodium 213mg.
Trout with Pastry Energy 475kcal/1978kJ; Protein 39.2g; Carbohydrate 7.6g, of which sugars 0.8g; Fat 32.2g, of which saturates 12.4g; Cholesterol 187mg; Calcium 101mg; Fibre 1.2g; Sodium 249mg.

Coulibiac

This wonderful salmon pie makes the ideal main course for the whole family.

Serves 4
50g/2oz/¼ cup butter
1 small onion, finely chopped
200g/7oz/1 cup long grain rice
350ml/12fl oz/1½ cups
   chicken stock
1 bay leaf
olive oil
175g/6oz button (white)
   mushrooms, sliced finely
450g/1lb ready-made puff pastry

2.25kg/5lb salmon, skinned
   and filleted
dash of dry white wine
chopped fresh fennel
3 eggs, boiled until firm and sliced
egg wash, made by whisking
   1 egg with a little milk
salt and ground black pepper

For the hollandaise sauce
3 egg yolks
30ml/2 tbsp white wine vinegar
115g/4oz/½ cup butter, diced
1.5ml/¼ tsp salt
pinch of ground black pepper

1 Preheat the oven to 180°C/350°F/Gas 4. In a small ovenproof pan, melt half the butter then cook the onion until translucent. Add the rice and stir. Add the stock and a pinch of salt. Bring to the boil and add the bay leaf. Cover and cook in the preheated oven for 20 minutes. When cooked, gently fluff up the rice with a fork and leave to cool.

2 Heat the remaining butter with a little olive oil in a second pan and quickly fry the mushrooms. Set aside to cool.

3 Roll out the puff pastry into a square, long enough for a fillet and leaving 2.5cm/1in at each end. Sprinkle half the rice in a strip across the centre. Cover with one salmon fillet, moisten with a little wine then season, and sprinkle with the fennel.

4 Cover the salmon with half the sliced egg and half the mushrooms and a few spoonfuls of the rice. Then lay the second fillet on top, adding another splash of wine and seasoning again. Place a layer of egg over the top, sprinkle the rest of the mushrooms over, and finish with the remaining rice.

5 Brush the edges of the pastry with the egg wash, fold the pastry over and seal. Decorate with any pastry trimmings, if you like, and brush egg wash all over. Allow to rest in a cool place for an hour. Preheat the oven to 220°C/425°F/Gas 7.

6 Bake the coulibiac in the preheated oven for about 40 minutes. If the pastry browns too quickly, turn down the heat. Allow to rest for 10 minutes before serving.

7 Make the hollandaise sauce. Put the egg yolks and vinegar in the top of a double boiler. Stir until combined. Place the pan on the base pan filled with hot, but not boiling, water and heat gently, stirring, until the yolks thicken. Add a piece of butter and whisk over a gentle heat until the butter has melted. Gradually add the remaining butter, whisking until the sauce thickens. Remove from the heat and stir in the salt and pepper.

8 Use a serrated bread knife to cut the coulibiac and slice across its width. Hot and moist, it is delicious served with salad or a green vegetable with the hollandaise sauce. It is also excellent cold with a fresh salad.

Fish Pie

The rather everyday title of fish pie does not do justice to this delicious dish.

Serves 4
1kg/2¼lb vendace or perch,
   cleaned, gutted and
   heads removed
150g/5oz sliced belly pork
15ml/1 tbsp salt
a little melted butter, to glaze

For the dough
25g/1oz fresh yeast
25ml/1½ tbsp milk, warmed
50g/2oz/¼ cup butter
450g/1lb/4 cups rye flour
5ml/1 tsp salt
500ml/17fl oz/generous 2 cups
   cold water
50g/2oz/½ cup plain
   (all-purpose) flour, plus extra
   for dusting

1 To make the dough, put the yeast in a small bowl, and pour the warm milk over the yeast. Blend together, then leave for 15 minutes until the yeast bubbles. Melt the butter in a pan and leave to cool. Put 400g/14oz/3½ cups of the rye flour in a large bowl, add the salt, milk and yeast mixture, water and melted butter and mix together to form a soft dough. Cover the bowl and leave at room temperature for 30 minutes until doubled in size.

2 Preheat the oven to 240°C/475°F/Gas 9. Add the remaining rye flour and the plain flour to the risen mixture to make a stiff dough. Turn on to a lightly floured surface and knead until smooth and elastic. Turn the dough on to baking parchment and roll out to a 20cm/8in rectangle, 1cm/½in in thickness. Place on a baking sheet.

3 Arrange the fish in layers in the centre of the dough, alternating with the slices of belly pork. Season each layer with salt. Lift the edges of the dough up and over the filling, overlapping them. Brush the edges of the pastry with water to moisten, then pinch together firmly to seal.

4 Bake the pie in the oven for 30 minutes. Lower the oven to 150°C/300°F/Gas 2. Brush with the cooled, melted butter and cover with baking parchment and then with foil. Bake for a further 3 hours. Remove from the oven and cover with a wet dish towel to soften the crust. Leave for 15 minutes if serving hot. If serving cold, chill overnight so that the filling sets.

Fish Pie Energy 862kcal/3634kJ; Protein 55.2g; Carbohydrate 95.5g, of which sugars 0.6g; Fat 31.6g, of which saturates 12.3g; Cholesterol 209mg; Calcium 126mg; Fibre 13.6g; Sodium 1711mg.
Coulibiac Energy 1005kcal/4190kJ; Protein 50.7g; Carbohydrate 77.9g, of which sugars 2.4g; Fat 56.6g, of which saturates 7.8g; Cholesterol 244mg; Calcium 139mg; Fibre 0.7g; Sodium 521mg.

Chicken and Leek Pies

Make these individual pies in small tart tins or in a four-hole Yorkshire pudding tin. Alternatively, as in the picture, make one large pie using a 20cm/8in tart tin or pie plate.

15g/½oz/1 tbsp butter
1 leek, thinly sliced
2 eggs
225g/8oz skinless chicken breast fillets, finely chopped
small handful of fresh parsley or mint, finely chopped
salt and ground black pepper
beaten egg, to glaze

Serves 4
400g/14oz shortcrust pastry, thawed if frozen

1 Preheat the oven to 200°C/400°F/Gas 6. Roll out the pastry on a lightly floured surface to a thickness of about 3mm/⅛in. Cut out four circles, each large enough to line an individual tart tin (pan) and line the four pans. Cut the remaining pastry into four slightly smaller circles ready to make lids for the pies.

2 Melt the butter in a pan, add the leek and cook gently for about 5 minutes, stirring occasionally, until soft but not brown.

3 Beat the eggs in a bowl and stir in the chicken, herbs and seasoning. Add the leek and its buttery juices from the pan, stirring until well mixed.

4 Spoon the mixture into the pastry cases (pie shells), filling them generously. Brush the edges of the pastry with beaten egg and place the lids on top, pressing the edges together to seal them. Brush the tops of the pies with beaten egg and make a small slit in the centre of each to allow steam to escape.

5 Put into the hot oven and cook for about 30 minutes, until golden brown and cooked through.

> **Variation**
> This pie tastes just as delicious made with puff pastry instead of the shortcrust pastry.

Chicken and Apricot Filo Pie

The filling for this pie features chicken combined with apricots, bulgur wheat, nuts and spices.

Serves 6
75g/3oz/½ cup bulgur wheat
75g/3oz/6 tbsp butter
1 onion, chopped
450g/1lb minced (ground) chicken
50g/2oz/¼ cup ready-to-eat dried apricots, finely chopped
25g/1oz/¼ cup blanched almonds, chopped
5ml/1 tsp ground cinnamon
2.5ml/½ tsp ground allspice
50ml/2fl oz/¼ cup Greek (US strained plain) yogurt
15ml/1 tbsp chopped fresh chives
30ml/2 tbsp chopped fresh parsley
6 large sheets filo pastry
salt and ground black pepper
chives, to garnish

1 Preheat the oven to 200°C/400°F/Gas 6. Put the bulgur wheat in a bowl with 120ml/4fl oz/½ cup boiling water. Soak for 5–10 minutes, until the water is absorbed.

2 Heat 25g/1oz/2 tbsp of the butter in a pan, and gently fry the onion and chicken until pale golden.

3 Stir in the apricots, almonds and bulgur wheat and cook for a further 2 minutes. Remove from the heat and stir in the cinnamon, allspice, yogurt, chives and parsley. Season to taste with salt and pepper.

4 Melt the remaining butter. Unroll the filo pastry and cut into 25cm/10in rounds. Keep the pastry rounds covered with a clean, damp dish towel to prevent drying.

5 Line a 23cm/9in loose-based flan tin (pan) with three of the pastry rounds, brushing each one with butter as you layer them. Spoon in the chicken mixture, cover with three more pastry rounds, brushed with melted butter as before.

6 Crumple the remaining rounds and place them on top of the pie, then brush over any remaining melted butter. Bake the pie for about 30 minutes, until the pastry is golden brown and crisp. Serve the pie hot or cold, cut in wedges and garnished with fresh chives.

Chicken and Apricot Filo Pie Energy 263kcal/1104kJ; Protein 21.9g; Carbohydrate 19.9g, of which sugars 3.8g; Fat 11.3g, of which saturates 5.2g; Cholesterol 70mg; Calcium 69mg; Fibre 1.6g; Sodium 106mg.
Chicken Pies Energy 588kcal/2459kJ; Protein 23.4g; Carbohydrate 48.4g, of which sugars 2.1g; Fat 34.9g, of which saturates 11.7g; Cholesterol 157mg; Calcium 133mg; Fibre 3.4g; Sodium 496mg.

Turkey and Cranberry Bundles

After the traditional Christmas or Thanksgiving meal, it is easy to end up with lots of turkey leftovers. These delicious filo pastry parcels are a marvellous way of using up the small pieces of cooked turkey.

Serves 6
450g/1lb cooked turkey, cut
  into chunks
115g/4oz/1 cup Brie, diced
30ml/2 tbsp cranberry sauce
30ml/2 tbsp chopped
  fresh parsley
9 sheets filo pastry, 45 x 28cm/
  18 x 11in each, thawed
  if frozen
50g/2oz/1/4 cup butter, melted
salt and ground black pepper
green salad, to serve

1 Preheat the oven to 200°C/400°F/Gas 6. Mix the turkey, diced Brie, cranberry sauce and chopped parsley. Season with salt and pepper.

2 Cut the filo sheets in half widthways and trim to make 18 squares. Layer three pieces of pastry together, brushing them with a little melted butter so that they stick together. Repeat with the remaining filo squares to give six pieces.

3 Divide the turkey mixture among the pastry, making neat piles on each piece. Gather up the pastry to enclose the filling in neat bundles. Place on a baking sheet, brush with a little melted butter and bake for 20 minutes, or until the pastry is crisp and golden. Serve hot or warm with a green salad.

> **Variation**
> These little parcels can be made with a variety of fillings and are great for using up left-over cooked meats. To make Ham and Cheddar Bundles, replace the turkey with ham and use Cheddar in place of the Brie. A fruit-flavoured chutney would make a good alternative to the cranberry sauce. Alternatively, to make Chicken and Stilton Bundles, use cooked chicken in place of the turkey and white Stilton instead of Brie. Replace the cranberry sauce with mango chutney.

Chicken and Mushroom Pie

Use wild mushrooms, such as ceps, to intensify the flavour of this family favourite.

Serves 6
50g/2oz/1/4 cup butter
30ml/2 tbsp plain (all-purpose) flour
250ml/8fl oz/1 cup hot chicken stock
60ml/4 tbsp single (light) cream
1 onion, coarsely chopped
2 carrots, sliced
2 celery sticks, coarsely chopped
50g/2oz fresh (preferably wild)
  mushrooms, quartered
450g/1lb cooked chicken, cubed
50g/2oz/1/2 cup frozen peas
salt and ground black pepper
beaten egg, to glaze

For the pastry
225g/8oz/2 cups plain
  (all-purpose) flour, plus extra
  for dusting
1.5ml/1/4 tsp salt
115g/4oz/1/2 cup cold butter, diced
65g/2 1/2oz/1/3 cup white
  vegetable fat (shortening), diced
90–120ml/6–8 tbsp chilled water

1 To make the pastry, sift the flour and salt into a bowl. Rub in the butter and white vegetable fat until the mixture resembles breadcrumbs. Sprinkle with 90ml/6 tbsp chilled water and mix until the dough holds together. Add more water if necessary. Gather the dough into a ball, wrap and chill for 30 minutes.

2 Preheat the oven to 190°C/375°F/Gas 5. To make the filling, melt half the butter in a heavy pan over low heat. Whisk in the flour. Whisk in the hot stock until the mixture boils. Cook for 2–3 minutes, then whisk in the cream. Season to taste and set aside.

3 Heat the remaining butter in a pan and cook the onion and carrots for 5 minutes. Add the celery and mushrooms and cook for 5 minutes. Add the chicken and peas and stir into the cream sauce. Spoon into a 2.5 litre/4 pint/10 cup oval baking dish.

4 Roll out the pastry on a floured surface to a thickness of about 3mm/1/8in. Cut out an oval 2.5cm/1in larger all around than the dish. Lay the pastry over the filling. Press around the edge of the dish to seal, then trim off the excess pastry.

5 Glaze the lid with beaten egg and cut several slits in the pastry. Bake the pie in the preheated oven for about 30 minutes, until the pastry has browned. Serve hot.

Chicken Pie Energy 600kcal/2501kJ; Protein 23.7g; Carbohydrate 38.8g, of which sugars 3.7g; Fat 40g, of which saturates 21.8g; Cholesterol 132mg; Calcium 92mg; Fibre 2.7g; Sodium 226mg.
Turkey Bundles Energy 304kcal/1274kJ; Protein 27.3g; Carbohydrate 16.6g, of which sugars 3.9g; Fat 14.3g, of which saturates 8.5g; Cholesterol 95mg; Calcium 91mg; Fibre 0.8g; Sodium 204mg.

Pork Empanada

This two-crust pie is famous because it is served at nearly all Spanish special occasions. It is good hot or cold.

Serves 8

75ml/5 tbsp olive oil, plus extra
    for greasing
2 onions, chopped
4 garlic cloves, finely chopped
1kg/2¼lb boned pork loin, diced
175g/6oz smoked gammon
    (smoked or cured ham), diced
3 red chorizo or other spicy
    sausages (about 300g/11oz)
3 (bell) peppers (mixed
    colours), chopped
175ml/6fl oz/¾ cup white wine
200g/7oz can tomatoes

pinch of saffron threads
5ml/1 tsp paprika
30ml/2 tbsp chopped
    fresh parsley
salt and ground black pepper

For the corn meal dough

250g/9oz/1½ cups cornmeal
7g/2 tsp easy-blend (rapid-rise)
    dried yeast
5ml/1 tsp caster (superfine) sugar
250g/9oz plain (all-purpose) flour,
    plus extra for dusting
5ml/1 tsp salt
200ml/7fl oz/scant 1 cup
    warm water
30ml/2 tbsp oil
2 eggs, beaten, plus 1
    for the glaze

1 Heat 60ml/4 tbsp oil in a pan and fry the onions, adding the garlic when they begin to colour. Transfer to a flameproof casserole. Fry the pork and gammon until coloured. Add to the casserole. Add 15ml/1 tbsp oil to the pan, fry the sausages and peppers and add to the dish. Deglaze the pan with the wine, and pour into the casserole. Add the tomatoes, saffron, paprika and parsley and season. Cook for 20–30 minutes. Leave to cool.

2 Meanwhile, put the cornmeal into a food processor. Add the dried yeast with the sugar. Gradually add the flour, salt, water, oil and 2 eggs and beat to a smooth dough. Put into a bowl, cover with a cloth and leave in a warm place for 40–50 minutes.

3 Preheat the oven to 200°C/400°F/Gas 6. Grease a baking dish 30 x 20cm/12 x 8in and line with half the dough, leaving the border hanging over the edge. Spoon in the filling. Roll out the lid and lay it in place. Fold the outside edge over the lid and seal. Prick and brush with beaten egg. Bake for 30–35 minutes, covering the edges if they brown too much. Cut into squares.

Leek, Bacon and Egg Pie

In this dish, leeks are used to make a sauce that is teamed with bacon and eggs to make a delicious family meal. Serve it with freshly cooked seasonal vegetables or a mixed salad.

Serves 4–6

15ml/1 tbsp olive oil
200g/7oz lean back bacon
    rashers (strips), trimmed of
    rinds and cut into thin strips

250g/9oz/2 cups leeks,
    thinly sliced
40g/1½oz/⅓ cup plain
    (all-purpose) flour
1.5ml/¼ tsp freshly
    grated nutmeg
425ml/¾ pint/scant 2 cups milk,
    plus extra for brushing
4 eggs
1 sheet ready-rolled puff pastry
salt and ground black pepper

1 Preheat the oven to 200°C/400°F/Gas 6. Put the oil and bacon in a pan and cook for 5 minutes, stirring occasionally, until the bacon is golden brown.

2 Add the leeks to the pan. Stir, cover and cook over medium heat for 5 minutes until softened, stirring once or twice.

3 Stir in the flour and nutmeg. Remove from the heat and gradually stir in the milk. Return the pan to the heat and cook, stirring, until the sauce thickens and boils. Season lightly.

4 Transfer the mixture into a shallow ovenproof pie dish, measuring about 25cm/10in in diameter. Using the back of a spoon, make four wells in the sauce and break an egg into each one.

5 Brush the edges of the dish with milk. Lay the pastry over the dish. Trim off the excess pastry and use it to make the trimmings. Brush the backs with milk and stick them on the top of the pie.

6 Brush the pastry with milk and make a small central slit to allow steam to escape. Put into the oven and cook for about 40 minutes until the pastry is puffed up and golden brown, and the eggs have set. Serve hot.

Pork Empanada Energy 704kcal/2944kJ; Protein 35.5g; Carbohydrate 58.6g, of which sugars 6.5g; Fat 35.6g, of which saturates 12.2g; Cholesterol 129mg; Calcium 97mg; Fibre 3.2g; Sodium 592mg.
Leek Pie Energy 202kcal/842kJ; Protein 13.4g; Carbohydrate 9.7g, of which sugars 4.4g; Fat 12.5g, of which saturates 4.2g; Cholesterol 149mg; Calcium 125mg; Fibre 1.1g; Sodium 592mg.

Rich Game Pie

This pie looks spectacular when baked in a fluted tin. Serve with steamed green vegetables and potatoes.

Serves 10
25g/1oz/2 tbsp butter
1 onion, finely chopped
2 garlic cloves, finely chopped
900g/2lb mixed boneless game
  meat, such as skinless pheasant
  and/or pigeon breast fillets,
  venison and rabbit, diced
30ml/2 tbsp chopped mixed fresh
  herbs such as parsley, thyme
  and marjoram
salt and ground black pepper

For the pâté
50g/2oz/¼ cup butter
2 garlic cloves, finely chopped

450g/1lb chicken livers, rinsed,
  trimmed and chopped
60ml/4 tbsp brandy
5ml/1 tsp ground mace

For the hot water crust pastry
675g/1½lb/6 cups strong plain
  (all-purpose) flour
5ml/1 tsp salt
115ml/3½fl oz/scant ½ cup milk
115ml/3½fl oz/scant ½
  cup water
115g/4oz/½ cup lard or white
  cooking fat, diced
115g/4oz/½ cup butter, diced
beaten egg, to glaze

For the jelly
300ml/½ pint/1¼ cups game or
  beef consommé
2.5ml/½ tsp powdered gelatine

1 Melt the butter in a pan, then add the onion and garlic, and cook until softened. Remove from the heat and mix with the game meat and the herbs. Season well, cover and chill.

2 To make the pâté, melt the butter in a pan. Cook the garlic and chicken livers until the livers are browned. Remove from the heat and stir in the brandy and mace. Purée the mixture in a blender or food processor until smooth. Set aside to cool.

3 To make the pastry, sift the flour and salt into a bowl and make a well in the centre. Place the milk and water in a pan. Add the lard or fat and butter and heat gently until melted, then bring to the boil and remove from the heat. Pour into the well and beat until smooth. Cover and leave to cool slightly.

4 Preheat the oven to 200°C/400°F/Gas 6. Roll out two-thirds of the pastry and use to line a 23cm/9in raised pie mould. Spoon in half the game mixture and press it down evenly. Add the pâté, and then top with the remaining game.

5 Roll out the remaining pastry to form a lid. Brush the edge of the pastry lining the tin with a little water and cover the pie with the lid. Trim any excess pastry and pinch the edges to seal. Make two holes in the lid and glaze. Bake for 20 minutes, then cover it with foil and bake for 10 minutes. Reduce the oven to 150°C/300°F/Gas 2. Glaze again and cook for 1¼ hours.

6 Remove the pie and leave for 15 minutes. Increase the oven to 200°C/400°F/Gas 6. Stand the tin on a baking sheet and remove the sides. Glaze the sides of the pie and cover with foil. Cook for 15 minutes, then cool completely and chill overnight.

7 To make the jelly, heat the consommé in a pan, whisk in the gelatine until dissolved and leave to cool until just setting. Using a small funnel, pour the jelly into the holes in the pie. Chill until set. The pie will keep in the refrigerator for three days.

Lamb and Currant Pie

This delicious sweet-savoury pie uses a crisp shortcrust pastry made with lard and butter. Serve with a salad of watercress, baby spinach leaves and red onion.

Serves 6
300g/11oz lean minced (ground)
  lamb, such as shoulder
75g/3oz/⅓ cup currants

75g/3oz/6 tbsp dark muscovado
  (molasses) sugar
salt and ground black pepper
milk for brushing

For the pastry
250g/9oz/2¼ cups plain
  (all-purpose) flour
75g/3oz/6 tbsp chilled lard, cut
  into small cubes
75g/3oz/6 tbsp chilled butter, cubed

1 To make the pastry, sift the flour and salt into a bowl. Add the lard and butter. With the fingertips, rub the fat into the flour until the mixture resembles fine breadcrumbs. Alternatively, you can process the mixture in a food processor.

2 Stir in about 60–75ml/4–5 tbsp cold water until the mixture can be gathered together into a smooth dough. Then wrap and refrigerate the dough for about 20–30 minutes.

3 Preheat the oven to 190°C/375°F/Gas 5. In a large bowl, mix together the lamb, currants and sugar with a little salt and ground black pepper.

4 On a lightly floured surface, roll out two-thirds of the dough into a circle. Use the rolled-out dough to line a 20–23cm/8–9in tart tin (pan).

5 Spread the lamb mixture over the pastry. Roll out the remaining pastry to make a lid and lay this on top of the lamb filling. Then trim off the excess pastry and pinch the edges together to seal them. Make a small slit in the centre of the pastry, and then brush the top with milk.

6 Place the pie into the preheated oven and bake for about 40 minutes, until the pastry is crisp and golden brown and the filling is cooked through. Serve the pie warm or leave to cool and serve at room temperature.

Rich Game Pie Energy 731kcal/3058kJ; Protein 44g; Carbohydrate 54.3g, of which sugars 2.5g; Fat 32g, of which saturates 17.9g; Cholesterol 223mg; Calcium 163mg; Fibre 2.3g; Sodium 444mg.
Lamb Pie Energy 527kcal/2206kJ; Protein 13.9g; Carbohydrate 54g, of which sugars 22.2g; Fat 29.9g, of which saturates 14.7g; Cholesterol 77mg; Calcium 88mg; Fibre 1.5g; Sodium 114mg.

Veal and Ham Pie

This classic pie is moist and
delicious with flavours that
marry perfectly. Serve with
mash and cabbage.

Serves 4
450g/1lb boneless shoulder of
   veal, diced
225g/8oz lean gammon
   (smoked or cured ham), diced
15ml/1 tbsp plain
   (all-purpose) flour
large pinch each of dry mustard
   and ground black pepper

25g/1oz/2 tbsp butter
15ml/1 tbsp sunflower oil
1 onion, chopped
600ml/1 pint/2½ cups chicken
   or veal stock
2 eggs, hard-boiled and sliced
30ml/2 tbsp chopped fresh parsley

For the pastry
175g/6oz/1½ cups plain
   (all-purpose) flour
75g/3oz/6 tbsp butter
iced water, to mix
beaten egg, to glaze

1 Preheat the oven to 180°C/350°F/Gas 4. Mix the veal and
gammon in a bowl. Season the flour with the mustard and pepper,
then add it to the meat. Heat the butter and oil in a flameproof
casserole, then cook the meat mixture in batches until golden.
Use a draining spoon to remove the meat. Cook the onion
until softened. Gradually stir in the stock, then replace the meat.
Cover and cook in the oven for 1½ hours.

2 To make the pastry, sift the flour into a bowl and rub in the
butter until the mixture resembles fine crumbs. Mix in enough
iced water to bind the mixture, then mix to make a dough.

3 Spoon the veal mixture into a 1.5 litre/2½ pint/6¼ cup pie
dish. Arrange the slices of egg on top and sprinkle with parsley.
Roll out the pastry on a lightly floured surface to 4cm/1½in
larger than the dish. Cut a strip from around the edge of the
pastry, dampen the rim of the dish and press the pastry strip
on it. Brush the rim with beaten egg and cover with the lid.

4 Press around the rim to seal and cut off any excess. Press
it down with your finger as you seal in the filling. Pinch the
pastry between your fingers to flute the edge. Brush the top
of the pie with beaten egg and bake for 30–40 minutes, or
until the pastry is golden brown. Serve hot.

Beef Wellington

This dish, which was popular
in the 19th century, is a fillet
of beef baked in puff pastry.
Start preparing the dish well
in advance to allow time for
the meat to cool before it is
wrapped in pastry.

Serves 6
1.5kg/3¼lb fillet of beef
45ml/3 tbsp sunflower oil

115g/4oz mushrooms, chopped
2 garlic cloves, crushed
175g/6oz smooth liver pâté
30ml/2 tbsp chopped
   fresh parsley
400g/14oz puff pastry, thawed
   if frozen
beaten egg, to glaze
salt and ground black pepper
fresh flat leaf parsley, to garnish

1 Preheat the oven to 220°C/425°F/Gas 7. Tie the beef at
regular intervals with string. Heat 30ml/½ tbsp of the oil in a
large frying pan, and fry the beef over a high heat for about
10 minutes, or until brown on all sides. Transfer to a roasting
pan, bake for 20 minutes. Cool.

2 Heat the remaining oil in a frying pan and cook the
mushrooms and garlic for about 5 minutes, stirring frequently.
Beat the mushroom mixture into the pâté with the parsley, and
season well. Set aside to cool.

3 Roll out the pastry into a sheet large enough to enclose the
beef, plus a strip to spare. Trim off the spare pastry, then trim
other edges to neaten. Spread the pâté mix down the middle of
the pastry. Untie the beef and lay it on the pâté.

4 Preheat the oven to 220°C/425°F/Gas 7. Brush the edges of
the pastry with beaten egg and fold the pastry over the meat to
enclose it in a neat parcel. Place the parcel on a baking tray with
the join in the pastry underneath. Cut leaf shapes from the
reserved pastry. Brush the parcel with beaten egg, garnish with
the pastry leaves and brush with egg. Chill for 10 minutes, or
until the oven is hot.

5 Bake in the oven for 50–60 minutes, covering it loosely with
foil after about 30 minutes to prevent the pastry from burning.
Serve cut into thick slices garnished with parsley.

Veal and Ham Pie Energy 621kcal/2595kJ; Protein 42.4g; Carbohydrate 39.2g, of which sugars 2.6g; Fat 33.8g, of which saturates 17.2g; Cholesterol 281mg; Calcium 128mg; Fibre 2.3g; Sodium 1007mg.
Beef Wellington Energy 511kcal/2131kJ; Protein 41.7g; Carbohydrate 19.3g, of which sugars 1.2g; Fat 30.6g, of which saturates 7.2g; Cholesterol 128mg; Calcium 41mg; Fibre 0.4g; Sodium 320mg.

Steak and Oyster Pie

Oysters are a luxury today, but they add a wonderful flavour to this tasty pie.

Serves 6
30ml/2 tbsp plain
  (all-purpose) flour
1kg/2¼lb rump (round) steak, cut
  into 5cm/2in pieces
45ml/3 tbsp oil
25g/1oz/2 tbsp butter
1 large onion, chopped
300ml/½ pint/1¼ cups beef stock
300ml/½ pint/1¼ cups brown
  ale or red wine
30ml/2 tbsp fresh thyme leaves
225g/8oz brown cap (cremini)
  mushrooms, halved if large
12 shelled oysters
375g/13oz puff pastry, thawed
  if frozen
beaten egg, to glaze
salt and ground black pepper

1 Preheat the oven to 150°C/300°F/Gas 2. Season the flour and toss the pieces of steak in it until well coated. Heat half the oil with half the butter in a flameproof casserole and quickly brown the meat in batches. Set it to one side.

2 Add the remaining oil and butter to the hot pan, stir in the onion and cook over medium heat, stirring occasionally, until golden brown and beginning to soften. Return the meat and any juices to the pan and stir in the stock, ale or wine and thyme. Bring to the boil, then cover the pan and cook in the oven for about 1½ hours, or until the beef is tender.

3 Using a slotted spoon, lift the meat and onion out of the liquid and put it into a 1.75 litre/3 pint/7½ cup pie dish. Bring the liquid to the boil and reduce to about 600ml/1 pint/2½ cups. Season to taste and stir in the mushrooms, then pour the mixture over the meat. Leave to cool. Add the oysters to the cooled meat, pushing them down into the mixture.

4 Roll out the pastry on a floured surface to 2.5cm/1in larger than the dish. Trim off a 1cm/½in strip all around the edge. Brush the rim of the dish with egg and lay the strip on it. Brush the strip with egg, lay the pastry sheet over the top, trim to fit and press the edges together to seal. Brush the top with egg. Bake in the hot oven for about 40 minutes, until the pastry is crisp and golden brown and the filling is piping hot.

Steak, Mushroom and Ale Pie

This recipe is a favourite at any traditional restaurant.

Serves 4
25g/1oz/2 tbsp butter
1 large onion, finely chopped
115g/4oz/1½ cups brown cap
  (cremini) or button (white)
  mushrooms, halved
900g/2lb lean beef in one piece,
  such as rump or braising steak
30ml/2 tbsp plain
  (all-purpose) flour
45ml/3 tbsp sunflower oil
300ml/½ pint/1¼ cups stout or
  brown ale
300ml/½ pint/1¼ cups beef
  stock or consommé
500g/1¼lb puff pastry, thawed
  if frozen
beaten egg, to glaze
salt and ground black pepper

1 Melt the butter in a large, flameproof casserole, add the onion and cook gently for about 5 minutes. Add the mushrooms and continue cooking for a further 5 minutes, stirring occasionally. Remove the onion mixture from the casserole and set aside.

2 Trim the meat and cut it into 2.5cm/1in cubes. Season the flour and toss the meat in it. Heat the oil in the casserole, then brown the steak in batches over a high heat to seal in the juices.

3 Replace the vegetables, then stir in the stout or ale and stock or consommé. Simmer for about 1 hour until the meat is tender. Season to taste and transfer to a 1.5 litre/2½ pint/6¼ cup pie dish. Preheat the oven to 230°C/450°F/Gas 8.

4 Roll out the pastry about 4cm/1½in larger all around than the dish. Cut a 2.5cm/1in strip from the edge of the pastry. Brush the rim of the dish with water and press the pastry strip on it. Brush the strip with beaten egg and cover the pie with the pastry lid. Press the lid in place and trim the excess from around the edge. Pinch the pastry between your fingers to flute the edge.

5 Make a hole in the middle of the pie, brush the top carefully with beaten egg and chill for 10 minutes to rest the pastry.

6 Bake the pie for 15 minutes, then reduce the oven temperature to 200°C/400°F/Gas 6 and bake for a further 15–20 minutes, or until the pastry is risen and golden.

Steak Pie Energy 689kcal/2874kJ; Protein 49.4g; Carbohydrate 29.8g, of which sugars 1g; Fat 39g, of which saturates 9.1g; Cholesterol 144mg; Calcium 145mg; Fibre 0.4g; Sodium 674mg.
Steak and Ale Pie Energy 1061kcal/4423kJ; Protein 58.8g; Carbohydrate 59.3g, of which sugars 7.6g; Fat 65.3g, of which saturates 24g; Cholesterol 164mg; Calcium 129mg; Fibre 3.2g; Sodium 622mg.

Hand-rolled Sushi

Roll your own filling in this fun way to enjoy sushi.

Serves 4–6
225g/8oz very fresh tuna steak
130g/4½oz smoked salmon
17cm/6½in cucumber cucumber
1 avocado, halved and stoned (pitted)
7.5ml/1½ tsp lemon juice
8 king prawns (jumbo shrimp), cooked and peeled
20 chives, trimmed and chopped into 6cm/2½in lengths
1 packet mustard and cress (fine curled cress), roots cut off

6–8 shiso leaves, cut in half lengthways

For the su-meshi
800g/1¾lb/2 cups Japanese short grain rice
75ml/5 tbsp rice vinegar
40ml/8 tsp caster (superfine) sugar
5ml/1 tsp salt

To serve
12 nori sheets, cut into four
mayonnaise
shoyu
45ml/3 tbsp wasabi paste
gari

1 To make the su-meshi, rinse the rice in plenty of water. Drain in a sieve (strainer) for 1 hour. Put the rice into a deep pan with 250ml/8fl oz/1⅛ cups water to each 200g/7oz /1 cup rice. Cover and bring to the boil. Simmer for 12 minutes. Remove from the heat and leave for 10 minutes. Transfer the rice to a large bowl. Mix in the vinegar, sugar and salt, and fluff the rice. Place in a large serving bowl and cover with a damp dish towel.

2 Slice the tuna, with the grain, into 5mm/¼in slices, then into 1 × 6cm/½ × 2½in strips. Cut the salmon and cucumber into strips the same size as the tuna. Cut the avocado into 1cm/½in long strips and sprinkle on the lemon juice.

3 Arrange the fish, shellfish, avocado and vegetables on a plate. Place the nori sheets on a plate and put the mayonnaise, shoyu, wasabi and gari into separate bowls. Half-fill a glass with water and place four to six rice paddles inside.

4 To roll the sushi, take a sheet of nori and spread 45ml/3 tbsp rice on the sheet. Spread some wasabi on the rice, and place a few strips of the fillings on top. Roll it up as a cone and dip the end into the shoyu. Have some gari between rolls to refresh.

Jewel-box Sushi

In this sushi, a bowl is filled with su-meshi, and colourful toppings decorate it.

Serves 4
2 eggs, beaten
vegetable oil, for frying
50g/2oz mangetouts (snow peas), trimmed
1 nori sheet, cut into small shreds
15ml/1 tbsp shoyu
15ml/1 tbsp wasabi paste
salt
30–60ml/2–4 tbsp ikura, to garnish

For the su-meshi
200g/7oz/1 cup Japanese short grain rice
40ml/8 tsp rice vinegar

20ml/4 tsp caster (superfine) sugar
5ml/1 tsp salt

For the fish toppings
115g/4oz very fresh tuna steak, skin removed
90g/3½oz fresh squid, body only, cleaned and boned
4 king prawns (jumbo shrimp), cooked and peeled

For the shiitake
8 dried shiitake mushrooms, stalks discarded and soaked in 350ml/12fl oz/1½ cups water for 4 hours
15ml/1 tbsp caster (superfine) sugar
60ml/4 tbsp mirin
45ml/3 tbsp shoyu

1 To make the su-meshi, see Hand-rolled Sushi (p. 168, step 1). Simmer the shiitake and the soaking water for 20 minutes. Add the sugar, mirin and shoyu. Drain and slice very thinly.

2 Beat the eggs in a bowl and add a pinch of salt. Heat a little oil in a frying pan and add enough egg to cover the pan thinly. Cook on both sides. Use the remaining egg to make several omelettes, roll into a tube and slice very thinly to make strands.

3 Slice the tuna across the grain into 7.5 × 4cm/3 × 1½in pieces, 5mm/¼in thick. Slice the squid crossways into 5mm/¼in strips. Par-boil the mangetouts for 2 minutes. Cut into 3mm/⅛in diagonal strips. Mix the nori with the shoyu and wasabi.

4 Place half the su-meshi in a bowl, cover with the nori mixture and the remaining su-meshi. Sprinkle over egg strands to cover the surface. Arrange the tuna slices in a fan shape with a fan of shiitake on top. Place the prawns and squid next to the tuna. Arrange the mangetouts and ikura decoratively on top.

Hand-rolled Sushi Energy 392kcal/1636kJ; Protein 29.3g; Carbohydrate 40.5g, of which sugars 0.2g; Fat 12.2g, of which saturates 2.1g; Cholesterol 77mg; Calcium 45mg; Fibre 0.1g; Sodium 86mg.
Jewel-box Sushi Energy 384kcal/1609kJ; Protein 23.1g; Carbohydrate 57.3g, of which sugars 7g; Fat 5g, of which saturates 1.3g; Cholesterol 203mg; Calcium 61mg; Fibre 0.4g; Sodium 1191mg.

Thick-rolled Sushi

You will need a makisu (a sushi rolling mat) to make these sushi, called *nori maki.*

Makes 16 pieces
2 nori sheets
wasabi, gari and shoyu, for dipping

For the su-meshi
200g/7oz/1 cup Japanese short
    grain rice
40ml/8 tsp rice vinegar
20ml/4 tsp caster (superfine) sugar
5ml/1 tsp salt

For the omelette
2 eggs, beaten

25ml/1½ tbsp dashi stock
10ml/2 tsp sake
2.5ml/½ tsp salt
vegetable oil, for frying

For the fillings
4 dried shiitake mushrooms, soaked
    in a bowl of water overnight
120ml/4fl oz/½ cup dashi stock
15ml/1 tbsp shoyu
7.5ml/1½ tsp caster (superfine) sugar
5ml/1 tsp mirin
6 large prawns (shrimp), cooked
    and peeled
4 asparagus spears, boiled for
    1 minute in lightly salted water
10 chives, ends trimmed

1 To make the su-meshi, see Hand-rolled Sushi (p. 168, step 1).

2 To make the omelette, mix the beaten eggs, dashi stock, sake and salt in a bowl. Heat a little oil in a frying pan on a medium-low heat. Pour in just enough egg mixture to cover the base of the pan thinly. As soon as the mixture sets, fold the omelette in half towards you and wipe the space left with a little oil.

3 With the first omelette still in the pan, repeat this process of frying and folding to make more omelettes. Each new one is laid on to the previous omelette, to form one multi-layered omelette. When all the mixture is used, slide the layered omelette on to a chopping board. Cool, then cut into 1cm/½in wide strips.

4 Put the shiitake, dashi stock, shoyu, sugar and mirin in a small pan. Bring to the boil, then reduce the heat to low. Cook for 20 minutes until half of the liquid has evaporated. Drain, remove and discard the stalks, and slice the caps thinly. Squeeze out any excess liquid, then dry on kitchen paper.

5 Make three cuts in the belly of the prawns to stop them curling up, and boil in salted water for 1 minute, or until they turn bright pink. Drain and cool, then remove the vein.

6 Place a nori sheet at the front edge of a makisu (sushi rolling mat). Scoop up half of the su-meshi and spread it on the nori. Leave a 1cm/½in margin at the side nearest you, and 2cm/¾in at the side furthest from you.

7 Make a shallow depression horizontally across the centre of the rice. Fill this with a row of half the omelette strips, then put half the asparagus and prawns on top. Place five chives alongside, and then put half the shiitake slices on to the chives.

8 When completed, gently roll the makisu on the chopping board to firm it up. Repeat the process to make another roll. Cut each roll into eight pieces, using a very sharp knife.

9 Serve the sushi on a tray with small dishes of wasabi, gari and shoyu for dipping.

Sushi with Smoked Salmon

This sushi, known as oshi-zushi, dates back almost a thousand years. The earliest forms of sushi were made as a means of preserving fish. The cooked rice was used as a medium to produce lactic acid and was discarded after one year. Only the marinated fish was eaten.

Makes about 12
175g/6oz smoked salmon,
    thickly sliced

15ml/1 tbsp sake
15ml/1 tbsp water
30ml/2 tbsp shoyu
1 lemon, thinly sliced into
    6 x 3mm/⅛in rings

For the su-meshi
200g/7oz/1 cup Japanese short
    grain rice
40ml/8 tsp rice vinegar
20ml/4 tsp caster
    (superfine) sugar
5ml/1 tsp salt

1 To make the su-meshi, see Hand-rolled Sushi (p. 168, step 1).

2 Lay the smoked salmon on a chopping board and sprinkle with a mixture of the sake, water and shoyu. Leave to marinate for an hour, then wipe dry with kitchen paper.

3 Line a 25 x 7.5 x 5cm/10 x 3 x 2in plastic box with a sheet of clear film (cling wrap), allowing the edges to hang over.

4 Spread half the smoked salmon to evenly cover the bottom of the plastic box. Add a quarter of the cooked rice and firmly press down with your hands dampened with rice vinegar until it is 1cm/½in thick. Add the remainder of the salmon, and press the remaining rice on top.

5 Cover the plastic box with the overhanging clear film. Place a weight, such as a heavy dinner plate, on top. Leave in a cool place overnight, or for at least 3 hours. If you keep it in the refrigerator, choose the least cool part.

6 Remove the compressed sushi from the container and unwrap. Cut into 2 cm/¾in slices and serve on a Japanese lacquered tray or a large plate. Quarter the lemon rings. Garnish with two slices of lemon on top of each piece and serve.

Thick-rolled Sushi Energy 107kcal/447kJ; Protein 3.8g; Carbohydrate 16.3g, of which sugars 1.3g; Fat 2.9g, of which saturates 0.6g; Cholesterol 52mg; Calcium 17mg; Fibre 0.2g; Sodium 112mg.
Sushi with Smoked Salmon Energy 68kcal/286kJ; Protein 4.7g; Carbohydrate 10.2g, of which sugars 0.2g; Fat 0.7g, of which saturates 0.1g; Cholesterol 5mg; Calcium 6mg; Fibre 0g; Sodium 452mg.

Rice and Potato Tortitas

Like miniature tortillas, these little rice pancakes are great served hot, either plain or with tomato sauce for dipping. They make an excellent scoop for any soft vegetable mixture or dip – a very Spanish way of eating.

Serves 4
30ml/2 tbsp olive oil
115g/4oz/1 cup cooked long grain white rice
1 potato, grated
4 spring onions (scallions), thinly sliced
1 garlic clove, finely chopped
15ml/1 tbsp chopped fresh parsley
3 large (US extra large) eggs, beaten
2.5ml/½ tsp paprika
salt and ground black pepper

1 Heat half the olive oil in a large frying pan and stir-fry the rice, with the potato, spring onions and garlic, over high heat for 3 minutes until golden.

2 Transfer the rice and vegetable mixture into a bowl and stir in the parsley and eggs, with the paprika and plenty of salt and pepper. Mix well.

3 Heat the remaining oil in the frying pan and drop in large spoonfuls of the rice mixture, leaving enough room for the mixture to spread. Cook the tortitas for about 1–2 minutes on each side.

4 Drain the tortitas on kitchen paper and keep hot in a warm oven while cooking the remaining mixture. Pile the cooked tortitas on a large serving platter or on individual plates and serve immediately.

> **Cook's Tip**
> These tortitas can be used as a base for a variety of dishes. Try using them in place of plain boiled rice or mashed potatoes for a change. Children love them just as they are, with a large dollop of tomato ketchup for dipping.

Artichoke Rice Cakes

These unusual little cakes contain artichoke in the rice mixture, and they break open to reveal a melting cheese centre. Manchego is made from sheep's milk and has a tart flavour that goes wonderfully with the delicate taste of these little rice cakes.

Serves 6
1 large globe artichoke
50g/2oz/¼ cup butter
1 small onion, finely chopped
1 garlic clove, finely chopped
115g/4oz/⅔ cup paella rice
450ml/¾ pint/scant 2 cups hot chicken stock
50g/2oz/⅔ cup grated fresh Parmesan cheese
150g/5oz Manchego cheese, very finely diced
45–60ml/3–4 tbsp fine cornmeal
olive oil, for frying
salt and ground black pepper
fresh flat leaf parsley, to garnish

1 Remove the stalks, leaves and choke to leave just the heart of the artichoke; chop the heart finely.

2 Melt the butter in a pan and gently fry the chopped artichoke heart, onion and garlic for 5 minutes until softened. Add the rice and cook for about 1 minute, stirring until the grains are well coated in butter.

3 Keeping the heat fairly high, gradually add the stock, stirring occasionally until all the liquid has been absorbed and the rice is cooked – this should take about 20 minutes. Season well, then stir in the Parmesan cheese. Transfer the mixture to a bowl. Leave to cool, then cover and chill for at least 2 hours.

4 Spoon about 15ml/1 tbsp of the mixture into the palm of one hand, flatten slightly, and place a few pieces of diced cheese in the centre. Shape the rice around the cheese to make a small ball. Flatten slightly, then roll the cake in the cornmeal, shaking off any excess. Repeat with the remaining mixture to make about 12 cakes.

5 Shallow fry the rice cakes in hot olive oil for 4–5 minutes until they are crisp and golden brown. Drain on kitchen paper and serve hot, garnished with flat leaf parsley.

Rice Tortitas Energy 185kcal/776kJ; Protein 6.8g; Carbohydrate 17.6g, of which sugars 1.2g; Fat 10.4g, of which saturates 2.1g; Cholesterol 143mg; Calcium 56mg; Fibre 1.3g; Sodium 63mg.
Rice Cakes Energy 354kcal/1469kJ; Protein 12g; Carbohydrate 21.8g, of which sugars 0.8g; Fat 23.6g, of which saturates 12.3g; Cholesterol 50mg; Calcium 299mg; Fibre 0.5g; Sodium 331mg.

Vegetable Rice Pot

Fresh seasonal vegetables are cooked in slightly spiced rice to make a delicious and healthy main course.

Serves 4

1 large aubergine (eggplant)
45ml/3 tbsp olive oil
2 onions, quartered and sliced
2 garlic cloves, finely chopped
1 red (bell) pepper, halved, seeded and sliced
1 yellow (bell) pepper, halved, seeded and sliced
200g/7oz fine green beans, halved
115g/4oz/1½ cups brown cap (cremini) mushrooms, halved
300g/11oz/1½ cups paella rice, washed and drained
1 dried chilli, seeded and crumbled
1 litre/1¾ pints/4 cups chicken stock
115g/4oz/1 cup peas
60ml/4 tbsp chopped fresh parsley
salt and ground black pepper
fresh parsley or coriander (cilantro) leaves, to garnish

1 Halve the aubergine lengthways, then cut it into slices. Spread them out in a large colander or on a draining board, sprinkle with salt and leave for about 30 minutes to drain, then rinse under cold running water and pat dry with kitchen paper.

2 Heat 30ml/2 tbsp olive oil in a wide flameproof casserole or sauté pan over high heat. Add the aubergine slices and sauté until slightly golden, stirring occasionally, then transfer to kitchen paper to drain.

3 Add the remaining oil to the pan and cook the onion and garlic until soft. Add the peppers, green beans and mushrooms and cook briefly.

4 Add the drained rice and stir for 1–2 minutes, then add the aubergine and stir. Add the chilli and stock and season to taste. Add the peas and parsley and mix together.

5 Bring to boiling point, cover and cook over low heat, for 20–25 minutes, checking the liquid level towards the end (the rice should absorb the liquid, but not burn). When the rice is tender, turn off the heat, cover the pan and leave to stand for 10 minutes for the remaining liquid to be absorbed. Garnish with parsley or coriander and serve.

Californian Citrus Fried Rice

As with all fried rice dishes, it is important to make sure the rice is cold. Add it after cooking everything else, and stir to heat it through.

Serves 4–6

4 eggs
10ml/2 tsp Japanese rice vinegar
30ml/2 tbsp light soy sauce
about 45ml/3 tbsp groundnut (peanut) oil
50g/2oz/½ cup cashew nuts
2 garlic cloves, crushed
6 spring onions (scallions), diagonally sliced
2 small carrots, cut into strips
225g/8oz asparagus, each spear cut diagonally into 4 pieces
175g/6oz/2¼ cups button (white) mushrooms, halved
30ml/2 tbsp rice wine
30ml/2 tbsp water
450g/1lb/4 cups cooked white long grain rice
about 10ml/2 tsp sesame oil
1 pink grapefruit or orange, segmented
thin strips of orange rind, to garnish

For the hot dressing

5ml/1 tsp grated orange rind
30ml/2 tbsp Japanese rice wine
45ml/3 tbsp oyster sauce
30ml/2 tbsp freshly squeezed pink grapefruit or orange juice
5ml/1 tsp medium/hot chilli sauce

1 Beat the eggs with the vinegar and 10ml/2 tsp of the soy sauce. Heat 15ml/1 tbsp of the oil in a wok and cook the eggs until lightly scrambled. Transfer to a plate and set aside. Add the cashew nuts to the wok and stir-fry for 1–2 minutes. Set aside.

2 Heat the remaining oil and add the garlic and spring onions. Cook over medium heat for 1–2 minutes until the onions begin to soften, then add the carrots and stir-fry for 4 minutes.

3 Add the asparagus and cook for 2–3 minutes, then stir in the mushrooms and stir-fry for a further 1 minute. Stir in the rice wine, the remaining soy sauce and the water. Simmer for a few minutes until the vegetables are just tender but still firm.

4 Mix the ingredients for the dressing, then add to the wok and bring to the boil. Add the rice, scrambled eggs and cashew nuts. Toss over low heat for 3–4 minutes, until the rice is heated through. Just before serving, stir in the sesame oil and the fruit segments. Garnish with strips of orange rind and serve.

Vegetable Rice Pot Energy 454kcal/1891kJ; Protein 11.8g; Carbohydrate 78.3g, of which sugars 13.2g; Fat 10.4g, of which saturates 1.5g; Cholesterol 0mg; Calcium 98mg; Fibre 7.4g; Sodium 13mg.
Californian Fried Rice Energy 264kcal/1107kJ; Protein 6.5g; Carbohydrate 32.3g, of which sugars 7.7g; Fat 12.6g, of which saturates 2.1g; Cholesterol 13mg; Calcium 48mg; Fibre 2.3g; Sodium 517mg.

Spiced Indian Rice with Spinach, Tomatoes and Cashew Nuts

This all-in-one, slow-cooked rice dish makes a delicious, nutritious vegetarian meal but can also accompany a spicy meat curry. Ghee, the clarified butter used in Indian cooking, is available from large supermarkets and Asian stores.

Serves 4
30ml/2 tbsp sunflower oil
15ml/1 tbsp ghee or unsalted (sweet) butter
1 onion, finely chopped
2 garlic cloves, crushed
3 tomatoes, peeled, seeded and chopped
275g/10oz/1½ cups easy-cook (converted) brown rice
5ml/1 tsp each ground coriander and ground cumin, or 10ml/2 tsp dhana jeera powder
2 carrots, coarsely grated
750ml/1¼ pints/3 cups boiling vegetable stock
175g/6oz baby spinach leaves, washed
50g/2oz/½ cup unsalted cashew nuts, toasted
salt and ground black pepper

1 Heat the oil and ghee or butter in a heavy pan, add the onion and fry gently for 6–7 minutes, until soft. Add the garlic and chopped tomatoes and cook for a further 2 minutes.

2 Rinse the rice in a sieve (strainer) under cold water, drain well and tip into the pan. Add the coriander and cumin or dhana jeera powder and stir for a few seconds. Turn off the heat and transfer the mixture to the ceramic cooking pot.

3 Stir in the carrots, then pour in the stock, season with salt and pepper and stir to mix. Switch the slow cooker on to high. Cover and cook for 1 hour.

4 Lay the spinach on the surface of the rice, replace the lid and cook for a further 30–40 minutes, or until the spinach has wilted and the rice is cooked and tender.

5 Stir the spinach into the rice and check the seasoning, adding a little more salt and pepper if necessary. Sprinkle the cashew nuts over the rice and serve.

Basmati and Nut Pilaff

Vegetarians will love this simple pilaff. Add wild or cultivated mushrooms, if you like.

Serves 4
15–30ml/1–2 tbsp sunflower oil
1 onion, chopped
1 garlic clove, crushed
1 large carrot, coarsely grated
225g/8oz/generous 1 cup basmati rice, soaked
5ml/1 tsp cumin seeds
10ml/2 tsp ground coriander
10ml/2 tsp black mustard seeds (optional)
4 green cardamom pods
450ml/¾ pint/scant 2 cups vegetable stock or water
1 bay leaf
75g/3oz/¾ cup unsalted walnuts and cashew nuts
salt and ground black pepper
fresh parsley or coriander (cilantro) sprigs, to garnish

1 Heat the oil in a large, shallow frying pan and gently fry the onion, garlic and carrot for 3–4 minutes. Drain the rice, and then add to the pan with the spices. Cook for 1–2 minutes more, stirring to coat the grains in oil.

2 Pour in the stock or water, add the bay leaf and season well. Bring to the boil, lower the heat, cover and simmer very gently for 10–12 minutes.

3 Remove the pan from the heat without lifting off the lid. Leave the rice to stand for about 5–8 minutes.

4 Check the rice. If it is cooked, there will be small steam holes on the surface of the rice. Remove and discard the bay leaf and the cardamom pods.

5 Stir in the nuts and check the seasoning. Spoon on to a platter, garnish with the parsley or coriander and serve.

> **Cook's Tip**
> Use whichever nuts you prefer in this dish – even unsalted peanuts taste good, although almonds, cashew nuts or pistachios are more exotic.

Spiced Rice Energy 473kcal/1989kJ; Protein 10.1g; Carbohydrate 72.1g, of which sugars 9.2g; Fat 18g, of which saturates 4.5g; Cholesterol 8mg; Calcium 111mg; Fibre 4.8g; Sodium 349mg.
Basmati and Nut Pilaff Energy 424kcal/1769kJ; Protein 8.4g; Carbohydrate 68.3g, of which sugars 14.5g; Fat 13g, of which saturates 4g; Cholesterol 14mg; Calcium 69mg; Fibre 1.7g; Sodium 48mg.

Cardamom-infused Lentils and Rice with Spiced Onions

This dish of rice and lentils is a classic Middle Eastern meal, popular from Egypt and Libya to Galilee and Greece. It is often eaten with a bowl of vegetables, accompanied by yogurt and a plate of crisp salad.

Serves 6–8
400g/14oz/1¾ cups large brown or green lentils

45ml/3 tbsp olive oil
3–4 onions, 1 chopped and 2–3 thinly sliced
5ml/1 tsp ground cumin
2.5ml/½ tsp ground cinnamon
6 cardamom pods
300g/11oz/1½ cups long grain rice, rinsed
about 250ml/8fl oz/1 cup vegetable stock
salt and ground black pepper
natural (plain) yogurt, to serve

1 Put the lentils in a pan with enough water to cover generously. Bring to the boil, then simmer for about 30 minutes, or until tender. Skim off any scum that forms on top.

2 Meanwhile, heat half the oil in a pan, add the chopped onion and fry for 10 minutes, or until softened and golden brown. Stir in half the cumin and half the cinnamon.

3 When the lentils are cooked, add the spicy fried onions to the pan, together with the cardamom pods, rice and stock. Stir well and bring to the boil, then reduce the heat, cover the pan and simmer gently until the rice is tender and all the liquid has been absorbed. If the mixture appears to be getting a little too dry, add some extra water or stock. Season with salt and pepper to taste.

4 Meanwhile, heat the remaining oil in a pan, add the sliced onions and fry for about 10 minutes, until dark brown, caramelized and crisp. Sprinkle in the remaining cumin and cinnamon just before the end of cooking.

5 To serve, pile the rice and lentil mixture on to a serving dish, then top with the browned, caramelized onions. Serve immediately, with yogurt.

Tomato Rice

Serve this tasty rice as a meal in itself or as a side dish.

Serves 4
30ml/2 tbsp sunflower oil
2.5ml/½ tsp onion seeds
1 onion, sliced
2 tomatoes, chopped
1 orange or yellow (bell) pepper, seeded and sliced

5ml/1 tsp crushed fresh root ginger
1 garlic clove, crushed
5ml/1 tsp chilli powder
1 potato, diced
7.5ml/1½ tsp salt
400g/14oz/2 cups basmati rice, soaked
750ml/1¼ pints/3 cups water
30–45ml/2–3 tbsp chopped fresh coriander (cilantro)

1 Heat the oil and fry the onion seeds for 30 seconds. Add the onion and fry for 5 minutes. Stir in the tomatoes, pepper, ginger, garlic, chilli powder, potato and salt. Stir-fry for 5 minutes.

2 Drain the rice, add to the pan and stir for 1 minute. Add the water and bring to the boil. Simmer, covered, for 12–15 minutes. Stir in the coriander and serve.

Oven-baked Porcini Risotto

This is a very simple and delicious risotto.

Serves 4
25g/1oz/½ cup dried porcini mushrooms, soaked in hot water for 30 minutes

30ml/2 tbsp garlic-infused olive oil
1 onion, finely chopped
225g/8oz/generous 1 cup risotto rice
salt and ground black pepper

1 Drain the mushrooms, reserving the soaking water. Dry on kitchen paper. Preheat the oven to 180°C/350°F/Gas 4.

2 Heat the oil in a roasting pan on the stove. Cook the onion for 4–5 minutes until softened. Stir in the rice for 1–2 minutes, then add the mushrooms and the soaking water. Season well. Bake in the oven for 30 minutes, stirring occasionally, until the stock has been absorbed and the rice is tender. Serve hot.

Cardamom Lentils Energy 394kcal/1656kJ; Protein 17.5g; Carbohydrate 68g, of which sugars 5.1g; Fat 6.6g, of which saturates 0.9g; Cholesterol 0mg; Calcium 54mg; Fibre 3.8g; Sodium 23mg.
Tomato Rice Energy 552kcal/2305kJ; Protein 12.7g; Carbohydrate 108.3g, of which sugars 4.8g; Fat 7g, of which saturates 1g; Cholesterol 0mg; Calcium 43mg; Fibre 3g; Sodium 10mg.
Porcini Risotto Energy 260kcal/1085kJ; Protein 4.8g; Carbohydrate 46.2g, of which sugars 0.9g; Fat 5.9g, of which saturates 0.8g; Cholesterol 0mg; Calcium 16mg; Fibre 0.5g; Sodium 2mg.

Risotto alla Milanese

This risotto, sprinkled with cheese and gremolata, makes a delicious light meal or accompaniment to a meaty stew or casserole.

Serves 4
For the gremolata
2 garlic cloves, crushed
60ml/4 tbsp chopped
   fresh parsley
finely grated rind of 1 lemon

For the risotto
5ml/1 tsp saffron strands
25g/1oz/2 tbsp butter
1 large onion, finely chopped
275g/10oz/1½ cups arborio rice
150ml/¼ pint/⅔ cup dry
   white wine
1 litre/1¾ pints/4 cups chicken
   or vegetable stock
salt and ground black pepper
Parmesan cheese shavings

1 To make the gremolata, mix together the garlic, parsley and lemon rind and reserve.

2 To make the risotto, put the saffron in a small bowl with 15ml/1 tbsp boiling water and leave to stand. Melt the butter in a heavy pan and gently fry the onion for 5 minutes.

3 Stir in the rice and cook for about 2 minutes until it becomes translucent. Add the wine and saffron mixture and cook for several minutes until the wine is absorbed.

4 Add 600ml/1 pint/2½ cups of the stock to the pan and simmer gently until the stock is absorbed, stirring frequently.

5 Gradually add more stock, a ladleful at a time, until the rice is tender. (The rice might be tender before you have added all the stock so add it slowly towards the end of cooking.)

6 Season the risotto with salt and pepper and transfer to a serving dish. Sprinkle lavishly with shavings of Parmesan cheese and the gremolata. Serve immediately.

> **Variation**
> Stir grated Parmesan cheese into the risotto, if you prefer.

Fresh Herb Risotto

Distinctive, nutty-flavoured wild rice is combined with arborio rice to create this creamy, comforting risotto. An aromatic blend of herbs gives the dish a light summery flavour.

Serves 4
90g/3½oz/½ cup wild rice
15ml/1 tbsp butter
15ml/1 tbsp olive oil
1 small onion, finely chopped
450g/1lb/2½ cups arborio rice

300ml/½ pint/1¼ cups dry
   white wine
1.2 litres/2 pints/5 cups
   vegetable stock
45ml/3 tbsp chopped
   fresh oregano
45ml/3 tbsp chopped
   fresh chives
60ml/4 tbsp chopped fresh flat
   leaf parsley
60ml/4 tbsp chopped fresh basil
75g/3oz/1 cup freshly grated
   Parmesan cheese
salt and ground black pepper

1 Cook the wild rice in boiling salted water according to the instructions on the packet.

2 Heat the butter and oil in a large heavy pan. When the butter has melted, add the onion and cook for 3 minutes, Add the arborio rice and cook for 2 minutes, stirring to coat it in the oil mixture.

3 Pour in the wine and bring to the boil. Reduce the heat and cook for 10 minutes until the wine is absorbed. Add the stock, a little at a time, and simmer, stirring, for 20–25 minutes until the liquid is absorbed and the rice is creamy. Season well.

4 Add the herbs and wild rice; heat for 2 minutes, stirring frequently. Stir in two-thirds of the Parmesan and cook until melted. Serve sprinkled with the remaining Parmesan.

> **Cook's Tip**
> Risotto rice is essential to achieve the right creamy texture in this dish. Other types of rice simply will not do. Fresh herbs are also a must, but you can use tarragon, chervil, marjoram or thyme instead of those listed here.

Fresh Herb Risotto Energy 632kcal/2637kJ; Protein 18g; Carbohydrate 109.3g, of which sugars 1.2g; Fat 12.8g, of which saturates 6.2g; Cholesterol 27mg; Calcium 280mg; Fibre 0.8g; Sodium 232mg.
Risotto alla Milanese Energy 397kcal/1650kJ; Protein 10.6g; Carbohydrate 46.8g, of which sugars 0.8g; Fat 18.3g, of which saturates 11.3g; Cholesterol 49mg; Calcium 204mg; Fibre 0.2g; Sodium 265mg.

Pumpkin and Pistachio Risotto

Vegetarians will love this elegant combination of creamy, golden saffron rice and orange pumpkin, and so will everyone else. It would look impressive served in the hollowed-out pumpkin shell.

Serves 4

1.2 litres/2 pints/5 cups vegetable
　stock or water
generous pinch of saffron strands
30ml/2 tbsp olive oil
1 onion, chopped
2 garlic cloves, crushed

900g/2lb pumpkin, peeled, seeded
　and cut into 2cm/³⁄₄in cubes
　(about 7 cups)
400g/14oz/2 cups risotto rice
200ml/7fl oz/scant 1 cup dry
　white wine
30ml/2 tbsp freshly grated
　Parmesan cheese
50g/2oz/¹⁄₂ cup pistachios,
　coarsely chopped
45ml/3 tbsp chopped fresh
　marjoram or oregano, plus
　leaves to garnish
salt, freshly grated nutmeg and
　ground black pepper

1　Bring the stock or water to the boil and reduce to a low simmer. Ladle a little of it into a small bowl. Add the saffron strands and leave to infuse.

2　Heat the oil in a large, heavy pan or deep frying pan. Add the onion and garlic and cook gently for 5 minutes until softened. Add the pumpkin and rice and stir to coat everything in oil. Cook, stirring constantly, for a few more minutes until the rice looks transparent.

3　Pour in the wine and allow it to bubble hard. When it has been absorbed, add a quarter of the hot stock or water and the saffron liquid. Stir until all the liquid has been absorbed. Gradually add the remaining stock or water, a little at a time, allowing the rice to absorb the liquid before adding more, and stirring constantly.

4　After 20–30 minutes the rice should be golden yellow, creamy and al dente. Stir in the Parmesan cheese, cover the pan and leave to stand for 5 minutes. To finish, stir in the pistachios and marjoram or oregano. Season to taste with a little salt, nutmeg and pepper; sprinkle over a few marjoram or oregano leaves and serve.

Rosemary Risotto with Borlotti Beans

Select a high-quality risotto in a subtle flavour as the base for this recipe. The savoury beans, heady rosemary and creamy mascarpone will transform a simple product into a feast. Serve with a simple salad of rocket and Parmesan shavings dressed with balsamic vinegar and plenty of black pepper.

Serves 3–4

400g/14oz can
　borlotti beans
275g/10oz packet vegetable
　or chicken risotto
60ml/4 tbsp mascarpone
　cheese
5ml/1 tsp finely chopped
　fresh rosemary

1　Drain the canned borlotti beans, rinse under cold running water and drain again.

2　Place about two-thirds of the beans in a food processor or blender and process to a fairly coarse purée. Set the remaining beans aside.

3　Make up the risotto according to the packet instructions, using the suggested quantity of water.

4　When the rice is cooked, stir in the bean purée. Add the reserved beans, with the mascarpone and rosemary, then season to taste.

5　Stir the risotto thoroughly, then cover the pan and leave to stand for about 5 minutes so that the risotto absorbs all the flavours fully, then serve.

> **Variation**
> Fresh thyme or marjoram can be used for this risotto instead of rosemary, if you like. One of the great virtues of risotto is that it lends itself well to many variations. Experiment with plain or saffron risotto and add different herbs to make your own speciality dish.

Pumpkin Risotto Energy 585kcal/2441kJ; Protein 14.4g; Carbohydrate 87.3g, of which sugars 5.7g; Fat 15.9g, of which saturates 3.5g; Cholesterol 8mg; Calcium 196mg; Fibre 3.2g; Sodium 151mg.
Rosemary Risotto Energy 419kcal/1752kJ; Protein 15.1g; Carbohydrate 68.8g, of which sugars 3.9g; Fat 6.2g, of which saturates 2.7g; Cholesterol 12mg; Calcium 198mg; Fibre 4.5g; Sodium 412mg.

Anchovy Pilaff

Packed full of anchovies and tender rice, this famous dish is from Turkey.

Serves 4–6

600g/1lb 6oz fresh anchovies, gutted, with heads and backbones removed
30ml/2 tbsp olive oil, plus extra for greasing
15ml/1 tbsp butter
1 onion, finely chopped
30ml/2 tbsp pine nuts
15ml/1 tbsp dried mint
5ml/1 tsp ground allspice
450g/1lb/2¼ cups long grain rice, rinsed and drained
1 small bunch of fresh dill, finely chopped
salt and ground black pepper
fresh dill fronds and lemon wedges, to serve

1 Rinse the anchovies and pat dry. Open them out like butterflies and sprinkle with salt. Lightly grease a dome-shaped ovenproof dish or bowl and line it with anchovies, skin side down. Reserve some anchovies for the top.

2 Heat the oil and butter in a heavy pan, stir in the onion and cook until soft. Add the pine nuts and cook until golden, then stir in the mint, allspice and rice. Season with salt and ground black pepper.

3 Pour in enough water to cover the rice by 2cm/¾in. Bring to the boil, lower the heat, partially cover and simmer for about 10–12 minutes, until the water has been absorbed. Preheat the oven to 180°C/350°F/Gas 4.

4 Turn off the heat under the pan and sprinkle the dill over the rice. Cover the pan with a dish towel, put the lid tightly on top and leave the rice to steam for 10 minutes.

5 Fluff up the rice with a fork to mix in the dill, then tip it into the anchovy mould. Lay the remaining anchovies, skin side up this time, over the rice. Splash a little water over the top and place the dish in the oven for about 25 minutes.

6 To serve, invert a serving plate over the dish and turn out the anchovy mould encasing the rice. Garnish with dill fronds and lemon wedges and serve.

Fish Paella with Aioli

Cooking rice in fish stock gives it a splendid flavour.

Serves 6

1.6kg/3½lb mixed fish on the bone, such as snapper, bream, grey or red mullet, or bass
45ml/3 tbsp olive oil
6 garlic cloves, smashed
1 ñora chilli or 1 hot dried chilli, seeded and chopped
250g/9oz ripe tomatoes, peeled, seeded and chopped
pinch of saffron threads (0.25g)
30ml/2 tbsp dry Martini or white wine
1 tomato, finely diced
30ml/2 tbsp chopped fresh parsley
400g/14oz/2 cups paella rice, washed
115g/4oz tiny unshelled shrimps
salt and ground black pepper

For the stock

1 onion, chopped
2 garlic cloves, chopped
1 celery stick, chopped
1 carrot, chopped
1 litre/1¾ pints/4 cups water

For the aioli

4 garlic cloves, finely chopped
2.5ml/½ tsp salt
5ml/1 tsp lemon juice
2 egg yolks
250ml/8fl oz/1 cup olive oil

1 Remove the heads from the fish. Working from the head end, cut the skin along the top of the back and work the fillets off the bone. Salt them lightly, cover and chill until required.

2 Make the fish stock. Put the bones, heads, tails and any other remaining bits into a large pan with the onion, garlic, celery, carrot and water. Bring to the boil, then reduce the heat, cover with a lid and simmer gently for about 30 minutes.

3 Make the aioli. Put the chopped garlic in a large mortar with the salt and lemon juice and reduce to a purée. Add the egg yolks and mix thoroughly. Gradually work in the oil to make a thick, mayonnaise-like sauce.

4 Put 15ml/1 tbsp of the olive oil in a small pan and add the whole smashed garlic cloves and dried chilli pieces. Fry for a few minutes until the garlic looks roasted. Add the chopped tomatoes halfway through, crumble in the saffron and cook to form a sauce. Pour into a blender and process until smooth.

5 Heat the remaining 30ml/2 tbsp oil in a large pan or a wide flameproof casserole and fry the fish pieces until they begin to stiffen. Strain the fish stock into a jug (pitcher), then add 900ml/1½ pints/3¾ cups stock and the tomato sauce to the fish. Cook the fish for 3–4 minutes, until slightly underdone.

6 Remove the fish pieces from the pan with a slotted spoon to a serving dish. Season lightly, sprinkle with the Martini or wine, diced tomato and parsley. Cover with foil and keep warm.

7 Add the rice to the stock, stir, season and bring to a simmer. Cook for 18–20 minutes. Before all the liquid is absorbed, stir in the shrimps. When the rice is tender, cover and turn off the heat. Stand until all the liquid is absorbed: about 5 minutes. Serve from the pan, accompanied by the aioli.

8 When the rice course is almost finished, uncover the fish. Stir the fish juices into the remains of the aioli, then pour over the fish. Eat on the same plates as the rice.

Anchovy Pilaff Energy 481kcal/2004kJ; Protein 19.5g; Carbohydrate 64g, of which sugars 3g; Fat 16g, of which saturates 3.1g; Cholesterol 37mg; Calcium 178mg; Fibre 0.8g; Sodium 1982mg.
Fish Paella Energy 378kcal/1581kJ; Protein 27.4g; Carbohydrate 35.8g, of which sugars 4.6g; Fat 13.4g, of which saturates 3.5g; Cholesterol 80mg; Calcium 77mg; Fibre 2.6g; Sodium 264mg.

Shellfish Paella

There are as many versions of paella. Some versions contain a lot of shellfish, while others feature chicken or pork. Here the only meat is the chorizo.

Serves 4
45ml/3 tbsp olive oil
1 Spanish (Bermuda)
   onion, chopped
2 fat garlic cloves, chopped
150g/5oz chorizo sausage, sliced
300g/11oz small squid, cleaned
1 red (bell) pepper, cut into strips

4 tomatoes, peeled, seeded
   and diced, or 200g/7oz can
   tomatoes
500ml/17fl oz/generous 2 cups
   chicken stock
105ml/7 tbsp dry white wine
200g/7oz/1 cup short grain
   Spanish rice or risotto rice
a large pinch of saffron threads
150g/5oz/1 cup frozen peas
12 large cooked prawns (shrimp),
   in the shell, or 8 langoustines
450g/1lb fresh mussels, scrubbed
450g/1lb medium clams, scrubbed
salt and ground black pepper

1 Heat the olive oil in a paella pan or wok, add the onion and garlic and cook until translucent. Add the chorizo and cook until lightly golden.

2 If the squid are very small, leave them whole, otherwise cut the bodies into rings and the tentacles into pieces. Add the squid to the pan and sauté over high heat for 2 minutes.

3 Stir in the pepper strips and tomatoes and simmer gently for 5 minutes, until the pepper strips are tender. Pour in the stock and wine, stir well and bring to the boil.

4 Stir in the rice and saffron threads and season well with salt and pepper. Spread the contents of the pan evenly. Bring the liquid back to the boil, then lower the heat and simmer gently for about 10 minutes.

5 Add the peas, prawns or langoustines, mussels and clams, stirring them gently into the rice. Cook the paella gently for a further 15–20 minutes, until the rice is tender and all the mussels and clams have opened. If any remain closed, discard them. If the paella seems dry, add a little more hot chicken stock. Gently stir everything together and serve piping hot.

Kedgeree

A popular breakfast dish, kedgeree has its origins in an Indian dish of rice and lentils. It is flavoured with curry powder, but this is mild.

Serves 4
500g/1¼lb smoked haddock
115g/4oz/generous ½ cup
   basmati rice
30ml/2 tbsp lemon juice

150ml/¼ pint/⅔ cup single
   (light) cream or sour cream
pinch of freshly grated nutmeg
pinch of cayenne pepper
2 hard-boiled eggs, peeled and
   cut into wedges
50g/2oz/4 tbsp butter, diced,
   plus extra for greasing
30ml/2 tbsp chopped
   fresh parsley
salt and ground black pepper

1 Put the haddock in a shallow pan, pour in just enough water to cover and heat to simmering point. Poach the fish for about 10 minutes, until the flesh flakes easily when tested with the tip of a sharp knife. Lift the fish out of the liquid, then remove any skin and bones and flake the flesh. Reserve the cooking liquid.

2 Pour the cooking liquid into a measuring jug (cup) and make up the volume with water to 250ml/8fl oz/1 cup.

3 Pour the measured liquid into a pan and bring it to the boil. Add the rice, stir, then lower the heat, cover and simmer for about 10 minutes, until the rice is tender and the liquid has been absorbed. Meanwhile, preheat the oven to 180°C/350°F/ Gas 4 and butter a baking dish.

4 When the rice is cooked, remove it from the heat and stir in the lemon juice, cream, flaked haddock, grated nutmeg and cayenne pepper. Add the egg wedges to the rice mixture and stir in gently.

5 Transfer the rice mixture into the prepared baking dish. Level the surface and dot with butter. Cover the dish loosely with foil and bake for about 25 minutes.

6 Stir the chopped parsley into the baked kedgeree and add seasoning to taste. Serve immediately.

Kedgeree Energy 320kcal/1336kJ; Protein 15.6g; Carbohydrate 46.6g, of which sugars 0g; Fat 7.6g, of which saturates 3.3g; Cholesterol 149mg; Calcium 39mg; Fibre 0g; Sodium 357mg.
Shellfish Paella Energy 585kcal/2445kJ; Protein 36.1g; Carbohydrate 60.9g, of which sugars 10.1g; Fat 20.4g, of which saturates 5.6g; Cholesterol 268mg; Calcium 132mg; Fibre 4.2g; Sodium 1055mg.

Salmon and Rice Gratin

This dish is ideal for informal entertaining as it can be made ahead of time and reheated for half an hour before being served.

Serves 6
675g/1½lb fresh salmon
   fillet, skinned
1 bay leaf
a few parsley stalks
1 litre/1¾ pints/4 cups water
400g/14oz/2 cups basmati rice,
   soaked in water for 30 minutes
30–45ml/2–3 tbsp chopped fresh
   parsley, plus extra to garnish
175g/6oz/1½ cups grated
   Cheddar cheese
3 hard-boiled eggs, chopped
salt and ground black pepper

For the sauce
1 litre/1¾ pints/4 cups milk
40g/1½oz/⅓ cup plain
   (all-purpose) flour
40g/1½oz/3 tbsp butter
5ml/1 tsp mild curry paste or
   Dijon mustard

1 Put the salmon in a wide, shallow pan. Add the bay leaf and parsley stalks, and season. Pour in the water and bring to a simmer. Poach the fish for 10–12 minutes until just tender.

2 Lift the fish out of the pan using a slotted spoon, then strain the liquid into a clean pan. Leave the fish to cool, then remove any visible bones and flake the flesh gently with a fork.

3 Drain the rice and add it to the fish-poaching liquid. Bring to the boil, then cover and simmer for 10 minutes. Remove from the heat and, without lifting the lid, leave to stand for 5 minutes.

4 Meanwhile, make the sauce. Mix the milk, flour and butter in a pan. Bring to the boil over low heat, whisking until the sauce is thick. Stir in the curry paste or mustard, and season. Simmer the sauce for 2 minutes, whisking occasionally.

5 Preheat the grill (broiler). Remove the sauce from the heat and stir in the chopped parsley and rice, with half the cheese. Using a large metal spoon, fold in the flaked fish and eggs.

6 Spoon into a shallow gratin dish and sprinkle with the rest of the cheese. Heat under the grill (broiler) until the top is bubbling. Serve in individual dishes, garnished with chopped parsley.

Trout with Rice, Tomatoes and Nuts

This recipe comes from Spain, where trout is very popular. If you fillet the fish before baking, it cooks more evenly and no bones get in the way of the stuffing.

Serves 4
2 fresh trout, about
   500g/1¼lb each
75g/3oz/¾ cup mixed unsalted
   cashew nuts, pine nuts,
   almonds and hazelnuts
25ml/1½ tbsp olive oil, plus extra
   for drizzling
1 small onion, finely chopped
10ml/2 tsp grated fresh
   root ginger
175g/6oz/1½ cups cooked white
   long grain rice
4 tomatoes, peeled and very
   finely chopped
4 sun-dried tomatoes in oil,
   drained and chopped
30ml/2 tbsp chopped
   fresh tarragon
2 fresh tarragon sprigs
salt and ground black pepper
dressed green leaves, to serve

1 Using a sharp knife, fillet the trout. Check the cavity of the fish for any remaining tiny bones and remove these with a pair of tweezers.

2 Preheat the oven to 190°C/375°F/Gas 5. Spread out the nuts in a baking tray and bake for 3–4 minutes, shaking the tray occasionally. Chop the nuts.

3 Heat the oil in a small frying pan and fry the onion for 3–4 minutes until soft. Stir in the ginger, cook for 1 minute more, then spoon into a mixing bowl.

4 Add the rice to the mixture in the bowl, then stir in the tomatoes, sun-dried tomatoes, toasted nuts and chopped tarragon. Season with plenty of salt and black pepper.

5 Place each of the trout in turn on a large piece of oiled foil and spoon the stuffing into the cavity. Add a sprig of tarragon and a drizzle of olive oil.

6 Fold the foil over to enclose each trout and put the parcels in a large roasting pan. Bake for 20–25 minutes until the fish is tender. Cut the fish into thick slices. Serve with the green salad.

Salmon Gratin Energy 752kcal/3137kJ; Protein 44.8g; Carbohydrate 66.5g, of which sugars 8.2g; Fat 33.5g, of which saturates 14.5g; Cholesterol 204mg; Calcium 492mg; Fibre 0.6g; Sodium 411mg.
Trout with Rice Energy 458kcal/1920kJ; Protein 45.1g; Carbohydrate 19.4g, of which sugars 5g; Fat 22.8g, of which saturates 3.4g; Cholesterol 160mg; Calcium 146mg; Fibre 3.2g; Sodium 161mg.

Malacca Fried Rice

There are many versions of this dish throughout Asia, all based upon leftover cooked rice. Ingredients vary according to what is available, but prawns are a popular addition.

Serves 4–6

2 eggs
45ml/3 tbsp vegetable oil
4 shallots or 1 onion, finely chopped
5ml/1 tsp chopped fresh root ginger
1 garlic clove, crushed
225g/8oz raw prawns (shrimp), peeled and deveined
5ml/1 tsp chilli sauce (optional)
3 spring onions (scallions), green part only, roughly chopped
225g/8oz/2 cups fresh or frozen peas
225g/8oz thickly sliced roast pork, diced
45ml/3 tbsp light soy sauce
350g/12oz/3 cups cooked white long grain rice, cooled
salt and ground black pepper

1 In a bowl, beat the eggs well with salt and ground black pepper to taste. Heat 15ml/1 tbsp of the oil in a large, non-stick frying pan, pour in the eggs and cook until set, without stirring. This will take less than a minute. Roll up the pancake, slide it on to a plate, cut into thin strips and set aside.

2 Heat the remaining vegetable oil in a preheated wok, add the shallots or onion, ginger, garlic and prawns, and cook for 1–2 minutes, stirring constantly and taking care that the garlic does not burn.

3 Add the chilli sauce, if using, the spring onions, peas, diced pork and soy sauce. Stir to heat through for a minute, then add the rice. Fry over medium heat, stirring frequently, for about 6–8 minutes. Spoon into a dish, decorate with the pancake strips and serve immediately.

> **Cook's Tip**
> There is no reason to wait until the day after you've served a Sunday roast to try this dish. Most delicatessens and supermarkets sell sliced roast pork.

Trout with Black Rice

Pink trout fillets cooked with ginger make a stunning contrast to black rice.

Serves 2

2.5cm/1in piece fresh root ginger, peeled and grated
1 garlic clove, crushed
1 fresh red chilli, seeded and finely chopped
30ml/2 tbsp soy sauce
2 trout fillets, about 200g/7oz each
oil, for greasing

For the rice

15ml/1 tbsp sesame oil
50g/2oz/³⁄₄ cup fresh shiitake mushrooms, stems discarded, caps sliced
8 spring onions (scallions), finely chopped
150g/5oz/³⁄₄ cup black rice
4 slices fresh root ginger or galangal
900ml/1¹⁄₂ pints/3³⁄₄ cups boiling water or chicken stock

1 Make the rice. Heat the sesame oil in a pan and fry the mushrooms with half the spring onions for 2–3 minutes.

2 Add the rice and sliced ginger to the pan and stir well. Cover with the boiling water or chicken stock and bring back to the boil. Reduce the heat, cover the pan and simmer for 25–30 minutes or until the rice is tender. Drain well and cover to keep warm, while you prepare the fish.

3 While the rice is cooking, preheat the oven to 200°C/400°F/Gas 6. In a small bowl, mix together the grated ginger, garlic, chilli and soy sauce.

4 Place the fish, skin side up, in a lightly oiled shallow baking dish. Using a sharp knife, make several slits in the skin of the fish. Spread the ginger paste all over the fillets, using your fingers to rub it in.

5 Cover the dish tightly with foil and cook in the preheated oven for about 20–25 minutes or until the trout fillets are cooked through.

6 Divide the rice between two warmed serving plates. Remove the ginger. Lay the fish on top and sprinkle over the reserved spring onions, to garnish.

Trout with Black Rice Energy 560kcal/2362kJ; Protein 45.6g; Carbohydrate 63.5g, of which sugars 3.3g; Fat 15.5g, of which saturates 1.4g; Cholesterol 0mg; Calcium 46mg; Fibre 2.3g; Sodium 1187mg.
Malacca Rice Energy 433kcal/1808kJ; Protein 23.5g; Carbohydrate 70.6g, of which sugars 5.8g; Fat 6.1g, of which saturates 3g; Cholesterol 158mg; Calcium 123mg; Fibre 3.2g; Sodium 189mg.

Mussel Risotto

The addition of freshly cooked mussels, aromatic coriander and a little cream to a packet of instant risotto can turn a simple meal into a decadent treat. Serve with a side salad for a splendid meal.

Serves 3–4
900g/2lb fresh mussels
275g/10oz packet risotto
30ml/2 tbsp chopped fresh coriander (cilantro)
30ml/2 tbsp double (heavy) cream
salt and ground black pepper

1 Scrub the mussels, discarding any that do not close when sharply tapped. Place in a large pan. Add 120ml/4fl oz/½ cup water and seasoning, then bring to the boil. Cover the pan and cook the mussels, shaking the pan occasionally, for 4–5 minutes, until they have opened.

2 Drain the mussels, reserving the liquid and discarding any that have not opened. Shell most of the mussels, reserving a few in their shells for garnish. Strain the mussel liquid.

3 Make up the packet risotto according to the instructions, using the cooking liquid from the mussels and making it up to the required volume with water.

4 When the risotto is about three-quarters cooked, add the mussels to the pan. Add the coriander and re-cover the pan without stirring in these ingredients.

5 Remove the risotto from the heat, stir in the cream, cover and leave to rest for a few minutes. Spoon into a warmed serving dish, garnish with the reserved mussels in their shells, and serve.

Cook's Tip
For a super-quick mussel risotto, use cooked mussels in their shells – the type sold vacuum packed ready to reheat. Just reheat them according to the packet instructions and add to the made risotto with the coriander and cream.

Crab Risotto

This simple risotto has a subtle flavour that makes the most of delicate crab. It makes a tempting main course or appetizer. It is important to use a good quality risotto rice, which will give a deliciously creamy result, but the cooked grains are still firm to the bite.

Serves 3–4
2 large cooked crabs
275g/10oz/1½ cups risotto rice
1.2 litres/2 pints/5 cups simmering fish stock
30ml/2 tbsp mixed finely chopped fresh herbs, such as chives, tarragon and parsley

1 One at a time, hold the crabs firmly and hit the underside with the heel of your hand. This should loosen the shell from the body. Using your thumbs, push against the body and pull away from the shell. Remove and discard the intestines and the grey gills.

2 Break off the claws and legs of the crabs, then use a hammer or crackers to break them open. Using a skewer or a small, pointed knife, remove the meat from the claws and legs. Place the meat on a plate.

3 Using a skewer, pick out the white meat from the body cavities and place with the claw and leg meat, reserving a little white meat to garnish. Scoop out the brown meat from the shell and add to the rest of the crab meat.

4 Place the rice in a pan and add one-quarter of the stock. Bring to the boil and cook, stirring, until the liquid has been absorbed. Adding a ladleful of stock at a time, cook, stirring, until about two-thirds of the stock has been absorbed.

5 Stir the crab meat and chopped herbs into the pan, and continue cooking, adding the remaining stock.

6 When the rice is almost cooked but still has some bite, remove it from the heat and adjust the seasoning. Cover and leave to stand for 3 minutes. Serve garnished with the reserved white crab meat.

Mussel Risotto Energy 439kcal/1833kJ; Protein 17.2g; Carbohydrate 56.6g, of which sugars 1.4g; Fat 11.3, of which saturates 3.5g; Cholesterol 37mg; Calcium 159mg; Fibre 0.2g; Sodium 146mg.
Crab Risotto Energy 496kcal/2060kJ; Protein 14.1g; Carbohydrate 56.4g, of which sugars 1.1g; Fat 18.7g, of which saturates 8.9g; Cholesterol 65mg; Calcium 25mg; Fibre 0.2g; Sodium 146mg.

Seafood Risotto

Seafood risotto is a warming dish all the family will enjoy.

Serves 4
60ml/4 tbsp sunflower oil
1 onion, chopped
2 garlic cloves, crushed
225g/8oz/generous 1 cup
   arborio rice

105ml/7 tbsp white wine
1.5 litres/2½ pints/6 cups hot
   fish stock
350g/12oz mixed seafood
grated rind of ½ lemon
30ml/2 tbsp tomato purée (paste)
15ml/1 tbsp chopped
   fresh parsley
salt and ground black pepper

1 Heat the oil in a pan, add the onion and garlic and cook. Add the rice and wine and cook until absorbed. Add a ladle of stock and cook until absorbed. Continue adding stock, stirring, until half is left.

2 Stir in the seafood and cook for 2–3 minutes. Add the stock as before, until the rice is creamy and cooked through. Stir in the lemon rind, tomato purée and parsley. Season and serve warm.

Risotto Nero

This unusual risotto is blackened by squid ink.

Serves 4
450g/1lb small cuttlefish or squid,
   with their ink, cut into rings
1.2 litres/2 pints/5 cups light
   fish stock

50g/2oz/¼ cup butter
30ml/2 tbsp olive oil
3 shallots, finely chopped
350g/12oz/1¾ cups risotto rice
105ml/7 tbsp dry white wine
30ml/2 tbsp chopped fresh
   flat leaf parsley
salt and ground black pepper

1 Add the ink to the fish stock. Bring to the boil. Heat the oil and half the butter in a pan. Cook the shallots for 3 minutes until soft. Add the seafood and cook gently for 5–7 minutes. Add the rice and stir well. Add in the wine and simmer until absorbed.

2 Add a ladle of stock and stir until absorbed. Continue in this way for 20–25 minutes. Season to taste, then stir in the parsley and butter. Spoon the risotto into four warmed dishes and serve.

Trout and Prosciutto Risotto Rolls

Risotto is a fine match for the robust flavour of these trout rolls.

Serves 4
4 trout fillets, skinned
4 slices prosciutto
caper berries, to garnish

For the risotto
30ml/2 tbsp olive oil
8 large raw prawns (shrimp),
   peeled and deveined

1 onion, chopped
225g/8oz/generous 1 cup
   risotto rice
about 105ml/7 tbsp white wine
about 750ml/1¼ pints/3 cups
   simmering fish or
   chicken stock
15g/½oz/¼ cup dried porcini
   or chanterelle mushrooms,
   soaked for 10 minutes in
   warm water to cover
salt and ground black pepper

1 To make the risotto, heat the oil in a heavy pan and cook the prawns very briefly until flecked with pink. Lift out using a slotted spoon and transfer to a plate. Keep warm. Add the chopped onion to the pan and cook gently for 3–4 minutes, or until soft. Add the rice and stir for 3–4 minutes to coat in the oil. Add 75ml/5 tbsp of the wine, and then the stock, a little at a time, stirring over a gentle heat and allowing the rice to absorb the liquid before adding more.

2 Drain the mushrooms, reserving the liquid, and cut the larger ones in half. Towards the end of cooking, stir the mushrooms into the risotto with 15ml/1 tbsp of the reserved liquid. Season to taste with salt and pepper. When the rice is al dente, remove from the heat and stir in the prawns. Preheat the oven to 190°C/375°F/Gas 5. Grease an ovenproof dish and set aside.

3 Take a trout fillet, place a spoonful of risotto at one end and roll up. Wrap each fillet in a slice of prosciutto and place in the prepared dish. Spoon any remaining risotto around the fish rolls and sprinkle over the remaining wine. Cover loosely with foil and bake for 15–20 minutes, or until the fish is cooked.

4 Spoon the risotto on to a warmed serving platter, arrange the trout rolls on top and garnish the dish with caper berries. Serve immediately.

Seafood Risotto Energy 404kcal/1693kJ; Protein 28.1g; Carbohydrate 56.3g, of which sugars 1.1g; Fat 3.9g, of which saturates 1.9g; Cholesterol 228mg; Calcium 200mg; Fibre 0.2g; Sodium 301mg.
Risotto Nero Energy 571kcal/2382kJ; Protein 24.1g; Carbohydrate 72.6g, of which sugars 1.1g; Fat 18.2g, of which saturates 7.8g; Cholesterol 280mg; Calcium 40mg; Fibre 0.2g; Sodium 201mg.
Trout Rolls Energy 397kcal/1662kJ; Protein 33g; Carbohydrate 43.6g, of which sugars 1.1g; Fat 7.6g, of which saturates 0.3g; Cholesterol 29mg; Calcium 37mg; Fibre 0.2g; Sodium 202mg.

Moroccan Paella

This version of paella has crossed the sea from Spain, and acquired some North African spicy touches.

Serves 6
2 large skinless chicken breast fillets
about 150g/5oz squid rings
275g/10oz cod or haddock fillets, skinned and cut into chunks
8–10 raw king prawns (jumbo shrimp), peeled and deveined
8 scallops, trimmed and halved
250g/9oz/1⅓ cups white long-grain rice
30ml/2 tbsp sunflower oil
5 spring onions (scallions), cut into strips
1 red (bell) pepper, cut into strips
2 small courgettes (zucchini), cut into strips
400ml/14fl oz/1⅔ cups chicken or vegetable stock
250g/8fl oz/1 cup passata (bottled strained tomatoes)
350g/12oz mussels, cleaned
salt and ground black pepper

For the marinade
2 fresh red chillies, seeded and roughly chopped
handful of fresh coriander (cilantro)
10–15ml/2–3 tsp ground cumin
15ml/1 tbsp paprika
2 garlic cloves
45ml/3 tbsp olive oil
60ml/4 tbsp sunflower oil
juice of 1 lemon

1 Mix the marinade ingredients with 5ml/1 tsp salt. Cut the chicken into bitesize pieces and place in a bowl. Place the fish and shellfish (apart from the mussels) in another bowl. Divide the marinade between the fish and chicken and stir. Cover with clear film (plastic wrap) and marinate for at least 2 hours.

2 Place the rice in a bowl, cover with boiling water and soak for 30 minutes. Drain the chicken and fish, and reserve the marinade. Heat the oil in a large pan and fry the chicken until lightly browned. Add the spring onions and pepper, fry for 1 minute, and then add the courgettes and fry for 3–4 minutes. Remove the chicken and vegetables to plates.

3 Scrape the marinade into the pan and cook for 1 minute, then stir in the rice. Add the stock, passata and chicken, and season. Bring to the boil, cover and simmer for 10–15 minutes until the rice is almost tender. Add the vegetables and place the fish and mussels on top. Cover and cook for 10–12 minutes. Discard any mussels that remain closed and serve.

Five Ingredients Rice

The Japanese love rice so much they invented many ways to enjoy it. Here, chicken and vegetables are cooked with short grain rice, making a healthy light lunch.

Serves 4
275g/10oz/1¼ cups Japanese short grain rice
90g/3½oz carrot, peeled
2.5ml/½ tsp lemon juice
90g/3½oz canned bamboo shoots, drained
225g/8oz/3 cups oyster mushrooms
8 fresh parsley sprigs
350ml/12fl oz/1½ cups water and 7.5ml/1½ tsp instant dashi powder
150g/5oz skinless chicken breast fillet, cut into 2cm/¾in chunks
30ml/2 tbsp shoyu
30ml/2 tbsp sake
25ml/1½ tbsp mirin (sweet rice wine)
pinch of salt

1 Put the rice in a large bowl and wash under cold running water until the water remains clear. Drain thoroughly and set aside for 30 minutes.

2 Using a sharp knife, cut the carrot into 5mm/¼in rounds, then cut the discs into flowers. Sprinkle with the lemon juice. Slice the canned bamboo shoots into thin matchsticks.

3 Tear the oyster mushrooms into thin strips. Chop the parsley. Put it in a sieve (strainer) and pour over hot water from the kettle to wilt the leaves. Allow to drain, and then set aside.

4 Heat the dashi stock in a large pan and add the carrots and bamboo shoots. Bring to the boil and add the chicken. Remove any scum that forms on the surface, then add the shoyu, sake, mirin and salt.

5 Add the rice and mushrooms and cover with a tight-fitting lid. Bring back to the boil, wait 5 minutes, then reduce the heat and simmer for 10 minutes.

6 Remove the pan from the heat without lifting the lid and leave to stand undisturbed for 15 minutes. Add the wilted herbs and serve immediately.

Moroccan Paella Energy 401kcal/1688kJ; Protein 46g; Carbohydrate 39.3g, of which sugars 4.4g; Fat 6.6g, of which saturates 1.1g; Cholesterol 200mg; Calcium 115mg; Fibre 1.4g; Sodium 343mg.
Five Ingredients Rice Energy 331kcal/1386kJ; Protein 16.2g; Carbohydrate 61.1g, of which sugars 5.5g; Fat 1.2g, of which saturates 0.2g; Cholesterol 26mg; Calcium 32mg; Fibre 1.5g; Sodium 567mg.

Rice Omelette Rolls

Rice omelettes make a great supper dish and are popular with children, who usually top them with a liberal helping of tomato ketchup.

Serves 4

1 skinless, boneless chicken thigh, about 115g/4oz, cubed
40ml/8 tsp butter
1 small onion, chopped
½ carrot, diced
2 shiitake mushrooms, stems removed and chopped
15ml/1 tbsp finely chopped fresh parsley
225g/8oz/2 cups cooked long grain white rice
30ml/2 tbsp tomato ketchup, plus extra to serve
6 eggs, lightly beaten
60ml/4 tbsp milk
5ml/1 tsp salt, plus extra to season
freshly ground black pepper

1 Season the chicken with salt and ground black pepper. Melt 10ml/2 tsp butter in a frying pan. Fry the onion, stirring frequently, for 1 minute, then add the chicken pieces and fry until the cubes are cooked.

2 Add the carrot and mushrooms to the pan, and stir-fry over medium heat until soft, then add the chopped parsley. Set this mixture aside.

3 Wipe the frying pan, then add a further 10ml/2 tsp butter and stir in the rice. Mix in the fried ingredients, ketchup and pepper. Stir well, adding salt to taste, if necessary. Keep the mixture warm. Beat the eggs with the milk in a bowl. Stir in the measured salt and add pepper to taste.

4 Melt 5ml/1 tsp of the remaining butter in an omelette pan. Pour in a quarter of the egg mixture and stir it briefly with a fork, then allow it to set for 1 minute. Top with a quarter of the rice mixture.

5 Fold the omelette over the rice and slide it to the edge of the pan to shape it into a curve. Slide it on to a warmed plate, cover with kitchen paper and press neatly into a rectangular shape. Keep warm while cooking three more omelettes from the remaining ingredients. Serve immediately, with tomato ketchup on the side.

Burritos with Chicken and Rice

The secret of a successful burrito is to have all the filling neatly packaged inside the tortilla for easy eating.

Serves 4

90g/3½oz/½ cup long grain rice
15ml/1 tbsp vegetable oil
1 onion, chopped
2.5ml/½ tsp ground cloves
5ml/1 tsp dried, or fresh oregano
200g/7oz can chopped tomatoes in tomato juice
2 skinless chicken breast fillets
150g/5oz/1¼ cups grated Monterey Jack or mild Cheddar cheese
60ml/4 tbsp sour cream (optional)
8 x 20–25cm/8–10in fresh wheat flour tortillas
salt
fresh oregano, to garnish (optional)

1 Bring a pan of lightly salted water to the boil. Add the rice and cook for 8 minutes. Drain, rinse and then drain again. Heat the oil in a large pan. Add the onion, with the ground cloves and oregano, and fry for 2–3 minutes. Stir in the rice and tomatoes and cook over low heat until the tomato juice has been absorbed. Set the pan aside.

2 Put the chicken fillets in a pan, pour in water to cover and bring to the boil. Simmer for 10 minutes until cooked through. Lift the chicken out of the pan, and leave to cool slightly.

3 Preheat the oven to 160°C/325°F/Gas 3. Shred the chicken by pulling the flesh apart with two forks. Add the chicken to the rice mixture, with the cheese. Add the sour cream, if using.

4 Wrap the tortillas in foil and place them on a plate. Stand the plate over boiling water for about 5 minutes. Alternatively, wrap in microwave-safe film and heat in a microwave on full power for 1 minute.

5 Spoon one-eighth of the filling into the centre of a tortilla and fold in both sides. Fold the bottom up and the top down to form a parcel. Secure with a cocktail stick (toothpick).

6 Put the filled burrito in an ovenproof dish, cover with foil and keep warm in the oven while you make seven more. Remove the cocktail sticks before serving, sprinkled with fresh oregano.

Rice Omelette Rolls Energy 322kcal/1347kJ; Protein 18.1g; Carbohydrate 22.8g, of which sugars 4.9g; Fat 18.5g, of which saturates 8.1g; Cholesterol 337mg; Calcium 80mg; Fibre 1.1g; Sodium 325mg.
Burritos Energy 754kcal/3130kJ; Protein 22.5g; Carbohydrate 58.6g, of which sugars 3.3g; Fat 54.1g, of which saturates 13.5g; Cholesterol 90mg; Calcium 53mg; Fibre 1.3g; Sodium 99mg.

Spicy Peanut Chicken Rice

Smooth peanut butter adds a delicious richness to this spicy, slow-cooker rice dish.

Serves 4

4 skinless chicken breast fillets, cut into thin strips
45ml/3 tbsp groundnut (peanut) or sunflower oil
1 garlic clove, crushed
5ml/1 tsp chopped fresh thyme
15ml/1 tbsp curry powder
juice of half a lemon
1 onion, finely chopped
2 tomatoes, peeled, seeded and chopped
1 fresh green chilli, seeded and sliced
60ml/4 tbsp smooth peanut butter
750ml/1¼ pints/3 cups boiling chicken stock
300g/10oz/1½ cups easy-cook (converted) white rice
salt and ground black pepper
lemon or lime wedges and sprigs of fresh flat leaf parsley, to garnish

1 Cut the chicken breast fillets into thin strips. In a bowl, mix together 15ml/1 tbsp of the oil with the garlic, thyme, curry powder and lemon juice. Add the chicken strips and stir well to combine. Cover with clear film (plastic wrap) and leave to marinate in the refrigerator for 1½–2 hours.

2 Meanwhile, heat the remaining oil in a frying pan, add the onion and fry for 10 minutes until soft. Transfer to the ceramic cooking pot and switch the slow cooker to high. Add the chopped tomatoes and chilli and stir to combine.

3 Put the peanut butter into a bowl, then blend in the stock, adding a little at a time. Pour the mixture into the ceramic cooking pot, season with salt and pepper and stir. Cover with the lid and cook for 1 hour.

4 About 30 minutes before the end of cooking time, remove the chicken from the refrigerator and leave it to come to room temperature. Add the chicken and the marinade to the ceramic cooking pot and stir to mix. Re-cover and cook for 1 hour.

5 Sprinkle the rice over the casserole, then stir to mix. Cover and cook for a final 45 minutes to 1 hour, or until the chicken and rice are cooked and tender. Serve immediately with lemon or lime wedges, and garnish with fresh parsley.

Chicken and Asparagus Risotto

Use thick asparagus, as fine spears overcook in this risotto. The thick ends of the asparagus are full of flavour and they become beautifully tender in the time it takes for the rice to absorb the stock.

Serves 4

50g/2oz/¼ cup butter
15ml/1 tbsp olive oil
1 leek, finely chopped
115g/4oz/1½ cups oyster mushrooms, sliced
3 skinless chicken breast fillets, cubed
350g/12oz asparagus
250g/9oz/1¼ cups risotto rice
900ml/1½ pints/3¾ cups boiling chicken stock
salt and ground black pepper
Parmesan cheese curls, to serve

1 Heat the butter with the oil in a pan until the mixture is foaming. Add the leek and cook gently until softened, but not coloured. Add the mushrooms and cook for 5 minutes. Remove the vegetables from the pan and set aside.

2 Increase the heat and cook the cubes of chicken until golden on all sides. Do this in batches, if necessary, and then replace them all in the pan.

3 Meanwhile, discard the woody ends from the asparagus and cut the spears in half. Set the fine tips aside. Cut the thick ends in half and add them to the pan. Replace the leek and mushroom mixture in the pan and stir in the rice.

4 Pour in a ladleful of boiling stock and cook gently, stirring occasionally, until the stock is absorbed. Continue adding the stock a ladleful at a time, simmering until it is absorbed, the rice is tender and the chicken is cooked.

5 Add the fine asparagus tips with the last ladleful of boiling stock for the final 5 minutes and continue cooking the risotto gently until the asparagus is tender.

6 Season the risotto to taste with salt and lots of ground black pepper and spoon it into individual warm serving bowls. Top each bowl with curls of Parmesan, and serve.

Peanut Chicken Energy 635Kcal/2677kJ; Protein 45.8g; Carbohydrate 70.7g, of which sugars 4.4g; Fat 20.8g, of which saturates 4.1g; Cholesterol 105mg; Calcium 65mg; Fibre 2.1g; Sodium 354mg.
Chicken Risotto Energy 496kcal/2072kJ; Protein 36.1g; Carbohydrate 50g, of which sugars 2.7g; Fat 16.1g, of which saturates 7.4g; Cholesterol 105mg; Calcium 53mg; Fibre 2.7g; Sodium 148mg.

Duck with Rice

This is a very rich dish, brightly coloured with tomatoes and fresh herbs.

Serves 4–6

4 duck breast fillets
1 Spanish (Bermuda) onion, chopped
2 garlic cloves, crushed
10ml/2 tsp grated fresh root ginger
4 tomatoes, peeled and chopped

225g/8oz Kabocha or onion squash, cut into 1cm/½in cubes
275g/10oz/1½ cups long grain rice
750ml/1¼ pints/3 cups chicken stock
15ml/1 tbsp finely chopped fresh coriander (cilantro)
15ml/1 tbsp finely chopped fresh mint
salt and ground black pepper

1 Heat a heavy frying pan or flameproof casserole. Using a sharp knife, score the fatty side of the duck breast fillets in a criss-cross pattern, rub the fat with a little salt, then dry-fry the duck, skin side down, for about 6–8 minutes to render some of the fat.

2 Pour all but 15ml/1 tbsp of the fat into a jar or cup, then fry the duck fillets, meat side down, in the fat remaining in the pan for 3–4 minutes until brown all over. Transfer to a board, slice thickly and set aside in a shallow dish. Deglaze the pan with a little water and pour this liquid over the duck.

3 Fry the onion and garlic in the same pan for 4–5 minutes until the onion is fairly soft, adding a little extra duck fat if necessary. Stir in the ginger, cook for 1–2 minutes more, then add the tomatoes and cook, stirring, for another 2 minutes.

4 Add the squash, stir-fry for a few minutes, then cover and allow to steam for about 4 minutes.

5 Stir in the rice and cook, stirring, until the rice is coated in the tomato and onion mixture. Pour in the stock, return the slices of duck to the pan and season with salt and pepper.

6 Bring to the boil, then lower the heat, cover and simmer gently for 30–35 minutes until the rice is tender. Stir in the coriander and mint and serve.

Duck Risotto

This makes an excellent lunch or supper dish with a green salad or mangetouts and sautéed red peppers.

Serves 3–4

2 duck breast fillets
30ml/2 tbsp brandy
30ml/2 tbsp orange juice
1 onion, finely chopped
1 garlic clove, crushed
275g/10oz/1½ cups risotto rice

1–1.2 litres/1¾–2 pints/4–5 cups duck or chicken stock, simmering
5ml/1 tsp chopped fresh thyme
5ml/1 tsp chopped fresh mint
10ml/2 tsp grated orange rind
40g/1½oz/½ cup freshly grated Parmesan cheese
salt and ground black pepper
strips of thinly pared orange rind, to garnish

1 Score the fatty side of the duck and rub them with salt. Put them, fat side down, in a heavy frying pan and dry-fry over medium heat for 6–8 minutes. Transfer the fillets to a plate. Discard the fat from the fillets and cut the flesh into 2cm/¾in wide strips.

2 Pour all but 15ml/1 tbsp of the duck fat from the pan into a bowl, then reheat the fat in the pan. Fry the duck slices quickly for 2–3 minutes until evenly brown but not overcooked. Add the brandy, heat to simmering point, and then ignite. When the flames have died down, add the orange juice and season with salt and pepper. Remove from the heat and set aside.

3 In a pan, heat 15ml/1 tbsp of the remaining duck fat. Fry the onion and garlic over a gentle heat until the onion is soft but not browned. Add the rice and cook, stirring all the time, until the grains are coated in oil and have become slightly translucent around the edges.

4 Add the stock, a ladleful at a time, waiting for each to be absorbed completely before adding the next. Just before adding the final ladleful, stir in the duck, with the thyme and mint. Cook until the risotto is creamy and the rice is tender.

5 Add the orange rind and Parmesan. Season to taste, then remove from the heat, cover and leave to stand for a few minutes. Serve garnished with the pared orange rind.

Duck with Rice Energy 754kcal/3130kJ; Protein 22.5g; Carbohydrate 58.6g, of which sugars 3.3g; Fat 45.1g, of which saturates 13.5g; Cholesterol 90mg; Calcium 53mg; Fibre 1.3g; Sodium 99mg.
Duck Risotto Energy 408kcal/1708kJ; Protein 24g; Carbohydrate 56.7g, of which sugars 1.5g; Fat 8.5g, of which saturates 3g; Cholesterol 93mg; Calcium 147mg; Fibre 0.2g; Sodium 193mg.

Pork and Rice Casserole with Chilli and Juniper Berries

This is a hearty marinated pork dish packed with vegetables and rice.

Serves 4–6
500g/1¼lb lean pork, such as
   fillet (tenderloin), cut into strips
60ml/4 tbsp corn oil
1 onion, chopped
1 garlic clove, crushed
1 green (bell) pepper, diced
about 300ml/½ pint/1¼ cups
   chicken stock
225g/8oz/1 cup long grain rice

150ml/¼ pint/⅔ cup double
   (heavy) cream
40g/1½oz/½ cup freshly grated
   Parmesan cheese
salt and ground black pepper

For the marinade
120ml/4fl oz/½ cup dry
   white wine
30ml/2 tbsp lemon juice
1 onion, chopped
4 juniper berries, lightly crushed
3 cloves
1 red chilli, seeded and sliced

1 Mix all the marinade ingredients, add the pork and set aside to marinate for 3–4 hours. Transfer the pork to a plate. Strain the marinade and set aside. Heat the oil in a heavy pan and brown the pork for a few minutes. Transfer to a plate.

2 Add the chopped onion, garlic and pepper to the pan and fry for 6–8 minutes, then return the pork to the pan. Pour in the reserved marinade and the stock. Bring to the boil and season with salt and black pepper, then lower the heat, cover and simmer for 10 minutes until the meat is nearly tender.

3 Preheat the oven to 160°C/325°F/Gas 3. Cook the rice in salted boiling water for 8 minutes or until three-quarters cooked. Drain. Spread half the rice over the bottom of a buttered baking dish. Make a neat layer of meat and vegetables on top, then spread the remaining rice over the top.

4 Stir the cream and 30ml/2 tbsp of the Parmesan into the liquid in which the pork was cooked. Pour this mixture over the rice and sprinkle with the remaining Parmesan cheese. Cover with foil, bake for 20 minutes, then remove the foil and cook for 5 minutes more, to brown the top. Serve immediately.

Crusted Paella with Chorizo and Chicken

This is an unusual paella with an egg crust that is finished in the oven. The crust seals in all the aromas until it is broken open at the table.

Serves 6
45ml/3 tbsp olive oil
200g/7oz chorizo, sliced
2 tomatoes, peeled, seeded
   and chopped

175g/6oz lean cubed pork
175g/6oz skinless chicken breast
   fillet or rabbit, cut into chunks
350g/12oz/1¾ cups paella rice
900ml–1 litre/1½–1¾ pints/
   3¾–4 cups hot chicken stock
pinch of saffron threads (0.2g)
150g/5oz/⅔ cup cooked
   chickpeas
6 large (US extra large) eggs
salt and ground black pepper

1 Preheat the oven to 190°C/375°F/Gas 5. Heat the oil in a flameproof casserole and fry the sausage for 6–8 minutes, stirring occasionally, until browned.

2 Add the chopped tomatoes to the pan and fry until reduced. Stir in the pork and chicken or rabbit pieces and cook for 2–3 minutes, stirring frequently, until all the meat has browned lightly.

3 Add the rice to the pan, stir over the heat for 1 minute to coat the grains in oil, then pour in the hot chicken stock. Add the saffron, season to taste with salt and ground black pepper, and stir well.

4 Slowly bring the mixture to the boil, then lower the heat and stir in the cooked chickpeas. Cover the casserole tightly with the lid and simmer over low heat for about 20 minutes or until the rice is tender.

5 Beat the eggs with a little water and a pinch of salt in a bowl and pour over the rice. Place the casserole, uncovered, in the preheated oven and cook for about 10 minutes, until the eggs have set and browned slightly on top. Serve the paella straight from the casserole.

Crusted Paella Energy 533kcal/2226kJ; Protein 29.1g; Carbohydrate 55.5g, of which sugars 1.7g; Fat 21.7g, of which saturates 6.3g; Cholesterol 242mg; Calcium 72mg; Fibre 1.5g; Sodium 436mg.
Pork Casserole Energy 490kcal/2040kJ; Protein 31.7g; Carbohydrate 33.3g, of which sugars 3g; Fat 23.9g, of which saturates 10.2g; Cholesterol 91mg; Calcium 342mg; Fibre 0.6g; Sodium 340mg.

Risotto with Bacon, Baby Courgettes and Peppers

This would make the perfect dish to come home to after an early show at the theatre. Creamy risotto topped with vegetables and crisp bacon is irresistible and easy to make.

Serves 4
30ml/2 tbsp olive oil
115g/4oz rindless streaky
  bacon rashers (strips), cut
  into thick pieces
350g/12oz/1¾ cups
  risotto rice
1.2 litres/2 pints/5 cups hot
  vegetable or chicken stock
30ml/2 tbsp single (light) cream
45ml/3 tbsp dry sherry
50g/2oz/⅔ cup freshly grated
  Parmesan cheese
50g/2oz/⅔ cup chopped
  fresh parsley
salt and ground black pepper

For the vegetables
1 small red (bell) pepper, seeded
1 small green (bell)
  pepper, seeded
25g/1oz/2 tbsp butter
75g/3oz field (portobello)
  mushrooms, sliced
225g/8oz baby courgettes,
  (zucchini) halved
1 onion, halved and sliced
1 garlic clove, crushed

1 Heat half the oil in a frying pan. Add the bacon and heat gently until the fat runs. Increase the heat and fry until crisp, then drain on kitchen paper and set aside.

2 Heat the remaining oil in a heavy pan. Add the rice, stir to coat the grains thoroughly, then ladle in a little of the hot stock. Stir until it has been absorbed. Gradually add the rest of the stock, a ladleful at a time, stirring constantly.

3 Cut the peppers into chunks. Melt the butter in a separate pan and gently fry the peppers, mushrooms, courgettes, onion and garlic for about 4–5 minutes or until the onion is just tender. Season well, then stir in the bacon.

4 When all the stock has been absorbed by the rice, stir in the cream, sherry, Parmesan, parsley and seasoning. Spoon the risotto on to individual plates and top each portion with fried vegetables and bacon. Serve immediately.

Smoked Pancetta Risotto with Broad Beans

This moist risotto makes a satisfying, balanced meal, especially when served with a mixed green salad. Add some fresh herbs and Parmesan shavings as a garnish, if you like.

Serves 4
175g/6oz smoked pancetta or
  streaky (fatty) bacon, diced
350g/12oz/1¾ cups
  risotto rice
1.5 litres/2½ pints/
  6¼ cups simmering
  herb stock
225g/8oz/2 cups frozen baby
  broad (fava) beans
salt and ground black pepper
chopped fresh herbs and
  Parmesan shavings (optional),
  to garnish

1 Place the pancetta or bacon in a non-stick or heavy pan and cook gently, stirring occasionally, for about 5 minutes, until the fat runs out of the meat.

2 Add the risotto rice to the pan and cook for 1 minute, stirring constantly to coat the grains in the fat.

3 Add a ladleful of the simmering stock to the pan and cook, stirring constantly, over a medium heat until the liquid has been absorbed by the rice.

4 Continue adding the simmering stock, a ladleful at a time, until the rice is tender, and almost all the liquid has been absorbed. This will take 30–35 minutes.

5 Meanwhile, cook the broad beans in a pan of lightly salted, boiling water for about 3 minutes until tender. Drain well and stir into the risotto. Season to taste. Spoon into a bowl, garnish with herbs and Parmesan, and serve immediately.

> **Cook's Tip**
> If the broad (fava) beans are large, or if you prefer skinned beans, remove the outer skin after cooking them.

Risotto with Bacon Energy 624kcal/2595kJ; Protein 19g; Carbohydrate 78.4g, of which sugars 7.8g; Fat 24.2g, of which saturates 10g; Cholesterol 49mg; Calcium 228mg; Fibre 3g; Sodium 549mg.
Pancetta Risotto Energy 444kcal/1858kJ; Protein 16.2g; Carbohydrate 77.9g, of which sugars 1.8g; Fat 7.2g, of which saturates 2.1g; Cholesterol 15mg; Calcium 76mg; Fibre 4.4g; Sodium 452mg.

Nasi Goreng

One of the most popular and best-known dishes from Indonesía, this is a marvellous way to use up left-over rice and meats.

Serves 4–6

350g/12oz/1¾ cups basmati rice
(dry weight), cooked and cooled
2 eggs
30ml/2 tbsp water
105ml/7 tbsp sunflower oil
10ml/2 tsp shrimp paste
2–3 fresh red chillies
2 garlic cloves, crushed
1 onion, sliced
225g/8oz fillet (tenderloin) of
pork or beef, cut into strips
115g/4oz cooked, peeled
prawns (shrimp)
225g/8oz cooked chicken, chopped
30ml/2 tbsp dark soy sauce
salt and ground black pepper
deep-fried onions (optional),
to serve

1 Separate the grains of the cooked rice with a fork. Place the rice in a large bowl, cover and set aside. Beat the eggs with the water and seasoning.

2 Heat 15ml/1 tbsp of the oil in a frying pan or wok, pour in about half the egg mixture and cook until set, without stirring. Roll up the omelette, slide it on to a plate, cut into strips and set aside. Make another omelette in the same way.

3 Put the shrimp paste and half the shredded chillies into a food processor or blender. Add the garlic and onion. Process to a smooth paste.

4 Heat the remaining sunflower oil in a wok or large frying pan. Stir-fry the spice paste, without browning, until it releases a spicy aroma.

5 Add the strips of pork or beef and toss the meat over the heat to seal in the juices. Cook the meat in the wok for about 2 minutes, stirring constantly.

6 Add the prawns to the wok, cook for 2 minutes, then add the chicken, rice and soy sauce, with salt and ground black pepper to taste, stirring constantly. Serve in bowls, garnished with omelette strips, shredded chilli and deep-fried onions, if using.

Spicy Lamb and Vegetable Pilaff

Tender lamb is served in this dish with basmati rice and a colourful selection of vegetables and cashew nuts. The dish is presented in cabbage leaf 'bowls'.

Serves 4

450g/1lb boned shoulder of
lamb, cubed
2.5ml/½ tsp dried thyme
2.5ml/½ tsp paprika
5ml/1 tsp garam masala
1 garlic clove, crushed
25ml/1½ tbsp vegetable oil
900ml/1½ pints/3¾ cups stock
large Savoy cabbage leaves,
to serve

For the rice
25g/1oz/2 tbsp butter
1 onion, chopped
1 medium potato, diced
1 carrot, sliced
½ red (bell) pepper, chopped
1 green chilli, seeded
and chopped
115g/4oz/1 cup sliced cabbage
60ml/4 tbsp natural (plain) yogurt
2.5ml/½ tsp ground cumin
5 green cardamom pods
2 garlic cloves, crushed
225g/8oz/generous 1 cup
basmati rice, soaked
and drained
50g/2oz/½ cup cashew nuts
salt and ground black pepper

1 Put the lamb cubes in a large bowl and add the thyme, paprika, garam masala and garlic, with plenty of salt and pepper. Stir, cover, and leave in a cool place for 2–3 hours.

2 Heat the oil in a pan and brown the lamb, in batches, over medium heat for 5–6 minutes. Stir in the stock, cover, and cook for 35–40 minutes. Using a slotted spoon, transfer the lamb to a bowl. Pour the liquid into a measuring jug (cup), topping it up with water if necessary to make 600ml/1 pint/2½ cups.

3 For the rice, melt the butter in a separate pan and fry the onion, potato and carrot for 5 minutes. Add the red pepper and chilli and fry for 3 minutes more, then stir in the cabbage, yogurt, spices, garlic and the reserved lamb stock. Stir well, cover, then simmer gently for 5–10 minutes, until the cabbage has wilted.

4 Stir the rice into the stew with the lamb. Cover and simmer over low heat for 20 minutes or until the rice is cooked. Sprinkle in the cashew nuts and season to taste with salt and pepper. Serve hot, cupped in cabbage leaves.

Nasi Goreng Energy 463kcal/1929kJ; Protein 27.3g; Carbohydrate 49.4g, of which sugars 2.1g; Fat 17.1g, of which saturates 2.7g; Cholesterol 151mg; Calcium 49mg; Fibre 0.5g; Sodium 288mg.
Spicy Pilaff Energy 751kcal/3135kJ; Protein 33.7g; Carbohydrate 86.3g, of which sugars 7.3g; Fat 30.1g, of which saturates 11.6g; Cholesterol 102mg; Calcium 88mg; Fibre 2.3g; Sodium 200mg.

Lamb Parsi

Serve this dish with a dhal or with spiced mushrooms.

Serves 6
900g/2lb lamb fillet, cubed
60ml/4 tbsp ghee or butter
2 onions, sliced
450g/1lb potatoes, cut into chunks
chicken stock or water (see method)
450g/1lb/2⅓ cups basmati rice, soaked
pinch of saffron threads, dissolved in 30ml/2 tbsp warm milk

fresh coriander (cilantro) sprigs, to garnish

For the marinade
475ml/16fl oz/2 cups natural (plain) yogurt
3–4 garlic cloves, crushed
10ml/2 tsp cayenne pepper
20ml/4 tsp garam masala
10ml/2 tsp ground cumin
5ml/1 tsp ground coriander

1 Make the marinade by mixing all the ingredients in a large bowl. Add the meat, stir to coat, then cover and leave for 3–4 hours in a cool place or overnight in the refrigerator.

2 Melt 30ml/2 tbsp of the ghee or butter in a large pan and cook the onions for 6–8 minutes. Transfer to a plate.

3 Melt a further 25ml/1½ tbsp of the ghee or butter in the pan. Cook the lamb, in batches, until brown. When all the lamb is browned, return it to the pan and add the remaining marinade.

4 Stir in the potatoes and add three-quarters of the cooked onions. Pour in stock or water to cover. Bring to the boil, then cover and simmer gently for 40–50 minutes, until the potatoes are cooked. Preheat the oven to 160°C/325°F/Gas 3.

5 Drain the rice. Cook it in a pan of boiling stock or water for 5 minutes. Meanwhile, spoon the lamb mixture into a casserole. Drain the rice and mound it on top of the lamb, then make a hole down the centre. Top with the remaining onions, pour the saffron milk over and dot with the remaining ghee or butter.

6 Cover the pan with a double layer of foil and a lid. Cook in the oven for 30–35 minutes, or until the rice is completely tender. Garnish with fresh coriander sprigs and serve.

Beef Biryani

This popular rice dish makes a delicious meal in itself.

Serves 4
2 large onions
2 garlic cloves, chopped
2.5cm/1in piece fresh root ginger, peeled and roughly chopped
½–1 fresh green chilli, seeded and roughly chopped
bunch of fresh coriander (cilantro)
60ml/4 tbsp flaked (sliced) almonds
30–45ml/2–3 tbsp water
15ml/1 tbsp ghee or butter, plus 25g/1oz/2 tbsp butter, for the rice
45ml/3 tbsp sunflower oil

30ml/2 tbsp sultanas (golden raisins)
500g/1¼lb braising or stewing steak, cubed
5ml/1 tsp ground coriander
15ml/1 tbsp ground cumin
2.5ml/½ tsp ground turmeric
2.5ml/½ tsp ground fenugreek
good pinch of ground cinnamon
175ml/6fl oz/¾ cup natural (plain) yogurt
275g/10oz/1½ cups basmati rice
about 1.2 litres/2 pints/5 cups hot chicken stock or water
salt and ground black pepper
2 hard-boiled eggs, quartered, to garnish
naan bread or chapatis, to serve

1 Roughly chop one onion and place it in a food processor or blender. Add the garlic, ginger, chilli, fresh coriander and half the flaked almonds. Pour in the water and process to a paste.

2 Slice the remaining onion into rings. Heat 75ml/1½ tsp ghee or butter with half the oil in a flameproof casserole and fry the onion rings for 10–15 minutes until golden brown. Transfer to a plate, then fry the remaining flaked almonds until golden and set aside. Fry the sultanas until they swell. Transfer to the plate.

3 Heat 75ml/1½ tsp ghee or butter in the casserole with a further 15ml/1 tbsp of the oil. Fry the meat, in batches, until evenly brown. Transfer to a plate and set aside.

4 Wipe the casserole clean with kitchen paper, heat the remaining oil and pour in the spice paste. Cook over medium heat for 2–3 minutes, stirring, until the mixture browns lightly. Stir in all the spices, season and cook for 1 minute more.

5 Lower the heat, then stir in the yogurt, a little at a time. When it has been incorporated into the spice mixture, return the meat to the casserole. Stir to coat, cover tightly and simmer over low heat for 40–45 minutes until the meat is tender. Soak the rice in a bowl of cold water for 15–20 minutes.

6 Preheat the oven to 160°C/325°F/Gas 3. Drain the rice, place in a pan and add the stock or water, together with a little salt. Bring back to the boil, cover and cook for 5–6 minutes.

7 Drain the rice and pile it in a mound on top of the meat in the casserole. Using the handle of a spoon, make a hole through the rice and meat mixture, to the bottom of the pan. Sprinkle the fried onions, almonds and sultanas over the top and dot with butter. Cover with a double layer of foil and a lid.

8 Cook the biryani in the oven for 30–40 minutes. To serve, spoon the mixture on to a warmed serving plate and garnish with the quartered hard-boiled eggs. Serve with naan bread or chapatis, if you like.

Lamb Parsi Energy 764kcal/3193kJ; Protein 41g; Carbohydrate 81.9g, of which sugars 9.8g; Fat 30.6g, of which saturates 16.1g; Cholesterol 147mg; Calcium 196mg; Fibre 1.5g; Sodium 295mg.
Beef Biryani Energy 778kcal/3240kJ; Protein 40g; Carbohydrate 70.4g, of which sugars 13.4g; Fat 37.4g, of which saturates 11.8g; Cholesterol 94mg; Calcium 164mg; Fibre 2.3g; Sodium 183mg.

Home-made Potato Gnocchi

These classic Italian potato dumplings are very simple to make.

2 eggs, beaten
10ml/2 tsp salt
150–175g/5–6oz/1¼–1½ cups plain (all-purpose) flour

Serves 2
900g/2lb floury potatoes, cut into large chunks

1 Cook the potatoes in salted, boiling water for 15 minutes, until tender. Drain well and return to the pan, set it over low heat and dry the potatoes for 1–2 minutes.

2 Mash the potatoes until smooth, then gradually stir in the beaten eggs and salt. Work in enough flour to form a soft dough.

3 Break off small pieces of the dough and roll into balls about the size of a walnut, using floured hands. Press the back of a fork into each ball to make indentations. Repeat the process until all the dough has been used. Leave the gnocchi to rest for 15–20 minutes before cooking.

4 Bring a large pan of water to a gentle boil. Add the gnocchi, about ten at a time, and cook for 3–4 minutes, or until they float to the surface. Drain and serve.

Semolina and Pesto Gnocchi

These gnocchi are cooked rounds of semolina paste, which taste wonderful with a home-made tomato sauce.

60ml/4 tbsp finely chopped sun-dried tomatoes
50g/2oz/¼ cup butter
75g/3oz/1 cup freshly grated Pecorino cheese

Serves 4–6
750ml/1¼ pints/3 cups milk
200g/7oz/generous 1 cup semolina
45ml/3 tbsp pesto sauce

2 eggs, beaten
freshly grated nutmeg
salt and ground black pepper
tomato sauce, to serve
basil, to garnish

1 Heat the milk in a large pan. When it is on the point of boiling, sprinkle in the semolina, stirring constantly until the mixture is smooth and thick. Simmer for 2 minutes.

2 Remove from the heat and stir in the pesto and tomatoes, with half the butter and half the Pecorino. Add the eggs, with nutmeg, and season. Spoon on to a shallow baking dish to a depth of 1cm/½in and level the surface. Leave to cool, then chill.

3 Preheat the oven to 190°C/375°F/Gas 5. Lightly grease a shallow baking dish. Using a 4cm/1½in pastry cutter, stamp out as many rounds as possible from the semolina pasta.

4 Place the leftover paste on the base of the dish and arrange the rounds on top in overlapping circles. Melt the remaining butter and brush it over the gnocchi. Sprinkle over the remaining Pecorino. Bake for 30–40 minutes until golden. Serve with tomato sauce and garnish with basil.

Potato Gnocchi with Tomato Sauce

Gnocchi make a substantial and tasty alternative to pasta. In this dish they are served with a very simple, but delicious, fresh tomato and butter sauce.

75g/3oz/¾ cup plain (all-purpose) flour, plus extra for dusting
60ml/4 tbsp finely chopped fresh parsley, to garnish
salt

Serves 4
675g/1½lb floury potatoes
2 egg yolks

For the sauce
25g/1oz/2 tbsp butter, melted
450g/1lb plum tomatoes, peeled, seeded and chopped

1 Preheat the oven to 200°C/400°F/ Gas 6. Scrub the potatoes, then bake them in their skins in the preheated oven for about 1 hour or until the flesh feels soft when pricked with a fork or skewer.

2 While the potatoes are still warm, cut them in half and gently squeeze out the flesh into a bowl, or use a spoon to scrape the flesh out of the shells. Mash the potato well, then season with a little salt. Add the egg yolks and mix lightly with a fork or spoon.

3 Add the flour to the potato mixture and mix to a form a rough dough. Place on a floured work surface and knead for 5 minutes until the dough is smooth and elastic. Shape the dough into small thumb-sized shapes by making long rolls and cutting them into segments. Press each of these with the back of a fork to give a ridged effect. Place the gnocchi on a floured work surface.

4 Preheat the oven to 140°C/275°F/Gas 1. Cook the gnocchi in small batches in barely simmering, slightly salted water for about 10 minutes. Remove with a slotted spoon, drain well and transfer into a dish. Cover and keep hot in the oven.

5 To make the sauce, heat the butter in a small pan for 1 minute, then add the tomatoes and cook over low heat until the juice starts to run. Sprinkle the gnocchi with chopped parsley and serve with the sauce.

Home-made Energy 687kcal/2916kJ; Protein 22.2g; Carbohydrate 140.5g, of which sugars 7.2g; Fat 8.1g, of which saturates 2.2g; Cholesterol 190mg; Calcium 179mg; Fibre 7.2g; Sodium 2087mg.
Semolina Gnocchi Energy 560kcal/2348kJ; Protein 25.8g; Carbohydrate 47.8g, of which sugars 9g; Fat 31.1g, of which saturates 15.3g; Cholesterol 159mg; Calcium 566mg; Fibre 1.1g; Sodium 484mg.
Potato Gnocchi Energy 278kcal/1174kJ; Protein 6.9g; Carbohydrate 45.3g, of which sugars 6g; Fat 9g, of which saturates 4.4g; Cholesterol 114mg; Calcium 57mg; Fibre 3.4g; Sodium 72mg.

Spiced Pumpkin Gnocchi

Pumpkin adds a sweet richness to these spicy potato gnocchi, which are superb on their own or served with meat.

Serves 4

450g/1lb pumpkin, peeled, seeded and chopped
450g/1lb potatoes, boiled
2 egg yolks
200g/7oz/1¾ cups plain (all-purpose) flour, plus more if necessary and extra for dusting
pinch of ground allspice
1.5ml/¼ tsp cinnamon
pinch of freshly grated nutmeg
finely grated rind of ½ orange

salt and ground black pepper
75ml/5 tbsp chopped fresh parsley, to garnish
50g/2oz/½ cup Parmesan cheese, freshly grated, to serve

For the sauce
30ml/2 tbsp olive oil
1 shallot, finely chopped
175g/6oz/2½ cups fresh chanterelles, sliced, or 15g/½oz/½ cup dried, soaked in warm water for 20 minutes, then drained
10ml/2 tsp almond butter
150ml/¼ pint/⅔ cup crème fraîche

1 Wrap the pumpkin in foil and bake at 180°C/350°F/Gas 4 for 30 minutes. Pass the pumpkin and cooked potatoes through a food mill into a bowl. Add the egg yolks, flour, spices, orange rind and seasoning and mix well to make a soft dough. If the mixture is too loose, add a little flour to stiffen it.

2 To make the sauce, heat the oil in a pan and fry the shallot until soft. Add the chanterelles and cook briefly, then add the almond butter. Stir to melt and stir in the crème fraîche. Simmer briefly, add the parsley and season to taste. Keep hot.

3 Flour a work surface. Spoon the gnocchi dough into a piping (pastry) bag fitted with a 1cm/1/2in plain nozzle. Pipe on to the flour to make a 15cm/6in sausage. Roll it in flour and cut crossways into 2.5cm/1in pieces. Repeat. Mark each piece lightly with a fork and drop into a pan of fast boiling salted water.

4 The gnocchi are done when they rise to the surface, after 3–4 minutes. Lift them out, drain and turn into bowls. Spoon the sauce over, sprinkle with Parmesan and parsley, and serve immediately.

Spinach and Ricotta Gnocchi

The success of this Italian dish lies in not overworking the mixture, to achieve delicious, light mouthfuls. Gnocchi is more usually made with semolina, or with potato that has been boiled and then put through a ricer, so this is quite an unusual recipe. The spinach not only gives the gnocchi great flavour, but the intense colour looks good, especially on white plates.

Serves 4

900g/2lb fresh spinach
350g/12oz/1½ cups ricotta cheese
60ml/4 tbsp freshly grated Parmesan cheese, plus extra to serve
3 eggs, beaten
1.5ml/¼ tsp grated nutmeg
45–60ml/3–4 tbsp plain (all-purpose) flour, plus extra for dusting
115g/4oz/½ cup butter, melted
salt and ground black pepper

1 Place the spinach in a large pan and cook for 5 minutes, until wilted. Leave to cool slightly, then squeeze out as much water as possible from the spinach.

2 Place the spinach in a food processor or blender. Process to a purée, then transfer to a bowl.

3 Add the ricotta, Parmesan, eggs and nutmeg. Season with salt and pepper and mix together. Add enough flour to make the mixture into a soft dough.

4 Remove from the bowl and place on a clean surface that has been lightly dusted with flour. Using your hands, shape the rolls into sausage shapes, each about 7.5cm/3in long, then dust lightly with flour.

5 Bring a large pan of salted water to the boil. Gently slide the gnocchi into the water and cook for 1–2 minutes, until they float to the surface.

6 Remove the gnocchi with a slotted spoon and transfer to a warmed dish. Pour over the melted butter and toss to coat, then sprinkle with Parmesan cheese. Serve immediately, with extra Parmesan in a separate bowl, if you like.

Pumpkin Gnocchi Energy 553kcal/2317kJ; Protein 15.6g; Carbohydrate 61.7g, of which sugars 5.9g; Fat 28.8g, of which saturates 14.7g; Cholesterol 156mg; Calcium 299mg; Fibre 4.5g; Sodium 166mg.
Spinach Gnocchi Energy 566kcal/2342kJ; Protein 24.2g; Carbohydrate 15.2g, of which sugars 6.4g; Fat 45.7g, of which saturates 26.4g; Cholesterol 251mg; Calcium 545mg; Fibre 5.1g; Sodium 651mg.

Broccoli and Chilli Spaghetti

The contrast between the chilli and the mild broccoli is delicious and goes perfectly with spaghetti.

Serves 4
350g/12oz dried spaghetti

450g/1lb broccoli, cut into
  small florets
150ml/¼ pint/⅔ cup garlic-
  infused olive oil
1 fat red chilli, seeded and
  finely chopped
salt and ground black pepper

1 Bring a large pan of lightly salted water to the boil. Add the spaghetti and broccoli and cook for 8–10 minutes, until both are tender. Drain thoroughly.

2 Using the back of a fork, crush the broccoli roughly, taking care not to mash the spaghetti strands at the same time.

3 Meanwhile, warm the oil and finely chopped chilli in a small pan over low heat and cook very gently for 5 minutes.

4 Pour the chilli and oil over the spaghetti and broccoli and toss together. Season to taste and serve immediately.

Italian Cold Pasta

Egg noodles are dressed with garlic, parsley and oil. Serve for lunch or supper.

Serves 4
250g/9oz dried egg noodles
30–60ml/2–4 tbsp extra virgin
  olive oil

3 garlic cloves, finely chopped
60–90ml/4–6 tbsp/¼–⅓ cup
  roughly chopped fresh parsley
25–30 pitted green olives, sliced
  or roughly chopped
salt

1 Cook the noodles in salted boiling water as directed on the packet, or until just tender. Drain and rinse under cold water.

2 Place the pasta in a bowl, then add the oil, garlic, parsley and olives and toss together. Chill overnight before serving.

Warm Pasta with Basil Tomatoes

It does not matter which type of pasta you use for this recipe – any kind in the kitchen will work well. It tastes marvellous with wheatfree rice noodles or long strands of spaghetti.

Serves 4
6 small ripe tomatoes, halved
45ml/3 tbsp extra virgin olive oil
a small handful of fresh
  basil leaves, torn
450g/1lb dried pasta
salt and ground black pepper

1 Put the tomatoes in a bowl and gently squash them until the juices run. Stir in the oil and basil. Season and mix well to combine. Cover the bowl with clear film (plastic wrap) and chill for 2–3 hours to allow the flavours to develop.

2 Cook the pasta according to the packet instructions. Let the tomato mixture come to room temperature. Drain the pasta, toss with the tomato mixture and serve immediately.

Pansotti with Walnut Sauce

Walnuts and cream make a great sauce for stuffed pasta.

Serves 4
90g/3½oz/scant 1 cup shelled
  walnuts or walnut pieces

60ml/4 tbsp garlic-flavoured oil
120ml/4fl oz/½ cup double
  (heavy) cream
350g/12oz fresh cheese and
  herb-filled pansotti
salt and ground black pepper

1 Put the walnuts and garlic oil in a food processor or blender and process to a paste, adding a little warm water to slacken the consistency. Spoon the mixture into a bowl and add the cream. Mix well, then season with salt and black pepper.

2 Cook the stuffed pasta according to the instructions on the packet. Meanwhile, put the walnut sauce in a large warmed bowl and add a ladleful of the pasta water to thin it.

3 Drain the pasta and transfer it into the bowl of walnut sauce. Toss well, then serve immediately.

Spaghetti Energy 396kcal/1678kJ; Protein 17.3g; Carbohydrate68.3g, of which sugars 6g; Fat 7.9g, of which saturates 0.8g; Cholesterol 0mg; Calcium 114mg; Fibre 5.6g; Sodium 24mg.
Cold Pasta Energy 352kcal/1476kJ; Protein 8.6g; Carbohydrate 45.3g, of which sugars 1.6g; Fat 16.4g, of which saturates 3.1g; Cholesterol 19mg; Calcium 86mg; Fibre 4.2g; Sodium 1244mg.
Warm Pasta Energy 552kcal/2336kJ; Protein 16.3g; Carbohydrate 96.9g, of which sugars 8.3g; Fat 13.8g, of which saturates 2g; Cholesterol 0mg; Calcium 65mg; Fibre 5.5g; Sodium 19mg.
Pansotti Energy 702kcal/2931kJ; Protein 14.3g; Carbohydrate 66.1g, of which sugars 4g; Fat 44.1g, of which saturates 13g; Cholesterol 41mg; Calcium 58mg; Fibre 3.3g; Sodium 11mg.

Pasta with Mushrooms

Slow-cooking a mixture of mushrooms, sun-dried tomatoes and garlic together with white wine and stock makes a rich and well-flavoured pasta sauce. Serve with warm ciabatta.

Serves 4

15g/¹/₂oz dried porcini
  mushrooms
120ml/4fl oz/¹/₂ cup hot water
2 cloves garlic, finely chopped
2 large pieces drained sun-dried
  tomato in olive oil, sliced
120ml/4fl oz/¹/₂ cup dry
  white wine
120ml/4fl oz/¹/₂ cup
  vegetable stock
225g/8oz/2 cups brown cap
  (cremini) mushrooms, sliced
450g/1lb/4 cups dried short
  pasta shapes, such as ruote,
  penne, fusilli or eliche
1 handful fresh flat leaf parsley,
  roughly chopped
salt and ground black pepper
rocket (arugula) and/or
  fresh flat leaf parsley,
  to garnish

1 Put the dried porcini mushrooms in a large bowl. Pour over the hot water and leave to soak for 15 minutes.

2 While the porcini mushrooms are soaking, put the garlic, tomatoes, wine, stock and brown cap mushrooms into the ceramic cooking pot and switch the slow cooker to high.

3 Transfer the porcini mushrooms into a sieve (strainer) set over a bowl, then squeeze them with your hands to release as much liquid as possible. Reserve the soaking liquid. Chop the porcini finely. Add the liquid and the chopped porcini to the ceramic cooking pot, and cover the slow cooker with the lid. Cook on high for 1 hour, stirring halfway through cooking time to make sure that the mushrooms cook evenly.

4 Switch the slow cooker to the low setting and cook for a further 1–2 hours, until the mushrooms are tender.

5 Cook the pasta in boiling salted water for 10 minutes, or according to the instructions on the packet. Drain the pasta and transfer it into a large bowl. Stir the parsley into the mushroom sauce and season with salt and pepper. Add the sauce to the pasta and toss well. Serve garnished with rocket and/or parsley.

Tagliatelle with Vegetable Ribbons

Narrow strips of courgette and carrot mingle well with tagliatelle to resemble coloured pasta. Serve with freshly grated Parmesan cheese handed around separately. Children may prefer grated Cheddar or Edam cheese.

Serves 4

2 large courgettes (zucchini)
2 large carrots
250g/9oz fresh egg tagliatelle
60ml/4 tbsp garlic-flavoured
  olive oil
salt and ground black pepper
freshly grated Parmesan cheese,
  to serve

1 Using a vegetable peeler, cut the courgettes and carrots into long thin ribbons.

2 Bring a large pan of lightly salted water to the boil, and then add the courgette and carrot ribbons. Bring the water back to the boil and blanch the vegetables for 30 seconds, then remove the courgettes and carrots with a slotted spoon and set them aside in a bowl.

3 Bring the water back to boiling point and cook the pasta for 3 minutes. Drain well and return it to the pan.

4 Add the vegetable ribbons, garlic-flavoured oil and seasoning and toss over medium to high heat until the pasta and vegetables are glistening with oil. Serve immediately with Parmesan cheese.

Variation
For a more substantial dish, try adding four bacon rashers (strips) that have been grilled (broiled) until crispy. Crumble the rashers on to the pasta before serving.

Cook's Tip
Garlic-flavoured olive oil is used in this dish. Flavoured oils, such as chilli or basil, are a quick and easy way of adding flavour to pasta dishes.

Tagliatelle Energy 397kcal/1663kJ; Protein 11.5g; Carbohydrate 52.4g, of which sugars 8.3g; Fat 17.1g, of which saturates 3.3g; Cholesterol 19mg; Calcium 80mg; Fibre 4.8g; Sodium 127mg.
Pasta with Mushrooms Energy 420kcal/1787kJ; Protein 15.1g; Carbohydrate 84.9g, of which sugars 5.1g; Fat 2.6g, of which saturates 0.3g; Cholesterol 0 mg; Calcium 61mg; Fibre 4.8g; Sodium 14mg.

Pasta with Slowly Cooked Onions, Cabbage, Parmesan and Pine Nuts

This is an unusual, but quite delicious, way of serving pasta. Cavolo nero, also known as Tuscan black cabbage, is a close relative of curly kale, with long leaves and a spicy flavour.

Serves 4
25g/1oz/2 tbsp butter
15ml/1 tbsp extra virgin olive oil, plus extra for drizzling (optional)
500g/1¼lb Spanish (Bermuda) onions, halved and thinly sliced
5–10ml/1–2 tsp balsamic vinegar
400–500g/14oz–20oz cavolo nero, spring greens (collards), kale or Brussels sprout tops, shredded
400–500g/14–20oz dried pasta, such as penne or fusilli
75g/3oz/1 cup freshly grated Parmesan cheese
50g/2oz/1½ cup pine nuts, toasted
salt and ground black pepper

1 Heat the butter and olive oil together in a large pan. Stir in the onions, cover and cook very gently, stirring occasionally, for about 20 minutes, until very soft.

2 Uncover, and continue to cook gently, until the onions have turned golden yellow. Add the balsamic vinegar and season well, then cook for a further 1–2 minutes. Set aside.

3 Blanch the cavolo nero, spring greens, kale or Brussels sprout tops in boiling, lightly salted water for about 3 minutes. Drain well and add to the onions, then cook over low heat for 3–4 minutes.

4 Cook the pasta in boiling, lightly salted water for about 8–12 minutes, or according to the packet instructions, until just tender. Drain, then add to the pan of onions and greens and toss thoroughly to mix.

5 Season well with salt and pepper and stir in half the Parmesan. Transfer the pasta to warmed plates. Sprinkle the pine nuts and more Parmesan on top and serve immediately, offering more olive oil for drizzling over to taste.

Pasta Bows with Mushrooms

Buckwheat, mushrooms and bow-shaped pasta are combined in the classic Jewish dish of kasha.

Serves 4–6
25g/1oz dried well-flavoured mushrooms, such as ceps
500ml/17fl oz/2¼ cups boiling stock or water
45ml/3 tbsp rendered chicken fat or vegetable oil, or 40g/1½oz/3 tbsp butter
3–4 onions, thinly sliced
250g/9oz/3 cups mushrooms, sliced
300g/11oz/1½ cups whole, coarse, medium or fine buckwheat
200g/7oz pasta bows
salt and ground black pepper

1 Put the dried mushrooms in a bowl, pour over half the boiling stock or water and leave to stand for 20–30 minutes, until reconstituted. Remove the mushrooms from the liquid, then strain and reserve the liquid.

2 Heat the chicken fat, oil or butter in a frying pan, add the onions and fry for 5–10 minutes until softened. Remove the onions to a plate, then add the sliced mushrooms to the pan and fry briefly. Add the soaked mushrooms and cook for 2–3 minutes. Return the onions to the pan and set aside.

3 In a large, heavy frying pan, toast the buckwheat over high heat for 2–3 minutes, stirring. Reduce the heat.

4 Stir the remaining boiling stock or water and the reserved mushroom soaking liquid into the buckwheat, cover the pan, and cook for about 10 minutes until the buckwheat is just tender and the liquid has been absorbed.

5 Meanwhile, cook the pasta according to the packet instructions, then drain. When the kasha is cooked, toss in the onions and mushrooms, and the pasta. Season and serve hot.

> **Variation**
> To cook kasha without mushrooms, omit both kinds and simply add all of the boiling stock in step 4.

Pasta Bows Energy 364kcal/1529kJ; Protein 10.3g; Carbohydrate 67g, of which sugars 4g; Fat 7.3g, of which saturates 3.6g; Cholesterol 14mg; Calcium 47mg; Fibre 2.2g; Sodium 48mg.
Pasta with Onions Energy 662kcal/2780kJ; Protein 25.7g; Carbohydrate 87.6g, of which sugars 13.5g; Fat 25.7g, of which saturates 8.4g; Cholesterol 32mg; Calcium 494mg; Fibre 8.3g; Sodium 269mg.

Linguine with Rocket

This fashionable lunch is very quick and easy to make at home. Rocket has an excellent peppery flavour that combines beautifully with the Parmesan cheese, but watercress leaves, which have a similar peppery taste, could be used in place of the rocket.

Serves 4
350g/12oz dried linguine
120ml/4fl oz/½ cup extra virgin
  olive oil
1 large bunch rocket (arugula),
  about 150g/5oz, stalks
  removed, shredded
75g/3oz/1 cup freshly grated
  Parmesan cheese
salt and ground black pepper

1 Cook the pasta in a large pan of lightly salted boiling water for 10–12 minutes, then drain thoroughly.

2 Heat about 60ml/4 tbsp of the olive oil in the pasta pan, then add the drained pasta and rocket. Toss over medium heat for 1–2 minutes, or until the rocket is just wilted, then remove the pan from the heat.

3 Transfer the pasta and rocket to a large warmed bowl. Add half the freshly grated Parmesan and the remaining olive oil to the bowl and mix well to combine. Add a little salt and black pepper to taste.

4 Toss the mixture quickly to mix all the flavours together and ensure the pasta is well coated with the oil. Serve immediately, sprinkled with the remaining Parmesan.

Cook's Tips
• Linguine is an egg pasta and looks rather like flattened strands of spaghetti.
• Dried pasta cooks in 10–12 minutes, but an even faster result can be obtained by using fresh pasta. Simply add it to a large pan of boiling, lightly salted water, making sure that all the strands are fully submerged, and cook for 2–3 minutes. The pasta is ready when it rises to the top of the pan and is tender to the taste, with a slight firmness in the centre.

Pasta with Pesto, Potatoes and Green Beans

This is one of the traditional ways to serve pesto in Liguria. Although the combination of pasta and potatoes may seem odd, it is delicious with the rich pesto sauce.

Serves 4
50g/2oz/½ cup pine nuts
2 large garlic cloves, chopped
90g/3½oz fresh basil leaves, plus
  a few extra leaves
90ml/6 tbsp extra virgin olive oil
  (use a mild Ligurian or French oil)
50g/2oz/⅔ cup freshly grated
  Parmesan cheese
40g/1½oz/½ cup freshly grated
  Pecorino cheese

For the pasta mixture
275g/10oz waxy potatoes,
  thickly sliced or cut into
  1cm/½in cubes
200g/7oz fine green beans
350g/12oz dried trenette,
  linguine, tagliatelle
  or tagliarini
salt and ground black pepper

To serve
extra virgin olive oil
pine nuts, toasted
Parmesan cheese, grated

1 Toast the pine nuts in a dry frying pan until golden. Place in a mortar with the garlic and a pinch of salt, and crush with a pestle. Add the basil and add a little oil as you work the mixture to a paste. Add the Parmesan and Pecorino and the remaining oil.

2 Bring a pan of lightly salted water to the boil and add the potatoes. Cook for 10–12 minutes, until tender. Add the green beans to the pan for the last 5–6 minutes of cooking.

3 Meanwhile, cook the pasta in boiling salted water for 8–12 minutes, or according to the packet instructions, until just tender. Times vary according to the pasta shapes.

4 Drain the pasta and potatoes and beans. Place in a large, warmed bowl and toss with two-thirds of the pesto. Season with black pepper and sprinkle extra basil leaves over the top.

5 Serve immediately with the rest of the pesto, extra olive oil, pine nuts and grated Parmesan.

Linguine with Rocket Energy 573kcal/2404kJ; Protein 19g; Carbohydrate 65.4g, of which sugars 3.5g; Fat 28g, of which saturates 6.9g; Cholesterol 19mg; Calcium 311mg; Fibre 3.3g; Sodium 260mg.
Pasta with Pesto Energy 658kcal/2760kJ; Protein 20g; Carbohydrate 78.6g, of which sugars 5.9g; Fat 31.5g, of which saturates 5.8g; Cholesterol 13mg; Calcium 240mg; Fibre 5.7g; Sodium 154mg.

Rustic Buckwheat Pasta and Fontina Cheese Bake

This bake is a deliciously spicy combination of nutty-flavoured buckwheat pasta, vegetables and Fontina cheese.

Serves 6

2 potatoes, cubed
225g/8oz/2 cups buckwheat
    pasta shapes, such as spirals
275g/10oz/2½ cups Savoy
    cabbage, shredded
45ml/3 tbsp olive oil, plus extra
    for greasing
1 onion, chopped
2 leeks, sliced
2 garlic cloves, chopped
175g/6oz/2½ cups brown cap
    (cremini) mushrooms, sliced
5ml/1 tsp caraway seeds
5ml/1 tsp cumin seeds
150ml/¼ pint/⅔ cup
    vegetable stock
150g/5oz/1¼ cups Fontina
    cheese, diced
25g/1oz/¼ cup walnuts,
    roughly chopped
salt and ground black pepper

1 Preheat the oven to 200°C/400°F/Gas 6 and oil a deep baking dish. Cook the potatoes in boiling, salted water for 8–10 minutes until tender, then drain and set aside.

2 Meanwhile, cook the pasta in boiling, salted water until it is only just cooked and is still very al dente. Add the cabbage in the last minute of cooking time. Drain, then rinse under cold running water.

3 Heat the olive oil in a large heavy pan and fry the onion and leeks over medium heat for 5–8 minutes, stirring frequently, until softened.

4 Add the garlic and mushrooms to the pan and cook for a further 3 minutes until tender, stirring occasionally. Stir in the spices and cook for 1 minute, stirring.

5 Add the cooked potatoes, pasta and cabbage and stir to combine, then season well. Spoon the mixture into the baking dish. Pour the stock over the vegetables, then sprinkle with the cheese and walnuts. Bake for 15 minutes or until the cheese is melted and bubbling. Serve immediately.

Fettucine all'Alfredo

This simple recipe was invented by a Roman restaurateur called Alfredo, who became famous for serving it with a gold fork and spoon. Since those heady days it has become one of the most popular pasta dishes around.

Serves 4

50g/2oz/¼ cup butter
200ml/7fl oz/scant 1 cup double
    (heavy) cream
50g/2oz/⅔ cup freshly grated
    Parmesan cheese, plus extra
    to serve
350g/12oz fresh fettucine
salt and ground black pepper

1 Melt the butter in a large pan. Add the cream and bring it to the boil. Simmer for 5 minutes, stirring constantly, then add the Parmesan, with salt and ground black pepper to taste, and turn off the heat under the pan.

2 Bring a large pan of lightly salted water to the boil over high heat. Add the pasta and cook for about 3 minutes, or until the fresh fettucine rises to the surface.

3 Turn the heat under the pan of cream to low. Drain the cooked pasta and add it to the pan all at once. Toss until it is coated in the sauce. Taste for seasoning and stir in more salt and pepper if needed. Serve immediately, with extra Parmesan cheese handed around separately.

Cook's Tip
A few drops of oil, added to the pan of water in which the fettucine is cooking, will help to prevent it from boiling over.

Variation
The original recipe for fettucine all'Alfredo did not contain cream, so the version above is already a slight variation on the traditional one. Some cooks add a little cream cheese, which thickens the coating sauce, or even some mashed blue cheese, such as Gorgonzola.

Buckwheat Pasta Energy 328kcal/1379kJ; Protein 11.5g; Carbohydrate 40.1g, of which sugars 6.1g; Fat 14.6g, of which saturates 4.6g; Cholesterol 18mg; Calcium 141mg; Fibre 3.9g; Sodium 374mg.
Fettucine Energy 697kcal/2912kJ; Protein 16.3g; Carbohydrate 65.8g, of which sugars 3.8g; Fat 42.8g, of which saturates 26g; Cholesterol 108mg; Calcium 199mg; Fibre 2.6g; Sodium 226mg.

Spaghetti with Raw Tomato and Ricotta Sauce

This straightforward pasta dish is ideal for a midweek family meal as it requires minimal preparation time and effort yet has delicious results. It is rich in plum tomatoes, which are high in vitamin A, vitamin C, potassium and iron.

Serves 4
500g/1¼ lb ripe Italian
  plum tomatoes
75ml/5 tbsp garlic-flavoured
  olive oil
350g/12oz dried spaghetti or
  pasta of your choice
115g/4oz ricotta cheese, diced
salt and ground black pepper

1 Coarsely chop the plum tomatoes, removing the cores and as many of the seeds as you can.

2 Put the tomatoes and oil in a bowl, adding salt and pepper to taste, and stir well. Cover and leave at room temperature for 1–2 hours to let the flavours mingle.

3 Cook the spaghetti in a large pan of water according to the packet instructions, then drain well.

4 Taste the sauce to check the seasoning before tossing it with the hot pasta, adding more salt and pepper if necessary. Sprinkle the diced cheese over the pasta and serve immediately.

Variation
This sauce goes well with many different kinds of pasta, both long strands such as spaghetti, tagliatelle or linguini, and short shapes such as macaroni, rigatoni or penne.

Cook's Tip
This dish is always at its best in summer when made with rich, sweet plum tomatoes that have ripened on the vine in the sun and have their fullest flavour.

Cheat's Lasagne with Mushrooms

This simple-to-assemble vegetarian version of lasagne requires neither baking nor the lengthy preparation of various sauces and fillings, but is no less delicious.

Serves 4
40g/1½oz/⅔ cup dried porcini
  mushrooms
50ml/2fl oz/¼ cup olive oil
1 large garlic clove, chopped
375g/13oz/5 cups mixed
  mushrooms, including brown
cap (cremini), field, shiitake and
  wild varieties, roughly sliced
175ml/6fl oz/¾ cup dry
  white wine
90ml/6 tbsp canned
  chopped tomatoes
2.5ml/½ tsp sugar
8 fresh lasagne sheets
40g/1½oz/½ cup freshly grated
  Parmesan cheese
salt and ground black pepper
fresh basil leaves, to garnish

1 Place the porcini mushrooms in a heatproof bowl and cover with boiling water. Set aside to soak for 15 minutes, then drain and rinse.

2 Heat the olive oil in a large frying pan and sauté the soaked mushrooms over high heat for 5 minutes until the edges are slightly crisp. Reduce the heat, then add the garlic and fresh mushrooms, and sauté for a further 5 minutes until tender, stirring occasionally.

3 Add the wine and cook for 5–7 minutes until reduced. Stir in the tomatoes, sugar and seasoning and cook over medium heat for about 5 minutes until thickened.

4 Meanwhile, cook the lasagne according to the instructions on the packet until it is al dente. Drain lightly – the pasta should still be moist.

5 To serve, spoon a little of the sauce on to each of four warm serving plates. Place a sheet of lasagne on top and spoon a quarter of the remaining mushroom sauce over each serving. Sprinkle with some Parmesan and top with another pasta sheet. Sprinkle with black pepper and more Parmesan and garnish with basil leaves.

Spaghetti Energy 496kcal/2087kJ; Protein 14g; Carbohydrate 69.6g, of which sugars 7.7g; Fat 19.9g, of which saturates 4.9g; Cholesterol 12mg; Calcium 31mg; Fibre 3.8g; Sodium 14mg.
Cheat's Lasagne Energy 331kcal/1397kJ; Protein 13.3g; Carbohydrate 47.7g, of which sugars 3.2g; Fat 7.9g, of which saturates 2.7g; Cholesterol 10mg; Calcium 147mg; Fibre 3.1g; Sodium 119mg.

Black Pasta with Squid Sauce

Tagliatelle flavoured with squid ink is sure to be a big hit with your family or dinner party guests because it looks amazing and tastes deliciously of the sea.

Serves 4

105ml/7 tbsp olive oil
2 shallots, chopped
3 garlic cloves, crushed
45ml/3 tbsp chopped
  fresh parsley
675g/1½lb cleaned squid, cut
  into rings and rinsed
150ml/¼ pint/⅔ cup dry
  white wine
400g/14oz can
  chopped tomatoes
2.5ml/½ tsp dried chilli flakes
  or powder
450g/1lb squid ink tagliatelle
salt and ground black pepper

1 Heat the oil in a pan and add the shallots. Cook for about 5 minutes, stirring frequently, until pale golden.

2 Add the garlic to the pan and cook for 3 minutes. When the garlic colours a little, stir in 30ml/2 tbsp of the chopped parsley.

3 Add the squid pieces to the pan and stir again. Cook for about 3–4 minutes, stirring, then add the wine and bring to simmering point.

4 Add the tomatoes and chilli flakes and season with salt and pepper. Cover and simmer gently for about 1 hour, until the squid is tender. Add more water if necessary.

5 Cook the pasta in plenty of boiling, salted water, according to the instructions on the packet, or until al dente. Drain and return the tagliatelle to the pan. Add the squid sauce and mix well. Sprinkle each serving with the remaining chopped parsley and serve immediately.

Cook's Tip
Watch out for squid ink pasta in good Italian delicatessens or in many large supermarkets.

Linguine with Anchovy Fillets and Capers

This is a fantastic recipe that can be made from ingredients that are often found in the kitchen. Serve with a rocket salad mixed with a lemon dressing for maximum impact.

Serves 4

450g/1lb dried linguine
8 anchovy fillets, drained
75ml/5 tbsp garlic-infused olive oil
30ml/2 tbsp salted capers,
  thoroughly rinsed and drained
salt and ground black pepper

1 Cook the linguine in plenty of salted, boiling water according to the instructions on the packet.

2 Meanwhile, finely chop the anchovy fillets and place in a small pan with the garlic-infused olive oil and some black pepper. Heat very gently for 5 minutes, stirring occasionally, until the anchovies start to disintegrate.

3 Drain the pasta and toss thoroughly with the anchovies, garlic-infused oil and capers. Season with a little salt and plenty of ground black pepper to taste. Divide between warmed bowls and serve immediately.

Cook's Tips
• Use salted capers if you can find them, as they have a better flavour than the bottled ones, but remember that you need to rinse them thoroughly before using.
• Be sure to chop the anchovy fillets finely so that they 'melt' into the sauce.

Variation
If you prefer, you can use fresh garlic rather than the garlic-infused olive oil for this dish. Peel and crush 1 large garlic clove or 2 smaller ones and add to the pan with the anchovy fillets in step 2.

Black Pasta Energy 738kcal/3112kJ; Protein 40.8g; Carbohydrate 90.2g, of which sugars 8.1g; Fat 24.6g, of which saturates 3.7g; Cholesterol 380mg; Calcium 88mg; Fibre 5.1g; Sodium 204mg.
Linguine Energy 516kcal/2176kJ; Protein 14.5g; Carbohydrate 83.4g, of which sugars 3.7g; Fat 16.1g, of which saturates 2.3g; Cholesterol 2mg; Calcium 40mg; Fibre 3.3g; Sodium 151mg.

Farfalle in Tomato Sauce with Tuna and Olives

This quick and easy pasta dish requires the minimum of effort but still tastes great. Serve it as a quick supper dish that will be enjoyed by all the family. Add a garnish of fresh oregano to this dish if you happen to have some.

Serves 4
400g/14oz/3½ cups dried farfalle
600ml/1 pint/2½ cups ready-made tomato sauce
8–10 pitted black olives, cut into rings
175g/6oz can tuna steak in olive oil
salt and ground black pepper

1 Cook the pasta in a large pan of lightly salted boiling water according to the instructions on the packet. Meanwhile, heat the tomato sauce in a separate pan until bubbling, and then stir in the black olive rings.

2 Drain the canned tuna and flake it with a fork. Add the tuna to the sauce with about 60ml/4 tbsp of the hot water used for cooking the pasta. Taste and adjust the seasoning.

3 Drain the pasta thoroughly and transfer it into a large, warmed serving bowl. Pour the tuna sauce over the top and toss lightly to mix. Serve immediately.

Variation
A variety of herbs can be added to simple pasta dishes like this one – choose from basil, marjoram or oregano – and use fresh herbs, as the short cooking time does not allow the flavour of dried herbs to develop fully.

Cook's Tip
Store-bought tomato sauce and canned tuna are endlessly versatile for making weekday suppers. Keep a supply in your kitchen for when you want a simple but tasty meal.

Pasta with Clams

This sensational dish is rather like paella made with pasta – just as nice, and a great deal easier. The milky flesh of clams contrasts wonderfully with the firmer pasta and fennel.

Serves 4–6
30ml/2 tbsp olive oil
1 large Spanish (Bermuda) onion, chopped
1 garlic clove, finely chopped
2 large ripe tomatoes
750ml/1¼ pint/3 cups fish stock
1kg/2¼lb clams, cleaned
120ml/4fl oz/½ cup anis spirit, such as Ricard or Pernod
120ml/4fl oz/½ cup dry white wine
juice of ¼ lemon
300g/11oz spaghetti, broken into 5cm/2in lengths
1 fennel bulb, sliced in thin strips
30ml/2 tbsp chopped fresh parsley
salt and ground black pepper
fennel fronds or fresh dill, to garnish

1 Heat the oil in a casserole big enough to contain all the ingredients. Fry the onion gently until soft. Add the garlic.

2 Put the tomatoes in a bowl, pour over boiling water and leave for 10 minutes. Peel the tomatoes on a plate and discard the seeds. Chop the flesh, add to the casserole and strain the tomato juices into the pan. Cook until reduced to a pulp, then add 250ml/8fl oz/1 cup of the stock.

3 Discard any open or cracked clams. Add the rest to the pan in three batches. As they open, remove most from the shells and transfer to a plate. Discard any clams that remain shut.

4 Add the anis spirit and white wine to the sauce, plus the remaining fish stock and lemon juice, to taste. Add the pasta and sliced fennel. Season and simmer, partially covered, for 10 minutes. Stir occasionally to separate the strands.

5 When the pasta is cooked, stir in the parsley and check the seasoning. Add the clams across the top and cover tightly. Leave to stand for 10 minutes, so the clams warm through and all the liquid is absorbed. Serve in bowls, sprinkled with the fennel fronds or dill.

Farfalle with Tuna Energy 459kcal/1949kJ; Protein 25.2g; Carbohydrate 78.6g, of which sugars 7.8g; Fat 7.1g, of which saturates 1.1g; Cholesterol 22mg; Calcium 53mg; Fibre 4.2g; Sodium 756mg.
Pasta Energy 358kcal/1501kJ; Protein 20.8g; Carbohydrate 45.2g, of which sugars 7g; Fat 5.4g, of which saturates 0.8g; Cholesterol 56mg; Calcium 104mg; Fibre 3.9g; Sodium 1014mg.

Spaghetti with Salmon and Prawns

This is a lovely, fresh-tasting pasta dish, perfect for an outdoor meal in the garden in summer. Serve it as a main course lunch with warm Italian bread and dry white wine.

Serves 4
300g/11oz salmon fillet
200ml/7fl oz/scant 1 cup dry white wine
a few fresh basil sprigs, plus extra basil leaves, to garnish
6 ripe Italian plum tomatoes, peeled and finely chopped
150ml/¼ pint/⅔ cup double (heavy) cream
350g/12oz/3 cups fresh or dried spaghetti
115g/4oz/⅔ cup peeled cooked prawns (shrimp), thawed and thoroughly dried if frozen
salt and ground black pepper

1 Put the salmon, skin side up, in a wide shallow pan. Pour over the wine, then add the basil. Sprinkle the fish with salt and pepper. Bring the wine to the boil, cover the pan and simmer gently for 5 minutes. Lift the fish out of the pan and set it aside to cool a little.

2 Add the tomatoes and cream to the liquid remaining in the pan and bring to the boil. Stir well, then reduce the heat and simmer, uncovered, for 10–15 minutes. Meanwhile, cook the pasta according to the instructions on the packet.

3 Flake the fish into large chunks, discarding the skin and any bones. Add the fish to the sauce with the prawns, shaking the pan until they are well coated. Check the seasoning.

4 Drain the pasta and put it in a warmed bowl. Pour the sauce over the pasta and toss to combine. Serve immediately, garnished with fresh basil leaves.

Cook's Tip
Check the salmon fillet carefully for small bones when you are flaking the flesh. Although the salmon is already filleted, you will always find a few stray 'pin' bones. Pick them out carefully using tweezers or your fingertips.

Lobster Ravioli

Use home-made pasta to obtain the delicacy of flavour that this superb filling deserves.

Serves 4
1 lobster, about 450g/1lb, cooked and taken out of the shell, cut into chunks
2 soft white bread slices, torn into small pieces, crusts removed
250ml/8fl oz/1 cup fish stock, made with the lobster shell
1 egg
250ml/8fl oz/1 cup double (heavy) cream
15ml/1 tbsp chopped fresh chives, plus extra to garnish
15ml/1 tbsp chopped fresh chervil
salt and ground white pepper

For the pasta dough
225g/8oz/2 cups plain (all-purpose) flour, plus extra for dusting
2 eggs, plus 2 egg yolks

For the mushroom sauce
a large pinch of saffron threads
25g/1oz/2 tbsp butter
2 shallots, finely chopped
200g/7oz/3 cups button (white) mushrooms, finely chopped
juice of ½ lemon
200ml/7fl oz/scant 1 cup double (heavy) cream

1 Make the pasta dough. Sift the flour with a pinch of salt. Put into a food processor with the eggs and extra yolks; process until it resembles coarse breadcrumbs. Turn out on to a floured surface; knead to a smooth dough. Wrap and chill for 1 hour.

2 Meanwhile, make the filling. Place the lobster meat in a bowl. Soak the bread pieces in 45ml/3 tbsp of the fish stock. Place in a food processor with half the egg and 30–45ml/2–3 tbsp of the cream and process until smooth. Stir into the lobster meat, then add the chives and chervil and seasoning.

3 Roll the ravioli dough to a thickness of 3mm/⅛in. Divide the dough into four rectangles and dust each rectangle lightly with flour. Spoon six heaps of filling on to a pasta sheet, leaving 3cm/1¼in between heaps. Lightly beat the remaining egg with a tablespoon of water and brush it over the pasta between the piles of filling. Cover with a second pasta sheet. Repeat with the other two sheets of pasta and remaining filling.

4 Press the top layer of dough down between the filling. Cut between the heaps with a 7.5cm/3in fluted pastry (cookie) cutter to make 12 ravioli. Place on a baking sheet, cover and chill.

5 Make the mushroom sauce. Soak the saffron in 15ml/1 tbsp warm water. Melt the butter in a pan and cook the shallots over low heat until soft. Add the mushrooms and lemon juice and cook until almost all the liquid has evaporated. Stir in the saffron, with its soaking water, and the cream, then cook gently, stirring occasionally, until the sauce has thickened. Keep warm.

6 In another pan, bring the remaining fish stock to the boil, stir in the rest of the cream and bubble until it thickens. Season and keep warm. Bring a large pan of salted water to a the boil. Drop in the ravioli and cook for 3–4 minutes, until just tender.

7 Place three ravioli on warmed serving plates, spoon over a little mushroom sauce and pour a ribbon of fish sauce around the edge. Serve immediately, garnished with chopped and whole fresh chives.

Spaghetti 701kcal/2941kJ; Protein 32.4g; Carbohydrate 70.4g, of which sugars 8.5g; Fat 30.6g, of which saturates 14.3g; Cholesterol 145mg; Calcium 94mg; Fibre 4.1g; Sodium 115mg.
Lobster Ravioli Energy 652kcal/2722kJ; Protein 23g; Carbohydrate 52.2g, of which sugars 3.1g; Fat 40.5g, of which saturates 22.2g; Cholesterol 361mg; Calcium 186mg; Fibre 2.9g; Sodium 298mg.

Seafood Lasagne

Choose the seafood for this dish based on the occasion.

Serves 8
350g/12oz monkfish
350g/12oz salmon fillet
350g/12oz smoked haddock
1 litre/1³/₄ pints/4 cups milk
500ml/17fl oz/2¹/₄ cups fish stock
2 bay leaves or a good pinch of
 saffron threads
1 small onion, halved
75g/3oz/6 tbsp butter, plus extra
 for greasing
45ml/3 tbsp plain (all-purpose) flour

150g/5oz/2 cups mushrooms, sliced
225–300g/8–11oz no pre-cook
 or fresh lasagne
60ml/4 tbsp grated Parmesan
salt, ground black pepper, grated
 nutmeg and paprika
rocket (arugula) leaves, to garnish

For the tomato sauce
30ml/2 tbsp olive oil
1 red onion, finely chopped
1 garlic clove, finely chopped
400g/14oz can chopped tomatoes
15ml/1 tbsp tomato purée (paste)
15ml/1 tbsp torn fresh basil leaves

1 Make the sauce. Heat the oil in a pan and fry the onion and garlic for 5 minutes, until soft. Stir in the tomatoes and purée and simmer for 20–30 minutes. Season and add the basil.

2 Put all the fish in a shallow flameproof dish or pan with the milk, stock, bay leaves or saffron and onion. Bring to the boil over medium heat; poach for 5 minutes, until almost cooked. Cool slightly, then place on a board. Strain the liquid and reserve it. Remove skin and any bones, then flake the fish.

3 Preheat the oven to 180°C/350°F/Gas 4. Melt the butter in a pan and stir in the flour. Cook for 2 minutes, stirring. Add the poaching liquid and bring to the boil. Add the mushrooms and cook for 2–3 minutes. Season with salt, pepper and nutmeg.

4 Grease a shallow ovenproof dish. Spread a thin layer of the mushroom sauce into the base. Stir the fish into the remaining sauce in the pan. Make a layer of lasagne, then a layer of fish and sauce. Add a layer of lasagne, then spread over all the tomato sauce. Continue, finishing with a layer of fish and sauce.

5 Top with Parmesan cheese and bake for 30–45 minutes, until bubbling. Sprinkle with paprika and garnish with rocket.

Smoked Trout Cannelloni

Cannelloni usually has a meat and tomato filling, or one based on spinach and ricotta cheese. Smoked trout makes a delicious change in this version.

Serves 4–6
1 large onion, finely chopped
1 garlic clove, crushed
60ml/4 tbsp vegetable stock
2 x 400g/14oz cans
 chopped tomatoes
2.5ml/¹/₂ tsp dried mixed herbs
1 smoked trout, about 400g/14oz,
 or 225g/8oz fillets

75g/3oz/¹/₂ cup frozen
 peas, thawed
75g/3oz/1¹/₂ cups fresh
 breadcrumbs
16 no pre-cook cannelloni tubes
25ml/1¹/₂ tbsp freshly grated
 Parmesan cheese
salt and ground black pepper

For the sauce
25g/1oz/2 tbsp butter
25g/1oz/¹/₄ cup plain
 (all-purpose) flour
350ml/12fl oz/1¹/₂ cups
 skimmed milk
freshly grated nutmeg

1 Put the onion, garlic clove and stock in a large pan. Cover and simmer for 3 minutes. Remove the lid and cook until the stock has reduced entirely.

2 Stir in the tomatoes and dried herbs. Simmer uncovered for 10 minutes, or until the mixture is very thick.

3 Skin the trout and flake the flesh, discarding any bones. Put the fish in a bowl and add the tomato mixture, peas and breadcrumbs. Mix well, then season with salt and pepper.

4 Spoon the filling into the cannelloni tubes and arrange them in an ovenproof dish. Preheat the oven to 190°C/375°F/Gas 5.

5 Make the sauce. Put the butter, flour and milk into a pan and cook over medium heat, whisking constantly, until the sauce thickens. Simmer for 2–3 minutes, stirring all the time. Season to taste with salt, freshly ground black pepper and grated nutmeg.

6 Pour the sauce over the stuffed cannelloni and sprinkle with the grated Parmesan cheese. Bake for 30–45 minutes, or until the top is golden and bubbling. Serve immediately.

Smoked Trout Energy 410kcal/1735kJ; Protein 23.4g; Carbohydrate 62.3g, of which sugars 12g; Fat 9.3g, of which saturates 2.1g; Cholesterol 21mg; Calcium 186mg; Fibre 4.5g; Sodium 919mg.
Seafood Lasagne Energy 411kcal/1724kJ; Protein 32.2g; Carbohydrate 29.8g, of which sugars 3.6g; Fat 18.9g, of which saturates 7.8g; Cholesterol 71mg; Calcium 143mg; Fibre 1.9g; Sodium 525mg.

Mixed Meat Cannelloni

Try to keep all the chopped stuffing ingredients the same size. Ready prepared cannelloni tubes have been used to make life simple.

Serves 4–8
60ml/4 tbsp olive oil
1 onion, finely chopped
1 carrot, finely chopped
2 garlic cloves, finely chopped
2 ripe tomatoes, peeled and
   finely chopped
2.5ml/½ tsp dried thyme
150g/5oz raw chicken livers
   or cooked stuffing
150g/5oz raw pork or cooked
   ham, gammon (smoked or
   cured ham) or sausage

250g/9oz raw or cooked chicken
25g/1oz/2 tbsp butter
5ml/1 tsp fresh thyme
30ml/2 tbsp brandy
90ml/6 tbsp crème fraîche or
   double (heavy) cream
16 no pre-cook cannelloni tubes
75g/3oz/1 cup grated fresh
   Parmesan cheese
salt and ground black pepper
green salad, to serve

For the white sauce
50g/2oz/¼ cup butter
50g/2oz/½ cup plain
   (all-purpose) flour
900ml/1½ pints/3¾ cups milk
fresh nutmeg, to taste

1 Heat the oil in a frying pan, and cook the onion, carrot, garlic and tomatoes, stirring, for 10 minutes until very soft. Chop the meats, keeping the fresh and cooked meat apart.

2 Add the butter, then the raw meat, to the centre of the frying pan and cook until coloured. Then add the remaining meats and sprinkle first with thyme, then with the brandy. Stir, then warm through and reduce the liquid. Pour in the crème fraîche or cream, season and leave to simmer for 10 minutes.

3 Preheat the oven to 190°C/375°F/Gas 5. Make the white sauce. Melt the butter in a pan, add the flour and cook, stirring, for 1–2 minutes. Gradually stir in the milk and simmer, stirring until the sauce is smooth. Grate in nutmeg, and then season.

4 Spoon a little sauce into a baking dish. Fill the cannelloni with the meat and arrange in a single layer. Pour over the remaining sauce, sprinkle with Parmesan, and bake for 35–40 minutes, or until tender. Leave for 10 minutes and serve with a green salad.

Creamy Pasta with Eggs and Bacon

This Italian classic, flavoured with pancetta and a garlic and egg sauce, is popular worldwide. It makes a great last-minute supper.

Serves 4
30ml/2 tbsp olive oil
1 small onion, finely chopped
1 large garlic clove, crushed

8 pancetta or rindless smoked
   streaky (fatty) bacon rashers
   (strips), cut into 1cm/½in strips
350g/12oz fresh or dried spaghetti
4 eggs
90–120ml/6–8 tbsp/½ cup
   crème fraîche
60ml/4 tbsp grated Parmesan
   cheese, plus extra to serve
salt and ground black pepper

1 Heat the oil in a large pan, add the onion and garlic and fry gently for about 5 minutes until softened.

2 Add the pancetta or bacon to the pan and cook for about 10 minutes, stirring frequently until evenly browned.

3 Meanwhile, cook the spaghetti in a large pan of salted boiling water according to the instructions on the packet until al dente.

4 Put the eggs, crème fraîche and grated Parmesan in a bowl. Stir in plenty of black pepper, then beat together well.

5 Drain the pasta thoroughly, transfer it into the pan with the pancetta or bacon and toss well to mix.

6 Turn off the heat under the pan, then immediately add the egg mixture and toss thoroughly so that it cooks lightly and coats the pasta.

7 Season to taste, then divide the spaghetti among four warmed bowls and sprinkle with ground black pepper. Serve immediately, with extra grated Parmesan handed separately.

Variation
You can replace the crème fraîche with either double (heavy) cream or sour cream, if you prefer.

Meat Cannelloni Energy 480kcal/2014kJ; Protein 27.4g; Carbohydrate 40.5g, of which sugars 8.9g; Fat 23.5g, of which saturates 11.4g; Cholesterol 148mg; Calcium 282mg; Fibre 1.9g; Sodium 473mg.
Pasta with Eggs Energy 535kcal/2257kJ; Protein 31.7g; Carbohydrate 66g, of which sugars 4g; Fat 18.1g, of which saturates 6.6g; Cholesterol 241mg; Calcium 165mg; Fibre 3.2g; Sodium 838mg.

Pasta with Hare and Mushrooms

This is a rich dish of hare, wine and mushrooms, flavoured with herbs and pine nuts.

Serves 6

800g/1¾lb hare meat and bone (the front legs and rib end)
200ml/7fl oz/scant 1 cup red wine
120–150ml/4–5fl oz/½–⅔ cup olive oil
150g/5oz smoked bacon lardons, or diced pancetta
2 onions, chopped
2 fat garlic cloves, finely chopped
8 baby (pearl) onions, peeled
4 carrots, diced
4 chicken thighs, halved along the bone and seasoned
seasoned plain (all-purpose) flour, for dusting
350g/12oz small open cap mushrooms
600ml/1 pint/2½ cups stock
5ml/1 tsp dried thyme
1 bay leaf
250g/9oz dried lasagne sheets
90ml/6 tbsp chopped parsley
30ml/2 tbsp pine nuts
salt and ground black pepper

1 Starting at least two days ahead, cut the hare into portions and put in a bowl. Pour over the red wine and 15ml/1 tbsp of the oil and leave in the refrigerator for at least 24 hours.

2 Heat 30ml/2 tbsp olive oil in a flameproof casserole, add the bacon or pancetta, chopped onion and garlic and fry until the onion is softened. Halfway through add the whole baby onions and diced carrots, and continue cooking, stirring occasionally.

3 Heat 45ml/3 tbsp oil in a large frying pan and fry the seasoned chicken pieces on both sides until golden brown. Transfer to the casserole.

4 Remove the hare from the red wine marinade, reserving the liquid. Blot the meat well on kitchen paper and dredge with the seasoned flour until well coated. Add more oil to the frying pan, if necessary, and fry the meat on all sides until browned.

5 Meanwhile, reserve eight of the smallest open cap mushrooms. Quarter the remaining mushrooms and add to the casserole. Continue cooking the hare in the frying pan, stirring every now and then, until browned.

6 When the hare is ready, arrange the pieces in the casserole. Pour the reserved marinade into the frying pan to deglaze it, then pour the juices into the casserole. Add the stock, dried thyme and bay leaf and season with salt and pepper. Cook over low heat for about 1½ hours, until the meat is tender. Leave to cool completely.

7 When ready to serve, bring plenty of water to the boil in a large roasting pan with 5ml/1 tsp salt and 15ml/1 tbsp oil. Break up the lasagne sheets and spread out the pieces in the pan. Cook for 7–8 minutes until soft, moving the pieces around to prevent them from sticking.

8 Remove all the meat from the bones and return the meat to the casserole with 60ml/4 tbsp of the parsley. Bring to a simmer. Stir the drained pasta into the sauce. Heat 15ml/1 tbsp oil in a small pan and fry the reserved mushrooms, then arrange them on top. Sprinkle with the remaining parsley and the pine nuts, and serve.

Pappardelle with Rabbit

This rich-tasting dish is ideal for entertaining as the sauce can be kept warm in the slow cooker until needed.

Serves 4

15g/½oz dried porcini mushrooms
150ml/¼ pint/⅔ cup warm water
1 small onion
½ carrot
½ celery stick
2 bay leaves
25g/1oz/2 tbsp butter or 15ml/1 tbsp olive oil
40g/1½oz pancetta or rindless streaky (fatty) bacon, chopped
15ml/1 tbsp roughly chopped fresh flat leaf parsley, plus extra to garnish
250g/9oz boneless rabbit meat
60ml/4 tbsp dry white wine
200g/7oz can chopped plum tomatoes or 200ml/7fl oz/ scant 1 cup passata (bottled strained tomatoes)
300g/11oz fresh or dried pappardelle
salt and ground black pepper

1 Put the dried mushrooms in a bowl, pour over the warm water and leave to soak for 15 minutes. Finely chop the vegetables, either in a food processor or by hand. Tear each bay leaf, so they will release their flavour when added to the sauce.

2 Heat the butter or oil in a frying pan until just sizzling. Add the vegetables, pancetta or bacon and the parsley and cook for 5 minutes. Add the rabbit and fry on both sides for 3–4 minutes. Transfer the mixture to the ceramic cooking pot and switch to high or auto. Add the wine and tomatoes or passata.

3 Drain the mushrooms and add the soaking liquid into the slow cooker. Chop the mushrooms and add to the mixture, with the bay leaves. Season to taste and stir well, cover with the lid and cook for 1 hour. Reduce the setting to low or leave on auto, and cook for a further 2 hours, or until the meat is tender.

4 Lift out the rabbit pieces, cut them into bitesize chunks and stir them back into the sauce. Remove and discard the bay leaves. Taste the sauce and season as necessary. The sauce is now ready, but can be kept hot in the cooker for 1–2 hours.

5 Cook the pasta according to the packet instructions. Drain and mix into the sauce. Serve sprinkled with parsley.

Pappardelle with Rabbit Energy 393kcal/1653kJ; Protein 23g; Carbohydrate 46g, of which sugars 4.9g; Fat 13.3g, of which saturates 5g; Cholesterol 46mg; Calcium 80mg; Fibre 1.1g; Sodium 128mg.
Pasta with Hare Energy 589kcal/2464kJ; Protein 42.4g; Carbohydrate 38g, of which sugars 7g; Fat 28.3g, of which saturates 6.2g; Cholesterol 152mg; Calcium 75mg; Fibre 3.5g; Sodium 430mg.

Sweet and Hot Vegetable Noodles

This noodle dish has the colour of fire, but only the mildest suggestion of heat. Ginger and plum sauce give it its fruity flavour.

Serves 4

130g/4½oz dried rice noodles
30ml/2 tbsp groundnut
   (peanut) oil
2.5cm/1in piece fresh root ginger,
   sliced into thin batons
1 garlic clove, crushed
130g/4½oz drained canned
   bamboo shoots, sliced in batons
2 medium carrots, sliced in batons

130g/4½oz/1½ cups beansprouts
1 small white cabbage, shredded
30ml/2 tbsp nam pla
30ml/2 tbsp soy sauce
30ml/2 tbsp plum sauce
10ml/2 tsp sesame oil
15ml/1 tbsp palm sugar
   (jaggery) or light muscovado
   (brown) sugar
juice of ½ lime
90g/3½oz mooli (daikon), sliced
   into thin batons
small bunch fresh coriander
   (cilantro), chopped
60ml/4 tbsp sesame
   seeds, toasted

1 Cook the noodles in a large pan of boiling water, following the instructions on the packet. Meanwhile, heat the oil in a wok or large frying pan and stir-fry the ginger and garlic together for 2–3 minutes over medium heat, until golden.

2 Drain the noodles and keep warm. Add the bamboo shoots to the wok, increase the heat to high and stir-fry for 5 minutes. Add the carrots, beansprouts and cabbage and stir-fry for a further 5 minutes, until they are beginning to char at the edges.

3 Stir in the sauces, sesame oil, sugar and lime juice. Add the mooli and coriander, toss to mix, and serve with the noodles in warmed bowls, sprinkled with toasted sesame seeds.

Cook's Tip
Use a large, sharp knife for shredding cabbage. Remove any tough outer leaves, if necessary, then cut the cabbage into quarters. Cut off and discard the hard core from each quarter, place flat side down, then slice the cabbage very thinly to make fine shreds.

Teriyaki Soba Noodles with Tofu and Asparagus

There is no need to buy ready-made teriyaki sauce as it is so easy to prepare at home using ingredients that are now readily available in supermarkets.

Serves 4

350g/12oz soba noodles
30ml/2 tbsp toasted sesame oil
200g/7oz asparagus tips
30ml/2 tbsp groundnut (peanut)
   or vegetable oil
225g/8oz block of tofu

2 spring onions (scallions),
   cut diagonally
1 carrot, cut into matchsticks
2.5ml/½ tsp chilli flakes
15ml/1 tbsp sesame seeds
salt and ground black pepper

For the teriyaki sauce
60ml/4 tbsp dark soy sauce
60ml/4 tbsp Japanese sake or
   dry sherry
60ml/4 tbsp mirin
5ml/1 tsp caster (superfine) sugar

1 Cook the noodles according to the instructions on the packet, then drain and rinse under cold running water. Set aside.

2 Heat the sesame oil in a griddle (grill) pan or in a baking tray placed under the grill (broiler) until very hot. Turn down the heat to medium, then cook the asparagus for 8–10 minutes, turning frequently, until tender and browned. Set aside.

3 Meanwhile, heat the groundnut or vegetable oil in a wok or large frying pan until very hot. Add the tofu and fry for 8–10 minutes until golden, turning it occasionally to crisp all sides. Carefully remove from the wok or pan and leave to drain on kitchen paper. Cut the tofu into 1cm/½in slices.

4 To prepare the teriyaki sauce, mix all the ingredients together, then heat the mixture in the wok or frying pan.

5 Toss in the noodles and stir to coat them in the sauce. Heat through for 1–2 minutes, then spoon into warmed individual serving bowls with the tofu and asparagus. Sprinkle the spring onions and carrot on top and sprinkle with the chilli flakes and sesame seeds. Season well and serve immediately.

Sweet Noodles Energy 368kcal/1530kJ; Protein 8.8g; Carbohydrate 45.8g, of which sugars 17.6g; Fat 16.5g, of which saturates 2.3g; Cholesterol 0mg; Calcium 200mg; Fibre 6.2g; Sodium 650mg.
Teriyaki Noodles Energy 794kcal/3356kJ; Protein 28g; Carbohydrate 135g, of which sugars 22.9g; Fat 19.5g, of which saturates 1.8g; Cholesterol 145mg; Calcium 155mg; Fibre 4.5g; Sodium 3278mg.

Noodles in Coconut Sauce

When everyday vegetables are given the Thai treatment, the result is a delectable dish that everyone is certain to enjoy.

Serves 4–6
30ml/2 tbsp sunflower oil
1 lemon grass stalk,
    finely chopped
15ml/1 tbsp Thai red curry paste
1 onion, thickly sliced
3 courgettes (zucchini),
    thickly sliced
115g/4oz Savoy cabbage,
    thickly sliced

2 carrots, thickly sliced
150g/5oz broccoli, stem sliced
    and head separated into florets
2 x 400ml/14fl oz cans
    coconut milk
475ml/16fl oz vegetable stock
150g/5oz dried egg noodles
15ml/1 tbsp Thai fish sauce
30ml/2 tbsp soy sauce
60ml/4 tbsp chopped fresh
    coriander (cilantro)

For the garnish
2 lemon grass stalks
1 bunch fresh coriander (cilantro)
8–10 small fresh red chillies

1 Heat the oil in a large pan or wok. Add the lemon grass and red curry paste and stir-fry for 2–3 seconds. Add the onion and cook over medium heat, stirring occasionally, for about 5–10 minutes, until the onion has softened but not browned.

2 Add the courgettes, cabbage, carrots and slices of broccoli stem. Toss the vegetables with the onion mixture. Reduce the heat and cook gently, stirring occasionally, for 5 minutes.

3 Increase the heat to medium, stir in the coconut milk and vegetable stock and bring to the boil. Add the broccoli florets and the noodles, then simmer gently for 20 minutes.

4 Meanwhile, make the garnish. Split the lemon grass stalks lengthways. Gather the coriander into a small bouquet and lay it on a platter, following the curve of the rim. Tuck the lemon grass halves into the bouquet and add chillies to resemble flowers.

5 Stir the fish sauce, soy sauce and chopped coriander into the noodle mixture. Spoon on to the platter, taking care not to disturb the herb bouquet, and serve immediately.

Buckwheat Noodles with Goat's Cheese

When you don't feel like doing a lot of cooking, try this good fast supper dish. Buckwheat is free from gluten so it is an excellent choice for anyone trying to avoid wheat. The earthy flavour of buckwheat goes well with the nutty, peppery taste of rocket leaves, offset by the deliciously creamy and tangy goat's cheese.

Serves 4
350g/12oz buckwheat noodles
50g/2oz butter
4 shallots, sliced
2 garlic cloves, finely chopped
75g/3oz hazelnuts,
    lightly roasted and
    roughly chopped
large handful rocket
    (arugula) leaves
175g/6oz goat's cheese
salt and ground black pepper

1 Cook the noodles in a large pan of boiling water until they are just tender, or according to the instructions on the packet. Drain well.

2 Heat the butter in a large frying pan. Add the shallots and cook for 2 minutes, stirring all the time, until they begin to soften and colour.

3 Add the chopped garlic to the pan and cook for about 2–3 minutes, stirring constantly.

4 Add the hazelnuts to the pan and fry for about 1 minute. Add the rocket leaves and, when they start to wilt, toss in the noodles and heat through.

5 Season well with salt and ground black pepper. Crumble the goat's cheese into the noodles and serve immediately in warmed bowls.

Variation
If you can't find any rocket (arugula), use the same amount of watercress. It has a similar peppery taste to the rocket.

Noodles Energy 293kcal/1235kJ; Protein 8.9g; Carbohydrate 44.7g; of which sugars 17.3g; Fat 10g; of which saturates 2.1g; Cholesterol 11mg; Calcium 131mg; Fibre 4.2g; Sodium 1007mg.
Buckwheat Noodles Energy 418kcal/1736kJ; Protein 14.4g; Carbohydrate 15g, of which sugars 2.8g; Fat 33.9g, of which saturates 15.2g; Cholesterol 67mg; Calcium 97mg; Fibre 2.2g; Sodium 342mg.

Stir-fried Noodles in Seafood Sauce with Asparagus

Recent discoveries along the Yellow River suggest that the Chinese were enjoying noodles made from millet some 4000 years ago! This dish features egg noodles with crab meat, asparagus and spring onions in a tasty seafood sauce.

Serves 4

225g/8oz Chinese egg noodles
8 spring onions (scallions),
    trimmed
8 asparagus spears, plus extra
    steamed asparagus spears,
    to serve
5cm/2in piece fresh root
    ginger, peeled
30ml/2 tbsp stir-fry oil
3 garlic cloves, chopped
60ml/4 tbsp oyster sauce
450g/1lb cooked crab meat
    (all white, or two-thirds white
    and one-third brown)
30ml/2 tbsp rice wine vinegar
15–30ml/1–2 tbsp light
    soy sauce

1 Put the egg noodles in a large pan, cover with lightly salted boiling water, cover and leave to simmer for 3–4 minutes, or for the time suggested on the packet. Drain well, transfer into a bowl and set aside.

2 Cut off the green spring onion tops and slice them thinly. Set aside. Cut the white parts into 2cm/¾in lengths and quarter them lengthways. Cut the asparagus spears on the diagonal into 2cm/¾in pieces, and slice the piece of fresh root ginger into very fine matchsticks.

3 Heat the stir-fry oil in a pan or wok until very hot, then add the ginger, garlic and white spring onion batons. Stir-fry over high heat for 1 minute.

4 Add the oyster sauce, crab meat, rice wine vinegar and soy sauce to taste. Stir-fry for about 2 minutes, until the crab meat and the sauce are hot. Add the noodles to the pan and toss until heated through.

5 At the last moment, toss in the spring onion tops and serve with a few extra asparagus spears.

Noodles with Sun-dried Tomatoes and Prawns

This noodle dish works particularly well with thin somen noodles.

Serves 4

350g/12oz somen noodles
45ml/3 tbsp olive oil
20 uncooked king prawns (jumbo
    shrimp), peeled and deveined
2 garlic cloves, finely chopped
45–60ml/3–4 tbsp sun-dried
    tomato purée (paste)
salt and ground black pepper

For the garnish

handful of basil leaves
30ml/2 tbsp sun-dried tomatoes
    in oil, drained and cut into strips

1 Cook the noodles in a large pan of boiling water until tender, following the directions on the packet. Drain well.

2 Heat half the oil in a large frying pan. Add the prawns and garlic and fry them over medium heat for 3–5 minutes, until the prawns turn pink and are firm to the touch.

3 Stir in 15ml/1 tbsp of the sun-dried tomato purée and mix well. Using a slotted spoon, transfer the prawns to a bowl and keep hot.

4 Reheat the oil remaining in the pan. Stir in the rest of the oil with the remaining sun-dried tomato purée. You may need to add a spoonful of water if the mixture is very thick.

5 When the mixture starts to sizzle, toss in the noodles. Add salt and pepper to taste and mix well. Return the prawns to the pan and toss to combine. Serve immediately garnished with basil and strips of sun-dried tomatoes.

Cook's Tip
Ready-made sun-dried tomato purée (paste) is readily available, however you can make your own simply by processing bottled sun-dried tomatoes with their oil. You can also add a couple of anchovy fillets and some capers, if you like.

Stir-fried Noodles Energy 385kcal/1622kJ; Protein 28.5g; Carbohydrate 45.9g, of which sugars 6.4g; Fat 10.9g, of which saturates 2.2g; Cholesterol 98mg; Calcium 167mg; Fibre 2.4g; Sodium 1233mg.
Noodles Energy 481kcal/2026kJ; Protein 19.2g; Carbohydrate 67.4g, of which sugars 2.9g; Fat 16.8g, of which saturates 1.6g; Cholesterol 98mg; Calcium 62mg; Fibre 2.8g; Sodium 99mg.

Noodles with Tomatoes, Sardines and Mustard

Serve this simple but delectable dish hot or at room temperature. The tomatoes and mustard are the perfect partner for the oily sardines.

Serves 4

350g/12oz broad egg noodles
60ml/4 tbsp olive oil
30ml/2 tbsp lemon juice
15ml/1 tbsp wholegrain mustard
1 garlic clove, finely chopped
225g/8oz ripe tomatoes,
  roughly chopped
1 small red onion, finely chopped
1 green (bell) pepper, seeded
  and finely diced
225g/8oz canned sardines
60ml/4 tbsp chopped
  fresh parsley
salt and ground black pepper
croûtons, made from 2 slices of
  bread, to serve (optional)

1 Cook the noodles in a large pan of boiling water for about 5–8 minutes until just tender, or follow the instructions on the packet. Drain well.

2 Meanwhile, to make the dressing, whisk the olive oil, lemon juice, wholegrain mustard and garlic in a small bowl with salt and ground black pepper to taste.

3 Transfer the drained noodles into a large bowl and toss with the dressing until the noodles are evenly coated.

4 Add the tomatoes, red onion and green pepper to the noodles and toss lightly to combine with the noodles.

5 Drain the can of sardines and add the fish to the noodles with the fresh parsley and toss lightly again. Season to taste and serve with crisp croûtons, if using.

> **Cook's Tip**
> It is useful to always have a can of sardines in the kitchen cupboard so you can prepare this fuss-free meal.

Seafood Laksa with Fish, Seafood and Fennel

Authentic laksa is spicy but cooled by the coconut milk.

Serves 4–5

3 fresh red chillies, seeded
4–5 garlic cloves
5ml/1 tsp mild paprika
10ml/2 tsp shrimp paste
25ml/1½ tbsp chopped fresh
  root ginger or galangal
250g/9oz small red shallots
25g/1oz fresh coriander (cilantro),
  with roots intact
45ml/3 tbsp groundnut
  (peanut) oil
5ml/1 tsp fennel seeds, crushed
2 fennel bulbs, cut into thin wedges
600ml/1 pint/2½ cups fish stock
300g/11oz thin vermicelli
  rice noodles
450ml/¾ pint/scant 2 cups
  coconut milk
juice of 1–2 limes
30–45ml/2–3 tbsp Thai fish sauce
450g/1lb firm white fish fillet,
  such as monkfish or snapper
450g/1lb large raw prawns (jumbo
  shrimp), shelled and deveined
small bunch of fresh basil
2 spring onions (scallions), sliced

1 Process the chillies, garlic, paprika, shrimp paste, ginger or galangal and two shallots to a paste in a food processor, blender or spice grinder. Remove the roots and stems from the coriander and add to the paste; chop and reserve the leaves. Add 15ml/1 tbsp of the oil and process until fairly smooth.

2 Heat the remaining oil in a large pan. Add the remaining shallots and the fennel seeds and wedges. Cook until lightly browned. Add 45ml/3 tbsp of the paste and stir-fry for about 1–2 minutes. Pour in the fish stock and bring to the boil. Reduce the heat and simmer for 8–10 minutes. Meanwhile, cook the noodles according to the packet instructions. Drain.

3 Add the coconut milk and the juice of one lime to the pan of shallots. Stir in 30ml/2 tbsp of the fish sauce. Bring to a simmer. Cut the fish into chunks and add to the pan. Cook for 2–3 minutes, then add the prawns and cook until pink. Chop most of the basil and add to the pan with the coriander.

4 Place the noodles in serving bowls. Ladle in the stew. Top with spring onions and the remaining basil leaves and serve.

Noodles Energy 603kcal/2533kJ; Protein 25.4g; Carbohydrate 69.8g, of which sugars 8g; Fat 26.9g, of which saturates 5.3g; Cholesterol 63mg; Calcium 353mg; Fibre 4.4g; Sodium 592mg.
Seafood Laksa Energy 524kcal/2199kJ; Protein 43.1g; Carbohydrate 65.1g, of which sugars 6.3g; Fat 10.1g, of which saturates 2g; Cholesterol 233mg; Calcium 162mg; Fibre 1.9g; Sodium 356mg.

Udon Pot

This noodle dish makes a substantial main meal, packed with lots of chunky, fresh vegetables, chicken pieces and large prawns.

Serves 4

350g/12oz dried udon noodles
1 large carrot, cut into
    bitesize chunks
225g/8oz chicken breast fillets or
    thighs, skinned and cut into
    bitesize pieces
8 raw king prawns (jumbo
    shrimp), peeled and deveined
4–6 Chinese leaves (Chinese
    cabbage), cut into short strips

8 shiitake mushrooms,
    stems removed
50g/2oz mangetouts (snow peas),
    topped and tailed
1.5 litres/2½ pints/6¼ cups
    chicken stock or instant
    bonito stock
30ml/2 tbsp mirin
soy sauce, to taste
1 bunch spring onions (scallions),
    finely chopped, 30ml/2 tbsp
    grated fresh root ginger, lemon
    wedges, and extra soy sauce,
    to serve

1 Cook the udon noodles until just tender in boiling water, following the instructions on the packet. Drain well, rinse under cold water and drain again.

2 Blanch the carrot pieces in a pan of boiling water for about 1–2 minutes, then drain well.

3 Spoon the noodles and carrot chunks into a large pan or flameproof casserole, and arrange the chicken breast fillets or thighs, prawns, Chinese leaves, mushrooms and mangetouts over the top.

4 Bring the chicken or bonito stock to the boil in a separate pan. Add the mirin and enough soy sauce to taste. Pour the heated stock over the noodles. Cover the pan or casserole, bring the mixture to the boil over medium heat, then simmer gently for about 5–6 minutes, stirring occasionally, until all the ingredients are cooked through.

5 Serve in warmed bowls with chopped spring onions, grated ginger, lemon wedges and a little soy sauce.

Chicken Chow Mein

Chow mein is arguably the best known Chinese noodle dish in the West. Noodles are stir-fried with meat, seafood or vegetables.

Serves 4

350g/12oz noodles
225g/8oz skinless chicken
    breast fillets
45ml/3 tbsp soy sauce

15ml/1 tbsp rice wine or dry sherry
15ml/1 tbsp dark sesame oil
60ml/4 tbsp vegetable oil
2 garlic cloves, finely chopped
50g/2oz mangetouts (snow peas),
    topped and tailed
115g/4oz beansprouts
50g/2oz ham, finely shredded
4 spring onions (scallions),
    finely chopped
salt and ground black pepper

1 Cook the noodles in a pan of boiling water until tender. Drain, rinse under cold water and drain well.

2 Slice the chicken into fine shreds about 5cm/2in in length. Place in a bowl and add 10ml/2 tsp of the soy sauce, the rice wine or sherry and sesame oil.

3 Heat half the vegetable oil in a wok or large frying pan over high heat. When it starts smoking, add the chicken mixture. Stir-fry for about 2 minutes, then transfer the chicken to a plate and keep it warm.

4 Wipe the wok clean and heat the remaining oil. Stir in the garlic, mangetouts, beansprouts and ham, stir-fry for another minute or so and add the noodles.

5 Continue to stir-fry until the noodles are heated through. Add the remaining soy sauce to taste and season with salt and pepper. Return the chicken and any juices to the noodle mixture, add the chopped spring onions and give the mixture a final stir. Serve immediately.

> **Variation**
> If you prefer you can use chicken thigh meat instead of breast fillet. Ask the butcher to debone the thigh as they can be fiddly.

Udon Pot Energy Energy 439kcal/1855kJ; Protein 28.8g; Carbohydrate 59.5g, of which sugars 3.9g; Fat 11.1g, of which saturates 1.8g; Cholesterol 225mg; Calcium 59mg; Fibre 2.9g; Sodium 1707mg.
Chow Mein Energy 593kcal/2494kJ; Protein 31.1g; Carbohydrate 67.9g, of which sugars 4.4g; Fat 22.6g, of which saturates 2.7g; Cholesterol 44mg; Calcium 44mg; Fibre 3.4g; Sodium 995mg.

Chiang Mai Noodles

An interesting dish that mixes soft, boiled noodles with crisp deep-fried ones.

Serves 4
250ml/8fl oz/1 cup coconut cream
15ml/1 tbsp Thai kroeung
 or magic paste
5ml/1 tsp Thai red curry paste
450g/1lb chicken thigh meat,
 chopped into small pieces
2 red (bell) peppers, seeded and
 finely diced

30ml/2 tbsp dark soy sauce
600ml/1 pint/2½ cups chicken
 or vegetable stock
90g/3½oz fresh or dried
 rice noodles

For the garnishes
vegetable oil, for deep-frying
90g/3½oz fine dried rice noodles
2 pickled garlic cloves, chopped
small bunch fresh coriander
 (cilantro), chopped
2 limes, cut into wedges

1 Pour the coconut cream into a large wok or frying pan and bring to the boil over medium heat. Continue to boil, stirring frequently, for 8–10 minutes, until the milk separates and an oily sheen appears on the surface.

2 Add the kroeung or magic paste and red curry paste and cook, stirring constantly, for 3–5 seconds. Add the chicken and toss until sealed on all sides. Stir in the peppers and soy sauce and stir-fry for 3–4 minutes. Pour in the stock. Bring to the boil, then simmer for 10–15 minutes, until the chicken is cooked.

3 Meanwhile, make the noodle garnish. Heat the oil in a pan or deep-fryer to 190°C/375°F or until a cube of bread, added to the oil, browns in 45 seconds. Break all the noodles in half, then divide them into four portions. Add one portion at a time to the hot oil. They will puff up on contact. As soon as they are crisp, lift out with a slotted spoon and drain on kitchen paper.

4 Bring a large pan of water to the boil and cook the fresh or dried noodles until tender, following the instructions on the packet. Drain well, divide among four warmed individual dishes, then spoon the curry sauce over them. Top each portion with a cluster of fried noodles. Sprinkle the chopped pickled garlic and coriander over the top and serve immediately, offering lime wedges for squeezing.

Wheat Noodles with Stir-fried Pork

Dried wheat noodles, sold in straight bundles like sticks, are versatile and robust. They keep well, so are handy items to have in the store cupboard, ready for quick and easy recipes like this one.

Serves 4
225g/8oz pork loin, cut into
 thin strips
225g/8oz dried wheat noodles,
 soaked in lukewarm water
 for 20 minutes
15ml/1 tbsp groundnut (peanut) oil

2 garlic cloves, finely chopped
2–3 spring onions (scallions),
 finely chopped
45ml/3 tbsp Thai kroeung or
 magic paste
15ml/1 tbsp fish sauce
30ml/2 tbsp unsalted roasted
 peanuts, finely chopped
chilli oil, for drizzling

For the marinade
30ml/2 tbsp fish sauce
30ml/2 tbsp soy sauce
15ml/1 tbsp peanut oil
10ml/2 tsp sugar

1 In a bowl, combine the ingredients for the marinade, stirring constantly until the all the sugar dissolves. Toss in the strips of pork, making sure that they are well coated in the marinade. Put aside for 30 minutes.

2 Drain the wheat noodles. Bring a large pan of water to the boil. Drop in the noodles, untangling them with chopsticks, if necessary. Cook for 4–5 minutes, until tender.

3 Drain the noodles thoroughly, then divide them among individual serving bowls. Keep the noodles warm until the dish is ready to serve.

4 Meanwhile, heat a wok or large frying pan. Add the oil and stir-fry the garlic and spring onions, until fragrant. Add the pork, tossing it around the wok for 2 minutes.

5 Stir the kroeung or magic paste and fish sauce into the wok or pan and cook for 2 minutes – add a splash of water if the pan gets too dry. Place the noodles in warmed serving bowls, then place the pork strips on top of the noodles. Sprinkle the peanuts over the top and drizzle with chilli oil to serve.

Chiang Mai Noodles Energy 245kcal/1034kJ; Protein 29.4g; Carbohydrate 27.6g, of which sugars 9g; Fat 1.8g, of which saturates 0.6g; Cholesterol 79mg; Calcium 35mg; Fibre 1.4g; Sodium 677mg.
Wheat Noodles Energy 340kcal/1435kJ; Protein 19.6g; Carbohydrate 46g, of which sugars 4.4g; Fat 9.9g, of which saturates 1.4g; Cholesterol 35mg; Calcium 23mg; Fibre 1.9g; Sodium 41mg.

Thai Curried Noodles

Chicken or pork can be used to make this tasty dish from southern Thailand. It is very quick and easy to prepare and cook.

Serves 2
30ml/2 tbsp vegetable oil
10ml/2 tsp Thai kroeung or
  magic paste
1 lemon grass stalk, finely chopped
5ml/1 tsp Thai red curry paste
90g/3½oz skinless chicken breast
  fillets or pork fillet (tenderloin),
  sliced into slivers
30ml/2 tbsp light soy sauce
400ml/14fl oz/1⅔ cups
  coconut milk
2 kaffir lime leaves, rolled into
  cylinders and thinly sliced
250g/9oz dried medium
  egg noodles
90g/3½oz Chinese leaves
  (Chinese cabbage),
  finely shredded
90g/3½oz spinach or watercress,
  stalks removed, shredded
juice of 1 lime
small bunch fresh coriander
  (cilantro), chopped

1 Heat the oil in a wok or large, heavy frying pan. Add the Thai kroeung or magic paste and lemon grass and stir-fry over a low to medium heat for 4–5 seconds, until they give off their aroma.

2 Stir in the curry paste, then add the chicken or pork. Stir-fry over a medium to high heat for 2 minutes, until the meat is coated in the paste and seared on all sides.

3 Add the soy sauce, coconut milk and sliced lime leaves. Bring to a simmer, then add the noodles. Simmer gently for 4 minutes, tossing the mixture occasionally to make sure that the noodles cook evenly.

4 Add the Chinese leaves and the spinach or watercress. Stir well, then add the lime juice. Spoon into a warmed bowl, sprinkle with the coriander and serve.

> **Cook's Tip**
> Kroeung or magic paste is a spice blend that includes garlic, coriander and pepper and is available from Asian markets.

Cellophane Noodles with Pork

Simple and satisfying, this is a great recipe for noodles.

Serves 2
200g/7oz cellophane noodles
30ml/2 tbsp vegetable oil
15ml/1 tbsp Thai kroeung or
  magic paste
200g/7oz minced (ground) pork
1 fresh green or red chilli, seeded
  and finely chopped
300g/11oz/3½ cups beansprouts
bunch spring onions (scallions),
  finely chopped
30ml/2 tbsp soy sauce
30ml/2 tbsp Thai fish sauce
30ml/2 tbsp sweet chilli sauce
15ml/1 tbsp light muscovado
  (brown) sugar
30ml/2 tbsp rice vinegar
30ml/2 tbsp roasted peanuts,
  chopped, to garnish
small bunch fresh coriander
  (cilantro), chopped, to garnish

1 Place the noodles in a large bowl, cover with boiling water and soak for 10 minutes. Drain the noodles and set aside.

2 Heat the oil in a wok or large, heavy frying pan. Add the kreung or magic paste and stir-fry for 2–3 seconds, then add the pork. Stir-fry the meat, breaking it up with a wooden spatula, for 2–3 minutes, until browned all over.

3 Add the chopped chilli to the meat and stir-fry for 3–4 seconds, then add the beansprouts and chopped spring onions, stir-frying for a few seconds after each addition.

4 Snip the noodles into 5cm/2in lengths and add to the wok, with the soy sauce, Thai fish sauce, sweet chilli sauce, sugar and rice vinegar.

5 Toss the ingredients together over the heat until well combined and the noodles have warmed through. Pile on to a platter or into a large bowl. Sprinkle over the peanuts and coriander and serve immediately.

> **Variation**
> This dish is also very good made with chicken. Replace the pork with the same quantity of minced (ground) chicken.

Thai Noodles Energy 702kcal/2965kJ; Protein 28.7g; Carbohydrate 101.6g, of which sugars 14.2g; Fat 23g, of which saturates 4.9g; Cholesterol 69mg; Calcium 187mg; Fibre 4.7g; Sodium 1564mg.
Cellophane Energy 720kcal/3009kJ; Protein 29.4g; Carbohydrate 99.9g, of which sugars 15.4g; Fat 21.6g, of which saturates 5.1g; Cholesterol 66mg; Calcium 58mg; Fibre 2.4g; Sodium 1933mg.

Crispy Noodles with Chilli Beef

When the rice vermicelli is deep-fried it expands to at least four times its size.

Serves 4

450g/1lb rump (round) steak
teriyaki sauce, for brushing
175g/6oz rice vermicelli
groundnut (peanut) oil, for
    deep-frying and stir-frying
8 spring onions (scallions),
    diagonally sliced
2 garlic cloves, crushed
4–5 carrots, cut into
    julienne strips
1–2 fresh red chillies, seeded
    and finely sliced
2 small courgettes (zucchini),
    diagonally sliced
5ml/1 tsp grated fresh
    root ginger
60ml/4 tbsp rice vinegar
90ml/6 tbsp light soy sauce
475ml/16fl oz/2 cups spicy stock

1 Beat the steak to about 2.5cm/1in thick. Place in a shallow dish, brush with the teriyaki sauce and set aside for 2–4 hours. Separate the rice vermicelli into manageable loops. Pour oil into a large wok to a depth of about 5cm/2in, and heat until a strand of vermicelli cooks as soon as it is lowered into the oil.

2 Add a loop of vermicelli to the oil. Almost immediately, turn to cook on the other side, then remove and drain on kitchen paper. Repeat with the remaining loops. Transfer the cooked noodles to a separate wok or serving bowl and keep warm.

3 Strain the oil from the wok into a heatproof bowl and set it aside. Heat 15ml/1 tbsp groundnut oil in the clean wok. When it sizzles, fry the steak for 30 seconds each side, until browned. Transfer to a board and cut into thick slices. The meat should be well browned on the outside but pink inside. Set aside.

4 Add a little extra oil to the wok. Fry the spring onions, garlic and carrots for 5–6 minutes, until the carrots are just soft. Add the chillies, courgettes and ginger and fry for 1–2 minutes. Stir in the rice vinegar, soy sauce and stock. Cook for 4 minutes, or until the sauce has thickened slightly. Return the slices of steak to the wok and cook for a further 1–2 minutes.

5 Spoon the steak, vegetables and sauce over the noodles and toss lightly and carefully to mix. Serve immediately.

Noodles with Hoisin Lamb

This tasty and substantial noodle dish features pieces of succulent lamb fillet that has been marinated overnight.

Serves 4

350g/12oz thick egg noodles
1kg/2¼ lb lean neck fillets
    of lamb
30ml/2 tbsp vegetable oil
115g/4oz fine green beans,
    trimmed and blanched
salt and ground black pepper
2 hard-boiled eggs, halved,
    and 2 spring onions
    (scallions), finely chopped,
    to garnish

For the marinade

2 garlic cloves, crushed
10ml/2 tsp grated fresh
    root ginger
30ml/2 tbsp soy sauce
30ml/2 tbsp rice wine
1–2 dried red chillies
30ml/2 tbsp vegetable oil

For the sauce

15ml/1 tbsp cornflour
    (cornstarch)
30ml/2 tbsp soy sauce
30ml/2 tbsp rice wine
grated rind and juice of ½ orange
15ml/1 tbsp hoisin sauce
15ml/1 tbsp wine vinegar
5ml/1 tsp soft light brown sugar

1 Bring a large pan of water to the boil and cook the noodles for about 3–5 minutes, or according to the instructions on the packet. Drain, rinse and drain again. Set aside.

2 Cut the lamb into 5cm/2in thick medallions. Mix the ingredients for the marinade in a large shallow dish. Add the lamb and leave to marinate for at least 4 hours or overnight.

3 Heat the oil in a heavy pan. Fry the lamb for 5 minutes until browned. Add just enough water to cover. Bring to the boil, skim, then simmer for 40 minutes or until the meat is tender.

4 Meanwhile, make the sauce. Blend the cornflour with the remaining ingredients in a bowl. Stir the sauce into the lamb and mix well.

5 Add the noodles and beans to the pan and simmer until cooked. Add salt and black pepper to taste. Divide among four large bowls, garnish with hard-boiled egg halves and spring onions and serve.

Noodles with Lamb Energy 605kcal/2545kJ; Protein 35.8g; Carbohydrate 62.8g, of which sugars 1.7g; Fat 25.3g, of which saturates 9g; Cholesterol 207mg; Calcium 48mg; Fibre 2.5g; Sodium 289mg.
Crispy Noodles Energy 493kcal/2052kJ; Protein 29.5g; Carbohydrate 43.4g, of which sugars 7.2g; Fat 21.9g, of which saturates 5.7g; Cholesterol 65mg; Calcium 43mg; Fibre 2g; Sodium 1697mg.

Pepper Soup with Parmesan Toasts

The secret of this soup is to serve it just cold, not over-chilled, topped with hot Parmesan toast dripping with cheese and butter.

Serves 4
1 onion, quartered
4 garlic cloves, unpeeled
2 red (bell) peppers, seeded and quartered
2 yellow (bell) peppers, seeded and quartered

30–45ml/2–3 tbsp olive oil
grated rind and juice of 1 orange
200g/7oz can chopped tomatoes
600ml/1 pint/2½ cups cold water
salt and ground black pepper
30ml/2 tbsp chopped fresh chives, to garnish (optional)

For the hot parmesan toast
1 baguette, halved lengthways and across into four pieces
50g/2oz/¼ cup butter
175g/6oz Parmesan cheese

1 Preheat the oven to 200°C/400°F/Gas 6. Put the onion, garlic and peppers in a roasting pan. Drizzle the oil over and mix well, then turn the pieces of pepper skin sides up. Roast for 25–30 minutes, until slightly charred, then allow to cool slightly.

2 Squeeze the garlic flesh into a food processor or blender. Add the vegetables, orange rind and juice, tomatoes and water. Process until smooth, then press through a sieve (strainer) into a bowl. Season well and chill for 30 minutes.

3 Make the Parmesan toasts when ready to serve the soup. Preheat the grill (broiler) to high. Spread the baguette pieces with butter. Pare most of the Parmesan into thin slices or shavings using a swivel-bladed vegetable knife or a small paring knife, then finely grate the remainder. Arrange the sliced Parmesan on the toasts, then dredge with the grated cheese.

4 Transfer the cheese-topped baguette pieces to a large baking sheet or grill (broiling) rack and toast under the grill for a few minutes until the topping is well browned.

5 Ladle the chilled soup into large, shallow bowls and sprinkle with the chopped fresh chives, if using, and plenty of ground black pepper. Serve the craggy hot Parmesan toast with the chilled soup.

Potato and Fennel Soup with Scones

Savoury scones are delicious with this lightly spiced soup.

Serves 4
75g/3oz/6 tbsp butter
2 onions, chopped
5ml/1 tsp fennel seeds, crushed
3 bulbs fennel, coarsely chopped
900g/2lb potatoes, thinly sliced
1.2 litres/2 pints/5 cups chicken stock
150ml/¼ pint/⅔ cup double (heavy) cream
salt and ground black pepper

handful of fresh herb flowers and 15ml/1 tbsp chopped fresh chives, to garnish

For the rosemary scones
225g/8oz/2 cups self-raising (self-rising) flour
2.5ml/½ tsp salt
5ml/1 tsp baking powder
10ml/2 tsp chopped fresh rosemary
50g/2oz/¼ cup butter
150ml/¼ pint/⅔ cup milk
1 egg, beaten, to glaze

1 Melt the butter in a pan. Add the onions and cook gently for 10 minutes, stirring occasionally, until very soft. Add the fennel seeds and cook for 2–3 minutes. Stir in the fennel and potatoes. Cover with wet baking parchment. Cover and simmer gently for 10 minutes, until very soft. Remove the paper. Pour in the stock, bring to the boil, cover and simmer for 35 minutes.

2 Meanwhile, make the scones. Preheat the oven to 230°C/450°F/Gas 8 and grease a baking tray. Sift the flour, salt and baking powder into a bowl. Stir in the rosemary, then rub in the butter. Add the milk and mix to form a soft dough.

3 Knead very lightly on a floured surface. Roll out to 2cm/¾in thick. Stamp out 12 rounds with a cutter and place on the baking tray. Brush with egg and bake for 8–10 minutes, until risen and golden. Cool on a wire rack until warm.

4 Purée the soup in a food processor or blender until smooth. Press through a sieve (strainer) into the rinsed-out pan. Stir in the double cream with seasoning to taste. Reheat gently but do not allow it to boil.

5 Ladle the soup in bowls, and sprinkle with a few herb flowers and chopped chives. Serve with the warm rosemary scones.

Pepper Soup Energy 529kcal/2209kJ; Protein 23.8g; Carbohydrate 39.6g, of which sugars 15.3g; Fat 31.7g, of which saturates 16.6g; Cholesterol 70mg; Calcium 605mg; Fibre 4.4g; Sodium 850mg.
Potato Soup Energy 797kcal/3331kJ; Protein 12.2g; Carbohydrate 84g, of which sugars 8.8g; Fat 48.1g, of which saturates 29.5g; Cholesterol 120.3mg; Calcium 315mg; Fibre 7.6g; Sodium 703mg.

Potato Soup with Garlic Samosas

Soup and samosas are the ideal partners. Bought samosas are given an easy, but clever, flavour lift in this simple recipe.

Serves 4

60ml/4 tbsp sunflower oil
10ml/2 tsp black mustard seeds
1 large onion, chopped
1 fresh red chilli, seeded
   and chopped
2.5ml/½ tsp ground turmeric
1.5ml/¼ tsp cayenne pepper
900g/2lb potatoes, cut into cubes

4 fresh curry leaves
750ml/1¼ pint/3 cups
   vegetable stock
225g/8oz spinach leaves, torn
   if large
400ml/14fl oz/1⅔ cups
   coconut milk
handful of fresh coriander
   leaves (cilantro)
salt and black pepper

For the garlic samosas
1 large garlic clove, crushed
25g/1oz/2 tbsp butter
6 vegetable samosas

1 Heat the oil in a large pan. Add the mustard seeds, cover and cook until they begin to pop. Add the onion and chilli and cook for 5–6 minutes, until softened.

2 Stir in the turmeric, cayenne, potatoes, curry leaves and stock. Bring to the boil, reduce the heat and cover the pan. Simmer for 15 minutes, stirring occasionally, until the potatoes are tender.

3 Meanwhile, prepare the samosas. Preheat the oven to 180°C/350°F/Gas 4. Melt the butter with the garlic in a small pan, stirring and crushing the garlic into the butter.

4 Place the samosas on an ovenproof dish – a gratin dish or quiche dish is ideal. Brush them lightly with the butter, turn them over and brush with the remaining butter. Heat through in the oven for about 5 minutes, until piping hot.

5 Add the spinach to the soup and cook for 5 minutes. Stir in the coconut milk and cook for a further 5 minutes.

6 Season and add the coriander leaves before ladling the soup into bowls. Serve with the garlic samosas.

Beef Chilli Soup with Nachos

Steaming bowls of beef chilli soup, packed with beans, are delicious topped with crushed tortillas and cheese. The soup can be finished by putting the bowls under the grill to brown the cheese.

Serves 4

45ml/3 tbsp olive oil
350g/12oz rump (round)
   steak, diced
2 onions, chopped
2 garlic cloves, crushed
2 fresh green chillies, seeded
   and chopped
30ml/2 tbsp mild chilli powder

5ml/1 tsp ground cumin
2 bay leaves
30ml/2 tbsp tomato
   purée (paste)
900ml/1½ pints/3¾ cups
   beef stock
2 x 400g/14oz cans mixed
   beans, drained and rinsed
45ml/3 tbsp chopped fresh
   coriander (cilantro)
salt and ground black pepper

For the topping
bag of plain tortilla chips,
   lightly crushed
225g/8oz Monterey Jack or
   Cheddar cheese, grated

1 Heat the oil in a large pan over a high heat and brown the meat all over until golden. Use a draining spoon to remove the meat from the pan. Reduce the heat and add the onions, garlic and chillies, then cook for 4–5 minutes, until softened.

2 Stir in the chilli powder and cumin, and cook for a further 2 minutes. Return the meat to the pan, then stir in the bay leaves, tomato purée and beef stock. Bring to the boil.

3 Reduce the heat, cover and simmer for about 45 minutes or until the meat is tender.

4 Put a quarter of the beans into a bowl and mash with a potato masher. Stir these into the soup to thicken it slightly. Add the remaining beans and simmer for 5 minutes. Taste the soup and adjust the seasoning.

5 When you are ready to serve the soup, stir in the chopped coriander. Ladle the soup into warmed bowls and sprinkle the tortilla chips over the surface. Pile the grated cheese over the tortilla chips and serve immediately.

Potato Soup Energy 658kcal/2744kJ; Protein 8.8g; Carbohydrate 63.4g, of which sugars 15.5g; Fat 42.8g, of which saturates 5.1g; Cholesterol 13mg; Calcium 184mg; Fibre 5.9g; Sodium 375mg.
Beef Chilli Soup Energy 631kcal/2629kJ; Protein 38.7g; Carbohydrate 25.6g, of which sugars 2.5g; Fat 41g, of which saturates 17.7g; Cholesterol 103mg; Calcium 500mg; Fibre 4.5g; Sodium 788mg.

Cabbage, Beetroot and Tomato Borscht

There are numerous versions of this classic soup, which originates in Eastern Europe. Beetroot and sour cream are the traditional ingredients in every borscht, but other ingredients tend to be many and varied. This slow-cooker version has a deliciously sweet and sour taste and can be served piping hot or refreshingly chilled on a hot day.

Serves 6
1 onion, chopped
1 carrot, chopped
6 raw or vacuum-packed (cooked, not pickled) beetroot (beets), 4 diced and 2 coarsely grated

400g/14oz can chopped tomatoes
6 new potatoes, cut into bitesize pieces
1 small white cabbage, thinly sliced
600ml/1 pint/2½ cups vegetable stock
45ml/3 tbsp sugar
30–45ml/2–3 tbsp white wine vinegar or cider vinegar
45ml/3 tbsp chopped fresh dill
salt and ground black pepper
sour cream and dill, to garnish
buttered rye bread, to serve

1 Put the onion, carrot, diced beetroot, tomatoes, potatoes and cabbage into the ceramic cooking pot and pour over the stock. Cover the cooking pot with the lid and cook on high for about 4 hours, or until the vegetables are just tender.

2 Add the grated beetroot, sugar and vinegar to the pot and stir to combine. Cook for a further hour until the beetroot is cooked.

3 Taste the soup, checking for a good sweet/sour balance, and add more sugar and/or vinegar if necessary. Season to taste with plenty of salt and ground black pepper.

4 Just before serving, stir the chopped dill into the soup and ladle into warmed soup bowls. Garnish each serving with a generous spoonful of sour cream and plenty more fresh dill, then serve with thick slices of buttered rye bread.

Celeriac Soup with Cabbage

Versatile, yet often overlooked, celeriac is a winter vegetable that makes excellent soup.

Serves 4
50g/2oz butter
2 onions, chopped
675g/1½lb celeriac, roughly diced
450g/1lb potatoes, roughly diced
1.2 litres/2 pints/5 cups vegetable stock
150ml/¼ pint/⅔ cup single (light) cream

salt and ground black pepper
sprigs of fresh thyme, to garnish

For the cabbage and bacon topping
1 small Savoy cabbage
50g/2oz/¼ cup butter
175g/6oz rindless streaky (fatty) bacon, roughly chopped
15ml/1 tbsp roughly chopped fresh thyme
15ml/1 tbsp roughly chopped fresh rosemary

1 Melt the butter in a pan. Cook the onions for 4–5 minutes, until softened. Add the celeriac. Cover with a wetted piece of baking parchment and the lid and cook gently for 10 minutes.

2 Remove the paper and stir in the potatoes and stock. Bring to the boil, then simmer for 20 minutes or until the vegetables are very tender. Leave to cool slightly. Using a draining spoon, remove half the celeriac and potatoes and set them aside.

3 Process the soup in a food processor or blender. Return it to the rinsed-out pan with the reserved celeriac and potatoes.

4 Prepare the cabbage and bacon mixture. Discard the tough outer leaves from the cabbage. Tear the remaining leaves, discarding any hard stalks, and blanch them in boiling salted water for 2–3 minutes. Refresh under cold water and drain.

5 Melt the butter in a large frying pan and cook the bacon for 3–4 minutes. Add the cabbage, thyme and rosemary, and stir-fry for 5–6 minutes, until tender. Season well.

6 Add the cream to the soup and season it well, then reheat gently until hot. Ladle into bowls and pile the cabbage mixture in the centre. Garnish with sprigs of fresh thyme.

Borscht Energy 125kcal/531kJ; Protein 3.5g; Carbohydrate 27.8g, of which sugars 7g; Fat 0.7g, of which saturates 0.1g; Cholesterol 0mg; Calcium 58mg; Fibre 3.2g; Sodium 357mg.
Celeriac Soup Energy 462kcal/1919kJ; Protein 12.3g; Carbohydrate 24.3g, of which sugars 7.3g; Fat 35.8g, of which saturates 20.4g; Cholesterol 97mg; Calcium 144mg; Fibre 4.3g; Sodium 954mg.

Wild Mushroom Soup with Polenta

This rich soup is delicious with Parmesan polenta.

Serves 6
20g/³/₄oz/scant ¹/₂ cup dried
  porcini mushrooms
175ml/6fl oz/³/₄ cup hot water
50g/2oz/¹/₄ cup butter
1 large red onion, chopped
3 garlic cloves, chopped
115g/4oz/1³/₄ cups mixed wild
  mushrooms, trimmed
120ml/4fl oz/¹/₂ cup light
  red wine

1.2 litres/2 pints/5 cups
  vegetable stock
2.5ml/¹/₂ tsp wholegrain mustard
salt and ground black pepper
chopped fresh parsley, to garnish

For the polenta
750ml/1¹/₄ pints/3 cups milk
175g/6oz/1 cup
  quick-cook polenta
50g/2oz/¹/₄ cup butter
50g/2oz/²/₃ cup freshly grated
  Parmesan cheese, plus extra
  to serve

1 Soak the porcini in the hot water for about 30 minutes. Drain, then strain the liquid through a fine sieve (strainer); reserve both the liquid and the mushrooms.

2 Melt the butter in a pan. Add the onion and garlic and cook for 4–5 minutes. Add the wild mushrooms and cook for a further 3–4 minutes. Add the dried mushrooms and strain in the soaking liquid through a sieve (strainer) lined with muslin (cheesecloth). Pour in the wine and stock, and cook for 15 minutes or until reduced by half.

3 Ladle half the soup into a food processor or blender and process until almost smooth. Pour the processed soup back into the soup remaining in the pan and set aside.

4 To make the polenta, bring the milk to the boil and pour in the polenta in a steady stream, stirring constantly. Cook for about 5 minutes, or until the polenta begins to come away from the pan. Beat in the butter, then stir in the Parmesan. Cover and keep warm.

5 Reheat the soup until just boiling. Stir in the mustard and season well. Divide the polenta among six bowls and ladle the soup around it. Sprinkle with grated Parmesan and parsley.

Cauliflower Soup with Broccoli and Bacon

Creamy cauliflower soup is given real bite by adding chunky cauliflower and broccoli florets and crusty bread piled high with melting Cheddar cheese.

Serves 4
1 onion, chopped
1 garlic clove, chopped
50g/2oz/¹/₄ cup butter
2 cauliflowers, broken into florets
1 large potato, cut into chunks

900ml/1¹/₂ pints/3³/₄ cups
  chicken stock
225g/8oz broccoli, broken
  into florets
150ml/¹/₄ pint/²/₃ cup single
  (light) cream
6 rindless streaky (fatty) bacon
  rashers (strips)
1 small baguette, cut in 4 pieces
225g/8oz/2 cups medium-mature
  (sharp) Cheddar cheese, grated
salt and ground black pepper
fresh parsley, chopped, to garnish

1 Melt the butter in a pan. Add the onion and garlic and fry for 4–5 minutes. Add half the cauliflower, all the potato and the stock. Bring to the boil, reduce the heat and simmer for 20 minutes.

2 Boil the remaining cauliflower for about 6 minutes, or until just tender. Use a draining spoon to remove the the florets and refresh under cold running water, then drain well. Cook the broccoli in the water for 3–4 minutes, until just tender. Drain, refresh under cold water, then drain. Add to the cauliflower.

3 Cool the soup slightly, then purée it until smooth and return it to the rinsed pan. Add the cream and seasoning, then heat gently. Add the cauliflower and broccoli and heat through.

4 Preheat the grill (broiler) to high. Grill (broil) the bacon until crisp, then cool slightly. Ladle the soup into flameproof bowls.

5 Place a piece of baguette in each bowl. Sprinkle grated cheese over the top and grill for 2–3 minutes, until the cheese is melted and bubbling. Take care when serving the hot bowls.

6 Crumble the bacon and sprinkle it over the melted cheese, then sprinkle the parsley over the top and serve immediately.

Mushroom Soup Energy 2117kcal/8817kJ; Protein 67.3g; Carbohydrate 176.6g, of which sugars 44.8g; Fat 118.3g, of which saturates 70.6g; Cholesterol 307mg; Calcium 1580mg; Fibre 7.9g; Sodium 1495mg.
Cauliflower Soup Energy 737kcal/3071kJ; Protein 34.8g; Carbohydrate 45.5g, of which sugars 9.2g; Fat 46.2g, of which saturates 26.4g; Cholesterol 121mg; Calcium 589mg; Fibre 6.6g; Sodium 1206mg.

Country-style Lamb Soup

Traditionally, Irish soda bread would be served with this hearty one-pot meal based on classic Irish stew.

Serves 4

15ml/1 tbsp vegetable oil
675g/1½lb boneless lamb chump chops, trimmed and cut into small cubes
2 small onions, quartered
2 leeks, thickly sliced
1 litre/1¾ pints/4 cups lamb stock or water
2 large potatoes, cut into chunks
2 carrots, thickly sliced
sprig of fresh thyme, plus extra to garnish
15g/½oz/1 tbsp butter
30ml/2 tbsp chopped fresh parsley
salt and ground black pepper
Irish soda bread, to serve

1 Heat the oil in a pan. Add the lamb and brown in batches. Use a slotted spoon to remove the lamb from the pan.

2 Add the onions and cook for 4–5 minutes, until browned. Return the meat to the pan and add the leeks. Pour in the stock or water, then bring to the boil. Reduce the heat, cover and simmer gently for about 1 hour.

3 Add the potatoes, carrots and thyme, and continue cooking for a further 40 minutes, until the lamb is tender. Remove from the heat and leave to stand for 5 minutes to allow the fat to settle on the surface of the soup.

4 Skim off the fat. Pour off the stock from the soup into a clean pan and whisk in the butter. Stir in the parsley and season well, then pour the liquid back over the soup ingredients.

5 Ladle the soup into warmed bowls and garnish with sprigs of fresh thyme. Serve with chunks of brown or Irish soda bread.

> **Variation**
> The vegetables in this rustic soup can be varied according to the season. Swede (rutabaga), turnip, celeriac and even cabbage can be added in place of some of the listed vegetables.

Lamb Shanks in Pearl Barley Broth

Succulent roasted lamb shanks studded with garlic and rosemary make a fabulous meal when served in a hearty vegetable, barley and tomato broth.

Serves 4

4 small lamb shanks
4 garlic cloves, cut into slivers
handful of fresh rosemary sprigs
30ml/2 tbsp olive oil
2 carrots, diced
2 celery sticks, diced
1 large onion, chopped
1 bay leaf
few sprigs of fresh thyme
1.2 litres/2 pints/5 cups lamb stock
50g/2oz pearl barley
450g/1lb tomatoes, peeled and chopped
grated rind of 1 large lemon
30ml/2 tbsp chopped fresh parsley
salt and ground black pepper

1 Preheat the oven to 150°C/300°F/Gas 2. Make small cuts all over the lamb and insert slivers of garlic and sprigs of rosemary into them.

2 Heat the oil in a flameproof casserole and brown the shanks two at a time. Remove and set aside. Add the carrots, celery and onion in batches and cook until lightly browned. Put all the vegetables in the casserole with the bay leaf and thyme. Pour in stock to cover, place the lamb shanks on top and roast in the oven for 2 hours.

3 Meanwhile, pour the remaining stock into a large pan. Add the pearl barley, then bring to the boil. Reduce the heat, cover and simmer for 1 hour, or until the barley is tender.

4 Remove the lamb shanks from the casserole using a slotted spoon. Skim the fat from the surface of the roasted vegetables, then add the vegetables to the broth. Stir in the tomatoes, lemon rind and parsley.

5 Bring the soup back to the boil. Reduce the heat and simmer for 5 minutes. Add the lamb shanks to the soup and heat through, then season with salt and pepper. Put a lamb shank into each of four large bowls, then ladle the barley broth over the meat and serve immediately.

Lamb Soup Energy 500kcal/2092kJ; Protein 38.2g; Carbohydrate 30.2g, of which sugars 12.2g; Fat 26g, of which saturates 11.3g; Cholesterol 136mg; Calcium 104mg; Fibre 6.1g; Sodium 197mg.
Roast Lamb Shanks Energy 287kcal/1199kJ; Protein 22.5g; Carbohydrate 19.5g, of which sugars 7.6g; Fat 13.7g, of which saturates 0.9g; Cholesterol 0mg; Calcium 35mg; Fibre 2.3g; Sodium 24mg.

Kidney and Bacon Soup

Although there is a modern twist in the seasonings, the two main ingredients of this meaty and substantial soup are very traditional.

Serves 4–6

225g/8oz ox (beef) kidney
15ml/1 tbsp vegetable oil
4 streaky (fatty) bacon rashers (strips), chopped
1 large onion, chopped
2 garlic cloves, finely chopped
15ml/1 tbsp plain (all-purpose) flour
1.5 litres/2½ pints/6¼ cups cold water
a good dash of Worcestershire sauce
a good dash of soy sauce
15ml/1 tbsp chopped fresh thyme, or 5ml/1 tsp dried
75g/3oz/¾ cup grated Cheddar cheese
4–6 slices fresh French bread, toasted
salt and ground black pepper

1 Wash the kidney in cold, salted water. Drain, dry well on kitchen paper and chop into small pieces.

2 Heat the vegetable oil in a large pan over medium heat. Add the chopped streaky bacon and sauté for a few minutes. Add the prepared kidney and continue cooking until nicely browned.

3 Add the chopped onion and chopped garlic into the pan, and cook, stirring occasionally, until the onion is just soft but not browned.

4 Add the flour and cook for 2 minutes. Gradually add the water, stirring constantly. Add the sauces, thyme and seasoning to taste. Reduce the heat and simmer gently for 30–35 minutes.

5 Sprinkle the cheese on to the toast and grill (broil) until it is bubbling. Pour the soup into bowls, and top with the bread.

> **Cook's Tip**
> *Ox kidneys are tougher than veal or lamb, so they need to be cooked more slowly.*

Braised Beef and Cabbage Soup

This is a main course in a bowl. Cook the beef as rare or as well done as you like.

Serves 6

butter, for greasing
900g/2lb red cabbage, finely shredded
2 onions, finely sliced
1 large cooking apple, peeled, cored and chopped
45ml/3 tbsp soft brown sugar
2 garlic cloves, crushed
1.5ml/¼ tsp grated nutmeg
2.5ml/½ tsp caraway seeds
45ml/3 tbsp red wine vinegar
1 litre/1¾ pints/4 cups beef stock
675kg/1½lb beef sirloin
30ml/2 tbsp olive oil
salt and ground black pepper
watercress, to garnish

For the horseradish cream
15–30ml/1–2 tbsp grated fresh horseradish
10ml/2 tsp wine vinegar
2.5ml/½ tsp Dijon mustard
150ml/¼ pint/⅔ cup double (heavy) cream

1 Preheat the oven to 150°C/300°F/Gas 2. Butter a casserole. Mix the cabbage, onions, apple, sugar, garlic, nutmeg, caraway seeds, red wine vinegar and 45ml/3 tbsp of the stock in the casserole. Season well, cover tightly and bake for 2½ hours. Stir every 30 minutes to ensure that the cabbage is not too dry. If necessary, add a few more tablespoons of the stock. Set aside.

2 Increase the oven temperature to 230°C/450°F/Gas 8. Trim excess fat from the meat, leaving a thin layer. Heat the oil in a frying pan and brown the beef thoroughly all over. Transfer to a roasting pan and roast for 15–20 minutes for a medium-rare result or 25–30 minutes for well-done beef.

3 To make the horseradish cream, mix the grated horseradish, wine vinegar, mustard and seasoning with 45ml/3 tbsp of the cream. Lightly whip the remaining cream and fold in the horseradish mixture. Chill until required.

4 Place the cabbage in a pan, pour in the remaining stock and bring to the boil. Set the roast beef aside to rest for 5 minutes before carving into slices. Ladle the cabbage soup into bowls, top with beef slices and add a little horseradish cream. Garnish with watercress and serve.

Beef Soup Energy 395kcal/1645kJ; Protein 29.4g; Carbohydrate 19.4g, of which sugars 18.5g; Fat 22.5g, of which saturates 11.1g; Cholesterol 92mg; Calcium 104mg; Fibre 3.8g; Sodium 97mg.
Kidney Soup Energy 379kcal/1592kJ; Protein 23.7g; Carbohydrate 34g, of which sugars 3.2g; Fat 17g, of which saturates 7.1g; Cholesterol 184mg; Calcium 225mg; Fibre 1.6g; Sodium 1167mg.

French Onion Soup

This is perhaps the most famous of all onion soups.

Serves 6
50g/2oz/¼ cup butter, plus extra
   for greasing
15ml/1 tbsp olive oil
2kg/4½lb onions, sliced
5ml/1 tsp chopped fresh thyme
5ml/1 tsp caster (superfine) sugar
15ml/1 tbsp sherry vinegar
1.5 litres/2½ pints/6¼ cups good
   vegetable stock

25ml/1½ tbsp plain
   (all-purpose) flour
150ml/¼ pint/⅔ cup dry
   white wine
45ml/3 tbsp brandy
salt and ground black pepper

For the croûtes
6–12 thick slices day-old French
   bread, about 2.5cm/1 in thick
1 garlic clove, halved
15ml/1 tbsp French mustard
115g/4oz Gruyère cheese, grated

1 Heat the butter and oil in a large pan. Add the onions and stir. Cook over medium heat for 5–8 minutes, stirring once or twice, until the onions begin to soften. Stir in the thyme. Reduce the heat to very low, cover and cook the onions for 20–30 minutes, stirring frequently, until very soft and golden.

2 Uncover the pan and increase the heat slightly. Stir in the sugar and cook for 5–10 minutes, until the onions start to brown. Add the sherry vinegar and increase the heat again, then continue cooking, stirring frequently, until the onions turn a deep, golden brown – this could take up to 20 minutes.

3 Bring the stock to the boil in another pan. Stir the flour into the onions and cook for 2 minutes, then gradually stir in the stock, wine, brandy and seasoning to taste. Bring to the boil, stirring, reduce the heat and simmer for 10–15 minutes.

4 For the croûtes, preheat the oven to 150°C/300°F/Gas 2. Place the bread on a greased baking tray and bake for 15–20 minutes, until lightly browned. Rub with the garlic and spread with mustard, then sprinkle with the cheese.

5 Preheat the grill (broiler) on the hottest setting. Ladle the soup into six flameproof bowls. Add the croûtes and grill (broil) until the cheese melts, bubbles and browns. Serve immediately.

Mussel Soup with Pumpkin

Pumpkin is excellent in this French mussel soup.

Serves 4
1kg/2¼lb mussels, cleaned
300ml/½ pint/1¼ cups dry
   white wine
1 large lemon
1 bay leaf
15ml/1 tbsp olive oil

1 onion, chopped
1 garlic clove, crushed
675g/1½lb pumpkin or
   squash, seeded, peeled and
   roughly chopped
900ml/1½ pints/3¾ cups
   vegetable stock
30ml/2 tbsp chopped fresh dill
salt and ground black pepper
lemon wedges, to serve

1 Discard any open mussels that do not shut when tapped sharply, and put the rest into a large pan. Pour in the wine.

2 Pare large pieces of rind from the lemon and squeeze the juice, then add both to the mussels with the bay leaf. Cover and bring to the boil, then cook for 4–5 minutes, shaking the pan occasionally until all the mussels have opened. Drain the mussels in a colander over a large bowl. Reserve the liquid.

3 Discard the lemon rind and bay leaf, and any mussel shells that have not opened. Set aside a few mussels in their shells for the garnish. Remove the remaining mussels from their shells. Strain the reserved cooking liquid through a sieve (strainer) lined with muslin (cheesecloth).

4 Heat the oil in a large, clean pan. Add the onion and garlic and cook for 4–5 minutes, until softened. Add the pumpkin flesh and the strained mussel cooking liquid. Bring to the boil and simmer, uncovered, for 5–6 minutes. Pour in the vegetable stock and cook for a further 25–30 minutes, until the pumpkin has almost disintegrated.

5 Cool the soup slightly, then process it in a food processor or blender until smooth. Return the soup to the rinsed-out pan and season well. Stir in the chopped dill and the shelled mussels, then bring just to the boil. Ladle the soup into warmed bowls. Garnish with the reserved mussels in shells. Serve lemon wedges with the soup.

French Onion Soup Energy 415kcal/1745kJ; Protein 13g; Carbohydrate 61.6g, of which sugars 12.6g; Fat 14.1g, of which saturates 6.7g; Cholesterol 25mg; Calcium 240mg; Fibre 4.1g; Sodium 1022mg.
Mussel Soup with Pumpkin Energy 126kcal/532kJ; Protein 13g; Carbohydrate 7.5g, of which sugars 4g; Fat 5g, of which saturates 0.8g; Cholesterol 40mg; Calcium 113mg; Fibre 2.5g; Sodium 245mg.

Mullet and Fennel Soup

Olives and tomato toasts are delicious in this soup.

Serves 4

25ml/1½ tbsp olive oil
1 onion, chopped
3 garlic cloves, chopped
2 fennel bulbs, thinly sliced
4 tomatoes, chopped
1 bay leaf
sprig of fresh thyme
1.2 litres/2 pints/5 cups fish stock
675g/1½lb red mullet or
  snapper, scaled and filleted
salt and ground black pepper

For the toasts

8 slices baguette, toasted
1 garlic clove
30ml/2 tbsp tomato
  purée (paste)
12 black olives, stoned (pitted)
  and quartered
fresh fennel fronds, to garnish

For the aioli

2 egg yolks
1–2 garlic cloves, crushed
10ml/2 tsp lemon juice
300ml/½ pint/1¼ cups extra
  virgin olive oil

1 Heat the olive oil in a large, heavy pan. Add the onion and garlic and cook for 5 minutes, until soften. Add the fennel and cook for 2–3 minutes. Stir in the tomatoes, bay leaf, thyme and stock. Boil, reduce the heat, cover and simmer for 30 minutes.

2 Meanwhile, make the aioli in a large bowl. Whisk the egg yolks, garlic, lemon juice and seasoning together. Whisk in the oil, drops at a time. As the mixture begins to thicken, add the oil in a slow trickle. Transfer to a large bowl and set aside.

3 Cut each mullet fillet into two or three pieces, then add them to the soup and cook gently for 5 minutes. Use a slotted spoon to remove the mullet and set aside.

4 Strain the cooking liquid, pressing the vegetables well. Whisk a ladleful of soup into the aioli, then whisk in the remaining soup in one go. Return the soup to a clean pan and cook very gently, whisking constantly, until the mixture is very slightly thickened. Add the mullet to the soup.

5 Rub the toasted baguette with garlic, spread with tomato purée and top with olives. Serve the soup topped with the toasts and garnished with fennel.

Bouillabaisse

Perhaps the most famous of all fish soups, this recipe originates from Marseilles in the south of France.

Serves 4–6

1.5 kg/3–3½ lb mixed fish and
  raw shellfish, such as red mullet,
  John Dory, monkfish, red snapper,
  whiting, large raw prawns
  (jumbo shrimp) and clams
225g/8oz well-flavoured tomatoes
pinch of saffron strands
90ml/6 tbsp olive oil
1 onion, sliced
1 leek, sliced
1 celery stick, sliced
2 garlic cloves, crushed
1 bouquet garni
1 strip orange rind
2.5ml/½ tsp fennel seeds
15ml/1 tbsp tomato
  purée (paste)
10ml/2 tsp Pernod
salt and ground black pepper
45ml/3 tbsp chopped fresh
  parsley and 4–6 thick slices
  French bread, to serve

1 Remove the heads, tails and fins from the fish and set the fish aside. Put the trimmings in a large pan with 1.2 litres/2 pints/5 cups water. Bring to the boil and simmer for 15 minutes. Strain and reserve the liquid.

2 Cut the fish into large chunks. Leave the shellfish in their shells. Scald the tomatoes, then drain and refresh in cold water. Peel them and chop roughly. Soak the saffron in 15–30ml/1–2 tbsp hot water.

3 Heat the oil in a large pan, add the onion, leek and celery and cook until softened. Add the garlic, bouquet garni, orange rind, fennel seeds and tomatoes, then stir in the saffron and its soaking liquid and the reserved fish stock. Season with salt and pepper, then bring to the boil and simmer for 30–40 minutes.

4 Add the shellfish and boil for about 6 minutes. Add the fish and cook for 6–8 minutes more, until it flakes easily.

5 Using a slotted spoon, transfer the fish to a warmed serving platter. Keep the liquid boiling, to allow the oil to emulsify with the broth. Add the tomato purée, Pernod, and seasoning.

6 Ladle into bowls, sprinkle with parsley and serve with bread.

Mullet Soup Energy 492kcal/2079kJ; Protein 41.2g; Carbohydrate 53.6g, of which sugars 10g; Fat 14.1g, of which saturates 1.2g; Cholesterol 0mg; Calcium 256mg; Fibre 6.1g; Sodium 965mg.
Bouillabaisse Energy 454kcal/1895kJ; Protein 53.8g; Carbohydrate 17g, of which sugars 6.4g; Fat 19.3g, of which saturates 3.1g; Cholesterol 135mg; Calcium 138mg; Fibre 2.5g; Sodium 345mg.

Salt Pork and Bean Soup

This classic Galician soup features salt pork and beans with young turnip tops, although purple sprouting broccoli makes a very pretty substitute. Make the soup ahead of time so that the flavours have a chance to blend. You will need to start making the soup at least a day in advance.

Serves 6
150g/5oz/⅔ cup haricot (navy) beans, soaked overnight in cold water and drained
1kg/2¼lb smoked gammon (cured or smoked ham) hock
3 potatoes, quartered
3 small turnips, sliced in rounds
150g/5oz purple sprouting broccoli
salt and ground black pepper

1 Put the drained beans and gammon into a casserole and cover with 2 litres/3½ pints/8 cups water. Slowly bring to the boil, skim off any scum, then turn down the heat and cook gently, covered, for about 1¼ hours.

2 Drain, reserving the broth. Return the broth to the casserole and add the potatoes, turnips and drained beans.

3 Meanwhile, strip all the gammon off the bone and return the bone to the broth. Discard the rind, fat and gristle and chop half the meat coarsely. Reserve the remaining meat for another recipe (see tip below).

4 Add the chopped meat to the casserole. Discard the hard stalks from the broccoli and add the leaves and florets to the broth. Simmer for 10 minutes. Season generously with pepper, then remove the bone and leave the soup to stand for at least half a day.

5 To serve, reheat the soup, add a little more seasoning if necessary, and ladle into soup bowls.

Cook's Tip
The leftover gammon can be chopped into bitesize pieces and added to rice or vegetable dishes, or tortillas.

Golden Chorizo and Chickpea Soup

Small uncooked chorizo sausages are available from Spanish delicatessens, but ready-to-eat chorizo can be cut into chunks and used.

Serves 4
115g/4oz/⅔ cup dried chickpeas, soaked overnight
pinch of saffron strands
45ml/3 tbsp olive oil
450g/1lb uncooked mini chorizo sausages
5ml/1 tsp dried chilli flakes
6 garlic cloves, finely chopped
450g/1lb tomatoes, roughly chopped
350g/12oz new potatoes, quartered
2 bay leaves
450ml/¾ pint/scant 2 cups water
60ml/4 tbsp chopped fresh parsley
salt and ground black pepper
30ml/2 tbsp extra virgin olive oil, to garnish
crusty bread, to serve

1 Place the chickpeas in a large pan. Cover with plenty of fresh water and bring to the boil, skimming off any scum. Cover and simmer for 2–3 hours, until tender. Add more boiling water, if necessary, to keep the chickpeas well covered. Drain, reserving the liquid. Soak the saffron strands in a little warm water.

2 Heat the oil in a large, deep frying pan. Add the chorizo and fry for 5 minutes, until a lot of oil has seeped out of the sausages and they are pale golden brown. Drain and set aside.

3 Add the chilli flakes and garlic to the fat in the pan and cook for a few seconds. Stir in the saffron with its soaking water, tomatoes, chickpeas, potatoes, chorizo and bay leaves. Pour in 450ml/¾ pint/scant 2 cups of the chickpea cooking liquor and 450ml/¾ pint/scant 2 cups water. Season to taste.

4 Bring to the boil, reduce the heat and simmer the soup for 45–50 minutes, stirring gently occasionally, until the potatoes are tender and the soup has thickened slightly.

5 Add the chopped parsley to the soup and adjust the seasoning. Ladle the soup into four large, warmed soup plates and drizzle a little extra virgin olive oil over each portion. Serve with crusty bread.

Pork Soup Energy 363kcal/1522kJ; Protein 37.5g; Carbohydrate 24.4g, of which sugars 4g; Fat 13.4g, of which saturates 4.4g; Cholesterol 38mg; Calcium 73mg; Fibre 4.4g; Sodium 1486mg.
Chorizo Soup Energy 642kcal/2674kJ; Protein 21.7g; Carbohydrate 42.3g, of which sugars 8.1g; Fat 44g, of which saturates 12.5g; Cholesterol 68mg; Calcium 174mg; Fibre 6.1g; Sodium 997mg.

Ribollita with Beans and Cabbage

This is a classic soup from Italy. Use cavolo nero cabbage, if you can, which is available in supermarkets.

Serves 4

115g/4oz/generous ½ cup cannellini beans, soaked overnight and drained
8 garlic cloves, unpeeled
30ml/2 tbsp olive oil
6 celery sticks, chopped
3 carrots, chopped
2 onions, chopped
400g/14oz can plum tomatoes, drained
30ml/2 tbsp chopped fresh flat leaf parsley
grated rind and juice of 1 lemon
800g/1¾lb cavolo nero cabbage, sliced
1 day-old ciabatta loaf
salt and ground black pepper
olive oil, to serve

1 Put the beans in a pan and cover with fresh water. Bring to the boil and boil for 10 minutes. Drain again. Cover generously with fresh cold water and add six garlic cloves. Bring to the boil, cover and simmer for 45–60 minutes, until the beans are tender. Set the beans aside in their cooking liquid.

2 Heat the oil in a pan. Peel and chop the remaining garlic and add it to the pan with the celery, carrots and onions. Cook gently for 10 minutes, until beginning to soften.

3 Stir in the tomatoes, parsley, lemon rind and juice. Cover and simmer for 25 minutes. Add the sliced cavolo nero cabbage and half the cannellini beans with enough of their cooking liquid to cover all of the ingredients. Simmer for 30 minutes.

4 Meanwhile, process the remaining beans with a little of their remaining cooking liquid in a food processor or blender until just smooth. Add to the pan and pour in boiling water to thin the mixture to the consistency of a thick soup.

5 Remove the crust from the ciabatta and tear the bread into rough pieces, then stir them into the soup. Season well. This soup should be very thick, but you may need to add a little more boiling water as the consistency varies depending on the bread. Ladle the soup into bowls and drizzle over a little olive oil. Serve immediately.

Sausage Soup with Borlotti Beans

A big-filler soup, perfect for a main meal. This recipe is based loosely on the famous French cassoulet. Toulouse sausages and Italian beans contribute lots of flavour and substance, and the soup is finished off with golden breadcrumbs.

Serves 6

250g/9oz/generous 1½ cups borlotti beans, soaked overnight and drained
115g/4oz pancetta, finely chopped
6 Toulouse sausages, thickly sliced
1 large onion, finely chopped
2 garlic cloves, chopped
2 carrots, finely diced
2 leeks, finely chopped
6 tomatoes, peeled, seeded and chopped
30ml/2 tbsp tomato purée (paste)
1.27 litres/2¼ pints/5⅔ cups vegetable stock
175g/6oz spring greens (collards), roughly shredded
25g/1oz/2 tbsp butter
115g/4oz/2 cups fresh white breadcrumbs
50g/2oz/⅔ cup Parmesan cheese, grated
salt and ground black pepper

1 Place the borlotti beans in a large pan. Cover with plenty of cold water and bring to the boil, then boil vigorously for 10 minutes. Drain well.

2 Heat a large pan. Dry-fry the pancetta until it is browned and yields its fat. Add the sausages and cook for 4–5 minutes, stirring occasionally, until beginning to brown. Add the onion and garlic and cook for 3–4 minutes until softened.

3 Stir in the beans, carrots, leeks, tomatoes, tomato purée and stock. Bring to the boil, reduce the heat and cover, then simmer for about 1¼ hours or until the beans are tender.

4 Stir in the spring greens and cook for 12–15 minutes more. Season well. Melt the butter in a frying pan and fry the breadcrumbs for 4–5 minutes, stirring, until golden, then stir in the Parmesan.

5 Ladle the soup into six bowls. Sprinkle the fried breadcrumb mixture over, then serve.

Ribollita Energy 104kcal/436kJ; Protein 5.7g; Carbohydrate 14.5g, of which sugars 6.9g; Fat 3g, of which saturates 0.5g; Cholesterol 0mg; Calcium 78mg; Fibre 5.9g; Sodium 218mg.
Sausage Soup Energy 574kcal/2405kJ; Protein 29g; Carbohydrate 47.7g, of which sugars 10.2g; Fat 31g, of which saturates 12.5g; Cholesterol 75mg; Calcium 284mg; Fibre 10.7g; Sodium 1179mg.

Pasta, Bean and Vegetable Soup

This is a Calabrian speciality and by tradition anything edible can go into it: use whatever beans and vegetables are to hand.

Serves 6

75g/3oz/scant ¹/₂ cup dried brown lentils
15g/¹/₂oz/¹/₄ cup dried mushrooms
15ml/1 tbsp olive oil
1 carrot, diced
1 celery stick, diced
1 onion, finely chopped
1 garlic clove, finely chopped
a little chopped fresh flat leaf parsley
a good pinch of crushed red chillies (optional)
1.5 litres/2¹/₂ pints/6¹/₄ cups vegetable stock
150g/5oz/1 cup each canned red kidney beans, cannellini beans and chickpeas, rinsed and drained
115g/4oz/1 cup dried small pasta shapes, such as rigatoni, penne or penne rigate
salt and ground black pepper
chopped flat leaf parsley, to garnish
freshly grated Pecorino cheese, to serve (optional)

1 Put the lentils in a pan, add 475ml/16fl oz/2 cups water and bring to the boil. Reduce the heat and simmer gently, stirring occasionally, for 15–20 minutes, or until tender. Soak the dried mushrooms in 175ml/6fl oz/³/₄ cup warm water for 20 minutes.

2 Drain the lentils, then rinse under cold water. Drain the soaked mushrooms and reserve the soaking liquid. Finely chop the mushrooms and set aside.

3 Heat the oil in a large pan and add the carrot, celery, onion, garlic, chopped parsley and chillies, if using. Cook over low heat, stirring constantly, for 5–7 minutes. Add the stock, then the mushrooms and their soaking liquid. Bring to the boil, then add the beans, chickpeas and lentils, with salt and pepper to taste. Cover, and simmer gently for 20 minutes.

4 Add the pasta and bring the soup back to the boil, stirring. Simmer, stirring frequently, for 7–8 minutes or until the pasta is al dente. Season, then serve hot in soup bowls, garnished with chopped parsley. Sprinkle with grated Pecorino, if you like.

Borlotti Bean Soup with Pasta

A complete meal in a bowl, this is a version of a classic Italian soup.

Serves 4

1 onion, chopped
1 celery stick, chopped
2 carrots, chopped
75ml/5 tbsp olive oil
1 bay leaf
1 glass white wine (optional)
1 litre/1³/₄ pints/4 cups vegetable stock
400g/14oz can chopped tomatoes
300ml/¹/₂ pint/1¹/₄ cups passata (bottled strained tomatoes)
175g/6oz/1¹/₂ cups pasta shapes, such as farfalle or conchiglie
400g/14oz can borlotti beans, drained
salt and ground black pepper
250g/9oz spinach
50g/2oz/²/₃ cup freshly grated Parmesan cheese, to serve

1 Place the onion, celery and carrots in a large pan with the olive oil. Cook over medium heat for 5 minutes.

2 Add the bay leaf, wine, vegetable stock, tomatoes and passata, and bring to the boil. Lower the heat and simmer for 10 minutes until the vegetables are just tender.

3 Add the pasta and beans, and bring the soup back to the boil, then simmer for 8 minutes until the pasta is al dente. Stir frequently to prevent the pasta from sticking.

4 Season to taste with salt and pepper. Remove any thick stalks from the spinach and add it to the soup. Cook for a further 2 minutes. Serve in heated bowls, sprinkled with Parmesan.

Variations

• For a delicious meaty version of this soup, you can add chunks of cooked spicy sausage or pieces of crispy cooked pancetta or bacon. The cooked meat needs to be piping hot before the soup is served, so add at the end of step 3 and stir frequently with the other ingredients.
• For vegetarians, you can use fried chunks of smoked or marinated tofu as an alternative to meat.

Pasta Bean Soup Energy 206kcal/874kJ; Protein 10.7g; Carbohydrate 36.7g, of which sugars 5g; Fat 2.9g, of which saturates 0.4g, Cholesterol 0mg; Calcium 72mg; Fibre 6.4g; Sodium 306mg.
Borlotti Bean Soup Energy 321kcal/1363kJ; Protein 15g; Carbohydrate 57.8g, of which sugars 12.7g; Fat 5g, of which saturates 0.8g; Cholesterol 0mg; Calcium 166mg; Fibre 9.9g; Sodium 762mg.

Meatballs in Pasta Soup

These meatballs are delicious in a hearty soup

Serves 4

400g/14oz can cannellini beans, drained and rinsed
1 litre/1³⁄₄ pints/4 cups vegetable stock
45ml/3 tbsp olive oil
1 onion, finely chopped
2 garlic cloves, chopped
1 small fresh red chilli, seeded and finely chopped
2 celery sticks, finely chopped
1 carrot, finely chopped
15ml/1 tbsp tomato purée (paste)
300g/11oz small pasta shapes

large handful of fresh basil, torn
salt and ground black pepper
basil leaves, to garnish
freshly grated Parmesan cheese, to serve

For the meatballs

1 thick slice white bread, crusts removed, made into crumbs
60ml/4 tbsp milk
350g/12oz lean minced (ground) beef or veal
30ml/2 tbsp chopped fresh parsley
grated rind of 1 orange
2 garlic cloves, crushed
1 egg, beaten
30ml/2 tbsp olive oil

1 For the meatballs, mix the bread, milk, meat, parsley, orange rind, garlic, egg and seasoning. Stand for 15 minutes, then shape into balls about the size of a large olive.

2 Heat the oil in a frying pan and fry the meatballs in batches for 6–8 minutes until browned all over. Use a draining spoon to remove them from the pan and set aside.

3 Purée the cannellini beans with a little of the vegetable stock in a food processor or blender until smooth. Set aside.

4 Heat the olive oil in a pan. Add the onion, garlic, chilli, celery and carrot. Cover and cook gently for 10 minutes, then stir in the tomato purée, bean purée and the remaining stock. Bring the soup to the boil and cook for about 10 minutes.

5 Stir in the pasta and simmer for 8–10 minutes, until the pasta is tender. Add the meatballs and basil and cook for 5 minutes. Season well before ladling it into warmed bowls. Garnish with basil and serve with Parmesan cheese.

Genoese Minestrone

This slow-cooker version of minestrone is packed with vegetables and makes a good vegetarian supper dish when served with bread.

Serves 4

30ml/2 tbsp olive oil
1 onion, finely chopped
2 celery sticks, finely chopped
1 large carrot, finely chopped
1 potato, weighing about 115g/4oz, cut into 1cm/¹⁄₂in cubes
1 litre/1³⁄₄ pints/4 cups vegetable stock
75g/3oz green beans, cut into 5cm/2in pieces
1 courgette (zucchini), thinly sliced

2 Italian plum tomatoes, peeled and chopped
200g/7oz can cannellini beans, drained and rinsed
¹⁄₄ Savoy cabbage, shredded
40g/1¹⁄₂oz dried 'quick-cook' spaghetti or vermicelli, broken into short lengths
salt and ground black pepper

For the pesto

about 20 fresh basil leaves
1 garlic clove
10ml/2 tsp pine nuts
15ml/1 tbsp freshly grated Parmesan cheese
15ml/1 tbsp freshly grated Pecorino cheese
30ml/2 tbsp olive oil

1 Heat the olive oil in a pan, then add the chopped onion, celery and carrot and cook, stirring, for about 7 minutes, until the vegetables begin to soften.

2 Transfer the fried vegetables to the ceramic cooking pot. Add the potato cubes and vegetable stock, cover the cooking pot with the lid, and cook on high for 1¹⁄₂ hours.

3 Add the green beans, courgette, tomatoes and cannellini beans to the pot. Cover and cook for 1 hour, then stir in the cabbage and pasta and cook for a further 20 minutes.

4 Meanwhile, place all the pesto ingredients in a food processor. Blend to a smooth sauce, adding 15–45ml/1–3 tbsp water through the tube to loosen the mixture if necessary.

5 Stir 30ml/2 tbsp of the pesto sauce into the soup. Check the seasoning, adding more if necessary. Serve hot, in warmed bowls, with the remaining pesto spooned on top.

Meatballs in Pasta Soup Energy 277kcal/1158kJ; Protein 19.9g; Carbohydrate 20.5g, of which sugars 1.4g; Fat 14g, of which saturates 6.1g; Cholesterol 89mg; Calcium 133mg; Fibre 1g; Sodium 731mg.
Genoese Minestrone Energy 263kcal/1098kJ; Protein 8.5g; Carbohydrate 25.1g, of which sugars 7g; Fat 14.9g, of which saturates 2.8g; Cholesterol 5mg; Calcium 103mg; Fibre 5.4g; Sodium 1034mg.

Red Curry Noodle Soup with Monkfish

This light and creamy coconut soup provides a base for a colourful fusion of red-curried monkfish and pad Thai, the classic stir-fried noodle dish of Thailand.

Serves 4
175g/6oz flat rice noodles
30ml/2 tbsp vegetable oil
2 garlic cloves, chopped
15ml/1 tbsp red curry paste
450g/1lb monkfish tail, cut into
  bitesize pieces
300ml/½ pint/1¼ cups
  coconut cream

750ml/1¼ pints/3 cups hot
  chicken stock
45ml/3 tbsp Thai fish sauce
15ml/1 tbsp palm sugar (jaggery)
60ml/4 tbsp roughly chopped
  roasted peanuts
4 spring onions (scallions),
  shredded lengthways
50g/2oz beansprouts
large handful of fresh Thai
  basil leaves
salt and ground black pepper
1 red chilli, seeded and cut
  lengthways into slivers,
  to garnish

1 Soak the noodles in boiling water for 10 minutes, or according to the packet instructions. Drain.

2 Heat the oil in a wok or pan over a high heat. Add the garlic and cook for 2 minutes. Stir in the curry paste and cook for 1 minute.

3 Add the monkfish pieces to the pan and stir-fry over high heat for 4–5 minutes, until just tender.

4 Pour in the coconut cream and stock. Stir in the fish sauce and sugar, and bring just to the boil. Add the drained noodles and cook for 1–2 minutes, until tender.

5 Stir in half the peanuts, half the spring onions, half the beansprouts, the basil and seasoning.

6 Ladle the soup into deep bowls and sprinkle over the remaining peanuts. Garnish with the remaining spring onions, beansprouts and the red chilli, and serve.

Red Onion and Vermicelli Laksa

Sliced red onions mimic flour noodles in this soup.

Serves 6
150g/5oz/2½ cups dried
  shiitake mushrooms
1.2 litres/2 pints/5 cups boiling
  vegetable stock
30ml/2 tbsp tamarind paste
250ml/8fl oz/1 cup hot water
6 large dried red chillies, stems
  removed and seeded
2 lemon grass stalks, finely sliced

5ml/1 tsp ground turmeric
15ml/1 tbsp grated fresh galangal
1 onion, chopped
5ml/1 tsp dried shrimp paste
30ml/2 tbsp oil
10ml/2 tsp palm sugar (jaggery)
175g/6oz rice vermicelli
1 red onion, very finely sliced
1 small cucumber, seeded and
  cut into strips
handful of fresh mint leaves,
  to garnish

1 Place the shiitake mushrooms in a large bowl and pour in enough boiling stock to cover them, then set aside to soak for 30 minutes. Put the tamarind paste into a bowl and pour in the hot water. Mash, then strain and reserve the liquid, discarding the pulp.

2 Soak the chillies in hot water to cover for 5 minutes, then drain, reserving the liquid. Place in a food processor and blend with the lemon grass, turmeric, galangal, onion and shrimp paste, adding a little soaking water to form a paste.

3 Heat the oil in a large, heavy pan and cook the paste over low heat for 4–5 minutes. Add the tamarind liquid and bring to the boil, then simmer for 5 minutes. Remove from the heat.

4 Drain the mushrooms and reserve the stock. Discard the stems, then halve or quarter the mushrooms, if large. Add the mushrooms to the pan with their soaking liquid, the remaining stock and the sugar. Simmer gently for about 25–30 minutes or until tender.

5 Put the rice vermicelli into a large bowl and cover with boiling water, then leave to soak for 4 minutes until softened. Drain well, then divide among six bowls. Top with onion and cucumber, then ladle in the boiling shiitake soup. Add a small bunch of mint leaves to each bowl and serve.

Red Onion Laksa Energy 161kcal/671kJ; Protein 4.1g; Carbohydrate 26.6g, of which sugars 2.7g; Fat 4.3g, of which saturates 0.6g; Cholesterol 4mg; Calcium 32mg; Fibre 0.2g; Sodium 41mg.
Red Curry Monkfish Soup Energy 379kcal/1589kJ; Protein 25.5g; Carbohydrate 41.2g, of which sugars 4.7g; Fat 12g, of which saturates 2g; Cholesterol 18mg; Calcium 49mg; Fibre 0.9g; Sodium 111mg.

Noodle, Pak Choi and Salmon Ramen

This lightly spiced noodle soup is enhanced by slices of seared fresh salmon and crisp vegetables.

Serves 4

1.5 litres/2½ pints/6 cups good
  vegetable stock
2.5cm/1in piece fresh root ginger,
  finely sliced
2 garlic cloves, crushed
6 spring onions (scallions), sliced
45ml/3 tbsp soy sauce
45ml/3 tbsp sake
450g/1lb salmon fillet, skinned
5ml/1 tsp groundnut (peanut) oil
350g/12oz ramen or
  udon noodles
4 small heads pak choi (bok
  choy), broken into leaves
1 fresh red chilli, seeded
  and sliced
50g/2oz/1 cup beansprouts
salt and ground black pepper

1 Pour the stock into a large pan and add the ginger, garlic, and a third of the spring onions. Pour in the soy sauce and sake. Bring the stock to the boil, then reduce the heat and simmer for 30 minutes.

2 Meanwhile, remove any pin bones from the salmon using tweezers, then cut the salmon on the slant into 12 slices, using a very sharp knife.

3 Brush a ridged griddle (grill) pan or frying pan with the oil and heat until very hot. Sear the salmon slices for 1–2 minutes on each side until tender and marked by the ridges of the griddle pan. Set aside.

4 Cook the ramen or udon noodles in a large pan of boiling water for 4–5 minutes or according to the instructions on the packet. Place into a colander, drain well and refresh under cold running water. Drain again and set aside.

5 Strain the broth into a clean pan and season, then bring to the boil. Add the pak choi. Using a fork, twist the noodles into four nests and put these into deep bowls. Divide the salmon slices, spring onions, chilli and beansprouts among the bowls. Ladle in the broth.

Crab and Chilli Soup

Prepared fresh crab is readily available, high quality and convenient – perfect for creating a soup in minutes.

Serves 4

45ml/3 tbsp olive oil
1 red onion, finely chopped
2 red chillies, seeded and
  finely chopped
1 garlic clove, finely chopped
450g/1lb fresh white crab meat
30ml/2 tbsp chopped fresh parsley
30ml/2 tbsp chopped fresh
  coriander (cilantro)
juice of 2 lemons
1 lemon grass stalk
1 litre/1¾ pints/4 cups good fish
  or chicken stock
15ml/1 tbsp Thai fish sauce
150g/5oz vermicelli or angel hair
  pasta, broken into 5–7.5cm/
  2–3in lengths
salt and ground black pepper

For the coriander relish
50g/2oz/1 cup fresh coriander
  (cilantro) leaves
1 green chilli, seeded
  and chopped
15ml/1 tbsp sunflower oil
25ml/1½ tbsp lemon juice
2.5ml/½ tsp ground roasted
  cumin seeds

1 Heat the oil in a pan and add the onion, chillies and garlic. Cook over a gentle heat for 10 minutes until the onion is very soft. Transfer this mixture to a bowl and stir in the crab meat, parsley, coriander and lemon juice, then set aside.

2 Lay the lemon grass on a chopping board and bruise it with a rolling pin or pestle. Pour the stock and fish sauce into a pan. Add the lemon grass and bring to the boil, then add the pasta. Simmer, uncovered, for 3–4 minutes or according to the packet instructions, until the pasta is just tender.

3 Meanwhile, make the coriander relish. Place the fresh coriander, chilli, oil, lemon juice and cumin in a food processor or blender and process to a coarse paste. Add seasoning.

4 Remove and discard the lemon grass from the soup. Stir the chilli and crab mixture into the soup and season it well. Bring to the boil, then reduce the heat and simmer for 2 minutes.

5 Ladle the soup into four deep, warmed bowls and put a spoonful of the relish in the centre of each. Serve immediately.

Crab and Chilli Soup Energy 228kcal/951kJ; Protein 23.6g; Carbohydrate 5.4g, of which sugars 5g; Fat 12.6g, of which saturates 3.7g; Cholesterol 90mg; Calcium 199mg; Fibre 1.1g; Sodium 767mg.
Noodle Ramen Energy 569kcal/2394kJ; Protein 34.6g; Carbohydrate 65.6g, of which sugars 4.1g; Fat 20.5g, of which saturates 4.3g; Cholesterol 83mg; Calcium 70mg; Fibre 3.5g; Sodium 746mg.

Chiang Mai Noodle Soup

This delicious noodle soup is similar to the famous Malaysian laksa.

Serves 4–6
600ml/1 pint/2½ cups coconut milk
30ml/2 tbsp Thai red curry paste
5ml/1 tsp ground turmeric
450g/1lb chicken thighs, boned and cut into bitesize chunks
600ml/1 pint/2½ cups chicken stock
60ml/4 tbsp Thai fish sauce
15ml/1 tbsp dark soy sauce
juice of ½–1 lime

450g/1lb fresh egg noodles, blanched briefly in boiling water
salt and ground black pepper

To garnish
3 spring onions (scallions), chopped
4 fresh red chillies, chopped
4 shallots, chopped
60ml/4 tbsp sliced pickled mustard leaves, rinsed
30ml/2 tbsp fried sliced garlic
coriander (cilantro) leaves
4–6 fried noodle nests (optional)

1 Pour about one-third of the coconut milk into a large, heavy pan or wok. Bring to the boil over medium heat, stirring frequently with a wooden spoon until the milk separates.

2 Add the curry paste and ground turmeric, stir to mix completely and cook until the mixture is fragrant.

3 Add the chunks of chicken and toss over the heat for about 2 minutes, making sure that all are coated with the paste.

4 Add the remaining coconut milk, the chicken stock, fish sauce and soy sauce. Season with salt and pepper to taste. Bring to simmering point, stirring frequently, then lower the heat and cook gently for 7–10 minutes. Remove from the heat and stir in lime juice to taste.

5 Reheat the fresh egg noodles in boiling water, drain and divide among four to six warmed bowls. Divide the chunks of chicken among the bowls and ladle in the hot soup. Top each serving with spring onions, chillies, shallots, pickled mustard leaves, fried garlic, coriander leaves and a fried noodle nest, if using. Serve immediately.

Chicken and Crab Noodle Soup

The chicken makes a delicious stock for this noodle soup with its hint of aromatic Chinese flavours.

Serves 6
2 chicken legs, skinned
1.75 litres/3 pints/7½ cups water
bunch of spring onions (scallions)
2.5cm/1in piece fresh root ginger, sliced
5ml/1 tsp black peppercorns
2 garlic cloves, halved

75g/3oz rice noodles
115g/4oz fresh white crab meat
30ml/2 tbsp light soy sauce
salt and ground black pepper
coriander (cilantro) leaves, to garnish

For the omelettes
4 eggs
30ml/2 tbsp chopped fresh coriander (cilantro) leaves
15ml/1 tbsp extra virgin olive oil

1 Put the chicken and water in a pan. Bring to the boil, then simmer gently for 20 minutes; skim the surface occasionally.

2 Slice half the spring onions and add to the pan with the ginger, peppercorns, garlic and salt. Simmer, covered, for 1½ hours. Meanwhile, soak the noodles in boiling water for 4 minutes, or according to the packet instructions. Drain and rinse under cold water. Shred the remaining spring onions and set aside.

3 To make the omelettes, beat the eggs with the coriander and seasoning. Heat a little of the oil in a small frying pan. Add a third of the egg and swirl the pan to coat the base evenly. Cook for 1 minute. Flip over and cook for 30 seconds. Turn out on to a plate and leave to cool. Repeat twice more. Roll up the omelettes tightly one at a time and slice thinly.

4 Remove the chicken from the stock and leave to cool. Strain the stock through a sieve (strainer) lined with muslin (cheesecloth) into a clean pan. When the chicken has cooled, remove and finely shred the meat, discarding the bones.

5 Bring the stock to the boil. Add the noodles, chicken, spring onions and crab meat. Simmer for 1–2 minutes. Stir in the soy sauce and season. Ladle into bowls and top each with sliced omelette and coriander leaves.

Chicken Noodle Soup Energy 159kcal/664kJ; Protein 13.5g; Carbohydrate 10.6g, of which sugars 0.4g; Fat 6.9g, of which saturates 1.7g; Cholesterol 157mg; Calcium 46mg; Fibre 0g; Sodium 526mg.
Chiang Mai Soup Energy 606kcal/2569kJ; Protein 39.5g; Carbohydrate 88.7g, of which sugars 10.1g; Fat 12.9g, of which saturates 3.7g; Cholesterol 135mg; Calcium 84mg; Fibre 3.3g; Sodium 1111mg.

Hot and Sour Prawn Soup

This salty, sour, spicy hot soup is a real classic. Cooking the stock in a slow cooker maximizes the flavour before the final ingredients are added.

Serves 4

450g/1lb raw king prawns (jumbo shrimp), thawed if frozen
900ml/1½ pints/3¾ cups near-boiling light chicken stock or water
3 lemon grass stalks
6 kaffir lime leaves, torn in half
225g/8oz straw mushrooms, drained
45ml/3 tbsp Thai fish sauce
60ml/4 tbsp fresh lime juice
30ml/2 tbsp chopped spring onion (scallion)
15ml/1 tbsp fresh coriander (cilantro) leaves
4 fresh red chillies, seeded and thickly sliced
salt and ground black pepper

1 Peel the prawns, reserving the shells. Using a sharp knife, make a shallow cut along the back of each prawn and use the point of the knife to remove the thin black vein. Place the prawns in a bowl, cover and chill until ready to use.

2 Rinse the reserved prawn shells under cold water, then put them in the ceramic cooking pot and add the chicken stock or water. Cover with the lid and switch the slow cooker to high.

3 Using a pestle, bruise the bulbous end of the lemon grass stalks. Lift the lid of the ceramic pot and quickly add the lemon grass stalks and half the torn kaffir lime leaves to the stock. Stir well, then re-cover with the lid and cook for about 2 hours until the stock is fragrant and aromatic.

4 Strain the stock into a large bowl and rinse out the ceramic cooking pot. Pour the stock back into the cleaned pot. Add the drained mushrooms and cook on high for 30 minutes.

5 Add the prawns to the soup and cook for a further 10 minutes until the prawns turn pink and are cooked.

6 Stir the fish sauce, lime juice, spring onion, coriander, chillies and remaining lime leaves into the soup. Taste and adjust the seasoning if necessary. It should be sour, salty, spicy and hot.

Pork and Egg Ramen-style Soup

This is a famous Japanese soup ideal for a tasty supper treat or a hearty lunch.

Serves 4
250g/9oz dried ramen noodles

For the stock
4 spring onions (scallions)
7.5cm/3in fresh root ginger, sliced
2 raw chicken carcasses
1 large onion, quartered
4 garlic cloves
1 large carrot, roughly chopped
1 egg shell
120ml/4fl oz/½ cup sake
60ml/4 tbsp shoyu or soy sauce
2.5ml/½ tsp salt

For the pot-roast pork
500g/1¼lb pork shoulder, boned
30ml/2 tbsp vegetable oil
2 spring onions (scallions), chopped
2.5cm/1in fresh root ginger, peeled and sliced
15ml/1 tbsp sake
45ml/3 tbsp shoyu or soy sauce
15ml/1 tbsp sugar

For the toppings
2 hard-boiled eggs
150g/5oz pickled bamboo shoots, soaked for 30 minutes, drained
½ nori sheet, broken into pieces
2 spring onions (scallions), chopped
ground white pepper
sesame oil or chilli oil

1 To make the stock, bruise the spring onions and ginger. Boil 1.5 litres/2½ pints/6¼ cups water in a wok. Add the chicken bones and boil for 5 minutes. Drain and rinse the bones. Bring another 2 litres/3½ pints/9 cups water to the boil. Add the bones and other stock ingredients, except the shoyu and salt. Simmer gently for up to 2 hours, until the liquid has reduced by half. Strain the stock, discarding the ingredients.

2 For the pork, roll the meat up tightly and tie. Heat the oil, stir in the spring onions and ginger. Add and brown the meat.

3 Sprinkle with sake and add 400ml/14fl oz/1⅔ cups water, the shoyu and sugar. Boil, then cover and cook for 25–30 minutes, turning every 5 minutes. Remove from the heat. Slice the pork.

4 Boil 1 litre/1¾ pints/4 cups soup stock. Add the shoyu and salt. Cook the noodles according to the packet instructions. Drain. Divide among four bowls. Cover with soup. Add the boiled eggs, pork, pickled bamboo shoots and nori. Sprinkle with spring onions. Serve with pepper and sesame or chilli oil.

Pork and Egg Soup Energy 521kcal/2193kJ; Protein 38.9g; Carbohydrate 55.6g, of which sugars 8.7g; Fat 17.5g, of which saturates 3.2g; Cholesterol 174mg; Calcium 57mg; Fibre 3g; Sodium 843mg.
Prawn Soup Energy 127kcal/536kJ; Protein 27g; Carbohydrate 1.4g, of which sugars 1.2g; Fat 1.4g, of which saturates 0.3g; Cholesterol 315mg; Calcium 133mg; Fibre 0.7g; Sodium 2715mg.

Salt Cod and Okra Soup with Yam

Inspired by the ingredients of the Caribbean, this chunky soup is served in deep bowls around a chive-flavoured sweet yam mash.

Serves 6

200g/7oz salt cod, soaked for
   24 hours, changing the water
   several times
15ml/1 tbsp olive oil
1 garlic clove, chopped
1 onion, chopped
1 green chilli, seeded
   and chopped
6 plum tomatoes, peeled
   and chopped
250ml/8fl oz/1 cup white wine
2 bay leaves
225g/8oz okra, trimmed and cut
   into chunks
225g/8oz callaloo or spinach
30ml/2 tbsp chopped
   fresh parsley
salt and ground black pepper

For the creamed yam
675g/1½lb yam, peeled and cut
   into chunks
juice of 1 lemon
50g/2oz/¼ cup butter
30ml/2 tbsp double
   (heavy) cream
15ml/1 tbsp chopped fresh chives

1 Drain and skin the cod, then rinse it under cold running water. Cut into bitesize pieces, removing bones, and set aside.

2 Heat the oil in a pan. Add the garlic, onion and chilli. Cook for 4–5 minutes until soft. Add the cod and cook for 3–4 minutes, until it begins to colour. Stir in the tomatoes, wine and bay leaves. Pour in 900ml/1⅓ pints/3¾ cups water, bring to the boil, reduce the heat and simmer for 10 minutes.

3 Add the okra and cook for 10 minutes. Stir in the callaloo or spinach and cook for 5 minutes, until the okra is tender.

4 Prepare the creamed yam. Place the yam in a pan with the lemon juice and add cold water to cover. Bring to the boil and cook for 15–20 minutes, until tender. Drain well, return to the pan and dry it out over the heat for a few seconds. Mash with the butter and cream, and season well. Stir in the chives.

5 Season the soup with salt and pepper and stir in the parsley. To serve, divide the creamed yam between six bowls and ladle the soup around it.

Rice and Bean Soup with Salt Cod

Based on the classic Caribbean dish of rice and peas, this soup is made with black-eyed beans, but kidney beans or, more traditionally, pigeon peas can be used.

Serves 6

15ml/1 tbsp sunflower oil
75g/3oz/6 tbsp butter
115g/4oz thick rindless bacon
   rashers (strips), cut into strips
1 onion, chopped
2 garlic cloves, chopped
1 fresh red chilli, seeded
   and chopped
225g/8oz/generous 1 cup long
   grain rice
2 fresh thyme sprigs
1 cinnamon stick
400g/14oz can black-eyed beans
   (peas), drained and rinsed
350g/12oz salt cod, soaked for
   24 hours, changing the water
   several times
plain (all-purpose) flour,
   for dusting
400g/14oz can coconut milk
175g/6oz baby spinach leaves
30ml/2 tbsp chopped
   fresh parsley
salt and ground black pepper

1 Heat the oil and 25g/1oz/2 tbsp of the butter in a large pan. Add the bacon and cook for 3–4 minutes, until golden. Stir in the onion, garlic and chilli and cook for a further 4–5 minutes.

2 Stir in the rice and cook for 1–2 minutes, until the grains are translucent. Stir in the thyme, cinnamon and black-eyed beans and cook for 1–2 minutes. Pour in 900ml/1⅓ pints/3¾ cups water and boil. Cook over low heat for 25–30 minutes.

3 Meanwhile, wash the soaked salt cod under cold running water. Pat dry with kitchen paper and remove the skin. Cut into large bitesize pieces and toss in the flour until evenly coated. Shake off the excess flour.

4 Melt the remaining butter in a large, heavy-based frying pan. Add the cod, in batches if necessary, and cook for 4–5 minutes until tender and golden. Remove the cod and set aside.

5 Stir the coconut milk into the rice and beans. Remove the cinnamon stick and cook the soup for 2–3 minutes. Stir in the spinach and cook for 2–3 minutes. Add the cod and parsley, season and heat through. Ladle the soup into bowls and serve.

Salt Cod Soup Energy 322kcal/1352kJ; Protein 10.7g; Carbohydrate 36.7g, of which sugars 5.3g; Fat 12.8g, of which saturates 6.6g; Cholesterol 40mg; Calcium 159mg; Fibre 4.6g; Sodium 137mg.
Rice Soup Energy 323kcal/1358kJ; Protein 10.7g; Carbohydrate 37g, of which sugars 5.6g; Fat 12.9g, of which saturates 6.7g; Cholesterol 40mg; Calcium 159mg; Fibre 4.6g; Sodium 138mg.

Soft-shell Crab and Corn Gumbo

A well-flavoured chicken and shellfish stock gives this dish the taste of a gumbo.

Serves 6

30ml/2 tbsp vegetable oil
1 onion, chopped
1 garlic clove, chopped
115g/4oz rindless streaky (fatty)
    bacon, chopped
40g/1 1/2oz/1/3 cup plain
    (all-purpose) flour
1 celery stick, chopped
1 red (bell) pepper, seeded
    and chopped
1 red chilli, seeded and chopped
450g/1lb plum tomatoes, chopped

2 large corn on the cob
4 soft-shell crabs, washed well
30ml/2 tbsp chopped fresh parsley
small bunch of spring onions
    (scallions), roughly chopped
salt and ground black pepper

For the stock

350g/12oz whole uncooked
    prawns (shrimp)
2 large chicken wings
1 carrot, thickly sliced
3 celery sticks, sliced
1 onion, sliced
handful of parsley stalks
2 bay leaves
1.5 litres/2 1/2 pints/6 1/4 cups water

1 To make the stock, peel the prawns and put the shells into a pan. Set the prawns aside. Add the remaining ingredients to the pan. Bring to the boil and skim. Cover and cook for 1 hour.

2 To make the gumbo, heat the oil in a large pan, add the onion and garlic and cook for 3–4 minutes. Add the bacon and cook for 3 minutes. Stir in the flour and cook for 3–4 minutes.

3 When the mixture is turning golden, strain in the stock, stirring constantly. Add the celery, pepper, chilli and tomatoes, bring to the boil and simmer for 5 minutes. Cut the corn cobs into 2.5cm/1in slices, and add to the gumbo.

4 To prepare the crabs, cut off the eyes and mouth, then cut across the face and push your fingers into the opening to hook out the stomach, a jelly-like sac. Turn the crab over and remove the tail flap. Lift up both sides of the shell and pull out the gills. Quarter the crabs, then add to the gumbo with the prawns.

5 Simmer for 15 minutes until the crabs and corn are cooked. Season, then stir in the parsley and spring onions, and serve.

Clam, Mushroom and Potato Chowder

The delicate, sweet shellfish taste of clams and the soft earthiness of wild mushrooms combine with slices of floury potatoes to make this soup a great meal on its own – and one that is fit for any occasion.

Serves 4

48 clams, scrubbed
50g/2oz/1/4 cup unsalted
    (sweet) butter
1 large onion, chopped
1 celery stick, sliced

1 carrot, sliced
225g/8oz assorted wild
    mushrooms, such as
    chanterelles, saffron milk-caps,
    chicken of the woods or
    St George's mushrooms, sliced
225g/8oz floury potatoes,
    thickly sliced
1.2 litres/2 pints/5 cups
    light chicken or vegetable
    stock, boiling
1 thyme sprig
4 parsley stalks
salt and ground black pepper
fresh thyme, to garnish

1 Place the clams in a large pan, discarding any that are open. Put 1cm/1/2in of water in the pan, cover, bring to the boil and steam over medium heat for 6–8 minutes until the clams open (discard any clams that do not open).

2 Drain the clams over a bowl, remove the shells, reserving a few clams in their shells for garnish. Chop the shelled clams. Strain the cooking juices into the bowl, add the chopped clams and set aside.

3 Add the butter, onion, celery and carrot to the pan and cook gently for about 10 minutes, until the vegetables are softened but not coloured.

4 Add the mixed mushrooms to the pan and cook for about 3–4 minutes until their juices begin to seep out.

5 Add the potatoes, the clams and their juices, the stock, thyme and parsley stalks to the pan and stir well.

6 Bring the soup to the boil, then reduce the heat, cover and simmer for 25 minutes, stirring occasionally. Season, ladle into bowls and garnish with the reserved clams and fresh thyme.

Crab and Corn Gumbo Energy 166kcal/694kJ; Protein 10.2g; Carbohydrate 11.1g, of which sugars 5.5g; Fat 9.3g, of which saturates 2.2g; Cholesterol 37mg; Calcium 94mg; Fibre 2.2g; Sodium 1280mg
Clam Chowder Energy 203kcal/848kJ; Protein 10.8g; Carbohydrate 15.8g, of which sugars 5.2g; Fat 11.2g, of which saturates 6.8g; Cholesterol 60mg; Calcium 66mg; Fibre 2.4g; Sodium 696mg

Mixed Seafood and Rice Gumbo

Gumbo is a soup served over rice as a main course.

Serves 6
450g/1lb fresh mussels, cooked and shelled, with cooking liquid
450g/1lb raw prawns (shrimp), with shells
1 cooked crab, about 1kg/2¼lb
small bunch of parsley, leaves chopped and stalks reserved
150ml/¼ pint/⅔ cup cooking oil
115g/4oz/1 cup plain (all-purpose) flour

1 green (bell) pepper, seeded and chopped
1 large onion, chopped
2 celery sticks, sliced
3 garlic cloves, finely chopped
75g/3oz smoked spiced sausage, skinned and sliced
275g/10oz/1½ cups white long grain rice
6 spring onions (scallions), shredded
cayenne pepper, to taste
Tabasco sauce, to taste
salt

1 Make the mussel liquid up to 2 litres/3½ pints/8 cups with water and place in a pan. Peel the prawns, reserving a few for the garnish. Put the shells and heads in the pan. Remove all the meat from the crab, separating the brown and white meat. Add the shell to the pan with 5ml/1 tsp salt. Bring to the boil, skimming. When there is no more froth, add the parsley stalks and simmer for 15 minutes. Cool, then strain the stock and make up to 2 litres/3½ pints/8 cups with water.

2 Heat the oil in a pan. Stir in the flour. Stir over medium heat until golden. Add the pepper, onion, celery and garlic. Cook for 3 minutes until softened. Stir in the sausage. Reheat the stock.

3 Stir the brown crab meat into the roux, then ladle in the hot stock, stirring until it is smoothly incorporated. Boil, partially cover, then simmer gently for 30 minutes.

4 Meanwhile, cook the rice in plenty of lightly salted boiling water until the grains are tender.

5 Add the prawns, mussels, white crab meat and spring onions to the gumbo. Return to the boil and season with salt, cayenne and a dash or two of Tabasco. Simmer for a minute, then add the chopped parsley. Serve immediately, ladled over the rice.

Corn and Potato Chowder

This creamy, yet chunky, soup is filled with the sweet taste of corn. Punchy Cheddar cheese rounds off the fabulous flavour.

Serves 4
1 onion, chopped
1 garlic clove, crushed
1 baking potato, chopped
2 celery sticks, sliced
1 small green (bell) pepper, seeded, halved and sliced

30ml/2 tbsp sunflower oil
25g/1oz/2 tbsp butter
600ml/1 pint/2½ cups vegetable stock or water
300ml/½ pint/1¼ cups milk
200g/7oz can flageolet (small cannellini) beans
300g/11oz can corn
good pinch of dried sage or a few small fresh sage leaves
salt and ground black pepper
Cheddar cheese or Monterey Jack, grated, to serve

1 Put the onion, garlic, potato, celery and green pepper into a large heavy pan with the oil and butter.

2 Heat until the ingredients are sizzling, then reduce the heat to low. Cover and cook gently for about 10 minutes, shaking the pan occasionally.

3 Pour in the stock or water, season with salt and pepper and bring to the boil. Reduce the heat, cover again and simmer gently for about 15 minutes or until the vegetables are tender.

4 Add the milk, beans and corn, including the liquor from the cans. Stir in the dried or fresh sage. Heat until simmering, then cook gently, uncovered, for 5 minutes. Check the seasoning before ladling the chowder into bowls. Sprinkle with cheese and serve immediately.

Variations
• Chickpeas are delicious with corn – add a can as well as the flageolet (small cannellini), or use them instead of the flageolet.
• For refreshingly spicy, zesty flavour, peel and chop a large chunk of fresh root ginger and cook it with the vegetables. Then add the grated rind of one lemon with the sage.

Seafood Gumbo Energy 559kcal/2336kJ; Protein 31.1g; Carbohydrate 57.6g, of which sugars 3.7g; Fat 23g, of which saturates 3.4g; Cholesterol 183mg; Calcium 145mg; Fibre 1.9g; Sodium 474mg.
Corn Chowder Energy 320kcal/1347kJ; Protein 9.4g; Carbohydrate 43.2g, of which sugars 15.7g; Fat 13.5g, of which saturates 5g; Cholesterol 18mg; Calcium 119mg; Fibre 5g; Sodium 500mg.

Succotash Soup with Chicken

Based on a vegetable dish from the southern states of the USA, this soup includes succulent fresh corn kernels, which give it a richness that perfectly complements the chicken.

Serves 4

750ml/1¼ pints/3 cups chicken stock
4 skinless chicken breast fillets
50g/2oz/¼ cup butter
2 onions, chopped
115g/4oz piece rindless smoked streaky (fatty) bacon, chopped
25g/1oz/¼ cup plain (all-purpose) flour
4 corn on the cob
300ml/½ pint/1¼ cups milk
400g/14oz can butter (lima) beans, drained
45ml/3 tbsp chopped fresh parsley
salt and ground black pepper

1 Bring the chicken stock to the boil in a large pan. Add the chicken breasts and bring back to the boil. Reduce the heat and cook for 12–15 minutes, until cooked through and tender. Use a slotted spoon to remove the chicken from the pan and leave to cool. Reserve the stock.

2 Melt the butter in a pan. Add the onions and cook for 4–5 minutes, until softened but not brown.

3 Add the bacon to the pan and cook for 5–6 minutes, until beginning to brown. Sprinkle in the flour and cook for 1 minute, stirring constantly.

4 Gradually stir in the hot stock and bring to the boil, stirring until thickened. Remove from the heat.

5 Using a sharp knife, remove the kernels from the corn cobs. Stir the kernels into the pan with half the milk. Return to the heat and cook, stirring occasionally, for 12–15 minutes, until the corn is tender.

6 Cut the chicken into bitesize pieces and stir into the soup. Stir in the butter beans and the remaining milk. Bring to the boil and cook for 5 minutes, then season well and stir in the parsley.

Chicken Broth with Dumplings

This is the classic comfort-and-cure recipe.

Serves 6–8

1–1.5kg/2¼–3¼lb chicken, cut into portions
2–3 onions, halved
3–5 carrots, thickly sliced
3–5 celery sticks, thickly sliced
1 small parsnip, cut in half
30–45ml/2–3 tbsp roughly chopped fresh parsley
30–45ml/2–3 tbsp chopped fresh dill
1–2 pinches ground turmeric
2 garlic cloves, finely chopped
salt and ground black pepper

For the dumplings
175g/6oz/¾ cup medium matzo meal
2 eggs, lightly beaten
45ml/3 tbsp vegetable oil
1 garlic clove, finely chopped
30ml/2 tbsp chopped fresh parsley, plus extra to garnish
½ onion, finely grated
salt and ground black pepper

1 Put the chicken, onions, carrots, celery, parsnip, parsley, half the dill and the turmeric in a pan. Add plenty of salt and pepper and 3–4 litres/5–7 pints/12–16 cups water.

2 Bring to the boil, then lower the heat and simmer, skimming scum that rises. Once it is removed, cover and simmer for 2–3 hours. Remove the chicken, discard skin and bones, dice the meat and add to the soup.

3 For the dumplings, combine the matzo meal with the eggs, oil, garlic, parsley, onion and salt and pepper. Add about 90ml/6 tbsp water, mixing the ingredients to a thick, soft paste. Cover and chill for 30 minutes to firm up the mixture.

4 Bring a pan of water to the boil, then regulate the heat so that it simmers when adding dumplings. Have a bowl of cold water and wet your hands. Dip a spoon in cold water, take a spoonful of matzo batter and roll it into a ball by hand, then add to the pan. Quickly shape and add all the mixture. Cover and simmer the dumplings gently for 15–20 minutes. Drain and transfer to a plate for about 20 minutes to firm up.

5 Reheat the soup. Add the garlic and remaining dill. Serve the soup ladled over the dumplings and garnish with parsley.

Succotash Soup Energy 539kcal/2267kJ; Protein 51.8g; Carbohydrate 37.4g, of which sugars 11.5g; Fat 21.4g, of which saturates 10.3g; Cholesterol 155mg; Calcium 155mg; Fibre 6.4g; Sodium 1120mg.
Chicken Broth Energy 266kcal/1115kJ; Protein 25.7g; Carbohydrate 24g, of which sugars 6.6g; Fat 7.5g, of which saturates 1.2g; Cholesterol 109mg; Calcium 48mg; Fibre 2.7g; Sodium 86mg.

Avocado, Orange and Almond Salad

A wonderful combination of creamy avocado with oranges and tomatoes.

Serves 4

2 tomatoes, peeled
2 small avocados
60ml/4 tbsp extra virgin olive oil
30ml/2 tbsp lemon juice
15ml/1 tbsp chopped fresh parsley
2–3 oranges, peeled and sliced
    into thick rounds
small onion rings
25g/1oz/¼ cup toasted almonds
10–12 black olives
salt and ground black pepper

1 Chop the tomatoes into quarters, remove the seeds and chop the flesh roughly. Cut the avocados in half, remove the stones (pits) and carefully peel away the skin. Cut into chunks. Mix the olive oil, lemon juice and parsley. Season, then toss the avocado and tomatoes in half of the dressing.

2 Arrange the sliced oranges on a plate and sprinkle with the onion rings. Drizzle with the remaining dressing. Spoon the avocados, tomatoes, almonds and olives on top and serve.

Asparagus and Orange Salad

All this tasty salad needs in the way of dressing is a good quality olive oil and a dash of sherry vinegar. Serve with chunks of crusty bread for a light lunch or healthy supper.

Serves 4

225g/8oz asparagus
2 large oranges
2 well-flavoured tomatoes, cut
    into eighths
50g/2oz romaine lettuce leaves,
    shredded
30ml/2 tbsp extra virgin
    olive oil
2.5ml/½ tsp sherry vinegar
salt and ground black pepper

1 Trim the asparagus. discarding the hard woody ends and cut the spears into 5cm/2in pieces. Cook the asparagus in boiling, salted water for 3–4 minutes, until just tender. Drain and refresh under cold water.

2 Grate the rind from half an orange and reserve. Peel all the oranges and cut into segments. Squeeze out the juice from the membrane and reserve the juice.

3 Put the asparagus, orange segments, tomatoes and lettuce into a salad bowl. Mix together the oil and vinegar and add 15ml/1 tbsp of the reserved orange juice and 5ml/1 tsp of the rind (left). Season with salt and pepper. Just before serving, pour the dressing over the salad and mix gently to coat.

> **Cook's Tip**
> For the best asparagus, buy it during the short growing season, rather than buying it out of season when it will have travelled many miles to get to the supermarket. Choose spears that are bright in colour and firm.

Date, Orange and Carrot Salad

A colourful salad for a light lunch featuring fresh dates and orange flower water.

Serves 4

1 Little Gem (Bibb) lettuce
2 carrots, finely grated
2 oranges
115g/4oz fresh dates, pitted and
    cut into eighths, lengthways
25g/1oz/¼ cup toasted whole
    almonds, chopped
30ml/2 tbsp lemon juice
5ml/1 tsp caster (superfine) sugar
1.5ml/¼ tsp salt
15ml/1 tbsp orange flower water

1 Separate the lettuce leaves and arrange them in the bottom of a salad bowl. Place the grated carrot in a mound on top.

2 Peel and segment the oranges and arrange them around the carrot. Pile the dates on top, then sprinkle with the almonds. Mix the lemon juice, sugar, salt and orange flower water and sprinkle over the salad. Serve chilled.

> **Variation**
> Cos or Little Gem (Bibb) lettuce can be used in place of the romaine lettuce, if you prefer.

Avocado Salad Energy 286kcal/1183kJ; Protein 3.5g; Carbohydrate 7.3g, of which sugars 6.4g; Fat 27.1g, of which saturates 4.4g; Cholesterol 0mg; Calcium 70mg; Fibre 4.4g; Sodium 575mg
Date Salad Energy 138kcal/582kJ; Protein 3.6g; Carbohydrate 21.8g, of which sugars 21.4g; Fat 4.7g, of which saturates 0.4g; Cholesterol 0mg; Calcium 90mg; Fibre 3.9g; Sodium 18mg
Asparagus Salad Energy 92kcal/384kJ; Protein 2.6g; Carbohydrate 7.1g, of which sugars 7.1g; Fat 6.1g, of which saturates 0.9g; Cholesterol 0mg; Calcium 46mg; Fibre 2.4g; Sodium 8mg

Raw Vegetable and Coconut Salad

This salad with its chilli and lime dressing is ideal for serving as a light meal on a banana leaf with rice, or with grilled or fried fish and meat. Try to vary the ingredients depending on what is in season. Serve it as a main course with a bowl of plain rice or some rustic bread, or serve it as a spicy accompaniment to meat, poultry or fish.

Serves 4–6

225g/8oz snake beans (yardlong beans) or green beans, cut into bitesize pieces

3–4 tomatoes, skinned, seeded and cut into bitesize chunks
4–6 spring onions (scallions), finely sliced
225g/8oz/1 cup beansprouts
½ fresh coconut, grated

For the dressing
1–2 red or green chillies, seeded and chopped
2 garlic cloves, chopped
25g/1oz galangal or fresh root ginger, grated
5–10ml/1–2 tsp shrimp paste
juice of 2–3 limes
salt and ground black pepper

1 First make the dressing. Using a mortar and pestle or a food processor, grind or process the chillies, garlic or galangal to a coarse paste.

2 Add the shrimp paste and juice of two limes. If the limes are not juicy, then squeeze the juice from the extra lime and add to the dressing. Alternatively, add a little water, so that it is of pouring consistency. Season the dressing with a little salt and pepper to taste.

3 Put the snake beans, tomatoes, spring onions, beansprouts and grated coconut into a large mixing bowl. Using your fingers or two spoons, mix the ingredients together until they are all well combined.

4 Pour the dressing over the vegetables in the bowl and mix thoroughly until everything is evenly coated in the dressing. Serve as part of a main meal to accompany meat, poultry or fish and bowls of fragrant boiled rice, or eat with lots of fresh bread for a meal in itself.

Chopped Vegetable Salad

This summery salad makes a lovely light meal when served with chunks of warm olive bread.

Serves 4–6

1 each red, green and yellow (bell) peppers, halved and seeded
1 carrot
1 cucumber
6 tomatoes
3 garlic cloves, finely chopped

3 spring onions (scallions), thinly sliced
30ml/2 tbsp chopped fresh coriander (cilantro) leaves
30ml/2 tbsp each chopped fresh dill, parsley and mint leaves
½–1 hot fresh chilli, chopped (optional)
45–60ml/3–4 tbsp extra virgin olive oil
juice of 1–1½ lemons
salt and ground black pepper

1 Using a sharp knife, finely dice the red, green and yellow peppers, carrot, cucumber and tomatoes and place them in a large mixing bowl.

2 Add the garlic, spring onions, coriander, dill, parsley, mint and chilli, if using, to the chopped vegetables in the mixing bowl and toss together to combine.

3 Pour the olive oil and lemon juice over the vegetables, season with salt and pepper to taste and toss together. Chill for at least 1 hour before serving.

> **Cook's Tip**
> A very popular dish in Israel, this colourful salad is best made in summer when there is an abundance of fresh herbs to give the salad its distinctive fresh taste.

> **Variation**
> This salad lends itself to endless variety: add olives, diced cooked beetroot (beet) or potatoes, omit the chilli, vary the herbs, use lime or lemon in place of the vinegar, or add a good pinch of ground cumin. It is always wonderful.

Raw Vegetable Salad Energy 141kcal/584kJ; Protein 4.5g; Carbohydrate 6.4g, of which sugars 5.1g; Fat 11g, of which saturates 9.1g; Cholesterol 8mg; Calcium 54mg; Fibre 4.6g; Sodium 86mg.
Chopped Vegetable Salad Energy 91kcal/378kJ; Protein 1.6g; Carbohydrate 7.8g, of which sugars 7.4g; Fat 6.1g, of which saturates 0.9g; Cholesterol 0mg; Calcium 35mg; Fibre 2.6g; Sodium 16mg

Globe Artichokes with Green Beans and Aioli

Just like the French aïoli, there are many recipes for the Spanish equivalent. This one is exceptionally garlicky, a perfect partner to freshly cooked vegetables.

Serves 4
For the aioli
6 large garlic cloves, sliced
10ml/2 tsp white wine vinegar
250ml/8fl oz/1 cup olive oil
salt and ground black pepper
crusty bread, to serve

For the salad
225g/8oz green beans
3 small globe artichokes
15ml/1 tbsp olive oil
pared rind of 1 lemon
coarse salt for sprinkling
lemon wedges, to garnish

1 To make the aïoli, put the garlic and vinegar in a blender or mini food processor. With the machine switched on, gradually pour in the olive oil until the mixture is thickened and smooth. (Alternatively, crush the garlic to a paste with the vinegar and gradually beat in the oil using a hand whisk.) Season with salt and pepper to taste.

2 To make the salad, cook the beans in boiling water for 1–2 minutes until slightly softened. Drain.

3 Trim the artichoke stalks close to the base. Cook the artichokes in a large pan of salted water for about 30 minutes, or until you can easily pull away a leaf from the base. Drain well.

4 Using a sharp knife, halve the artichokes lengthways and ease out the choke using a teaspoon.

5 Arrange the artichokes and beans on serving plates and drizzle with the oil. Sprinkle with the lemon rind and season with coarse salt and a little pepper. Spoon the aïoli into the artichoke hearts, garnished with lemon wedges, and serve warm with fresh, crusty bread. To eat artichokes, pull the leaves from the base one at a time and use to scoop a little of the sauce. It is only the fleshy end of each leaf that is eaten as well as the base or heart of the artichoke.

Grilled Onion and Aubergine Salad with Garlic and Tahini Dressing

This is a deliciously smoky salad that balances sweet and sharp flavours. It makes a light lunch when served with hot pitta bread.

Serves 6
3 aubergines (eggplants), cut into 1cm/½ in thick slices
675g/1½lb onions, thickly sliced
75–90ml/5–6 tbsp olive oil
45ml/3 tbsp roughly chopped flat leaf parsley
45ml/3 tbsp pine nuts, toasted
salt and ground black pepper

For the dressing
2 garlic cloves, crushed
150ml/¼ pint/⅔ cup light tahini paste
juice of 1–2 lemons
45–60ml/3–4 tbsp water

1 Place the aubergines on a rack or in a colander and sprinkle generously with salt. Leave to drain for 45–60 minutes, then rinse under cold running water and pat dry with kitchen paper.

2 Preheat the grill (broiler). Thread the onions on to skewers or place them in an oiled wire grill (broiler) cage.

3 Brush the aubergines and onions with about 45ml/3 tbsp of the oil and grill (broil) for 6–8 minutes on each side. Brush with more oil, if necessary, when you turn the vegetables. The vegetables should be browned and soft.

4 Arrange the grilled (broiled) vegetables on a serving dish and season with salt and black pepper to taste. Sprinkle with the remaining oil if they seem dry.

5 To make the dressing, crush the garlic in a mortar with a pinch of salt and gradually work in the tahini. Gradually work in the juice of 1 lemon, then the water. Taste and add more lemon juice if necessary. Thin with more water as required to make it fairly runny.

6 Drizzle the dressing over the salad and leave for 30–60 minutes, then sprinkle with the chopped parsley and pine nuts. Serve immediately at room temperature, not chilled.

Globe Artichokes Energy 299kcal/1232kJ; Protein 1.1g; Carbohydrate 1.7g, of which sugars 1.4g; Fat 22.7g, of which saturates 4.5g; Cholesterol 0mg; Calcium 39mg; Fibre 1.4g; Sodium 418mg.
Grilled Onion Salad Energy 294kcal/1216kJ; Protein 7.2g; Carbohydrate 11.8g, of which sugars 8.6g; Fat 24.6g, of which saturates 3.5g; Cholesterol 0mg; Calcium 224mg; Fibre 6g; Sodium 13mg.

Pumpkin Salad

Wine vinegar brings out the sweetness of the pumpkin. No leaves are used, just lots of fresh parsley.

Serves 4

675g/1½lb pumpkin, peeled and cut into 4cm/1½ in pieces
1 large red onion, thinly sliced
200ml/7fl oz/scant 1 cup olive oil
60ml/4 tbsp red wine vinegar
40g/1½oz/¾ cup fresh flat leaf parsley leaves, chopped
salt and ground black pepper
fresh flat leaf parsley sprigs, to garnish (optional)

1 Put the pumpkin in a large pan of salted water. Bring to the boil, then simmer gently for 15–20 minutes. Drain well.

2 Mix the onion, oil and vinegar in a large bowl. Season and stir well. Add the pumpkin to the bowl and toss lightly. Stir in the parsley. Serve, garnished with parsley sprigs, if you like.

Chilli Salad Omelettes with Hummus

These delicate omelettes are filled with salad and served chilled to make a refreshing lunch. Try to include as wide a variety of vegetables as possible.

Serves 6

4 eggs
15ml/1 tbsp cornflour (cornstarch)
15ml/1 tbsp stock or water
115g/4oz/1 cup shredded salad vegetables, such as crisp lettuce, carrot, celery, spring onion (scallions) and (bell) peppers
60ml/4 tbsp chilli salad dressing (or add a few drops of chilli sauce to your favourite salad dressing)
60–75ml/4–5 tbsp hummus
4 crisply cooked bacon rashers (strips), chopped
salt and ground black pepper

1 Break the eggs into a bowl. Add the cornflour and stock or water and beat well. Heat a lightly oiled frying pan and pour a quarter of the egg mixture into the pan, tipping it to spread it out to a thin, even layer.

2 Cook the omelette gently to avoid it colouring too much or becoming bubbly and crisp. When cooked, remove from the pan and make a further three omelettes in the same way. Stack between sheets of baking parchment, then cool and chill.

3 When ready to serve, toss the shredded salad vegetables together with 45ml/3 tbsp of the dressing. Season to taste.

4 Spread half of each of the four omelettes with hummus, top with the salad vegetables and chopped bacon and fold in half. Drizzle the rest of the chilli salad dressing over the filled omelettes before serving.

> **Variation**
> These omelettes can be filled with a whole range of ingredients. Try using taramasalata instead of hummus, or fill the omelettes with ratatouille or mixed roasted vegetables.

White Beans with Green Peppers

Tender beans are delicious in this spicy sauce with the bite of crunchy pepper.

Serves 4

750g/1⅔lb tomatoes, diced
1 onion, finely chopped
½–1 fresh chilli, finely chopped
1 green (bell) pepper, seeded and chopped
pinch of sugar
4 garlic cloves, chopped
400g/14oz can cannellini beans, drained
45–60ml/3–4 tbsp olive oil
grated rind and juice of 1 lemon
15ml/1 tbsp cider vinegar or wine vinegar
salt and ground black pepper
chopped fresh parsley, to garnish
toasted pitta bread, to serve

1 Put the tomatoes, onion, chilli, green pepper, sugar, garlic, cannellini beans, salt and plenty of ground black pepper in a large bowl and toss together until well combined.

2 Add the olive oil, grated lemon rind, lemon juice and vinegar to the salad and toss lightly to combine. Chill before serving, garnished with chopped parsley. Serve with toasted pitta bread.

Chilli Salad Energy 173kcal/719kJ; Protein 11.8g; Carbohydrate 5.7g, of which sugars 0.8g; Fat 11.7g, of which saturates 3.1g; Cholesterol 204mg; Calcium 45mg; Fibre 0.6g; Sodium 558mg.
Pumpkin Salad Energy 404kcal/1663kJ; Protein 1.7g; Carbohydrate 5.2g, of which sugars 4g; Fat 42g, of which saturates 6.1g; Cholesterol 0mg; Calcium 73mg; Fibre 2.4g; Sodium 4mg.
White Beans Energy 226kcal/947kJ; Protein 8.8g; Carbohydrate 27.6g, of which sugars 12.9g; Fat 9.6g, of which saturates 1.5g; Cholesterol 0mg; Calcium 92mg; Fibre 9g; Sodium 409mg.

Warm Salad with Poached Eggs

Soft poached eggs, chilli, hot croûtons and cool, crisp salad leaves make a lively and unusual combination. This simple salad is perfect for a mid-week supper. Poached eggs are delicious with salad leaves as the yolk runs out when the eggs are pierced and combines with the dressing in the most delightful way.

Serves 2

½ small loaf wholemeal
  (whole-wheat) bread
45ml/3 tbsp chilli oil
2 eggs
115g/4oz mixed salad leaves
45ml/3 tbsp extra virgin olive oil
2 garlic cloves, crushed
15ml/1 tbsp balsamic or
  sherry vinegar
50g/2oz Parmesan cheese, shaved
ground black pepper

1 Carefully cut away the crust from the wholemeal loaf and discard it. Cut the bread into neat slices, and then into 2.5cm/1in cubes.

2 Heat the chilli oil in a large frying pan. Add the bread cubes and cook for about 5 minutes, tossing the cubes occasionally, until they are crisp and golden brown all over.

3 Meanwhile, bring a pan of water to the boil. Break each egg into a measuring jug (cup) and carefully slide into the water, one at a time.

4 Gently poach the eggs in the simmering water for about 4 minutes until they are lightly cooked.

5 Meanwhile, divide the salad leaves between two plates. Using a slotted spoon, remove the croûtons from the pan and arrange them over the leaves.

6 Wipe the pan clean with kitchen paper. Then heat the olive oil in the pan, add the garlic and vinegar and cook over high heat for 1 minute, stirring constantly. Pour the warm dressing over the salads.

7 Place a poached egg on each salad. Top with thin Parmesan shavings and a little ground black pepper. Serve immediately.

Peppery Egg, Watercress and Chilli Salad

Chillies and eggs may seem unlikely partners, but actually work very well together. The peppery flavour of the watercress makes it the perfect foundation for this tasty salad.

Serves 2

15ml/1 tbsp groundnut
  (peanut) oil
1 garlic clove, thinly sliced
4 eggs
2 shallots, thinly sliced
2 small fresh red chillies, seeded
  and thinly sliced
½ small cucumber, finely diced
1cm/½in piece fresh root ginger,
  peeled and grated
juice of 2 limes
30ml/2 tbsp soy sauce
5ml/1 tsp caster (superfine) sugar
small bunch coriander (cilantro)
bunch watercress or rocket
  (arugula), coarsely chopped

1 Heat the oil in a frying pan. Add the garlic and cook over low heat until it starts to turn golden.

2 Crack the eggs into the pan. Break the yolks with a wooden spatula, then fry until the eggs are almost firm. Remove from the pan and set aside.

3 In a bowl, mix together the shallots, chillies, cucumber and ginger until well blended.

4 In a separate bowl, whisk the lime juice with the soy sauce and sugar. Pour this dressing over the vegetables and toss lightly.

5 Set aside a few coriander sprigs for the garnish. Chop the rest and add them to the salad. Toss it again.

6 Reserve a few watercress or rocket sprigs and arrange the remainder on two serving plates. Cut the fried eggs into slices and divide them between the watercress or rocket mounds.

7 Spoon the shallot mixture over the eggs and serve immediately, garnished with the reserved coriander and watercress or rocket.

Warm Salad Energy 697kcal/2907kJ; Protein 25.9g; Carbohydrate 41.3g, of which sugars 2.8g; Fat 49g, of which saturates 11.5g; Cholesterol 215mg; Calcium 408mg; Fibre 6.3g; Sodium 914mg.
Peppery Egg Salad Energy 215kcal/894kJ; Protein 14.2g; Carbohydrate 2.4g of which sugars 2.2g; Fat 16.9g, of which saturates 4.2g; Cholesterol 381mg; Calcium 112mg; Fibre 0.8g; Sodium 1223mg.

Springtime Salad with Quail's Eggs

Enjoy some of the best early season garden vegetables in this crunchy green salad. Quail's eggs add a touch of sophistication and elegance.

Serves 4

175g/6oz broad (fava) beans
175g/6oz fresh peas
175g/6oz asparagus
175g/6oz very small new potatoes, scrubbed
45ml/3 tbsp good lemon mayonnaise
45ml/3 tbsp sour cream or crème fraîche
½ bunch fresh mint, chopped, plus whole leaves for garnishing
8 quail's eggs, soft-boiled and peeled
salt and ground black pepper

1 Cook the broad beans, peas, asparagus and new potatoes in separate pans of lightly salted boiling water until just tender. Drain, refresh under cold water, and drain again.

2 When the vegetables are completely cold, mix them lightly together in a large bowl.

3 Mix the mayonnaise with the sour cream or crème fraîche and chopped mint in a bowl. Stir in salt and ground black pepper, if needed.

4 Pour the dressing over the salad and toss to coat.

5 Add the quail's eggs and whole mint leaves and toss very gently to mix. Serve immediately.

> **Cook's Tip**
> To make your own lemon mayonnaise, combine two egg yolks, 5ml/1 tsp Dijon mustard, and the grated (shredded) rind and juice of half a lemon in a blender or food processor. Add salt and pepper to taste. Process to combine. With the motor running, add about 250ml/8fl oz/1 cup mild olive oil (or a mixture of olive oil and sunflower oil) through the lid or feeder tube, until the mixture emulsifies. Trickle the oil in at first, then add it in a steady stream.

Fennel and Egg Tabbouleh with Herbs

This Middle-Eastern classic is given a different twist with the addition of aniseed-flavoured fennel and tangy black olives.

Serves 4

250g/9oz/1½ cups bulgur wheat
4 small eggs
1 fennel bulb
1 bunch of spring onions (scallions), chopped
25g/1oz/½ cup drained sun-dried tomatoes in oil, sliced
45ml/3 tbsp chopped fresh parsley
30ml/2 tbsp chopped fresh mint
75g/3oz/½ cup black olives
60ml/4 tbsp olive oil
30ml/2 tbsp garlic oil
30ml/2 tbsp lemon juice
50g/2oz/½ cup chopped hazelnuts, toasted
1 open-textured loaf or 4 pitta breads, warmed
salt and ground black pepper

1 Put the bulgur wheat into a large bowl. Add enough cold water to come 2.5cm/1in above the level of the wheat. Leave to soak for approximately 30 minutes.

2 Turn the soaked bulgur wheat into a sieve (strainer) lined with a clean dish towel. Drain the wheat well and use the dish towel to squeeze out any excess water. Leave to cool.

3 Cook the eggs in boiling water for 8 minutes. Cool under running water, peel and quarter.

4 Halve and finely slice the fennel. Boil in salted water for 6 minutes, then drain and cool under running water. Drain again thoroughly.

5 Combine the eggs, fennel, spring onions, sun-dried tomatoes, parsley, mint and olives with the bulgur wheat.

6 Put the olive oil, garlic oil and lemon juice in a small bowl and whisk together with a fork. Add to the bulgur wheat salad, toss well, then add the nuts. Season with salt and pepper to taste, then tear the bread into pieces and add to the salad. Serve the salad immediately.

Springtime Salad Energy 256kcal/1067kJ; Protein 12.5g; Carbohydrate 19.3g, of which sugars 3.6g; Fat 14.9g, of which saturates 3.7g; Cholesterol 110mg; Calcium 100mg; Fibre 6.1g; Sodium 101mg.
Fennel Tabbouleh Energy 842kcal/3521kJ; Protein 25g; Carbohydrate 106g, of which sugars 5.7g; Fat 37.6g, of which saturates 5.5g; Cholesterol 190mg; Calcium 273mg; Fibre 6g; Sodium 946mg.

Tomato, Mozzarella and Onion Salad

Sweet tomatoes and the heady scent of basil capture the essence of summer in this simple salad. Vine-ripened tomatoes usually have the best flavour. Use local ones if possible.

Serves 6
5 large ripe tomatoes, peeled if liked
2 buffalo mozzarella cheeses, drained and sliced
1 small red onion, chopped

For the dressing
½ small garlic clove, peeled
15g/½oz fresh basil
30ml/2 tbsp chopped fresh flat leaf parsley
25ml/5 tsp small capers in brine, rinsed
2.5ml/½ tsp mustard
75–90ml/5–6 tbsp extra virgin olive oil
5–10ml/1–2 tsp balsamic vinegar
ground black pepper
fresh basil leaves and parsley sprigs, to garnish

1 First make the dressing. Put the garlic, basil, parsley, half the capers and the mustard in a food processor or blender and process briefly to chop. Then, with the motor running, gradually pour in the olive oil through the feeder tube to make a smooth purée with a dressing consistency. Add the balsamic vinegar to taste and season with pepper.

2 Slice the tomatoes. Arrange the tomato and mozzarella slices on a plate.

3 Sprinkle the onion over the tomatoes and mozzarella, and season the salad with a little freshly ground black pepper.

4 Drizzle the dressing over the salad, then sprinkle the basil leaves, parsley sprigs and remaining capers on top. Leave for 10–15 minutes before serving, if possible.

> **Cook's Tip**
> When making the dressing, it is a good idea to use the pulse facility for first chopping the garlic, parsley and capers together. Add the mustard and give the ingredients a quick blitz before beginning to pour in the olive oil.

Leek and Grilled Pepper Salad with Goat's Cheese

This is a perfect dish for entertaining, as the salad actually benefits from being made in advance.

Serves 6
675g/1½lb young leeks
15ml/1 tbsp olive oil
2 large red (bell) peppers, halved and seeded
few fresh thyme sprigs, chopped
4 x 1cm/½in slices goat's cheese

75g/3oz/1½ cups fine dry white breadcrumbs
vegetable oil, for shallow frying
45ml/3 tbsp chopped fresh flat leaf parsley
salt and ground black pepper

For the dressing
75ml/5 tbsp extra virgin olive oil
1 small garlic clove, finely chopped
5ml/1 tsp Dijon mustard
15ml/1 tbsp red wine vinegar

1 Preheat the grill (broiler). Bring a pan of lightly salted water to the boil and cook the leeks for 3–4 minutes. Drain, cut into 10cm/4in lengths and place in a bowl.

2 Add the olive oil to the leeks, toss to coat, then season to taste with salt and ground black pepper. Place the leeks on a grill (broiling) rack and grill (broil) for 3–4 minutes on each side.

3 Set the leeks aside. Place the peppers on the grill rack, skin side up, and grill until blackened and blistered. Place them in a bowl, cover with crumpled kitchen paper and leave for 10 minutes. Rub off the skin and cut the flesh into strips. Place in a bowl and add the leeks, thyme and a little pepper.

4 To make the dressing, shake all the ingredients together in a screw-top jar, adding salt and pepper to taste. Pour the dressing over the leek mixture, cover and chill for several hours.

5 Roll the cheese slices in the breadcrumbs, pressing them in gently so that the cheese is well coated. Chill the cheese in the refrigerator for 1 hour. Heat a little oil and fry the cheese until golden on both sides. Drain and cool, then cut into bitesize pieces. Toss the cheese and parsley into the salad and serve at room temperature.

Tomato Salad Energy 232kcal/960kJ; Protein 10.3g; Carbohydrate 3.6g, of which sugars 3.3g; Fat 19.7g, of which saturates 8.3g; Cholesterol 29mg; Calcium 206mg; Fibre 1.4g; Sodium 208mg.
Leek Salad Energy 265kcal/1100kJ; Protein 5.7g; Carbohydrate 17g, of which sugars 6.5g; Fat 19.7g, of which saturates 3.9g; Cholesterol 8mg; Calcium 60mg; Fibre 3.7g; Sodium 174mg.

Salad of Roasted Shallots and Butternut Squash with Feta Cheese

This is especially good served with a grain or starchy salad, based on rice or couscous, for example. Serve with plenty of good bread to mop up the juices.

Serves 4–6

75ml/5 tbsp olive oil
15ml/1 tbsp balsamic vinegar, plus a little extra to taste
15ml/1 tbsp sweet soy sauce
350g/12oz shallots, peeled but left whole
3 fresh red chillies
1 butternut squash, peeled, seeded and cut into chunks
5ml/1 tsp finely chopped fresh thyme
15g/½oz flat leaf parsley
1 small garlic clove, finely chopped
75g/3oz walnuts, chopped
150g/5oz feta cheese
salt and ground black pepper

1 Preheat the oven to 200°C/400°F/Gas 6. Beat the oil, vinegar and soy sauce together in a large bowl, then season with salt and pepper.

2 Toss the shallots and two of the chillies in the oil mixture and turn into a large roasting pan or ovenproof dish. Roast for 15 minutes, stirring once or twice.

3 Add the butternut squash and roast for a further 30–35 minutes, stirring once, until the squash is tender.

4 Remove from the oven, stir in the chopped thyme and set the vegetables aside to cool.

5 Chop the parsley and garlic together and mix with the walnuts. Seed and finely chop the remaining chilli.

6 Stir the parsley, garlic and walnut mixture into the vegetables. Add chopped chilli to taste and adjust the seasoning, adding a little extra balsamic vinegar to taste.

7 Crumble the feta cheese and add to the salad. Transfer to a serving dish and serve immediately.

Warm Broad Bean and Feta Salad

This recipe is loosely based on a typical medley of fresh-tasting Greek salad ingredients – broad beans, tomatoes and feta cheese. It's lovely as a light lunch, served warm or cold. It is the sort of dish that would go down very well at a party, so next time you are invited to one of those occasions where every guest brings a contribution, this would be an ideal choice.

Serves 4–6

900g/2lb broad (fava) beans, shelled, or 350g/12oz shelled frozen beans
60ml/4 tbsp olive oil
75g/3oz plum tomatoes, halved, or quartered if large
4 garlic cloves, crushed
115g/4oz firm feta cheese, cut into large, even chunks
45ml/3 tbsp chopped fresh dill, plus extra to garnish
12 black olives
salt and ground black pepper

1 Cook the fresh or frozen broad beans in lightly salted boiling water until just tender. Drain and refresh, then set aside.

2 Meanwhile, heat the oil in a heavy frying pan and add the tomatoes and garlic. Cook until the tomatoes are beginning to colour and the garlic is pungent.

3 Add the feta cheese to the pan and toss the ingredients together for 1 minute.

4 Mix the tomatoes, garlic and feta with the drained beans, dill, olives and salt and pepper. Serve garnished with chopped dill.

Variations

• For a special treat, pop the shelled broad (fava) beans out of their skins and use only the bright green beans inside. This is a fiddly business, and doesn't yield much in terms of weight of beans, but as a bonus, the appearance and flavour is superb.
• Instead of broad beans, use extra-fine green beans, French beans or even runner beans. A mixture of green and yellow beans would look good, when the latter are in season.
• Use tiny cocktail tomatoes instead of plum tomatoes.

Salad of Shallots Energy 275kcal/1136kJ; Protein 7.7g; Carbohydrate 9.3g, of which sugars 7g; Fat 23.2g, of which saturates 5.6g; Cholesterol 18mg; Calcium 165mg; Fibre 2.9g; Sodium 541mg.
Warm Bean Salad Energy 175kcal/727kJ; Protein 7.9g; Carbohydrate 8g, of which sugars 2g; Fat 12.6g, of which saturates 3.9g; Cholesterol 13mg; Calcium 109mg; Fibre 4.3g; Sodium 471mg.

Panzanella with Anchovies

In this lively Italian speciality, a sweet tangy blend of tomato juice, rich olive oil and red wine vinegar is soaked up in a colourful salad of roasted peppers, anchovies and toasted ciabatta bread.

Serves 4

225g/8oz ciabatta
(about ⅔ loaf)
150ml/¼ pint/⅔ cup olive oil
3 red (bell) peppers
3 yellow (bell) peppers
50g/2oz can anchovy fillets
675g/1½lb ripe plum tomatoes
4 garlic cloves, crushed
60ml/4 tbsp red wine vinegar
50g/2oz capers
115g/4oz/1 cup pitted
black olives
salt and ground black pepper
basil leaves, to garnish

1 Preheat the oven to 200°C/400°F/Gas 6. Cut the ciabatta into 2cm/¾in chunks and drizzle with 50ml/2fl oz/¼ cup of the oil. Toast the bread chunks lightly under a hot grill (broiler) until just golden.

2 Put the peppers on a foil-lined baking sheet and bake in the preheated oven for about 45 minutes until the skin begins to char. Remove from the oven, cover with a cloth and leave to cool slightly.

3 Pull the skin off the peppers and cut them into quarters, discarding the stalk ends and seeds. Drain and then roughly chop the anchovies. Set aside.

4 To make the tomato dressing, peel and halve the tomatoes. Scoop the seeds into a sieve (strainer) set over a bowl. Using the back of a spoon, press the tomato pulp in the sieve to extract as much juice as possible. Discard the pulp from the sieve and add the remaining oil, the garlic and vinegar to the pressed tomato juice.

5 Layer the toasted bread, peppers, tomatoes, anchovies, capers and olives in a large salad bowl. Season the tomato dressing with salt and pepper and pour it over the salad. Leave to stand for about 30 minutes. Serve garnished with plenty of basil leaves.

Leek Salad with Anchovies, Eggs and Parsley

This salad makes a good light main dish that can be finished with a tomato salad, a potato salad or some crusty bread.

Serves 4

675g/1½lb thin or baby
leeks, trimmed
2 large (US extra large) or
3 medium (US large) eggs
50g/2oz good-quality anchovy
fillets in olive oil, drained
15g/½oz flat leaf parsley, chopped
a few pitted black olives (optional)
salt and ground black pepper

For the dressing

5ml/1 tsp Dijon mustard
15ml/1 tbsp tarragon vinegar
75ml/5 tbsp olive oil
30ml/2 tbsp double
(heavy) cream
1 small shallot, very
finely chopped
pinch of caster (superfine)
sugar (optional)

1 Cook the leeks in boiling salted water for 3–4 minutes. Drain, plunge into cold water, then drain again. Squeeze out excess water, then pat dry.

2 Place the eggs in a pan of cold water, bring to the boil and cook for 6–7 minutes. Drain, plunge into cold water, then shell and chop the eggs.

3 To make the dressing, whisk the mustard with the vinegar. Gradually whisk in the oil, followed by the cream. Stir in the shallot, then season to taste with salt, pepper and a pinch of caster sugar, if liked.

4 Leave the leeks whole or thickly slice them, then place in a serving dish. Pour most of the dressing over them and stir to mix. Leave for at least 1 hour, or until ready to serve, bringing them back to room temperature first, if necessary.

5 Arrange the anchovies on the leeks, then sprinkle the eggs and parsley over the top. Drizzle with the remaining dressing, season with black pepper and dot with a few olives, if using. Serve immediately.

Panzanella Energy 360kcal/1500kJ; Protein 8.6g; Carbohydrate 33.7g, of which sugars 14.8g; Fat 22.1g, of which saturates 3.3g; Cholesterol 5mg; Calcium 103mg; Fibre 5.2g; Sodium 977mg.
Leek Salad Energy 265kcal/1099kJ; Protein 9.4g; Carbohydrate 6.3g, of which sugars 4.8g; Fat 22.7g, of which saturates 5.6g; Cholesterol 113mg; Calcium 107mg; Fibre 4.1g; Sodium 533mg.

Roasted Peppers with Tomatoes and Anchovies

This is a Sicilian-style salad, using some typical ingredients from the Italian island. The flavour improves if the salad is made and dressed an hour or two before serving.

Serves 4
1 red (bell) pepper
1 yellow (bell) pepper
4 sun-dried tomatoes in
  oil, drained
4 ripe plum tomatoes, sliced
2 canned anchovies, drained
  and chopped
15ml/1 tbsp capers, drained
15ml/1 tbsp pine nuts
1 garlic clove, very thinly sliced

For the dressing
75ml/5 tbsp extra virgin olive oil
15ml/1 tbsp balsamic vinegar
5ml/1 tsp lemon juice
chopped fresh mixed herbs
salt and ground black pepper

1 Cut the peppers in half. Remove the seeds and stalks and cut into quarters. Preheat the grill (broiler).

2 Cook the pepper quarters, skin side up, under the hot grill until the skins blacken and blister. Transfer to a bowl and cover with a plate. Leave to cool. Peel the peppers and cut into strips.

3 Thinly slice the sun-dried tomatoes. Arrange the peppers and fresh tomatoes on a serving dish. Sprinkle over the anchovies, sun-dried tomatoes, capers, pine nuts and garlic.

4 To make the dressing, mix together the olive oil, vinegar, lemon juice and chopped herbs and season with salt and pepper. Pour over the salad just before serving.

> **Cook's Tip**
> Many of the ingredients in this salad have a long shelf life, such as the canned anchovies, the capers and the sun-dried tomatoes. Keep your kitchen stocked up with these ingredients so you can prepare this salad for any occasion without too much fuss.

Caesar Salad

This is a well-known and much enjoyed salad invented by a chef called Caesar Cardini. Be sure to use crisp lettuce and add the very soft eggs at the last minute.

Serves 6
175ml/6fl oz/¾ cup olive oil
115g/4oz French or Italian bread,
  cut into 2.5cm/1in cubes
1 large garlic clove, crushed or
  finely chopped
1 cos or romaine lettuce
2 eggs, soft-boiled for 1 minute
120ml/4fl oz/½ cup lemon juice
50g/2oz/⅔ cup freshly grated
  Parmesan cheese
6 canned anchovy fillets, drained
  and finely chopped (optional)
salt and ground black pepper

1 Heat 50ml/2fl oz/¼ cup of the oil in a large frying pan. Add the bread cubes and garlic. Cook over medium heat, stirring constantly, until the bread cubes are golden brown all over. Drain well on kitchen paper. Discard the garlic.

2 Tear large lettuce leaves into smaller pieces. Put all the lettuce in a bowl.

3 Add the remaining oil to the lettuce and season with salt and plenty of ground black pepper. Toss well with your hands to coat the leaves.

4 Break the eggs on top of the dressed lettuce leaves. Sprinkle with the lemon juice. Toss thoroughly again to combine all the ingredients. Add the Parmesan cheese and anchovies, if using. Toss gently to mix.

5 Sprinkle the fried bread cubes evenly on top of the salad and serve immediately.

> **Variation**
> For a tangier dressing, mix 30ml/2 tbsp white wine vinegar, 15ml/1 tbsp Worcestershire sauce, 2.5ml/½ tsp mustard powder, 5ml/1 tsp sugar, salt and pepper in a screw-top jar, then add the oil and shake well.

Roasted Peppers Energy 235kcal/973kJ; Protein 3g; Carbohydrate 11.2g, of which sugars 10.9g; Fat 20.1g, of which saturates 2.8g; Cholesterol 1mg; Calcium 24mg; Fibre 3.2g; Sodium 78mg.
Caesar Salad Energy 782kcal/3251kJ; Protein 49.6g; Carbohydrate 8.6g, of which sugars 1.2g; Fat 62.4g, of which saturates 15.6g; Cholesterol 1342mg; Calcium 354mg; Fibre 1g; Sodium 785mg.

Exotic Fruit and Vegetable Salad

This substantial salad makes an ideal main course.

Serves 6–8

115g/4oz green beans, trimmed
2 carrots, cut into batons
115g/4oz/2 cups beansprouts
¼ head Chinese leaves (Chinese cabbage), shredded
½ small cucumber, cut into thin strips
8 spring onions (scallions), sliced diagonally
6 cherry tomatoes, halved
12–16 cooked tiger prawns (shrimp)
1 small mango
1 small papaya
225g/8oz rice, compressed into cubes
4 hard-boiled eggs, quartered
fresh coriander (cilantro)

For the peanut dressing
120ml/8 tbsp crunchy or smooth peanut butter
1 garlic clove, crushed
300ml/½ pint/1¼ cups coconut milk
15ml/1 tbsp tamarind water or juice of ½ lemon
15–30ml/1–2 tbsp light soy sauce
hot chilli sauce, to taste

1 First, make the dressing. Place all the ingredients except the chilli sauce in a pan and heat the mixture, stirring all the time, until it is very hot and smooth. Stir in chilli sauce to taste. Keep the dressing warm, or allow to cool and reheat before serving.

2 Cook the beans and carrots in boiling water for 3–4 minutes until just tender. Drain, then refresh under cold water and drain again. Boil the beansprouts for 2 minutes, then drain and refresh.

3 Arrange the carrots, beans and beansprouts on a large, attractive platter, with the shredded Chinese leaves, cucumber strips, spring onions, tomatoes and prawns.

4 Peel the mango and cut the flesh into cubes. Quarter the papaya, remove the skin and seeds, then slice the flesh. Add to the salad platter, with the compressed rice. Garnish with the egg quarters and fresh coriander.

5 Reheat the dressing, if necessary. Pour it into a serving bowl. Place the bowl in the centre of the salad and serve. Guests help themselves to salad, adding as much dressing as they like.

Thai Prawn Salad

In this salad, sweet prawns and mango are covered in a garlic dressing with the hot taste of chilli.

Serves 4–6

675g/1½lb prawns (shrimp), peeled and deveined, with tails intact
finely shredded rind of 1 lime
½ fresh red chilli, seeded and finely chopped
30ml/2 tbsp olive oil, plus extra for brushing
1 ripe firm mango, stoned (pitted)
2 carrots, cut into long thin shreds
10cm/4in piece cucumber, sliced
1 red onion, halved and thinly sliced
a few fresh mint sprigs
a few coriander (cilantro) sprigs
45ml/3 tbsp roasted peanuts, coarsely chopped
4 large shallots, thinly sliced and fried until crisp in 30ml/2 tbsp groundnut (peanut) oil
salt and ground black pepper

For the dressing
1 large garlic clove, chopped
10–15ml/2–3 tsp caster (superfine) sugar
juice of 2 limes
15–30ml/1–2 tbsp Thai fish sauce
1 red chilli, seeded and chopped
5–10ml/1–2 tsp light rice vinegar

1 Place the prawns in a glass dish with the lime rind, chilli, oil and seasoning. Toss to mix and leave for 30–40 minutes.

2 Make the dressing. Place the garlic in a mortar with 10ml/2 tsp of the sugar. Pound until smooth, then add in three-quarters of the lime juice, followed by 15ml/1 tbsp of the Thai fish sauce. Transfer the dressing to a bowl. Stir in half the chopped red chilli and the light rice vinegar to taste.

3 Cut the mango flesh into strips and cut off any flesh still adhering to the stone. Place the strips of mango in a bowl with the carrots, cucumber slices and red onion.

4 Pour about half the dressing over the ingredients in the bowl and mix. Arrange the salad on four to six individual serving plates or in bowls. Heat a griddle (grill) pan until hot. Brush with oil, then sear the prawns for 2–3 minutes on each side.

5 Arrange the prawns on the salads. Pour the remaining dressing over and garnish with the mint and coriander, the remaining chopped chilli, the peanuts and crisp-fried shallots.

Exotic Salad Energy Energy 260kcal/1090kJ; Protein 13.7g; Carbohydrate 27.1g, of which sugars 15.5g; Fat 11.3g, of which saturates 2.9g; Cholesterol 144mg; Calcium 89mg; Fibre 4.2g; Sodium 319mg.
Thai Prawn Salad Energy 292kcal/1222kJ; Protein 33.5g; Carbohydrate 13.4g; of which sugars 11.8g; Fat 11.9g, of which saturates 2g; Cholesterol 329mg; Calcium 160mg; Fibre 2.7g; Sodium 596mg.

Potato, Mussel and Watercress Salad

The creamy, well-flavoured dressing enhances all the ingredients in this tasty and substantial salad.

Serves 4
675g/1½lb salad potatoes
1kg/2¼lb mussels, scrubbed and beards removed
200ml/7fl oz/scant 1 cup dry white wine
15g/½oz fresh flat leaf parsley, chopped
1 bunch of watercress or rocket (arugula)
salt and ground black pepper
chopped fresh chives or spring onion (scallion) tops, to garnish

For the dressing
105ml/7 tbsp olive oil
15–30ml/1–2 tbsp white wine vinegar
5ml/1 tsp strong Dijon mustard
1 large shallot, finely chopped
15ml/1 tbsp chopped fresh chives
45ml/3 tbsp double (heavy) cream
pinch of caster (superfine) sugar (optional)

1 Boil the potatoes in salted water for 15–20 minutes, or until tender. Drain, cool, then peel. Slice the potatoes into a bowl and toss with 30ml/2 tbsp of the oil for the dressing.

2 Discard any open mussels. Bring the white wine to the boil in a large, heavy pan. Add the mussels, cover and boil vigorously, shaking the pan occasionally, for 3–4 minutes, until the mussels have opened. Discard any that do not open. Drain and shell the mussels, reserving the cooking liquid.

3 Boil the reserved mussel cooking liquid until reduced to about 45ml/3 tbsp. Pour through a fine sieve (strainer) over the potatoes and toss to mix.

4 Make the dressing. Whisk together the remaining oil, 15ml/1 tbsp of the vinegar, the mustard, shallot and chives. Add the cream and whisk again to form a thick dressing. Adjust the seasoning, adding more vinegar and/or a pinch of sugar to taste.

5 Toss the mussels with the potatoes, then gently mix in the dressing and chopped parsley. Arrange the watercress or rocket on a serving platter and top with the salad. Serve sprinkled with extra chives or a little spring onion.

Seafood Salad with Fragrant Herbs

This is a spectacular salad. The luscious combination of prawns, scallops and squid, makes it the ideal choice for a special celebration.

Serves 4–6
250ml/8fl oz/1 cup fish stock or water
350g/12oz squid, cleaned and cut into rings
12 raw king prawns (jumbo shrimp), peeled, with tails intact
12 scallops
50g/2oz cellophane noodles, soaked in warm water for 30 minutes
½ cucumber, cut into thin batons
1 lemon grass stalk, finely chopped
2 kaffir lime leaves, finely shredded
2 shallots, thinly sliced
30ml/2 tbsp chopped spring onions (scallions)
30ml/2 tbsp fresh coriander (cilantro) leaves
12–15 fresh mint leaves, coarsely torn
4 fresh red chillies, seeded and cut into slivers
juice of 1–2 limes
30ml/2 tbsp Thai fish sauce
fresh coriander sprigs, to garnish

1 Pour the fish stock or water into a medium pan set over a high heat and bring to the boil. Cook each type of seafood separately in the stock for 3–4 minutes. Remove with a slotted spoon and set aside to cool.

2 Drain the noodles. Using scissors, cut them into short lengths, about 5cm/2in long. Place them in a serving bowl and add the cucumber, lemon grass, kaffir lime leaves, shallots, spring onions, coriander, mint and chillies.

3 Pour the lime juice and fish sauce over the noodle salad. Mix well, then add the seafood. Toss lightly. Garnish with the fresh coriander sprigs and serve immediately.

> **Cook's Tip**
> To peel the large prawns (shrimp), gently pull off the head, then peel off the body shell, pulling up from the legs. Using a sharp knife, gently prise (pry) out the black vein running down the back.

Mixed Seafood Salad

This is a very pretty arrangement of fresh mussels, prawns and squid rings served on a colourful bed of salad vegetables. Do not be tempted to chill the salad or the delicate flavours will be blunted.

Serves 6

115g/4oz prepared squid rings
12 fresh mussels, scrubbed and
 beards removed
1 large carrot
6 crisp lettuce leaves
10cm/4in piece cucumber,
 finely diced
115g/4oz cooked, peeled
 prawns (shrimp)
15ml/1 tbsp drained
 pickled capers

For the dressing

30ml/2 tbsp freshly squeezed
 lemon juice
45ml/3 tbsp virgin olive oil
15ml/1 tbsp chopped fresh parsley
salt and ground black pepper

1 Put the squid rings into a metal sieve (strainer) or vegetable steamer. Place the sieve or steamer over a pan of simmering water, cover with a lid and steam the squid for 2–3 minutes until it just turns white. Cool under cold running water and drain on kitchen paper.

2 Discard any open mussels that do not close when tapped. Cover the base of a large pan with water, add the mussels, then cover and steam for a few minutes until they open. Discard any mussels that stubbornly remain shut.

3 Using a swivel-style vegetable peeler, cut the carrot into wafer-thin ribbons. Tear the lettuce into pieces and arrange on a serving plate. Sprinkle the carrot ribbons on top, then sprinkle over the diced cucumber.

4 Arrange the mussels, prawns and squid rings over the salad and sprinkle the capers over the top.

5 Make the dressing. Put all the ingredients in a small bowl and whisk until they are well combined.

6 Drizzle half the dressing over the salad. Serve at room temperature with the remaining dressing.

Salad Niçoise

Made with the freshest of ingredients, this classic salad makes a simple yet unbeatable summer dish.

Serves 4

115g/4oz green beans, trimmed
 and cut in half
115g/4oz mixed salad leaves
½ small cucumber, thinly sliced
4 ripe tomatoes, quartered
4 eggs, hard-boiled
1 tuna steak, about 175g/6oz
olive oil, for brushing
50g/2oz can anchovies
½ bunch small radishes,
 trimmed
50g/2oz/½ cup small
 black olives
salt and ground black pepper

For the dressing

90ml/6 tbsp extra virgin olive oil
2 garlic cloves, crushed
15ml/1 tbsp white wine vinegar

1 To make the dressing, whisk together the extra virgin olive oil, garlic and white wine vinegar and season to taste with salt and pepper. Set aside.

2 Cook the French beans in a pan of boiling water for 2 minutes until just tender, then drain.

3 Mix together the salad leaves, sliced cucumber, tomatoes and French beans in a large, shallow bowl. Halve the anchovies lengthways and shell and quarter the eggs.

4 Preheat the grill (broiler). Brush the tuna with oil and sprinkle with salt and black pepper. Grill (broil) for 3–4 minutes on each side until cooked through. Cool, then flake.

5 Sprinkle the flaked tuna, anchovies, quartered eggs, radishes and olives over the salad. Pour over the dressing and toss together lightly to combine. Serve immediately.

> **Variation**
> Opinions vary on whether salad Niçoise should include potatoes but, if you like, include a few small cooked new potatoes and some chopped celery.

Seafood Salad Energy 91kcal/379kJ; Protein 7.5g; Carbohydrate 1.5g, of which sugars 1g; Fat 6.2g, of which saturates 0.9g; Cholesterol 84mg; Calcium 29mg; Fibre 0.4g; Sodium 86mg.
Salad Niçoise Energy 351kcal/1457kJ; Protein 21.7g; Carbohydrate 5.3g, of which sugars 5g; Fat 27.3g, of which saturates 5g; Cholesterol 210mg; Calcium 114mg; Fibre 2.6g; Sodium 876mg.

Skate with Bitter Salad Leaves

Skate has a delicious sweet flavour, enhanced here by orange. It contrasts well with any bitter leaves – buy a bag of mixed salad leaves for contrasting textures and flavours.

Serves 4
800g/1¾lb skate wings
15ml/1 tbsp white
　wine vinegar
4 black peppercorns
1 fresh thyme sprig
1 orange

175g/6oz bitter salad leaves, such
　as frisée, rocket (arugula),
　radicchio, escarole, lamb's
　lettuce (corn salad)
　and watercress
2 tomatoes, peeled, seeded
　and diced
crusty bread, to serve

For the dressing
15ml/1 tbsp white wine vinegar
45ml/3 tbsp extra-virgin olive oil
1 bunch spring onions (scallions),
　whites finely chopped
salt, paprika and black pepper

1 Put the skate wings into a large shallow pan, cover with cold water and add the vinegar, peppercorns and thyme. Bring to the boil, then poach gently for 8–10 minutes, until the flesh comes away easily from the bones.

2 Pare of a few strips of rind from the orange, then cut the rind into fine shreds and reserve. Remove the remaining peel from the orange, taking care to remove all the pith. Slice the orange flesh into thin rounds.

3 To make the dressing, whisk together the vinegar, oil and spring onions and season with salt, paprika and pepper. Put the salad leaves in a large bowl, pour over the dressing and toss.

4 Flake the fish, discarding the bones, and add to the salad. Add the reserved orange rind, the orange slices and tomatoes, toss gently and serve with crusty bread.

> **Cook's Tip**
> Skate is a flat fish and the 'wings' contain many bones, but once cooked, the flesh falls off easily and it tastes succulent.

Seafood Salad with Olives

This salad is a wonder to behold, but is easy to make.

Serves 6
1 lolla green lettuce
50g/2oz cured, sliced chorizo or
　in a piece skinned and diced
4 thin slices Serrano ham
130g/4½oz can sardines
　in oil, drained
130g/4½oz can albacore tuna
　steak in oil, drained
8 canned white asparagus
　spears, drained
2–3 canned palm hearts, drained
115g/4oz/⅔ cup arbequina olives

115g/4oz/⅔ cup big gordas
　or queen olives, preferably
　purple ones
10 medium red tomatoes, peeled,
　seeded and quartered
15ml/1 tbsp chopped fresh
　parsley, to garnish

For the vinaigrette
1 garlic clove, split lengthways
30ml/2 tbsp sherry vinegar
30ml/2 tbsp red wine vinegar
60ml/4 tbsp olive oil
60ml/4 tbsp extra virgin olive oil
salt and ground black pepper

1 Make the vinaigrette. Wipe the cut side of the garlic around a bowl and discard. Whisk the other ingredients in the bowl. Select eight lettuce leaves and break off the stem ends. Toss the leaves in the vinaigrette. Arrange around a large serving plate.

2 Place the chorizo on one side of the plate. Roll the ham and arrange opposite. Arrange the sardines and tuna across the plate, in a cross, then place the asparagus, spears outwards, and the palm hearts (split lengthways), on opposite sides of the plate. Pile the two types of olive in the remaining spaces.

3 Arrange the tomatoes, round side up, in the centre of the plate, just touching all the prepared sections. Prepare more tomatoes as they are needed. Arrange them in a flower shape, each new ring just overlapping the previous one. The final ring, in the centre of the pile, should make a flower shape.

4 Brush a little vinaigrette dressing over the tomatoes, palm hearts and asparagus spears and season lightly with salt and ground black pepper. Sprinkle the chopped fresh parsley very discreetly on the tomatoes and white vegetables. Serve the salad at room temperature.

Skate Energy 230kcal/965kJ; Protein 31.6g; Carbohydrate 4.8g, of which sugars 4.8g; Fat 9.5g, of which saturates 1.3g; Cholesterol 0mg; Calcium 118mg; Fibre 1.5g; Sodium 247mg.
Seafood Salad Energy 638kcal/2671kJ; Protein 74.6g; Carbohydrate 9.8g, of which sugars 9.8g; Fat 33.7g, of which saturates 7.3g; Cholesterol 218mg; Calcium 183mg; Fibre 3.1g; Sodium 4618g.

Chicken Salmagundi

Salads, with the ingredients elaborately arranged, were fashionable in 17th-century England, containing chopped meat, anchovies and eggs, garnished with onions, lemon juice, oil and other condiments. This variation of the dish is a classic example of these hearty dishes.

Serves 4–6

1 large chicken, weighing about
  2kg/4¹/₂lb
1 onion
1 carrot
1 celery stick
2 bay leaves
large sprig of thyme

10 black peppercorns
500g/1¹/₄lb new or
  baby potatoes
225g/8oz carrots, cut into
  small sticks
225g/8oz sugar snap peas
4 eggs
¹/₂ cucumber, thinly sliced
8–12 cherry tomatoes
8–12 green olives stuffed
  with pimento

For the dressing
75ml/5 tbsp olive oil
30ml/2 tbsp lemon juice
2.5ml/¹/₂ tsp sugar
1.5ml/¹/₄ tsp ready-made English
  (hot) mustard
salt and ground black pepper

1 Put the chicken in a deep pan with the onion, carrot, celery, bay leaves, thyme and peppercorns. Add water to cover. Bring to the boil and simmer gently for 45 minutes or until the chicken is cooked. Leave to cool in the stock for several hours.

2 Whisk together all the ingredients for the dressing in a medium bowl. Set aside.

3 Using a separate pan for each, cook the potatoes, carrots and peas in lightly salted boiling water until just tender. Drain and rinse under cold water. Halve the potatoes. Hard-boil the eggs, cool, shell and cut into quarters.

4 Lift the chicken out of the stock, remove the meat and cut or tear into bitesize pieces.

5 Arrange the vegetables, chicken and eggs on a large platter, or in a large bowl, and add the tomatoes and olives. Just before serving, drizzle the salad dressing over the top.

Grilled Spiced Quail with Mixed Leaf and Mushroom Salad

This is a perfect supper dish for autumnal entertaining. Quail is at its best when the breast meat is removed from the carcass, so that it cooks quickly and can be served rare.

Serves 4

8 quail breast fillets
50g/2oz/¹/₄ cup butter
5ml/1 tsp paprika
75g/3oz/generous 1 cup
  chanterelle mushrooms,
  sliced if large

25g/1oz/2 tbsp butter to cook the
  mushrooms
25g/1oz/3 tbsp walnut
  halves, toasted
115g/4oz mixed salad leaves

For the dressing
60ml/4 tbsp walnut oil
30ml/2 tbsp olive oil
45ml/3 tbsp balsamic vinegar
salt and ground black pepper

1 To make the dressing, whisk the oils with the balsamic vinegar, then season with salt and pepper and set aside.

2 Preheat the grill (broiler). Arrange the quail breast fillets on the grill rack, skin side up. Dot with half the butter and sprinkle with half the paprika and a little salt.

3 Grill (broil) the quail breast fillets for 3 minutes. Turn them over and dot with half the remaining butter, then sprinkle with the remaining paprika and a little salt. Grill for a further 3 minutes, or until cooked. Transfer the fillets to a warmed dish, cover and leave to stand while preparing the salad.

4 Heat the remaining butter until foaming and cook the chanterelles for about 3 minutes, or until just beginning to soften. Add the walnuts and heat through. Remove from the heat.

5 Thinly slice the cooked quail fillets and arrange them on four serving plates with the warmed chanterelle mushrooms, toasted walnuts and mixed salad leaves. Drizzle the oil and balsamic vinegar dressing over the salad and serve warm.

Salmagundi Energy 397kcal/1664kJ; Protein 41.2g; Carbohydrate 24.9g, of which sugars 8.7g; Fat 15.5g, of which saturates 3g; Cholesterol 220mg; Calcium 63mg; Fibre 4.6g; Sodium 155mg.
Grilled Quail Energy 443kcal/1837kJ; Protein 25.6g; Carbohydrate 0.9g, of which sugars 0.8g; fat 37.5g, of which saturates 12.3g; Cholesterol 110mg; Calcium 24mg; Fibre 0.7g; Sodium 176mg.

Chicken and Mango Salad

This is a hearty, fresh salad, perfect for a main meal.

Serves 4

15ml/1 tbsp sunflower oil
1 onion, chopped
1 garlic clove, crushed
30ml/2 tbsp red curry paste
10ml/2 tsp apricot jam
30ml/2 tbsp chicken stock
about 450g/1lb cooked chicken, cut into small pieces
150ml/¼ pint/⅔ cup natural (plain) yogurt
60–75ml/4–5 tbsp mayonnaise
1 mango, cut into 1cm/½in dice
fresh flat leaf parsley sprigs, to garnish
poppadums, to serve

For the orange rice

175g/6oz/scant 1 cup white long grain rice
225g/8oz carrots, grated
1 large orange, cut into segments
40g/1½oz/⅓ cup roasted flaked (sliced) almonds

For the dressing

45ml/3 tbsp olive oil
60ml/4 tbsp sunflower oil
45ml/3 tbsp lemon juice
1 garlic clove, crushed
15ml/1 tbsp chopped mixed fresh herbs (tarragon, parsley, chives)
salt and ground black pepper

1 Heat the oil in a frying pan and fry the onion and garlic for 3–4 minutes until soft. Stir in the curry paste, cook for about 1 minute, then lower the heat and stir in the apricot jam and stock. Mix well, add the chicken and stir until coated in the paste. Spoon the mixture into a large bowl and leave to cool.

2 Meanwhile, boil the rice in plenty of lightly salted water until just tender. Drain, rinse under cold water and drain again. When cool, stir into the carrot, the orange segments and almonds.

3 Make the dressing by whisking all the ingredients together in a bowl. Set aside. When the chicken mixture is cool, stir in the yogurt and mayonnaise, then add the mango, stirring it in carefully so as not to break the flesh. Chill for about 30 minutes.

4 When ready to serve, pour the dressing into the rice salad and mix well. Spoon on to a platter and mound the cold curried chicken on top. Garnish with flat leaf parsley and serve with poppadums.

Warm Duck Salad with Poached Eggs

These golden duck skewers look and taste wonderful.

Serves 4

3 skinless duck breast fillets, thinly sliced
30ml/2 tbsp soy sauce
30ml/2 tbsp balsamic vinegar
30ml/2 tbsp groundnut (peanut) oil
1 shallot, finely chopped
115g/4oz/1½ cups chanterelle mushrooms
4 eggs
50g/2oz mixed salad leaves
salt and ground black pepper
30ml/2 tbsp extra virgin olive oil, to serve

1 Put the duck in a shallow dish and toss with the soy sauce and balsamic vinegar. Cover and chill for 30 minutes. Meanwhile, soak 12 bamboo skewers (about 13cm/5in long) in water for 30 minutes to help prevent them from burning during cooking.

2 Preheat the grill (broiler). Thread the duck slices on to the skewers, pleating them neatly. Place the skewers on a grill (broiling) pan and cook for 3–5 minutes, then turn the skewers and cook for a further 3 minutes, or until the duck is golden brown.

3 Meanwhile, heat the groundnut oil in a large frying pan and cook the chopped shallot, stirring frequently, until softened. Add the mushrooms to the pan and cook over high heat for 5 minutes, stirring occasionally.

4 While the chanterelles are cooking, half-fill a frying pan with water, add a little salt and heat until simmering. Break the eggs one at a time into a cup, then gently tip into the water. Poach the eggs gently for about 3 minutes, or until the whites are set. Use a slotted spoon to transfer the eggs to a warm plate, pat them dry with kitchen paper, then trim off any untidy white.

5 Arrange the salad leaves on four individual plates, then add the chanterelles and skewered duck. Place the poached eggs on the plates. Drizzle the salad with olive oil, season with pepper and serve immediately.

Chicken Salad Energy 776kcal/3245kJ; Protein 35.9g; Carbohydrate 60.2g, of which sugars 21.1g; Fat 45.3g, of which saturates 6.4g; Cholesterol 93mg; Calcium 172mg; Fibre 4.5g; Sodium 206mg.
Warm Duck Salad Energy 271kcal/1132kJ; Protein 29.2g; Carbohydrate 1.5g, of which sugars 1.1g; Fat 18.6g, of which saturates 3.9g; Cholesterol 314mg; Calcium 51mg; Fibre 0.7g; Sodium 196mg

Egg and Bacon Caesar Salad

The key elements of this popular salad are sweet lettuce, crisp croûtons and a mayonnaise-like dressing.

Serves 4–6

3 × 1cm/½in thick slices
   white bread, cubed
45ml/3 tbsp olive oil
1 large garlic clove, finely chopped
3–4 Little Gem (Bibb) lettuces or
   2 larger cos or romaine lettuces
12–18 quail's eggs

115g/4oz thinly sliced Parma,
   San Daniele or Serrano ham
40–50g/1½–2oz/½–⅔ cups
   Parmesan cheese, grated
salt and ground black pepper

For the dressing

1 large egg (US extra large)
1–2 garlic cloves, chopped
4 anchovy fillets in oil, drained
120ml/4fl oz/½ cup olive oil
10–15ml/2–3 tsp lemon juice or
   white wine vinegar

1 Preheat the oven to 190°C/375°F/Gas 5. Toss the bread cubes with the oil and garlic. Season to taste with salt and pepper. Turn on to a baking tray and bake for 10–14 minutes, stirring once or twice, until golden brown all over.

2 Meanwhile, to make the dressing, boil the egg for 90 seconds, then plunge into cold water. Shell and put in a food processor or blender. Add the garlic and anchovy fillets and process to mix. With the motor still running, gradually add the olive oil in a thin stream until creamy. Add the lemon juice or vinegar and season to taste with salt and pepper.

3 Separate the lettuce leaves and tear up if large. Place in a large salad bowl.

4 Put the quail's eggs in a pan, cover with cold water, then bring to the boil and boil for 2 minutes. Plunge the eggs into cold water, then part-shell them. Grill (broil) the ham for 2–3 minutes on each side, or until crisp.

5 Toss the dressing into the lettuce with 25g/1oz/⅓ cup of the Parmesan until the lettuce is well coated. Add the croûtons. Cut the quail's eggs in half and add them to the salad. Crumble the ham into large pieces and sprinkle it over the salad with the remaining cheese.

Salad with Ham, Egg and Asparagus

When you think it is too hot for pasta, try serving it in a warm salad. Here it is combined with ham, eggs and asparagus, with a tangy mustard dressing made from the asparagus stems.

Serves 4

450g/1lb asparagus
450g/1lb dried tagliatelle pasta
225g/8oz cooked ham, in
   5mm/¼ in thick slices,
   cut into fingers

2 hard-boiled eggs, peeled
   and sliced
50g/2oz fresh Parmesan
   cheese, shaved
salt and ground black pepper

For the dressing

50g/2oz cooked potato
75ml/5 tbsp extra virgin olive oil
15ml/1 tbsp lemon juice
10ml/2 tsp Dijon mustard
120ml/4fl oz/½ cup
   vegetable stock

1 Trim and discard the tough woody part of the asparagus. Cut the spears in half and cook the thicker stems in boiling salted water for 12 minutes. After 6 minutes add the tips. Drain, then refresh under cold water until warm.

2 Finely chop 150g/5oz of the thick asparagus pieces. Place in a food processor with all the dressing ingredients and process until smooth.

3 Cook the pasta in a large pan of lightly salted boiling water according to the instructions on the packet, until al dente. Refresh under cold running water until just lukewarm, then drain well.

4 Toss the pasta with the asparagus sauce and divide between four warmed serving plates. Top with the ham, boiled eggs and asparagus tips. Serve with a generous sprinkling of fresh Parmesan cheese shavings.

> **Variation**
> Try using thin slices of softer Italian cheese, such as Fontina, in place of the Parmesan, if you like.

Egg and Bacon Salad Energy 318kcal/1320kJ; Protein 13.8g; Carbohydrate 6.8g, of which sugars 0.7g; Fat 26.5g, of which saturates 5.8g; Cholesterol 180mg; Calcium 149mg; Fibre 0.3g; Sodium 546mg.
Ham Salad Energy 696kcal/2928kJ; Protein 35g; Carbohydrate 88g, of which sugars 6.3g; Fat 25.1g, of which saturates 6.3g; Cholesterol 140mg; Calcium 224mg; Fibre 5.1g; Sodium 852mg.

Pasta Salad with Salami

This salami and charcoal-roasted peppers salad is simple to make and it can be prepared in advance for a perfect and satisfying one-dish main course.

Serves 4

225g/8oz dried fusilli pasta
275g/10oz jar charcoal-roasted
  peppers in oil
115g/4oz/1 cup pitted
  black olives
4 sun-dried tomatoes, quartered
115g/4oz Roquefort
  cheese, crumbled
10 slices peppered salami,
  cut into strips
115g/4oz packet mixed
  leaf salad
30ml/2 tbsp white wine
  vinegar
30ml/2 tbsp chopped
  fresh oregano
2 garlic cloves, crushed
salt and ground black pepper

1 Cook the pasta in a large pan of lightly salted boiling water according to the instructions on the packet, until al dente. Drain thoroughly and rinse with cold water, then drain again.

2 Drain the peppers and reserve 60ml/4 tbsp of the oil for the dressing. Cut the peppers into long, fine strips and mix them with the olives, sun-dried tomatoes and Roquefort in a large bowl. Stir in the pasta and peppered salami.

3 Divide the salad leaves between four individual bowls and spoon the pasta salad on top. Whisk the reserved oil with the wine vinegar, oregano and garlic in a bowl. Season with salt and ground black pepper to taste, then spoon over the salad and serve immediately.

> **Cook's Tip**
> Be careful not to overcook the pasta; it must still retain bite.

> **Variation**
> Use chicken instead of the salami and cubes of Brie in place of the Roquefort.

Waldorf Rice Salad

Waldorf Salad takes its name from the Waldorf Hotel in New York, where it was first made. The rice makes this salad slightly more substantial than usual. Serve with a selection of cold meats for a really hearty meal.

Serves 2–4

115g/4oz/generous ½ cup white
  long grain rice
1 red apple
1 green apple
60ml/4 tbsp lemon juice
3 celery sticks
2–3 slices thick cooked ham
90ml/6 tbsp good quality
  mayonnaise, preferably
  home-made
60ml/4 tbsp sour cream
generous pinch of saffron,
  dissolved in 15ml/1 tbsp
  hot water
10ml/2 tsp chopped fresh basil
15ml/1 tbsp chopped fresh parsley
several romaine or iceberg
  lettuce leaves
50g/2oz/½ cup walnuts,
  roughly chopped
salt and ground black pepper

1 Cook the rice in plenty of boiling salted water until tender. Drain and set aside in a bowl to cool.

2 Cut the apples into quarters, remove the cores and finely slice one red and one green apple quarter. Place the slices in a bowl with half the lemon juice and reserve for the garnish. Peel the remaining apple quarters and cut into fine sticks. Place in a separate bowl and toss with another 15ml/1 tbsp of the fresh lemon juice.

3 Cut the celery into thin strips. Roll up each slice of ham, slice finely and add to the apple sticks, with the celery.

4 Mix together the mayonnaise, sour cream and saffron water. Stir in salt and ground black pepper to taste. Stir into the rice with the herbs. Add the apple and celery and the remaining lemon juice.

5 Arrange the lettuce leaves around the outside of a salad bowl and pile the rice and apple mixture into the centre. Sprinkle with the chopped walnuts and garnish with fans of the apple slices.

Pasta Salad Energy 429kcal/1797kJ; Protein 17.8g; Carbohydrate 46.7g, of which sugars 6.6g; Fat 20.3g, of which saturates 8.9g; Cholesterol 37mg; Calcium 188mg; Fibre 3.9g; Sodium 1341mg.
Waldorf Rice Salad Energy 523kcal/2178kJ; Protein 24.7g; Carbohydrate 32.4g, of which sugars 9.3g; Fat 32.9g, of which saturates 6.4g; Cholesterol 84mg; Calcium 111mg; Fibre 3.2g; Sodium 1331mg

Chilli Beef Salad with Shiitake Mushrooms

All the ingredients for this Thai dish are available in larger supermarkets.

Serves 4
675g/1½lb beef fillet or rump (round) steak
30ml/2 tbsp olive oil
2 red chillies, seeded and sliced
225g/8oz/3¼ cups fresh shiitake mushrooms, stems removed and caps sliced

For the dressing
3 spring onions (scallions), finely chopped
2 garlic cloves, finely chopped
juice of 1 lime
15–30ml/1–2 tbsp Thai fish sauce
5ml/1 tsp soft light brown sugar
30ml/2 tbsp chopped fresh coriander (cilantro)

To serve
1 cos or romaine lettuce, in strips
175g/6oz cherry tomatoes, halved
5cm/2in piece cucumber, peeled, halved and thinly sliced
45ml/3 tbsp toasted sesame seeds

1 Preheat the grill (broiler) to medium, then cook the steak for 2–4 minutes on each side, depending on how well done you like it. Leave to cool for at least 15 minutes.

2 Slice the beef fillet or rump steak as thinly as possible (freezing it for 30 minutes before slicing will help make this easier). Place the slices in a bowl.

3 Heat the olive oil in a small frying pan. Add the seeded and sliced red chillies and the sliced shiitake mushroom caps. Cook for 5 minutes, stirring occasionally. Turn off the heat and add the steak slices to the pan. Stir well to coat the beef slices in the chilli and mushroom mixture.

4 Make the dressing by mixing all the ingredients in a bowl, then pour it over the meat mixture and toss gently.

5 Arrange the lettuce, tomatoes and cucumber on a serving plate. Spoon the steak mixture in the centre and sprinkle the sesame seeds over. Serve immediately.

Marinated Beef and Potato Salad

The beef steak needs to marinate overnight, but once that has been done, this dish is very quick to assemble and makes a substantial main meal.

Serves 6
900g/2lb sirloin steak
3 large white potatoes
½ red (bell) pepper, seeded and diced
½ green (bell) pepper, seeded and diced
1 small red onion, finely chopped
2 garlic cloves, crushed
4 spring onions (scallions), diagonally sliced
1 small cos or romaine lettuce, leaves torn
salt and ground black pepper
olive oil, to serve
Parmesan cheese shavings, to serve

For the marinade
120ml/4fl oz/½ cup olive oil
120ml/4fl oz/½ cup red wine vinegar
90ml/6 tbsp soy sauce

1 Place the beef in a large, non-metallic container. Mix the marinade ingredients together. Season with pepper and pour over the meat.

2 Cover the meat and leave to marinate for several hours, or preferably overnight.

3 Drain the marinade from the meat and pat the joint dry. Preheat the frying pan, cut the meat carefully into thin slices and fry for a few minutes until just cooked on each side, but still slightly pink. Set aside to cool.

4 Using a melon baller, scoop out rounds from each potato. Boil in lightly salted water for 5 minutes or until just tender.

5 Drain the potato and transfer to a bowl. Add the peppers, onion, garlic, spring onions and lettuce leaves. Season with salt and pepper and toss together.

6 Transfer the potato and pepper mixture to a plate with the beef. Drizzle with a little extra olive oil and serve topped with Parmesan shavings.

Chilli Beef Salad Energy 381kcal/1588kJ; Protein 39.7g; Carbohydrate 4g; of which sugars 3.8g; Fat 23g; of which saturates 6.6g; Cholesterol 103mg; Calcium 105mg; Fibre 2.4g; Sodium 352mg.
Marinated Beef Energy 296kcal/1247kJ; Protein 38g; Carbohydrate 20.1g; of which sugars 5g; Fat 7.6g; of which saturates 3.2g; Cholesterol 77mg; Calcium 40mg; Fibre 2.3g; Sodium 120mg

Beef and Sweet Potato Salad

This salad makes a good main dish for a summer buffet, especially if the beef has been cut into strips.

Serves 6–8
800g/1¾lb fillet of beef
5ml/1 tsp black peppercorns, crushed
10ml/2 tsp chopped fresh thyme
60ml/4 tbsp olive oil
450g/1lb orange-fleshed sweet potato, peeled and sliced
salt and ground black pepper

For the dressing
1 garlic clove, chopped
15g/½oz flat leaf parsley
30ml/2 tbsp chopped fresh coriander (cilantro)
15ml/1 tbsp small salted capers, rinsed
½–1 fresh green chilli, seeded and chopped
10ml/2 tsp Dijon mustard
10–15ml/2–3 tsp white wine vinegar
75ml/5 tbsp extra-virgin olive oil
2 shallots, finely chopped

1 Roll the beef fillet in the crushed peppercorns and thyme, then set aside to marinate for a few hours. Preheat the oven to 200°C/400°F/Gas 6.

2 Heat half the olive oil in a frying pan. Add the beef and brown it all over, turning frequently, to seal it. Place on a baking tray and cook in the oven for 10–15 minutes. Remove from the oven, and cover with foil, then leave to rest for 10–15 minutes.

3 Meanwhile, preheat the grill (broiler). Brush the sweet potato with the remaining olive oil, season to taste with salt and pepper, and grill (broil) for about 5–6 minutes on each side, until browned. Cut into strips and place them in a bowl. Cut the beef into slices or strips and toss with the sweet potato.

4 To make the dressing, process the garlic, parsley, coriander, capers, chilli, mustard and 10ml/2 tsp of the vinegar in a food processor until chopped. With the motor still running, gradually pour in the oil to make a smooth dressing. Season and add more vinegar, to taste. Stir in the shallots.

5 Toss the dressing into the sweet potatoes and beef and leave to stand for up to 2 hours before serving.

Seared Beef Salad in a Lime Dressing

Versions of this dish are enjoyed all over South-east Asia. Strips of seared beef are flavoured with lime and chilli, then tossed with crunchy beansprouts and fresh herbs to make a salad suitable for a main course.

Serves 4
about 7.5ml/1½ tsp vegetable oil
450g/1lb beef fillet, cut into steaks 2.5cm/1in thick
115g/4oz/½ cup beansprouts

1 bunch each fresh basil and mint, stalks removed, leaves shredded
1 lime, cut into slices, to serve

For the dressing
grated (shredded) rind and juice (about 80ml/3fl oz) of 2 limes
30ml/2 tbsp Thai fish sauce
30ml/2 tbsp raw cane sugar
2 garlic cloves, crushed
2 lemon grass stalks, finely sliced
2 fresh red Serrano chillies, seeded and finely sliced

1 To make the dressing, beat the lime rind, juice and fish sauce in a bowl with the sugar, until the sugar dissolves. Stir in the garlic, lemon grass and chillies and set aside.

2 Pour a little oil into a heavy pan and rub it over the base with a piece of kitchen paper. Heat the pan and sear the steaks for 1–2 minutes each side.

3 Transfer the seared steaks to a board and leave to cool a little. Using a sharp knife, cut the meat into thin slices. Toss the slices in the dressing, cover and leave the meat to marinate for 1–2 hours.

4 Drain the meat of any excess juice and transfer it to a wide serving bowl. Add the beansprouts and herbs and toss it all together. Serve with lime slices to squeeze over.

> **Cook's Tip**
> It is worth buying an excellent-quality piece of tender fillet steak for this recipe as the meat is only just seared.

Seared Beef Salad Energy 233kcal/979kJ; Protein 26g; Carbohydrate 12g, of which sugars 9g; Fat 9g, of which saturates 3g; Cholesterol 69mg; Calcium 74mg; Fibre 0.5g; Sodium 400mg.
Beef Salad Energy 300kcal/1253kJ; Protein 21.9g; Carbohydrate 12g, of which sugars 3.2g; Fat 18.6g, of which saturates 4.6g; Cholesterol 61mg; Calcium 18mg; Fibre 1.4g; Sodium 67mg.

Index